Project Management Using Earned Value

Second Edition

Gary C. Humphreys

First edition published 2002. Second edition 2011

Printed in the United States of America

ISBN 0-9708614-0-0

Humphreys & Associates, Inc.
3111 North Tustin Street, Suite 250
Orange, CA 92865 USA
(714) 685-1730
humphreys@humphreys-assoc.com
www.humphreys-assoc.com

Table of Contents

List of Figures

Chapter 10 Considerations for Developing a Useful, Quality Schedule

Chapter 11 Crashing the Network

Chapter 17 Schedule Risk Assessment

Chapter 18 Scheduling in a Performance Measurement Environment

Chapter 36 Implementation of the Project Management Process

Preface

This book is about project management. It is not about all aspects of project management but it includes some of the most important aspects. This book is about how the planning, control, and management of projects can be improved through the use of the concept called Earned Value.

This book is intended for anyone who desires to know more about project planning and control and how to improve these processes through the use of Earned Value. Intended readers include project and program managers, project control personnel, project technical personnel, procurement activity personnel and the stakeholders and owners of projects. While it is intended for a wide range of readers, each is assumed to have a basic familiarity with the requirements and the disciplines of project management. Readers new to this arena would be well advised to supplement this reading with a basic but general work on Project Management.

The material in this book as been drawn from the collective experiences of the author and many of the professional personnel of Humphreys & Associates, Inc., consultants in project and program management for over forty years. This material has been presented in seminars, workshops and successfully used assisting our clients in the United States and around the world. While introductory theory is explained, time tested samples are provided. Samples are presented from specific industries. Please do not conclude that a sample does not apply to those of you in the construction, software, or other industries.

To facilitate the learning experience, the topics covered are linked together in a process flowchart. This flowchart is displayed at the beginning of each chapter and the elements of the flowchart addressed in that chapter are highlighted. In addition, the chapters have been grouped into Sections. Each Section represents a major activity in the planning and control process, Organization, Scheduling, Estimating, and Earned Value. These are supplemented by a Section on Implementation (of project planning and control) and by a Conclusion and an Appendix.

To further aid the reader, a series of questions about chapter content are found at the conclusion of each chapter. The answers are provided in the Appendix. In addition, at the end of each Section there is a Section Quiz. Again the answers are provided in the Appendix. Finally, the majority of chapters contain one or more Case Studies. These are practical exercises that have been drawn from our consulting experiences and presented in Humphreys & Associates, Inc. seminars and workshops. The Case Studies have been found to reinforce the participants learning. Suggested solutions to these Case Studies can be found on our website at: www.humphreys-assoc.com.

Acknowledgments

I should like to express my heartfelt thanks and appreciation for the collaborative efforts by the Humphreys & Associates, Inc's staff and consultants who were very instrumental in developing this second edition of Project Management Using Earned Value.

Special thanks goes to Paul Bolinger, Paul Bosakowski, Steve Osborn, Ken Pastor, Lynn Sandberg, Harry Stuart, and Buck Wilkerson for their Scheduling and Risk Management expertise; and Doug Fisher, Tim Kruzic, and Lynn Sandberg for their keen Earned Value insights and updates. I also want to thank the reviewers' contributions made by Will Eldridge, Chris Humphreys, Hugh Langford, Barbara Minke, Harvey Mymit, and Barbara Wever; and for the review, formatting, and final book production provided by Joan Ugljesa.

My deepest gratitude and thanks go to Lynn Sandberg for her countless hours of dedication and professionalism in creating, editing, and updating the entire book; as well as her tireless energy to meet the completion objectives with the creative team.

Finally, to all our clients over the past thirty-five years who challenged us, prodded us, and encouraged us to provide the most comprehensive and complete Earned Value process possible, thank you.

Gary C. Humphreys
Orange, CA
December, 2010

EARNED VALUE PROJECT MANAGEMENT AND ORGANIZATION

SECTION 1

EARNED VALUE PROJECT MANAGEMENT AND ORGANIZATION

Initial considerations for a project are project definition and organization. One of the first challenges faced in the overall Earned Value Management process is selecting the appropriate level of detail for adequate visibility and effective control. An important selection criterion is the amount of associated risk. Therefore, the question of technical risk identification and quantification must be considered. Once work scope is well defined, the next step is responsibility assignment. Responsibility assignment includes the identification of "control accounts" that display the intersection points of work scope and responsibility for accomplishing the work. An important factor in the assignment of responsibility is the application of the work team concept to projects. Incorporating work teams directly affects the selection of control accounts. More importantly, work teams should promote improved project communication and morale.

The topics covered in this section form an infrastructure for all of the succeeding topics in the Earned Value Management process. A flowchart is displayed at the start of each chapter. The segments highlighted are the subjects being addressed in that particular chapter. It is entitled "Earned Value Project Management: The Process," and is illustrated in Figure 1-8 and described in Chapter 1.

Chapter **1**

PROJECT MANAGEMENT USING EARNED VALUE

Objectives of this Chapter:

1. Define "project" and project management.

2. Describe the performance-oriented approach using an Earned Value Management System and explain why it is superior to actual versus budget comparisons.

3. Discuss factors affecting the appropriate level of detail for Earned Value implementation.

4. Introduce the process flowchart for the Earned Value Project Management process.

What is a Project?

Before delving into the intricacies of the Earned Value Management process, projects and Earned Value Management need to be defined first. A project consists of a defined objective to develop or produce a new product, capability, or to expand capacity within a specified time frame and budget. Examples of projects include large capital-intensive efforts such as highway construction, new commercial buildings, power plants and petrochemical plants, water treatment plants, flood control, dams, bridges, hospitals, schools, prisons, and churches. These are the obvious, highly visible projects.

They are not the only types of projects; however, as new product development is also a project. A new automobile, engine, or communication satellite is a project. Other projects include research and development, definition of new information systems, design and installation of communication systems, creation of new software programs, and computer hardware advances.

Projects are so widespread that it is difficult to get through the day without being involved in some way with a project, whether it is sitting in traffic while road work continues, finding a more effi-cient information flow for office communication, or managing a home improvement.

The Project Management Institute (PMI) defines a project as:

> *A project is a temporary endeavor undertaken to create a unique product, service, or result. The temporary nature of projects indicates a definite beginning and end. The end is reached when the project's objectives have been achieved or when the project is terminated because its objectives will not or cannot be met, or the need for the project no longer exists.*[1]

A well conceived project could also be characterized as any endeavor that has a well-defined scope of work and optimistic yet achievable schedule and cost objectives.

The words "project" and "program" are sometimes used interchangeably in industry, resulting in some confusion. A program is made up of individual projects to be accomplished. For example, the inertial guidance system for an aircraft may be a separate project on a program. Because

---

1. Project Management Institute. *A Guide to the Project Management Body of Knowledge (PMBOK), Fourth Edition.* Newton Square, PA: Project Management Institute, 2008, 5.

projects and programs share the same characteristics they can be treated in a similar manner. For that reason, throughout this text, the term "project" will be used generically to refer to both projects and programs.

Now that project has been defined, what is Earned Value Management? It is the process of defining and controlling the project so that defined objectives are met. The controlling aspect includes scope control, schedule control, and budget control. It also includes the process of identifying and minimizing risk. There are many aspects involved in Earned Value Management, including development of the Earned Value Management System. An Earned Value Management System is a set of processes and tools used to facilitate the management of a project.

Managing Projects

Many projects result in highly successful completions. Successful projects contain many common characteristics: they were well defined and organized, had a closely monitored work scope, had optimistic yet achievable schedule and budget from the time of initiation, and were closely monitored and managed. Many projects have been successful for another reason: they benefited from mistakes on other projects. The primary factor observed on successfully managed projects is managing performance. The common thread throughout all of the topics in this textbook is exactly that.

The approaches and techniques that will be discussed have a performance measurement orientation, because the better something can be measured, the better it can be managed.

In a performance measurement system, cost and schedule targets are assigned to each activity planned in a project and to the project itself; progress (performance) is measured against these targets. Deviations from the activity targets and the causes of the deviations are identified and action is taken to minimize adverse consequences to the project.

Projects require expertise from many disciplines. Close coordination and communication are essential parts of successful execution of a

project. To achieve these, a separate "project team" is typically assembled for accomplishing the project's scope of work. This team is organized using individuals from various disciplines such as accounting, purchasing, engineering, manufacturing, testing, operations, finance, contracts, construction, project controls, and may also include subcontractors. Some people provide part time support to a project. These might include any of those mentioned above and others such as the legal department, record retention, financial services, and executive management.

The job of managing all of these organizations and people is typically assigned to a full time senior individual who is designated as the project manager. A project manager should meet several specific qualifications: many years of experience in the type of project being managed to be technically qualified; a degree to be academically qualified; and stamina to be physically qualified. In addition, project managers must have good processes and tools to effectively manage the people and the project.

The project manager must orchestrate the entire project to achieve the technical, schedule, and cost objectives. If a project is an internal endeavor, then a project manager's role is to manage the internal departmental interfaces and contractors, and possibly other owners and customers, in addition to all of the internal staff.

Unlike normal functional organizations, a project has a specific duration. Even as a project is initiated, its purpose is to accomplish defined objectives and disband. A project team's job is to quickly accomplish the technical scope of work, resource as efficiently as possible, and then move on to the next project. The project manager's job is, therefore, inherently complex and challenging. Besides the interfaces that must be managed on a daily basis, he or she must often be a motivational expert since the many players involved may have different goals. For many reasons, a project manager has a great need for accurate status information. Only with reliable indication of project status can concerns be surfaced early enough to allow corrective action, preventing potential concerns from becoming real concerns that adversely impact technical, schedule, and cost objectives.

Examples used throughout this text are extracted from actual experiences. Frequently it is easier to illustrate a concept by showing what can or will happen if certain fundamentals are ignored than what happens if they are followed. If the principles in this text are followed, there is a good probability of executing a well-managed project. If they are ignored, unpleasant, career-limiting, unsuccessful experiences can occur.

Depending on project risk, project duration, and cost, (technical, schedule, and cost), certain aspects may be implemented less stringently. The principles do not change. It is still necessary to define the scope of work, have a plan for accomplishing the work, and to manage the plan. However, the level of detail of the implementation can vary. Unsuccessful applications of these principles have also happened when organizations went overboard on the level of detail of implementation. If common sense is forgotten, it is possible to create a management system that requires so much effort that it requires and extensive staff just to provide the production and distribution of data. The cost of the management system is then not worth the additional insight received regarding project status.

The Earned Value Management tools that are recommended in this book have been effectively used to improve management on numerous projects. By selectively employing tools, the practitioner will improve management on current and future projects and thus, the prospects for project success.

There are several other topics related to Earned Value Management that are not directly covered. These include contract administration, project administration, and material and subcontract management. These are, however, incorporated within the discussions of related subjects generally performed by these functions.

The contract type has an impact on the extent of Earned Value Management implementation, but all of the basic information is still necessary to ascertain project status regardless of the contracting arrangement. Experience shows that too much attention is placed on the type of contract rather than incorporating all of the information, but at a different level of detail.

The human aspects of Earned Value Management must not be forgotten either. As mentioned before, the project manager needs to be a motivational expert. The project manager also needs a strong supporting staff. No single person can successfully perform all of the work involved in a major project. He or she must rely on the support of many others. This makes the project a team effort. Even the best systems will be less effective in the hands of individuals who do not cooperate with each other and do not work towards a common goal. An underlying assumption is that effective management tools will facilitate better management of a project and minimize the confusion that results from a project that is not well defined and planned.

Background

In the past few decades, many large projects in numerous industries experienced significant schedule delays and cost overruns. Nuclear power projects stretched for years beyond their original schedule and more than tripled in cost. Software development projects in most companies required so much lead-time that the intended users had to find alternative ways of accomplishing their goals. In other cases, competitors beat software development firms to the marketplace and millions of dollars were wasted. Water treatment and sewer treatment plants soared in cost, with immediate impact on the consumer's water bill. Research and development projects and military projects were cancelled because of continually escalating schedule and cost projections. The U.S. auto industry suffered from a perceived lack of quality and unit prices increased. Many of these cases became highly visible to a large number of people.

For the project managers, the owners, and customers of these projects, this was not the objective envisioned in the project plan. How did this happen?

Causes were both internal and external. Scope changes occurred without being recognized and incorporated into a revised plan for accomplishing the work. Customer needs changed, sometimes because of a delay in finishing a product, thus resulting in obsolescence. Delays in material delivery occurred without properly reflecting the impact to other work activities. Regulations changed, frequently affecting the time needed to acquire permits or authority to proceed. Lack of coordination between contributing groups meant delays because of missing information, design or otherwise. When these and other disruptions occurred, resulting schedule slippage had large cost impacts because of high rates of escalation. Every delay was penalized with a significant negative economic consequence.

Typically a domino effect is observed. First, a technical problem occurs. This is followed by a negative schedule variance and ultimately a negative cost variance. Sometimes the dominos fall very fast, but problems could evolve over months.

Regardless of the source of difficulty, the underlying problem was that impacts were not recognized quickly enough when conditions changed. In some cases, project managers were ignoring variances from the plan and failing to take action because they did not believe the variances were real. In others, they were not informed well enough about the variances. The situation was much like that shown in Figure 1-1.

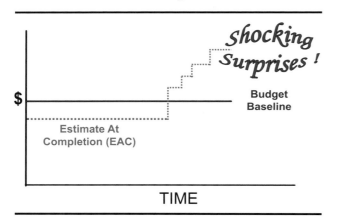

Figure 1-1 Shocking Surprises

In Figure 1-1, the Estimate at Completion (EAC) is below budget throughout most of the life of the project. While challenges were faced daily in the management process, there was no way to quantitatively assess the impact in a timely manner. By the time a schedule slip or an overrun was forecast, it was too late to do anything to mini-

mize its impact. The result was shocking surprises.

This scenario occurred often enough that there was a heightened awareness of the technical, schedule and cost risk associated with projects. Because of this risk, many organizations reacted by creating better management systems. These systems provided the capability of integrating all of the available data into a cohesive form so that better visibility would result. One of the greatest challenges for these systems was timeliness. If information were not available until after the fact, all that would be accomplished from its use was a well documented history of what went wrong rather than an effective tool for management during the life of the project. This improved visibility must allow for earlier identification of trends so that situations like the one pictured in Figure 1-1 can be prevented.

Most projects develop a time phased plan to accomplish the work. This resembles an S-curve shape. In the early stages, staffing and progress may be slow. In the middle part of the curve, both staffing and progress should be at their peak. At the end of the curve, progress slows while actual staffing may still be at peak or near-peak levels. The implications are obvious: identify and address the problems earlier in the project life and there is a much greater chance of avoiding schedule slips and large cost overruns. Early in the project, it takes very few additional resources to accelerate and resolve variant conditions. At the peak of the project activity, it takes enormous resources just to stay even with the progress curve, making catch-up very difficult. Even worse, at the end of a project, even great cost expenditures may do little to accelerate technical and schedule progress. Improved early visibility is a primary objective of any project management system.

The Performance-Oriented Approach

Every company has some sort of tracking system to indicate how it is performing. Unfortunately, in many cases, the tracking may have been no more sophisticated than what is shown in Figure 1-2, Budget Plan versus Actual Cost. This was the traditional approach used for many years in companies and is still used in too many organizations.

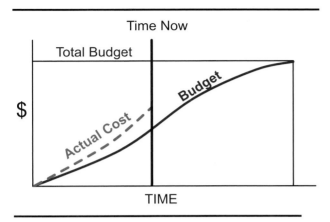

Figure 1-2 Budget Plan vs. Actual Cost

Actual costs are collected and compared with budgeted costs. This is done in the only common denominator available for resources - dollars in the U.S., Canada, and Australia, or the corresponding local currency in other countries. Does this approach provide improved visibility?

A good system must provide status and, therefore, the necessary visibility into progress. The graph shown in Figure 1-2 at least allows comparison of expenditures with what was planned to be spent. However, there is no assurance that project status is known. Actual cost to date is higher than planned, but does that indicate a cost overrun or is the project ahead of schedule? This situation is shown in Figure 1-3.

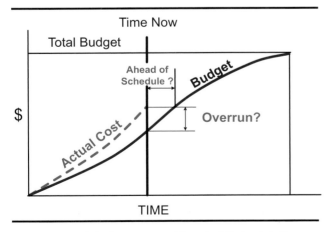

Figure 1-3 Overrun or Ahead of Schedule?

A budget versus actual comparison is shown in Figure 1-4. This may appear to indicate that a cost underrun is occurring. However, there is no basis for projecting what status will be at project completion. It may be that the project is incurring a cost underrun, but it may also be that the project is behind schedule and future expenditures will accelerate significantly. This is shown in Figure 1-5.

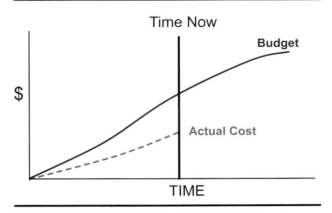

Figure 1-4 Underrun or Behind Schedule?

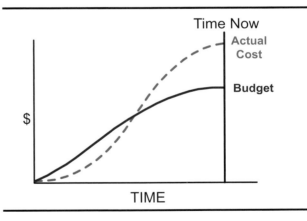

Figure 1-5 Significant Overrun or Accelerated Schedule?

What is missing from the comparison shown in Figures 1-4 and 1-5? There is no measure of what has actually been accomplished for what has been spent. The fact that money was being spent slower than planned could mean that there would be a cost underrun. It could just as easily mean that the project is behind schedule, or both, or neither.

The key to knowing what the true progress and status actually are requires the addition of a third line to the curve that reflects the dollar value for the work that has been completed.

This third line results from a "performance-oriented" approach. This approach shifts the emphasis from expenditures to work accomplishment. The project objective should be to accomplish all of the work rather than to spend all of the money.

When using a performance oriented approach, work scope and associated responsibilities must be defined in the initial planning phase of the project. This is a far better approach than defining responsibility in some form of finger-pointing exercise of guilt determination after a crisis occurs. It allows the person responsible for an emerging variance to take action before it becomes a problem. The entire organization benefits from this approach. If action cannot be taken in time to entirely avoid a problem, at least the impact can be accurately assessed if there were an objective method of measuring progress. By setting variance standards or "thresholds", the system can be used as a high level Management by Exception indicator. A result is the ability to develop improved forecasts of technical performance, scheduled completion, and final cost earlier in the project. The third line that represents work accomplishment has been added to Figure 1- 6.

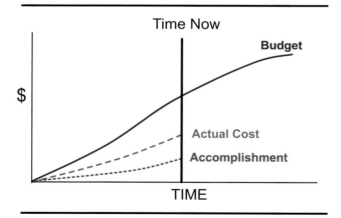

Figure 1-6 A Performance Oriented Approach Provides Better Visibility

Now there is a completely different picture of the project status. This graphic depicts the value of

the work scheduled to be accomplished, the value of the work accomplished, and how much the accomplished work actually cost. Actual costs to date are still below the budget line, but the value of work accomplished is even less. In other words, cost is not underrunning, but in fact is overrunning relative to the value of the work accomplished. Similarly, a behind schedule condition is apparent. The various methods for measuring the accomplishment of work will be presented in later chapters of this text, but the important point is that it can be measured and compared with an approved plan.

With this type of information, it is possible to project schedule slippage and cost overrun in early stages of the effort. This early warning feature is one of the most important advantages of including a measure of work accomplished. Figure 1-7 illustrates how these projections might be represented.

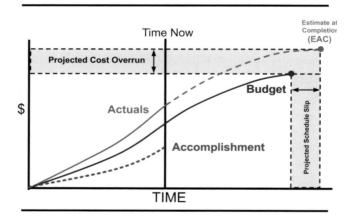

Figure 1-7 Cost and Schedule Impacts

Summary Implementation Concerns

The Earned Value Management process concepts are appropriate in any single project or multi-project environment. On any type of project in any industry, regardless of how small it is, a project must be effectively defined to be effectively accomplished. A project cannot be completed if its scope is not understood. Individuals or organizations must be identified with responsibility for completing the work, and a time frame must be established for accomplishing that work.

Budgets and other resources that are allocated to the project need to be identified. In other words, a plan for accomplishing the work is needed. Then progress must be measured against that plan. When variances are identified, corrective action should be identified, evaluated, and implemented in the most cost effective manner. These are standard techniques that apply in any situation.

Experience shows small, short duration projects are often managed far worse than the large projects that have high visibility. Because small projects are considered less significant towards the overall profit picture, they are sometimes overlooked with very unfavorable results. When small projects ignore basic management concepts, they commonly miss their budgets by 100 to 300 percent. The accumulation of absolute dollars may be more than a large project that misses its budget by 10 percent. The point is that the summation of many poorly managed small projects could exceed the impact of a large project.

A convenient aspect of the performance oriented approach is that it works in all environments including research and development, manufacturing, testing, construction, procurement, software development, and design. It also works on all types of contracts, regardless of whether they are firm fixed price, cost plus, or some other type between these two extremes. However, these factors play an important part in deciding on the level of detailed implementation to be used.

Factors Affecting System Implementation Detail

Among the factors that will impact the selection of project controls for a particular application, are the following:

- Project size and duration.
- Technical, schedule and cost risk.
- Project contract environment.
- Management involvement level.

The size and duration of a project are critical considerations when making key decisions on desired management system characteristics.

Because of the complexity of long duration, high cost projects, it is not surprising when it takes six months to develop a detailed plan for accomplishing the project objectives. Smaller projects often do not have a total of six months duration. This does not suggest that the smaller project needs no plan, but rather that it will have a less detailed plan featuring the same general requirements. Similarly, it will not make sense to set up an elaborate monthly reporting scheme with variance analysis reports and corrective action plans since the project will be completed before such a program can even be properly established. Variances still need to be identified and actions taken to correct them, but it will be a far less formal process, probably involving little documentation.

Risk is another important consideration and relates to maturity of the technology involved. If the project were the tenth in a long series of similar products or services, some simple indicators of progress over time may be all that is required. But if it were the development of a new technology, greater detail will be needed for monitoring and managing progress against the goal.

The project contract environment may impact the emphasis of controls. On a firm fixed price contract, cost monitoring and evaluation is typically not emphasized by the customer. However, the contractor will be very cost conscious, since it is responsible for any overruns when this contract type is used. From a customer's perspective, technical and schedule considerations are also very important for firm fixed price contracts with its support contractors, especially on a multiple contractor program as the interfaces between contractors and projects must be managed. Productivity may still be a concern since it will relate to whether the schedule can be met. In a cost reimbursable environment, cost controls are a paramount consideration since the contractor can maximize income by increasing the hours required to complete the work. The level of detail for cost and schedule control systems will vary in detail accordingly.

The level of management involvement is another contributing factor to decisions regarding implementation detail. In many cases, both owner/customer and contractor will have their own systems for determining project status. The contractor responsible for accomplishing the work will need a detailed system. However, the owner/customer should need a far less involved reporting system and could track progress on a higher level. There are exceptions to this as well. If the owner/customer were hiring the labor for the project and operating in a hands-on management situation, then detailed controls may be needed in the owner's/customer's organization.

Common sense and reason must be used when developing and implementing Earned Value Management Systems. Implementing systems at too low a level of detail and with unnecessary complexity has probably caused nearly as many problems as having no system at all. While that may be a slight exaggeration to make a point, the objective of improved visibility can be clouded just as easily by too much data (and not enough information) as it can by lacking enough input.

Earned Value Management System Recognition

The techniques developed and explained throughout this text were implemented widely only after it became apparent that they were necessary. They have not always been enthusiastically embraced by all project participants for various reasons. Some do not want extra visibility into the status of their work if that same information is in the hands of their boss and/or their customer. Typically, managers prefer to attempt resolution of problems before they are discovered by others. While this is understandable from a human nature standpoint, it is entirely unacceptable from a project manager's viewpoint. If problems are hidden and not satisfactorily resolved, they will later have increasingly substantial impacts to project cost and schedule. It is essential that the project manager has the information and tools to assess status accurately, allowing more rapid, effective management decisions.

The Earned Value Management Process

Successful management of a project involves many concepts and implementation concerns. A project is any endeavor that has a well under-

stood statement of work and optimistic, yet achievable, schedule and cost targets. An Earned Value Management System is a tool set used to facilitate management of a project. There are many considerations in this complex discipline. A series of flowcharts are used throughout the text to exhibit how the various chapters interrelate.

The master flowchart is shown in Figure 1-8, "Earned Value Project Management: The Process". This chart is repeated at the beginning of each chapter to show where that chapter fits in the overall process. Individual blocks will be expanded as necessary into lower level, more detailed flowcharts for the more involved topics. This will help assure that a proper understanding of each concept is achieved.

The fundamental concept of this entire book is that the Earned Value Management process should be logical, well-defined, and integrate all of the pertinent information relating to a project's status into a comprehensive picture. Every organization implements many of the concepts; few of them integrate those concepts into a unified status. That is the primary challenge: to use all of the tools in the tool box in a coordinated manner so that they meet the objective of improved project visibility, allowing earlier management decisions based on accurate information. This provides a project manager the best opportunity to meet project schedule and cost objectives while achieving the technical requirements.

The following is an overview of the process steps in Figure 1-8.

The Process Steps

Step 1 – Project Objectives

The first step in the process is definition of the project objectives. These objectives include a general description of the technical requirements of the project, its budget, and the time frame for the work to be completed. A targeted starting date and a completion date are included in this description. There may even be some guidance provided as to whether this is a technical, schedule and/or cost critical project. These can be critical pieces of information: as an example, at one

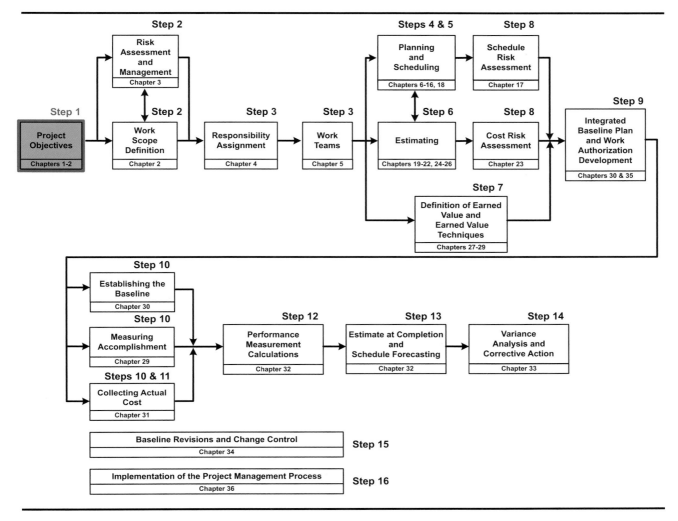

Figure 1-8 Earned Value Project Management: The Process

of the major auto manufacturers a project to design a new bumper system was being initiated. The time for this product to reach the market was critical, with a goal of eight and a half months. However, the contractor's project manager assumed that the project was more cost critical than schedule critical. This resulted in the project plan being stretched to 18 months to lower the peak cost requirements.

When the owners and customers reviewed the contractor's plan, they realized that the primary objectives had not been explained clearly enough. The contractor was sent back to completely redo the plan to support the eight and a half-month requirement. If this project had been managed to the 18-month plan, it would have lost much of its commercial appeal.

The project plan is the set of documentation and directives that formalize the entire management process described in this text, including project objectives, general scope, project organization, desired schedule/cost goals, and a description of management systems and procedures to be used in completing the project. The project plan reflects the project specific internal as well as customer management, reporting, and analysis requirements. The approach used to code and organize the project data is an important up front activity to establish a standard approach to integrate the technical, schedule, cost, and risk data to generate reliable information for effective management, reporting, and analysis for the life of the project.

Step 2 – Work Scope Definition, Risk Assessment and Management

Once the project objectives have been defined, the next function that must be fulfilled is to delineate, capture, and define the entire scope of the project. This is the best opportunity to assure understanding among the various project participants. It also is the best chance to avoid later nightmares with numerous scope changes and possible litigation. The work breakdown structure (WBS) and work breakdown structure dictionary are the tools used to segregate the work into manageable components and to define each component.

A risk assessment of the technical goals is an important part of this process. Risks are identified and mitigation plans are developed. After the organization is assigned in Step 3, additional risks may be identified and the risk plans updated.

Step 3 – Responsibility Assignment, Work Teams

Once the scope is crisply defined, the next step is to document who is responsible for the work. Each component of work defined in the work breakdown structure will have one individual assigned who will be responsible for the scope, schedule and budget for that work.

It takes an entire project team working together to make the project a success, but only a single individual to cause it to fail. This explains some of the reason for the growing popularity of work teams that help break down the traditional barriers between functional work areas (i.e. departments which can also include subcontractors) and encourage a team spirit.

Work teams are composed of the functional elements necessary to develop or produce the end product. This work team structure has advantages in that fewer management accounts are needed, there is improved communication and efficiency, and potential risks often are surfaced earlier.

Step 4 – Planning

Once the work definition and organizational concerns have been addressed, the particulars of the Earned Value Management process must be developed. These include the functions of scheduling, estimating, budgeting, and performance measurement. These elements must all be performed and integrated for the baseline plan to be developed.

Step 5 – Planning and Scheduling

The scheduling process is defined as what must be done, and when it must be done, to accomplish the project objectives on time.

Step 6 – Estimating

The estimating process is defined as a forecast of how much it will cost to perform the work.

Step 7 – Definition of Earned Value and Earned Value Techniques

Determining performance measurement is accomplished through the use of Earned Value techniques, which is the key concept of the entire Earned Value Management process. While this definition has been given earlier, it is important enough to repeat here. It provides a critical element of information when project status is assessed by providing insight to what has actually been accomplished for the money that has been spent. This can also be compared with what was planned to be accomplished to allow an accurate picture of the current cost and schedule position.

Earned Value is determined through numerous techniques. The techniques selected for a project will depend on each application, but objective guidelines are available to help the selection process.

Step 8 – Schedule and Cost Risk Assessment

A topic of growing importance is that of risk assessment. This Earned Value Management process includes three components: technical risk, schedule risk, and cost risk. Each of these has its own considerations and impacts. Like the overall Earned Value Management process, these are also interrelated. There has been some tendency over the years for managers to ignore the possibilities of identifying and especially quantifying risk because the results may be disconcerting. However, ignoring risk does not lessen its impact, and will most likely increase its effects. As profit margins become slimmer in a highly competitive environment, the topic of risk assessment must be addressed.

Step 9 – Integrated Baseline Plan and Work Authorization Development

Next we come to the center of the flowchart for a concept that is central to the overall process: performance measurement baseline development. The performance measurement baseline is the official, documented plan that shows in detail how the project objectives are to be achieved. All of the activities described thus far and the processes displayed on the Figure 1-8 flowchart are needed to achieve a well-planned performance measurement baseline. At the completion of this step, the technical, schedule, and budget baselines have been established and integrated; the schedule reflects the time frame where all of the detailed work scope is planned to be performed and the budgets are time phased based on the schedule requirements. The work is authorized to the responsible manager and the technical work commences.

Subcontract management is a critical element for many projects. The subcontractor's technical, schedule, and budget baseline must be integrated with the prime contractor baseline. Since the integrated baseline must include this element, a separate chapter on subcontract management (Chapter 35), is included in this step.

Step 10 – Establishing the Baseline Plan, Measuring Progress

At this point, there is a shift from the planning phase of baseline establishment to the control phase of the Earned Value Management process. Once the performance measurement baseline has been established, the main concern from that point on is the determination of progress. Progress is measured using the same earned value techniques that were established as part of the planning process. The techniques used when the performance measurement baseline (PMB) was established must be applied consistently when progress is determined. Progress is compared with the plan, and this comparison, in turn, provides the schedule variance.

Step 11 – Collecting Actual Costs

All projects will have a system for collection of actual costs. Regardless of how unsophisticated a system may be this component must be included. The challenge in this area is to define account structures that can be used for consistently comparing budgets, actuals, and performance. This could mean modification to existing accounting structures. Actual costs are necessary so that they can be compared with progress, and this comparison, in turn, provides the cost variance.

Step 12 – Performance Measurement Calculations

After progress is measured against the plan and the actual cost is entered, the three points necessary for data analyses are available. There are many calculations that aid in assessing the project status and assist the manager in targeting problem areas for corrective action. These calculations also assist in the Estimate at Completion and Variance Analysis reporting.

Step 13 – Estimate at Completion and Schedule Forecasting

Organizations are very concerned with bottom line performance. One of the essential pieces of corollary information needed to evaluate an ongoing project is, "When is it going to finish and what is it finally going to cost?" This answer will be used for many purposes, ranging from reward of project participants with better positions on new projects to project cancellation. The "Estimate at Completion" is so important that it can become a highly political number. A well-defined Earned Value Management System will have objective means of determining and evaluating estimates at completion to improve their accuracy even in the early stages of a project. This can only be achieved with defined performance factors that provide an accurate picture of what has happened to date and what is forecast to happen.

Step 14 – Variance Analysis and Corrective Action

Variance analysis and corrective action are very important to the overall process. Much time and effort are invested in baseline establishment, and now the baseline information can be used as a basis for determining the course of the project. The tools defined in the previous two Steps directly feed variance analysis and corrective action. By comparing earned value to budget, schedule variances can be determined. By comparing earned value to actual cost, cost variances can be determined. The second element, corrective action, is a critical part of the control phase. At this point in the process, there is a strong basis for determining the project's true position versus the approved plan so that exceptions can be addressed. The carefully defined system will provide immediate feedback as to whether the corrective action was successful.

Step 15 – Baseline Revisions and Change Control

An essential aspect of the Earned Value Management process is managing change. After all of the effort that goes into developing the baseline plan and determining current status, it is always a disruption to change that plan. Nevertheless, changes are a part of every project and must be addressed as to how they will be reviewed, approved, and incorporated into the plan. Procedures are required to manage the change control process or, over time, the project's reports will relate less and less to the current scope, schedule, and budget as well as the true status. One guideline stipulates that as much attention is needed for processing baseline changes as was used in developing the original baseline plan.

Step 16 – Implementation of the Project Management Process

Now that the system design is complete, there are still some ways to streamline the information flow. These include topics such as paperless systems and electronic data integration. There are also programs available for automating much of the data reduction and analysis, with built-in sanity checks to catch obvious errors. These topics are discussed in the final chapter of this book.

Conclusion

A project is any endeavor that has a scope of work and optimistic yet achievable schedule and cost targets. A project is typically managed by a single individual known as a project manager, who must be able to coordinate a multi-functional team towards the achievement of all of the project objectives. One of the greatest needs of the project manager is accurate, reliable, and timely information to enable effective management decisions. The information needs to include a valid assessment of project progress and status. Projects were historically monitored by comparing planned expenditures against actual expenditures.

This approach lacks the most important element of status: a measure of work accomplished. This shortcoming can be overcome by including a third data element that determines an objective value of work completed. This is known as the performance oriented approach. The performance oriented approach allows early identification of trends that indicate if a project's objectives are in jeopardy. This "early warning system" allows a timely response on the part of management to mitigate unfavorable outcomes by making informed decisions.

It is important that the tradeoff between adequate project status visibility and excessive data collection be recognized and addressed. This is accomplished by setting an appropriate level of detail in the implementation process. Factors that affect level of detail include project size and duration, risk (technical, schedule and cost), type of contract, and desired level of management involvement.

The entire process of managing projects must be a logical one. Each of the steps of the Earned Value Management process is illustrated by the flowchart in Figure 1-8 and will be discussed in detail in subsequent chapters.

Chapter 1 Review Questions

1-1. Explain the difference between a project and a program.

1-2. What aspects of a project are managed during the controlling phase of Earned Value Management?

1-3. How is a project organized differently from a functional organization?

1-4. What are some frequent causes of project delays?

1-5. Why is a comparison of actual costs to date versus budgeted costs not adequate from an Earned Value Management standpoint?

1-6. List at least three factors that will affect the level of detail appropriate for implementation of earned value on a project.

True or False

1-7. The Earned Value Management process is only applicable for large projects.

1-8. The fact that more money has been spent at a point in time than was planned to be spent means that an overrun in final cost is indicated.

1-9. A program may be made up of multiple projects.

1-10. Performance measurement can be successfully applied in engineering, construction, manufacturing, and software development applications, among others.

1-11. Using a measure of performance allows earlier indication of potential increases in final cost.

1-12. From the customer's viewpoint, a firm fixed price contract suggests the need for tight cost controls.

The answers to these questions can be found in Section 6, Solutions.

Chapter 2

DEFINITION OF SCOPE, WORK BREAKDOWN STRUCTURE (WBS) AND WBS DICTIONARY

Objectives of this Chapter:

1. Explain the three aspects of project objectives (technical performance, schedule, and cost), and illustrate these with an example.

2. Define the Work Breakdown Structure (WBS) and its application in work scope definition.

3. Provide guidance in developing an effective WBS.

4. Provide examples of sample WBS content for various types of applications/projects.

5. Explain the WBS Dictionary and its role in defining the scope of each WBS element.

Project objectives and the scope of work form the basis of a project. Project objectives are the key parameters that must be achieved for the project to be considered successful. Project objectives address technical, schedule, and cost aspects of the project. Often, one of the three parameters must be compromised to meet the other two. For example, to meet a certain schedule objective, more resources may be required which causes the cost objective to become unachievable. Similarly, to meet both cost and schedule, key technical parameters may have to be compromised. Work scope is the written definition of the project's technical parameters. Work scope can be included in a Technical Specification, Statement of Work, Project Plan, and combinations of documents. Work scope and project objectives are typically defined by the customer and documented in the Request for Proposal and/or contract documentation. An effective Earned Value Management system uses the key external inputs of work scope and project objectives as the foundation of the planning process. Conversion of the contractual project objectives and work scope into logical and manageable units of work consti-

tutes the work definition process of the Earned Value Management system.

The work definition process consists of three steps. The first step is the creation of a technical statement of work that includes the technical objectives of the project and defines the specifications and major work products. In many cases, the customer has provided specifications, and development of the technical statement of work is the consolidation of all of the customer's requirements into a form that can be communicated to all of the project participants. The technical statement of work is used as the starting point for the second step which is developing a Work Breakdown Structure (WBS). The WBS logically displays subdivisions of the complete project into smaller, more manageable, pieces of work. Finally, the third step is preparation of a WBS Dictionary to define the work included within each WBS element. The WBS Dictionary serves as the specific statement of the project scope for each WBS element. Further, the WBS and the WBS Dictionary serve as structure that will be used to budget the work, collect and report earned value, and collect actual cost. A WBS

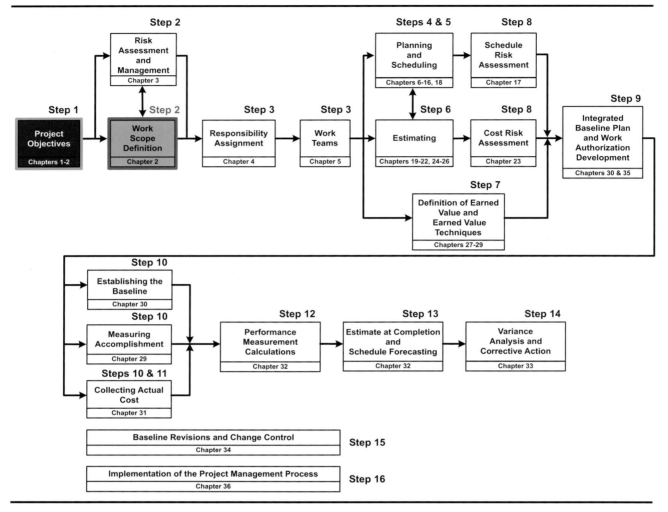

Figure 2-1 Earned Value Project Management: The Process

integrates technical scope, schedule and budget, and a WBS Dictionary documents the scope of work.

An important consideration in determining the proper level of detail for the WBS is technical, schedule, and cost risk. Risk is discussed in Chapters 3, 17 (schedule), and 23 (cost).

Defining Project Objectives

Before work scope can be defined, the project objectives must be known. The first and most critical objectives are the technical objectives that define what the project is required to produce or accomplish. Examples of technical objectives are:

Mission:

Design a new automobile that combines economy with high performance.

Objectives:

Fuel economy = 20 mpg for the city and 28 mpg on highways.

Acceleration = 0-60 miles per hour in less than 8.0 seconds.

Range without refueling = 500 miles.

Braking distance at 50 miles per hour = 110 feet (on dry pavement, excluding driver reaction time).

Seat 4 passengers.

The above items constitute the customer's technical objectives, and it should be easy to verify whether each of these has actually been met. In most U.S. Department of Defense (DoD) projects, the systems engineering process is instituted to manage and track the technical objectives. Therefore, the WBS definition process in the Earned Value Management system works in tandem and integrates with the systems engineering process. While the technical objectives described above provide a starting point for the design team, a technical concept must be developed. Lower level attributes of the technical concept might include seemingly obvious items such as the number of wheels, number of cylinders in the engine, or key components that may be purchased from a supplier. Additionally, the technical concept should identify subsystems or components of the end item that the project will produce.

During the development of the technical concept, trade-offs among the technical objectives are considered. Some of these trade-offs address competing objectives, such as fuel economy and acceleration. To achieve the fuel economy, it may be difficult to provide the power needed. If fuel economy were the prime objective, then acceleration may have to be modified. If performance is the main concern, then fuel economy and range without refueling may be affected. The key point is that the customer's technical objectives must be converted into internal work scope documentation that describes the project's end item in terms meaningful to the design team, estimators, schedulers, and managers who plan the project. Once the objectives are defined and understood, it is possible to begin defining the scope of work.

In addition to the technical work scope, it is important to understand schedule and cost objectives. The customer's schedule objective may be as simple as specifying a project completion date. During development of the internal work scope, definition of intermediate schedule objectives is useful in the planning process. Intermediate schedule objectives include items such Preliminary Design Review, Critical Design Review, Fabrication Completion, Integration & Assembly Completion, Testing Completion, End Item Completion. These intermediate schedules objectives help planners organize the scope of work tasks into the appropriate time frame as well as time phasing cost estimates/budgets. Cost objectives, such as the total project cost or the end item cost are useful for conducting trade-off analyses.

The Work Breakdown Structure (WBS)

The Work Breakdown Structure (WBS) is the tool in Earned Value Management that organizes and defines the work scope. The WBS is typically displayed as a tree diagram, similar to a family tree. Each level of the WBS can have many elements; however, elements must sum to only one higher level element. The WBS should reflect a product-oriented logical subdivision of products, equipment, services and all other tasks, and it should contain all work being performed on the project. The WBS serves as a common framework for cost and schedule planning as well as definition of work scope.

The work scope defined in the internal work scope documentation provides the basis for WBS elements. For example, if the work scope documentation defines three subsystems within the end item, each of these subsystems should become a WBS element under the end item WBS element. In U.S. Department of Defense projects, the systems engineering process defines hardware and software configuration items. Defining configuration items in the WBS provides an excellent basis for a product-oriented breakdown and ensures integration with the systems engineering process.

The WBS elements should progressively decompose the work scope until manageable units of work are defined. A manageable unit of work is a task that can be assigned to a responsible organization. For example, consider a "leg" of the WBS that consists of a system, subsystem, sub-subsystem, and configuration item. The configuration item will require work effort from mechanical engineering, design & drafting, and manufacturing. The configuration item is a logical level to terminate the WBS decomposition because control accounts can be assigned to each of the responsible organizations for their respective work efforts within the configuration item.

One of the common misapplications of a WBS is to use it to reflect the organization assigned to accomplish the work rather than the work itself. The WBS is not an organization chart of the project team. The project team is represented within an Organizational Breakdown Structure (OBS) or simply by an organization chart. It is important to remember that a WBS displays what the work is, not who is to accomplish that work.

Considerations in Developing a WBS

The WBS includes the following characteristics:

1. Is product-oriented.

2. Includes all work: equipment, hardware, software and services, and each element logically aggregates those below it.

3. Supports historical cost collection for future cost estimating purposes.

If these guidelines are not followed, the WBS will not be an effective project management tool.

In any type project, it is always a challenge to maintain the proper level of detail in a WBS for effective project control. Many examples illustrate how WBS structures can go far beyond the necessary or even useful level. One nuclear power project featured a 13-level WBS, with level 12 consisting of detail such as individual pieces of office furniture and level 13 being individual drawers in a desk!

Initial implementation of a WBS can easily get out of control. The progression that frequently occurs within an organization implementing its first WBS is resistance to the concept, followed by understanding of its potential use, to breaking down the work as low as it can possibly be done. The logic was that if level 5 were good then level 6 is twice as good. This is considered illogical thinking because it may drive the cost of the system up exponentially.

It is not apparent, when creating that first WBS, just how much extra effort is involved with each additional level of detail. The effort escalates for developing it, for defining the scope of the accounts, and for later cost collection and variance analysis. By the time the extra cost is evident, it may be too late to redo the structure. At that point, it is easy to draw the wrong conclusion that the WBS concept is flawed or not cost effective, when in it was the implementation that was flawed.

Also, it should be noted that different legs of the WBS need not be defined to the same level of detail.

WBS Examples

A Work Breakdown Structure can be used to define any scope of work. The highest level, identified as Level 1, is the total project. It is the summarization point for all of the detailed information (technical scope, schedule, and cost) collected and analyzed at the lower levels. Level 1 defines total project scope while Level 0 may be used to summarize a total program or company with multiple projects. Level 2 represents the major subdivisions of the project.

An example is shown in Figure 2-2.

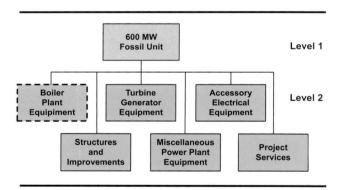

Figure 2-2 600 Megawatt WBS

For construction of a power plant, Level 2 items might include categories such as Structures and Improvements (which would include all buildings and associated civil work), Boiler Plant Equipment, Project Services, Turbine Generator Equipment, Miscellaneous Power Plant Equipment, and Accessory Electrical Equipment. Because of their size, Boiler and Turbine associated work are individually categorized rather than being included with "Miscellaneous Power Plant Equipment" or "Accessory Electrical Equipment."

These are the two most expensive individual items in such a plant and are critical to the schedule of designing or constructing any electric generating station. Project Services support all of the other identified areas, and consequently, can logically be tracked separately rather than prorated arbitrarily across the other Level 2 elements.

Each of these Level 2 elements should then be further subdivided logically according to the work components that comprise it. As an example, "Boiler Plant Equipment" in Level 2, might be broken down into Level 3 elements such as those shown in Figure 2-3.

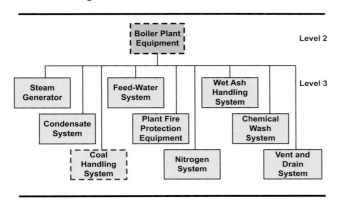

Figure 2-3 Boiler Plant Equipment WBS

Such subdivisions would continue until each element is represented by a scope of work that could be comfortably managed by a single responsible person. For the Level 3 "Coal Handling System", Level 4 could include items such those shown in Figure 2-4.

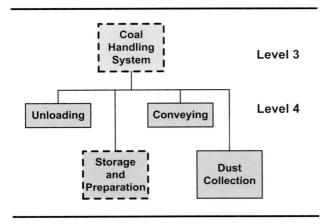

Figure 2-4 Coal Handling System WBS

Level 4 could be broken down further into Level 5, as shown in Figure 2-5, the further breakdown of the "Storage and Preparation" block.

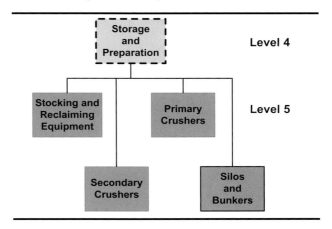

Figure 2-5 Storage and Preparation WBS

This level of detail is justified since the Level 5 WBS elements in this example still represent high dollar equipment items and significant work efforts that will require months of labor content. On smaller cost, shorter duration projects, five levels of detail could prove to be excessive.

The breakdown described here is not the only possible one but is an example.

The negotiations among project teams members to create and agree upon a WBS can range from straight forward to very frustrating. Any number of possible configurations can be made to work successfully, as long as the guidelines previously described are followed. At some point, the lowest practical level of WBS extension is reached. For the purpose of this example, the fifth level is the lowest level necessary.

A WBS can be generated for nearly any kind of effort. Examples of WBS applications to various types of projects are shown on the following pages.

They include an example of a sewer treatment plant (3 levels of detail) in the following Figure 2-6, a floor coverings WBS (3 levels) in Figure 2-7, a training and consulting WBS (2 levels) in Figure 2-8, a Department of Energy Summary WBS (Levels 1-3) with Contract WBS extended down to Levels 4-6 in Figure 2-9, and a software development WBS (5 levels) in Figure 2-10.

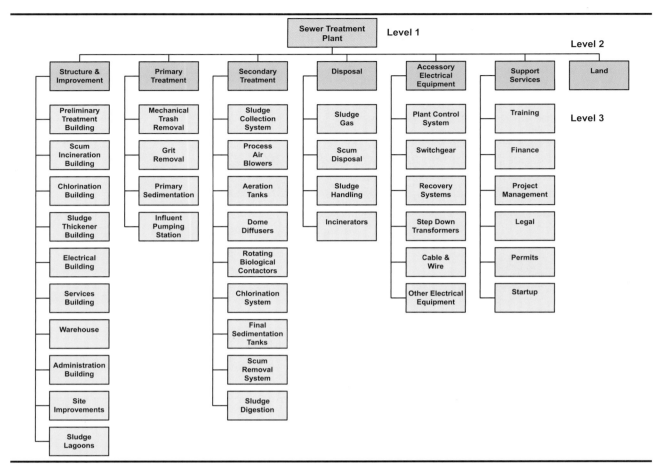

Figure 2-6 Sewer Treatment Plant WBS

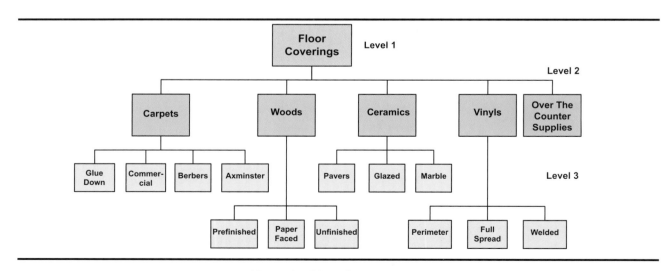

Figure 2-7 Floor Covering WBS

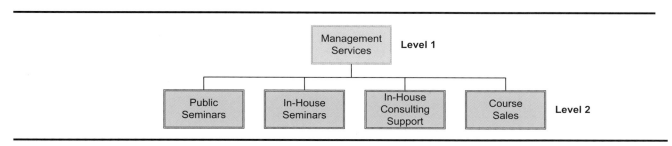

Figure 2-8 Consulting WBS

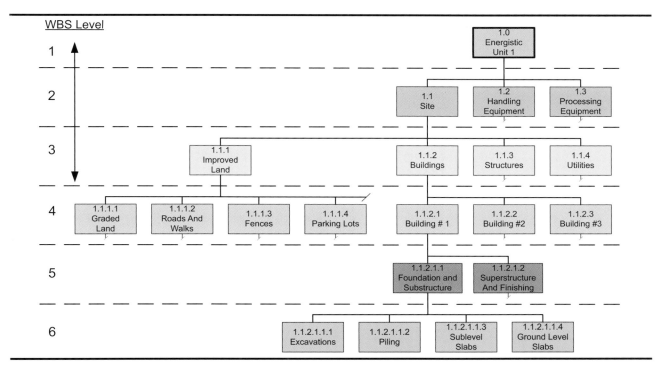

Figure 2-9 DOE Project Summary WBS

One point to remember is that the lowest appropriate level of detail is not consistent across the entire WBS. Each leg of the WBS should end at that level where it is appropriate to assign managerial responsibility related to the functional elements of work required to produce that particular product. Some Level 2 elements, such as project services, may need very little additional breakdown (if any).

Figure 2-10 illustrates a WBS for a software development project.

Figure 2-11 represents the situation when multiple software products ("builds") are required during the development process and each of these builds is a deliverable.

Figure 2-12 is a sample WBS structure that results when multiple builds are planned to support the development process, but they are not deliverables. Notice that the number of required levels in the WBS decreases by one. The term "control account" shown in Figures 2-11 and 2-12 will be explained in Chapter 4, "Relating Organizations, Responsibility, and Work Scope."

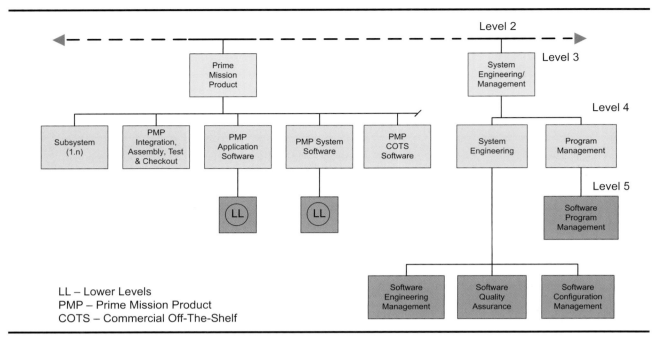

LL – Lower Levels
PMP – Prime Mission Product
COTS – Commercial Off-The-Shelf

Figure 2-10 Sample Project WBS Software Development Project

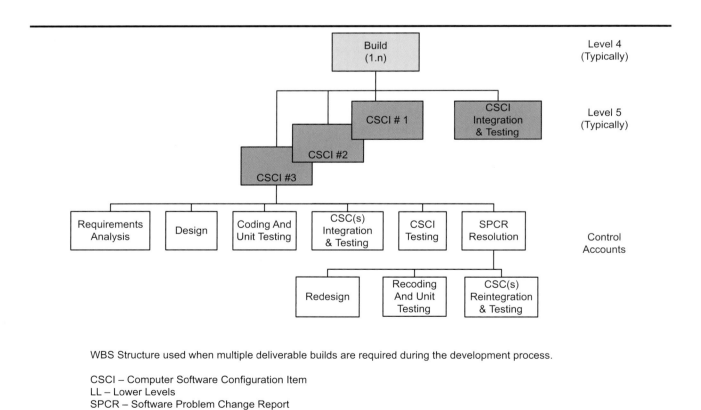

WBS Structure used when multiple deliverable builds are required during the development process.

CSCI – Computer Software Configuration Item
LL – Lower Levels
SPCR – Software Problem Change Report

Figure 2-11 Sample Project WBS Software Development Project details

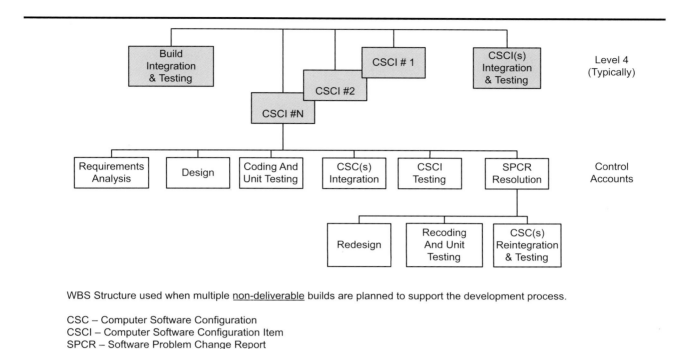

WBS Structure used when multiple <u>non-deliverable</u> builds are planned to support the development process.

CSC – Computer Software Configuration
CSCI – Computer Software Configuration Item
SPCR – Software Problem Change Report

Figure 2-12 Sample Project WBS

WBS Dictionary

Subdividing the total project scope of work within a WBS does not specifically define work. To ensure effective communication and mutual understanding among project team members, each WBS element must be described individually. This grouping of WBS element descriptions is the "WBS Dictionary." The WBS Dictionary is critically important to the success of scope definition and subsequent project control. The contract/project scope is what is referred to when discussing the scope of work. Because there is not always a one-for-one relationship between WBS elements and contract line items, it is very important to have the scope fully sorted and covered for each element of the WBS. Many organizations receive funds by contract line item. It may be that ten work scope statements are combined in a single WBS element or a single scope statement (or paragraph of scope in the contract) is subdivided into ten WBS elements. Consequently, the cross-referencing between the contract scope and the WBS elements in the WBS Dictionary becomes critical.

Matching the contract scope with the WBS Dictionary can be ensured by the owner/customer during the bidding and contracting process if the bid and subsequent contract includes a WBS Dictionary. This approach has many advantages, such as:

1. Easier for the owner/customer to evaluate bids. Bid values are truly comparable by line item since each entry is based on the same scope boundaries.

2. Promotes better understanding between the contractor and owner/customer regarding the contract's scope.

3. Guarantees the early availability of the WBS and Dictionary, which also expedites earlier detailed planning.

The WBS Dictionary contains the scope of work for each WBS element. This is preferable to having an independent work scope that allows for the possibility of a mismatch to the WBS. Mismatches between these elements can lead to situations ranging from the humorous to very serious. On one major maintenance project, the same work was to be performed on two identical units. Because of confusion on scope, only one unit was bid by one of the bidders. The exact opposite situation occurred on a bid for construction of two new petrochemical facilities. The estimate for equipment was prepared for two units, but assigned as a single number to a WBS element that was not well defined. When the overall proposal coordinator saw the number, the assumption was made that it was for a single unit and the value was doubled. The resulting mismatch made that bid the high bid.

Both of these errors would have been quickly noticed if a WBS Dictionary that defined the scope and boundaries for each element had been in place.

The WBS Dictionary thus becomes a valuable tool in documentation of the scope for each element. The dictionary also aids in the careful identification of those closely related items that have not been included in that WBS element. An example of a WBS element description from a WBS Dictionary is shown in Figure 2-13. Note that it identifies the element title and number, the project name and contract, the element to which it is summarized, and a description of the scope of work, including boundaries.

These descriptions should be prepared by the responsible technical person in conjunction with a representative from the Earned Value Manage-ment organization. The representative is necessary as technical people may not be familiar with the requirements of WBS Dictionary development and content. Since the task of creating a WBS dictionary may not be their highest priority, some mechanism is needed to ensure consistency among the descriptions prepared by different departments or organizations.

Other Considerations in WBS Development

Why must the WBS be product-oriented? With the product orientation in the first example, Boiler Plant Equipment and Turbine Plant Equipment were shown to be two of the logical Level 2 WBS elements. This distinction is appropriate since questions relating to the status of the project will inevitably demand a status of the boiler and turbine areas.

If a cost-element orientation, such as that shown in Figure 2-14 had been used, a fragmentation of the boiler and turbine status to multiple control accounts would result. Summarizing status for these two key areas of the project would become difficult or impossible because data would be added from numerous element of cost legs to obtain a total status for a subset of a project

Contract Work Breakdown Structure Dictionary		Project: Sewer Teatment "A"	Ref No. 1.3.6 Contract No. M12	Date: 5/18/Year01
Levels of CWBS	CWBS Elements	CWBS Definition		
3	Chlorinating System	This element includes the mechanical equipment within the Chlorine room, including evaporators, chlorinators, contact tanks, flash mechanical mixers, and effluent water pumps. It also includes the individual equipment foundations and interconnecting piping and associated valves and pipe supports/hangers. Related Work Excluded: Chlorination Building (element 1.2.5), electrical connections (element 1.7.5) and hydrostatic testing of pipe (element 1.5.5).		

Figure 2-13 CWBS Dictionary and Contract

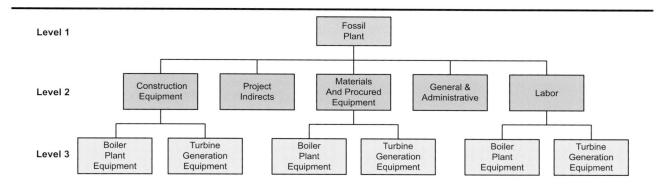

This figure illustrates a work breakdown structure organized around elements of cost. Note that the Boiler Plant Equipment is contained in three places in this WBS, therefore causing the necessity of adding items together across the WBS to reach the total cost related to one product. A WBS should not be constructed this way.

Figure 2-14 Element of Cost Orientation

(such as Boiler Plant Equipment). If an organizational orientation were used WBS and organization structure contain redundant information. It is easy to get status by organization through the matrix of WBS to OBS and other functional cost reports. Therefore, no added value accrues from having an organizationally structured WBS.

If the project under consideration has multiple phases, it may be necessary to structure the WBS by phase. This allows the WBS to be properly oriented for all phases. An example can be seen in any project that includes engineering, design, Research and Development, construction, or manufacturing. Work in the design phase is accomplished by system (e.g. guidance system, propulsion system, heating and ventilation system). However, when the project shifts to construction or production the system orientation no longer makes sense for management of the effort since construction and production are organized by physical plant area (e.g. west wing of a hospital, mid-fuselage of an airplane, rear of a motor scooter).

The changing emphasis from system to phase can be accommodated by having a different WBS for each phase of the project. This allows the engineering and start-up work to be managed in the same way that it is performed and allows production and construction work to do the same. This is done in practice by beginning with the first subdivision of a total project into phases with separate major legs of a structure built around each phase, as in Figure 2-15.

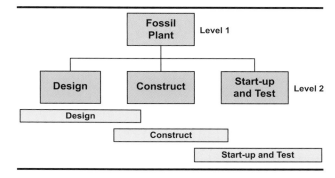

Figure 2-15 Phase Orientation

It may be possible to use the same leg for design, start-up, and test since they are accomplished on a system basis.

Can a single WBS be used for all project phases? Yes, but not without major compromises in selecting WBS elements. One multi-year engineering contract required the combining of all project phases in a single WBS. The results were predictable. Neither engineering nor production were satisfied with the final product.

In many cases, an element was included because of the needs of one participant while a counterpart argued that such an element was meaningless. They were both right. A single WBS element that was too large for production effort could be too small for engineering effort. There were examples where a single WBS element contained $50 million of material, $10 million of production labor, and $2,000 of engineering cost. It cost more than $2,000 for engineering to keep track of the paperwork, and production clearly needed a much more detailed breakdown to effectively control its work.

These are challenges that inevitably occur when "force fitting" different types of work into the same structure. Of course, the WBS still includes the entire project, but Level 2 may define the phases of the project while Level 3 breaks the work down in accordance with how it is to be performed.

An engineering or design WBS will differ from a production/construction WBS, as has been illustrated. The next examples illustrate the engineering WBS. The corresponding construction examples were presented in Figures 2-2 through 2-5. The design/engineering example shown in Figure 2-16 has a notably different Level 2 than the first example in this chapter for construction (Figure 2-2).

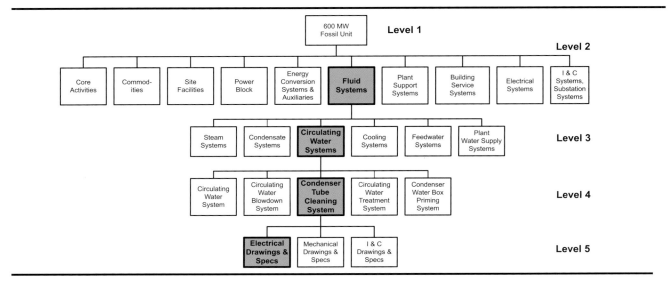

Figure 2-16 Engineering/Design WBS

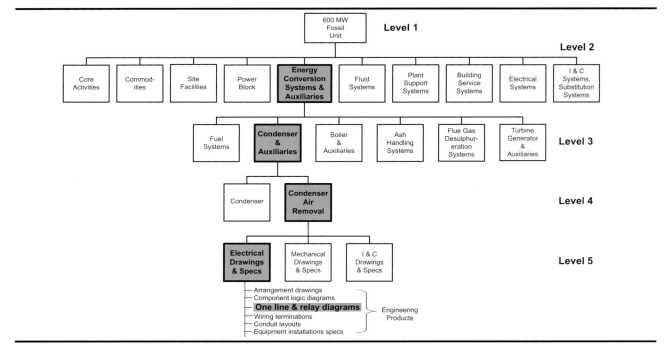

Figure 2-17 Engineering/Design WBS

The Level 2 block that is subdivided further in Figure 2-16 is "Fluid Systems". This refers to all of the piping and mechanical systems on the project. The Level 3 block, "Circulating Water System", was selected for the example for further breakdown at Level 4 and so on. The lowest level would consist of the detailed work products such as drawings and specifications in an engineering phase oriented WBS.

Another similar example is shown for another leg of the engineering WBS. In the example shown in Figure 2-17, the Level 2 element "Energy Conversion Systems & Auxiliaries" is subdivided into more detail. The lowest WBS element would likely be the "Condenser Air Removal" block at Level 4, with the items listed below being part of the WBS element description in the WBS Dictionary. The engineering work products (as listed) should be visible in the Dictionary.

There is one other issue that should be addressed as separate legs in the WBS are created for engineering and construction/production. If these legs are not integrated in the same WBS elements, how is the interface going to be managed? Construction (or manufacturing) packaging must be implemented.

Simply stated, the work products in design or engineering are "mapped" to the construction contracts that they must support. An example is shown in Figure 2-18. The work products listed would include technical specifications, equipment lists, design drawings, engineering system descriptions and associated studies. This assumes that there are multiple contracts that need to be supported.

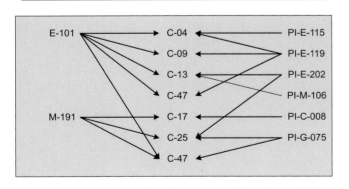

Figure 2-18 Product - User Mapping

If there were only a single contract (i.e. a general contractor), then the mapping would be done to production or construction WBS elements. In either case, this cross-referencing is necessary from a scheduling standpoint to ensure that all of the required design products will be available when needed in the manufacturing or construction process.

The Contract Work Breakdown Structure (CWBS)

The CWBS developed and used by the contractor for the management of the contract scope of work typically extends the higher level program WBS supplied by the owner or customer. The CWBS must support the higher level WBS that was provided without any allocation of costs to two or more summary level WBS elements.

Scope Verification

Many ways exist to verify that all scope has been included within the appropriate project documents. Most of these verifications consist of crosschecks. One check includes comparing the statement of work to the WBS, to the WBS Dictionary, and schedule activities. Another check verifies the estimates against the schedule activities, or compares the WBS Dictionary products against the products estimated. In an integrated system, all components must be related to each other.

Another important consideration is that there is consistent understanding between the contractor and the owner/customer regarding the scope. This can be accomplished during the establishment of the schedule baseline (Chapter 12) and the performance measurement baseline (Chapter 30). However, an earlier opportunity exists to achieve this understanding. At the time of bid submittal the understanding can be reached if the bids are required to be broken down in a manner consistent with the highest levels of the WBS. This is one of the fastest ways to verify the bidders' understanding of the scope. While this may seem to be an unlikely scenario, it is not uncommon to find an element that Bidder A estimates at $1 million, Bidder B estimates at $800,000, Bidder C bids $925,000, and Bidder D bids $0. Whatever it is, Bidder D should be contacted to find out why no estimate was included. Sometimes the answer is surprising, and is based on a wholly unsubstantiated assumption. This indicates an obvious misunderstanding of the intended scope.

In the example described, consider what happens if the bids are not submitted in detailed accounts. All four bidders submit their bottom line total cost and Bidder D wins the contract. When the baseline is being developed and approved, it becomes apparent that Bidder D did not accurately estimate the cited effort. The assumptions are explained, and Bidder D now believes that more budget (and funds) are required to incorporate this "scope change" that was not considered in the original bid. No matter how the dispute is resolved, the interface between contractor and the customer/owner is strained. Maintaining a positive interface is an important reason for having the bid submitted in detail. Obviously, the more important reason for this practice is to facilitate better evaluation and comparison of the bids.

The scenario described above occurred in the southwest United States. So-called "Bidder D" estimated zero dollars for software with the understanding it would be provided "by others". When Bidder D was told that software was indeed part of the scope of the contract, the bid was amended. Without the scope definition provided with a WBS Dictionary from the owner/customer, Bidder D may have received the contract solely because an important part of the contract scope had been omitted. Had no review of the proposed scope been conducted, the result would have later caused problems for both sides.

Conclusion

There are three major steps in defining the work for a project. The first step in planning a project is to define the project objectives. These objectives can include technical performance, schedule and cost. A technical statement of work is created that includes the technical objectives of the project and defines the specifications and the major work products. This is used for the second step, developing the Work Breakdown Structure.

The Work Breakdown Structure (WBS) logically displays subdivisions of the project into smaller, more manageable segments of work. The WBS is a product-oriented logical subdivision of products, equipment, services and all other tasks that comprise a project. The WBS is the framework for management of the project and is the common basis for cost and schedule planning as well as control of work scope.

The third step is preparation of the Work Breakdown Structure Dictionary. The Dictionary is used to define the work included in each WBS element. The scope of work is defined in detail and cross checked against the contract to ensure that all work has been included in the planning when establishing the baseline. The WBS Dictionary is a valuable communication tool for the program team and the customer/owner.

Chapter 2 Review Questions

2-1.   Describe the function of a Work Breakdown Structure (WBS).

2-2.   List guidelines to be considered when developing a WBS.

2-3.   Explain the role of the WBS Dictionary.

2-4.   Why does a WBS oriented by element of cost or organizational element cause problems when used for Earned Value Management?

2-5.   Identify methods for verifying that all scope has been included within the WBS.

True or False

2-6.   One approach to developing a WBS is to represent the organizations that will be performing the work.

2-7.   There is a high correlation between the level of detail within the WBS and the cost of maintaining an Earned Value Management system.

2-8.   It is acceptable to have multiple Work Breakdown Structures for a single project.

2-9.   A WBS Dictionary will usually include enough detail to list the individual work products.

2-10.   All project scope must be included within a WBS, including those activities that may not be directly identified to any particular work product.

The answers to these questions can be found in Section 6, Solutions.

2.1 WORK BREAKDOWN STRUCTURE PART 1

MOR-DED Motor Scooter Project

Background

The Army Tank and Automotive Command has issued a Request for Proposal (RFP) for the MOR-DED Project. This project includes the design, development and production of a new Army Standard Motor Scooter.

The RFP describes a two phased project. Phase A will be a Cost Plus Incentive Fee (CPIF) contract for the design, development, and production of 10 prototypes of the MOR-DED vehicle, associated support hardware and the necessary services. Phase B will be a Fixed Price Incentive (FPI) production contract for 10 lots of 2,000 vehicles each, support hardware and services. The current RFP requires a WBS for Phase A only.

Problem Statement

The Cushperson Corporation is responding to the MOR-DED RFP. A special team has been appointed to develop a Work Breakdown Structure (WBS) for inclusion in the proposal. You are a member of that team.

Your team is to prepare a recommended Work Breakdown Structure (WBS) for the MOR-DED Motor Scooter Project, Phase A. Attachment 1 is the MOR-DED Motor Scooter Work Statement (furnished by the Army in the RFP). Attachment 2 is the MOR-DED Hardware Breakdown. These attachments are furnished to help you develop the WBS. Also attached is a form for your use in preparing your WBS. The form includes the elements of the WBS furnished by the Army in the RFP.

1. Expand the furnished WBS to the levels that you think will be necessary to manage the Phase A contract.

2. Choose a team spokesperson to describe your WBS.

The solution to this case study can be found on the Humphreys & Associates, Inc. web site.
www.humphreys-assoc.com

ATTACHMENT 1
MOR-DED Motor Scooter Project
Work Statement

ITEM

Phase A

0001   Design, develop, fabricate, and test 10 prototype MOR-DED Motor Scooters in accordance with Specification USATA-78-754A, Revision 1.

0002   Develop and provide data in accordance with the contract requirements.

0003   Design, develop, fabricate and test 1 prototype Depot Test Set in accordance with specification USATA-78-763A, Revision 1.

0004   Provide all related Systems/Engineering Management required to meet the requirements of Reliability, Availability and Maintainability (RAM), Safety & Human Factors, Transportability, Weight analysis; and support all program reviews, Configuration Management, and Quality Assurance requirements.

Phase B

0005   Option Item - Fabricate and deliver MOR-DED Motor Scooters in accordance with technical specification accepted at the end of Phase A. The initial requirement is 10 lots of 2,000 each.

0006   Option Item - Furnish all supporting engineering services required for Configuration Item Verification Review (CIVR) and associated engineering functions. Furnish the necessary tooling and factory test equipment to produce Item 0005 above.

0007   Option Item - Fabricate and deliver Depot Maintenance Test Set equipment in accordance with technical specification accepted at the end of Phase A. The initial requirement is 50 sets.

0008   Option Item - Furnish Production data in accordance with the production contract requirements.

0009   Option Item - Furnish initial spare parts for item 0005 and 0007.

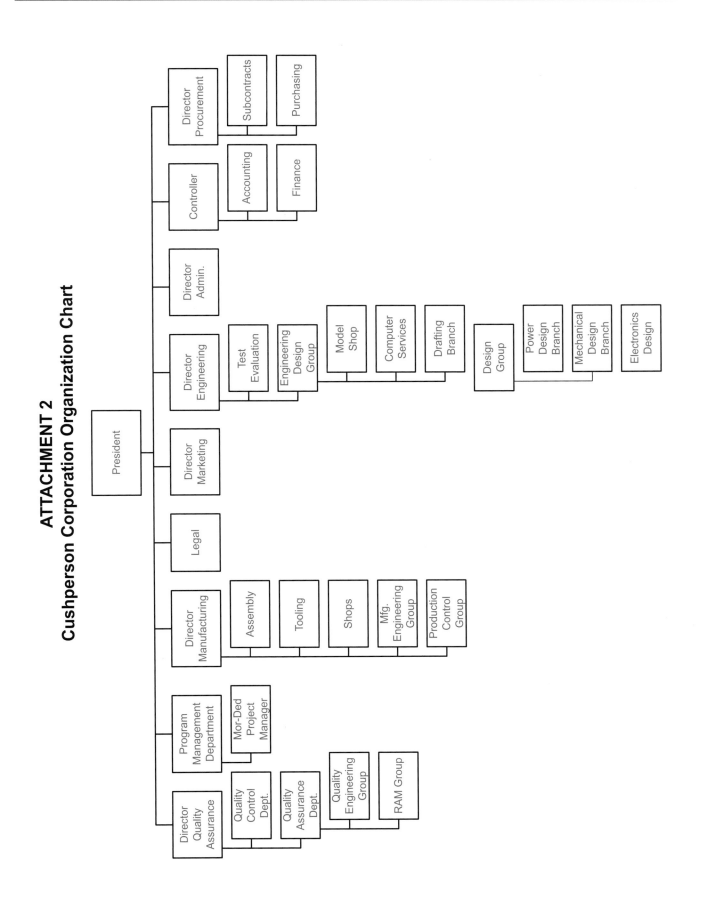

ATTACHMENT 2
Cushperson Corporation Organization Chart

ATTACHMENT 3 MOR-DED Vehicle Hardware Breakdown						
Part Level						
1	2	3	4	5	6	Title
X						Vehicle
	X					Power Source & Transmission
		X				Engine
			X			Engine Block Assembly
				X		Engine Block Head
				X		Engine Block
				X		Crank Shaft Assembly
				X		Piston/Rod Assembly
					X	Piston
					X	Rod Assembly
					X	Pin
				X		Valve Assemblies
				X		Cam Shaft
				X		Valve Covers
				X		Oil Pan
			X			Lubrication System
				X		Oil Pump Assembly
				X		Oil Lines
				X		Oil Filter Assembly
			X			Fuel-Air System
				X		Carburetor Assembly
				X		Air Filter Assembly
					X	Air Filter Structure
					X	Air Filter
				X		Fuel Filter
				X		Fuel Lines
			X			Ignition System
				X		Distributor Assembly
				X		Alternator
				X		Spark Plugs
				X		Ignition Wiring Harness
			X			Instrumentation
				X		Oil Pressure Gage Assembly
				X		Fuel Gage Assembly
				X		Speedometer
				X		Instrumentation Wiring Harness
		X				Power Transmission

ATTACHMENT 3 MOR-DED Vehicle Hardware Breakdown						
Part Level						
1	2	3	4	5	6	Title
			X			Clutch Assembly
				X		Clutch Body
				X		Pressure Plate
				X		Clutch Operator Controls
					X	Clutch Pedal
					X	Clutch Cable
			X			Transmission Assembly
				X		Transmission Housing
				X		Gear Train
				X		Transmission Housing Cover
				X		Transmission Operator Controls
					X	Transmission Selector Levers
					X	Transmission Levers
	X					Frame Assembly
		X				Frame
			X			Front Fork Attachment
			X			Upper Frame Structure
			X			Lower Frame Structure
			X			Seat Post Assembly
			X			Suspension Attachments
			X			Engine/Transmission Attachments
		X				Seat
		X				Fenders
			X			Fender Body
			X			Fender Attachment Rods
		X				Foot Pegs
	X					Suspension
		X				Shock Absorber Assemblies
		X				Wheels
			X			Rim
			X			Wheel Body
			X			Tire
			X			Valve
		X				Axles
		X				Steering Assembly
			X			Fork
			X			Handlebar

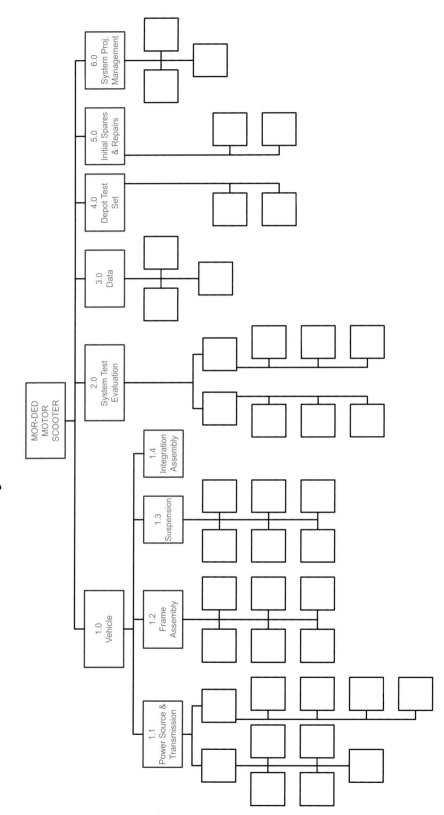

MOR-DED Project Work Breakdown Structure

2.2 WORK BREAKDOWN STRUCTURE PART 2

Automated Interdiction System (AIS) Workstation Project

Karen began to think about observing the results of her plans. She knew that cost data was collected by control account and that control accounts were grouped under Work Breakdown Structure (WBS) elements. Karen also knew that the WBS submitted with the proposal was not defined in sufficient detail to permit a meaningful analysis. The Coast Guard had provided two levels with the RFP, and TDS added one level in their proposal. Unsure of her latitude in extending the WBS, Karen called Broud Stearman and arranged a meeting.

Her meeting with Broud was enlightening. Broud agreed that the WBS had to be extended; he was unwilling to extend it by more than one level. Broud was convinced that too much granularity clouded perspective. Also, the availability of too much detail could result in problems with the customer. There was nothing to hide. On the other hand, Broud liked the law of large numbers in formal reporting.

Karen retrieved the Statement of Work (Attachment 1), the preliminary Configured Item Breakdown (Attachment 2), and the WBS (Attachment 3) submitted with the proposal. Several hours later Broud walked into Karen's office and offered to help with the extension - he also had a stake in the outcome of her work. Unfortunately, Broud was unfamiliar with software development activities.

Using the SOW, the preliminary Configured Item Breakdown and the preliminary WBS:

1. Expand the WBS to provide better visibility of progress.

2. Do you agree with Broud that the WBS should be extended by only one level?

3. How should multiple builds be handled?

4. Choose a spokesperson to present your results.

The solution to this case study can be found on the Humphreys & Associates, Inc. web site.
www.humphreys-assoc.com

ATTACHMENT 1
Automated Workstation
Statement of Work

ITEM

0001   Design, develop, fabricate and test twenty (20) Automated Workstation Consoles in accordance with specification.

0002   Design, develop and test Automated Workstation Software in accordance with specification. Includes Display Processor, Man-Machine Interface Processor and System as defined in the specification.

0003   Design, develop, fabricate and test one (1) Automated Workstation Test Set and associated operating software in accordance with the specification.

0004   Develop and deliver data in accordance with DD 1423.

0005   Provide project management functions required for the successful execution of the contract. Software management shall be reported separately to the Contacting Officer.

0006   Provide System engineering functions required for the successful execution of the contract. Software engineering management, software configuration management and software quality assurance shall be reported separately to the Contracting Officer.

0007   Provide all support functions required for the successful execution of the contract, including but not limited to, system specialty engineering and logistics support.

ATTACHMENT 2 Automated Workstation Configured Item Breakdown						
Part Level					Part Title	Make/Buy
1	2	3	4	5		
X					Automated Workstation	M
	X				Console	M
		X			Display Processor (DP)	M
			X		DP Hardware	M
				X	CRT Assembly	M
				X	DP Circuit Cards	M
				X	Card Drawer	M
				X	Console Harness	M
			X		DP CSCI	M
				X	DP Firmware	B
				X	DP Software	M
		X			Man-Machine Interface (MMI)	M
			X		MMI Hardware	M
				X	Trackball Assembly	B
				X	Joystick Assembly	B
				X	LCD Assembly	B
				X	Switch - Indicator Assembly	B
				X	Keyboard Assembly	B
				X	MMI Circuit Cards	M
			X		MMI CSCI	M
		X			Interface Processor (IP)	M
			X		IP Hardware	M
				X	Hard Disk Assembly	B
				X	CD-ROM Assembly	B
				X	IP Circuit Cards	M
			X		IP CSCI	M
		X			Subsystem Integration and Test	M
			X		Build Integration and Test	M
			X		CSCI Integration and Test	M
		X			System Software	M
			X		System Firmware	M
			X		System Software	M

ATTACHMENT 3
Work Breakdown Structure (WBS)

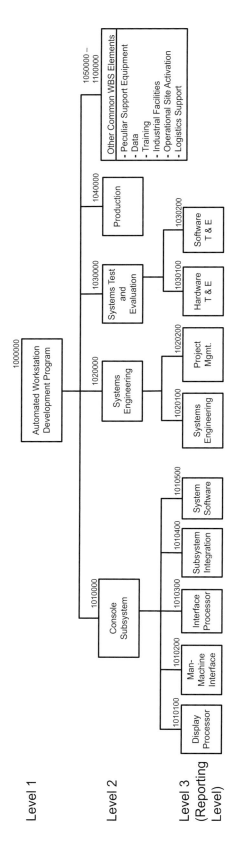

Case Study

2.3 WBS ELEMENT DESCRIPTION

The WBS Dictionary is being prepared to define the scope of work to be included within the WBS elements of an engineering work breakdown structure.

Five examples of scopes of work for engineering the extraction steam system for a coal fired electric generating station are attached for your review. Be prepared to comment on which one you think is most appropriate for defining WBS element scope, with reasons for your selection.

What changes in emphasis might there be if these were scopes of work for construction WBS elements instead of engineering?

The solution to this case study can be found on the Humphreys & Associates, Inc. web site.
www.humphreys-assoc.com

Example 1

WBS Element Title: Extraction Steam System	**WBS Element No:** 6.1.4
Parent WBS No: 6.1 **Parent WBS Title:** Steam System	**WBS Level:** 4
Project: 600 MW Fossil Unit	**Originator:** J. Jones

WBS Element Description:

The scope of this element includes all engineering and design effort required for the development of the extraction steam system.

Revision No:	**Page** 14
Revision Date:	**Of** 27

Example 2

WBS Element Title:	WBS Element No:
Extraction Steam System	6.1.4
Parent WBS No: 6.1	**WBS Level:**
Parent WBS Title: Steam System	4
Project:	**Originator:**
600 MW Fossil Unit	J. Jones

WBS Element Description:

The scope of this element includes all engineering work related to piping systems, mechanical equipment, electrical power, instrumentation and control for the extraction steam system. This includes determination of design pressures and temperatures, pipe sizes, wall thickness, pipe material, insulation requirements, pipe supports, and control schemes. The scope of this element includes all supporting studies and calculations used in determination of the previously mentioned design definition.

Related Work Excluded:
1. Associated supervision (included in WBS Element 3.16).
2. System Design Review (included in WBS Element 3.20).
3. Engineering input to schedule logic development (included in WBS Element 4.11).

Revision No:	**Page** 14
Revision Date:	**Of** 27

Example 3

WBS Element Title:	WBS Element No:
Extraction Steam System	6.1.4
Parent WBS No: 6.1 **Parent WBS Title:** Steam System	**WBS Level:** 4
Project: 600 MW Fossil Unit	**Originator:** J. Jones

WBS Element Description:

The scope of this element includes the engineering and design effort for the extraction steam system, as defined in the control element work products defined below.

System Descriptions
    SD101 - Extraction Steam.

Procurement Packages
    None.

Drawings
    Control Logic Diagram CLD101 - Extraction Line Control, LP and HP Heaters.
    Control Logic Diagram CLD102 - Extraction Line Control, Deaerator P&ID101 - Extraction Steam.
    Electrical Elementary Diagram EED101 - Extraction Line Control, LP & HP Heaters.
    Electrical Elementary Diagram EED102 - Extraction Line Control, LP & HP Deaerator.
    Piping Drawing PD101 - First, Second & Third Point Extraction Steam Piping.
    Piping Drawing PD102 - Fourth & Fifth Point Extraction Steam Piping.
    Piping Isometric PI101 - First, Second & Third Point Extraction Steam Isometric.
    Piping Isometric PI102 - Fourth & Fifth Point Extraction Steam Isometric.
    Pipe Supports PS101 - Supports for First, Second & Third Point Extraction Steam Piping.
    Pipe Supports PS102 - Supports for Fourth & Fifth Point Extraction Steam Piping.

Calculations
    Pressure drops for Extraction Steam Lines.

Related Work Excluded:
1. Associated supervision (included in WBS Element 3.16).
2. System Design Review (included in WBS Element 3.20).
3. Engineering input to schedule logic development and review (included in WBS Element 4.11).

Revision No:	**Page** 14
Revision Date:	**Of** 27

Example 4

WBS Element Title:	WBS Element No:
Extraction Steam System	6.1.4
Parent WBS No: 6.1	**WBS Level:**
Parent WBS Title: Steam System	4
Project:	**Originator:**
600 MW Fossil Unit	J. Jones

WBS Element Description:

The scope of this element includes all engineering work related to the extraction steam system piping from the cold reheat system to the first point heaters, from the intermediate pressure turbine stage to the second point heaters, from the intermediate pressure turbine exhaust to the deaerator and boiler feed pump turbines and auxiliary steam system, as well as from the turbine to the fourth point and fifth point heaters. The design conditions for first point extraction are 650º F, 675 psia; second point extraction 800º F, 300 psia; third point extraction 700º F, 160 psia; fourth point extraction 525º F, 75 psia; fifth point extraction 300º F, 25 psia.

Related Work Excluded:
    Condenser neck piping, included piping to the sixth and seventh point.

Revision No:	**Page** 14
Revision Date:	**Of** 27

Example 5

WBS Element Title:	WBS Element No:
Extraction Steam System	6.1.4
Parent WBS No: 6.1 **Parent WBS Title:** Steam System	**WBS Level:** 4
Project: 600 MW Fossil Unit	**Originator:** J. Jones

WBS Element Description:

The scope of this element includes the engineering and design effort for the extraction steam system, as defined in the WBS element work products defined below.

System Descriptions - 1, estimated 50 pages long.

Procurement Packages - 0.

Drawings - 73 Sheets, as broken down below.
- 15   sheets control logic diagrams
- 2   sheets P&ID
- 21   sheets elementary wiring diagrams
- 26   sheets piping - drawings
- 5   sheets piping isometrics
- 4   sheets pipe support drawings

Revision No:	**Page** 14
Revision Date:	**Of** 27

Chapter **3**

MANAGING PROJECT RISKS

Objectives of this Chapter:

1. Explain the Process Flow Diagram.

2. Define project risk management terms.

3. Explain the project risk management process.

4. Provide an example of a risk management document.

5. Describe risk management evaluation techniques.

6. Describe the importance of ongoing risk awareness.

Inherent in any undertaking is the issue of risk containment and responses to managing that risk in order to complete the undertaking with minimum disruption. Consider the analogy to a journey in an automobile. Prior to any journey, there is a plan for the route; provisions for adequate resources to complete the journey; along with provisions to observe speed limits, to wear seat belts, to have auto and trip insurance, and emergency tactics such as verifying that the spare tire is inflated. One might also arrange emergency phone contacts for family members and carry a list of medications and medical histories of those on the journey.

While the journey itself is the undertaking, identifying the attendant risk is also prudent; just in case. This chapter addresses the "Just in Case" part of an undertaking.

Introduction to Managing Project Risks

The topic of Risk Management is broad, pervasive and cuts across many human activities from investment to medicine. Often, when the initial attempt is made to apply its tenets to project management, the presumed beneficiaries and sometimes the practitioners can become bogged down and bewildered by both its terminology and some of its more sophisticated quantitative tools. Even the concept of "Risk" can be a challenge to explain fully. This may sometimes lead to the conclusion that the benefits are outweighed by the effort to conduct project risk management. On the other hand, the idea of "a risk" to a project's success is straightforward and project risks can be identified and managed in a systematic manner. Therefore, this chapter focuses on the process of managing project risks.

A risk is easily defined. A risk is something that has not happened, but if it does happen, it will impact the project's ability to meet the planned objectives. At that point, it becomes an issue. Each issue must be resolved before the project's objectives can be met. As it turns out, a risk can have either a positive or a negative impact on a project. The negative impact is most common and is called a threat. For example, a risk that the project's funding will not be continued could jeopardize the project's completion. A positive risk is called an opportunity. Opportunities are not as common as threats. An example of a positive risk is a technical solution to an existing

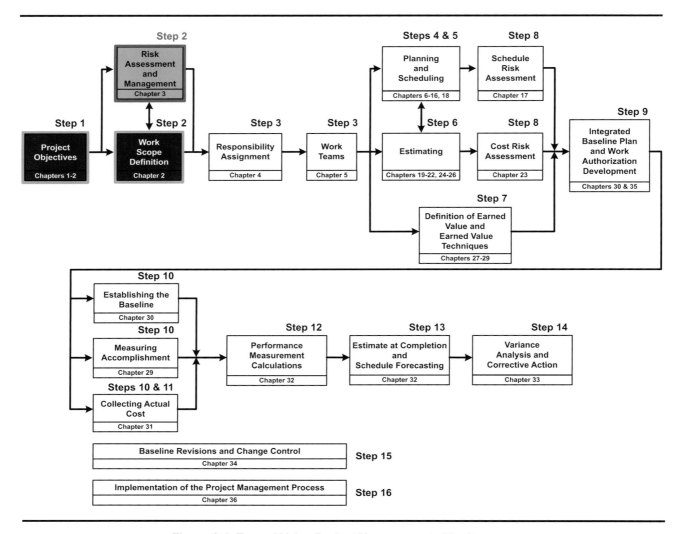

Figure 3-1 Earned Value Project Management: The Process

problem that could also have a favorable environmental impact that results in lower costs to the project.

Each risk has two attributes. First, since a risk has not occurred, there is a likelihood or probability that it will occur. Second, if the risk does occur, the result will be a consequence that impacts the project. Much of the work of managing project risks is focused on assessing and quantifying these attributes.

Managing project risks prioritizes the severity of the identified risks so that risks with greater impact and a higher probability of occurring receive a greater share of resources and attention. Some projects attempt to classify the impact of project risks in order to facilitate prioritization. The most common classifications are technical,

schedule, and cost. Another useful risk classification is external or internal. External risks originate outside of the project, and the project has little control over the occurrence of the risk but bears the impact. Examples of external risks include funding limitations, changes to laws or regulations, and public relations situations. Internal risks originate within the project, and the project manager can exert some degree of control or influence. Examples of internal risks include aspects of the technical approach, subcontractors, and availability of resources. Regardless of classification, all risks that are realized ultimately become project costs.

As project risks are prioritized, projects begin to develop measures to reduce the likelihood that an individual risk will occur or reduce the impact on the project if it does occur, or both. When these efforts are added to the determination of what actions might be taken if the risks actually occur, this part of the process is called risk mitigation.

Essential to any good management practice is communication, and the key to communication is good documentation. To manage project risks properly, information is needed about the project's objectives, assumptions, management processes and the project's risks themselves. A risk management plan is the vehicle for communicating the risk management process for the project.

The Process Flow Diagram

If the management of project risks can be accomplished in a systematic manner, then the process should fit into a flow diagram. In Figure 3-2, Managing Project Risks: The Process, such a diagram is provided and explained below.

Traditionally, Risk Management was divided into four stages: Risk Planning, Risk Identification, Risk Assessment, and Risk Implementation. More recently, the Project Management Institute (PMI) has increased the number of steps to six: Risk Management Planning, Risk Identification, Risk Qualification, Risk Quantification, Risk Response Planning, and Risk Monitoring and Control. While the PMI steps are certainly more descriptive of the underlying activities, the activities themselves are not materially changed. Some companies still describe their risk management process using the traditional four-step approach. In addition, not all companies apply all risk steps to all projects. For example, some

companies delay the initiation of Risk Planning and reduce the requirement for Risk Quantification on smaller projects.

A. Determine the Project Objectives, Priorities and Assumptions

The determination of Project Objectives was discussed in Chapter 2, Definition of Scope. This activity is even more important to managing project risks. Without a complete understanding of the project objectives, project personnel will be unable to determine which events, if they occur, will impact those objectives. The project objectives should be clearly stated, documented, approved and distributed by the project manager to project stakeholders. A statement of the Project Objectives can be a standalone document, but, ultimately, it should also be incorporated into a project risk management plan.

Project priorities are also important. These priorities are used to determine the direction of the mitigation of the risks. Is schedule more important than cost? Is cost more important than technical performance? These decisions will allow trade-offs to be made when conflicting alternatives are available in the development of mitigation plans.

Explicit knowledge of the project assumptions is essential to identifying project risks and to developing the path forward when a risk becomes reality. The assumptions themselves may be a source of project risks. Suppose one of the assumptions proves to be suspect or incorrect? Assumptions must be validated and thus the list of assumptions is a good place to start the search for project risks.

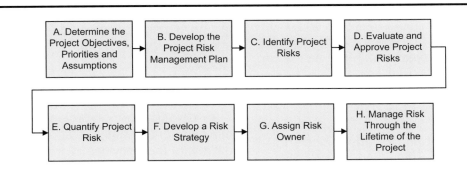

Figure 3-2 Managing Project Risks: The Process

B. Develop the Project Risk Management Plan

The Project Risk Management Plan is, as the name implies, a plan for managing the risks on the project. It provides, in one place, the information necessary for project personnel to identify and execute their risk management responsibilities.

The content of the plan will be driven by any company risk management guidelines or procedures and by any customer requirements identified in the contract for the project. At a minimum, however, the plan should include:

- The criteria for use of risk management on the project, including the conduct, timing, level, and extent.

- The roles and responsibilities of the project personnel with regard to project risks.

- The processes for the identification of project risks.

- Identification of risk management documents and reports required, along with their development cycle and approval authority.

- Any guidance or reference to guidance, for the conduct of qualitative and quantitative risk assessments.

- The description of the risk assessment and process maintenance tools to be used on the project.

- A glossary and a definition of abbreviations and acronyms.

The use criteria should include the customer requirements to be met by the project as well the company guidelines and procedures.

The risk management roles and responsibilities should identify the project manager as having overall responsibility for managing project risks. The document should identify the process and procedure for identifying project risks among project personnel and the procedure for approving a project risk. The roles and responsibilities should include the identification of individual risk owners. Any risk planning document should outline the establishment and use of project risk specialists or specialist teams along with their ongoing

responsibilities. Finally, project risk review and reporting responsibilities should be identified.

The project risk identification discussion should identify any formal processes that will be used for the identification of project risks as well as suggest informal ones. The historical sources of project risks should also be identified, especially any project unique sources such as extreme weather conditions.

The project risk management documents and reports will be presented later in the chapter; but should include documents to help identify new risks, to display the approved risks, to report the qualitative or quantitative assessment of risks, to identify any mitigation or contingency plans, to report the occurrence of risks, and to detail the disposition of risks. These instructions may also include the description of risk management activity in a report of lessons learned.

Qualitative or, especially, quantitative assessments of risks may require special or company/ project specific procedures or guidance. These procedures should be identified or referenced in the risk management plan. Any special or specific tools available for the conduct of risk assessments and the maintenance of risk management information should be identified and referenced.

Like most specialty disciplines, the management of project risks is usually accompanied by a myriad of unique terms, abbreviations, and acronyms. What, for example, is a Schedule Risk Assessment (SRA) or what is the difference between a risk analysis and a risk assessment? The risk management plan should address these and other such challenges with a glossary and a definition of abbreviations and acronyms.

Finally, the risk management plan should be subject to a risk document revision procedure and should be approved and distributed by the project manager.

C. Identify Project Risks

The identification of project risks is the single most important activity, and, arguably, the most difficult of the activities of managing project risks. Participation in the activity of risk identification provides each participant with a degree of risk awareness. Doing so supports the notion that there are additional project risks yet to be discovered and, with diligence, these new risks may be discovered in time to enact a mitigation plan.

As described in the risk management plan, the identification of project risks is the responsibility of every member of the project team. Initial identification may include not only project personnel, but also others whose association with the project may be only supportive in nature. Thus, every stakeholder, along with others who have a vested interest in the outcome of the project, is encouraged to participate.

The identification of project risks begins at the inception of the project, preferably when the project is being proposed. As the project progresses from inception to execution, the risks identified in the earlier phases should be conveyed to the succeeding project personnel.

While everyone on the project is encouraged to identify project risks, as a practical matter, the actual identification captured in the risk register most often results from the experience of the project personnel. Personnel new to a discipline or operating outside of their expertise are unlikely to be as proficient as those with more familiarity and experience. While contributions can always be made, it would not be productive to ask persons who have never visited China, for example, to identify the risks of working there. A sample Risk Register is illustrated in Figure 3-3.

How long does the risk identification activity last? Answer, it lasts as long as the project is active. Although the majority of the formal identification occurs in the beginning of the project, even in the latest stages of a project, new or evolving risk events can impact meeting project objectives.

Identifying project risks can take many paths. Some aids to the activity include:

- The project assumptions.

- Lists of risks experienced on previous similar projects.

- Industry sources.

- Expert opinion.

- Earned Value Management System Variance Analysis Reports.

- "Lessons learned" on similar projects.

- Brainstorming.

- Delphi analysis.

- Company risk management guidance and procedures.

The identified project risks should be recorded in a list. The lists of risk events experienced from previous projects are an excellent source of risk exposure for the present project. As will be seen, these lists can contain, in addition to the risks themselves, substantial information about each risk including its impact(s) along with successful mitigation strategies. This information will be useful later in characterizing the current risks.

Industry sources include just about any information sources from professional journals to the Wall Street Journal. The Internet is also a good source. Professional conferences and workshops address project risks and provide the

Project Risk Register										
Risk No.	Risk Area	Risk Description	Trigger	EMV			Response Strategy	Assigned To	Current Status	Disposition
				Impact	Probability	EMV				

Figure 3-3 Sample Risk Register

added benefit of a description of how the risks were managed.

Expert opinion refers to anyone with greater experience or expertise than the person looking for help. An expert may have studied particular projects or processes or may have experienced them firsthand. Firsthand experience may be invaluable if it were from one's own company.

As will be seen later in this text, variance analysis reports are a product of a well functioning Earned Value Management System. When performance is compared to plan, deviations or variances are often noted. When these variances become significant, they must be explained. The explanations include the cause of the variance, the impact of the variance, and the corrective action to be planned or taken. As such, they provide a window into what went wrong, or right, and into what was done about the problem. From this information, possible project risks may be identified. Sometimes the variance is caused by the occurrence of a previously identified risk.

Lessons learned in other projects are another excellent source of what went wrong and what went right. The only limitation is the conspicuous absence of their identification in many company and customer organizations.

Brainstorming can be another source of risk identification. Brainstorming is a process in which project personnel, usually working with a facilitator, seek to spontaneously identify risks by offering whatever risks come to mind in an open and positive atmosphere. This technique allows one risk to suggest another. When the initial risks are deemed to be exhausted, the group attempts to further define and develop those risks judged most credible. This process, and the Delphi technique that follows, may offer the only credible alternatives in a ground-breaking project or technology.

Delphi analysis or the Delphi technique is similar to brainstorming except that the participants are not present in the same room. Instead, an initial list of risks is consolidated by the facilitator and returned without attribution to each participant for comment and expansion. Participants can add comments, agree, modify or disagree with the consolidated list, and return the list to the facilita-

tor. The process continues until a consensus of the experts forms. While this technique avoids the clash of opinions and offers more deliberation than brainstorming, it obviously takes more time.

Company risk management guidance and procedures may contain lists of previously identified project risks for the consideration of the new project. These lists, if they exist, were probably developed using any or all of the sources described above and can be immeasurably helpful when time is short.

Identification of project risks should also include identification of the "risk trigger" - the precursor event that suggests that a risk event is about to occur. If, for example, a supplier's plant experiences a labor stoppage for any reason then a schedule delay for materials is also likely.

D. Evaluate and Approve Project Risks

Not all identified risks will be approved for inclusion in the project risk register. Approval connotes formal recognition that a project risk is to be managed on the project. A terrorist act may be a risk to the successful meeting of the project objectives, but it may also be considered outside the scope of actions the project is charged with addressing. On the other hand, it may be an event that the project must secure itself against. There must be an authority to approve all project risks, be it the project manager, the project risk manager, or a project risk committee. Some forward-thinking organizations include risk management as a corporate oversight function.

Before project risks can be approved, they must be described and evaluated in sufficient detail to allow the decision maker to make an informed decision. As a practical matter, oral discussions will dispose of those potential risks unlikely to be included. But for those serious risk candidates, a standard risk identification document should be prepared.

The information to be contained on the risk identification document should include the title, a description of the risk, and a description of its potential impact on meeting the project objective. The project risk register should include an initial identification of the likelihood of occurrence.

E. Quantify Project Risks

Using the risk register, the team should develop an approximation of the impact of each identified risk. Time-related risks result in direct and indirect cost impacts. Thus any schedule delay will incur the actual cost, the expected monetary value (EMV), of the delay plus the additional indirect costs of supervision, equipment, rental costs, etc.

The objective of this risk analysis is to identify the impact and the probability of each risk event identified on the risk register. The expected monetary value is the product of the impact and the probability of the event.

There are two types of risk quantification: qualitative and quantitative. Either approach is perfectly acceptable. The difference lies in the amount of information available to attach a numeric evaluation to each risk.

Qualitative assessment uses a less rigorous approach that categorizes both the impact and the probability in terms of high, medium and low risk. Thus it is possible to establish an overall EMV even if numeric impacts or probabilities are difficult to produce.

Consider this example: a project team has determined that the completion of the project depends on the fabrication and delivery of a certain piece of equipment. This is known prior to the development of a detailed CPM network; therefore it is difficult to evaluate the numeric value of the risk in terms of days of delay. By assessing the risk in terms of qualitative measurement, the team can progress towards development of the risk strategies without debating specific numeric data. The danger of a Qualitative assessment lies in its subjectivity; what is a high impact and high probability risk sometimes exists in the eye of the beholder. For this reason, those who participate in the development of the risk register need to reach consensus and there needs to be an overall owner of the risk process, as established in the risk management plan, who will make the final decision on the register content.

The second method of risk quantification, quantitative, is more rigorous. When a specific risk can be evaluated numerically, the quantitative approach is desirable.

Consider this example: in the Widget project, a control account has been identified to have a potential to slip because the resources needed to execute the work as planned were insufficient at the time of the proposal. Thus the control account manager has estimated a cost impact of $20,000 in overtime to recover lost time. However, the probability of the resources not being available is only 40%. Thus, the EMV assigned to that specific risk is 40% of $20,000, or $8,000. The EMV of $8,000 becomes the quantified amount assigned to the risk register.

The Risk Register illustrating how these two risks are entered is shown in Figure 3-4.

A couple of important points need to be made concerning the EMV assigned in a risk register.

Project Risk Register									
Risk No.	Risk Area	Risk Description	Trigger	EMV			Response Strategy	Assigned To	Current Status	Disposition
				Impact	Probability	EMV				
2931	Vendor XYZ	Vendor cannot meet shipping date of 9/28/y2	Inspection Reports	High	High	High	Close inspection intervals; Assist with shipping	PBOS	Active	
2932	Engineering	Sufficient number of qualified engineers are not available during the critical design period of 7/5/y2 – 5/8/y3	Schedule Slip	$20,000	40%	$8,000	Overtime authorized; Use schedule float	HSTU	Active	

Figure 3-4 Widget Project Risk Register

First, it is extremely unlikely that all risks identified as critical events will occur exactly as postulated and that each risk has 100% probability of occurring. (If a risk has 100% probability, it should be included in the estimate for the project because it is not a risk.) Second, risks in the risk register often intersect with one another or address different facets of the same problem. Therefore, it is usually misleading to declare that the dollarized risk for the project equals the sum the EMVs in the risk register.

Who should estimate the impact and the probability of the individual risk elements? The person with the most knowledge of the risk event should make the assessment. The content of the entire risk register should be a consensus effort, subject to final approval as specified in the risk management plan.

F. Develop a Risk Strategy

Now that the risk register includes a listing of risks with accompanying expected monetary values, it is time to develop a strategy to mitigate each of the risks. What can be done to manage each of the risks? Risk strategies fall into four generic categories:

- **Avoidance.** Find a different approach to avoid the risk. Using the previous example of a control account with insufficient resources, the account manager may elect to extend the duration of the task to assure completion with fewer resources.

- **Control.** Find a way to minimize the impact and/or the probability of the event. Injuries on a construction project can be reduced with protective equipment along with a vigorous safety program.

- **Transfer.** Covering the potential risk event with insurance or subcontracting another risk to an entity that specializes in, for example, data base development as opposed to creating the data base in-house is a responsible risk strategy.

- **Acceptance.** Recognizing that a risk is either insignificant (in monetary terms) or completely unavoidable leads the company to accept that the risk will become a reality. When using this mitigation strat-

egy, financial budgets and/or projections should include the estimated dollar value of the risk until the risk occurs. All projects contain risks that can be accepted as the normal part of doing business.

Innovative use of the four generic strategies helps to develop risk mitigation plans for each risk listed on the register.

G. Assign Risk Owner

Overall ownership of risk belongs to the program/project manager. The PM leads the risk management process, but needs help to manage individual risks. Thus, it is customary to delegate specific risk elements to the individual most capable of recognizing the risk trigger and closest to the work to execute the risk strategy.

H. Manage Risk through the Lifetime of the Project

Once the project risk register has been developed and approved, it must become a living document subject to periodic review, preferably monthly. During each review, it is also good practice to convert qualitative risk assessments to quantitative ones as more information about the specifics of each risk line item becomes available. Over the life of any project, some risks are mitigated as part of the risk management process, some do not materialize either through good luck or outstanding project execution, and the risk register must reflect the remaining risk exposure accurately. A good question directed periodically to any responsible project manager should be: "What are the remaining risks this project is exposed to?"

It is also true that new risks appear during project execution for any number of reasons. All of these risks have occurred after implementation of the initial project risk register:

- Loss of a key project employee.

- Damage to equipment and/or materials while in transit.

- An engineering mistake not discovered until installation.

- Labor unrest at the jobsite or in a key vendor's facility.

- New environmental regulations made retroactive.
- Poor project execution including insufficient project control tools.

It is vitally important that the final component of a vigorous and effective risk management process includes a periodic review of the risk register. As mentioned previously, a review of risks on previous projects, especially how the risks were managed, is a credible input for future undertakings.

The final column on the risk register form, Disposition, provides the ability to assess the risk line item retrospectively: what strategy worked, which did not, was there a risk lesson learned that will benefit another project in the future?

Implementing a structured risk management process helps the project foster a healthy sense of risk awareness for all project stakeholders. The project will benefit when potential decisions are accompanied by the question "What are the risks associated with this decision?"

Relationship of Risk Management to the Earned Value Management System

Project risk management intersects with the Earned Value Management System in numerous ways: Schedule Risk Analysis (Chapter 17), Development of Estimates (Chapter 21), Budgets (Chapter 30), Management Reserve (Chapter 30), and Estimates at Completion (Chapter 32), and Variance Analysis (Chapter 33).

Development of Estimates

As part of estimate development, most organizations attempt to mitigate risks. Actions include substitution of lower risk approaches (system, subsystems, parts, or vendors), estimating additional labor hours for perceived risk items, studies or pilot projects to mitigate perceived risks, and including contingency amounts in the estimate. Prior to submission of the final proposal to the customer, many organizations develop a qualified or quantified risk assessment. Using this data, actions are taken to reduce high risks to medium or low risks by including the cost of mitigation

activities in the estimate. The resulting proposal and associated cost estimate that form the basis for the contract value therefore should have both identified risks and included the cost of mitigation measures for some risks.

Quantitative Schedule Risk Analysis

Modern scheduling systems are based on network logic schedules. These network logic schedules provide the infrastructure of activities and logic to perform quantitative schedule risk analysis. There are software tools that work in tandem with network logic schedules to process most likely, best case, and worst case estimates using Monte Carlo simulations to provide risk-based estimates of key milestones and project completion.

Budgets

Budgets should be based on the estimates developed for the project. Accordingly, any tasks included in the estimate to mitigate risks should be included in the project budget. These budgeted tasks represent risk mitigation measures in the risk management plan.

Management Reserve

Management Reserve is a budget set aside for future dispersal to budget the performance of in-scope tasks that were unknown at the time the project budget was established. Management reserve can be applied to new tasks for mitigating existing risks or newly identified risks.

Variance Analysis

As variances occur, managers should determine the root cause of the problem, which is often a risk coming to fruition. The variance analysis process and variance analysis reports (VARs) document the conversion of a risk to an issue.

Estimates at Completion

Estimates at Completion are the updated projections of the project's final costs. As it becomes clear that a risk will become an issue, estimated costs for the risk should be included in the estimate at completion. Some companies have instituted procedures that when the probability of occurrence of a risk identified in the risk register exceeds a certain percentage, the risk must be incorporated into next version of the estimate at completion.

Conclusion

Managing risk requires a plan, dedicated adherence to the plan, and participation by those who will execute the project and all its components. The first step is to determine the project objectives, priorities and assumptions. The project objectives must be understood or the project personnel will be unable to determine any impact on those objectives. The project risk management plan must be created and project risks identified. Then follows risk identification, the most important and difficult activity in the process. Risks must be approved for inclusion in the project risk register since not every identified risk might be pertinent to the project. Using the risk register, the team will develop a numeric approximation of the impact of each identified risk. Then a strategy is developed to manage each of the risks. A risk owner, who is closest to the work, is appointed to execute the risk strategy. Finally, the risks are managed throughout the life of the project.

Chapter 3 Review Questions

3-1.   What is the definition of a project risk?

3-2.   What is the importance of the project objectives to managing project risks?

3-3.   What is a risk threat?

3-4.   What is a risk opportunity?

3-5.   Who has the overall responsibility for managing project risks?

3-6.   Who has the responsibility for identifying project risks?

3-7.   What is the purpose of the risk register?

3-8.   What is the last activity in managing project risks?

3-9.   What are the responsibilities of the risk owner?

3-10.   What alternatives are there to managing "excessive" risks?

True or False

3-11.   The schedule impact is more important than the performance impact.

3-12.   The risk owner decides whether a risk is approved.

3-13.   An action plan is usually undertaken when a risk is rated "low".

3-14.   The risk manager maintains the risk register for the project manager.

3-15.   Three levels of qualitative risk rating are positive, negative and neutral.

3-16.   An excessive risk can be treated as if it will occur.

3-17.   Delphi analysis takes more time than "brainstorming".

3-18.   A risk management program should not raise risk awareness.

3-19.   Once the risk horizon has passed, a risk can be removed from the risk register.

3-20.   Managing project risks requires risk specialists.

The answers to these questions can be found in Section 6, Solutions.

.

Case Study

3.1 USING THE RISK REGISTER

A primary project has a contractual requirement to be able to demonstrate to their customer that they are using and Earned Value Management System (EVMS) to manage the performance on the project. A subproject has been established to conduct the earned value training for a primary project. The objective of the subproject has been established as:

"To enable each Control Account Manager to successfully demonstrate his/her knowledge and use of Earned Value Management policies, procedures, processes, software tools and their respective responsibilities in a formal review of the Project EVMS by the customer."

A primary project time line includes the following activities:

Day 01 -	Contract "go-ahead"
Day 02 - 20	Develop EV Concepts Policy
Day 02 - 20	Develop EV Concepts Training Plan
Day 15 - 20	Identify and Assign fifty (50) Control Account Managers (CAMs)
Day 21 - 25	Review and Approve EV Concepts Training Plan
Day 21 - 60	CAMs Implement EV Management System at CAM level
Day 16 - 30	Develop Software Tools Training Plan
Day 31 - 35	Review and Approve Software Tools Training Plan
Day 41 - 60	Develop EV Concepts Training
Day 41 - 60	Develop Software Tools Training
Day 41 - 60	Write EV Policy Guide
Day 60 - 66	Review and Approve EV Policy Guide
Day 65 - 66	Conduct EV Concepts Training for fifty (50) CAMs.
Day 72 - 76	Conduct "practice" customer review
Day 90 - 96	EVMS Review conducted by Customer

Identify and enter into the Project Risk Register worksheet any significant risks to meeting the subproject objective. "Significant risks" are those risks that could be expected to be "approved".   Include in the register all risk information by the column headings.   For the Risk Rating use the Likelihood times the highest Impact.

Continue the Risk Register form for your answers.

The solution to this case study can be found on the Humphreys & Associates, Inc. web site.
www.humphreys-assoc.com

Project Risk Register

Risk ID	Risk Title/ Type	Risk Description	Likelihood		Performance Impact		Schedule Impact		Cost Impact		Risk Rating
			Quantitative	Qualitative	Quantitative	Qualitative	Quantitative	Qualitative	Quantitative	Qualitative	
1	Poor CAM Training Attendance. Threat	CAMs do not understand Earned Value because they have not taken training.	5	CAMs have many other job related reasons to avoid training classes.	5	Untrained CAMs will be unable to understand or perform CAM duties and unable to pass CAM interview.	3	Additional CAM training Classes must be scheduled resulting in delay of customer's EV review.	3	Additional CAM training classes will require additional project resources.	5 x 5 = 25

Chapter 4

RELATING ORGANIZATIONS, RESPONSIBILITY, AND WORK SCOPE

Objectives of this Chapter:

1. Explain that an Organization Breakdown Structure (OBS) must be defined as precisely as the Work Breakdown Structure (WBS).

2. Demonstrate how an Organization Breakdown Structure (OBS) and Work Breakdown Structure (WBS) can be integrated into a single matrix known as a Responsibility Assignment Matrix (RAM).

3. Define the control account and explain its role in the project management process.

4. Provide guidelines for establishing the control account at the proper level of detail.

After work has been defined, the next step in the process is to identify the individuals responsible for performing the work.

Organization charts exist in every company, even if only informally, and they support this step in the development of the project management system. The company organization chart displays the pool from which the project organization is assigned. The project organization chart is the Organization Breakdown Structure (OBS).

A matrix can be formed by the intersection of the Work Breakdown Structure and the Organization Breakdown Structure; this is the tool for assigning work responsibility. An "X" can be placed in each intersection block to indicate which part of the overall project organization is responsible for each part of the project scope. This intersection is called the control account. This matrix is commonly referred to as a Responsibility Assignment Matrix, or RAM.

Sometimes, because they already exist, organization charts are overlooked in the project management process relative to their integration with a Work Breakdown Structure. The organization chart needs the same type of precise definition as the Work Breakdown Structure. This definition is accomplished through a charter of functions and responsibilities. Creating a charter of functions and responsibilities is a prerequisite for the next step in system development: identifying who will be responsible for accomplishment of what project scope.

To be useful, formalized organization charts must be accompanied by specific descriptions of the mission and objectives of each organizational element. Further definition is then developed for the specific responsibilities of that organization in support of the project.

A separate document may be required to describe a specific project's organization. Like its multi-project higher level counterpart, it consists of an organization chart accompanied by written descriptions of specific project responsibilities for each participating organization, team, or department assigned to the project. Organizational roles and responsibilities may be defined in a

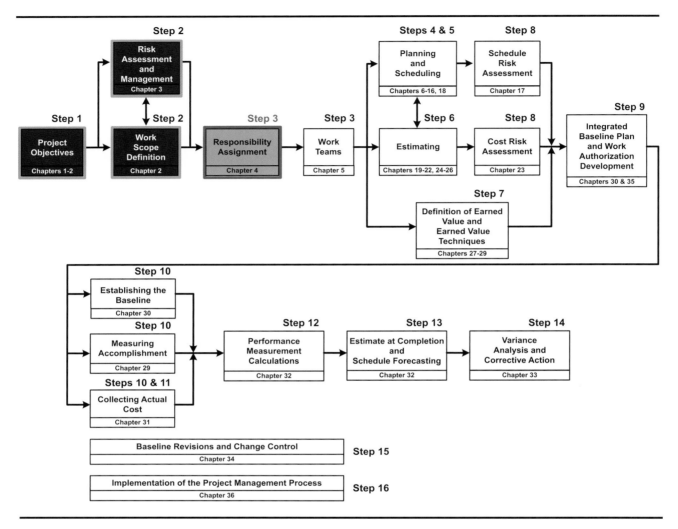

Figure 4-1 Earned Value Project Management: The Process

project organization procedure as part of the project plan.

Organizational Structures

The Project Management Institute identifies the following types of organization structures:

1. Functional Organization.

2. Projectized Organization.

3. Weak Matrix.

4. Balanced Matrix.

5. Strong Matrix.

6. Composite Organization.[1]

The Project Management Institute further describes the functional organization as:

... a hierarchy where each employee has one clear superior. Staff members are grouped by specialty, such as production, marketing, engineering, and accounting at the top level. Specialties may be further subdivided into functional organizations, such as mechanical and electrical engineering. Each department in a functional organization will do its project work independent of other departments.[2]

1.   Project Management Institute. *A Guide to the Project Management Body of Knowledge (PMBOK), Fourth Edition.* Newtown Square, PA: Project Management Institute, 2008, 28.
2.   PMBOK, 28.

Figure 4-2 illustrates the above definition of functional organizations. Examples of the functions include Engineering, Manufacturing, Operations, Human Resources, and Finance/Accounting.

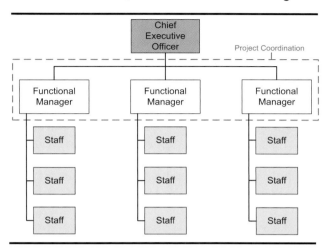

Figure 4-2 Functional Organization

A projectized organization is pictured in Figure 4-3. The organization is structured along project lines, with the project manager invested with significant authority and autonomy in project matters. Note the absence of functional managers. Each project manager has a dedicated staff whose entire scope of work consists of supporting that specific project.

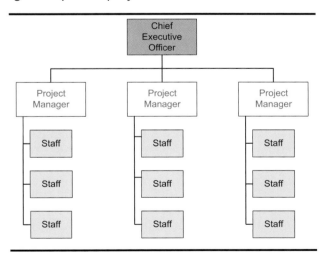

Figure 4-3 Project Organization

Matrix organizations are a hybrid of functional and project organizations. They may be weak (Figure 4-4), strong (Figure 4-5), or balanced (Figure 4-6). As indicated in these figures, they

vary in structure from very close to a functional organization to nearly a fully projectized organization.

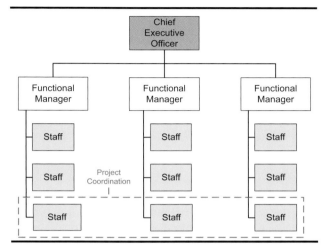

Figure 4-4 Weak Matrix

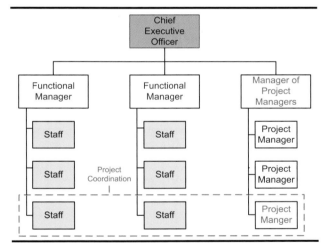

Figure 4-5 Strong Matrix

The Weak Matrix, pictured in Figure 4-4, closely resembles the functional organization. Functional managers direct the operations of the company, with no formal project manager position. Projects may be formed of loose alliances of functional staff members whose duties include project support activities. As pictured in Figure 4-4, individual staff members are selected and assigned from each functional area. While the diagram indicates a single staff member from each functional area, multiple personnel from each discipline may be used. On a large project, for example, all nine organization boxes marked

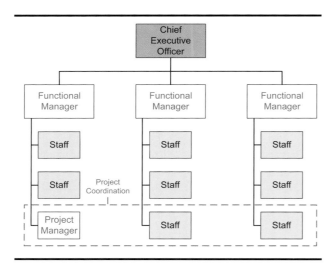

Figure 4-6 Balanced Matrix

"staff" may be assigned to that single project. Or, some staff may be assigned to one project while other staff is designated for other projects or non-project activities. While there may be a project manager designated, the role of this position is primarily one of coordination and/or expediting.

A Strong Matrix organization, as shown in Figure 4-5, features a Manager of Project Managers who is on an equal level with the functional managers. Individual project managers are then assigned to specific projects, with staff assigned from the various functional areas. Besides having a separate project organization, there may be separate operating procedures different from those of the functional organization. These separate procedures would usually require tighter controls or project specific requirements.

In some organizations, the position of Manager of Project Managers is on a higher level than the functional managers, with the individual project managers on the same organizational level as the functional managers. The project managers are provided with whatever support is necessary from the various functional organizations. This support could consist of the dedication of key staff, the assignment of multiple people who can fulfill the project's requirements, or a mix of staff within the functions that perform different specialties. Some functions may not require a dedicated full time person assigned to the project. In these instances, a person is assigned part time and splits work duties between the project and other projects or non-project activities.

The Balanced Matrix organization as shown in Figure 4-6, has a full-time project manager assigned to direct a project. However, unlike the Strong Matrix organization, the project manager reports to one of the functional managers. This reduces the authority and autonomy of the project manager compared with the Strong Matrix. While the project manager is fully responsible for directing the project, he or she is still subject to the priorities of a single functional organization. In effect, the project manager is part of one of the organizational "silos" rather than spanning responsibility for all organizations as an independent entity. When controversy arises, difficulties are likely to be addressed from the point of view of the functional manager who provides a home for the project manager. This may not always be the best solution from a project standpoint or from an overall organization standpoint. In the worst case, the functional manager for the project manager may end up acting as the real project manager. This arrangement is unlikely to properly balance the needs of the project.

Modern organizations frequently resemble Figure 4-7, the Composite Organization. This organizational structure features portions of the organization aligned with functional formats while other parts of the organization are aligned as purely project organizations. Staffing for projects is carved out of the existing functional organizations, and some part time project personnel may support more than one project simultaneously. The relative strength of projects versus functions will vary over time as the number and importance of projects rise and fall. Another important factor will be the strength of personality, charisma, or style of the project manager. The project manager must actively compete with the other project managers for the best available people.

Some levels of management have been removed from Figures 4-2 through 4-7 to clarify the differences between organization types. Typically organizations have far more levels of management than shown in these figures, particularly between the Chief Executive Officer and the functional managers and project managers.

The specialized contribution of the project controls organization also should be considered. This group, which directly supports the project

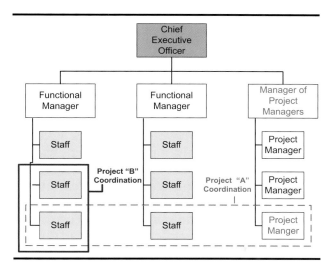

Figure 4-7 Composite Organization

manager, may be called project management, project controls, or the project/program office. Sometimes it is designated as "planning and control". Like the project manager, the project controls manager has responsibility that extends across all functional organizations assigned to the project. It is the responsibility of the project controls to accurately assess project status and report those findings to the project manager. This individual sometimes has to face the difficult situation of not having the value of his or her daily contribution to the project's success recognized. When evaluating organizations, there is an important question to be answered: Is it because the person in the position is ineffective or is it because the importance of project controls is not recognized?

In one pharmaceutical organization, a project team meeting was held that included at least 25 individuals, but not the project controls manager. When the project controls manager was asked about this apparent oversight, he revealed that he had asked the project manager about attending and was told there was nothing in the meeting that would concern him. Nothing of concern to project controls, but there were items of concern for engineering, purchasing, accounting, production, quality assurance, material management, start-up and test, project administration, records management and expediting. One has to question what the role of project controls was on that project.

Since project controls' work affects everyone on the project, excluding them from important project meetings can create problems. The schedule is for the entire project and includes everyone's activities. Consequently, excluding a key team member may result in miscommunications or faulty direction. On one design project, the lead scheduler was forced to determine status unilaterally while being excluded from weekly engineering status meetings. It is easy to anticipate what happened. The scheduler would show design activities behind schedule and announce gloom and doom in later higher level project meetings. The engineering representative would then stand up and announce that engineering had already resolved that concern in its weekly working meeting and had found a way to maintain schedule. The new schedule network logic, durations, and possibly even varied technical requirements were decided unilaterally by engineering without consultation with project controls. Their assumptions, such as faster delivery of external design information, sometimes had little basis in fact. Worse than that, the project documentation still reflected the original assumptions because no one was responsible for updating it (remember the need for organization charters). It would not take many meetings such as this until no one on the project would know the "real" status.

Responsibility Assignment Matrix (RAM)

After the project organization is well defined, a common understanding exists of the element definition of the Organization Breakdown Structure (OBS). This definition of the project's organizational elements is analogous to the previously described work scope content in the WBS elements. At this point, an infrastructure exists that will allow the integration of the two structures into a cohesive management tool.

With the work defined and the project organization known, the development of a matrix that correlates scope of work with the organization ensures proper assignment of specific responsibilities. Further planning can proceed in the area of defining specific accounts or elements that can be used to control the work. These are called control accounts. The identification of control accounts is pictured in Figure 4-8.

The matrix of responsibility versus scope of work is referred to as a Responsibility Assignment Matrix, or RAM. This matrix shows the WBS on one axis and the OBS on the other. The intersection of these axes allows the designation of who is responsible for what products or services. By marking the intersection of the WBS and the OBS with an "X", the responsibility is identified. This arrangement allows for specific designation of responsibility for each managerially significant piece of work. This matrix could also be used to indicate who is allowed to charge which accounts and/or the amount of resources budgeted. After the final budgets have been approved, the RAM is usually "dollarized". The Xs are replaced with the authorized budgets so that the budgets can be totaled for both the WBS and the OBS. Whenever an authorized change to the budgets is made, the "dollarized" RAM is updated. This provides an excellent management tool to ensure that budgets are not over-allocated and that the budgets are traceable to the reporting system

This matrix not only helps ensure that someone is responsible for all items of work; it also verifies that there is only one individual assigned with responsibility for that work. The challenges presented in the last chapter regarding development of the WBS to the proper level of detail also apply to the RAM. As the number of levels of the WBS increase and the number of levels in the OBS increase, the number of potential intersection points increases dramatically. Projects have burdened themselves with matrices that show a potential for thousands of possible intersection points. Even though a software tool can handle this structure, the project team should not burden itself with unnecessary accounts. The owner/customer often requires a rather detailed level for its visibility. This occurs when the owner/customer says, "We do not want to burden your systems unnecessarily, so just provide the level of detail you would ordinarily use for managing your projects. However, we do need you to summarize to our WBS." The clincher is when the owner/customer provides a WBS that is more detailed than the contractor would ever use and then politely asks for information to be "summarized" to the lowest level.

This type of situation occurred on an international project when the owner/customer-supplied WBS

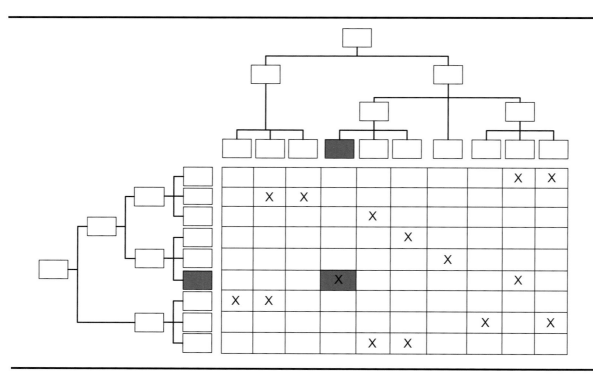

Figure 4-8 Responsibility Assignment Matrix (RAM)

extended to 5 levels. This resulted in approximately 600 WBS elements to be defined and interfaced with the OBS. The contractor was then told to "extend the WBS to whatever appropriate level it would need to manage the project". The contractor responded that 4 levels of WBS would have been sufficient. The result was that the contractor had to expand the level of detail just to support the "summary" reporting requirements of the owner/customer. It also meant that the contractor had little additional detail to answer the owner/customer's questions than the owner/customer already possessed. A good rule of thumb for project management is that the contractor needs at least one level of detail greater for internal control than for external reporting. Otherwise, it is very difficult to provide much additional insight into control account cost and schedule variances.

Control Account Establishment

Establishment of the control account is one of the key concepts in the entire project management process. The control account is established to manage the technical, schedule, and cost performance of a managerially significant element of the work. It focuses responsibility for the work in such a way that cost and schedule performance data can be gathered, monitored, and assigned to a control account manager (CAM). The control account is placed in the matrix where work scope and responsibility are integrated. Sample control account establishment is shown pictorially in Figure 4-9.

In this illustration, a turbine engine contract is subdivided to level 5 in the WBS where it is integrated with the OBS at level 4. Note that there is no requirement for perfect symmetry. The training WBS element, for example, stops at level 2. While this is not a complete sample, it displays another concept that will be discussed in future chapters: the work package and planning package. For now, the purpose is control account establishment.

Clearly, establishing the control account at the proper level of detail is an important factor in the success or failure of any project management control system. Control accounts are created at

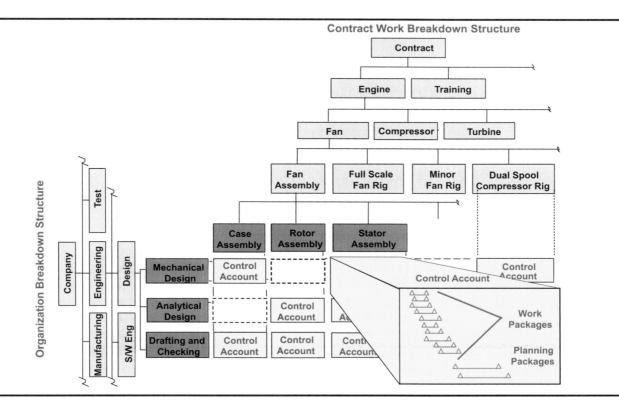

Figure 4-9 Responsibility Assignment Matrix and Control Account Structure

the intersection of the WBS and organization structures. The way they are established depends on work scope, associated risk, duration of the account, dollar value, performing organization, contract framework, and information objectives.

A control account is the lowest level in the WBS/OBS matrix, where all of the data elements and management activities exist. Specifics of the data elements are discussed in subsequent chapters. Management of the project can occur on an exception basis at more summary levels of the WBS and OBS, but all significant variances will eventually be traced at least to the control account level.

Control account management responsibilities include schedule planning and status, measurement of accomplishment, actual cost collection, variance analysis and resultant corrective action, and estimating costs at completion. It is the point where technical scope, schedule, and budget are integrated.

Control accounts are often established at too low a level of detail resulting in subdivisions that are not managerially significant. Figures 4-10 through 4-13 detail four different ways control accounts could be established. For illustration purposes, levels of the OBS and WBS are deleted, as shown in gray, and the next higher level is then used in control account establishment. The examples are for the same scope of work, starting with one at too low a level of detail.

Control Account Example 1 in Figure 4-10 illustrates how a control account may be established at a very low level in the WBS and OBS structure. To understand this illustration using the Condenser WBS element, assume that each lowest level organization element has some effort in each lowest level WBS element. Accordingly, every single intersection of the OBS and WBS results in a control account, which means this illustration defines 35 control accounts for the Condenser alone. Perhaps some of these lowest level organizations have very minor effort in some of the WBS elements. While this approach provides the maximum visibility, it will cost more to set up and administer the planning, statusing, and cost collection functions for such a detailed structure. Additionally, the potential for inaccu-

rate charges increases with the number of control accounts.

Figure 4-10 Control Account Example 1

Control Account Example 2 in Figure 4-11 displays the impact of a more summary approach to control account definition. The lowest level of detail shown in Figure 4-10 has been elevated to the next higher level. In the OBS, the Boiler Superintendant and Cooling System Superintendant become the Control Account Managers, and the WBS Level 5 detail for the Condenser was eliminated. This approach results in a total of two control accounts for the Condenser. Both sides of the matrix have been raised to a higher level, reducing the amount of insignificant subdivisions and the associated planning and administration costs. However, there can be a corresponding loss of visibility. Variances that may be readily identified in Control Account Example 1 (Figure 4-10) are obscured in combination with other efforts in Control Account Example 2 (Figure 4-11). While recognizing that there may be less visibility than in the previous case, the judgment must be made as to whether or not this additional visibility is warranted. Managing at too low of a level of detail is not cost effective.

Reducing the number of control accounts may result in decreased reporting visibility but it does not eliminate information from the project management system. This is because a control account is composed of work packages, which are defined in Chapter 29, "Measuring Accomplishment". Work packages are detailed, short duration tasks that are part of the control account's identified scope of work. Higher level control accounts can still have visibility into the details by planning an increased number of work

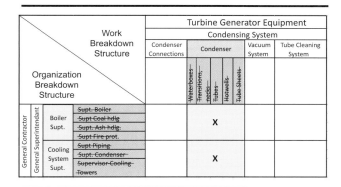

Figure 4-11 Control Account Example 2

packages within each control account. When a variance is identified at the control account level, it is still possible to trace it to its source at the work package level.

Control Account Example 3 in Figure 4-12 shows the impact of eliminating a level of WBS detail while maintaining the original OBS elements. This approach results in seven control accounts for the Condenser, which falls between Control Account Examples 1 and 2. Using this approach implies that it is more important to plan and control the lowest level organizational elements rather than to know the performance details of the Condenser WBS element.

Work Breakdown Structure / Organization Breakdown Structure				Turbine Generator Equipment						
				Condensing System						
				Condenser Connections	Condenser					Vacuum System	Tube Cleaning System
					Waterboxes	Transitions, necks	Tubes	Hotwells	Tube Sheets		
General Contractor	General Superintendant	Boiler Supt.	Supt. Boiler				X				
			Supt Coal hdlg				X				
			Supt. Ash hdlg.				X				
			Supt Fire prot.				X				
		Cooling System Supt.	Supt Piping				X				
			Supt. Condenser				X				
			Supervisor-Cooling Towers				X				

Figure 4-12 Control Account Example 3

Control Account Example 4 in Figure 4-13 shows the impact of eliminating a level of OBS detail while maintaining the original WBS elements. This approach results in 10 control accounts for the Condenser WBS element and may represent the best tradeoff between visibility and detail. If the Condenser WBS element were defined to a lower level of detail than the other Condensing

System elements because of higher perceived risk, this approach would maintain the needed visibility. Additionally, most company labor accumulation systems include the lowest level organizational element code in the time reporting source documents, so the OBS actual cost data should exist in the accounting system if needed for detailed analysis.

Work Breakdown Structure / Organization Breakdown Structure				Turbine Generator Equipment						
				Condensing System						
				Condenser Connections	Condenser					Vacuum System	Tube Cleaning System
					Waterboxes	Transitions, necks	Tubes	Hotwells	Tube Sheets		
General Contractor	General Superintendant	Boiler Supt.	Supt. Boiler								
			Supt Coal hdlg		X	X	X	X	X		
			Supt. Ash hdlg.								
			Supt Fire prot.								
		Cooling System Supt.	Supt Piping								
			Supt. Condenser		X	X	X	X	X		
			Supervisor Cooling Towers								

Figure 4-13 Control Account Example 4

To summarize Control Account Examples 1-4, any of these examples could be an appropriate approach for a project. The point often compromised by many company systems or project control practitioners is that lowest level elements in the WBS do not have to be defined at the same level. Similarly, the lowest level OBS elements do not have to correspond to the same organizational level. One organizational element may assign a Vice President as the Control Account Manager while another organizational element may assign a line supervisor as the Control Account Manager.

Control account dollar value and duration should also be considered in the establishment of control accounts. While there is no absolute rule for "typical" control account size and duration, experience has shown that a control account is usually 9 to 12 months in duration and represents at least $1,000,000 of direct budget for a research and development project. Those dollar values include labor, material, and other direct cost. For a production or construction project, control accounts tend to be longer (13 to 18 months) and represent at least $3,000,000 of budget in direct costs. While budget value is not the only consideration in establishing control accounts, it is a value that is readily available and very helpful in the establishment of control accounts; however, the scope and the cost element content needs to be considered. High dollar material items or subcontracts often result in larger control account values.

Conclusion

An important element of project management is the identification of who is responsible for the accomplishment of specific work items. The Organization Breakdown Structure (OBS) defines the project's organization. Assignment of responsibility for the products and services to be provided as part of the scope of work is then accomplished by creating a matrix from the intersection of the Work Breakdown Structure (WBS) and the project Organization Breakdown Structure (OBS). This matrix is known as the Responsibility Assignment Matrix (RAM). The

intersection points between the WBS and OBS are called control accounts.

The control account is the basic building block of the project management process. It is the control point where technical scope, schedule, and cost parameters are integrated. The control account is also the point where work progress is measured, where actual costs are collected, where variance analysis occurs, and where corrective action is initiated. The selection of the proper level of detail for the control account is a key factor in the success of the system application. If the control accounts are at a very summary level, adequate management visibility will not exist. If control accounts are too numerous, the cost of operating the system increases dramatically and the data produced may overwhelm the users and be less effective for project management. Guidelines for selecting the proper level of detail for control accounts include technical, schedule, cost, risk, and information objectives.

Chapter 4 Review Questions

4-1.   Explain the role of the Responsibility Assignment Matrix, or RAM, in the project management process.

4-2.   What is the fundamental difference between a WBS and an OBS?

4-3.   What is the role of the control account in the project management process?

4-4.   What is the primary tradeoff to be considered in the establishment of control accounts?

4-5.   Name at least five factors that go into the determination of the proper level of detail for control accounts.

True or False

4-6.   Since the Responsibility Assignment Matrix can be maintained in an automated system that indicates which accounts are valid charge numbers, there is not much cost impact if there were a large number of control accounts.

4-7.   The Organization Breakdown Structure (OBS), is really just another name for the company's organization chart.

4-8.   Use of a Responsibility Assignment Matrix (RAM) helps to ensure that someone is responsible for all elements of work while simultaneously ensuring that there is no duplication of responsibility.

4-9.   A control account is the lowest level in the WBS/OBS matrix.

The answers to these questions can be found in Section 6, Solutions.

Case Study

4.1 Control Account Definition Part 1

Background

The Cushperson Corporation was awarded the MOR-DED Motor Scooter Phase A Contract. Mr. James Wagner was appointed the Project Manager. One of the contract clauses required the contractor to be validated for Earned Value Management under EVMSG. Mr. Wagner had been to a seminar on Earned Value Management, and he thought the next step was to integrate the Cushperson Organization with the CWBS to identify control accounts. Wagner recognized the excellent job that the special WBS development team did in its first assignment and felt that their familiarity with the WBS would help them in recommending the control accounts for the MOR-DED Phase A Contract.

Problem Statement

Your team is to identify a recommended set of control accounts for the MOR-DED Motor Scooter Phase A contract. Use the "Assumptions for Control Account Selection" (Figure 1) and "Make or Buy Plan" (Figure 2) to develop your recommendation and the Control Account Matrix to record your analysis.

1. Identify individual intersections on the matrix that you think represent control accounts by marking with an "X". If you wish to gather more than one intersection into a single control account, mark each one with an "X" and then circle those that go together.

2. Choose a team spokesperson to describe your control account selections.

The solution to this case study can be found on the Humphreys & Associates, Inc. web site.
www.humphreys-assoc.com

FIGURE 1

Assumptions for Control Account Selection

1. Purchasing Department will be responsible for control accounts for purchased materials.

2. Tooling is only needed for Engine Block, Fuel Air System and Lubrication System during Phase A.

3. The frame will be developed in the Model Shop.

4. Assembly Department does only final vehicle assembly. Component subassembly is performed by Shops.

5. Production Control, Manufacturing Engineering, and Quality Control activities related to the vehicle components are too small to be individual component level control accounts. Control accounts for these activities are placed in Integration and Assembly.

6. All Computer Services effort on this project will be part of any Engineering Data delivered to the customer.

7. All Drafting efforts are consolidated into either Engineering Data or Integration & Assembly.

8. The Project Manager will be responsible for the Management Data, Systems Management, and Program Management.

9. Reporting elements required for the Contract Performance Report (CPR) are identified as "*". All control accounts must summarize into these elements.

10. Some organizational elements may be considered as indirect and/or G & A. No control accounts should be identified for these elements.

FIGURE 2
Cushperson Corporation
Make or Buy Plan
Project: MOR-DED Motor Scooter Phase A

WBS NO.	TITLE	MAKE	BUY	REMARKS
1.1.1.1	Engine Block	X		Purchase Casting/Machine In-house
1.1.1.2	Fuel-Air System	X		
1.1.1.3	Ignition System		X	In-house Specifications/Subcontract
1.1.1.4	Lubrication System		X	
1.1.1.5	Instrumentation		X	In-house Specifications/Subcontract
1.1.2.1	Clutch	X		Purchase Components/In-house Sub-assembly
1.1.2.2	Trans Assembly		X	Purchase Components/In-house Sub-assembly
1.2.1	Frame	X		
1.2.2	Seat	X		
1.2.3	Fenders	X		
1.2.4	Foot Pegs	X		
1.3.1	Shock Absorbers	X		
1.3.2	Wheels	X		
1.3.3	Axles	X		
1.3.4	Steering Assembly		X	In-house Specifications/Subcontract
1.4	Integration Assembly	X		
2.1.1	Test Planning	X		
2.1.2	Reliability Tests	X		
2.1.3	Road Test	X		
2.2	Test & Evaluation Support	X		
3.1	Technical Manuals	X		
3.2	Engineering Data	X		
3.3	Management Data	X		
4.0	Depot Test Set	X		
5.0	Initial Spares & Repairs			Phase 'B' Decision
6.1	Project Management	X		
6.2	Systems Management	X		
6.3	Quality Assurance	X		

MOR-DED Motor Scooter Control Account Matrix (Part 1)

Work Breakdown Structure

Organization Breakdown Structure

MOR-DED MOTOR SCOOTER

1.0 Vehicle

- 1.1 Power Source & Transmission *
  - 1.1.1 Engine
    - 1.1.1.1 Engine Block
    - 1.1.1.2 Fuel-Air System
    - 1.1.1.3 Ignition System
    - 1.1.1.4 Lubrication System
    - 1.1.1.5 Instrumentation
  - 1.1.2 Power Trans
    - 1.1.2.1 Clutch
    - 1.1.2.2 Trans Assembly *
- 1.2 Frame Assembly *
  - 1.2.1 Frame
  - 1.2.2 Seat
  - 1.2.3 Fenders
  - 1.2.4 Foot Pegs
- 1.3 Suspension
  - 1.3.1 Shock Absorbers
  - 1.3.2 Wheels
  - 1.3.3 Axles
  - 1.3.4 Steering Assembly *
- 1.4 Integration Assembly *

Organization Breakdown Structure (P R E S I D E N T):

- Procurement Director *
  - Purchasing
  - Subcontracts
- Controller
  - Finance
  - Accounting
- Director Administration
- Legal
- Marketing Director
- Engineering Director *
  - Design Group
    - Electronics Design
    - Power Design Branch
    - Mechanical Design Branch
  - Test & Evaluation
  - Engineer Design Group
    - Drafting Branch
    - Computer Services
    - Model Shop
- Director Manufacturing *
  - Production Control Group
  - Manufacturing Engineering Group
  - Tooling
  - Shops
  - Assembly
- Director Quality Assurance *
  - Quality Assurance Department
    - RAM Group
    - Quality Engineering Group
  - Quality Control Department
- Prog. Management Department *
  - MOR-DED Project Manager

* CUSTOMER REPORTING LEVEL

MOR-DED Motor Scooter Control Account Matrix (Part 2)

Work Breakdown Structure (columns, under MOR-DED MOTOR SCOOTER)

- 2.0 System Test & Evaluation
  - 2.1 Dev Test
    - 2.1.1 Test Planning
    - 2.1.2 Reliability Tests
    - 2.1.3 Road Test
  - 2.2 Test & Evaluation Support *
- 3.0 Data
  - 3.1 Technical Manuals
  - 3.2 Engineering Data
  - 3.3 Management Data *
- 4.0 Depot Test Set *
- 5.0 Initial Spares & Repairs *
- 6.0 System Project Mgmt.
  - 6.1 Project Management *
  - 6.2 Systems Management *
  - 6.3 Quality Assurance *

Organization Breakdown Structure (rows)

PRESIDENT

- Procurement Director *
  - Purchasing *
  - Subcontracts
- Controller
  - Finance
  - Accounting
- Director Administration
- Legal
- Marketing Director
- Engineering Director *
  - Design Group *
    - Electronics Design
    - Power Design Branch
    - Mechanical Design Branch
  - Test & Evaluation
  - Engineer Design Group
    - Drafting Branch
    - Computer Services
    - Model Shop
- Director Manufacturing *
  - Production Control Group *
  - Manufacturing Engineering Group
  - Tooling
  - Shops
  - Assembly
- Director Quality Assurance *
  - Quality Assurance Department *
    - RAM Group
    - Quality Engineering Group
  - Quality Control Department
- Program Management Department *
  - MOR-DED Project Manager

* CUSTOMER REPORTING LEVEL

Case Study

4.2 CONTROL ACCOUNT DEFINITION PART 2

With the WBS structure in place for the Automated Interdiction System (AIS) Workstation Project, Karen was ready to progress to the next step - defining the control account structure. She did not want to infringe on the responsibilities of the Control Account Managers. Nevertheless, she wanted to make sure that control accounts were sufficiently granular to ensure traceability, without becoming burdensome to administrators.

Using the WBS, the program organization chart and the guidelines provided by administration, Karen constructed a form that could be used by her and her staff to select control accounts. The chart could also provide insight into the participation required of other organizations in each control account.

Control Account Selection Guidelines

1. Procurement is responsible for managing control accounts containing purchased materials that exceed $25,000.

2. Production Engineering is responsible for all control accounts containing production tooling.

3. The Program Manager is responsible for Management Data (sent to customer) and all elements of Program Management.

4. The Quality Organizations and Hardware Configuration Management charge a relatively small amount to each WBS item. These efforts should be aggregated into control accounts in the most appropriate WBS elements.

5. The Software Configuration Management effort should be distributed to the WBS elements where the work is performed.

6. Organizations that are in the overhead or G&A pools and are considered indirect should not be identified in control accounts.

7. A control account can be identified with one and only one WBS element.

Exercise

Using Karen's form and the guidelines provided by administration:

1. Identify a set of control accounts to be used for Software Configured Item development and for WBS elements associated with Subsystem Integration and Test, System Software and System Engineering.

2. Since each control account can contain numerous work packages, what is the trade-off in using control accounts versus work packages?

The solution to this case study can be found on the Humphreys & Associates, Inc. web site.
www.humphreys-assoc.com

Work Breakdown Structure

Organization Breakdown Structure

Project Manager Broud Stearman

Automated Workstation Development Project - 10000000

Work Breakdown Structure (columns):

- Console Subsystem 1010000
  - Display Processor (DP) 1010100
    - DP CSCI - 1010101
    - DP HWCI - 1010102
  - Man Machine Interface 1010200
    - MMI CSCI - 1010201
    - MMI HWCI - 1010202
  - Interface Processor (IP) 1010300
    - IP CSCI - 1010301
    - IP HWCI - 1010302
  - Subsystem Integration and Test 1010400
    - Build Integ. & Test - 1010401
    - CSCI Integ. & Test - 1010402
  - System Software 1010500
    - System Software - 1010501
    - System Firmware - 010502
- System Engineering 1020000
  - Systems Engineering 1020100
    - Software Eng. Mgmt. - 1020101
    - Software QA - 1020102
    - Software Conf. Mgmt. - 1020103
    - Specialty Engineering - 1020104
  - Project Management 1020200
    - Project Management - 1020201
    - Software Proj. Mgmt. - 1020202
- Sys T&E 1030000
  - Hardware Test and Evaluation - 1030100
  - Software Test and Evaluation - 1030200
- Production - 1040000
- Peculiar Support Equipment - 1050000
- Data - 1060000
- Training - 1070000
- Industrial Facilities - 1080000
- Operational Site Activation - 1090000
- Logistics Support - 1100000

Organization Breakdown Structure (rows):

- Systems Engineering
  - System Development
  - System Design
  - Test & Evaluation
  - Software Systems Engineering
  - Specialty Engineering
- Product Engineering
  - Electrical Design
  - Mechanical Design
- Software Engineering
  - Software Design
  - Software CM
- Manufacturing
  - Production Engineering
  - Production
- Procurement
  - Purchasing
  - TAS - Trackball Subcontract
  - JAS - Joystick Subcontract
  - DPFS -DP Firmware Subcontract
  - LCDS - LCD Subcontract
  - SIAS - Switch - Indicator Subcontract
- Product Assurance
  - Hardware QA
  - Software QA
- Project Management
  - Administration
  - Technical Director
  - Hardware CM

Chapter 5

WORK TEAMS

Objectives of this Chapter:

1. Define the work team concept.

2. Explain the benefits of work teams realized in many applications.

3. Illustrate how the work team concept can be used to greatly reduce the number of control accounts, thus reducing the operating cost of the project management system.

4. Define the role of the work team lead.

In the previous step of the project management process, control accounts were established as the basic element for project control activities. The next step involves work teams, which allow the number of control accounts to be greatly reduced while providing the necessary visibility into project status. The work team approach has rapidly gained popularity because it helps to eliminate the barriers between functional organizations. Many additional benefits also result from the use of work teams, further encouraging their application.

Work teams are also known by other names. Frequently they are called "Integrated Product Teams" (or IPTs). Some organizations identify them as "work cells" and associates on a team are consequently known as "cellmates". In this text, the generic term "work team" is used.

The Work Team

The work team is defined as a group of people who have the shared responsibility to produce a specific end product or to provide a specific service that has been previously authorized. A team is composed of individuals drawn from the various functional organizations that provide input to the work being performed. The team may be from a single functional organization or from mul-

tiple disciplines, but the greatest potential gains are in the multi-discipline environment. An example of multiple disciplines would be the production of a product that required support from mechanical design, fabrication and assembly, and testing for the completion of the project. Part of the advantage is that early input from those at the end of the production cycle will improve the design of the product.

The traditional barriers between functional organizations have impeded successful project management. While the assignment of a full time project team to a large project forces some organizational integration, there are still notable barriers. Project teams are assigned temporarily until their effort on a project is complete, meaning that team members must be assigned from a "home base". This base is a functional organization and the result is matrix management. Project team members report to two bosses, one from the home base functional organization and the other from a project; this often results in competing priorities. What is best for the project sometimes violates the turf of one or more functional organizations and vice versa.

When using work teams, the concepts of the Work Breakdown Structure (WBS) and the Organization Breakdown Structure (OBS) remain the same. The project is still divided into its compo-

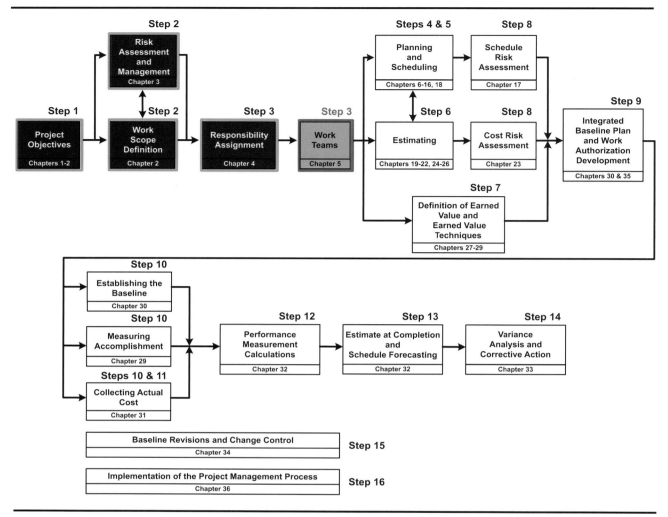

Figure 5-1 Earned Value Project Management: The Process

nent parts and responsibility assigned to each of those parts. The work team takes it a step further by organizing around the end objectives. It also assigns a single individual, from this multi-discipline environment, with overall team responsibility.

In the absence of work teams, it may be a formidable challenge to overcome the "silo" management that exists within pure functional organizations. A case from an automotive firm illustrates some of those challenges. A technical problem arose on the production floor because of faulty design completed six months earlier. The problem was passed up the chain of direct management (the silo) to the vice president of production. The first opportunity to address this situation occurred three and a half weeks later when the Vice President of Production met her counterpart, the Vice President of Engineering, on the golf course. The issue was discussed between the two and some of the technical details were incorrectly conveyed. A resolution was agreed upon and the wrong solution, resulting from the technical misinformation, flowed back to the engineering and production organizations. When the engineers familiar with the detailed design heard of the proposed resolution, they recognized that it did not correctly address the problem. Therefore, a special meeting was called with production and engineering in attendance to produce a better solution. The new solution had a $3 million positive cost impact to the company profit.

With the work team concept, this entire scenario could have been avoided. Production and engineering would have been on the same team on a daily basis and would have discovered and resolved the technical challenge as it occurred. Collaboration would have minimized the cost impact of the resolution, as well as saved numerous hours of meeting time.

Work teams often include owner/customer, contractor, and subcontractor personnel working side by side, particularly for end products and services that involve several different companies in product or service development. The composition of the work team will vary depending on the contract phase. To be effective, the work team must have decision-making ability including the authority to direct its own activities. Decentralized execution is a feature of the work team approach.

Work teams are applied in virtually all industries and on many different types of projects. One of the early applications of work teams occurred on the design and production of a satellite project. The project team consisted of an integrated group of contractor and owner/customer personnel all working toward a common objective without concern for traditional organizational boundaries. This second unit of a two-unit project was one of the most successful of that era in the United States.

Beginning in the 1990s, the United States Department of Defense (DoD) has organized most of its acquisition management around work teams. This emphasis on work teams by the DoD has influenced defense contractors to organize in work teams to align with their customers' expectations and enhance communications. In some cases, DoD contracts require the use of work teams to align with the DoD management organization.

Work teams have been developed to their greatest extent in Sweden. The entire culture successfully supports the team building concept. Children are encouraged to cooperate rather than compete from the earliest age. School children do not receive grades until the third grade. Teams are part of the total culture, not just the corporate culture. Major corporations such as Volvo, Saab, Celsiustech, and Ericsson Radar have proved themselves to be very well managed organizations.

Generals Sven-Olof Hokborg and Gunnar Lindstrom coached the multi-organizational teams on the Gripen Aircraft project. Electronic communications, such as e-mail and video teleconferencing, achieved the equivalent of co-location. All challenges on this very complex project were dealt with essentially in "real time". It was possible to interface the working levels where there was an appreciation for the technical/schedule/cost corrective actions. Using work teams on such a project minimizes the potential for confusion and misdirection. They also help to ensure that objectives remain crystal clear and communicated on a continuing basis. Team members feel good about their involvement in a project when they truly are responsible members of a team. When an employee has a direct input to the way that daily work is performed, that employee feels appreciated and respected.

Breaking down the barriers between organizations also has side benefits such as cross training between groups that were previously territorial. Improvements occur in appreciation for the talents of others within the organization. As engineering learns of the problems of the tool and die people and, conversely, production realizes the challenges that engineering faces, the likelihood increases of respecting each other's expertise and ingenuity.

Countries with a less homogeneous society than Sweden face additional challenges. While the greater diversity of countries such as the United States requires additional effort in developing effective interfaces among differing cultures and traditions, greater rewards can be achieved through integration of ideas and viewpoints.

Advantages of Work Teams

So what is special about the work team approach? Numerous benefits have been attributed to the use of work teams, including the following:

- Improved communication.
- Improved efficiency.
- Team spirit - "synergy".

- Increased productivity.

Reduced overall time to provide a product or service to a customer is an important goal. Reduced cost and improved quality are other important benefits desired by management. Side benefits accrue as well. All team members have the opportunity to contribute to decisions, resulting in an increase in the level and range of employee skills. Work teams dissolve or diminish territorial boundaries common in the functional or matrix management approaches, which leads to elimination of some of the distrust and hostility that frequently occurs among organizations worried about protecting their "turf". Industry experience with work teams has also shown increased morale and decreased absenteeism. Best of all, as illustrated in our earlier anecdote about executives trading incorrect information on the golf course, communication is improved.

Peter F. Drucker describes a leading cause of the breakdown of communication:

> **Communications** *are fairly good in the small functional organization. They break down once the functional organization reaches even moderate size. Even within the individual functional unit, e.g., the marketing department, communications weaken if the unit becomes large or complex. People are then increasingly specialists and interested primarily in their own narrow specialty.*[1]

This communications challenge is representative of those encountered on projects. The nature of the endeavor is large and complex or a project team would not have been assigned to accomplish the project in the first place. The work team is an effective approach to reduce and/or eliminate the mindset of isolated specialists. Drucker addresses organizations in general, but the following statement applies very well to project organizations in particular:

> *An organization should enable everyone to* **understand the common task, the task of the entire organization**. *Each member of the organization, in order to relate his efforts to the common good, needs to understand how his task fits in with the task of the whole and, in turn, what the task of the whole implies for his own task.... Communications therefore need to be helped rather than hindered by organizational structure.*[2]

The application of work teams to the project environment helps eliminate the barriers between silos of functional management and facilitates team member understanding of the individual's role in support of the common project objectives. The organization can either help or hinder the successful accomplishment of objectives. To demonstrate how this concept works in the project management process, Figure 5-2 shows a typical RAM, as discussed in Chapter 4. Individual responsibilities are designated with an "X" in the applicable control account boxes.

In the typical functional alignment shown in Figure 5-2, the individual in charge of the control account usually reports back to the responsible parent organization and receives program direction from the program organization.

Figure 5-3 illustrates the potential radical reduction in the number of control accounts that is possible using a work team alignment. All of the people contributing to a single end product or service are on one team, e.g. the Engine Work Team. Figure 5-3 readily shows that Purchasing, Subcontracts, Electronics Design, Power Design Branch, Mechanical Design Branch, Tooling, and Shops are all part of a single work team. These individuals would typically all be part of separate (sometimes competing) organizations. A count of the "X"s reveals that the number of control accounts has been reduced from 41 to 11 using the work team approach.

However, Figure 5-3 is just one of a number of possible groupings.

Another possibility, identified as Potential Work Team Alignment 2 in Figure 5-4, results in 12 control accounts. In this alignment, changes are made in the Quality Assurance and Project Management areas. If the decision were made instead to put the Reliability, Availability and

---

1. Drucker, Peter F. *Management: Tasks, Responsibilities, Practices.* New York, NY: Harper & Row, 1974, 561.

2. Drucker, 455.

Organizational Elements			1.1.1 Engine	1.1.2 Power Trans	1.2 Frame Assy.*	1.3 Sus-pension*	1.4 Integ. Assy.*	2.1 Dev Tests	2.2 T & E Suppt.	3.0 Data*	4.0 Depot Test Set*	5.0 Initial Spares And Repairs*	6.1 Sys Eng	6.2 Proj Mgt
			1.1 Power Source & Trans*					2.0 System Test & Eval*					6.0 System/ Project Mgmt.*	
			1.0 Vehicle											
			Mor-Ded Motor Scooter											
President – Procure-Ment Director*	Purchasing		X	X	X	X			X		X	X		
	Subcontracts		X			X								
Eng. Director*	Design Group	Electronics Design	X					X			X			
		Power Design Branch	X					X			X			
		Mech. Design Branch	X	X	X	X								
	Test & Evaluation							X	X	X				
	Engineer Design Group	Drafting Branch								X				
		Computer Services								X				
		Model Shop							X					
Manufact uring Director*	Production Control Group													
	Manufacturing Engr. Group											X		
	Tooling		X									X		
	Shops		X	X	X	X								
	Assembly						X					X		
Director Quality Assurance*	Quality Assurance Dept	R & M Group						X					X	
		Quality Engr. Group											X	
	Quality Control Department						X					X		
Prog. Mgt Dept*	Mor-Ded Program Manager									X				X

* Customer Reporting Level

Figure 5-2 Typical Responsibility Matrix - Functional Alignment

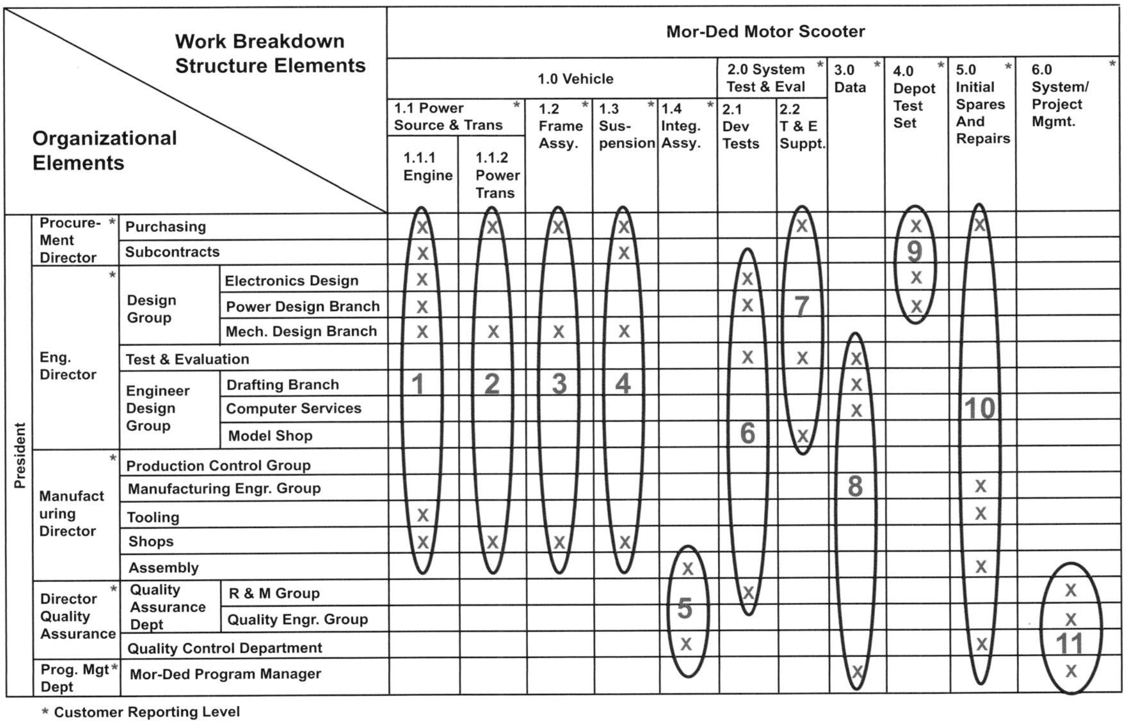

Figure 5-3 Potential Work Team Alignment - 1

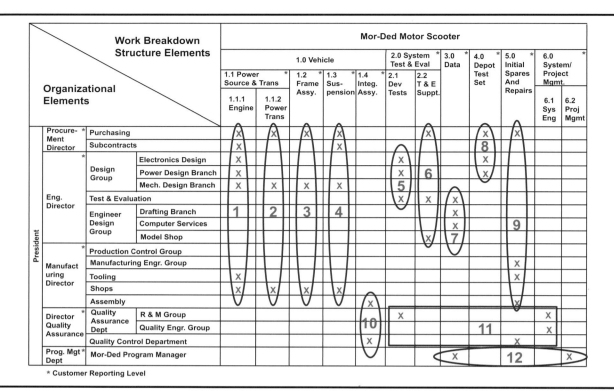

Figure 5-4 Potential Work Team Alignment - 2

Maintainability effort with the Systems Engineering effort, then the Development Tests (WBS 2.1) would be reduced in scope, schedule, and budget accordingly while Systems Engineering (WBS 6.1) would be accordingly increased. The resultant plans would align to a revised WBS Dictionary, cost estimates, and charge numbering scheme so that a team would not cross WBS elements in the final control account structure.

Still other arrangements are possible. Potential Work Team Alignment 3 in Figure 5-5 assigns work teams by discipline: Procurement, Design, etc. Although this dramatically increases the number of control accounts relative to alignments 1 and 2, there would still be 34% fewer control accounts than a typical RAM, as Figure 5-2, displays.

The approach shown in Figure 5-5 exists when strong-willed, non-flexible functional organizations will not relax their traditional "stove pipe silo" management style. This result is often observed when a strong single functional orientation exists that will not allow working with what bosses perceive to be non-team members.

Figures 5-6 through 5-8 contain additional examples of work team applications. Figure 5-6 shows the traditional interface of a propulsion/engine contractor. This would typically result in many control accounts that average about $1,000,000 each. This may be viewed as dividing the effort into too many finite pieces so the trend is to combine them into a more integrated work team approach.

Figure 5-7 combines accounts into work teams so that they average $3,000,000. This is triple the size of those shown in Figure 5-6, so there are one third of the accounts to manage. This is a more integrated management approach.

Figure 5-8 illustrates three levels of work teams on a multi-billion dollar project. The lowest level teams, represented by the blue circles, are within the contractor's organization and consists of those actually charged with performing the technical work. The highest level team, represented by the green circle, is the Integrated Project Management Team (IPMT) that provides the overall objectives for the effort and is composed primarily of customer/owner personnel. The IPMT is also represented by all appropriate functional dis-

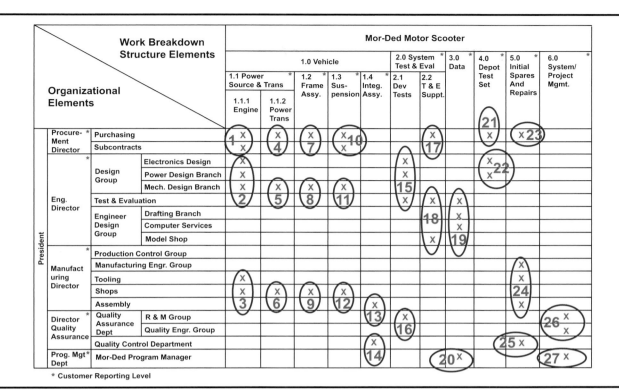

Figure 5-5 Potential Work Team Alignment - 3

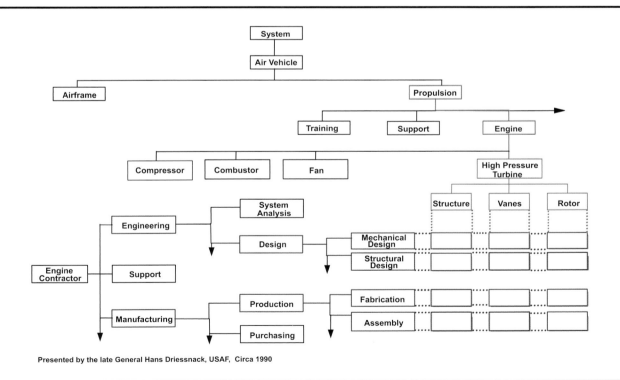

Presented by the late General Hans Driessnack, USAF, Circa 1990

Figure 5-6 Work Team Application - Example 1

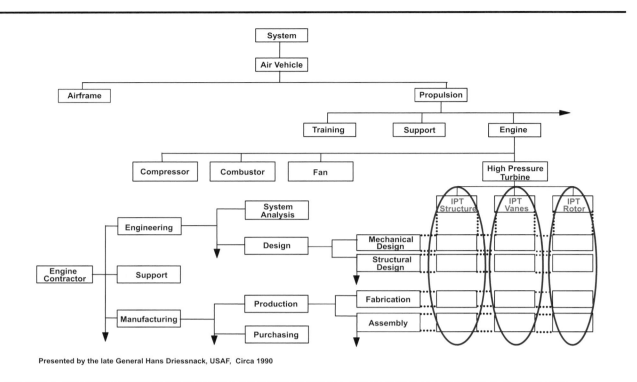

Presented by the late General Hans Driessnack, USAF, Circa 1990

Figure 5-7 Work Team Application - Example 2

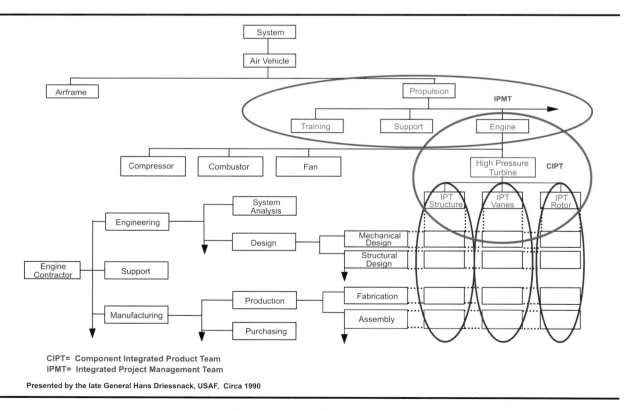

CIPT= Component Integrated Product Team
IPMT= Integrated Project Management Team

Presented by the late General Hans Driessnack, USAF, Circa 1990

Figure 5-8 Work Team Application - Example 3

ciplines, but at a higher organizational level than for the contractor IPT/work team. The Component Integrated Product Team (CIPT), designated by the red circle, is the interface organization between the IPT/work team and the IPMT.

The composition of the various teams must be well defined. The team lead of each of the IPTs/work teams forms the Component Integrated Product Team. In this case, the lead for the structure team, the vanes team, and the rotor team would all be members of the Component Integrated Product Team. The team lead of the CIPT becomes an automatic member of the Integrated Product Management Team. This degree of formality and team organization structure exists because this example is for a very large, long duration project.

The Work Team Lead

A work team lead is selected for each group. This individual has overall responsibility and authority for the success of the group. The team lead may be appointed by management or elected by the work team to manage the team's efforts. However, the team lead facilitates the decision making process rather than making unilateral decisions. The individual team members actively contribute to the process. This leaves the work team lead more in the role of coach than as manager or decision-maker for the team. The team lead will typically be the one assigned overall responsibility for a control account, but the success of the team is dependent on its ability to work together to contribute to the overall project objectives. Because team members participate in decisions to meet objectives, they will usually more enthusiastically embrace the direction of the team.

The work team lead can also change over time. On a large project that includes both design and production, the work teams would include engineering design and manufacturing personnel. The initial design phase could be led by the engineering manager and when transitioning to production, the manufacturing manager could then also transition to become the work team lead.

An underlying concept is illustrated here:

No organization can depend on genius; the supply is always scarce and unreliable. It is the test of an organization to make ordinary human beings perform better than they seem capable of, to bring out whatever strength there is in its members, and to use each man's [sic] strength to help all the other members perform. It is the task of organization at the same time to neutralize the individual weaknesses of its members. The test of an organization is the spirit of performance. [3]

The work team lead is responsible for bringing this concept to life within the work team.

This concept may be extended upwards in the WBS. Teams can be formed for these higher level elements to allow important cost, schedule, technical, and risk tradeoffs to be addressed at a level above the control account so that a work team lead could have more than one control account manager reporting to him or her. In this case, a work team lead is commonly referred to as a WBS element manager.

Conclusion

Work teams have increased in popularity and extended to numerous applications. The concept of a work team is to organize a group of people charged with the responsibility and authority to produce a particular end product shown on the WBS. They work together to accomplish that objective regardless of their functional affiliation. A work team lead is selected for each group. It is the role of the work team lead to assume overall responsibility and authority for the success of the group. Besides fostering improved teamwork and communication, this approach also reduces the number of control accounts needed to manage the project which has a substantial associated cost savings.

---

3.   Drucker, 455.

Chapter 5 Review Questions

Note: There may be more than one answer to a question.

5-1.   List four advantages of using the work team concept.

5-2.   Which of the following is true about work teams?

    A. They are composed of individuals drawn from various functions.

    B. They substantially reduce the number of control accounts for managing the project.

    C. They have a team lead.

    D. All of the above are true.

True or False

5-3.   Work teams are organized in the RAM along the lines of the Organization Breakdown Structure (OBS).

5-4.   Every work team has a work team lead.

5-5.   A work team lead is always assigned by management.

5-6.   The work team concept has been limited in its application to federal government contracts in the aerospace industry.

5-7.   The work team approach looks at what the objective is (an end product or service) and organizes along those lines.

5-8.   Some work teams are still applied along strictly functional lines because of inflexibility in the functional organizations.

5-9.   Work teams are typically organized along a Work Breakdown Structure (WBS) because that is the manner of organizing work into manageable subdivisions.

The answers to these questions can be found in Section 6, Solutions.

Case Study

5.1 ORGANIZATION CHART AND RESPONSIBILITY ASSIGNMENT MATRIX

On the Automated Interdiction System (AIS) Workstation Project, Karen found that the development planning process she was going through was raising questions faster than she found answers. Early one morning, about a week after she started on the program, Karen began to think about the people who were asking to join her development team. She was not ready to assign work yet, and Broud Stearman had made it clear that she could not start until she had a reasonably well defined plan.

Karen had a good idea about how to run the development. Now she needed to start thinking about people. For one thing, she needed help. Also, the situation had changed somewhat. A new Engineering Manager, Ilene Turkel, had been hired. She had a well rounded background; computer literate, systems and hardware engineering experience, quite familiar with software. She had even asked about the Software Engineering Institute's (SEI) Capability Maturity Model (CMM).

Karen began the development of an organization chart.

Considering the following four examples Karen had observed on other projects, and using the partially completed organization chart provided, please create a suggested organization chart and Responsibility Assignment Matrix (RAM) for Karen.

The solution to this case study can be found on the Humphreys & Associates, Inc. web site.
www.humphreys-assoc.com

Pure Functional Organizations

Organization Breakdown Structure		Work Breakdown Structure	1.0 Total Project							
			1.1			1.2			1.3	
			1.1.1	1.1.2	1.1.3	1.2.1	1.2.2	1.2.3	1.3.1	1.3.2
Top Level Organization	Org. A	Organization A1	X			X			X	
		Organization A2			X			X		X
		Organization A3								
	Org. B	Organization B1				X	X			
		Organization B2	X		X			X		
	Org. C	Organization C1	X							X

Pure Integrated Product Team (IPT) Organizations

Organization Breakdown Structure		Work Breakdown Structure	1.0 Total Project							
			1.1			1.2			1.3	
			1.1.1	1.1.2	1.1.3	1.2.1	1.2.2	1.2.3	1.3.1	1.3.2
Top Level Organization	Summary IPT 1.1	IPT A	X							
		IPT B		X						
		IPT C			X					
	Summary IPT 1.2	IPT D				X				
		IPT E					X			
		IPT F						X		
	Summary IPT 1.3	IPT G							X	
		IPT H								X

Alternate RAM for Pure Integrated Product Team (IPT) Organizations

Work Breakdown Structure/ Integrated Product Teams (IPTs)	1.0 Total Project							
	1.1			1.2			1.3	
	1.1.1	1.1.2	1.1.3	1.2.1	1.2.2	1.2.3	1.3.1	1.3.2
	IPT A	IPT B	IPT C	IPT D	IPT E	IPT F	IPT G	IPT H

Hybrid of Functional Organizations and Integrated Product Team (IPT)

Organization Breakdown Structure / Work Breakdown Structure			1.0 Total Project							
			1.1			1.2			1.3	
			1.1.1	1.1.2	1.1.3	1.2.1	1.2.2	1.2.3	1.3.1	1.3.2
Top Level Organization	Org. A	Organization A1				X			X	
		Organization A2			X			X		X
		Organization A3		X						
	Org. B	Organization B1				X	X			
		Organization B2			X			X		
	Integrated Product Team A		X							
	Integrated Product Team B							X		
	Org. C	Organization C1								X

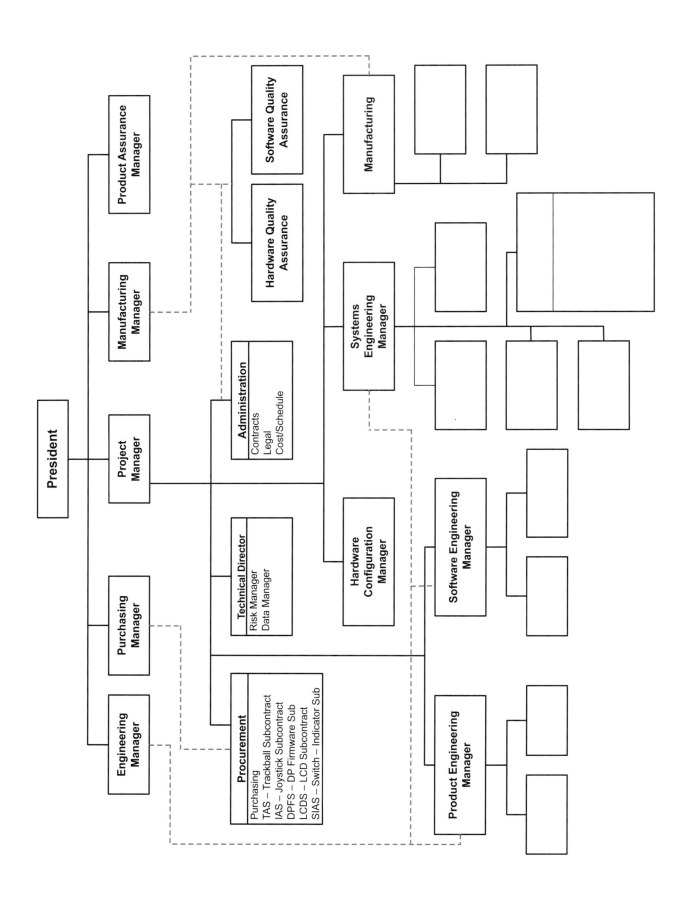

Work Breakdown Structure

Automated Workstation Development Project - 10000000

Console Subsystem 1010000
- Display Processor (DP) 1010100
  - DP CSCI - 1010101
  - DP HWCI - 1010102
- Man Machine Interface 1010200
  - MMI CSCI - 1010201
  - MMI HWCI - 1010202
- Interface Processor (IP) 1010300
  - IP CSCI - 1010301
  - IP HWCI - 1010302
- Subsystem Integration and Test 1010400
  - Build Integ. & Test - 1010401
  - CSCI Integ. & Test - 1010402
- System Software 1010500
  - System Software - 1010501
  - System Firmware - 1010502

System Engineering Management 1020000
- Systems Engineering 1020100
  - Software Eng. Mgmt. - 1020101
  - Software QA - 1020102
  - Software Conf. Mgmt. - 1020103
  - Specialty Engineering - 1020104
- Project Management 1020200
  - Project Management - 1020201
  - Software Proj. Mgmt. - 1020202

Sys T&E 1030000
- Hardware Test and Evaluation - 1030100
- Software Test and Evaluation - 1030200

- Production - 1040000
- Peculiar Support Equipment - 1050000
- Data - 1060000
- Training - 1070000
- Industrial Facilities - 1080000
- Operational Site Activation - 1090000
- Logistics Support - 11000000

Organization Breakdown Structure

Systems Engineering
- System Development
- System Design
- Test & Evaluation
- Software Systems Engineering
- Specialty Engineering

Product Engineering
- Electrical Design
- Mechanical Design

Software Engineering
- Software Design
- Software CM

Manufacturing
- Production Engineering
- Production
- Purchasing

Procurement
- TAS - Trackball Subcontract
- JAS - Joystick Subcontract
- DPFS - DP Firmware Subcontract
- LCDS - LCD Subcontract
- SIAS - Switch - Indicator Subcontract

Product Assurance
- Hardware QA
- Software QA

Project Management
- Administration
- Technical Director
- Hardware CM

Project Manager: Broud Stearman

SECTION 1 QUIZ

Note: There may be more than one answer to a question.

1. What is the WBS Dictionary?
    A. A document listing specific contract acronyms.
    B. A set of instructions for completing a work package.
    C. A document that describes each WBS element.
    D. A document which defines the role of the control account manager.

2. A control account has four major characteristics. What are they?
    A. Labor, material, other direct costs, budget.
    B. Statement of work, budget, schedule, responsible person.
    C. Organization, planning, accounting, analysis.
    D. Thresholds, approval, date, WBS reference.

3. A Work Breakdown Structure is:
    A. A graphical representation of organizational responsibility for a project.
    B. A product oriented subdivision of hardware, software, services, and facilities for a project.
    C. The intersection of control accounts and work packages.
    D. A method of comparing budgets and actual costs.

4. A Responsibility Assignment Matrix (RAM) is a matrix that depicts the intersection of the:
    A. WBS and the statement of work.
    B. Functional organization and the contractor's management structure.
    C. WBS and the contractor's organization.
    D. Control accounts with work packages.

5. Control account levels are to be established where the contractor will actually manage the work.
    A. True.
    B. False.

6. List three factors that will impact the selection of project controls for a particular project application:
    A.
    B.
    C.

7. The use of a firm fixed price contract will shift the emphasis from cost control to schedule control for the contractor.
    A. True.

   B. False.

8.   What is needed even before the project work scope is identified?
      A. Project objectives.
      B. A signed contract.
      C. A letter of understanding.
      D. A project manager.
      E. A schedule and a budget.

9.   Cost and schedule objectives are more important than technical objectives.
      A. True.
      B. False.

10.   The biggest impact of contract type is on the appropriate level of control for:
      A. Cost.
      B. Schedule.
      C. Technical scope.
      D. Cash flow.

11.   One of the biggest advantages of including a measure of accomplishment is the ability to forecast potential cost overruns and schedule slips early in the project.
      A. True.
      B. False.

12.   Work Breakdown Structures are only appropriate for large construction projects.
      A. True.
      B. False.

13.   Which of the following statements are true about the Work Breakdown Structure Dictionary?
      A. It documents the scope of each WBS element.
      B. It is a valuable communication tool.
      C. It serves as a framework for understanding changes in scope.
      D. All of the above.

14.   The problem with an element of cost orientation for the WBS is:
      A. Most accounting systems are designed to collect costs by element of cost.
      B. This makes it too difficult to track costs when a project goes from one phase to the next.
      C. Costs associated with specific work scope end products are scattered throughout the WBS, complicating analysis.
      D. There is nothing wrong with this approach.

15.   The fact that engineering/construction efforts shift from an emphasis on systems to physical areas and back to systems again suggests that the best WBS approach would be:
      A. A common WBS for all project phases.
      B. A different WBS for each project phase.
      C. A single project WBS with different legs (Level 2 WBS elements) corresponding to various project phases.
      D. To abandon the WBS approach for this type of project.

16.   A company should revise its organization structure in order to better support development of the Responsibility Assignment Matrix (RAM).

A. True.

B. False.

17.   The lowest level in the RAM is:

A. The bottom level of the WBS.

B. The bottom level of the organization structure.

C. The control account.

D. The schedule task.

18.   Selecting the proper level for the control account depends on:

A. Work scope, associated risk, and performing organization.

B. Dollar value and account duration.

C. Contract framework and information objectives.

D. All of the above.

19.   Summarizing the OBS to too high of a level causes problems because there is lost visibility of the status of the end products.

A. True.

B. False.

20.   Use of work teams places more emphasis on organizational work areas than on end product development.

A. True.

B. False.

21.   The use of work teams typically produces:

A. Increased productivity.

B. Increased number of control accounts.

C. Improved communication.

D. More accurate measures of accomplishment.

22.   Which are the first three steps in the project management process?

A. Work scope definition, scheduling, and budgeting.

B. Baseline establishment, progress measurement, and variance analysis.

C. Definition of project objectives, estimating, and scheduling.

D. Definition of project objectives, work scope definition, and responsibility assignment.

23.   A program may be made up of several projects.

A. True.

B. False.

The answers to these questions can be found in Section 6, Solutions.

SCHEDULING

SECTION 2

SCHEDULING

Up to this point, Earned Value Project management has been discussed in relation to work definition and organizational considerations: work scope, work teams, and project organizations. Now, the other components of the project management process will be addressed, beginning with scheduling, because scheduling drives so many of the other implementation processes.

Experienced schedulers will be the first to point out that planning should be discussed first, and scheduling should be considered the most important product of planning. The initial planning phase has an impact on much of the project and how it will be executed. When a potential project is identified, there is no defined cost. However, there is usually a defined boundary for when the project can start and when it must be finished. Depending on how challenging is the duration for completing the project work, decisions will be made as to the schedule, staffing requirements, cash flow requirements and total cost. As the schedule is developed and resources applied, a total cost is developed. The cost cannot be precisely defined until the execution strategy and general outline of the schedule is available. These two activities, strategy and schedule outline, are part of the planning process.

The process of scheduling should be done to provide complete and accurate information regarding the overall project status along with recommendations to take advantage of favorable situations as well as how to resolve unfavorable situations. The Earned Value Project Management flowchart of this book shows three topics in a vertical row. These three areas are highly interrelated and are usually performed concurrently. The estimate is needed to develop the duration for the activities in the schedule. The schedule can then be used to develop the cash flow and the total cost. For manufacturing, hardware, or construction applications, the quantity of items to be produced and the amount of material needed on the project will define the material cost and labor hours that, in turn, will determine the activity durations and labor cost. The schedule also directly affects the amount of services needed to support the project. This iterative process requires careful coordination between an organization's cost and schedule functions and its executing functions.

The Planning and Scheduling flowchart (Figure 6-2) is divided into two major areas, both of which will be covered in detail in succeeding chapters. These two areas are the scheduling process (fundamentals of scheduling) and implementation of schedules on projects. The scheduling process will address the need for a schedule and then present the various types of schedules/presentation formats and their appropriate application. Network diagrams will be explained in detail, including their application in Critical Path Method (CPM) scheduling. This includes specific instruction in the calculations performed to determine the critical path and the relative criticality of all schedule activities. Finally, the application of resources on schedule activities will be outlined. Methods for summary presentation of resource requirements will be developed, and the role of resource leveling in achieving a realistic plan will be discussed. Manufacturing/production environments may use an alternative approach to scheduling; such as, Line of Balance (LOB), or a derivative thereof. This topic will also be addressed in detail later as one of the scheduling techniques to be considered for certain project applications.

The implementation portion of the planning and scheduling flowchart immediately addresses considerations in developing a schedule for a particular project. Various strategies for schedule development are explored and their outcomes investigated. Techniques are presented for accelerating the project schedule when the initial schedule does not satisfy the project's objectives. A summation of all information presented is then incorporated in the topic of schedule baseline establishment. One requirement of the baseline schedule is that all schedule documents must be consistent, i.e. they must exhibit traceability.

The implementation portion next considers a series of topics related to the continuing use of the schedule throughout the duration of the project. The process of updating schedules is discussed and differentiated from approved schedule changes. Specific techniques for resolving behind schedule conditions ("negative float") are presented. Various techniques may be used in Critical Path Method (CPM) scheduling that do not always provide accurate status information. These are identified, explained, and solutions are presented for detecting and avoiding these scheduling abuses.

Technical risk assessment was discussed in Section 1, Chapter 3. Schedule risk assessment and its application to CPM will be discussed in this section. The concept of the highest schedule risk path now supplements the idea of critical path to provide improved insight into status for more effective schedule control.

The implementation portion of the flowchart is completed with discussions on automation of the scheduling process and evaluation considerations. Specific applications of scheduling are considered in two areas: (1) the specialized requirements for scheduling on contracts using the Earned Value Management System Guidelines (EVMSG), and (2) considerations when using CPM schedules to resolve claims for additional funds based on schedule impact from other contractors/ suppliers/customers.

This comprehensive coverage of the scheduling topic provides both the fundamentals and advanced scheduling considerations, and serves as a basis for future topics in the integrated project management process.

Throughout this text there will be references to several government initiatives and standards. One of the standards is the Generally Accepted Scheduling Principles (GASP). The GASP has been embodied in the newly published Planning and Scheduling Excellence Guide (PASEG). The GASP is based on eight essential principles, divided into two basic groups: five valid schedule and three effective schedule principles.

Valid Schedules meet these five Generally Accepted Scheduling Principles:

- Complete: Schedules represent authorized discrete effort for the entire contract, with essential subcontracted or other external work or milestones integrated yet distinguishable from internal work.

- Traceable: Schedules reflect realistic and meaningful network logic that horizontally and vertically integrates the likely sequence for project execution. Schedules are coded to relate tasks or milestones to source or dependent documents, tools, and responsible organizations.

- Transparent: Schedules provide full disclosure of project status and forecast and include documented ground rules, assumptions, and methods for building and maintaining schedules. Documentation includes steps for analyzing the critical paths, incorporating risks and opportunities, and generating schedule health and performance metrics.

- Statused: Schedules reflect consistent and regular updates of completed work, interim progress, achievable remaining durations relative to the status date, and accurately maintained logic relationships.

- Predictive: Schedules accurately forecast the likely completion dates and impacts to the project baseline plan through valid network logic and achievable task durations from the status date through project completion.

Effective schedules also meet these three additional Principles:

- Usable: Schedules produce meaningful metrics for timely and effective communication and tracking and improving performance, mitigating issues and risks, and capturing opportunities.

Schedules are robust and functional to help stakeholders manage different levels, groupings, or areas as needed. Schedules are developed and maintained at a size, level, and complexity such that they are timely and enable effective decision-making.

- Resourced: Resources align with the schedule baseline and forecasts to enable the stakeholders to view and assess the time-phased labor and other costs required to achieve project baseline and forecast targets. Each project is unique and uses varying techniques to load, baseline, and maintain the time-phased resources at levels that are practical and produce meaningful and accurate projections. When resource loaded schedules are used they enable flexible updates to resource requirements as conditions change. Whether or not resource loaded schedules are used, cost and schedule data are integrated for internal and external reporting.

- Controlled: Schedules are baselined and maintained using a rigorous, stable, and repeatable process. Schedule additions, deletions, and updates conform to this process and result in valid and accurate results for sound schedule configuration control and maintenance.

Another emerging standard for schedule health is the Government Accounting Office's best scheduling practices. These practices were developed by industry and the GAO representing non-DOD United States Government Agencies. In general, the GAO Best Scheduling Practices align with the GASP with one exception; GAO's Best Practice number eight suggests that the procuring activity conduct a Schedule Risk Analysis to determine a level of confidence in meeting a program's completion date. More discussions of the SRA process and products can be found in Chapter 17.

The Earned Value Management System Guidelines (EVMSG) is a set of 32 guidelines established by the ANSI/EIA-748 (latest revision) that define the requirements that an Earned Value Management System must meet. The 32 EVMS Guidelines incorporate best business practices for project management systems that have proven to provide strong benefits for project or enterprise planning and control. The processes include integration of project scope, schedule, and cost objectives, establishment of a baseline plan for accomplishment of project objectives, and use of earned value techniques for performance measurement during the execution of a project. The system provides a sound basis for problem identification, corrective actions, and management replanning as required.

Throughout the scheduling portion of this text, the eight core principles of GASP, the best practices of the GAO, and the ANSI/EIA-748 (latest revision) EVMS Guidelines will be addressed as applicable.

Chapter **6**

WHAT IS SCHEDULING? SCHEDULE TYPES

Objectives of this Chapter:

1. Define scheduling and explain why scheduling is necessary.

2. Determine the data requirements to develop a schedule.

3. Discuss processing of scheduling data.

4. Describe how the results of an effective scheduling system may be used to assist in the management of a project.

The complexity involved in the scheduling process requires the use of a separate flowchart to supplement the overall Earned Value Project Management flowchart. This more detailed flowchart will be referenced for the remainder of the scheduling sections to show where each chapter fits within that sub-process. The chart is divided into two sections: scheduling fundamentals and implementation. The scheduling process begins in this chapter with an overview of the function that addresses the "why" of scheduling.

Project Scheduling

One of the first activities to occur in the development of any project execution plan is definition of a high level schedule, including the identification of major milestones to show the timing of key events, accomplishments and interfaces. This high level schedule initiates a discipline of scheduling for the duration of the project, an important tool for its management. Project managers rely on the schedule for primary management of a project. At the other extreme, project managers may despair of getting any useful information from their schedules because the schedule was either improperly constructed or used. The principles of scheduling are straight forward and facil-

itate understanding for all project personnel. Nevertheless, scheduling requires a dedicated effort and familiarity with many subtle factors that affect its analysis.

At one time, the scheduling function was treated with a lack of appreciation by those responsible for the technical portion of the work, such as engineers and construction personnel. Since scheduling was not the main goal of these personnel, they viewed it as an intrusion on their work, which was performing the engineering or directing the design, production, or construction. Over time, companies realized that scheduling was a specialized area that required a dedicated staff. So they purchased software, hired or redirected people and called them schedulers. That did not work well either because a scheduler must understand the overall objectives of a project and how those objectives can best be accomplished in order to be a truly effective scheduler. In other words, it is beneficial if they have an appreciation for what is involved in engineering if they plan to schedule engineering work. Some engineering organizations will not accept a scheduler unless that person is a graduate engineer and sits in the same area as the engineering personnel, so the scheduler will feel the pulse of the daily activities. They believe that there is

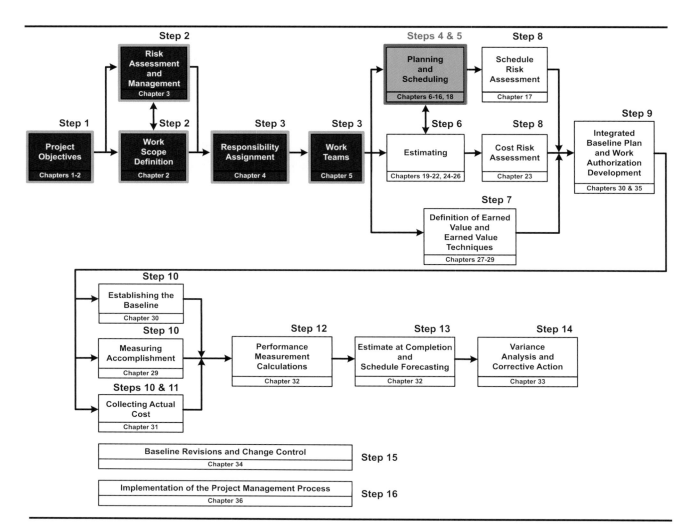

Figure 6-1 Earned Value Project Management: The Process

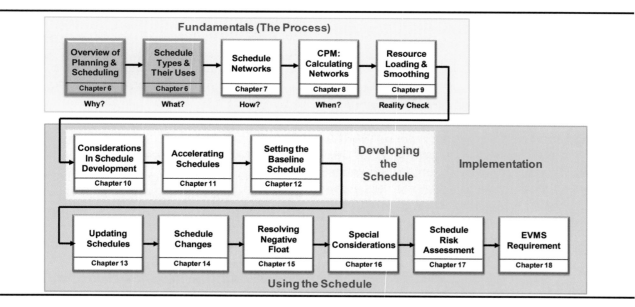

Figure 6-2 Planning and Scheduling

more to interpreting the schedule position than reading output reports.

The scheduling function will be examined in detail. Many people who view themselves as schedulers do not fully understand the concepts. This is a natural result of assigning people to the scheduling discipline, loading a scheduling software package on their computers, training them in the commands to use the program, and calling the training process completed. The fallacy of this practice was illustrated too well at a training class for a major scheduling software package some years ago. There were about a dozen people attending the class. As the software instructor patiently explained what the features of the program were and what commands initiated certain functions, the only questions were of a more general nature. "Why do we need to load resources?" "What is the importance of float?" "Is it important to level resources as my company doesn't do it?" "What happens when the schedule is longer than the time available?"

The software instructor did not have a clue what the answers were to these questions. The usual response was, "It is a feature of the program. You can use it if you want or not use it. We have to support a lot of different needs for our clients and some of them want this feature." What these people needed was training in the fundamentals of scheduling, not training in how to use a particular software program. Ideally, new users should first be introduced to the concepts and only later trained in how to use a particular software solution. Scheduling tools should also be taught by instructors that are adept in the scheduling concepts.

The bottom line is that while it takes hard work to set up and properly operate a scheduling system, it is also a straightforward effort. It is possible to set up a system that will provide useful, accurate, and timely information; and it becomes inexcusable not to initiate such a program with the tight management of all projects in these days of corporate belt-tightening.

What is a Schedule and Why Use One?

A simple definition of a schedule is a document that defines what work must be done, and when, in order to accomplish project objectives on time. It is the time-phased portion of the total plan. When combined with the technical plan (the scope of the project) and the financial plan (the budget or cost), it forms the project plan.

The schedule is developed as part of the total project plan; it is also used to measure performance against the plan. There are two sides to the answer of "why schedule?" The first is the positive benefit that can be derived from a disciplined scheduling approach, while the flip side is the negative results or penalties that occur without a well-defined schedule. The benefits will be discussed first.

Development and maintenance of a schedule provides an excellent vehicle for communication throughout the duration of a project. Communication includes sharing what the overall plan is, how the plan is to be achieved, who will complete which activities, in what time frames the activities will be completed, and what resources will be required to support the schedule dates. Many project managers say that the initial planning required for development of a baseline schedule justifies creation of a detailed schedule. The schedule also facilitates communication on the status of the project, and is an important link for feedback from the technical disciplines to the project management office. Equally important, the use of a schedule can provide a basis for management by exception by allowing attention to be focused on those activities that are deviating significantly from the original plan or on those activities that are most important towards achieving the project objectives.

Other advantages to good scheduling exist as well. With a formal schedule in place, resources can be applied, analyzed, and allocated or leveled as necessary. The exploration of project execution alternatives is possible through the investigation of "what-if" scenarios, and time/cost tradeoffs are possible through project acceleration/delay studies.

Conversely, negative results are associated with the absence of a scheduling process. It is impossible to know if a planned completion date is realistic or even achievable without a formal schedule. Without advance knowledge of how many resources will be needed, their type, and their timing, it is highly unlikely that they will be available when needed. Coordination of work becomes difficult as each project team member works according to his/her own internal schedule rather than a defined project plan. Without coordinated internal schedules, the true effect of individual delivery dates and resource requirements cannot be evaluated and do not represent an achievable plan to support the project objectives. An unachievable plan eventually shows slippages in the false schedule, resulting in major cost impacts. For example, as project durations are extended, costs for administrative and other services rise because of the longer duration of service provision. Cost escalation impacts are also felt, particularly if there is a long delay or it occurs during a period of high inflation. If material delivery dates are incorrect, it can impact storage costs or further delays because of material shortages. All of these are consequences of an unachievable schedule and impact the most important goal of all: a delayed or diminished return on investment. Lost revenue because of lack of product availability or lost award fees can amount to hundreds of thousands of dollars a day or more. These considerations make the comparatively inexpensive cost of operating a scheduling system a wise financial investment.

Data Requirements

In the schedule development process, certain specific and consistent data are required for all projects. They include:

- The scope of work, defined to the activity level.
- Activity interrelationships.
- Activity duration.
- Resource requirements.
- Assigned responsibilities.

The first requirement is a detailed scope of work. The development of an adequate schedule is impossible without an adequate scope definition. The second requirement is that relationships between activities need to be identified so that the input and output of each activity is known in relationship to the other project activities, and the impact of a slip in one activity on the schedule can be determined. The third and fourth requirements, activity duration and resource requirements, are interrelated since most durations are a function of the amount of resources assigned. This is especially true in a production environment. Lastly, knowing who is responsible for particular activities is a requirement so that he or she can provide data on their status. Responsibility definition is essential very early in the process, since the responsible person provides the other inputs (activity interrelationships, duration, and resource requirements).

Two reasons make it important to actively involve those responsible for the activities in the generation of the schedule: (1) they are the ones most familiar with the work that needs to be accomplished and thus provide the best input, and (2) their involvement ensures their participation in the process and ownership of the product. The standard response from a person who is late in completing an activity, but was not involved in the scheduling process, is "I never agreed to that date."

Previous work should be used as a reality check on inputs gathered from those responsible for the current work. A well documented historical data base can be a valuable asset to anyone developing a schedule for a new project, as well as to anyone reviewing that schedule.

Data Processing

Four factors affect the amount of effort required for data processing. First, the level of detail in the schedule directly impacts the amount of information generated by the scheduling system as well as the number of people needed to maintain it. Second, the scheduling methods must be selected. This will be discussed at length in the following chapters. Another decision regards the role of automation in the scheduling process. While it is anticipated that all scheduling systems will have a component of automation, many also include a manual aspect, such as manually prepared high level summary documents. There is a need for procedures in that instance to ensure that the manual and automated schedules remain consistent. However, most modern scheduling tools can directly produce summarized information consistent with its detail. The fourth and final question related to data processing is how the information is to be displayed. Information display includes not only format, but also a directory of who gets specific information.

Using Results

The point of having a scheduling system is to use the results. Specific purposes of the system include:

1. Development of a realistic baseline plan.

2. Priority definition.

3. Status reporting.

4. Problem area identification.

5. Problem impact analysis.

6. Corrective action plan support.

The baseline plan is the starting point and must accurately reflect the scope of work and the resources available. The best crafted and logically correct schedule is not achievable unless resources are considered. After the plan is established, it is possible to prioritize work activities based on scheduling and risk assessment techniques.

The primary purpose of a schedule should be as a communication tool. Priorities are determined by identifying the schedule drivers: those items that directly affect the total length of the schedule. Once the plan is established, the next use of the schedule is to employ it as a status reporting document. The comparison of this status with the baseline plan supports identification of problem areas. An effective scheduling system does more than just identify problems; it also identifies the impacts of the problem on project delivery dates and costs. Once problems and impacts have been identified, the schedule helps determine if the development of alternative plans were warranted. If they are, then the schedule is ana-

lyzed to find the alternatives and implement the most effective option.

A carefully developed schedule requires discipline and time, but it provides a capable management tool for the life of the project. Without it, successful management of the project is severely hampered.

Schedule Types

The objectives of this section are to:

1. Present commonly used schedule formats.

2. Describe the strengths and weaknesses of each format.

3. Discuss the type of applications in which a particular format will most likely be used.

4. Demonstrate that network scheduling provides much more information and analysis capability than any other approach.

Formats for schedules extend from the rudimentary that contain little information, to the advanced, that provide information that can greatly assist the effective management of any project. Different schedule formats serve various objectives, and it is likely that every project will have more than one schedule presentation format. The usefulness of a given schedule application is enhanced by the selection of the proper type and format. In this chapter, different types of schedules are presented, giving attention to their advantages and limitations. Finally, guidance as to their proper application is provided.

Numerous techniques and graphical representations are used to create and report schedules. The various scheduling approaches will be presented from an historical perspective, starting with early Gantt and bar charts and advancing to more recent techniques such as network diagramming.

Gantt Charts

One of the oldest and simplest forms of scheduling is the Gantt Chart. This form of scheduling traces back to World War I and a man named

Henry L. Gantt, who worked in the Frankford Arsenal in 1917. The logistics demands of the war indicated a need for better information to assist the flow of supplies and material. Mr. Gantt therefore devised the scheduling technique that still bears his name.[1]

The Gantt Chart has received widespread use over the years because it is easy to understand and requires a minimum of time to develop and update. An example of a Gantt Chart is pictured in Figure 6-3. Time is represented on the horizontal axis and groups of activities are shown on the vertical axis. The "time now" line is represented by the inverted triangle shown on September 1. Status is shown by either filling the bar or by adding another bar below the original, as illustrated. While it takes little effort to produce this type of schedule, it provides little information as well. There are serious shortcomings with this scheduling approach. It does not show critical activities or interdependencies between activities.

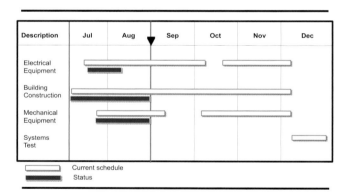

Figure 6-3 Gantt Chart

That means if one activity were late, there is no indication as to the effect on other activities. Status reporting of progress can also be very misleading. There is no indication of the actual start or finish date for any activity.

This format only depicts that an activity has started and finished, but not when it happened or even if it occurred on schedule. There is no possibility of early warning of future schedule slippages.

1. Fleming, Bronn, and Humphreys. *Project & Production Scheduling.* Chicago, IL: Probus Publishing Company, 1987, 37-38.

Milestone Chart

Another scheduling technique that arose from the early Gantt Chart efforts is the Milestone Chart. It shows only the point in time for the milestone, without indication of the driving activities. It is very useful, however, for reporting status to executive management. Like the Gantt Chart, it is easy to generate and simple to interpret. Milestone Charts also have some additional information not contained in a Gantt Chart, such as indication of schedule slippage and the provision for forecasting completion dates of future milestones.

Description	Jan	Feb	Mar	Apr	May	Jun	Jul	Aug	Sep
Contract Signed	▲								
Program Planned	▲								
Bill of Material Finalized			▲						
Subcontracts Signed			▲ ▽						
System Specs Completed				▽ △					
Design Reviewed					△				
Subsystem Tested						△			
1st Unit Delivered							△		
Production Plan Completed								△	
Program Phase 1 Completed									△

Figure 6-4 Milestone Chart

In Figure 6-4 it is immediately apparent that the milestone "Subcontracts signed" was achieved about two weeks late. This caused the next milestone ("System Specs Completed") to also have a two week forecasted slip. The symbols associated with subsequent milestones imply that they are not affected by the slips of the earlier milestones. The convention of filling in the triangles of completed milestones is used, so that it is possible at a glance to tell what has been achieved and what has not been completed. Inverted triangles are used to show rescheduled dates. Milestone Charts make good summaries, but may not be representative of schedule status if there were no underlying system that supports the forecasted dates.

Bar Chart

At first glance, the Bar Chart example shown in Figure 6-5 closely resembles the Gantt Chart. However, it embodies some improvements over that earlier technique. Individual activities are shown on their own lines rather than grouped as on the Gantt Chart. This allows a more accurate display of status. Another improvement is the display of the true start and finish dates, with forecasts of future starts and finishes also indicated. This is a very popular display type, and is frequently used to provide a quick picture of more complex information contained within advanced scheduling systems. As with the Milestone Chart, the information presented here should be supported by an underlying scheduling system. This format does not allow identification of significant problems or a formal early warning capability. The Bar Chart still has the same serious drawback as the Gantt Chart: the inability to reflect status of partially completed activities. Filling in the bar as "time now" advances is not an accurate method for reflecting real progress.

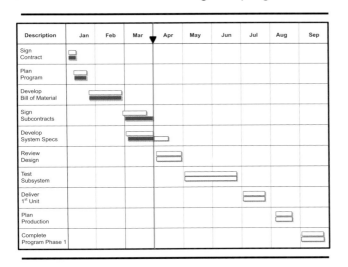

Figure 6-5 Bar Chart

Combination Chart

As its name implies, this schedule format attempts to combine the advantages of the Milestone Chart and the Gantt Chart to allow for better representation of status. By adding objective milestones along the schedule bars, it is possible to more accurately indicate partial completion of activities.

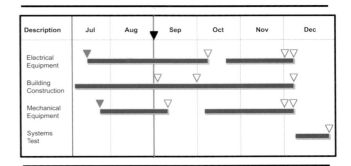

Figure 6-6 Combination Chart

For example, the "Building Construction" bar in Figure 6-6 would not be permitted to be filled in as actual progress beyond the first indicated milestone unless that milestone had been accomplished. This means that the bars are primarily used to indicate start and stop dates, as well as durations, but progress is determined primarily by the accomplishment of milestones. This schedule presentation technique has most of the other shortcomings that limit the usefulness of the Gantt Chart and Bar Chart. Specifically, this format does not allow identification of significant problems or a formal early warning capability. This format also fails to reflect the status of partially completed activities.

Modified Gantt/Milestone Chart

A further refinement of the Gantt and Milestone Charts is shown in Figure 6-7. Major relationships between milestones have been added, providing even greater visibility into schedule status. With this representation, probable delays in the future based on current schedule slips can be anticipated. While this format contains considerably more information than those previously presented, it also requires more effort to develop and is more difficult to interpret. The most difficult part in both development and interpretation is the logic between bar chart lines. Since the detailed plan for accomplishing the work will have many more interrelationships, it is difficult to decide which few will be included on a summary chart like this. It is impossible to accurately represent the real logic between all activities in this format, so accurate status is compromised for the sake of a readable presentation.

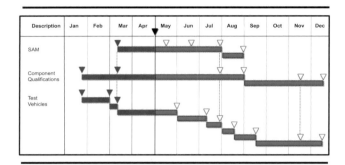

Figure 6-7 Modified Bar/Milestone Chart

Flow Process Chart

Figure 6-8 depicts a Flow Process Chart, one of the first steps toward network diagrams. Notice that it shows events and relationships between events rather than activities independently displayed. This is a completely different approach than the Gantt Chart.

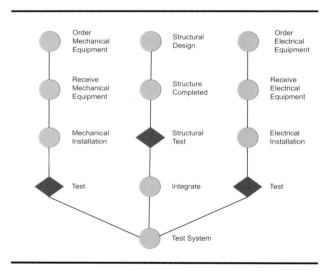

Figure 6-8 Process Flowchart

Set Back Chart

The Set Back Chart is a supporting tool for the Line of Balance scheduling technique that will be addressed next. It is the most advanced technique yet discussed, since it includes activities, logic between the activities, lead times, and total project duration.

There is a time axis, as shown in Figure 6-9, but it runs backwards from the final delivery date. The amount of lead time to support each operation is determined, and then time is counted backwards

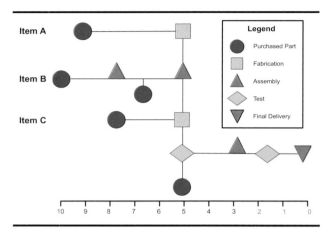

Figure 6-9 Set Back Chart

to find out when the previous operation had to have occurred. This approach is used in manufacturing operations and also in procurement processes. It is primarily suited for repetitive operations, such as production.

Line of Balance

The Line of Balance scheduling technique uses an 'objective chart' to display cumulative unit requirements over time. A brief explanation here will suffice. Figure 6-10 depicts the required completion of events (horizontal line) versus actual completions (vertical bars) in production operations.

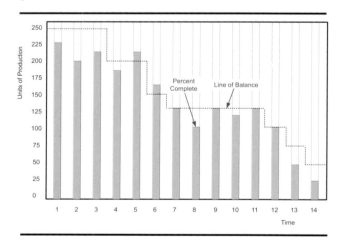

Figure 6-10 Line of Balance Chart

This method is used in conjunction with the Set Back Chart and provides an early warning system for schedule problems. The Line of Balance is not applicable to many projects, because efforts that involve programming, engineering, design or construction of a single plant are best addressed by the network techniques that will be introduced next. Line of Balance best fits the manufacturing environment or other repetitive task schedules, where a certain defined delivery schedule of similar items must be maintained.

Network Diagrams

The latest and most advanced scheduling technique is schedule networks, and most of the scheduling section of this book will focus on this method. Network techniques were introduced on multiple fronts in the late 1950s as Program Evaluation and Review Technique (PERT) and the Critical Path Method (CPM), both of which will be discussed in more detail in later chapters. Network techniques have been applied in virtually every industry and have been most successfully used in the hands of scheduling professionals trained in its use. As the complexity of the project and the scheduling methodology increases, the need for trained schedulers becomes more critical. Many schedules have suffered because of insufficient preparation of schedulers who were not trained on the value of the network in the scheduling system.

Network diagramming provides the most detailed status information by far of any of the techniques presented here. However, it is also the most complicated, most difficult to interpret, and requires the most training for staff. Network diagramming offers a complete listing of activities as well as interrelationships between those activities. It provides a method for identifying which activities are most critical. It facilitates easy trend analysis and provides an early warning of likely impacts to the project completion date. Network diagramming gives the project team the ability to analyze resources, to perform studies of alternative scenarios for completing the work, and to analyze time/cost tradeoffs. Finally, it creates a good starting point for determining who was responsible for a schedule delay.

Two different types of networks are shown in Figure 6-11: Arrow Diagramming Method (ADM) and Precedence Diagramming Method (PDM). ADM uses lines for activities and circles as events to depict the project logic, but is not commonly in use today. The PDM uses boxes as

activities and lines to depict activity relationships and is the network capabilities basis of almost every commercial scheduling tool today.

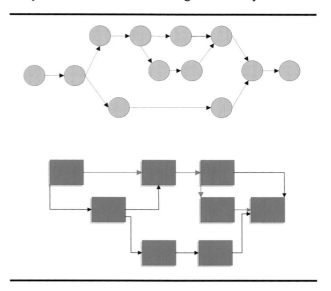

Figure 6-11 Network Diagrams

With so many different types of schedules and since more than one type probably will be used on a single project, it is important to consider the use for which a particular schedule is intended. Is it for the project manager or is it a working tool for the scheduler? Those with detailed information needs should receive different formats than a project manager. Manufacturing may need different scheduling tools than construction.

While there are many ways of presenting schedule data in different formats, it is important to match the format with the audience and the intended use of the information. One near-disaster occurred on a ten-year construction project that had about 20,000 activities in its schedule database. A giant, 50-foot long printout of all the time-phased network logic had been printed on a weekly time scale and hung in the longest hallway available in the area. Of course, because of the time scale and the number of activities and associated logic ties, it resembled nothing more than a giant spider web. The activity descriptions were minuscule, and virtually invisible to all but those with extraordinary eyesight. It was impossible to decipher what line went where without tracing each line with brightly colored markers. Unfortunately, that had not yet been done.

As fate would have it, the Vice President of Construction happened to pass through that hallway on that particular day. As he stood there in speechless amazement, looking at what the scheduling group was producing for him, he asked the nearest scheduler, "What in the world is this?" Undaunted, the scheduler responded, "Sir, that is what we are using to control your latest project." In less than a heartbeat, the VP answered, "Not on my project."

During the next year, it was a remarkable period of damage control. The VP never did recover from that initial shock as he readily recognized that the format confronting him was useless for just about anything. It could have been a useful format for an initial schedule baseline review that was occurring on that fateful day, if it had been put on a shorter time scale. But under no circumstances was it going to be used as the primary or even the secondary tool for controlling the project. Nevertheless, the first impression had been made and from then on the perception was that the project controllers were building a dynasty of confusion that only they could interpret. Consequently, a lesson learned: the format used for presenting information can make or break the entire project control/project management effort.

Conclusion

Many possible approaches to scheduling the work for a project are possible. Schedule types range from simple techniques, such as Bar Chart representations, to complex techniques such as the Critical Path Method (CPM). The value of a schedule tool is directly related to the amount of time and effort invested in its development. Thus while there are many simple presentations that provide a picture of schedule progress, they are of limited value in the actual management of a project; e.g., simplicity is achieved at the expense of accuracy. Nevertheless, such easy to understand formats are of use when summarizing status to top management providing they have a more detailed foundation. On any project, multiple schedule formats are needed to serve differing objectives.

While CPM is the most complex of the scheduling types discussed, it provides far more information than any other approach. Among the additional capabilities that CPM schedules provide are: an objective method for prioritizing activities, easy trend analysis, identification of impacts from individual activity slippages, early warning of possible delays to project completion, the ability to analyze resources, and a mechanism for analyzing time/cost tradeoffs.

A schedule is a document that defines what work must be done, and when, to accomplish the project objectives on time. A schedule is needed as part of the total project plan and provides an excellent vehicle for communication of status and problems throughout the life of a project. Without a formal schedule, it is impossible to know if a planned completion date is realistic or even achievable.

Development of a schedule presupposes certain data items: detailed scope of work, activity durations, activity relationships, resource requirements and assigned responsibilities at the activity level. Automated tools are almost universally used for processing the large amount of data available from a scheduling system. The output of an effective scheduling system is a powerful tool for project management through priority definition, status reporting, problem area identification, problem impact analysis, and support of corrective action planning.

Chapter 6 Review Questions

6-1.   Describe the functions of a schedule.

6-2.   What are the advantages of a formalized scheduling system?

6-3.   What are three ways in which schedule delays cause an increase in costs?

6-4.   What are five information prerequisites for developing a valid schedule?

6-5.   What are potential uses of scheduling system information in a project?

6-6.   Describe how the "Combination Chart" is an improvement over the Milestone Chart or the Bar Chart for schedule status reporting.

6-7.   Name at least three shortcomings of the Bar Chart when used for schedule status determination.

6-8.   Describe at least four types of information available from network scheduling systems that are not available from simpler scheduling techniques.

6-9.   Which of the following schedule techniques provide some indication of interrelationships between activities?

     A. Combination Chart.

     B. Modified Gantt/Milestone Chart.

     C. Flow Process Chart.

     D. Network Diagrams.

     E. B, C, and D.

     F. All of the above.

True or False

6-10.   The first objective in the development of a project plan is preparation of a detailed schedule that includes all of the anticipated work activities.

6-11.   Staffing requirements for supporting a scheduling system are affected most strongly by the level of detail selected for the schedule.

6-12.   Past similar jobs can be a "reality check" for current project schedules.

6-13.   Schedules should initially be developed by the most experienced schedulers.

6-14.   Schedule status should be compared with an approved schedule baseline plan to identify variances.

6-15.   The simplest schedule reporting techniques also tend to be the least useful for successful management of a project.

6-16.   One of the oldest and simplest forms of scheduling is the Gantt Chart.

6-17.   The Bar Chart has no mechanism for forecasting revised completion dates.

6-18.   The Combination Chart combines useful traits of the Bar Chart and of schedule networks.

6-19.   In the Modified Gantt/Milestone Chart, true schedule status is compromised for the sake of a readable presentation.

6-20.   The Line of Balance scheduling technique is usually applied in the manufacturing environment.

6-21.   One good application of a Bar Chart is to represent more complex information in a simple format, usually at a summary level.

6-22.   PDM is a variation of the Line of Balance approach to scheduling.

The answers to these questions can be found in Section 6, Solutions.

Case Study

6.1 DEVELOPING A PERSONAL SCHEDULE

Basic steps in developing a schedule:

1. List the activities (time-consuming and resource-consuming tasks) and events (point-in-time items or milestones) to be accomplished between the start and finish of the "project".

2. Sequence the activities and events in time order.

3. Put start and finish times on each activity and time on each event.

4. Convert the activities/events into graphic form as shown in Figure 6.1-1.

5. Status and revise the schedule on a periodic basis. Note the types of changes made to the schedule and why the changes were made.

Case Study Requirements

Develop a schedule of the activities and events. Use the guidelines above.

1. Choose a 'project' to schedule – something like flying a light plane from one city to another – or anything else you feel comfortable with. In the form shown in Figure 6.1-2, the Activity/Event Planning Form, list up to 13 activities and events. The initial list need not be in sequence. Provide activity/event numbers or codes.

2. Indicate the sequence of the activities/events and record the planned start and finish times. Use only one time for events (since they have no duration).

3. In Figure 6.1-3, the Time-Scaled Chart, record all the activities/events in graphic form as shown in Figure 6.1-1. Indicate the durations of the activities.

Personal Schedule
Common Schedule Display Methods

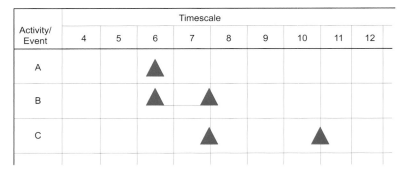

Figure 6.1-1

Activity/Event Planning Form

Responsible Person:

Activity/ Event Number	Sequence Number		Planned Start Time	Planned Finish Time

Figure 6.1-2

Time Scaled Chart

Activity/ Event	Time Scale												Hours Required
	7am	8am	9am	10am	11am	12am	1pm	2pm	3pm	4pm	5pm	6pm	

Figure 6.1-3

Chapter 7

INTRODUCTION TO NETWORK LOGIC DEVELOPMENT

Objectives of this Chapter:

1. Name and describe the two basic components of Precedence Diagramming Method (PDM) diagrams.

2. Describe the four types of relationships between activities in PDM.

3. Present the options for time phasing PDM networks.

This chapter presents the network-based method of schedule development called the Precedence Diagramming Method, or PDM.

Prior to PDM, the Arrow Diagramming Method, or ADM, was used as the notation for schedule development. Initially scheduling was used almost exclusively for construction where complex networks were not required. These early schedules tended to have a definite sequence of activities: excavation must occur before the foundation work is done, the foundation must be complete before walls are erected, and the walls finished before the roof is installed, and so on. However, since all projects have some overlapping activities, and projects in engineering and research and development have many activities that overlap, consequently, over time ADM fell out of favor. It has been replaced almost entirely by PDM.

This chapter introduces the network development concept and the next chapter will present new techniques for interpreting the logic network. Because of its functionality and importance, the bulk of the scheduling section is devoted to expanding on the theory and practice of network diagramming.

Precedence Diagramming Method

There are two basic components used in creating logic networks. One is the activity and the other is the logic or relationship between activities. Events, which are zero duration activities, are entered as milestones. A milestone is a point in time that does not have a resource assignment since work cannot be performed in zero time. The PDM convention is shown in Figure 7-3. Activities are shown as boxes and relationships are shown as lines between the boxes. The box contains all of the information about the activity: code, description, duration, resource identifier, and any other special references desired. It could also include a WBS reference. The relationship line shows how the start or finish of one activity is related to the start or finish of another. Several types of relationships can be used, and each of these will be discussed in turn. Milestones are shown as triangles in this text notation. Some scheduling software differentiates between start or finish milestones and will generate the appropriate start or finish date based on the activity to which they are related.

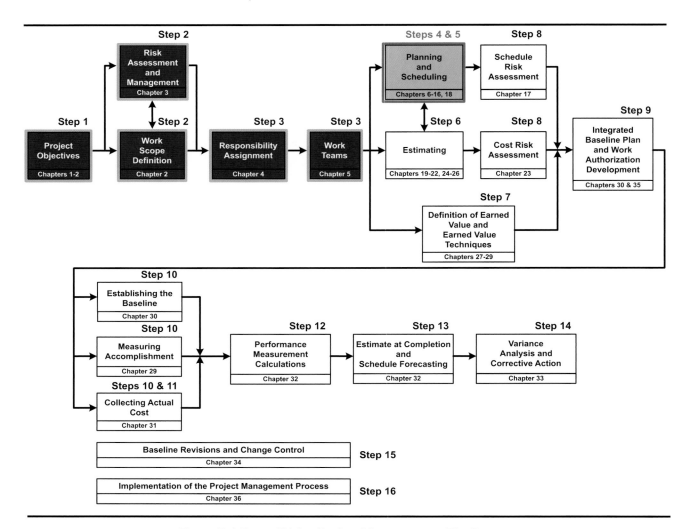

Figure 7-1 Earned Value Project Management: The Process

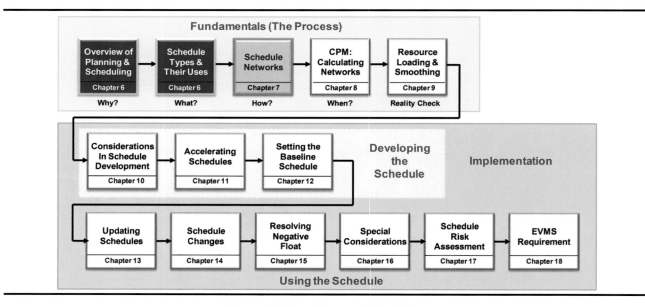

Figure 7-2 Planning and Scheduling

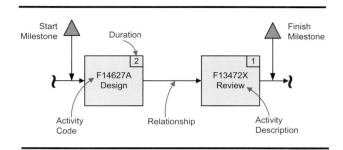

Figure 7-3 PDM Networks

Activity Relationships

Activity pairs are connected together by one of four relationships:

1. Finish-to-Start (FS).
2. Finish-to-Finish (FF).
3. Start-to-Start (SS).
4. Start-to-Finish (SF).

The activity relationships are used so that the scheduler can model the sequence of tasks from the real world of the project into the project schedule. Careful application of the activity relationships allows the network schedule to properly represent the project flow of work as it should be accomplished. When used as a management tool, a properly modeled schedule can control the initiation of work.

The first [finish-to-start (FS) relationship] is the standard logic tie that is used with the majority of activities. It is represented in Figure 7-4. It simply states that Activity B cannot start until Activity A finishes. This is the most common relationship, and will typically include about 90% of all relationships in a network.

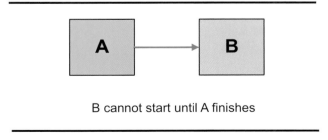

B cannot start until A finishes

Figure 7-4 Finish to Start

There are many possible examples of finish-to-start. The possession of a permit before beginning work is one example. In other words, the permitting process must be finished before the work can begin. Another example requires that the walls of a building be finished before the roof can be installed. An item or sub-item must be manufactured before testing can be performed.

The next relationship, pictured in Figure 7-5, is the finish-to-finish (FF). This relationship says that Activity B cannot finish until Activity A finishes; said another way, when A finishes, B can finish. It does not say that Activity B will finish when Activity A finishes, only that it can finish no earlier. In this type of relationship, there is not necessarily a tie between the beginning of Activities A and B. Note that the activities overlap in this type of relationship. During part of their durations, A and B are occurring concurrently. There are many examples of this type of relationship in engineering and design activities.

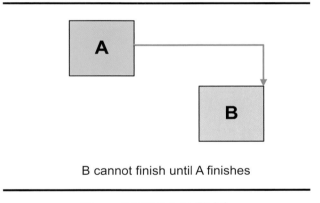

B cannot finish until A finishes

Figure 7-5 Finish to Finish

It may be possible to start design of a system without vendor information available for some component, but the design cannot be completed until all the information is available. The system design cannot be finished until the vendor's finish; the receipt of information. Construction examples are also helpful to illustrate finish to finish. Once pipe is installed, it can be insulated. These two activities ("install pipe" and "insulate pipe") can proceed simultaneously, but the installation must be finished before the pipe insulation can be finished.

A more obvious every-day example would be the process of washing and drying dishes. The two activities under discussion are "wash dishes" and "dry dishes". Assuming that the dishes are being washed and dried by hand, the washing and drying of dishes can proceed concurrently. However, the drying clearly cannot be completed until the washing has been completed. The washing must finish before the drying can finish. If this had been a finish-to-start relationship, it would have been necessary for all the dishes to be completely washed before drying the first dish could begin. It should be apparent that the use of all FS activities will make the total project duration longer than if overlapping activities are planned.

The start-to-start (SS) relationship, shown in Figure 7-6, states that Activity B cannot start until after Activity A starts. So when A starts, B can start. Note that this logic does not state that B will start once A starts, only that it can start. This is another example of overlapping activities. A start-to-start relationship does not imply any relationship between the completion of the two activities in question.

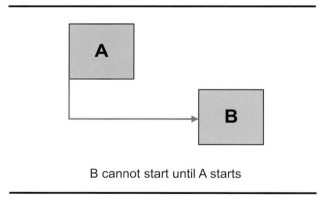

B cannot start until A starts

Figure 7-6 Start to Start

One example of a SS relationship is that the beginning of design allows the beginning of purchasing material for whatever product is being designed. Clearly, purchasing cannot start until the start of design for what is being manufactured or installed. However, purchasing does not have to start as soon as design starts.

Often there is a delay between one start and the next start, which is called a lag. In the example just given, purchasing likely would not begin until some delay after the start of design. Lag is discussed further in Chapter 10. Lags are frequently

employed in FF relationships as well when there is a time delay between the completion of one activity and completion of another that depends on the first activity.

The previous example of dish washing and drying also illustrates the SS relationship. Drying the dishes cannot start until after the washing activity starts. The activities then proceed in parallel until completion, at which time there is a finish-to-finish relationship between washing and drying as well. The start-to-start and finish-to-finish relationships may occur together between the same two activities to show parallel relationships. However, some schedule software packages may not allow both of these relationships on the same two activities.

Note that an activity with only a start-to-start successor is a problem. If only the start of the activity has a purpose, then what is depending on the output of the activity? An activity that has only a start-to-start successor is referred to as a "hanging activity". Hanging activities should be avoided as they generally represent a weakness or defect in the logic.

Start-to-start and finish-to-finish each comprise about 10%-15% of the relationships in a typical network.

A final point for consideration is that the selection of the appropriate activity relationship depends on the level of detail for the schedule. Relationships such as start-to-start and finish-to-finish predominate in summary level schedules. Because the activities are general in nature, there will be many overlapping conditions. Very detailed schedules, on the other hand, will have a higher percentage of finish-to-start activity relationships. In the dish washing and drying example, all of the activities would be FS if the planning and scheduling is done on the detailed level. The schedule would become: "wash dish #1", "dry dish #1", "wash dish #2", "dry dish #2", and so on. Each of these would be finish-to-start.

The final relationship type, the start-to-finish (SF), is the rarest type by far. Many network logic diagrams will not contain a single example of this activity relationship. This relationship type says that activity A must start before its preceding activity B can finish. In other words, B will continue until A starts. If A has not started, B cannot finish. Most applications of this relationship are incorrect representations of the very common finish-to-start. Start-to-finish is pictured in Figure 7-7.

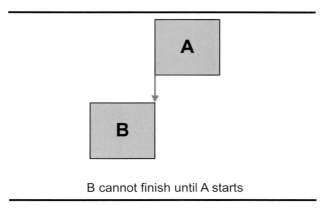

B cannot finish until A starts

Figure 7-7 Start to Finish

While a start-to-finish relationship is possible, it is very unlikely. It can be argued that this type of relationship is unnecessary since the logic should be able to be represented in another way. Some schedule software packages do not even allow for this type of activity relationship. However, a few examples deserve mention and illustrate why SF relationships have been included.

A simple example of a start-to-finish relationship is the 'watchman' scenario. The watchman on duty for shift #1 cannot finish his shift until the replacement watchman for shift #2 arrives and starts his shift.

A more complex example relates to flight testing of new aircraft. When a new design is initiated, extensive wind tunnel tests are conducted. These tests continue throughout the design and production phases of the project, and do not stop until these tests are replaced with the actual aircraft flight tests. So what is the start-to-finish relationship? The wind tunnel tests are not completed until the flight tests are begun. In this case, the start of a succeeding activity (flight testing) is necessary before the completion of a prior activity (wind tunnel testing) occurs. However, the reverse is not true, i.e. finish-to-start: the end of the wind tunnel testing would have no effect on the flight testing. This is an example of the SF relationship.

Software engineering provides the framework for another example. When programming new software, there may be continual revisions and improvements to the program over time. These improvements continue until program testing begins. The start of program verification and testing finishes the programming phase. This is a requirement or the test is to no avail. As can be seen, this is analogous to the flight testing example previously presented.

Representations of Logic in Time-Phased Formats

There are two options that are used. The first is to show the activity (box) as a fixed length, with the left side of the box corresponding to the starting date. With a fixed length there is no relationship between the right side of the box and the finish date. Alternatively, the right side of the activity box could be made to correspond to the completion date, but then there is no relationship between the left side of the box and the starting date.

A formerly popular display technique, shown in Figure 7-8, is to elongate the boxes to show the proper start and finish dates. This is sometimes referred to as the "variable box length display," but the name used depends on the software package. However, most current scheduling tools no longer offer this option. Because of the extra length of each box, the charts produced were required to be taller, making it almost impossible to produce a usable display of a network with over 500 activities.

Because of the size and complexity issues of the variable length network chart, the most popular display technique has always been the Bar Chart as presented in Chapter 6. Non-schedulers are very comfortable with information displayed this way, and it is entirely accurate because it reflects the details contained within a CPM network logic. The usual type of display is shown in Figure 7-9. The activity boxes are stretched to correspond to the activity duration. This display should be sorted by start date, then by finish date, to produce a "tumble-down" or "waterfall" display such as the one pictured.

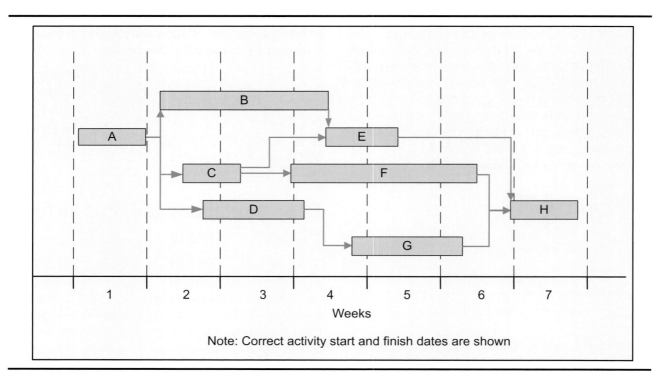

Figure 7-8 Time-Phased Diagrams - Variable Box Length

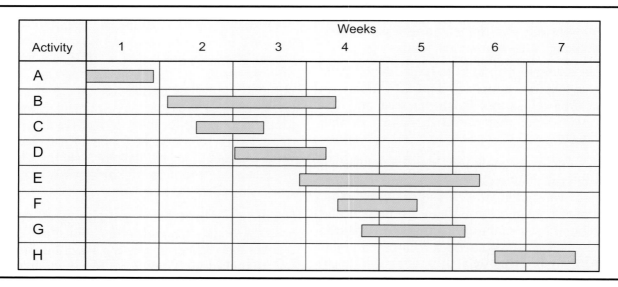

Figure 7-9 Time Phased Bar Chart

Conclusion

The Precedence Diagramming Method (PDM) uses two basic components in the creation of network logic: activities and activity relationships. Its ability to represent every conceivable relationship between activities has won it favor on all types of projects, but especially on projects with many overlapping activities. The four types of relationships employed are finish-to-start (FS), start-to-start (SS), finish-to-finish (FF), and start-to-finish (SF). Overlapping activities are accommodated by SS and FF relationships.

There are several options for time-phasing networks, but the most popular is still the classic bar chart with relationships displayed. It provides the flexibility of aligning bars with time and relationships, while defining additional information on the table portion of the chart.

Chapter 7 Review Questions

7-1.   Explain the difference between finish-to-start and start-to-finish logic relationships. Which is more common?

7-2.   What are the four types of logic relationships?

True or False

7-3.   A start-to-start relationship means that the successor activity must start at the same time as its predecessor.

7-4.   Both milestones and activities must have resources assigned to them.

The answers to these questions can be found in Section 6, Solutions.

7.1 CONSTRUCTING A NETWORK DIAGRAM

Arrange the following activities into a logic diagram using the Precedence Diagramming Method.

1. Activities A and B start the project and may proceed concurrently.

2. Activity A must be completed before C begins.

3. Activity B precedes activities D and E.

4. Activity C precedes activity F.

5. Activity E precedes activity G.

6. Activity G cannot start until activity D is completed.

7. When activities F and G are finished, the project is completed.

Use the following notation to complete the diagrams.

Chapter 8

CRITICAL PATH METHOD FUNDAMENTALS

Objectives of this Chapter:

1. Define the meaning of critical path.

2. Define the method of performing a "forward pass" and "backward pass" and their use in the critical path method schedule technique.

3. Define and explain total float and free float.

4. Describe the different implications of total float and free float.

5. Learn how to identify the schedule critical path.

6. Describe the impact of directed dates and the meaning of positive or negative float on the critical path.

The significance of the Critical Path Method (CPM) has been so profound that its terminology has become part of everyday vocabulary. People who have no background in the scheduling fundamentals presented in this text still talk about important activities being on the "critical path," or ask someone to allow them some "slack" when an activity is late. It is a statement of importance to be able to brag (or admit), "Right now, I'm on the critical path."

While the terminology has become part of the lexicon, it sometimes causes confusion. The terms can be used in contexts that are not always technically correct. The term "critical path" has a very specific meaning; and it does not always correspond to the items that are most technically critical. "Critical" is not a temporary condition used to attract attention to a specific set of activities at a specific time or to attract the attention of contractor or owner senior management. The terms "slack" and "float" are used interchangeably, and they are interchangeable. Slack was a PERT (Program Evaluation and Review Technique) term while float is the proper CPM term for the same concept.

The Critical Path Method is neither magical, with the ability to solve all project problems, nor is it incomprehensible. It is a logical calculation tool that allows the determination of several important aspects of schedule network logic. It allows identification of the earliest possible date and the latest possible date that an activity can be worked while still allowing overall project objectives to be met. The CPM also allows management by exception. It highlights those activities that are most time critical, that is, have the least amount of flexibility (or "float") between their earliest and latest dates.

The techniques used to calculate networks will be explained in this chapter. It is important to understand the underlying concepts even though these calculations are always done on computers. Knowing and being able to explain the principles of CPM is similar to understanding mathematics versus knowing how to use a calculator.

The last chapter presented types of logic networks used to represent project schedules. Now it is time to find out how networks can be used to determine information about the schedule. The

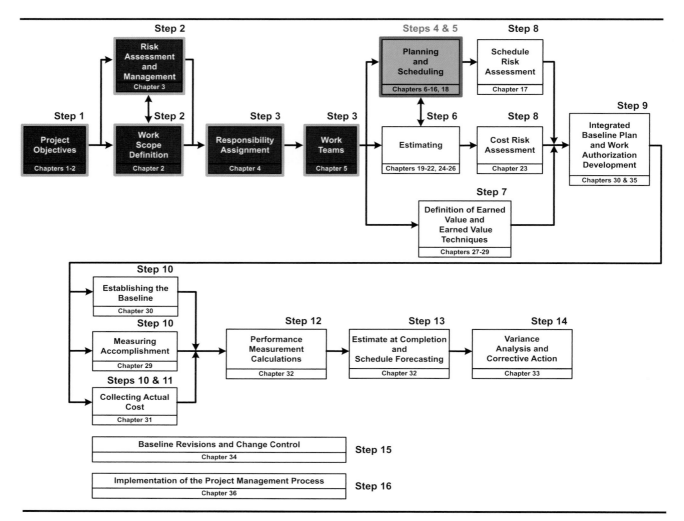

Figure 8-1 Earned Value Project Management: The Process

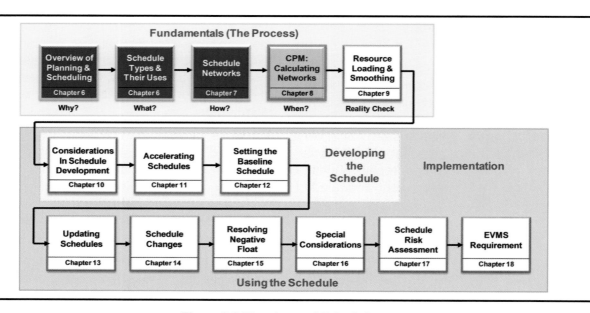

Figure 8-2 Planning and Scheduling

technique used to analyze networks is known as the Critical Path Method, or CPM. Once the logic for the schedule has been defined and durations added to each of the activities, a series of calculations can be performed to determine the total duration of the project, what its "critical path" is, and how much flexibility there is in the schedule. Understanding CPM is the key to understanding and interpreting network scheduling. Virtually everything contained in the next ten chapters, and some material after that as well, requires a solid understanding of the information contained in this chapter.

The Critical Path Method

The Critical Path Method is defined as a methodology or management technique that makes analytical use of information regarding the critical path and other sequential activity paths through the network. The Integrated Master Schedule (IMS) Data Item Description DI-MGMT-81650 that is part of the Department of Defense Earned Value Management Policy defines the critical path as "a contiguous path of activities in a network having the longest total duration and thus defining the minimum duration of the project". This path is usually the path with the lowest float value. That may seem like a contradiction in terms, but all paths through the network must be completed for the project to be completed. Thus, the longest one sets the overall project duration, as the project is not complete just because some of the shorter paths have been finished.

At this point, it is worthwhile to recognize the implications of the critical path definition. Non-schedulers sometimes confuse critical path with technically critical activities. Critical path is not synonymous with technical difficulty. A very difficult technical activity may or may not be on the critical path. It is all a function of whether or not the activity in question resides on the longest path through the network.

If an activity were technically challenging and has a high degree of uncertainty regarding its initial success, it could be on the highest risk path without being on the critical path. See Chapter 17, "Schedule Risk Assessment."

Critical Path Example

A network example will help to illustrate the general concepts of critical path. The determination of the critical path will be explained later in this chapter. For now, the focus is on the path itself.

The network in Figure 8-3 has three paths within it, each having a different total duration. The duration is indicated in the box in the upper right hand corner of each activity. The path across the top of the diagram, indicated by activities A-B-C-D-H, is 25 days long. The middle path, A-B-E-H, is 19 days long. The path across the bottom, described by the activities A-F-G-H, is 22 days long. With nothing more than this information, it is possible to identify the critical path as the one that is 25 days long. This path defines the duration of the project; the project cannot be finished any sooner using this logic and these durations. However, the other paths are shorter, and this means that there is some scheduling flexibility on these paths.

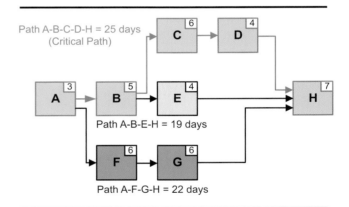

Path A-B-C-D-H = 25 days
(Critical Path)

Path A-B-E-H = 19 days

Path A-F-G-H = 22 days

Figure 8-3 Critical Path

With durations and logic, it is possible to convert the information to start and completion dates for each activity. This calculation will initially consider only workday numbers rather than calendar dates in order to avoid the confusion associated with weekends and holidays. Using the previous sample network, the calculations look like this:

Activity	Duration	Start	Finish
A	3	1	3
B	5	4	8
C	6	9	14

Activity	Duration	Start	Finish
D	4	15	18
E	4	9	12
F	6	4	9
G	6	10	15
H	7	19	25

Why did activity A finish on day 3 in this example?

Welcome to the "AM-PM" convention. Since there is no such thing as "day zero" this means that the activity starts at the first instant of day 1 (AM) and ends at the last instant of day 3 (PM). Total time consumed is 3 days. There are other conventions, but modern scheduling software products most frequently use this one. All starts are assumed to be at the start of the day, and all completions are assumed to occur at the end of the day. After all, when the IRS says income taxes are due April 15, it does not mean they must be filed by the first thing in the morning. Some people will actually wait until just before midnight to take full advantage of the day it is due. A due date of Friday implies the end of day on Friday. The AM-PM convention recognizes this fact.

Network Calculations

While it was easy to see the critical path in the last example, most project networks are so large and complex that it is impossible to determine the critical path and the flexibility in other paths by visual inspection. Therefore, some other procedures are necessary to find the critical path for the cases that will be encountered in day-to-day work. To make the necessary determinations, two "passes", or calculation runs, through the network must be performed. The forward pass starts at the beginning of the project and works left to right, determining the earliest dates each activity can be started and completed based on the logic and given durations. The backward pass starts at the end of the project and calculates from right to left to determine the latest possible dates that each activity can start and finish while still supporting the required completion date of the overall project. The standard notation used

in this text to represent the activity dates is shown in Figure 8-4. The activity will be shown as a box with its name or identifier (in this case, "A") in the box.

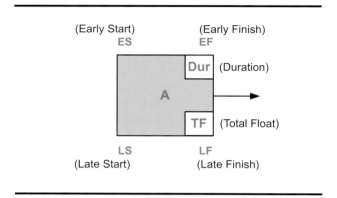

Figure 8-4 Standard Notation

The activity duration will always be shown in a small box in the upper right hand corner. Then four dates, all calculated from the forward and backward passes, are placed in the corners. These dates are Early Start (ES) and Early Finish (EF) on the top, and Late Start (LS) and Late Finish (LF) on the bottom. The difference between ES and EF is determined by the activity's duration, as is the difference between LS and LF. Used later in this text, the total float (TF) will be shown in the bottom right-hand corner.

To produce the early dates, the forward pass is performed, as shown in Figure 8-5. Day 1 is the early start for the first activity. When the duration (DUR) is added and one is subtracted, the early finish results. The subtraction of one is because of the AM-PM convention that was explained earlier. The result is an early start of day 1 (AM) and an early finish of day 6 (PM). This is a total duration of six working days.

When computing the start of the next activity, one is added to the early finish of the previous activity. This is shown in Figure 8-6. What is shown here is that activity A finishes at the end of day 6 and activity C starts at the beginning of day 7. The calculations continue in a similar manner throughout all of the paths in the network.

The only complication occurs when two or more activity paths join together at a common activity, as shown in Figure 8-7. The logic indicates that both activities (F & G) must be completed before

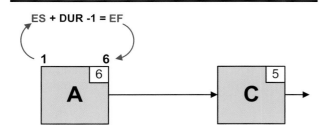

ES + DUR -1 = EF

Activity A spans from the beginning
of day 1 to the end of day 6.

Figure 8-5 Forward Pass (Activity Early Dates)

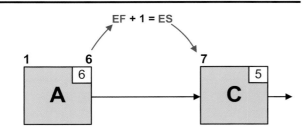

EF + 1 = ES

Activity A finishes at the end of day 6 -
Then Activity C will start at the beginning of day 7.

**Figure 8-6 Forward Pass (Activity Relationship
Early Dates)**

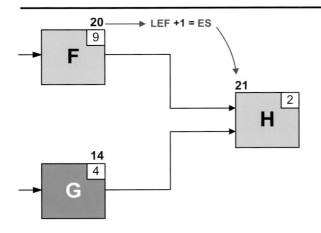

LEF +1 = ES

On the Forward Pass, use the LATEST Early Finish (LEF)

**Figure 8-7 Forward Pass (Early Dates -
Converging Paths)**

activity H can begin. Both activities are not complete until the latest one is done, so the latest finishing activity is the driving force in the calculation of the following activity.

The next example (Figure 8-8) demonstrates a complete forward pass (i.e. from left to right) of a simple CPM network. As always, the first activity (activity A) is defined as starting on the morning of day 1. Since it is 6 days long, it completes on the end of day 6. This allows activity C to start on the morning of day 7. Note that there is a start-to-start relationship between activities A and B, so B can also start as early as the morning of day 1. By continuing on in this way, the start and completion day numbers for each activity can be determined. From the forward pass, it is determined that the earliest the project can finish is on the end of day 22.

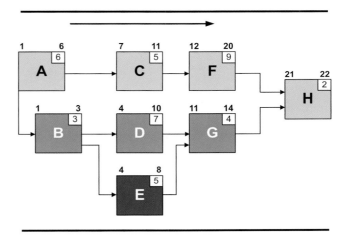

Figure 8-8 Forward Pass

The next step is to perform the backward pass. This calculation establishes the latest possible finish and start dates for the task without impacting the completion of the project or the next major milestone if the project is large. If the forward pass establishes the earliest possible schedule dates based on activity durations and relationships, the backward pass establishes what dates for each activity are necessary to accomplish the project on time.

The calculations are performed in reverse of the forward pass (i.e. from right to left) and a sample calculation is indicated in Figure 8-9. This example shows the process in the middle of the network. In reality, the backward pass starts from the last activity and works from right to left from the end toward the start of the network. The duration is subtracted from the late finish and one is added to the total to generate the late start. Once again, this is because of the AM-PM convention. Activity C has a five day duration: all of days 7, 8, 9, 10, and 11.

One important principle needs to be noted before the backward pass can be calculated: the early finish of the last activity determines the project length and thus the total project duration. Therefore, the early finish is also the late finish, and the late finish value is the starting point for the backward pass.

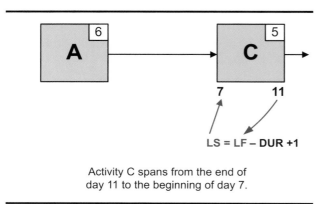

Activity C spans from the end of
day 11 to the beginning of day 7.

Figure 8-9 Backward Pass (Activity Late Dates)

After the late start is calculated, the next step is to subtract one to get the late finish of the previous activity. This is just the opposite of the forward pass. An example of this is shown in Figure 8-10.

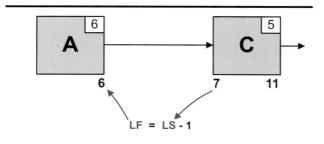

Activity C starts at the beginning of day 7-
Then Activity A will finish at the end of day 6.

Figure 8-10 Backward Pass (Activity Relationship Late Dates)

The same challenge as the forward pass exists when considering multiple activities coming

together or converging. The situation is, of course, reversed. Now a single activity is a prerequisite for two or more subsequent activities. So the earliest of the late start dates is used to determine the late finish of the preceding activity. Instead of trying to memorize the formula, think logically.

In Figure 8-11 the logic states that when B is finished, D and E may both start. Since D can start no later than day 10 and E can start no later than day 12, and B must support both D and E, then B must finish no later than day 9, otherwise, it will not be available when activity D needs its input. Since day 10 is the latest that D can start and still support the project completion date, finishing B after day 9 means the end date will be impacted. Thus the earlier late start date from D and E must be used.

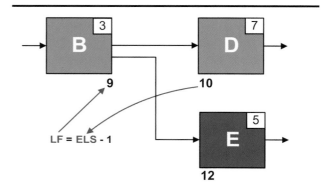

On the Backward Pass, use the EARLIEST Late Start (ELS)

Figure 8-11 Backward Pass (Late Dates - Converging Paths)

Figure 8-12 summarizes the results of the entire backward pass of the previous example in Figure 8-8. Start with the earliest completion date (the end of day 22) and use that as the late finish date. The process then continues as through the past few examples.

Note that the early finish may not always equal the late finish. As will be shown later, a project-required date may override the late date. Nevertheless, that is the procedure for initial CPM calculation of a network.

The information from the backward pass is then combined with the forward pass results to produce the network displayed in Figure 8-13. The

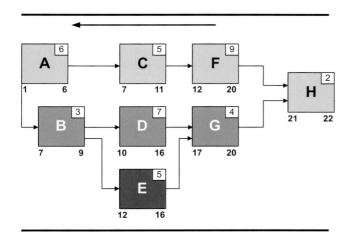

Figure 8-12 Backward Pass

critical path has been marked with a heavier red line and goes through the path A-C-F-H. How is the critical path determined?

By the calculation of the total float which is the difference between the early and late dates. The critical path is then the longest contiguous path through the network. This path also has the lowest total float value, as is usually the case, and adheres to the critical path definition as outlined earlier.

Total float (TF) is the difference between the early start and the late start, or the difference between the early finish and the late finish. The formula is expressed as:

$$TF = LF - EF \text{ or } TF = LS - ES.$$

Total float is a key concept of CPM. This value defines the amount of time an activity can be delayed or expanded before the finish date of the project is affected. Activity D, in Figure 8-13, can be expanded or delayed up to six days before it impacts project completion. But if activity D were delayed, even though it does not impact the project finish, it may impact another activity. For that reason, a second type of float is important.

Before proceeding any further, one clarification is in order. The terms "float" and "slack" are frequently used interchangeably. "Slack" was initially a term associated with PERT, another early network diagramming technique that will be covered later when schedule risk is discussed in Chapter 17, "Schedule Risk Assessment." "Float" has always been the CPM terminology. The term "slack" is nevertheless used frequently in some scheduling software vendors' literature in reference to CPM. The two terms refer to the same concept; the degree of flexibility in the schedule for that particular activity.

One final concept needs to be understood: total float is a shared value in a path. Activity D above has a total float of six days, as do activities B and G, the other activities in the same path. If activity D uses the entire six days, either by delay or by extending its duration by six days, the total float is consumed and activity G has no total float left. The total float for G and all subsequent activities in the path would then be zero.

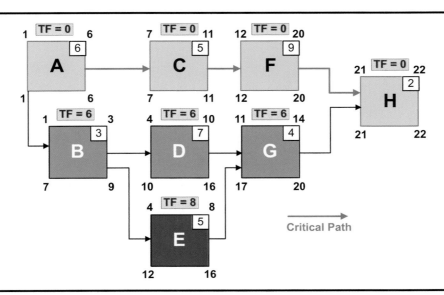

Figure 8-13 Early, Late Dates and Total Float - the Critical Path

Free Float

Free float (FF) is the second type of float. Free float is the amount of time an activity can be delayed or expanded before it impacts the next activity. Free float is calculated by taking the early start of the succeeding activity minus the early finish of the preceding activity, minus one. Looking at a portion of the network shown in Figure 8-13, activity E has a free float of 2 while activity D does not have any free float since it is driving activity G, as shown in Figure 8-14. Free float is always associated with a single activity: the preceding activity in a sequence. If activity E were delayed or expanded by more than two days, activity G would then be affected.

Since free float relates to the amount of time the activity can be delayed without impacting the very next activity, it also represents the amount of possible delay without impacting any other activity in the entire network. This is an important difference from total float, since using total float affects the entire string of network activities associated with the delayed activity. Note: free float exists only at a point of convergence and is never on the critical path.

All of the network calculations are now illustrated in Figure 8-15 including the early dates, late dates, total float, and free float for each activity. All of the relevant information needed for subsequent analysis is now available: the listing of

- The amount of time an activity can be delayed or expanded before it impacts the next activity
- The Early Finish Date of an activity subtracted from the Early Date of the next activity, minus 1
- Free Float for D = 11 - 10 - 1 = 0
- **Free Float for E = 11 - 8 - 1 = 2**

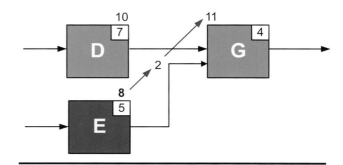

Figure 8-14 Free Float Calculation

activities, the activity relationships and durations, the measures of flexibility and impact, the critical path and project duration. At least this is all that is needed from a time management standpoint. Resources still need to be addressed in the network. That subject will be discussed in a subsequent chapter.

Reinforcing the point made earlier, notice that the activity path B-D-G has a total float of 6. This float value is a shared value along the path. If B is delayed by two days, its float will decrease to 4. More importantly, D and G will also have their float reduced to 4. Activity E has a free float of 2

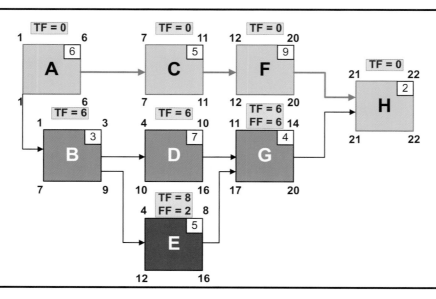

Figure 8-15 Total and Free Float

as well as a total float of 8. The concept of free float is easy to visualize here. Activities D and E are in parallel and have different durations.

Whether E takes 5 days or 7 has no impact on the start of G, since it needs both D and E complete before it can start. This is the two days of free float associated with E. Free float is not shared along an activity path as total float is. It is "owned" by a single activity only.

One inevitable result of the methodology used so far is that the total float on the critical path will always be zero (or lower, as discussed later). This is a result of setting the late finish date equal to the early finish date when the backward pass is initiated. A common misconception is that the critical path is the path with zero total float. However, this will not be the case when there is a directed date for project finish, or on tasks within the project, which is the normal situation.

Directed Dates

Directed dates, or constraints, are applied in several ways. Most of these will be defined and explained in detail in Chapter 16, "Special Networking Considerations." For this example, however, the "Not-Later-Than" constraint will be addressed. It is being applied to the last activity, the overall project completion. This type of constraint changes the calculations done in the backward pass by using a date that is manually input.

In the example in Figure 8-15, it would replace the late finish date of day 22.

Why would such a thing be done? The primary reason is that day 22 was calculated from the network, but may not meet the requirements of the project. What if this is a project that must be finished in 17 days or it will not be undertaken? Suppose this is a response to a request for bids, and late bids will not be accepted. Finishing the project five days late is as bad as not even responding at all. For now, assume that the "drop dead" date is day 17. That means that the latest the project can finish is day 17. This would therefore replace the late finish date of the project of day 22 as shown in Figure 8-16.

When this occurrence happens, all float calculations through the entire network, including the critical path, lose five days of float based upon the revised late dates from the backward pass.

Since the total float definition remains the same, the total float of the critical path would now be a negative 5 days. What does this mean? It indicates that based on current logic and durations, the required project finish date cannot be achieved. Now a decision must be made. Will the project still be initiated? If it is, how can five missing days be accommodated? Will there be overtime? Will additional resources be assigned to the project? Can any of the activity durations be shortened? Can the logic be changed? Can

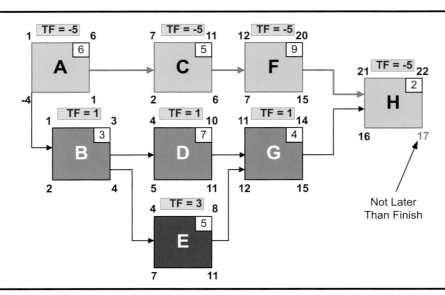

Figure 8-16 Impact of Directed Finish Date - Negative Float

the scope be changed? The answers to questions such as this will be covered in detail in Chapters 11 and 15, "Crashing the Network" and "Resolving Negative Float." The point is that a critical path definition of zero float does not always make sense.

Less likely, but also a possibility, would be an outcome where the completion was not required until later than the calculated date. If a "Not-Later-Than" date of day 29 were imposed on this same network logic, it would now mean the late finish for the project was day 29 instead of day 22. This would add seven additional days of float to every activity, including those on the critical path. The critical path would now be indicated as the path with +7 days of float. The implication of positive float on the critical path is that activities may be delayed or extended without impacting the required finish date. Resources could be realigned for better overall results. This could mean a lower peak staffing requirement and better supervision, with improved productivity. Figure 8-17 shows how the float calculations in the example would be changed for every activity.

No matter what type of directed dates are placed, and even if there are no directed dates, the critical path is the longest contiguous path through the network and usually the path with the lowest total float (negative, positive, or zero).

Critical Path Characteristics

Four statements will always be true about the critical path:

1. It is the longest path in the network.

2. It is the path that defines the earliest date for project completion.

3. It is usually the path with the least total float.

4. It is the path on which any activity expansion or delay will lengthen the total project duration.

A Final Note

This chapter often raises a question: "Why bother to go through all these calculations when a computer program will automatically take care of this?" A flippant answer would be that this is a computer appreciation chapter. However, the real reason goes much deeper than that. Scheduling is not a discipline of producing reports. It should be a dedicated effort to analyze the status of the project, identify specific areas that need immediate attention, and make recommendations regarding how to resolve problems. Scheduling requires a real understanding; not only of the project and its technical content, but also a complete understanding of what exactly it is that the computer is doing when it produces all of those

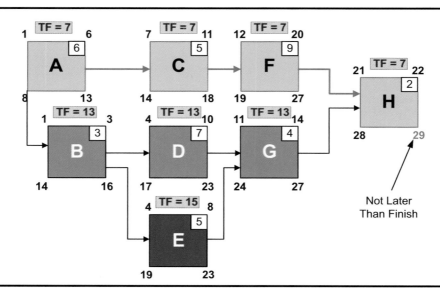

Figure 8-17 Impact of Directed Finish Date - Positive Float

impressive reports. Those impressive reports have caused management personnel to lose credibility because the scheduling or cost experts blindly accepted something that made no practical sense simply because it came out of a computer. The questions any scheduler needs to ask when inundated with data are, "Does this answer make sense? Is this believable?"

Frequently those questions are as important as the questions about method and procedure for developing the answer. If a conclusion does not make sense, then it is even more necessary to know the logic behind how the answer was developed to spot the hidden flaw in the logic.

An example drawn from the many stories relating to critical path will help to illustrate the importance of understanding the logic behind the computer programs. One lead scheduler on a fossil-fueled power plant project prepared a critical path analysis for review at a meeting with the project team. At this meeting, a room full of technical experts were told that the critical path for the project was installation of handrails. It is important to note that two key areas during construction are the boiler and turbine installation. A critical path that never touches either of these two areas is quite likely incorrect. Conversely, putting up handrails is something that can be done quickly as construction proceeds and is a trivial activity in terms of labor hours and dollars. The loss in credibility was incalculable and the scheduler soon resigned. It is easy to see how this happened though: handrails are not scheduled in detail because they are trivial to the overall completion of the project and so they were probably input as a single, long duration activity. They would be installed throughout the duration of the project as the various levels were constructed. How is the critical path defined? That is easy to answer: the longest contiguous path through the network. By now it should be easy to imagine the trap that occurred. The situation is the same as if the critical path were to be defined as managing the project. That will also last a long time but it is not the work product, it merely supports it.

So what was the mistake? The question, "Does this make sense?" was never asked. The computer had spoken. The longest path was handrail installation and so that was the area that had to be watched most closely and be carefully expedited.

Similar problems occur with schedule resources. When a schedule is proposed that meets the required end date but requires three times as many people as are available and there is a hiring freeze, one has to question the validity of the schedule despite the agreeable dates. It is difficult or impossible to intelligently critique a cost or schedule output report if the reviewer does not have some idea of what the answer should be before seeing the report. This chapter may appear clerical in nature, but it establishes the foundation for the analysis that comes later.

Conclusion

Critical path is a methodology that allows analysis of a logic network diagram and provides information about the activities in that schedule. Start and completion dates for each activity are calculated, as well as an indication of how much flexibility (float) there is in the start or completion of that activity. The objective is to implement a management by exception approach by focusing attention on those activities that are most critical to the successful achievement of the project completion date.

The critical path itself is the longest contiguous path through the network logic. It may or may not correspond to the most technically challenging critical portion of the project. It is determined by means of a "forward pass" and "backward pass" through the network. These calculations define the earliest and latest dates for each activity based on the network logic and stated activity durations. They also define the total float, the amount of time an activity can slip before impacting the project completion date. Free float is also calculated and indicates the amount an activity can slip without impacting any of the other network activities. Using directed dates can alter all of the forward pass and backward pass calculations. The use of such directed dates changes the network calculations and must be considered before analysis is performed.

Chapter 8 Review Questions

8-1.   Explain the forward pass through a network and what its results mean.

8-2.   Describe the backward pass through a network and what its results mean.

8-3.   How do "total float" and "free float" differ?

8-4.   List three absolute statements that are always true about the critical path.

True or False

8-5.   "Critical path" refers to those activities that are most technically critical.

8-6.   On the forward pass through a network, converging paths require the use of the earliest early finish of the converging activities for the succeeding activity.

8-7.   Expending the total float of an activity has no impact on subsequent activities.

8-8.   "Slack" is another term for "float".

8-9.   Changing the completion date for a project will affect the total float values for every activity in the entire network.

8-10.   It is possible to have positive total float on the critical path.

8-11.   Moving the completion date for the project network seven days earlier will result in all activities losing seven days of total float.

8-12.   Free float and total float do not have to be equal for the same activity.

8-13.   The total float for any activity can be calculated by subtracting the early finish date from the late finish date.

The answers to these questions can be found in Section 6, Solutions.

Case Study

8.1 A MORE COMPLEX NETWORK

A. Arrange these activities in logical sequence using PDM.

   1. Activity A initiates the project.

   2. Activity B can start 1 day after activity A finishes.

   3. Activity A precedes activity C.

   4. Activity D can start after B finishes, but cannot finish until 2 days after C finishes.

   5. Activity E can start 1 day after activity C starts.

   6. Activity F is preceded by activities D and E.

   7. Activity X runs the life of the project.

   Activity Durations

   A = 5

   B = 2

   C = 3

   D = 4

   E = 3

   F = 2

B. Perform the forward and backward path calculations to determine the critical path.

C. What are the options for handling activity X?

The solution to this case study can be found on the Humphreys & Associates, Inc. web site.
www.humphreys-assoc.com

8.2 CPM NETWORK CONSTRUCTION

Shown on the following pages are the activities and logic details one would expect to complete in the development of a project schedule. All relationships are finish-to-start.

Your job is to create a PDM network diagram using the activities and their relationships. Do not attempt to calculate dates or float yet. This will be done in Case Study 8.3. Draw the network diagram.

PDM

Activity List

Activity	Description
A	Define general project scope.
B	Develop detailed project scope, including a master list of all products.
C	Develop a master schedule.
D	Determine appropriate level of schedule detail.
E	Define detailed activities.
F	Define responsibility assignments to individual network activities.
G	Develop detailed schedule logic.
H	Assign resources to activities.
I	Preliminary determination of activity times.
J	Determine preliminary lead times.
K	Review activity durations based on available resources.
L	Calculate early and late dates by processing the network with no resource or end date restrictions.
M	Check feasibility and efficiency of resource profiles.
N	Compare calculated dates for milestones with required dates.
O	Revise detailed logic and durations if necessary to support required master schedule dates.
P	Resource level the schedule.
Q	Review the network for inclusion of all activities.
R	Revise the network as necessary.
S	Review activity responsibility assignment.
T	Revise responsibility assignments as necessary.
U	Review network logic.
V	Revise network logic as necessary.
W	Final review of resource profiles.
X	Revise resource plan as necessary.
Y	Approve schedule baseline.

Network Logic

1. Activity A initiates the project.

2. Activity A precedes activities B and C, which may proceed concurrently.

3. Activity B precedes activity D.

4. Activity C and F precede activity G.

5. Activity D precedes activity E.

6. Activity E precedes activity F.

7. Activity G precedes activities H, I and J, which may proceed concurrently.

8. Activities H and I precede activity K.

9. Activities J and K precede activity L.

10. Activity L precedes activities M and N, which may proceed concurrently.

11. Activities M and N both precede activity O.

12. Activity O precedes activity P.

13. Activity P precedes activities Q and W, which may proceed concurrently.

14. Activity Q precedes activity R.

15. Activity R precedes S and U, which may proceed concurrently.

16. Activity W precedes activity X.

17. Activity S precedes activity T.

18. Activity U precedes activity V.

19. Activities T, V and X precede activity Y.

20. Activity Y completes the project.

Note: All relationships are finish-to-start.

Case Study

8.3 DATE, FLOAT AND CRITICAL PATH CALCULATION

Using the network developed in Case Study 8.2, and the activity durations provided on the next page, calculate the following for each activity:

- Early Start (ES)
- Early Finish (EF)
- Late Start (LS)
- Late Finish (LF)
- Total Float (TF)
- Free Float (FF)

Use day numbers only and start with day 1. For example, activity A will start on day 1 and finish on day 2. For now, do not consider weekends and holidays.

Record your answers on the answer sheet provided for Case Study 8.4 or on the answer form provided with this case. Mark the critical path on the network diagram and circle the critical activities on the answer sheet.

The solution to this case study can be found on the Humphreys & Associates, Inc. web site.
www.humphreys-assoc.com

Activity Durations (In days)

A	2
B	10
C	4
D	1
E	4
F	2
G	8
H	3
I	2
J	4
K	2
L	1
M	1
N	1
O	2
P	5
Q	1
R	1
S	1
T	1
U	1
V	1
W	1
X	4
Y	1

Date and Float Calculation

Activity	Early Start	Early Finish	Late Start	Late Finish	Total Float	Free Float
A						
B						
C						
D						
E						
F						
G						
H						
I						
J						
K						
L						
M						
N						
O						
P						
Q						
R						
S						
T						
U						
V						
W						
X						
Y						

Case Study

8.4 CONSTRUCTING A BAR CHART

Using the activities' early dates and total float from the solution of Case Study 8.3, construct a bar chart. Use the forms following on the next pages and configure the chart as shown below.

Order the activities by early start date. When the early start dates are the same, show the critical activities first, then order by finish date. In other words, if two or more non-critical activities have the same early start, use the one with the shortest duration first.

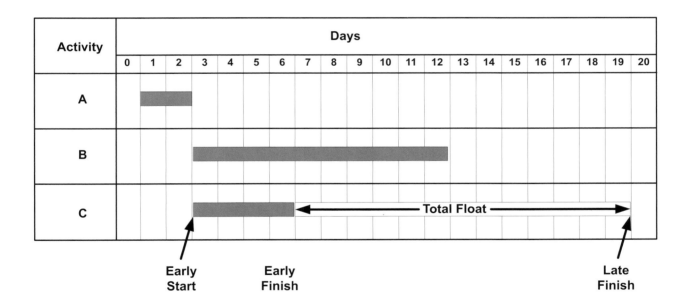

The solution to this case study can be found on the Humphreys & Associates, Inc. web site.
www.humphreys-assoc.com

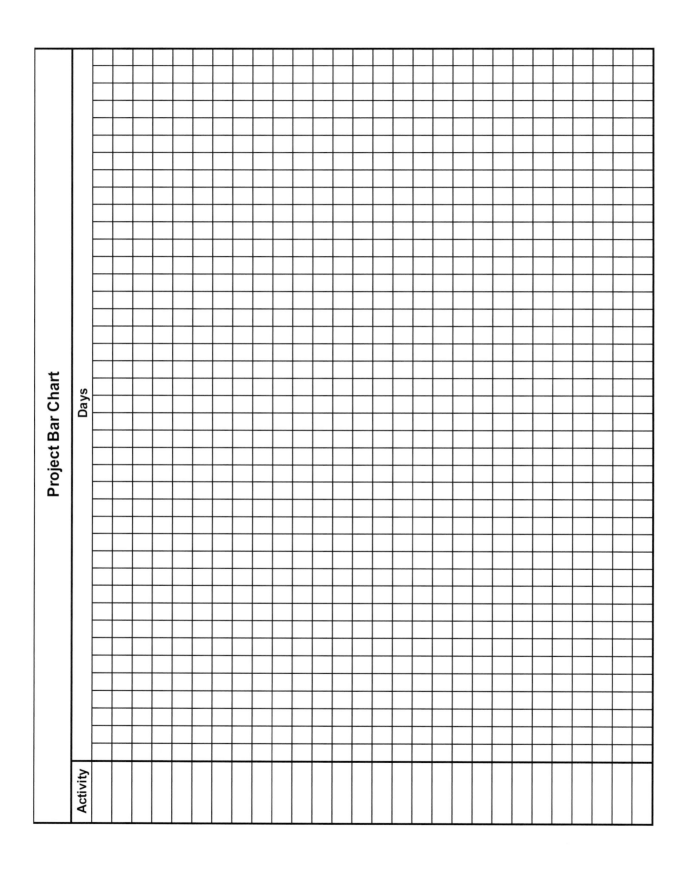

Project Bar Chart

Days

Activity

Case Study

8.5 PATH ANALYSIS USING TOTAL FLOAT

In the table below, four weeks of total float data are shown for the ten "most critical" paths (series of activities) of a project.

Float was determined by statusing the network at the end of each of the weeks.   Analyze the data and answer the following:

1.   Which are the four most important paths that management attention should be directed to each week? That is, which paths as of the end of Week 1, then at the end of Week 2, etc.

2.   List the reasons float could change more than five days in one week.

Total Float (in Days) as of the End of the Week				
Activity Path	Week 1	Week 2	Week 3	Week 4
11-1	5	8	3	-2
11-2	4	2	3	-4
26-1	3	5	5	5
27-1	7	5	4	16
29-1	5	8	7	3
32-1	4	30	30	31
32-2	6	7	8	2
35-1	6	Finished	Finished	Finished
43-1	7	7	7	2
43-2	4	18	4	-4

The solution to this case study can be found on the Humphreys & Associates, Inc. web site.
www.humphreys-assoc.com

Chapter 9

RESOURCE LOADING AND LEVELING THE SCHEDULE

Objectives of this Chapter:

1. Define the term resource as it applies to scheduling.

2. Discuss how resources are applied to a schedule.

3. Discuss the purpose and process of resource leveling.

4. Identify considerations for establishing priority rules for resource leveling.

5. Explain how the "leveled start" and "leveled finish" dates relate to the early start/finish and late start/finish dates.

6. Discuss the use of resource curves to assess resource risk.

This chapter is the last associated with the theory of the network scheduling process. Since the activity durations needed to calculate the critical path are dependent on the resources available, the CPM calculations performed in the last chapter are not sufficient to conclude the scheduling process. The schedule may be logically correct, in agreement with the estimate, and devoid of time constraints. But the schedule may not be achievable until resources are applied and verified as available. Once resources are applied to the schedule and leveled, there is a firm basis for finalizing an approved project plan. As resources are applied to the activities, it is possible to sum these and learn the staffing requirements, as well as equipment requirements, if appropriate, for supporting the schedule. If these resource requirements exceed the quantity that can be made available, then the schedule must be adjusted to reflect these realities.

Even if resources are available consistent with the plan, their use may not be efficient. It is not logical to have a plan that has wildly oscillating staffing or other resource needs. Thus, there is a need not only to identify and apply resources, but also to level them over the life of the project.

All of the discussion so far has centered on the time aspect of scheduling. Calculations have proceeded as if there were unlimited resources available to support the dates required. This assumption is not realistic, although for many years organizations developed schedules in exactly that way, with no regard for the resources needed to accomplish the work. It is virtually impossible to know if the defined dates can actually be met, even with a CPM schedule, unless resource needs and availability are considered. There are realistic limitations on how quickly staff can be added, and not having a resource plan almost assures that the necessary resources will not be available to meet the demand.

So, what exactly is a 'resource'? Resources can include installed equipment, subcontractors, facilities, people, permits and specific tests/acceptance documents, among others. Unavailability of a heavy lift crane can cause a scheduled event

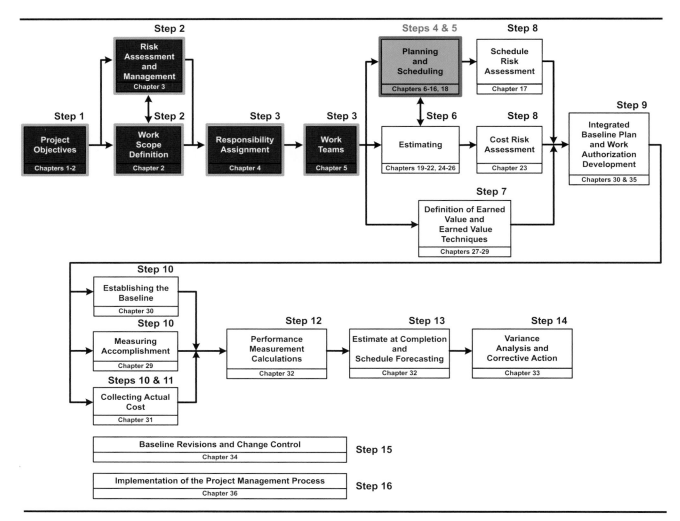

Figure 9-1 Earned Value Project Management: The Process

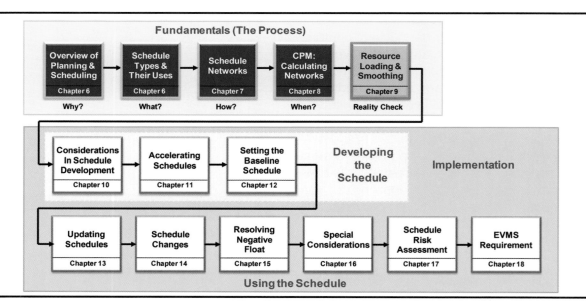

Figure 9-2 Planning and Scheduling

to be delayed. Experienced project managers and scheduling personnel will always ask themselves this question: what human or other resource is driving this schedule?

Resource loading and leveling in some form is done in nearly all organizations today. There is nearly universal recognition that resource reassessment is an essential part of the planning process. Resource loading and leveling would be important even without the existence of a CPM schedule and it certainly is true with one as well. The critical path is driven by activity durations, and the number and amount of resources available largely determine durations.

Advances in computer hardware and software have also made it much easier and faster to perform the task of resource analysis. It is still a challenging venture, however, as priorities should be defined by the executing organization rather than by the computer.

There is a dual objective to the resource loading process: ensuring that the necessary resources will be available and then ensuring that they will be used efficiently. This requires realistic staffing curves that are time-phased consistent with the project needs.

The Resource Loading Process

The resource loading process is initiated by loading resource requirements on individual activities. For labor resources, loading could be done by assigning a certain number of full time equivalent people to each activity. If the activities are summary in nature, this approach provides only summary headcount requirement profiles independent of skill set or costs. By identifying the number of labor hours of each resource required to complete each task, the schedule can more accurately forecast specific requirements and associated cost for project labor (the preferred method) more accurately.

Resources need not be assigned linearly, but nonlinear spreads of labor hours are, in most cases, a refinement that is neither necessary nor accurate. Few organizations have available records that would support nonlinear staffing. In addition, as long as the activities are kept short in duration, such fine-tuning is really more for show than for control.

Resource profiles can be generated by scheduling software in spreadsheet format such as the one shown in Figure 9-3. This representation displays the number of full time equivalent people needed for each activity. The timing of those resource requirements is therefore defined by the timing of the activity. Summing up the require-

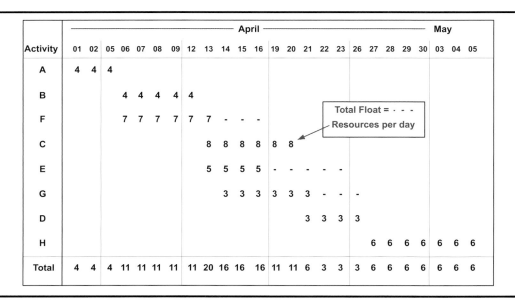

Figure 9-3 Resource Profile

ments for all activities reveals the staffing needs for the entire project. If the activity has some float, it will allow resources to be adjusted to create a smooth staffing distribution. Notice that the x-axis is now displaying calendar dates, rather than project day numbers, that do not reflect the impact of weekends, holidays, and vacations.

This calculation summary is done internally in the computer when the user sets up the particular project calendar, defining all work periods as well as those periods when no work will be scheduled.

The focus of Figure 9-3 is the bottom line total. This resource summary is not an efficient staffing plan because of the sudden swings in staff requirements. It is impractical to have a plan that calls for 11 people one day, 20 the very next day, and then 16 the day after that. It is obvious, even before the project starts that multiple activities will have to be delayed on April 13, the day with 20 people.

If the resource usage curve were plotted, sometimes called a skyline chart for obvious reasons, a pattern may emerge such as that shown in Figure 9-4. Of course this curve would not just be needed for the total project, but also for the time-phased totals of each skill code or resource. This type of picture provides a quick indication of the project staffing demands that are being placed on the executing organization before the leveling process occurs.

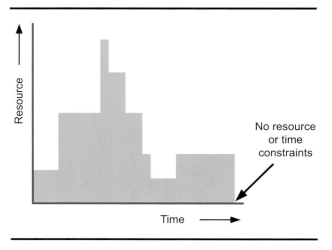

Figure 9-4 Skyline Chart

Figure 9-4 was prepared assuming no constraints, either time or resource. This is the first step in the resource process.

The very next step is to add a touch of realism by adding the actual restraints faced by the project: time and/or resource limitations. This is shown in Figure 9-5.

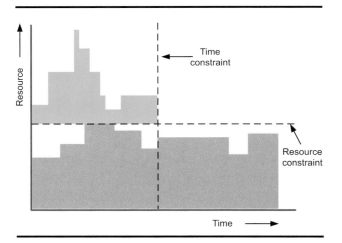

Figure 9-5 Time and/or Rersource Constraints

Two types of constraints are shown in Figure 9-5. The first is the resource availability constraint represented by the horizontal line. As resource availability lowers, the project end date extends. The second is the time constraint, indicated by the vertical line. As the time constraint moves to the left (earlier), more resources are required in each time period to support the project. The question that must ultimately be asked when resource leveling problems occur is whether the project is time critical or cost critical. In other words, which of these limiting conditions will rule: hold resources to a predetermined maximum and let the end date slide or hold the end date at all costs? The answer to this question sets the resource leveling strategy.

Priority Rules and Strategies for Resource Leveling

The process of leveling the time phased resources requires definition of the rules for determining which activities are to be delayed and in what order.

There are many possible rules for this process, but the first steps taken should be fairly standard. Based on the definitions of total float and free float, it is apparent how these should be ordered. An example of possible rule setting might be:

1. Free float (delay activities with the highest values first, minimize impact to other activities).

2. Total float (delay activities with the highest values first, minimize impact to the critical path).

3. Long versus short activities (delay the shorter activities first).

4. Early versus late activities (delay the activities starting later rather than current activities).

5. High versus low resource requirements (delay activities with the highest resource requirements first since it will smooth the curve more quickly).

Combinations of these and other rules are usually used to create an algorithm to facilitate the leveling process. Most software programs also allow a priority to be assigned to individual activities so that users can prevent certain tasks from being delayed. This strategy may be necessary because of a particular resource's criticality independent of the CPM criticality.

The first step in leveling should always be to use the entire free float. Since this float is associated with a single activity and affects no other activities in the network, the impact of the delay is minimal. Unfortunately, only a small percentage of the network activities will have free float, so using this strategy alone will not ordinarily resolve the leveling concerns.

The next strategic consideration is total float. While using total float impacts multiple activities, it does not delay the project completion date. Another strategic priority consideration may be the duration of the activity. What is the advantage to starting longer activities before shorter ones? Since it is usually easier to control and complete shorter tasks, longer more complicated tasks should be started first.

The last consideration is the amount of resources allotted to the activity. If high resource activities are moved first, doing so will more quickly resolve leveling concerns. This could reduce the total number of activities that must be delayed within their available float. All of these rules may be used in combination or supplemented with additional guidelines.

There is no perfect answer to the resource leveling question. Tests have been run by a number of individuals and results show that just about every software program on the market will level the same schedule differently.

There are other alternatives available besides delaying activities to level resources. Activity splitting is one such alternative. If a critical resource were available in March and May but not in April, one option would be to perform part of the effort in March, pause for April, and then resume in May. Unfortunately, in many cases, this cannot be done efficiently. This is particularly true of intellectual assignments that may be largely forgotten in the interim and require a period of familiarization when reactivated. Activities may also be stretched in lieu of outright delay. A stretched activity should take longer with fewer available resources, but it may be able to start earlier if it is performed at a lower level of intensity than if it is delayed because of lack of a full resource complement.

Additional Considerations

While most project emphasis is on total resources, usually because of bottom line funding limitations, it is equally important to ensure that each discipline or resource code is also individually leveled. An example from an aerospace company illustrates the need for individual leveling. At the time this example took place, the company involved was quite advanced since few aerospace contractors effectively used CPM schedules, and fewer still used resource loaded and leveled schedules. Everything looked good throughout the review until resources were analyzed. Even that was apparently textbook perfect with an almost too good to be true resource leveled total project resource curve. When the consultants for the project asked to see the resource curves by individual department, the hesitation was evident. The reason for the hesitation soon became obvious.

The profiles for each resource code included staffing levels varying from 28 to 65 to 14 in successive reporting periods. What was worse, all of the various skill levels had similar profiles. The profiles balanced wonderfully at the project total line because as one resource surged upward, another plummeted to cancel it out. Unless today's civil engineer was yesterday's welder and would be tomorrow's electrical supervisor, there was no way to support the staffing plan, even though the total looked reasonable. Nevertheless, the resource profile looked good on the bottom line totals. The rule of reason must prevail when considering skill availability.

Leveled Start and Finish

Once resources have been addressed and leveled, a new set of activity start and finish dates will be created. These are called the leveled dates: leveled start and leveled finish. The resulting early start and early finish dates now represent the leveled dates. Ideally, the leveled start is between the early start and late start dates, and the leveled finish is between the early finish and late finish dates. Is there still any float remaining? Have the critical path or near critical paths been driven to negative float? That depends on how much the start of the activity was delayed during the leveling process.

The early start date and early finish date now represent the slide to the right, if any, based on the leveling process. The late start and finish still represent what is necessary to meet the schedule objectives of the milestones or the project and determine the new float values. If the resource leveling process develops negative float in the schedule, then the schedule is telling the project that the resource requirements, resource availability and network logic predict a problem with timely completion. In this event, any or all of the above should be changed manually and thoughtfully to produce an achievable plan. When the changes have been made, everyone on the project should be working to accomplish the new leveled dates once they have been approved.

Resource Curves

Resource usage is not limited to display in a spreadsheet format such as the one shown in Figure 9-3.

Another useful format, allowing additional analysis, is displayed in Figure 9-6. The S-curve display shows the cumulative total of resources (usually work hours) versus time. Much information can be gleaned from this type of presentation when cumulative resource curves are drawn for early schedules and late schedules. The example shown here has a third curve: the cumulative resource requirement according to the leveled start. The basis for these curves is as follows:

The "Early Start Curve" defines the resource requirement if all activities started on their earliest possible date.

The "Late Start Curve" defines the resource requirement if all activities started on their latest possible date (without delaying project completion).

The "Leveled Start Curve" defines the resource requirement if all activities started exactly as planned on the resource leveled schedule.

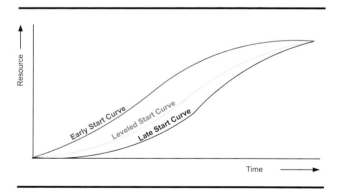

Figure 9-6 Resource Boundaries

The location of the cumulative leveled start curve provides some insight into the reasonableness of the plan.

If the leveled start were too close to the late start curve, it would be a plan for disaster. It will take very little slip before the leveled start curve will shift to the right and will cross the late start curve. Once that happens, the project completion date is in serious jeopardy. If the leveled start were too close to the early start curve, it would be an overly optimistic schedule and would likely have many dates that are missed. Ideally, the leveled curve should be in the center of the envelope defined by the early and late curves, but a little closer to the early curve than the late curve.

There is additional information contained within the set of curves in Figure 9-6. In fact, even without the leveled start curve there is valuable insight that can be gained just from the early and late curves.

Figure 9-7 provides definition of other types of "float" as it relates to resources. The shape of these curves provides information on the degree of flexibility for resources on the project, much as total float provides insight into the degree of flexibility from a time standpoint. These curves are called time float and resource float. Time float indicates how much time variation exists before reaching a specified resource level while still supporting the schedule objectives of the project. It may indicate, for example, that a staffing level of 100 people must be reached somewhere between month seven and month eleven of the project. That would correspond to a "time float" of four months for that level of resources. It would also indicate that if a staffing level of 100 is reached before month seven, people are not being used efficiently on the project based on the schedule logic. Even if every single network activity began on the earliest possible date, and the assigned resources were correct, there would not be a need for that level of staffing before month seven. If staffing were not reached by month eleven, however, it could be concluded that the project end date was in serious danger. When staffing is outside of the envelope described by the late start curve, it indicates that a higher staffing level would be needed to support the project completion date (even if one were willing to wait until the last possible instant to start every network activity).

The same type of comment applies to the vertical dimension on this chart, the "resource float." This value indicates at a given point in time, such as "time now", what the variation in staffing levels may be while still supporting the resource loaded schedule plan. It may indicate, for example, that current staffing levels may be between 65 and

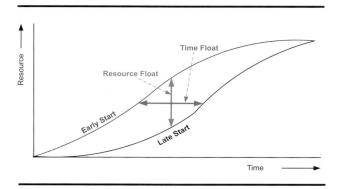

Figure 9-7 Resource Boundaries - Time and Resource Floats

130 and still be acceptably supporting the overall objectives. If staffing levels are above or below these levels, a problem is indicated.

Are there exceptions to these general conclusions? Of course there are. The conclusions are based on the assumption that the staffing levels used in the schedule are correct and that work is being accomplished as efficiently as planned. If work accomplishment were 20% less than planned, for example, it could mean that staffing levels need to rise faster than anticipated to compensate for decreased productivity. Also, remember that these curves are based on the earliest and latest possible dates. Once a schedule plan has been developed, the intent is to staff according to the scheduled start curve that should be midway between these curves.

The shape of these boundaries still provides important planning input. Figure 9-8 illustrates this example. Both of the curves have exactly the same total number of resource units and the same time frame in which to use them. However, two very different pictures of resource criticality emerge from these two graphs.

It should be apparent that the resource skill in the right curve is far more critical than the resource represented in the curve on the left. That is because of the great variation in the amount of flexibility each curve has.

Use of resource curves such as these can be a powerful analytical tool to evaluate staffing criticality and priorities. This can be done on an exception basis as well. One company used resource curves on a complex project and two resource-critical disciplines were easily identified

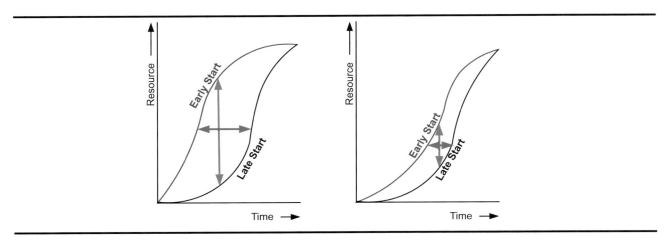

Figure 9-8 Resource Boundaries - Less and More Critical Curves

out of twenty or more other aspects of the project. As a result, very close attention was focused on these particular resource providers to verify that necessary staffing increases would be supported. Thanks to close monitoring, staffing proceeded according to plan and the project remained on schedule.

Other Applications

It is not always possible to level and control resources neatly. A prime example is maintenance, scheduled or unscheduled. With unscheduled maintenance, there is an immediate need for resources to return the process or equipment to an operational status. This is not a condition that can be scheduled and resource loaded in advance. Even with scheduled maintenance, resource leveling may not be possible. One example comes from the United States Navy and its ship maintenance and repair operations. Ships do not always need overhaul at the precise time when resources are available to support it. The result is often large peaks in staffing requirements that can only be supported with overtime, double shifting, and the addition of contract maintenance personnel. This dilemma makes the resource management process much more difficult, but it does not eliminate the need for managing resources. Resource loading may be even more important in applications such as these, when resource leveling is impossible. At least the magnitude of the resource challenge can be assessed and addressed.

Conclusion

Schedule durations are based on available resources, so the schedule plan should reflect this fact. The process of resource loading and leveling a schedule is the method for fine-tuning the overall project execution plan. Resource loading includes defining the necessary resources required for accomplishing each activity within the stated time duration. Summing labor requirements, for example, allows creation of a project staffing plan. Cumulative staffing requirements can be determined from the early start schedule and from the late start schedule. A plan can then be implemented that stays within these boundaries. The same approach can be used for material and equipment requirements.

While resource loading is straightforward, resource leveling is more challenging. Rules and strategies should be developed for stretching activities or delaying them based on the project priorities. These rules may be based on total float, free float, resource criticality, or a host of other alternatives. Resource leveling is not as simple as developing a smooth total project staffing plan. The same type of effort is needed for each project skill category, since staff will not be used interchangeably. Even in applications when resource leveling is not practical (such as unscheduled maintenance), resource loading is a critical element in successful completion of the effort.

Chapter 9 Review Questions

9-1.   Define several different types of resources.

9-2.   Why is resource loading necessary as part of the schedule development process?

9-3.   Explain the difference between resource loading and resource leveling.

9-4.   What is meant by the statement, "This project is time critical"? How does this differ from being resource critical?

9-5.   How does the leveled start/completion date relate to the early and late dates for the same activities?

True or False

9-6.   Resource leveling is primarily a concern at the total project level.

9-7.   The process and purpose of resource leveling is to help ensure that the necessary resources will be available when needed and that they can be used efficiently.

9-8.   The use of nonlinear resource spreads on individual activities is usually not warranted.

9-9.   When resources are initially loaded in the schedule, the assumption should be that unlimited resources are available.

9-10.   In order for resource leveling to be achieved, it will be necessary to delay the start and completion of some activities within the network.

9-11.   An "early start" curve is a cumulative resource profile that represents what the resource requirements would be if all activities started on their earliest possible date.

The answers to these questions can be found in Section 6, Solutions.

Case Study

9.1 RESOURCE LEVELING

Part A

One resource has been loaded on the activities of a small network. These resources are shown in spreadsheet format in the table below. All activities are at their early start dates. This means that while they may be rescheduled to the right (later in time), they may *not* be moved to the left (earlier in time).

Your requirement is to manually reschedule the activities so that no more than *100 resource units* are used in any one week. It would be preferable to use not more than *90 resource units* per week if that is possible. Also consider efficiency in the use of the resource.

You may not change the activity duration or the configuration of the resource within an activity. Use the table on this page. Use of a pencil instead of a pen is recommended.

Activity	Week									
	1	2	3	4	5	6	7	8	9	10
A	50	50	50	50	....	....	....	....	....	....
B		20	20	40	....	....	....	....	....	....
C	30	30	....	....	....	....	....	....	....	....
D		60	60	60	60	....	....	....	....	....
E	50	50	....	....	....	....	....	....	....	....
F		20	30	20	....	....	....	....	....	....
G			10	10	10	....	....	....	....	....
H		10	20	10	....	....	....	....	....	....
Total	130	240	190	190	70	0	0	0	0	0

The solution to this case study can be found on the Humphreys & Associates, Inc. web site.
www.humphreys-assoc.com

Resource Leveling Part A - Worksheet

Activity	Week									
	1	2	3	4	5	6	7	8	9	10
A										
B										
C										
D										
E										
F										
G										
H										
Total										

Part B

Resource level the network again, but this time use additional restrictions:

1. Activities E, F, and H are critical and also have no Total Float.
2. Other Total Float limitations: A has 6 weeks, B has 2 weeks, C and D have 3 weeks, and G has 5 weeks.
3. Activities B, F and H require the same sub-resource, design drafters. Design drafters can work on any activity, but are required for these activities. This category cannot exceed a total of 50 units per week.
4. Total resource units may not exceed 110 in any week, but that should be held to 100 if possible. Also consider efficiency of usage.

Activity durations and resource patterns are fixed: No splitting, stretching or re-profiling. You might try scheduling the subcategory first, then the others.

Activity	Week									
	1	2	3	4	5	6	7	8	9	10
A	50	50	50	50	....	....	....	....	....	....
B (r)		20	20	40	....	....	....	....	....	....
C	30	30				....	....	....	....	....
D		60	60	60	60	....	....	....	....	....
E (c)	50	50	....	....	....	....	....	....	....	....
F (c,r)		20	30	20	....	....	....	....	....	....
G			10	10	10	....	....	....	....	....
H (c,r)		10	20	10	....	....	....	....	....	....
Total	130	240	190	190	70	0	0	0	0	0

r = Sub-resource category

c = Critical activity

Resource Leveling Part B - Worksheet

Activity	Week									
	1	2	3	4	5	6	7	8	9	10
A										
B (r)										
C										
D										
E (c)										
F (c,r)										
G										
H (c,r)										
Total										

r = Sub-resource category

c = Critical activity

Chapter **10**

CONSIDERATIONS FOR DEVELOPING A USEFUL, QUALITY SCHEDULE

Objectives of this Chapter:

1. Explain the differing considerations in top-down versus bottom-up scheduling.

2. Explain the development of the Integrated Master Plan (IMP).

3. Discuss the integration of the Integrated Master Plan (IMP) with the Integrated Master Schedule (IMS).

4. Discuss the use of hammocks, summary activities and grouping as methods of producing concise reporting.

5. Define the characteristics and application of templates in the schedule development process.

6. Explain the role of lags and date constraints in schedule logic development.

7. Explain the use of Schedule Margin in accommodating schedule contingencies.

8. Discuss the advantages/disadvantages of conservative and aggressive scheduling.

9. Discuss the pros and cons of project schedules versus organizational schedules.

10. Discuss the importance of properly choosing the level of detail for a schedule.

11. Examine the metrics, based on the scheduling attributes that should be performed to ensure a quality schedule.

12. Display the correlation between the 14-point health check and the 8 principles of GASP (Generally Accepted Scheduling Principles).

This chapter begins the implementation portion of scheduling. The theory of the past few chapters has served as a technical base for the scheduling process, but the focus is now on application realities. Many decisions must be made when a project schedule is being developed, and these decisions profoundly affect how the schedule will be used throughout the life of the project. In this chapter, some of the key decisions will be investigated as well as how they affect analysis.

Many decisions that affect the utility of a schedule are made as it is developed. These decisions are not questions of what scope to include, since all scope must be represented, but how that scope will best be portrayed to produce a useful analytical and control document. Some of these questions relate to the philosophical approach, such as the question of conservative versus aggressive schedule durations. How much detail will be represented? What shortcuts are available to speed network development or to simplify analysis of the progress? What gimmicks are used to "fix" a schedule? How can the schedule be used as an effective communication tool for the project

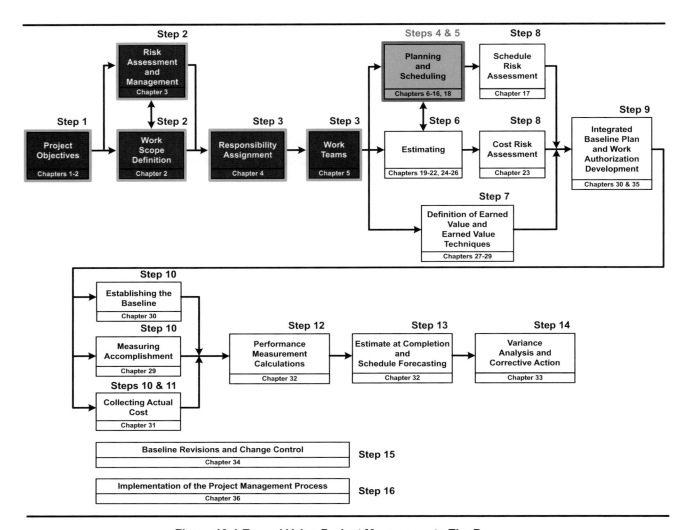

Figure 10-1 Earned Value Project Management: The Process

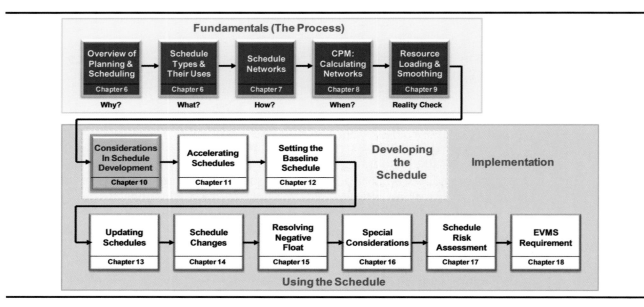

Figure 10-2 Planning and Scheduling

team? Finally, what procedural approach will be used to generate the initial schedule document: top-down or bottom-up?

Network Development Techniques: Top-Down

The first question to be addressed relates to initial network development. A popular subject for debate for many years among schedulers was whether schedules were developed "top-down" or "bottom-up." This always made an interesting discussion since it had to be done both ways to get a consistent multi-level schedule. This chapter will address the considerations that affect this discussion, including an explanation of exactly what is meant by each of these terms.

Top-down scheduling is most frequently used in the early phases of a project, such as during proposal preparation. The top-down approach uses high-level milestones to identify key project schedule requirements or events that must occur in certain sequences and time frames. These milestones may include contract authorization, preliminary design reviews, system design reviews, important material deliveries, or delivery of the end product(s) to support customer/owner specified dates. Using these milestones as a guideline, the span of time allowed to complete supporting activities is easily determined.

If the project were intended for Federal procurements, the contract would call for the creation of an Integrated Master Plan (IMP) that would be integrated with the Integrated Master Schedule (IMS). The IMP has a top-down strategy and is described in further detail later in this chapter.

How does top-down planning work? The Widget Project contract has just been signed. The contract calls for the design and manufacture of 3 widget units with deliveries starting at the end of July of this year. An example of the first high level schedule is portrayed in Figure 10-3. This displays the project-level contractual milestones for the delivery of units A, B, & C. Note that the time axis is in months and years only. This is only a starting point, because this format has many disadvantages associated with it. There is no indication of work needed to support these

dictated dates, nor is there any comfort level that they can even be achieved. Other questions remain unanswered: when does the design effort have to be completed to support these delivery dates? What are the resource requirements? Who is responsible for ensuring that supporting work is completed on time? How will status be indicated during the months when there are no milestones? These are reasons why the top-down process cannot stop once the highest level is complete; there are too many unanswered questions.

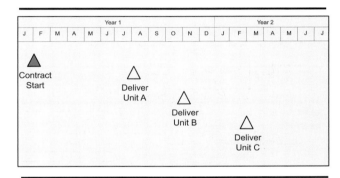

Figure 10-3 Top Level Schedule - Contractual Milestones

Because of these questions and many others, the next step is to expand the detail of the schedule by defining the supporting activities that are needed to achieve the milestones. A sample is shown in Figure 10-4.

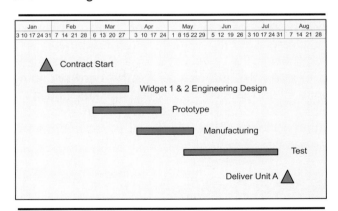

Figure 10-4 'Unit A' Top Level Schedule

This plan is still at a high level, but it illustrates the basic work areas that will be needed to support that next milestone, delivery of Unit A. Similar detail would need to be developed for support of Unit B and Unit C delivery.

There are a few things to note about Figure 10-4. As the detail has expanded, so has the time axis. Now the horizontal axis is expressed in weeks and months rather than months and years. This expanded schedule definition is oriented to areas of functional responsibility: design, manufacturing, and testing. The expansion is appropriate since there is a sequential nature to these functions and the time required for each should be planned and scheduled.

A number of the questions expressed for the higher schedule level still apply here, and so further breakdown is required. The Widget 1 & 2 Engineering Design breakdown is shown in Figure 10-5.

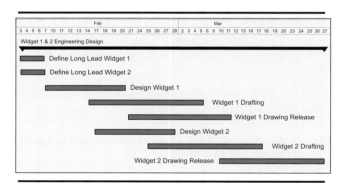

Figure 10-5 'Unit A' Widgets 1 and 2 Engineering Schedule

The detail has been further expanded in Figure 10-5 to show individual products included within the umbrella of activity "Widget 1 and 2 Engineering Design" in Figure 10-4. Similar expansions of detail would be developed for the other activities in Figure 10-3, as well as for the corresponding units B and C. At this point, the time intervals along the horizontal axis have been expanded again so that now activities are scheduled by day if need be.

Network Development Techniques: Bottom-Up

The bottom-up scheduling technique begins schedule development at the lowest level of the end item activity and is consolidated or summarized at progressively higher levels. It is applied when there is enough visibility of activity requirements to clearly define what is needed to com-

plete the task; in other words, the scope of work is fully defined and understood and detailed planning can precede the development of the schedule with very few uncertainties. This low level of definition allows for the assignment of specific resources (junior programmer, senior designer, mechanical engineer, etc.). It clearly illustrates the activities required to complete an established goal or milestone, and identifies interim milestones that could affect the final outcome of the project. See Figure 10-6 for a detailed schedule equivalent to the earlier examples of top-down scheduling.

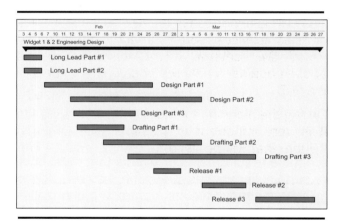

Figure 10-6 'Unit A' Widget 1 Engineering Schedule

Network Development Techniques: IMP/IMS

As mentioned above, an Integrated Master Plan/Integrated Master Schedule (IMP/IMS) approach is usually required for projects where the customer is the Federal Government. The IMP is an event-based plan consisting of a hierarchy of project events, with each event being supported by specific accomplishments, and each accomplishment associated with specific criteria to be satisfied for its completion. The use of the IMP is normally part of the contract and thus contractually binding.

The IMP is a narrative explaining the overall management of the project. An IMP event is a project assessment point that occurs at the culmination of significant project activities, accomplishments, and criteria. An accomplishment is the desired result(s) prior to or at completion of an event that indicates a level of the project's progress. Criteria provide definitive evidence that a specific accomplishment has been completed. Entry criteria reflect what must be done to be ready to initiate a review, demonstration, or test. Exit criteria reflect what must be done to clearly ascertain the event has been successfully completed. Unlike an IMS, the IMP does not contain any dates.

Assume that the Widget Project, as shown in Figure 10-4, was being performed as a result of a government contract that specifies an IMP/IMS environment. The IMP for the project might have started like the one shown in Figure 10-7.

The IMP is expanded in the IMS to incorporate all detailed activities required to accomplish the individual IMP criteria. The activities are then applied against a networked schedule to develop the IMS.

During the planning for the IMP/IMS environment, it is very important to consider the numbering system that will be used for the project. Design-ing a single numbering scheme aids cross referencing with the IMP, IMS, and WBS which is essential when there is an Earned Value requirement and an integrated cost and schedule system is being established. Figure 10-8 demonstrates how an activity ID in the IMS can be composed of the WBS element ID, the IMP ID, and a sequential number to make the activity ID unique within the IMS. This coding scheme gives complete visibility from the summary levels within the WBS down to the elementary level of an activity in the schedule.

Not all scheduling software uses an activity ID field and therefore a concatenated activity ID, as shown in Figure 10-8, is not possible. Regardless of what software is used for the IMS, all the code fields from the WBS, SOW, Integrated Product Team (IPT)/Work Team, CAM (Control Account Manager) and other company specific fields should always be fully populated in order to ensure that reporting from the IMS is always accurate and complete and that the information is

WBS Ref	IMP	Event
		Accomplishment
		Criteria
	B	Widget 1 & 2 Engineering PDR
	B01	Widget 1 Detail Design Completed
110	B01A	Final Review of Widget 1 Design
110	B01B	Validation of Widget 1 Design
110	B01C	Widget 1 Drawings Completed
	B02	Widget 2 Detail Design Completed
120	B02A	Final Review of Widget 2 Design
120	B02B	Validation of Widget 2 Design
120	B02C	Widget 2 Drawings Completed
	C	CDR
	C01	Critical Design Review Completed
400	C01A	CDR Preparation Completed
400	C01B	CDR Meeting Conducted
400	C01C	Widget 1 Drawings Released

Figure 10-7 Integrated Master Plan for the Widget Project

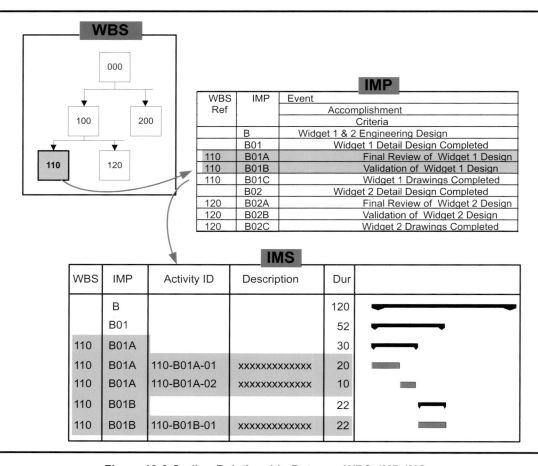

Figure 10-8 Coding Relationship Between WBS, IMP, IMS

Concerns in the Schedule Development Process

transferred correctly to the integrated cost system. Later in this chapter, how health checks can be performed to ensure that all critical code fields are present in the schedule will be shown.

One of the problems frequently associated with top-down scheduling is that it tends to result in schedules that are too short in total duration. Such schedules are unrealistic and make a poor plan, but certain agencies and organizations encourage this practice and even have a euphemistic term for it: "success oriented schedules." The approach is to force detailed activities to fit within the proposed project milestones, regardless of the actual time needed to complete the intended scope of work. This practice tends to lead to underestimation of schedule durations and associated resources, resulting in the cre-

ation of an unrealistic baseline plan. This practice will be discussed in more detail later in this chapter under the topic of "Schedule Approaches".

Another drawback of top down scheduling is that people want to "fill up" the time between milestones even though they may not all require that much time. This results in schedules that are difficult to analyze because they have many parallel activities that do not represent realistic durations.

Conversely, bottom-up scheduling many times leads to overestimating the requirements. This, of course, is no better than the top-down concern. Over estimation occurs when each activity tends to be considered by itself rather than as part of the whole network. Completion of certain activities provides information that will benefit other activities. If this were not considered in the durations, then the total schedule duration would become longer than required.

Using Hammocks, Summary Activities and Grouping for Concise Reporting

Large, complex networks can contain tens of thousands of activities. Developing such a network, as well as presenting its status to management, can prove to be quite challenging. Three techniques, frequently used to make large networks more manageable, are the use of hammocks, summary activities, and a facility available in most scheduling software, grouping.

A hammock task can be defined as either a summary task that aggregates a related set of activities, or an actual ongoing activity whose start and finish is driven by other activities or milestones that may or may not be related.

A hammock is unique. Hammocks are calculated from the duration and dates from detail activities. There is one and only one hammock or parent activity for an associated group of detailed activities. Each hammock has a single start and end point. The starting date of a hammock activity is determined by the earliest start date of any of the detailed activities that it summarizes. The completion is likewise dictated by the latest completion date of any of the detailed activities. The technique of using hammocks can be beneficial in performing "what-if" analysis because it limits the number of activities that must be analyzed. However, many scheduling software packages have difficulties handling hammocks properly and may not calculate the duration of the summary activity correctly.

Figure 10-9 shows the relationship of a hammock to a portion of a schedule. The hammock assumes the ES and LS of activity D and the EF and LF of activity H. The hammock length adjusts to any variation in length of the activities that define it.

Summary activities are created by code structure. The activities they summarize may not be contiguous or directly related to one another. In Figure 10-10, activities are summarized by the IMP code. The summarized activities need not be directly related to one another, unlike activities in hammocks.

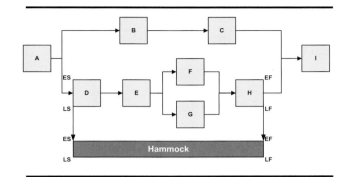

Figure 10-9 Hammock

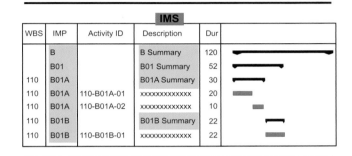

Figure 10-10 Summaries Using Code Fields

Many scheduling tools have a feature that allows users to group activities based on their specifications. This allows the grouping of activities or resources based on the user's criteria. Figure 10-11 illustrates sample output. The report displays the activities that have been assigned to the control account managers in total float order, from the most critical to the least critical. The grouping facility is the most flexible method of producing targeted reporting. Further benefits can be gained with careful design of project-specific code fields that will allow the intelligent selection of information to enhance the display options.

Templates

Templates are standardized network modules to describe a specific activity or series of activities used repetitively as needed in the development of a network. Since templates are fragments of networks, templates used to be referred to as fragnets. There are many advantages in using templates, especially in large networks. By defining standard activity sequences once, groups of

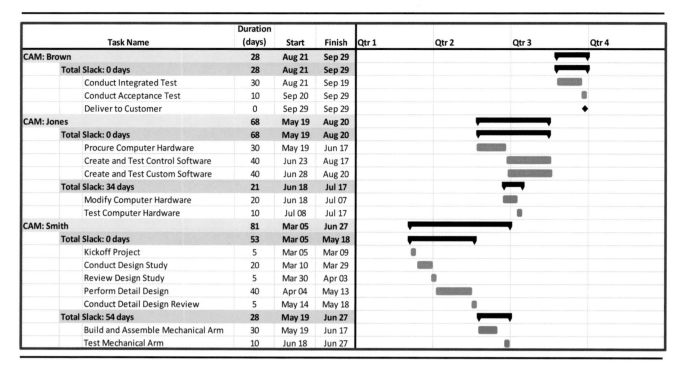

Task Name	Duration (days)	Start	Finish	Qtr 1	Qtr 2	Qtr 3	Qtr 4
CAM: Brown	28	Aug 21	Sep 29				
Total Slack: 0 days	28	Aug 21	Sep 29				
Conduct Integrated Test	30	Aug 21	Sep 19				
Conduct Acceptance Test	10	Sep 20	Sep 29				
Deliver to Customer	0	Sep 29	Sep 29				
CAM: Jones	68	May 19	Aug 20				
Total Slack: 0 days	68	May 19	Aug 20				
Procure Computer Hardware	30	May 19	Jun 17				
Create and Test Control Software	40	Jun 23	Aug 17				
Create and Test Custom Software	40	Jun 28	Aug 20				
Total Slack: 34 days	21	Jun 18	Jul 17				
Modify Computer Hardware	20	Jun 18	Jul 07				
Test Computer Hardware	10	Jul 08	Jul 17				
CAM: Smith	81	Mar 05	Jun 27				
Total Slack: 0 days	53	Mar 05	May 18				
Kickoff Project	5	Mar 05	Mar 09				
Conduct Design Study	20	Mar 10	Mar 29				
Review Design Study	5	Mar 30	Apr 03				
Perform Detail Design	40	Apr 04	May 13				
Conduct Detail Design Review	5	May 14	May 18				
Total Slack: 54 days	28	May 19	Jun 27				
Build and Assemble Mechanical Arm	30	May 19	Jun 17				
Test Mechanical Arm	10	Jun 18	Jun 27				

Figure 10-11 Grouping Facility Showing Total Float by CAM

activities can be re-used quickly and accurately. This process helps standardize the schedules and the quality is improved by providing consistency in the naming and linking of the activities in standard processes.

Use of templates provides for standard stages of work. If, for example, there are many documents to be created on a project and reviewed by the customer, use of a template with these standard activities can help:

1. Draft the document.

2. Peer Review the Document.

3. Revise the document.

4. Provide for Customer Review.

5. Respond to Customer comments and revise.

6. Release.

With many documents moving through this process, the team knows how many documents are in each stage of the process, for example, how many and which are in review by the customer.

In one recent proposal effort, a two person team built a 3500 line schedule in two days using templates. The schedule was then provided to the technical team for adjustment of durations and logic as needed; but these changes were under control of the proposal manager.

Some companies have taken this a step further and defined standard durations as well as activity sequences. However, some durations must be activity specific such as lead times for equipment delivery. Figure 10-12 conceptually illustrates the use of templates. Each DRWG activity would be replaced with the 5-activity template. Depending on requirements, each reuse of the template activities might involve some modifications in the activity attributes such as duration, descriptions, etc.

Templates, like hammocks, contain single start and completion dates. However, a single template may summarize to many different "parent" activities. Since many parents are represented in the main network, development of a template can save schedule preparation and status time. Examples where templates can be successfully employed include drawing preparation, procurement processes, repetitious activities of any kind such as manufacturing, construction, testing, or software project development.

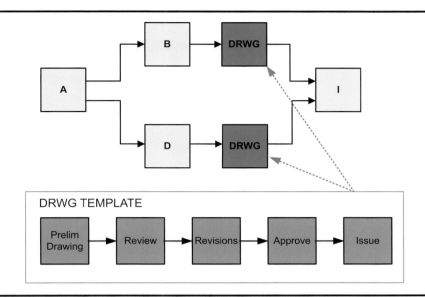

Figure 10-12 Templates

One case for template usage is the procurement cycle for materials or equipment. This cycle can be described by anything from one to seventeen or more activities. When this number is multiplied by the total number of procurement packages on a large project, the variability in the final total number of activities is considerable. The greatest time saving occurs when there is a requirement for the extra detail of the large standard sequences.

Here is a specific example for specification and procurement of equipment. The "parent" activity would be "Specify and Procure Widget A." Two levels of template detail are presented to illustrate the point:

1. Prepare bid list.
2. Prepare specification for Widget A.
3. Issue request for proposal.
4. Evaluate bids.
5. Award purchase order.
6. Deliver Widget A.
7. Incorporate Widget A into integrated design.

The above list allows the act of specifying and procuring Widget A to be planned and tracked based on the seven activities listed. These would be used repeatedly throughout the network for procuring Widget B, Widget C, etc. The durations may not always be the same, but the activity sequence and logic would be identical. Certain activities such as "prepare bid list" should be a standard duration for every item procured. An activity such as "delivery", however, is product specific and may vary with every order. The level of visibility into the process of procurement is established by the number of activities used to track the process.

The standard template for procurement may instead look like this:

1. Identify potential bidders.
2. Complete bid list.
3. Prepare draft specification.
4. Review draft specification.
5. Incorporate comments to draft specification.
6. Approve and issue specification.
7. Issue Requests For Proposal (RFPs).
8. Pre-bid meeting.
9. Receive bids.
10. Review bids.
11. Evaluate bids and make recommendations.

12. Award purchase order/contract.

13. Receive vendor drawings.

14. Review and approve vendor drawings.

15. Deliver material/equipment.

While this latter approach may seem like overkill, it does provide far more visibility into the process. For example, receiving vendor drawings is a common delay point that impacts schedule. That could be carefully tracked in the 15-item template but it does not even appear in the 7-item template. The correct selection of template detail depends on the criticality of the project and the desired reporting visibility.

A template could be changed once to cause changes in many locations in the network, and the actual durations from historical records can be used for refining future estimates of required schedule time. The greatest use of templates observed was a company that had 1500+ templates in their library. The templates were applied to a project and the project team could not add, remove activities, or change logic from the standard without permission. However, the duration and resource assignments could be changed.

Lags, Leads and Date Constraints

Logic development is more than just interconnecting individual activities. Lags and leads, imposed milestones that affect network calculations, date constraints, and resource availability must be considered.

A lag is a specified amount of time, or duration, applied to a logical relationship. In Chapter 8, logical relationships were used to calculate dates of interrelated activities. Dates for succeeding activities were calculated "as soon as" the preceding activity was started or completed, depending on the relationship type: FS, SS or FF. A lag may be applied to any relationship type and, in certain cases, to both the SS and FF relationships between a pair of activities. Lags are typically shown as positive values. A lag of +2 days applied to an FS relationship indicates that the succeeding activity must wait at least 2 days after the completion of the preceding activity before it can start. Negative values of lags, called leads,

are sometimes used to indicate overlapping activities. The use of leads is discouraged by the Generally Accepted Scheduling Principles (GASP), since there are better alternatives for handling these activities. Lags, in general, are looked upon with suspicion, since they are frequently used to influence the outcome of the CPM process. This use of lags constitutes an abuse of the CPM process and should be completely avoided.

Because of the way that lags are treated in CPM scheduling, they should be short and extremely certain as to their duration. Lags represent activity; that activity may be benign and not "worthy" of inclusion in a network, in which case the lag simply represents the unspecified activity. Examples of such passive activities include the cure time for concrete, chemicals or coatings; short lead times for materials or equipment; or clean up time of workspace or equipment between activities.

The legend for the examples that follow is shown in Figure 10-13.

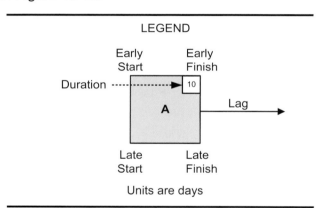

Figure 10-13 Legend for the Examples

Figure 10-14 shows a Finish to Start relationship with a +1 day lag. Notice that the early start of Activity B is 2 days after the finish of Activity A, not the next day.

Lags may be applied to Start to Start or to Finish to Finish relationships. For SS relationships, the start of the succeeding activity is delayed beyond the start of the preceding activity by the value of the lag. Similarly, for FF relationships, the finish of the succeeding activity is delayed past the end of the preceding activity.

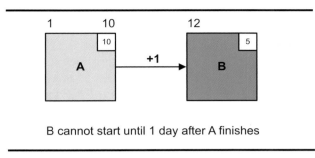

B cannot start until 1 day after A finishes

Figure 10-14 Finish to Start with Lag

Figure 10-15 shows a Start to Start relationship with a +2 day lag. Notice that the early start of Activity B is 2 days after the start of Activity A.

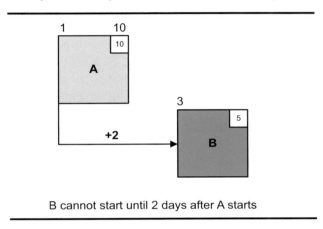

B cannot start until 2 days after A starts

Figure 10-15 Start to Start with Lag

In this case, the lag represents a part of the Activity A scope that must be completed prior to the beginning of Activity B. This lag must be documented and defended in a "Notes" type of field in the scheduling software or in supporting documentation. Best practice indicates limited use of lags and completely discourages the use of negative lags, also called leads.

Figure 10-16 shows a Finish to Finish relationship with a +3 day lag. The early finish of Activity B is 3 days after the finish of Activity A.

In this case, the lag represents a part of the Activity B scope that must be completed after the completion of Activity A. This lag must be documented and defended in a "Notes" type of field in the scheduling software or in supporting documentation.

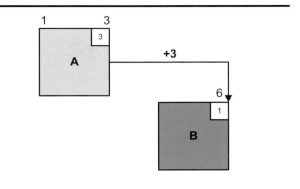

B cannot finish until 3 days after A finishes

Figure 10-16 Finish to Finish with Lag

Not all scheduling software will support multiple relationships between activity pairs such as described in the following examples.

Figure 10-17 shows a Start to Start and a Finish to Finish relationship between Activity A and Activity B. Each of the relationships includes a positive lag as well. This arrangement is frequently called a "forced parallel", since Activity B is forced by the logic to be in parallel with or "shadow" Activity A. Forced parallel activities are pairs of activities that are closely related but distinctive in scope, such as an assembly activity and an associated inspection activity. The SS lag allows some of the assembly to take place prior to the start of inspection. The FF lag allows inspection to be performed on the last of the items assembled in the driving activity.

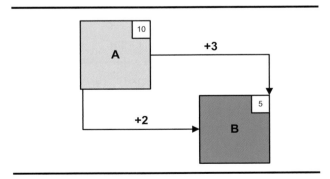

Figure 10-17 Parallel Start to Start and Finish to Finish Relationships with Lags

Figure 10-18 shows the date calculations that result from the SS relationship line of logic between Activities A and B. Assuming that Activity A begins the project, its ES is day 1. Applying the +2 day lag to the beginning of Activity B, its ES is day 3, 2 days after the start of Activity A. Considering the 5 day duration of Activity B, its EF is day 7.

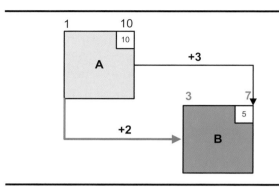

Figure 10-18 CPM Calculations - Start to Start Relationship

Now, applying the CPM process to the FF relationship line of logic, the EF of Activity A is day 10. Applying the +3 day lag between the end of Activity A and the finish of Activity B produces an EF of day 13 for Activity B. When the duration of 5 days is subtracted from the EF of Activity B, the resulting ES date of day 9 is calculated.

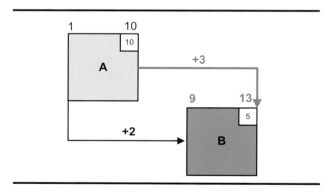

Figure 10-19 CPM Calculations - Finish to Finish Relationship

An interesting dilemma is produced by the foregoing two calculation sets. Two different ES and EF pairs are calculated, depending on which line of logic is used. Figure 10-20 shows the dilemma.

Following the SS + 2 line of logic from Activity A, the ES of Activity B is day 3 and the EF is day 7. Following the FF + 3 line of logic, the EF of Activity B is day 13 and the ES is, therefore, day 9.

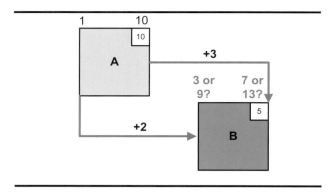

Figure 10-20 CPM Calculations - Activity B Date Possibilities

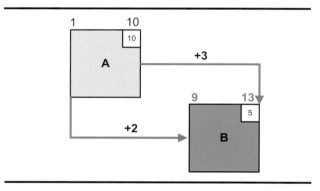

Figure 10-21 CPM Calculations - Activity B Dates

For the dates to be valid, both lines of logic must be satisfied. The resulting dates for Activity B are shown in Figure 10-21.

Studying the foregoing closely, a valid case can be made for stating that the ES of Activity B in reality is day 3. However, the EF, driven by the FF logic, would still be day 13. This implies that the duration of Activity B, 13 – 3 + 1, would be 11 days, not 5 as indicated. In order to take advantage of the earlier ES date and comply with the existing EF date, Activity B should be reconfigured in one of several ways. There are now 11 days in which to do work that was estimated to take 5 days. The 5 day estimate may have been based on the resources applied to the activity. It may be possible to reduce the number and/or quality of the resources, thus increasing the duration of Activity B to as many as 11 days, or it may be possible to split Activity B's work to occur over 11 days, but not continuously. Either of these scenarios would only be undertaken if there were economic, efficiency, resource leveling or other

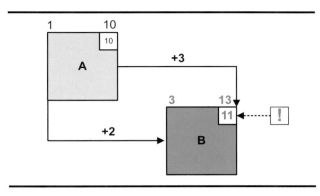

Figure 10-22 CPM Calculations - Effective Duration for Activity B

advantages. The resulting network would look like that shown in Figure 10-22.

Lags can and should be used instead of activities to diagram delays, down time, or to ensure proper interfaces between organizations. Possible uses of lags might include the following situations:

1. Concrete curing (3 days).

2. Issue RFP and receipt of bids.

3. Lead time for equipment delivery.

4. Time allowance for obtaining a permit.

5. Interface point between contractors (schedule contingency).

An example related to item 1 in the above list is the use of resilient mounts under a ship's engines. A 15-day "cure time" is used, which amounts to an aging process of the foundation with load on it. This must occur before final engine alignment is done.

An example of item 5 in the above list was a built in delay of 30 days used between the completion of one contractor and the start of the subsequent contractor on several projects. The idea behind this was to ensure that there were no claims for damages because of delays in the schedule. The overall General Contractor or owner representative managing the interfaces between contractors could then control that interface. If Contractor A had a schedule slip, there would still be an option to either expedite progress or allow the slip to stand if it did not exceed the 30-day window. A similar example of using lag to represent sched-

ule contingency was that on some of these same projects, a 90-day lag was built in between when material was defined as being needed on site and when it would actually be used. Unavailability of material is one of the leading causes of nonproductive time. Without some schedule allowance to overcome this problem, cost overruns because of lack of productivity will accompany the time delays associated with waiting for materials.

However, lags can easily be abused by applying them throughout the network to position activities in the desired place. Lags are not intended to be used to "fix" activities in certain time slots, just because the logic did not work out right the first time. Since the logic for doing the project will be a factor in all future analysis, it should be done carefully and correctly. On one recent project, the entire schedule was set by using start-to-start relationships with lags. In effect, there was no CPM. Instead, there was an initiating event and a barrage of start-to-start ties with lags used to fix each activity in its "appropriate" time frame. This is a bar chart in disguise.

Consideration should also be given to the impact of using lags when the schedule is used as a communication tool. When a lag is used, the reason for the lag should be specified: is the lag used to represent a resource constraint; a "curing time"; a planned delivery delay; or for some other reason? Any schedule that uses lags indiscriminately or without explanation can frustrate the reviewers, other users, other schedulers, or all of the intended users. Without explaining lags, users can become impatient and can dismiss the schedule entirely as being "unreadable".

Date constraints are useful for customer directed dates. Constraints applied to milestones should only be entered after the initial baseline is developed. It is important to develop the initial baseline without constraints to give an idea of how realistic the schedule actually is. The other consideration is that date constraints may cause reworking of the logic, as certain activities become negative solely because of their presence. All date constraints should be monitored and limited to absolute requirements. Date constraints are discussed in detail in Chapter 16.

Schedule Margin

Schedule margin (or schedule reserve) is the establishment and management of a margin of time in the schedule. The Government IMS Data Item Description DI-MGMT-81650 defines a schedule margin as being "the difference between the contractual milestone dates and the contractor's planned dates of accomplishment". When the baseline is created, it consists of a resource loaded and leveled schedule. At that stage, the float belongs to the project manager.

There are two methods for creating a schedule margin: using the buffer task method or the baseline finish variance method.

Buffer Activity Method

The ability to use this method depends on the capability of the scheduling tool. An understanding of the scheduling tool's features and limitations is essential.

In Figure 10-23, a 'buffer of time' has been set up prior to the required date of a contractual milestone. This buffer is defined by an unresourced activity and is problematic for government contractors' schedules. This and other issues surrounding this method are discussed below. The schedule margin is considered to be part of the baseline and so the same work and buffer activities exist both in the current and baseline schedules. This schedule represents the work required before a Preliminary Design Review (PDR). The second to the last activity is 'Get Ready for the

PDR'. The end of this activity is the date that the project manager has mandated as the end date for the work and is followed by a 10-day buffer activity.

The buffer has no assigned resources and is under the control of the project manager. It is managed to allow up to 10 days of schedule deterioration without impacting the contractual milestone and without the knowledge of the other activity owners.

As mentioned earlier, this method does present some issues. For government contractors' schedules, it should be noted that there is opposition to this method since it could interfere with the calculation of the critical path. Also, some customers do not allow unbudgeted activities in the schedule. Since the buffer activity must be statused, managing, for example, 200 buffer activities in a large schedule might become very burdensome. When statusing the schedule, the Schedule Performance Index (SPI), a measure of the ratio of the earned value to the planned value or budget (reference Chapter 32) might be negatively affected and affect fees and incentives if they are tied to the Schedule Performance Index.

Alternatively to a buffer activity, the margin can be set with a date-constrained milestone placed on the end of the Ready for PDR activity. The milestone is anchored with a Finish-Not-Later-Than directed date, or a Defense Contract Management Agency (DCMA) suggested 'Deadline date' that is available in some scheduling tools, and replaces the 10-day buffer activity. No sta-

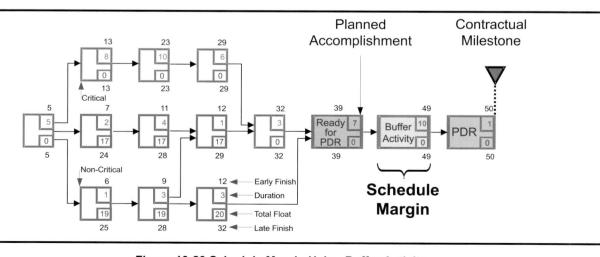

Figure 10-23 Schedule Margin Using Buffer Activity

tusing of the milestone is required except for an actual finish date or any modification of the milestone date to accommodate schedule slippage into the margin.

Baseline Finish Variance Method

In this method, the baseline schedule duration encompasses the entire 50 days of the work and the buffer, as shown in Figure 10-23. However, the current schedule forecast is only for the period of time where work is scheduled, 40 days. Thus the margin is defined by the difference between the baseline and current schedules, known as the Baseline Finish Variance, or just the Finish Variance.

Monitoring the Finish Variance gives an indication as to whether the schedule will complete on time. If the Finish Variance stays negative, the forecast will be that the schedule will complete early. If positive, the forecast is that the margin has been exhausted and that the schedule will be late.

This method has some benefits over the buffer activity method. There is no extra work inserting and managing buffers and normal operations yield management data, specifically the baseline finish variance and schedule variance. Note: for projects subject to a DCMA review, there should be no unbudgeted activities in the baseline.

One caveat: there is some software that reverses the Finish Variance calculation. Consequently, the schedule will indicate late when the variance is negative and early when it is positive. The user should be aware of the calculation nuances in the software.

Resource Application

Unlimited resources should be assumed in the first phase of schedule planning and preparation to allow the true picture of schedule position to emerge. Once resource constraints are applied, it may be necessary to reexamine the schedule logic and possibly even revise the scope and/or overall duration.

If resources are not loaded on schedule networks, a true schedule baseline cannot be established. Even after resources are loaded, the work is not done. While most scheduling software

packages will allow resource loading, using their automated resource leveling algorithms may produce a less than ideal result. Resource leveling is a very complex process. The leveling of one resource may impact other activities, and their resources, that would then have to be leveled. A far more desirable result will be obtained by manually leveling the schedule thus allowing a greater degree of control by the scheduler.

Until the schedule is resource leveled, and not just leveled at the bottom line total, a schedule should not be proposed as a baseline schedule because its 'achievability' has not been validated. The topic of schedule baselines will be examined in more detail in Chapter 12, "Setting a Traceable Schedule Baseline".

Schedule Approaches

This section contrasts the use of conservative schedules and aggressive schedules, as well as examining the organizational schedule approach versus the project schedule.

A conservative approach to schedule development will build in float or pad durations to allow for contingencies. The advantage of building a conservative schedule is the ability to handle slips without having to always develop alternative work around plans. Since assumptions used in the development of the schedule may not later match reality, it is likely that there will be variations from what was originally intended.

A major drawback to a conservative schedule is that a sense of urgency to complete the job may be lost because the schedule is not challenging. If unexpected contingencies arise later in the project, the float may have all been used because of the relaxed approach to fulfilling the planned dates.

Frequently there is no option to use a conservative schedule, because it is far too long to meet the target schedule objectives. Another difficulty is that conservative schedules include contingency by definition, which confuses the analysis of schedule risk. Chapter 17, "Schedule Risk Assessment," explains that risk assessment must be conducted on a CPM network with no built in contingency. A conservative schedule may therefore require an extra step in analysis to identify and remove the contingency.

An aggressive or success oriented schedule is a schedule that assumes perfect conditions, unrestricted resources, and sometimes even the ability to perform minor miracles. One of the major problems created by an aggressive schedule is that it can become unrealistic very early in the project and, as a result, often abandoned as a working plan. More often than not, this results in the development of unofficial internal operating schedules that do not support the official project schedule or coincide with the information reported to the owner/customer.

An overly aggressive schedule commonly results in disruption of the project. Before long, comments begin to surface such as, "So what if I'm six weeks behind schedule? Everyone else is nine weeks behind. I'm doing great." Another comment might be, "Of course we're behind schedule, but everyone knew from the start that we had no chance of supporting that schedule." Once there is no commitment to the plan, there is no plan. Forcing people to work according to a completely unrealistic plan invalidates all of the good efforts that go into a project management system.

When organizational schedules are employed, low level schedules are created within the functional organizations independent of each other, resulting in conflicting objectives and confused communication. One person's need date for information from another organization may not match when that organization is planning to provide it. This will make it very difficult to have visibility into total project status and impacts of delays.

Organizational schedules also have limitations when it comes to implementation. One schedule application within a transmission and distribution organization of an electric utility allowed for the scheduling of a hundred or more individual small projects within a calendar year. However, each organization maintained its own schedule based on its own needs, available resources, and priorities. Since the schedules were not integrated, it was not unusual for someone to arrive ready to install a transformer and find that there was no foundation to put it on. The foundation was

scheduled to be done later by another group. Similarly, a work crew would arrive to connect a transformer and find that no transformer was there to connect.

The use of organizational schedules with no overall integrated project schedule was also the bane of an aerospace hardware subcontractor. Each hardware support group had its schedule, all of which supported the required project completion date. Of course, each of these independent schedules had information needs from the other groups.

The problem was that in many cases the source of the information was planning on providing information to the succeeding group much later than the succeeding group was assuming its availability. The result was predictable when the schedule was finally integrated as part of a baseline effort. Suddenly the overall schedule was much longer than allowed, and the completion date was in jeopardy. It took several weeks of intense effort to revise the individual organizational schedules so that they supported each other and resulted in an acceptable completion date. Some projects never go through that agonizing step and continue to work with non-integrated schedules until disaster occurs.

A variation of the organizational schedule problem occurred at a higher level on another aerospace project. The scope of work was split between two organizations with a relative split of 75%/25%. The contractor with the 25% split recognized the schedule risk involved with the overall project and went through a perfect application of the principles enumerated in this text for producing an accurate baseline schedule. When this contractor was prepared to interface its effort with the other organization that had the 75% split, it was told that there would be no detailed schedule on that portion of the work. While the baseline was still a useful control tool for the 25% contractor, it did little to ensure a successful completion of the overall project.

The Program/Project Schedule approach creates a single total project schedule, with all project activities maintained in a single network. This practice facilitates proper identification of interfaces between all organizations and allows for total project analysis with relative ease. The drawback to the project wide network is that it can become too large and hard to manage if the activities are at the level needed for adequate visibility. If the network size were limited, the activities would be forced to a more summarized level and may not provide acceptable control of the project. A single, integrated project schedule tends to be so large that it involves more time for creating and maintaining the schedule.

The situations encountered relative to excessive schedule detail rival those associated with excessive Work Breakdown Structure detail. On one eight year engineering project, the activities in the CPM file included items on a single topic such as: "write memo", "approve memo", "issue memo". The durations were listed as two hour items or less. Of course, there are instances when activity durations of fractions of an hour are expected, such as in critical maintenance work.

This is especially true for outage or "turnaround" work. The cost in terms of lost revenue associated with extended down time more than justifies this extra care in planning and controlling the work. Such detail may also be used for very critical, highly visible work. During the 1960s when the Apollo space program was in full swing, daily activities were scheduled to the quarter hour. The person in charge of project controls on that program stated that no one was supposed to go home until all of the scheduled activities for that day were complete. When asked how that was possible, considering the inevitable job interruptions that always occur, he said that the work was indeed completed each day. Then there was the punch line: "Of course, it usually took 16 hours to accomplish all of the work we had scheduled for each 8 hour day."

How big is big when it comes to schedule networks? On eight to 10 year long projects, it is not unusual to see integrated schedules (including engineering, construction, and testing startup) of 20,000 to 40,000 individual activities. One of the largest schedule networks encountered, however, was for a new fighter aircraft where the CPM schedule consisted of over one million activities.

Schedule Visibility Versus Risk

The main function of a schedule is to provide a management tool that allows for proactive rather than reactive management. Therefore, the level of detail to which a schedule needs to be developed depends on the amount of risk involved with meeting the project goals. In other words, a greater level of detail will be required on a development project with many unknowns than on a manufacturing effort that has been successfully operating for years.

The final schedule, ready for approval, should already have defined and sequenced the discrete activities required to meet both long and short-term objectives. If activities are maintained at too high of a level, progress measurement becomes subjective and priorities become hard to establish. Suppose that different engineering drawings are needed to support the manufacture of widgets 1 and 2. The additional complexity of widget 2 requires that it go into production two weeks in advance of widget 1.

If the drawings are not maintained as individual activities, it is impossible to tell if the right drawings are being completed to support the schedule. Some companies control the size of the CPM while still tracking important information such as this by maintaining a separate scheduling document for each drawing sheet while limiting the CPM activities to the drawing series. The two are then related through a hammock arrangement.

Determining Detail

While the level of detail that must be built into a schedule depends on many project specific considerations, reporting requirements may override everything else. If there were a requirement for detailed reporting, this would force the schedule to a lower level. If the reverse were true and only summary reporting were required, then a level could be selected based on what is actually needed to control the project. The primary factors affecting level of detail include project size, project duration, and associated risk. A summary of qualitative selection criteria for level of schedule detail is shown in Figure 10-24.

Project Size	Project Duration	Project Risk	Activity Level of Detail
Small	Short	Low	High detail
Small	Short	High	Low detail
Small	Long	Low	Moderate detail
Small	Long	High	Low detail
Large	Short	Low	Moderate detail
Large	Short	High	Low detail
Large	Long	Low	Low detail
Large	Long	High	Low detail

Figure 10-24 Qualitative Selection Criteria for Schedule Detail

The high, moderate and low levels of detail refer to whether the project is composed of many short duration activities (high detail), fewer longer duration activities (low detail), or somewhere in-between (moderate detail). While it is apparent that most of the entries in the previous table correspond to "low" level of detail, meaning large networks, it should be recognized that there are fewer projects, on a percentage basis, that fall in these categories. Said another way, there are many more short, small projects than there are giant, long-term projects. In reality, many projects will not require the behemoth schedules of the career projects.

Creating and Maintaining Quality Schedules

As with any other aspect of a Project Management System, it is not only important to establish rules for schedule management, but it is equally important to follow up the schedule construction activity with verification of compliance with those rules. Those rules should reflect both general scheduling practices and contractual requirements.

A complete schedule review is not just a one-time event. A schedule is a dynamic database from creation to completion. Schedule audits should be performed not only at critical junctures of the schedule process but on a regular basis so that the consumers of the schedule information receive reassurance in the quality of the information.

Schedule audits focus on four primary areas:

- Schedule Health Checks consist of metrics designed to indicate potential problems in the schedule. Out of tolerance indications can help an auditor focus on areas of concern even on very large projects where the auditor has limited knowledge of the project details. Health checks should be performed on a regular basis and are described below.

- Whether dealing with high-risk development projects or a project effort that has been performed numerous times, there are basic scheduling practices that apply to all schedules. The auditor should review the practices of all participants in the schedule and make sure the practices are aligned with industry and professional standards.

- The schedule must be aligned with corporate standards (if any) and with the customer expectations and contractual requirements.

- Finally, the EVM System must be aligned with the schedule through the Budgeted Cost for Work Scheduled (BCWS) and the Estimate to Complete (ETC). There is no requirement for electronic linkages, but the dates and codes of the work packages, control accounts, milestones, WBS, OBS, and IMS summary bars should be the same in both systems.

As with any of the schedule metrics, the data can be broken down by organization, work team lead or CAM, WBS, subcontractor, or other elements to help pinpoint problems and focus management attention.

Some software packages treat some of the date constraints differently than other packages. On a large-scale project with multiple team partners each using their own internal scheduling system, special attention must be paid to ensuring that any constraint used in one system will translate and function exactly the same way when the data is transferred to the total project IMS. Failure to do so may inject differences between the local schedule and the IMS, requiring time and effort to fault isolate and correct.

In an era of larger and broader-reaching enterprise database schedules, it has become even more important that common rules are established and followed by all participating subcontractors, agencies and personnel. The first step is to perform a needs assessment and make sure everyone agrees with the outcome. The second step is to architect a solution to fulfill those needs. Part of that process is the identification and location of common code structures, agreement on the handling of Level of Effort in the schedule, and agreement on what features of the scheduling packages will and will not be used, among other things.

If the schedule were designed to be integrated with the EVM system, the above items would represent some of the basic areas that should be checked. The schedule should be the basis for the EVMS data. If mistakes exist in the schedule, they are magnified in the EVMS and will produce undesirable results.

The fourteen points discussed below have target thresholds developed by the Defense Contract Management Agency (DCMA) and are used by them to evaluate government contractor schedules. They could be considered to be a mechanism to help ensure that schedule best practices are attained. Schedules are tested using filtering tools of the scheduling software, home-grown analytical software, or other commercially available software. There are some metrics, however, that will have to be tested using customized filters or other 'back-door' techniques since the data being verified is unique to that project.

Fourteen Point Schedule Health Check

1. Missing Logic

A method to test the 'completeness' of the schedule is to measure the ratio of activities to relationships. It only stands to reason that if there is one starting point and one finish point in a schedule, every activity, except the first and the last activity, should have at least one predecessor and one successor. Therefore, for discrete activities, the ratio should be at least 1:1. Smaller ratios of relationships to activities may indicate a less flexible schedule rigged with date constraints and/or a great deal of positive float because of multiple ends without successors.

This metric helps to see how well the activities in the schedule are linked together. A schedule with more than 5% of its activities missing predecessors or successors may indicate problems with its logic. The links should be examined to make sure that they make sense. Hanging activities, or those without a successor, can cause serious miscalculations of float throughout the schedule. Many organizations find it useful to run filters in their schedule software that isolate those activities without successors (and those without predecessors) to be able to correct the logic prior to submitting the schedule for review. Figure 10-25 shows activities with missing logic. The percentage of activities that have missing logic is calculated by this formula:

((# of Activities Missing Logic) / (# of Incomplete Activities)) x 100 = %

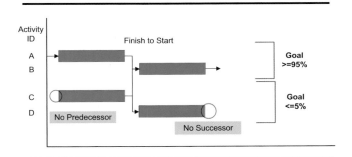

Figure 10-25 Missing Logic - Goal: 5% or Less

2. Activities with Leads

Of special interest is the use of leads (negative lags). Generally speaking, negative lags indicate that the schedule is either not detailed enough or the scheduler is attempting to "fix" activity dates. Large numbers of activities using lags, or activities with large positive or negative lags, should draw attention to the integrity of the schedule.

Having leads (negative lags) in a schedule makes it harder to analyze the critical path, distorts the total float in a schedule, and may cause resource conflicts. For these reasons, using leads in a schedule, as shown in Figure 10-26, with activity B overlapping activity A with a Finish to Start relationship and a negative lag, is not encouraged and the goal is 0%. The scheduler could use a Start to Start relationship with a positive lag to simulate this requirement.

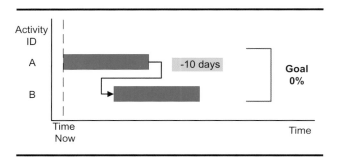

Figure 10-26 Leads - Goal: 0%

3. Activities with Lags

With relationships between activities comes the ability to offset those activities using lags. While lags have their legitimate uses, excessive lags can complicate a schedule to a point of not being maintainable and render it ineffective in forecasting future dates.

Having lags in a schedule, as demonstrated in Figure 10-27, with activity B following activity A after a 10 day delay, makes it harder to analyze the critical path and can be used to manipulate float or constrain the schedule. The goal is 5% or less.

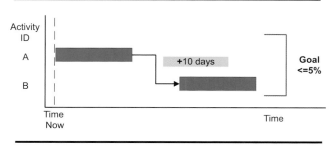

Figure 10-27 Lags - Goal: 5% or Less

4. Relationship Types

In order to examine the quality of integration of the schedule activities, relationship metrics are developed to look for common problems. For example, most new projects should start out with a vast majority of relationships using the Finish to Start technique. The use of Start to Start and Finish to Finish is usually minimal on new projects, but more common in more mature projects as serial activities are replanned in parallel to shorten the schedule. The use of Start to Finish is prohibited by many companies and should only be used sparingly and with specific justification.

As shown in Figure 10-28, the Finish-to-Start relationship should account for at least 90% of the links between activities. Finish-to-Finish and Start-to-Start relationships should be used sparingly (goal: < 10% combined). Start-to-Finish relationship types should only be used with good justification (goal: 0%).

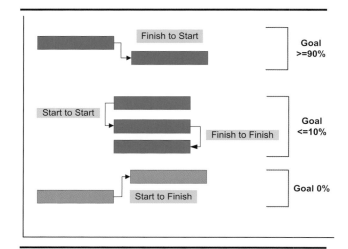

Figure 10-28 Relationship Goals

5. Hard Constraints

One of the most common abuses of a schedule is the overuse of date constraints. While the constraints are necessary to reflect milestone deadlines, material and subcontractor availability dates and other functions, overuse of them will 'harden' the schedule and limit its ability to forecast the future.

In addition to identifying quantities of activities with date constraints, it is also important to identify the types of date constraints. Most constraints should be either Start Not Earlier Than, representing the earliest availability of the activity or the resources assigned to the task, or Finish Not Later Than, representing due dates for the task. Where available, a Deadline date should be substituted for Finish Not Later Than date since many Government review agencies, including the DCMA, have classified the latter as a hard constraint, meaning that it impacts the calculation of the critical path. Other constraints should be used sparingly and with documentation in the activity notes field commenting on why the constraint was assigned.

The use of Hard Constraints, prevents the schedule from being driven by links and should only be used with good justification. The number of activities with hard constraints should not exceed 5%. However, many companies allow none. Figure 10-29 shows two activities that are constrained by dates that are immovable. This reduces the flexibility of the preceding and succeeding activities and may cause unintended variations in total float and the critical path.

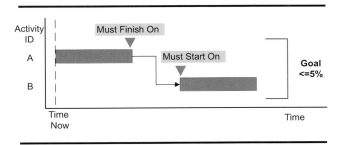

Figure 10-29 Hard Constraints - Goal: 5% or Less

6. High Float

Float cannot only show the critical path, but indicate the health of the schedule infrastructure. Excessive amounts of positive float may indicate incomplete schedule logic or an unstable network. On the other hand, large negative float values may be the result of the scheduler simply entering the wrong year into the date constraint instead of the year required to support the schedule.

According to the DCMA, if more than 5% of activities have float higher than 44 working days the network might not have the proper logic. The float value of 44 should be considered in the con-

text of the project and many times a higher value can be justified. Figure 10-30 shows two activities that have total float exceeding the maximum of 44 work days. The percentage of activities that have high float is calculated by this formula:

((# of Activities w/ High Float) / (# of Incomplete Activities)) x 100 = %

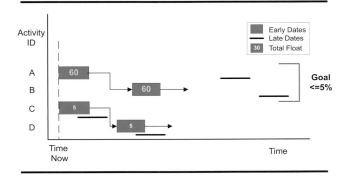

Figure 10-30 High Total Float of 44 Working Days or More - Goal: 5% or less

7. Negative Float

No more than 5% of activities should have negative float (less than 0 working days). If the goal were exceeded, there should be a corrective action plan to mitigate the negative float. Some organizations do not tolerate negative float at all and demand that it be eliminated by replanning any paths where it appears. In Figure 10-31, activities A and B have negative total float and activities C and D have positive total float. The percentage of activities that have negative float is calculated by this formula:

((# of Activities w/ Negative Float) / (# of Incomplete Activities)) x 100 = %

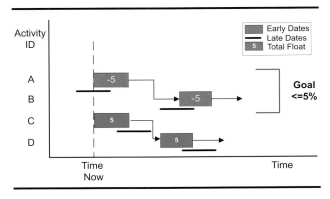

Figure 10-31 Negative Float - Goal: 5% or Less

8. High Duration

Activity durations are another area of focus during the schedule analysis. In some software packages, an activity with duration may be displayed as a milestone. Other software requires the scheduler to identify the milestone as either a start or a finish milestone. Incorrect identification of the milestone type can affect date calculations.

One method of evaluating project management interest in the schedule is by the perceived accuracy of the durations. For example, if a significant number of the activity durations are at or near the maximum corporate mandated duration, it may be assumed that there was not as much thought put into the durations by the estimators (guesses); that the estimators have padded some internal float into the duration, or conversely, they think the duration for the activities should be longer, but are limited by the rule.

According to the DCMA, if more than 5% of activities have a duration of greater than 44 working days, the project may be difficult to manage. The activities should be broken up into two or more discrete activities. Figure 10-32 shows two activities that exceed the 44 work day limit. The percentage of activities that have high duration is calculated by this formula:

((# of Activities w/ High Duration) / (# of Incomplete Activities)) x 100 = %

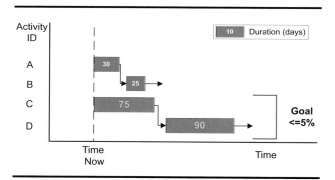

Figure 10-32 Durations Greater than 44 Working Days - Goal: 5% or less

9. Invalid Dates

Activities that have not started should not have projected start or finish dates before the status date. If they do, those dates are wrong. For the same reason, there should not be any actual start dates after the status date. The goal for both metrics is 0%. Figure 10-33 demonstrates activities with invalid dates; activity A shows completed dates in the future while activity B shows forecast dates in the past.

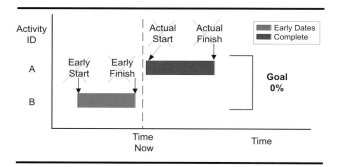

Figure 10-33 Invalid Dates - Goal: 0%

10. No Assigned Resources

Projects that have an EV requirement will generally need the schedule activities to be resource loaded. The unit of measure for labor is generally hours. Material resources use an appropriate unit of measure such as cubic yards for concrete, dollars for purchased parts, etc. The estimates are then transferred to the cost system and rates applied to create budgets. If a schedule were not resource loaded, then budgets must be directly loaded into the cost system. Changes in the schedule would not be directly reflected in cost and there would be an attendant increase in maintenance to keep the systems synchronized.

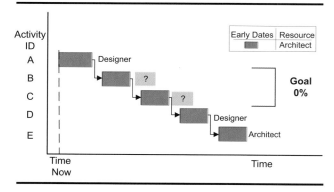

Figure 10-34 Missing Resources on Activities with Durations of 1 Day or More - Goal: 0%

Activities that have at least one day of duration should have baseline work and/or cost assigned. Otherwise, cost projections for the project will not be valid.   Figure 10-34 displays a schedule in which resources have not been assigned to two activities that are on the critical path. The goal for missing resources is 0%.

11. Missed Activities

This metric tests for the number of activities that have missed their baseline finish dates and therefore are not meeting the baseline plan. If the activity baseline finish date were less than or equal to the status date and the activity actual finish date or projected finish date were greater than the baseline finish date, the activity would be deemed to be late. If more than 5% of activities were missed, the schedule is not adequately meeting the baseline plan.

Figure 10-35 shows two missed activities. Activity A has an actual finish date later than the baseline date and activity B is projecting that the early finish date will be greater than the baseline finish date.

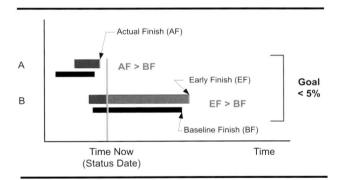

Figure 10-35 Missed Activities - Goal: < 5%

12. Critical Path Test

This test must be run manually. The purpose of the test is to check the integrity of the critical path by making sure a delay introduced into the path has the appropriate impact on the end date. After determining the early finish of the project, an activity on the project critical path is temporarily modified with a large duration such as 600 days. After reanalyzing the network, the end date of the project should move in concert with the induced delay.

If activity E slipped by 600 days, the critical path is sound and this test passes. If activity E did not slip by 600 days, it is likely that there are one or more problems affecting the integrity of the critical path.   The final activity on the critical path should slip one-for-one.

Figure 10-36 demonstrates the before and after successful test of the critical path with activity B being extended to 600 days.

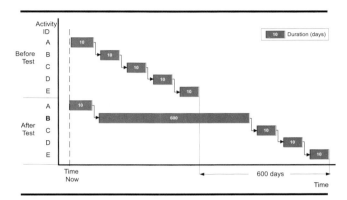

Figure 10-36 Critical Path Test, Before and After

13. Critical Path Length Index (CPLI)

The CPLI is an indicator on the likelihood of completing the schedule on time. The target is to have a CPLI of 1.00 with a threshold of 0.95. The CPLI is a measure of the relative efficiency required to complete the schedule on time.

A CPLI of 1.00 means the project must accomplish one day's worth of work for every day that passes. A CPLI less than 1.00 means the project schedule is inefficient with regard to the schedule completion (i.e., slipping from the baseline date). Likewise, a CPLI greater than 1.00 means that the project schedule is running efficiently in relationship to the schedule end (i.e., finishing before the baseline date). The CPLI will usually be calculated to contract completion, but may be calculated for an interim milestone.

Figure 10-37 shows a schedule with a CPLI on or above the threshold of .95 in January, February, and June.

The CPLI is calculated by this formula:

(Critical Path Length + Total Float) / Critical Path Length

14. Baseline Execution Index (BEI)

The Baseline Execution Index measures the activities that were completed as a percentage of

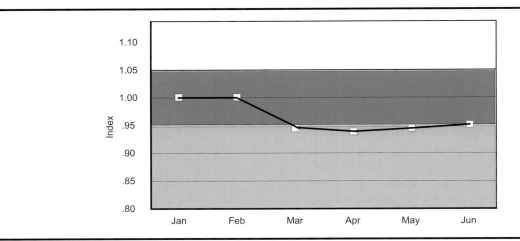

Figure 10-37 CPLI Graphic Highlighting the .95 Threshold

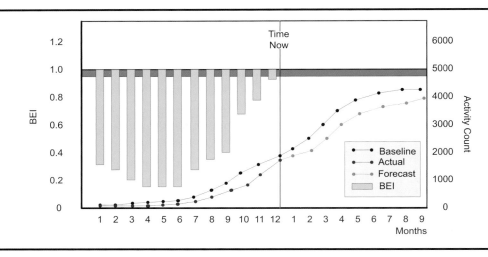

Figure 10-38 Baseline Execution Index

the activities that should have been completed per the original (baseline) plan. The goal is to have a BEI of 0.95 or greater. Figure 10-38 displays the incremental Baseline Execution Index and the cumulative baseline, actual, and forecast activity count.

In the past, many of these tests were performed on a less frequent basis because of the unavailability of analysis tools or the lack of will to maintain a quality schedule. With the emphasis more and more on quality, many companies are including schedule analysis in their reporting rhythms.

Fourteen Point Schedule Health Check – Correlation with GASP

The Generally Accepted Scheduling Principles were outlined in Chapter 6. Figure 10-39 displays the correlation between the eight GASP principles and the 14 point assessment (or health) checks.

GASP		14 Point Assessment
Valid	Complete	8. High Duration - activities with Duration > 44 working days (goal <5%)
	Traceable	1. Logic - activities without predecessors and/or successors (goal <5%) 4. Relationship Types - Finish to Start (FS) should be the most common (goal >90%)
	Transparent	2. Leads - (negative lag) distorts the critical path (goal 0%) 3. Lags - (positive lag) excessive size and/or usage distorts the critical path (goal <5%)
	Statused	9. Invalid Dates - Activities with invalid forecast (incomplete activities to the left of time now) or actual start/finish dates (completed activities in the future) (goal 0%) 11. Missed Activities - Activities not complete or forecasted to complete as planned (goal <5%) 14. Baseline Execution Index (BEI) - Activities completed as a ratio to those activities that should have been completed to date according to the baseline plan (goal >.95)
	Predictive	6. High Float - Activities with Total Float > 44 work days (goal <5%) 7. Negative Float - Activities with Total Float <0 work days (goal 0%) 12. Critical Path test - Tests the logic in the critical path (goal 'pass') 13. Critical Path Length Index (CPLI) - Measures the 'realism' of the critical path (goal >.95%)
Effective	Usable	5. Hard Constraints - Activities not designated as As Soon As Possible (ASAP), Start Not Earlier Than (SNET), or Finish Not Earlier Than (FNET) (goal <5%)
	Resourced	10. Resources - If loaded, activities without dollars or hours assigned (goal 0%)
	Controlled	--

Figure 10-39 Health Check/GASP Correlation

Conclusion

Many factors affect the development of a useful project schedule. Different scheduling approaches may have to be integrated to achieve the desired result. Scheduling may be initiated in a top-down format, but it will need to be verified in a bottom-up confirmation of the dates. The philosophies of conservative versus aggressive scheduling can be a driving factor in the ability to create an achievable plan.

Aggressive scheduling may invalidate the plan before the project even begins, but incorporation of contingency into the schedule may result in a longer total duration than justified. What is needed is a realistic, challenging and achievable plan, neither a purely conservative nor aggressive approach.

The use of independent organizational schedules will make analysis difficult or even impossible, but the use of a single project schedule often makes the network almost too large to manage. The use of hammocks, outlines, grouping and templates can provide the solution to this dilemma. How much detail is enough and when is it too much? Consideration of reporting needs, risk, duration, and cost (size) all contribute to the answer to this question.

One simple answer is this: If it takes all of the staff's time to maintain and update the schedule with no time remaining for analysis and action, then the network is too large for that application, or the staff is too small.

On large schedules, it is possible that hundreds of activities are modified with progress information or other network changes specified by the activity owners.

To complicate the situation further, there may be multiple schedulers modifying the same schedule. To maintain a quality schedule, schedulers perform these analyses after each update to increase the probability of correcting improperly entered data.

Chapter 10 Review Questions

10-1.   Describe the "Top-Down" approach to schedule development.

10-2.   How does the "Bottom-Up" approach serve to validate the Top-Down schedule?

10-3.   Explain the differences between a hammock, a summary activity and a template.

10-4.   How does a lag affect the network calculation?

10-5.   What does a negative lag between activities mean?

10-6.   What scheduling considerations are important when assessing the value of a project schedule versus the use of organizational schedules?

10-7.   Describe the advantages and disadvantages of using a conservative approach to developing the baseline schedule.

10-8.   What is the major concern with use of an aggressive scheduling philosophy in baseline establishment?

10-9.   What is the definition of an IMP?

10-10. How is it possible to recognize qualitatively that a schedule is too detailed (i.e. has too many activities)?

10-11. List the factors that must be considered when planning how detailed a schedule should be.

10-12. What is one technique often used to limit the total number of activities maintained in a given project schedule file?

10-13. What is the best way to ensure that schedule quality is maintained over the life of a project?

10-14. In the 14 point health check, what do leads, start to finish relationships and activities that start or finish in the future have in common?

True or False

10-15. Schedules that are developed using the "Top-Down" approach typically are too long in total duration.

10-16. A "hammock" is a standardized network module used to describe a specific activity or series of activities.

10-17. Templates are used repeatedly within a large network file.

10-18. Unlimited resources should be assumed in the first phase of resource loading.

10-19. Resource loading a schedule assures efficient planning of staffing levels.

10-20. Including contingency in schedule durations provides a further complication when schedule risk assessment is performed.

10-21. The level of detail to which a schedule should be developed depends on the amount of risk involved.

10-22. Development of a schedule baseline requires a decision to either employ "top-down" scheduling or "bottom-up" scheduling.

10-23. Using a single, integrated project schedule helps keep the network small.

10-24. When a schedule is being created, it is recommended that 90% or more of the activity relationships be start to finish.

10-25. Leads and lags should be limited to no more than 5% of the total number of activities in a schedule.

10-26. No more than 5% of activities should have a duration of greater than 44 days.

The answers to these questions can be found in Section 6, Solutions.

10.1 BUILD A NETWORK SCHEDULE

The Robotic Arm project has been presented to you. In conjunction with the team, you are to build a schedule. The initial meeting with them was rushed and informal and you walked away with a narrative and promised to deliver them an initial discussion schedule the next day.

Here are your notes:

[X] = Activity Identifier.

All relationships are FS unless otherwise noted.

- A 5 day **project kick-off** activity to enable project organization [A].

- A **design study** that will take 20 days [B].

- A **review** of the study over a 5-day period [C].

- 40 days of **detail design** [D] followed by a 5-day **design review and drawing release** [E].

- Material for the mechanical arm is in inventory. The **mechanical arm** can then be **built and assembled** (30 days) [F] and **tested** (10 days) [G] during which the following will occur:

  - **Computer Hardware** must be **procured** from a vendor. It is anticipated that this will take 30 days [H].

  - Once the computer hardware is delivered, it must be **modified**, a 20 day job [J]. The modifications must be **tested** for 10 days [K].

  - Also, 5 days after the hardware is delivered, the **control software** can be **created and tested** [L] – a 40 day effort. **Custom application software creation and testing** [M] starts 5 days after the control software starts and is 40 days long.

- Finally, when the hardware is tested, the software is tested and the arm is tested, a 30 day **system integrated test** [N] will take place followed by a 10 day **acceptance test** [O] and **delivery to the customer** [P].

The solution to this case study can be found on the Humphreys & Associates, Inc. web site.
www.humphreys-assoc.com

There are two templates in the library that can be used in this schedule.

Control software template [CS]

Activity ID	Description	Duration	Predecessor	Successor
C1	Internet interface control	10 days		C2
C2	UPS control	8 days	C1	C3
C3	Fail safe control	12 days	C2	C4
C4	Integrated test	10 days	C3	

Custom software template [CK]

Activity ID	Description	Duration	Predecessor	Successor
K1	Vertical module	15 days		K3
K2	Horizontal module	18 days	K1 SS	K3
K3	Overload control	12 days	K1, K2	K4
K4	Integrated test	10 days	K3	

This is a high priority contract and therefore work will be scheduled 7 days a week. There are sufficient resources with the right skill sets to allow this. Resource effort is estimated at 8 hours/day.

Resources:

   [RR] = Resource Identifier.

The PM has given the following resource assignments to the scheduler:

 •   Software Engineers [SE] have been assigned to these activities:
     K1, K2, K3, C1, C2, C3, A, B, C, O (50%).

 •   Computer Hardware Engineers [HE] have been assigned to these activities:
      A, B, C, J, O (50%).

 •   Mechanical Engineers [ME] have been assigned to these activities:
     A, B, C, F, O (50%).

 •   Testers [T] have been assigned to these activities:
     C4, K4, K, N, O.

 •   Designers [D] have been assigned to these activities:
     A, B, C, D, E.

The project will start on day 1.

The project must be completed by day 180 at the latest.

Templates CS and CK are standard networks held in the scheduling library.

 •   Substitute Template CS for activity L.

 •   Substitute Template CK for activity M.

Attach a build and test hammock [X] to measure the duration from the start of the mechanical build until just before the start of the System Integrated Test.

You will use the following notation to complete the schedule diagram:

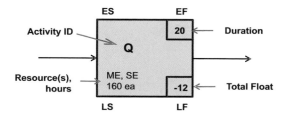

You will supply your team with a schedule showing the critical path.

But there are a few questions that will arise during your presentation; see if you can prepare for them.

1. What is the Total Float of the critical path?
2. How many hours per resource?
3. What is the ES and EF of the Hammock?
4. Would any of the 14 point quality health check thresholds be exceeded? If so, which ones and what are their values?

Chapter **11**

CRASHING THE NETWORK

Objectives of this Chapter:

1. Define "network crashing".

2. Describe the procedure used for network crashing.

3. Explain the process of crashing a sample network, developing cost/time tradeoff data and an objective duration for the network activities.

4. Define other schedule acceleration techniques.

Occasionally it happens that after all of the care that goes into the development of the project schedule, it still takes more time than can be allowed. Another possibility is that the completion date is advanced for any number of reasons. When any of these conditions occur, it is time for a revised plan, which accelerates the schedule. This chapter assumes that the schedule is still too long even after all of the usual ways of shortening it have been implemented. Therefore, cost/time tradeoffs are investigated to see how they can be quantified and used to best advantage.

In the first draft of the project schedule, it is fairly common to find that the required duration is longer than the time actually available. Even if the initial schedule does satisfy the required completion date, management direction may result in the need for a shorter schedule. In either of these cases, the next step is to find a way to shorten the schedule. This process is called "crashing" the network. This also refers to the discussion in Chapter 9 on resource loading schedules, where the statement was made that it may eventually be necessary to decide if a project is time critical or resource critical. This chapter covers the time critical case, where the cost is of secondary importance when compared to finishing the schedule within a given time frame.

The real issue is cost/time tradeoffs because almost every time the schedule changes, the cost changes. To shorten the duration normally required for individual activities, additional cost is usually incurred. This cost increase may be a result of overtime pay at premium rates, additional costs paid to expedite vendors when shops are full and orders are backlogged, using more expensive labor, or it may be a result of reduced productivity because of the need to work excessive hours. Whatever the cause, an intelligent decision cannot be made about schedule acceleration until the cost for shortening the schedule is known. Cost impact is determined by developing the cost slope, as shown in Figure 11-3. The known points on this graph at the start of the exercise are the normal time and normal cost. These data are already included in the network details. Notice that this process assumes that a CPM network is in place. The procedure presented in this chapter is only possible if a critical path has been identified.

The intention is to shorten the schedule and the critical path identifies the total project duration. Therefore, only the critical activities need to be scrutinized for compression. Compressing activities that are not on the critical path is a waste of effort and resources.

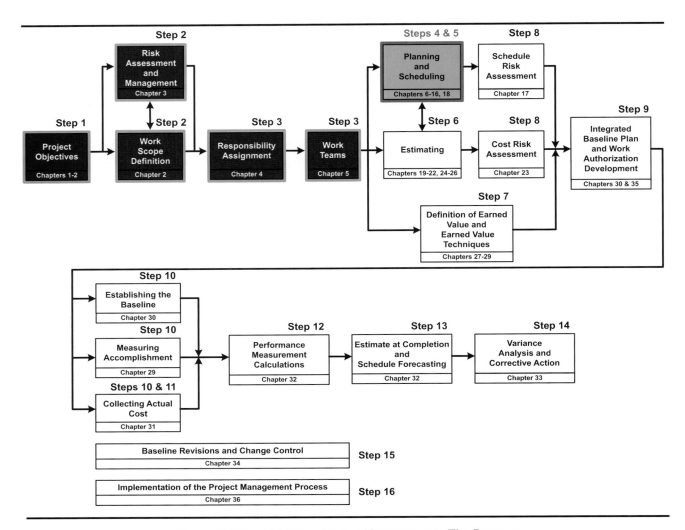

Figure 11-1 Earned Value Project Management: The Process

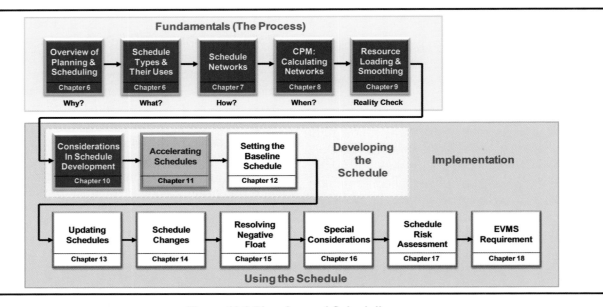

Figure 11-2 Planning and Scheduling

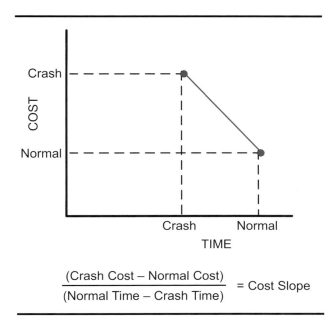

$$\frac{(\text{Crash Cost} - \text{Normal Cost})}{(\text{Normal Time} - \text{Crash Time})} = \text{Cost Slope}$$

Figure 11-3 Activity "Crashing" Concept

The "Crashing" Procedure

This procedure is a straightforward seven-step process as identified below.

1. Compute the network critical path.

2. Establish the objective total duration.

3. Identify the crash time/cost for each activity selected for compression.

4. Prioritize critical path activities, with lowest cost duration reductions first.

5. Invoke the lowest cost alternative by shortening that activity and comparing the revised project duration with the objective duration.

6. Recheck the critical path(s).

7. Continue steps 5 and 6 until the objective is reached or a critical path becomes "fully crashed."

Step 1 is necessary because the critical path will be shortened. The objective total duration referred to in step 2 is the goal. The next data points that must be gathered are the shortest time periods in which each activity can possibly be completed, and how much it will cost to achieve those compressed durations. This infor-

mation should be collected from the same individuals who provided the original activity logic and durations: the people responsible for performing the work. This information will be needed for every activity since the critical path will change as the schedule is compressed. Step 5 could be eliminated, but only at the expense of unnecessary cost. One approach would be to shorten all activities to their "crash" time, which would also mean that the cost for all activities would be increased.

Shortening activities not on the critical path is wasted expense, since only the critical path activities need to be shortened to accomplish a reduction of the total project duration. Therefore, the value in step 5 is that only those activities that really need to incorporate the premium cost will be selected for acceleration.

Another result of compression could be a change in the critical path or multiple critical paths. While multiple critical paths would be unexpected in the initial network, the crashing procedure could increase the number of critical paths. As the acceleration process progresses, there may be two or more options to pursue. With the cost slopes determined for all activities, it is possible to consistently choose the lowest cost alternative. This alternative will become apparent as a detailed example is presented.

Steps 5 and 6 are pursued until the objective is reached or a critical path becomes "fully crashed" (step 7). Shortening the critical path cannot go on indefinitely. Eventually, all activities on at least one critical path will be at their lowest possible duration, regardless of cost. At this point, the network can be classified as "fully crashed." While expenditures can continue in order to accelerate other activities, the project duration cannot be shortened any further.

An Example of Network Crashing

Figure 11-4 illustrates a simple logic network that will be used to demonstrate the crashing process. Activities A-B and A-C are start-to-start and activities F-G are in a finish-to-finish relationship.

There are four separate paths through the logic with varying durations. The durations are repre-

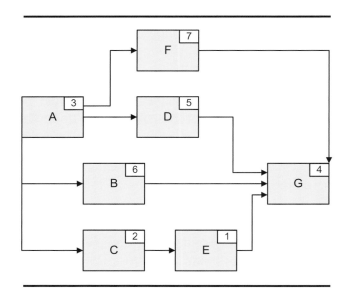

Figure 11-4 "Crashing" a Network - An Example

sented by the numerical values in the blocks in the upper right hand corner of each activity. Even a glance reveals that there will be float available on a number of the activities.

Figure 11-5 shows the first two steps for this example. Step 1: The critical path is calculated (A-D-G) and is found to be 12 weeks long. Step 2: The highly challenging objective is to cut the

total duration in half and complete the project in six weeks. After a backward pass is calculated using CPM analysis, the critical path would have negative 6 weeks of float.

Step 3 in the process is to collect all of the information that is contained in Figure 11-6. By interviewing those responsible for the network activities, the costs associated with schedule acceleration can be listed in a table such as the one shown. In this example, the cost of completing the project at the "normal" rate of 12 weeks is $92,000. To fully crash all activities, the same project would cost $139,000, which amounts to more than a 50% increase in total cost. However, as previously mentioned, it will not be beneficial to reduce all activity durations.

Figure 11-7 presents the cost slope for Activity A, which is $5,000 per week. That is the cost penalty associated with compressing that activity. Since a two week duration is the crash time for "A", spending anything greater than $15,000 will not reduce it below two weeks.

In the sample network, activity path A-D-G is 12 weeks long. Activity path A-F is 10 weeks long, as is path B-G. The remaining path, C-E-G, is

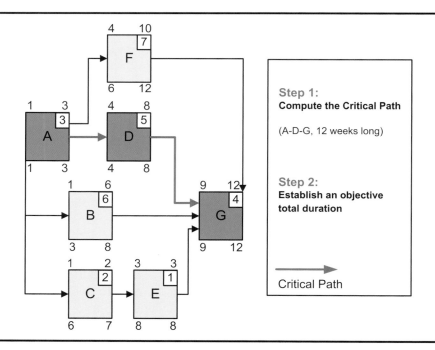

Figure 11-5 Step 1 and Step 2: "6 Weeks"

Activity	Normal		Crash		Cost Slope ($000/week)
	Duration	Cost ($000)	Duration	Cost ($000)	
A	3	10	2	15	5
B	6	22	4	34	6
C	2	8	1	10	2
D	5	14	3	22	4
E	1	9	1	9	-
F	7	17	5	23	3
G	4	12	2	26	7
		92		139	
		$92,000 Normal Cost		$139,000 All Crash Cost	

Figure 11-6 Step 3 - Identify Crash Time and Crash Costs for Each Activity

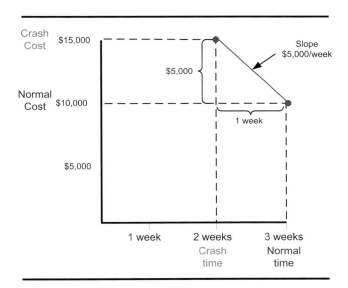

Figure 11-7 Cost of Crashing Activity "A"

seven weeks in duration. The next step (step 4) is to shorten either Activity A, D, or G.

The costs associated with these reductions are displayed in Figure 11-8.

With the information structured properly, it is easy to see that the preferred alternative is to shorten Activity D by one week. One reason for presenting this case in a systematic manner is so that total costs associated with each project duration

will then be available. If it were not possible to reach the six week objective, management may opt for an eight or nine week duration. Or if the six weeks is possible, but costs twice as much as a seven week project, management might decide that the seven week duration is more practical. Since Activity D has been reduced by one week, the critical path has been shortened to 11 weeks and the cost has been increased by $4,000 to a revised total of $96,000. The critical path remains the same, as shown in Figure 11-9.

Since Activity D is still the cheapest alternative to shorten the critical path A-D-G, and it can be shortened by another week before reaching its minimum possible duration, it is shortened by another week. This will increase the total cost by another $4,000 while shortening the path by another week. This is shown in Figure 11-10.

After completing this first sequence of actions, the critical path must again be checked. The situation has now become more complex because there are now three critical paths: A-D-G as before, A-F-G, and path A-B-G. Each of these paths has a duration of 10 weeks. Now it is not just a matter of reducing a single activity; multiple activities must be addressed simultaneously. There are three alternatives, as shown in Figure 11-11.

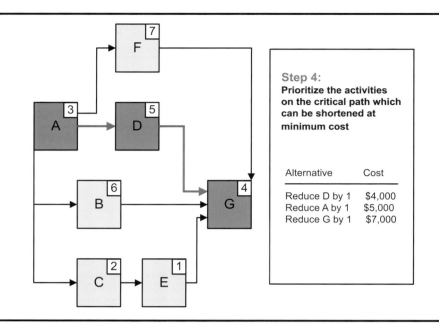

Figure 11-8 Step 4

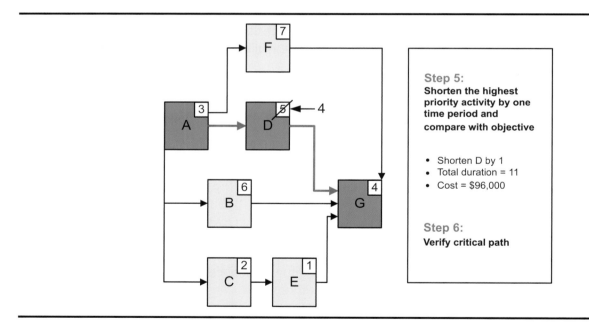

Figure 11-9 Step 5 and Step 6

Once again, the least expensive alternative is selected. The results of this action are shown in Figure 11-12.

In Figure 11-13, all three critical paths have now been shortened to 8 weeks, but the cost has grown to $118,000. Another factor is that Activities A, E, and G cannot be shortened further, thus reducing the number of options to shorten the project.

The only remaining step is to implement the most expensive alternative, summarized in Figure 11-14. This allows the total project to now be compressed to 7 weeks, with a cost of $131,000. Now Activities A, D, E, F, and G have reached their fully crashed durations.

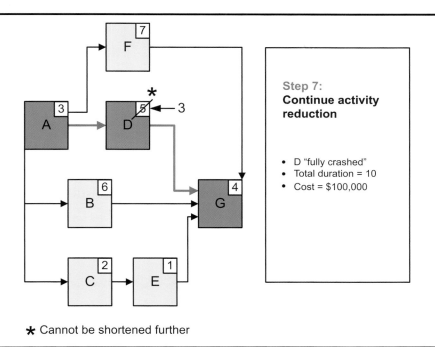

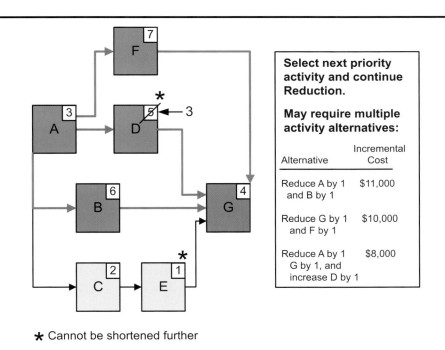

* Cannot be shortened further

Figure 11-10 Step 7

* Cannot be shortened further

Figure 11-11 Alternatives

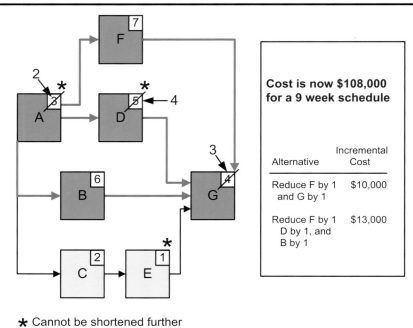

Figure 11-12 9 Weeks Cost

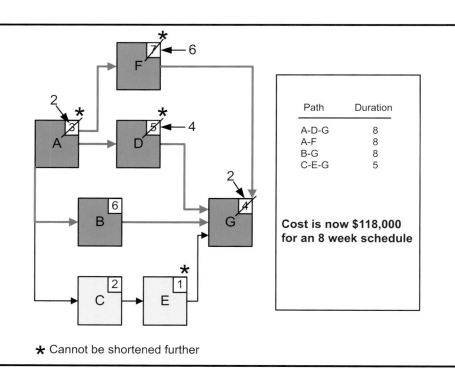

Figure 11-13 8 Weeks Cost

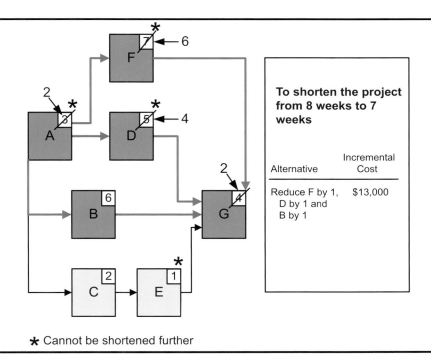

To shorten the project from 8 weeks to 7 weeks

Alternative	Incremental Cost
Reduce F by 1, D by 1 and B by 1	$13,000

* Cannot be shortened further

Figure 11-14 7 Weeks Schedule

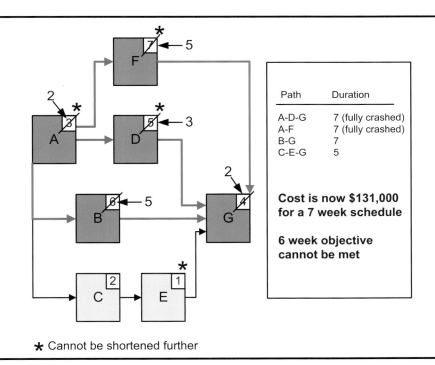

Path	Duration
A-D-G	7 (fully crashed)
A-F	7 (fully crashed)
B-G	7
C-E-G	5

Cost is now $131,000 for a 7 week schedule

6 week objective cannot be met

* Cannot be shortened further

Figure 11-15 7 Weeks Cost

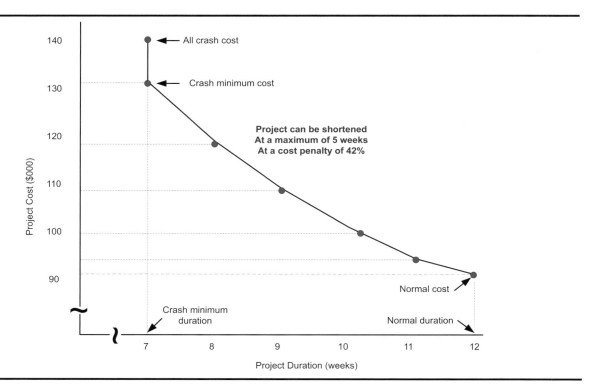

Figure 11-16 Project Cost vs. Time Relationship - The Tradeoff Curve

That also means that activity paths A-D-G and A-F-G have reached their fully crashed condition (see Figure 11-15). Thus, it is impossible to shorten the total project below the current 7 weeks.

The conclusion is that the 6 week objective cannot be met. The analysis of the crashing process in which the schedule was compressed to 7 weeks from 12 weeks can be seen in the Tradeoff Curve in Figure 11-16.

While a 6-week schedule cannot be achieved for this scope of work, it might be possible to accomplish it in other ways. Some examples include: if the scope were reduced or if more experienced resources could perform the activities faster and cheaper than the currently assigned resources or if activities can be performed in parallel. The last consideration is whether the revised duration (with its increased cost) can be supported by the available resources or any non-critical activities delayed to allow the needed resources to be used on critical path activities instead. In any event, management now has the information to make an informed decision regarding schedule duration.

Other Schedule Acceleration Techniques

While the schedule crashing techniques described above are a methodical means of shortening schedules based on the focused application of additional resources to critical path tasks, there are several other methods of accomplishing the same goals.

Fast Tracking is a technique that changes the relationships of some tasks so they are performed in parallel instead of the original serial plan. Care must be taken to ensure that the increased resource requirements necessary to perform activities in parallel are available.

Streamlining is another method requiring the team to replan the effort based on reuse and innovation. With streamlining comes the potential for increased risk of creating a new plan to meet the revised dates, not to perform the scope of work.

Finally, a technique known as Focused Work is based on resources being dedicated to tasks on the critical path in order to reduce the durations of those tasks and thus shortening the schedule. To support the focused efforts, other work assigned to those performing the critical work must be assigned to others.

Conclusion

Whether overcome by events, changes in scope, or project execution issues, there are times when the plan does not meet the current date requirements of the contract. When this happens, the project team must use one of four basic methods for schedule acceleration.

The most structured of these processes, crashing the schedule, is a step-by-step approach that relies on the idea of time/cost tradeoffs, and can be implemented logically. The process can be controlled in that a tradeoff curve can be established for reduced project duration versus increased cost, and any point can be selected on the curve. Other techniques exist to accelerate the schedule, including Fast Tracking, Streamlining, and Focused Work. All of the techniques depend on abbreviating the critical path activities.

Chapter 11 Review Questions

11-1.   Why is it important to recheck the critical path during a network crashing exercise?

11-2.   What does it mean when the critical path is "fully crashed"?

11-3.   Define "crash time" and "crash cost".

11-4.   Explain why the cost slope is significant when performing a network crashing exercise.

11-5.   What two occurrences will signal the end of a network crashing effort?

True or False

11-6.   The network critical path must be known before a crashing exercise is begun.

11-7.   Crashing a network is an effort of quantifying time/cost tradeoffs.

11-8.   Shortening a standard activity duration typically will cost less than the historical duration.

11-9.   A cost slope of $6,000 per week indicates that $6,000 will be saved for each week that the associated activity is shortened.

11-10.   Crashing all activities in a network will result in a higher cost than necessary for a fully crashed project schedule.

The answers to these questions can be found in Section 6, Solutions.

Case Study

11. 1 CRASHING THE NETWORK OR "WHAT IF"

Using the network developed in Case Study 8.1, study the following new requirements added by management:

- Activity L must begin on or before Day 30.
- Activities Q, W, and X use the same facility, therefore no two can be performed at the same time.

Use the following to make decisions:

Activity	Normal Duration	Normal Cost	Crash Duration	Crash Cost
C	4	$8,400	2	$9,600
G	8	$12,000	5	$24,000
H	3	$3,000	1	$4,500
I	2	$6,000	1	$8,000
J	4	$8,500	3	$10,000
K	2	$3,800	1	$6,000

Recommend the solution that has the minimum time and cost impact while conforming to the new requirements. Be prepared to justify your solution.

The solution to this case study can be found on the Humphreys & Associates, Inc. web site.
www.humphreys-assoc.com

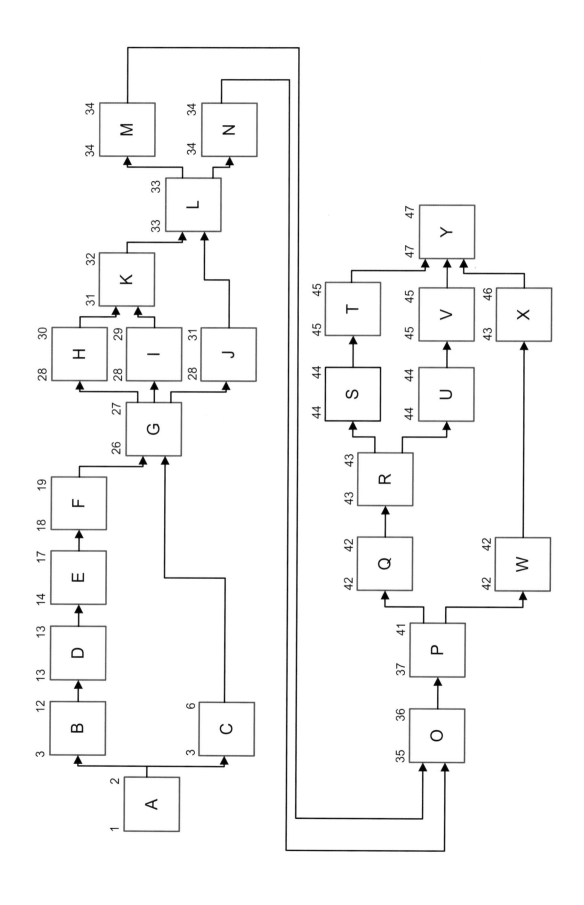

Chapter 12

SETTING A TRACEABLE SCHEDULE BASELINE

Objectives of this Chapter:

1. Define a schedule baseline and explain why it is necessary.

2. Define schedule traceability.

3. List two types of schedule traceability and describe why each is important.

4. Describe the use of meaningful milestones in the scheduling process.

5. Discuss potential problem areas in achieving traceability.

6. Describe the step-by-step process for establishing a schedule baseline.

7. Discuss the timing of baseline establishment.

8. List appropriate reasons for revising the schedule baseline.

9. Describe the differences between the current schedule and the baseline schedule, and how both are used for controlling a project.

There has been a great deal of effort in the schedule development process. The initial planning has occurred, the schedule types have been selected, the logic networks have been developed, computed, resource loaded and leveled, and adjustments have been made by schedule acceleration to produce a plan that meets project schedule objectives.

However, there is another step that must be taken before the plan can be approved so that it can be used for tracking and managing progress. The schedule must be traceable both horizontally and vertically.

Schedule traceability overlaps the two major divisions of the scheduling flowchart: developing the schedule and using the schedule. If multiple scheduling tools are used in the project, effort must be made to ensure consistency between them.

In addition to the automated scheduling system, there may be manually prepared summary format schedules that are independent of the schedule data base and used for executive reporting. When the baseline schedule is approved, there must be just one project schedule and it must be integrated among all of the project participants. This is part of the process as the baseline is being established and approved.

The challenge of traceability is that the job is not over once the approved schedule baseline has been established. Often it is more difficult to maintain consistency among schedules after progress is being reported and it may be necessary to indicate progress on multiple schedule documents in a uniform manner.

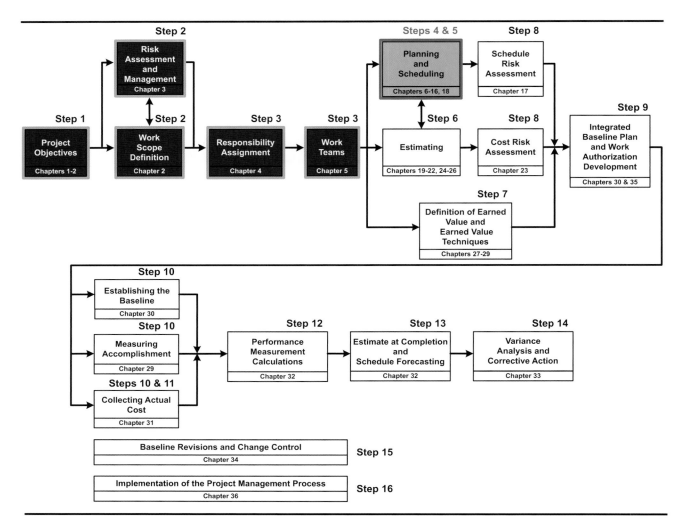

Figure 12-1 Earned Value Project Management: The Process

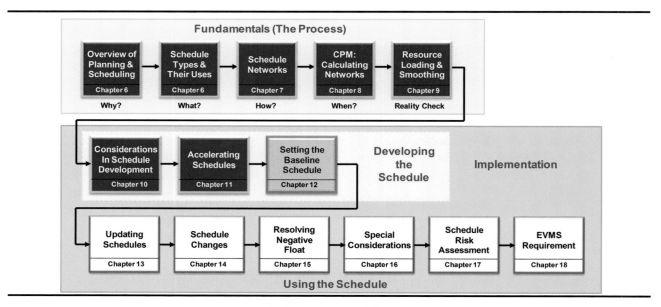

Figure 12-2 Planning and Scheduling

Schedule Traceability

Schedule traceability is consistency between schedule dates, status, and revisions at all levels of schedule detail and between schedules at the same level of detail. When different organizations maintain their own schedules, the interface points must be consistent. There are three considerations to this subject: horizontal traceability, vertical traceability and historical traceability.

Traceability is the second of the eight Generally Accepted Scheduling Principles (GASP) presented in the Scheduling Overview. It is also number six in the GAO's Best Scheduling Practices. The schedule is vertically aligned and the schedule logic is horizontally integrated and cross-referenced to key documents and tools.

Horizontal traceability means that schedules independently maintained by different divisions or departments, or between subcontractors, must each have the same dates at interface points as other schedules prepared at the same level of detail. This is not a concern on projects that use a single integrated project schedule encompassing all project participants.

However, some projects allow organizations to maintain separate schedules at the detailed level that summarize to a master schedule used for external reporting. Ensuring that these detailed schedules actually interface smoothly can be a challenge. An example of what is meant by horizontal traceability is shown in Figure 12-3.

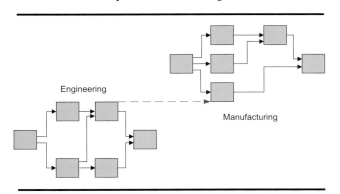

Figure 12-3 Horizontal Traceability Between Same Level of Detail

Traceability seems as if it should be an assumed condition, but surprises often appear. Horizontal traceability is the degree to which the work of many teams is linked into one schedule. The required inputs of one team are the outputs from another. Activities feed activities. Horizontal traceability task starts can be achieved on a project through the use of integrating events in which the various teams or CAMs are brought together and the needs of each team are discussed. Every needed input is defined and the provider of that input identified. An agreement is reached and documented about who is providing what and when it will be provided. An example might be: "CAM A agrees to provide a draft specification for a certain item to Team B 15 working days after the preliminary design task starts". This yields a SS+15 link between their work, a horizontal traceability link.

Having an Integrated Master Plan (IMP) (reference Chapter 10, Considerations for Developing a Useful, Quality Schedule) means all teams are working to the same master plan and that enhances the horizontal traceability. Since the IMP is already hierarchical it then helps enforce vertical traceability.

Vertical traceability is an easier concept. It simply means that higher level schedule dates are consistent with the dates shown in lower level schedules. An example is shown in Figure 12-4.

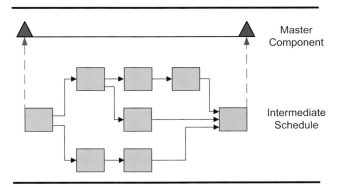

Figure 12-4 Vertical Traceability Btween Different Levels of Detail

The most common way to ensure consistency is to define a series of meaningful milestones and to identify them clearly on all schedules. "Meaningful" suggests that they be clearly defined, observable events that are understood, well documented, and agreed upon. The IMP provides an organized, hierarchical milestone set for the project. Then a specific date is set for each milestone, and these dates can be verified as the same on each level of schedule and within each organizational schedule. To aid in the verification task, the milestone identification code should be the same on every schedule. An example of how this can be accomplished is shown in Figure 12-5.

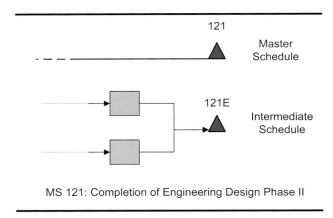

MS 121: Completion of Engineering Design Phase II

Figure 12-5 Milestones

The example in Figure 12-5 shows how coding clarity can assist in verifying vertical traceability. Completion of engineering design phase II always carries the root code 121 on all schedules, although it may have varying suffixes depending on the level or organization schedule on which it appears.

There also needs to be a disciplined system of status and change reporting. Status reporting should always be reported at the lowest working level of the schedule. This status should then be summarized vertically. If a milestone date slips on the detailed schedule level, then the milestone date on the higher level schedules must be modified to the corresponding date as well.

Change reporting can be an upward or downward flow. If direction were provided by the owner/customer via an approved scope change, for example, this would be shown on the master schedule and reflected downward into the more detailed schedules. The impact of this change on future activities and milestones is measured on the detailed schedule and those dates are then reported upwards, if any subsequent milestones are impacted.

Another major challenge may be to integrate manual and automated methods of schedule reporting. In some systems, the highest and/or lowest level of the schedule is maintained manually. The intermediate levels are depicted in a fully automated CPM. Maintaining date consistency is obviously more difficult in a manual system than one that is fully automated.

Achieving schedule traceability can be difficult on large projects with many organizations, but it is a requirement of proper project management. The Data Item Description (DID) DI-MGMT-81650, Integrated Master Schedule (IMS), specifies that the IMS must be vertically traceable to the Integrated Master Plan (where applicable), the Contract Work Breakdown Structure (CWBS) and the Statement of Work (SOW). The IMS should have a numbering system that provides traceability to the IMP. Figure 12-6 demonstrates a coding schema that provides a vertical traceable link from the activity level of the IMS to the IMP and CWBS.

Historical traceability is the ability to trace baseline changes back to the beginning of the project. This is achieved through a formal Baseline Change Request (BCR), or similar change management tracking process that documents the changes from the original baseline, and all revisions, to the most recent baseline. The reasons why a baseline would be modified are delineated later in this chapter. The BCR process involves establishment of a paper or electronic trail consisting of why, when, how, and by whom the baseline was modified. Impacts on time and cost are also considered before the project manager approves the change and it is implemented. A sample Baseline Change Request form is displayed in Figure 12-7.

Once implemented, BCRs are filed along with other project documentation as part of the historical files, to enable later analysis and as proof that the baseline was updated in the approved manner.

A Solution

The most direct way of achieving horizontal and vertical traceability is through the use of integrated CPM schedule software. The Critical Path

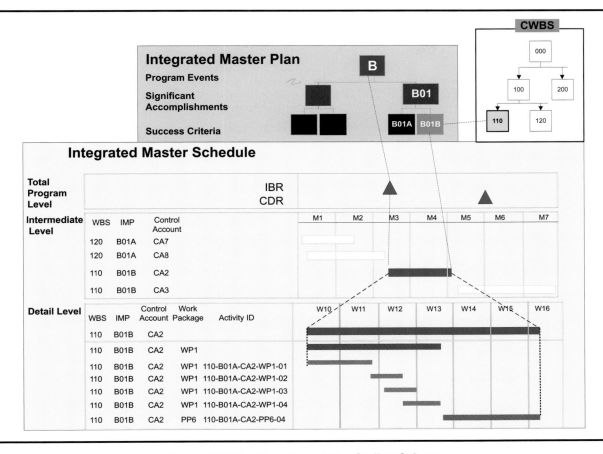

Figure 12-6 Vertifcal Traceability Coding Schema

Method requires the identification of all interface points when the network logic is constructed. Doing so assures horizontal traceability. If all intermediate and summary level schedules are produced from the same detailed CPM database, schedule dates will automatically be consistent on all schedule levels. This assures vertical traceability. This discussion assumes that the scheduling software has hammock or other summarization technological capability and can calculate the summary dates of the detail work accurately and consistently. Use of an integrated CPM is rapidly becoming the scheduling system approach chosen to simplify schedule maintenance and to enforce traceability.

Defining the Schedule Baseline

The formally approved schedule plan that will be used for monitoring and managing progress is the schedule baseline. It is a resource loaded and leveled schedule record of how project objectives will be accomplished on time. The schedule baseline will also include any approved changes to that plan, from the owner/customer or through management approved internal changes.

The most basic reason for a schedule baseline is that a project cannot be controlled if there were not a target against which to control it. Another factor is that there can be no assurance that contract required dates can be met unless there is a plan to demonstrate how those dates will be achieved. The baseline serves to document the scope, logic, durations, resources and assumptions that went into the plan's development. Having a baseline plan is not enough; it must also be controlled in a disciplined way throughout the life of the project. If the baseline were to change based on status, then the project would be managed against a moving target and trend analysis would be meaningless.

BASELINE CHANGE REQUEST

PROJECT TITLE	PROJECT NO.	CAM	ORGN	BCR NO. 11
XYZ	86-1900	L. R. SMITH	6000	

CWBS NO.	CONTROL ACCOUNT NO.	TITLE:	DATE: 4 APRIL YR 03
1.4.5	600-1234	COMPONENT ENVIRONMENTAL TESTS	PAGE 1 OF 1

DESCRIPTION OF CHANGE: (ATTACH REVISED CAP)

1. ADD WORK PACKAGE NO. 6 "CONDUCT FOUR ENVIRONMENTAL TESTS ON XYZ SUBASSEMBLY".

2. WORK CURRENTLY INCLUDED IN PLANNING PACKAGE NO. 1.

3. NO CHANGE TO CONTROL ACCOUNT BUDGET OR PERIOD OF PERFORMANCE.

REASON FOR CHANGE

1. ROUTINE "ROLLING WAVE" PLANNING PACKAGE TO WORK PACKAGE CONVERSION

REQUESTED BUDGET CHANGE				REQUESTED SCHEDULE REVISION		
COST ELEMENT	CURRENT AUTHORIZATION	REQUESTED CHANGE	NEW BUDGET	MILESTONE	FROM	TO
LABOR HOURS	1410	0	1410	SEE CAP FOR WORK PACKAGE PERFORMANCE MEASUREMENT MILESTONES		
LABOR DOLLARS	$25,380	0	$25,380			
MATERIAL DOLLARS	0	0	0			
SUBCONTRACT DOLLARS	0	0	0			
ODC DOLLARS	0	0	0			
TOTAL DOLLARS:	$25,380	0	$25,380			

BUDGET SOURCE				
UNDISTRIBUTED BUDGET		MANAGEMENT RESERVE	XX	OTHER: CONTROL ACCT PLNG PKG

CONTROL ACCOUNT MANAGER	DATE	COST CONTROL SECTION	DATE
L.R. SMITH	4/7/Y3	JENNY JOHNSON	4/7/Y3
FUNCTIONAL MANAGER	DATE	BUSINESS MANAGER	DATE
ROBERT ROBINSON	4/7/Y3	BEN BENSON	4/8/Y3
SCHEDULING SECTION	DATE	PROGRAM MANAGER	DATE
NELS NELSON	4/8/Y3	LINDA LARSON	4/8/Y3

Figure 12-7 Baseline Change Request

Schedule Baseline Establishment

There is a logical procedure to develop a schedule baseline plan. It is a series of 17 steps, some of which may have to be repeated more than once to achieve the desired result. Not all of these steps will be enumerated in all schedule baseline procedures and some of the steps may be performed in a different sequence.

1. Define the general bid proposal scope.

2. Develop the Master Schedule (including any associated milestones).

These first two steps will always be performed as part of the bidding process. They are essential to prepare even a preliminary estimate for a new project. In many companies, all of the following steps may be performed before a formal bid is submitted.

3. Develop detailed activities.

4. Assign responsibility for each activity.

5. Establish activity durations.

6. Develop the detailed network logic.

This sequence of tasks relates to the specification of the proposed project schedule. The objectives of the project are considered in more detail to allow specific schedule requirements to be recognized. The assignment of individual responsibility is very important, since these people are the ones most knowledgeable of the processes they will use in completing the work tasks. More simply, a schedule is most effective, and has a higher probability of success, when the people who will be executing the schedule are involved in its planning and development. In addition, this will help ensure that those responsible are in agreement with the activities and logic developed.

7. Perform CPM calculations.

Notice all of the steps that preceded this one. Only now are dates established for the CPM activities. This may raise a challenge, since there is no guarantee that these dates will be consistent with those previously established in the bid documents. The next step should be obvious.

8. Verify consistency of schedule at all levels of detail and revise as necessary.

This is one of the steps that may require multiple iterations. If the detailed schedule does not support the required dates, it will be necessary to investigate alternative ways of completing the work within the specified time frame. Even after the dates are consistent, it still has not been established that the work can actually be supported with available staff.

9. Load resources at activity level.

10. Check resources for efficiency/availability.

11. Define priorities for resource leveling.

12. Resource level schedule.

This is the point where some scheduling systems fail. Many of the reasons were discussed in Chapter 9, "Resource Loading and Leveling the Schedule." It is important to note that the software used for scheduling allows some freedom to establish the priorities for leveling the resources. Each project is different, and differing emphases may be placed on the cost and time objectives from one project to the next. A single set of resource rules will therefore not suffice. "One size does not fit all."

Resource loading and date consistency between schedule levels are two of the reasons many companies are now investing much more time and money in the development of detailed schedules in the bidding stage. Some companies literally plan the entire project in the bidding stage, an activity that previously was not done until after a contract award. The reason is simple, especially for a firm fixed price contract; the possibility of committing to an unrealistic plan cannot be afforded. Profit margins are too tight to realize after contract award that the available budget will not support the contract dates and/or intermediate contract milestones. One company actually produced a 25,000 activity CPM network as a part of preparing the bid. This would have been unheard of even a few years ago. Others have produced a proposed Performance Measurement Baseline as part of the bid process.

While the work is not yet done as far as schedule baseline establishment is concerned, it is nearly so, at least in terms of number of steps.

13. Team review of proposed schedule baseline for:

a. Inclusion of all work.

b. Responsibility assignment.

c. Logic.

d. Durations.

  e. Resource plan practicality.

14. Revise as necessary.

15. Ensure that the schedule is both horizontally and vertically traceable.

16. Perform schedule health checks.

17. Approve schedule baseline.

Step 13 is a major commitment of time and effort. Step 14 may require a month or longer after extensive reviews with significant comments. Step 15 is a check that the master schedule milestones are logically and correctly supported by their detail support activities. It is also a check that any independently maintained schedules by other divisions or departments, or between subcontractors, have the correct date alignment at the same level of detail. Step 16 should be performed continually during the creation of the schedule to ensure that it conforms to both corporate standards and scheduling best practices. Once step 17 is reached, the resource leveled dates created during the resource leveling process have replaced the previous early and late dates. These are the dates that will now be monitored, managed, used to determine performance, and will replace the early and late dates originally calculated.

Preparing a resource loaded and leveled schedule is not a trivial task. For resource leveling to be done correctly, the process requires that all project participants take part in the development process. Since everyone is busy in the early stages of a project, and becomes even busier when the project is in full swing, finding the time to create the resource loaded schedule is one of the challenges faced.

It is essential that this effort be undertaken very early in the project. This means the effort must be initiated within the first month or two after contract award on a long multi-year project. If the project were two years or less in duration, the baseline should be established in the first month after contract award. Also, the owner/customer for the project often includes a contract requirement that an approved baseline be established

within a specified number of days after contract award. Usual lead times for longer projects would be 60 or 90 days after contract award.

Another helpful tip is to perform the team review of the proposed baseline at a neutral site away from the immediate work area and to involve all disciplines from both the customer and contractor organizations. This ensures incorporation of the best available information. A poor plan causes added difficulty in managing the project, so the effort invested is worthwhile.

More than one organization has found the best plan is to hold the baseline review in a local hotel and have the project participants stay there while working whatever hours are required to expedite completion of the process. One such effort went from 7:00 A.M. to 7:00 P.M. every workday for a week. Lunch was catered, allowing work to continue. All of the involved project leaders, from every discipline on the contractor's side and the owner's side, were available full time until the baseline was agreed to and formalized. This resulted in the best possible baseline in the shortest possible time. Up front planning requires concentrated and dedicated effort, but it will pay dividends for the remainder of the project.

Once the baseline has been approved, the emphasis for project schedule control is on the leveled start curve (reference Chapter 9). The late start/finish curve may still be monitored for current status, particularly if the leveled dates are not being met, but the early dates no longer have significance unless conditions requiring schedule acceleration occur.

Realism and Schedule Detail

There are limits to how much detail should be put into the baseline schedule of a long project. An example comes from a meeting with a scheduling software vendor to look at a top of the line scheduling product. A baseline schedule for an actual project was used for demonstration purposes, and the vendor displayed a visually overwhelming presentation of capabilities.

As the schedule was being sliced and diced every possible way, suddenly the total project duration appeared on the screen. It was 8 years,

2 months, 1 week, 3 days, and 11 minutes. Who would schedule a project more than eight years long to the minute? With tongue in cheek, one of the observers said, "Gee, 8 years, 2 months, 1 week, 3 days, and 11 minutes? Are you sure about the 11 minutes?" The software presenter missed the point and jumped right in. "Oh yes. There is detail to support the duration to the minute, and, I can show you how it is developed."

The point was not the capability of the software. It was the ability and lack of maturity of the people doing the input to actually develop and imply that level of precision. It would be similar to pulling out an old wooden yardstick and boldly announcing that your child was now 4 feet, 3.0895249 inches last week. The statement may or may not be true, but the measuring instrument will never be able to verify it. Just because a calculator or computer will accept eight-digit accuracy does not make the input accurate to eight decimal places.

Timing of Schedule Baseline Establishment

The contract details should identify when a proposed schedule baseline is required to be submitted to the owner/customer for review and approval. A typical requirement is 60-90 days after contract award. Prior to that, a summary schedule would be used for tracking performance while the baseline schedule is developed. One of the first schedules produced may be a schedule to develop the baseline schedule. Mature companies also employ a deliverable-oriented interim schedule that establishes priorities and measures progress toward project goals during the baseline development work process. The schedule baseline should be resource loaded and leveled and, as such, serve as a primary input to the development of the integrated cost and schedule baseline. This is discussed in more detail later in Chapter 30, "Establishing the Performance Measurement Baseline."

The recommended best practice is to initiate the scheduling process during the bid process, increase the detail after contract award, and acquire approval of the plan as soon as is rea-

sonable or as required by the contract. This allows formal variance analysis and corrective action to begin when it has the best chance of success; sooner rather than later. Unfortunately, it does not always work that way. On one subcontract in the aerospace industry, consultants were called in one year after contract award to develop a schedule baseline.

To further complicate the situation, the original, undocumented plan had been revised a few months earlier. This meant the task included defining the original baseline, the revised baseline, and then assessing current status against the revised baseline. If this were not challenging enough, there was virtually no one currently on the project who had participated in the original planning. This is an example where the subcontractor would have benefited from using consulting help in the planning phase instead of waiting until problems arose.

A well documented set of procedures is another item that should not be forgotten until the last minute. One of the first things that system reviewers look for in any industry is the documentation: Are procedures established? Are people aware of them and have they been trained in their use? Are they being followed?

A software development company had intended to develop scheduling procedures and had indicated to its client that the procedures were in place. When the client, the United States Air Force, announced its intention to review the scheduling procedures the following week, panic calls went out to consulting firms to assist in the immediate development of a book of procedures. Four days later, after long nights and a weekend, the procedures were in place. Was everyone aware of the content of those procedures and were they being followed? Those are separate questions. The point is that procedures, while not part of the baseline per se, must be in place at the same time, since they provide instructions to the project schedulers on how to carry out their mission of maintaining the schedule baseline while still reflecting current status. They should also explain the process of schedule analysis, review, and the methods for proposing corrective action.

Schedule Baseline Revisions

The approved baseline must change when there are approved changes to the scope of work. However, many other reasons may cause change. What if an activity takes longer than planned to be completed? What if other activities finish early? What if an activity that could not be completed according to the schedule logic is reported as complete? This last case happens regularly in schedules that do not reflect the true logic, when activities are shown as sequential (finish-to-start), and when they should be shown as overlapping or parallel (start-to-start or finish-to-finish). All of these instances, from early completion to delay, reflect the current status of the project and do not indicate a baseline change. This is one of the more difficult points of implementation; when is a change a baseline change? Are logic changes to the current schedule baseline considered changes? It is impossible to consider in some schedule software since baseline logic is not even captured. There are many possibilities for change in a large schedule; therefore, procedures are required to guide the decisions. Baseline revisions are usually limited to just six cases:

1. The schedule is impacted by approved scope changes.

2. The project is delayed or accelerated or other owner/customer direction is received, sometimes based on funding constraints.

3. Rolling wave planning takes place where planning packages that approach the current period are converted to detailed work packages.

4. Management Reserve or Undistributed Budget is applied to the project and scheduling adjustments result.

5. When the schedule is replanned within the existing budget based upon updated knowledge of the scope, project conditions, new ideas, etc.

6. When unrecoverable slippage has occurred, and with owner approval, an over target schedule (OTS) is developed to the new schedule dates. If an OTS

were necessary, it would also be possible that an over target baseline (OTB) would require approval and implementation at the same time. If that were the case, the project would be replanned to the revised target dates and budgets. This is known as formal reprogramming.

The first five cases are examples of revised baseline situations. In all of these, the project has changed in a significant way. In the first, it has grown or decreased in scope, so it is no longer the same project. In the second, the project objectives have changed, and therefore the plan for achieving those objectives must also change. The third is common in large projects where future activities are entered in summary form and then detail planned as they near their planned start date. This process is termed the "rolling wave" and both the baseline and current schedules are modified accordingly. The fourth case is to allocate contractual scope that has been held in Undistributed Budget or internal scope changes allocated from Management Reserve. Again, both the baseline and current schedules are modified. The fifth case keeps the door open for changing the project plan based on new ideas or conditions.

The last is often controversial and may be difficult to justify. In essence, the claim is made that the plan is no longer achievable and therefore no longer serves as a valid basis for controlling the project. This can certainly be true in some instances. But there is a hidden danger with this logic. The problem is that the plan is being changed to match performance, instead of changing performance to match the plan. This may become a moving target, in which case analysis has little meaning and the plan is no longer used to control the project. That is why prior approval by the owner/customer is required in these instances. Formal processes using Baseline Change Requests initiate all such baseline changes.

Are there cases when a schedule baseline revision may be advisable? Yes, but they must be considered on a case-by-case basis. The objective of the schedule plan, as well as of the overall project management plan, is to provide clear targets to achieve and monitor performance to ensure that those targets are achieved. Changing the targets continually will not provide any measure of control, but neither will measurement against a plan that cannot possibly be achieved. In either instance, the main objective of effective project monitoring, managing, and control is endangered. The evaluation of which is the lesser evil of these two choices must be made jointly by the contractor and the owner/customer.

The Baseline Schedule Versus the Current Schedule

There is always an underlying conflict with the use of the scheduling system. Having a fixed baseline schedule is critical to be able to analyze status fairly and consistently. Without baseline control, it is impossible to meaningfully analyze the schedule update reports. In conflict with this requirement is the need for the schedule to contain the latest information in order to be useful. This results from such things as changes in material and equipment lead times, or other delays encountered, which must be reflected in the schedule status or the schedule will not serve as a tool for continuing control of the project.

There are two different objectives: status and performance. Status contains information about where the project is and allows planning of current work. Performance expresses how well the project is doing against the original plan and helps the planning of future work. Both of these objectives can be satisfied within the scheduling system using two separate schedules. The baseline schedule is fixed and never changed except when there are approved changes. When there is a valid baseline update, the original baseline is archived for historical purposes. The current schedule is regularly updated with status, progress and changes. By comparing these two schedules, a picture can be developed showing how current status compares with the baseline plan. Graphical presentations of this type of information in bar chart format are extremely popular.

The information in baseline schedules is not necessarily maintained in the same way by various scheduling systems. In one scheduling tool, the baseline schedule is a separate stand alone schedule containing the same data fields as the current schedule and can, therefore, be analyzed and displayed separately. For historical purposes, multiple versions can be saved as separate schedules. In another scheduling tool, the baseline schedule and up to 10 prior versions are contained within the current schedule file as adjuncts. Activity logic is not maintained and any logic shown for a baseline belongs to the current schedule. Thus one system has more complete information saved if the need for a forensic analysis ever occurs.

Why go through the extra effort of maintaining two separate schedules? Because there really is no choice if both objectives of an effective scheduling system are to be met. Why not just measure performance against the current schedule? Since the current schedule is a moving target, trend information would be meaningless since it would encourage rescheduling to match performance rather than altering performance to match schedule.

Conclusion

Schedule traceability means consistency of information among all schedule levels, formats and types of schedules. This is usually divided into horizontal, vertical, and historical traceability. Horizontal traceability means that schedules maintained by different organizations must reflect the same schedule dates among schedules at the same level of detail. Vertical traceability means that lower level detail schedule dates must support the achievement of higher level, summary schedules. Said another way, there must be date consistency among different levels of schedules. Historical traceability means that there is the capability to trace the origin of all baseline changes, providing information as to the reasons, the date and cost impacts and the requestors of the changes.

The use of meaningful milestones, consistently identified on all schedules and levels, helps verify traceability. A scheduling system is of little use if the dates are inconsistent among organizational interfaces or among various levels of detail. Which one is then the "real" schedule? Even schedules that satisfy the requirement for traceability can become disconnected as changes or status updates are incorporated. Ensuring traceability should therefore be a prime concern of the scheduler.

Challenges arise with traceability for numerous reasons. Among them are a mix of automated and manual schedules maintained by different organizations, a lack of identified meaningful milestones, and inadequate procedures for ensuring that schedule updates are reflected consistently on all schedule documents.

The schedule baseline is the approved schedule plan for accomplishing the scope of work for the project. Developing an approved schedule baseline should be one of the first priorities on any new project. It is not a quick process, but it is a logical one that can be defined and followed. A successful baseline requires the input of all project participants, including all functions/depart-ments that are part of the project on both the contractor's side and the owner/customer's side. The extra effort in assuring that all parties understand the project scope and how it will be accomplished will minimize scope changes and delay claims later. This initial forced communication among all team members will initiate the project in a positive direction.

The schedule baseline should be revised when approved scope changes impact the schedule, whenever the project schedule objectives change, or if unrecoverable slippage has occurred and its recovery is approved by the owner/customer. Status is not recorded in the baseline schedule; rather it is maintained within a separate current schedule. The current schedule can be compared against the baseline schedule at any time to determine schedule performance.

Chapter 12 Review Questions

12-1.   Define horizontal traceability.

12-2.   Define vertical traceability.

12-3.   Explain why traceability is important from a scheduling and management standpoint.

12-4.   Define what is meant by a "meaningful" milestone.

True or False

12-5.   Once the schedule baseline has been approved, the emphasis for project schedule control should be on the late start curve.

12-6.   Baseline schedule dates should be revised if an activity starts later than planned.

12-7.   Repeated revising of schedule dates results in a moving target and meaningless trend indicators.

12-8.   A true schedule baseline should include resources so that verification is available that required staffing to support the schedule can actually be met.

12-9.   Typically, requirements are for a schedule baseline to be in effect within 60-90 days after contract award.

The answers to these questions can be found in Section 6, Solutions.

Case Study

12.1 VERTICAL AND HORIZONTAL SCHEDULE TRACEABILITY

The three phases of a project have been planned and scheduled without giving consideration to each other. The logic network and early start bar chart for each phase are provided. The Work Breakdown Structure reference for each activity is noted in the activity box and on the bar chart.

Your assignment is to integrate the three phases into a project schedule using the following additional logic:

Activity E (Phase 1) precedes Start Milestone 1 (Phase 2)

Activity 5 (Phase 2) precedes Start Milestone R (Phase 3)

Requirements:

1. Recalculate early dates for each activity after integrating the three phases.

2. Produce a detail bar chart for each phase after integration.

3. Produce an intermediate bar chart for each phase by using the WBS.

4. Produce a master schedule bar chart for the project by using the WBS.

Phase 1 Logic Network

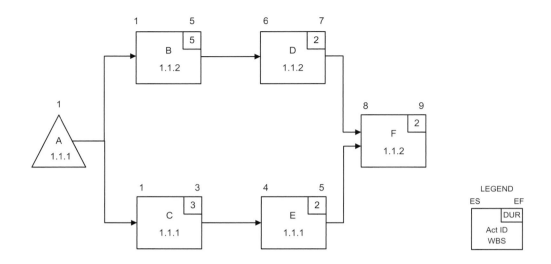

Phase 1 Early Start Bar Chart (Before Integration)

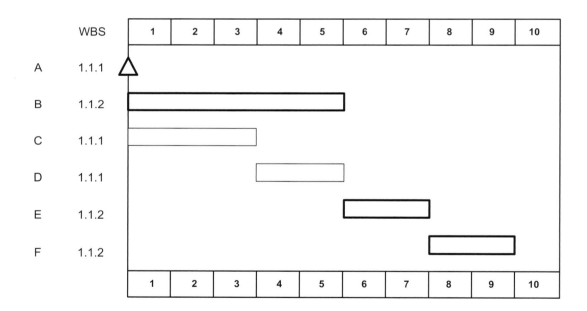

Phase 2 Logic Network

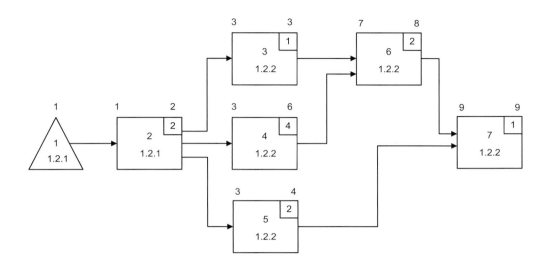

Phase 2 Early Start Bar Chart (Before Integration)

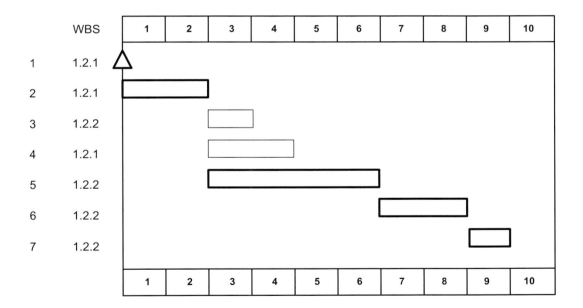

Phase 3 Logic Network

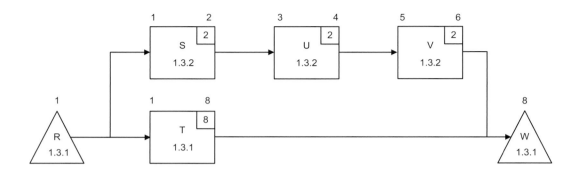

Phase 3 Early Start Bar Chart (Before Integration)

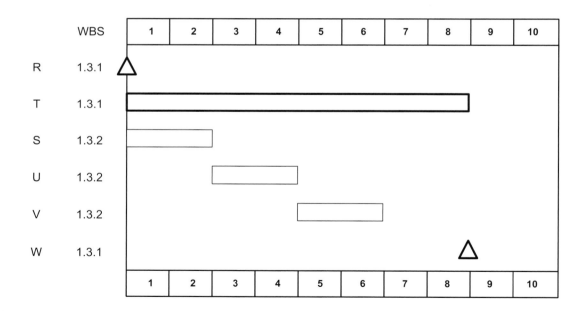

Chapter **13**

UPDATING THE SCHEDULE

Objectives of this Chapter:

1. Present the various methods used for updating schedules to include current progress.

2. Demonstrate how total float is impacted because of the update process.

3. Explain two common approaches used by scheduling software programs to address reported schedule progress that is out of sequence with the established logic.

4. Demonstrate the impact on network total float calculations depending on which out-of-sequence technique is used.

The baseline schedule has been established and approved, but now the actual progress is deviating from the plan. How can the status be incorporated? What information is needed to support the schedule update process? What if the logic were wrong or has changed, and work is being performed in a different sequence than was planned? Lastly, how do all of these things affect analysis? These are all issues once the approved schedule has been established and the work team lead/control account manager begins to evaluate progress against the baseline plan.

A significant amount of time and effort has been spent covering the basics of developing a schedule. While this is a formidable and worthwhile task, the schedule will be changing from the time of the first update cycle. The process of updating schedules is addressed here, as well as the types of things that happen when activities are not performed in the same sequence in which they were planned. How will the act of updating the schedule to include the latest status affect the analysis?

Certain data are needed to update the schedule. Many of these items are interrelated and so only some of these need to be manually reported and the others can be calculated (by scheduling software). The key status considerations include:

1. "Time now" - All schedule calculations depend on this information. Status is only valid for the single date on which it is reported. This date is "time now". This is also known as the "data date" or the "status date".

2. "Actual Start Date" - When a network is created, all of the start and completion dates are projected based on the network logic and activity durations. This information is no longer relevant for an activity once actual status is reported. A reported actual start date will cause the network to be recalculated on its next update based on this actual start date.

3. "Actual Finish Date" - The same comments apply as for "Actual Start Date."

4. "Remaining Duration" - This is the key piece of information for any activity that has started but not completed. Even "Actual Start" is not as important, because the network calculations will be based on Time Now plus Remaining Duration. This input must be based on the best estimate of the time required to complete the activity, and should not be determined by

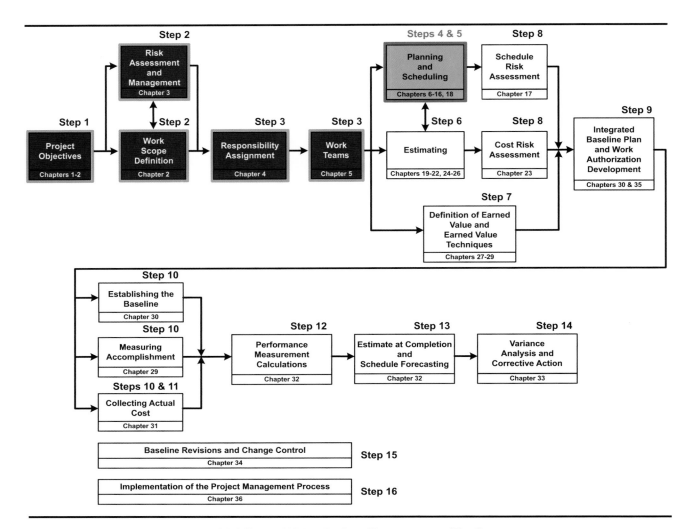

Figure 13-1 Earned Value Project Management: The Process

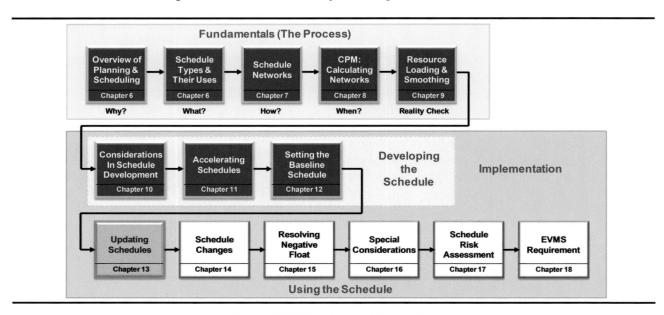

Figure 13-2 Planning and Scheduling

subtracting the elapsed time from the total duration. Since this input is used to evaluate current schedule position, it should be more than a mere calculation.

5. "Percent Complete" - This is the least useful of all the status indicators. It matters little if an activity is 99% complete if, for any reason, the last 1% will require six months. The important information is the six months remaining, not the 99% complete. This consideration is sometimes used in conjunction with earned value determination and reporting.

6. "Physical Percent Complete" - This metric is commonly used to calculate earned value for resource loaded tasks in the schedule. It is maintained separately in the schedule from the "Percent Complete" that is duration based, not effort based. This is sometimes called "Work % Complete".

Two notes of caution:

1. Actual start and actual completion dates should never be later than "time now." If they are, then that is a forecast date rather than an actual date and it should be treated as remaining duration. However, scheduling software typically will have an error check that will not permit such status to occur.

2. "Time now" has two interpretations in scheduling software. If, for example, the reporting week runs from Monday through Sunday and the company desires to include all the hours worked until 11:59:59 PM on Sunday, then time now (the status date) would be the Sunday date in one software package but the next day (Monday) in another software package. A software package might consider time now to be the end of the last day of the period while another considers it to be the beginning of the first day of the next period. It is essential to understand how time now is handled in the scheduling software.

In the examples used in this chapter, time now is defined as being the last day of the reporting period; Friday of each week. Therefore, any work performed on the weekend will be counted in the following week.

A sample statused activity will help to illustrate the six status considerations defined above. To be able to make sense of the float analysis, a calendar is needed for the months involved. The calendar is displayed in Figure 13-3.

This is the current and, in this case, the baseline schedule activity information:

- Early Start = Friday June 12.
- Early Finish = Thursday July 2.
- Duration = 15 days.
- Float = 10 days.

The status information is as follows:

(Note: calculations based on time now being the last day of the reporting week)

- Time Now = Friday June 26.
- Actual Start = Wednesday June 17.

June 20xx								July 20xx						
S	M	T	W	T	F	S		S	M	T	W	T	F	S
	1	2	3	4	5	6					1	2	3	4
7	8	9	10	11	12	13		5	6	7	8	9	10	11
14	15	16	17	18	19	20		12	13	14	15	16	17	18
21	22	23	24	25	26	27		19	20	21	22	23	24	25
28	29	30						26	27	28	29	30	31	

Figure 13-3 Calendar

- Remaining Duration = 12 days.

- Percent Complete = 40% based on duration.

- Physical Percent Complete = 50% based on the amount of work completed; this has no bearing on float calculation.

First look at the information reported. The activity resource was reported with an actual start of June 17, a difference of 3 workdays from the planned start date. Also reported was a remaining duration of 12 days. Most schedule tools will automatically calculate a remaining duration of the original duration minus the actual duration. In this case, that would be 15 − 8 leaving 7 days remaining. However, the reporting entity re-estimated the remaining duration to be 12 days and that overrode the tool calculation.

Reported data included two percent complete numbers. The Percent Complete is duration-based and can either be entered instead of remaining duration or calculated by the schedule tool according to the formula:

Actual Duration (8 days) divided by Duration (Actual Duration of 8 days + Remaining Duration of 12 days) multiplied by 100 thus calculating 40%.

If either Percent Complete or Remaining Duration were reported, the system would calculate the other. However, from a best practice perspective, reporting Remaining Duration is a far more reliable indicator of progress since it requires a thought process that gauges the time to completion of an activity rather than a more subjective assessment of how much has been completed expressed as a percentage.

Physical Percent Complete is a quantity that can be supplied as a gauge of how much work has been completed and is used as input to the cost system where Earned Value can be calculated. It has no impact on total float or remaining duration unless an option, available in some scheduling tools, allows it to be substituted for duration Percent Complete.

Now, what has happened to the float? Three days of float were lost because of the start occurring later than planned. The actual start was June 17 versus a planned early start of June 12.

As of time now, June 26, a remaining duration of 12 days is reported. (These are 12 working days rather than 10 calendar days.) With a time now of June 26 (PM), the 12 working days includes, June 29 - July 2, and July 6 - 10 and July 13 - 15. The Fourth of July holiday falls on a weekend and the holiday will be observed on the Friday before. But even if the holiday were observed on the following Monday, there would not be any difference in this case.

The early finish date is therefore recalculated as July 15 (end of day) based on the 12 day remaining duration. Since the revised total duration for the activity is now 20 days (12 days remaining and 8 days elapsed), 5 days of float have also been lost because of an extended activity duration (20 versus 15).

The situation on float looks like this:

- Original baseline float = 10 days.

- Float lost because of late start = 3 days.

- Float lost because of extended duration = 5 days.

- Revised total float available = 2 days.

This scenario can be more readily understood by referring to the graphical view in Figure 13-4.

A scheduling program ordinarily performs these calculations, not because this example is so difficult to understand, but because there are so many changes that occur throughout the network file when status is reported.

The calculated dates and float will vary based on the actual calendar. If this or any activity were being performed on a different work week, such as six or seven days per week, the results would change. Work weeks and holidays are defined in the calendar of the scheduling tool and are automatically employed by software for each activity according to how the calendar was planned.

The example just completed addressed activities that have started but are not yet completed. Completed activities, with a reported actual finish date, are not part of any further network calculations. However, what about activities that have not started yet? To ensure an accurate forecast, activities that have not yet started should not be ignored. Specifically, new information about

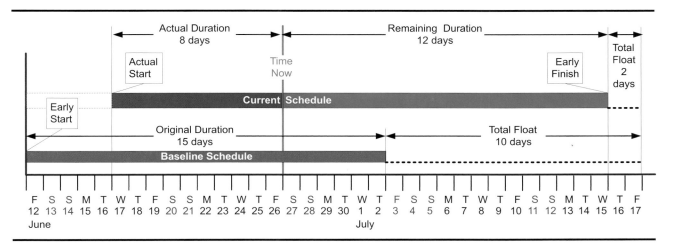

Figure 13-4 Impact of Status on Duration and Float

future activities is important if it were known that durations should be changed, new date constraints added, or revised plans for accomplishing the work result in changed logic. This scenario could happen because of schedule slips and the development of "work-around" plans.

Successful Schedule Update Process

One of the most trying aspects of schedule updates is to get changes incorporated and analyzed in a timely fashion, allowing the results to be used for managing the project. A very successful application occurred on a major construction project at a Lighting & Power Company that was performing a weekly schedule status update. (Usually it is a challenge to keep up with all of the status tracking, reporting, analysis and follow-up, even with a monthly update cycle.)

Because of good planning and good role definition this project was able to provide current status, with all analysis complete, the very next working day after a weekend. Weekly meetings were held with the project manager, construction manager, contractor staff and the owner's/customer's staff to report on current problems and also to lay out the next three weeks of planned work at a greater level of detail than maintained in the CPM network. This was a fully resource loaded and leveled schedule. Scheduling personnel were ready to address the issues, including identification of problem areas on the job and

even to recommend solutions to the problems. The information was so accurate that the project manager came to rely on this input almost exclusively for jobsite status. The concern about timeliness of data had been overcome dramatically and completely.

Anyone who has ever worked in scheduling should be asking themselves, "How was that possible?" The secret was timing and hard work. The timing related to the contractor's work schedule that consisted of four 10 hour days (Monday through Thursday) while the owner's/customer's personnel were working a standard five day work week of eight hours per day. The contractor was required to submit up-to-date status before leaving on Thursday.

This protocol allowed the owner/customer personnel to input and digest this information all day Friday without interruption (as well as Saturday and Sunday, if needed). This is where the hard work came in. First of all, the "eight hour" days were rarely eight hours. Secondly, the weekends were a key part of the update cycle.

The meetings were held first thing Monday morning. That was the first working day after close of business Thursday, so the information presented was literally right up to the minute.

There was another key component of this success story. The individual in charge of the scheduling effort was an experienced engineer with a construction background who was supported by an energetic and talented staff of three, in other words, the project had an adequate staff. They knew what the status on the job was before receiving any reports from the contractor.

On a monthly basis, even more information was available. Besides critical path analysis and scope change impact definition, considerable resource analysis was available. These analyses included planned versus actual staffing by area of work as well as by type of labor skill (e.g. carpenter, welder, electrician, etc.). The staff also compared completed work with work scheduled to be completed.

"What-if" analyses were conducted on a regular basis to provide the project manager with all of the information needed to make risk related decisions regarding schedule extensions, staffing, or budget adjustments.

It is unusual for a scheduling group to wield this kind of power, especially on a construction site. But all of the elements came together: work schedule, an effective system, highly motivated personnel, and a project manager who trusted the system output and the people who were analyzing it. The result was effective project management.

Additional Statusing Considerations

Schedulers expect to status the activities in the timing sequences provided by the logic network. However, it is not unusual for progress to be measured on successor activities prior to the start of a predecessor activity. This situation, called "out of sequence work", can be caused by unexpected changes in resource availability, the elimination of constraints, or technical changes to the project. Whenever out-of-sequence progress is indicated in the network, the scheduler must determine the best way to recalculate the network.

Note, however, metrics that determine schedule health include the identification of out-of-sequence progressing. If later activities are to be executed ahead of their predecessors, the scheduler should consider modifying the logic so that those activities are performed in parallel rather than in series with their predecessors. Out of

sequence activities should be kept to an absolute minimum.

Methods for Addressing Out-Of-Sequence Logic Status

The situation that must be assessed when activities are performed out-of sequence in a network is whether the logic needs revision or simply that an anomaly has occurred that should not require any revision. The options available within software packages are Retained Logic and Progress Override. Most scheduling software packages will have one or the other of these options selected as a default condition. This selection may need to be changed on a project-by-project or case-by-case basis.

Retained Logic is the correct choice if the scheduler wishes to maintain the initial logic as much as possible because the out-of-sequence progress results from an unusual situation. Using this Retained Logic option minimizes the change to the network calculations but still requires that the scheduler be aware of what out-of-sequence progress means in the analysis.

Progress Override reflects the belief that the out-of-sequence condition correctly reflects the new network logic. With Progress Override, the predecessor relationship is still maintained but will have little effect on the successor. As with all software default conditions, the program will assume an approach that must be understood if the output were to be correctly interpreted.

Retained Logic

An example of how Retained Logic works will add clarification. Figure 13-5 displays a sample network prior to statusing. When networks are calculated using the Retained Logic methodology, the logic for the predecessor to the activity along with the out-of-sequence progress is taken into consideration and the overall network logic maintained as much as possible. With the Retained Logic, the in-process, out-of-sequence activity cannot be completed until the predecessor has been completed. Changes that occur could include changes to the critical path and to the float on other paths.

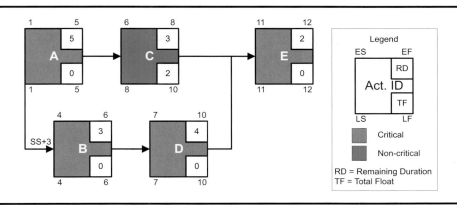

Figure 13-5 PDM Network

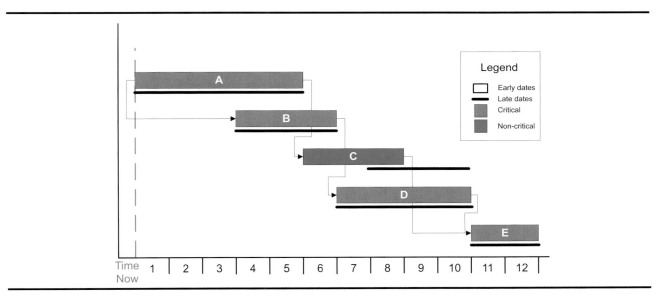

Figure 13-6 Schedule Bar Chart

The PDM network can more easily be understood when displayed as a bar chart as shown in Figure 13-6.

In Figure 13-7 the reported status to the network is shown in the block at the lower right hand corner and Figure 13-8 shows the bar chart view of the same. The activity that is being performed out of sequence is Activity D, which only has one day remaining until completion while its predecessor activity (Activity B) has not even begun. The way that a scheduling program would handle this situation (when Retained Logic is used) is shown.

The data date (or "Time Now") is Day 2 at the end of the day. Activity A has a remaining duration of

3 days reported that corresponds to days 3-4-5. The Early Start that now corresponds to the data date becomes Day 3 and the completion of Activity A remains unchanged from its original plan.

Activity D, the offending activity, has a reported Actual Start of Day 1 and has a remaining duration of one day. This situation would suggest that Activity D would end at the end of Day 3.

However, with the Retained Logic option, the predecessor activity (Activity B) must be considered first. Since Activity B has no change reported, and it is a 3 day activity constrained by a 3 day lag after the start of Activity A, it cannot begin until Day 4 at the earliest and cannot finish until Day 6. If Activity B finishes on Day 6, the remain-

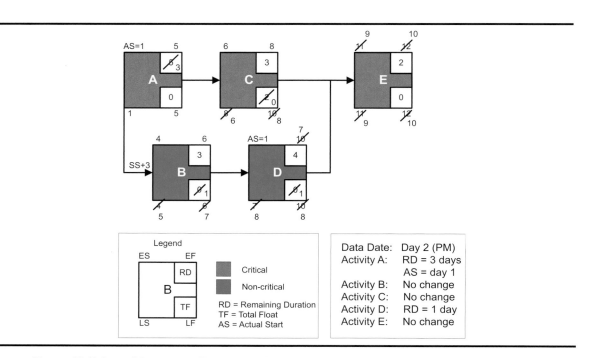

Figure 13-7 Out-of-Sequence Progress - Retained Logic Option (PDM Network)

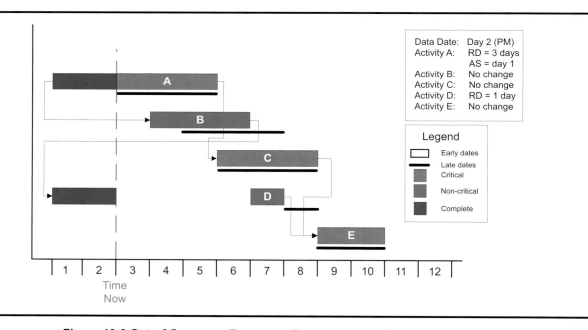

Figure 13-8 Out-of-Sequence Progress - Retained Logic Option (Bar Chart)

der of D cannot begin until Day 7. Activity D has one day remaining duration, suggesting that its finish will be on Day 7 if B must finish before D. Working backwards, that means the late finish (LF) for B is Day 7 and the Late Start (LS) is Day 5. This results from the duration of Activity B (3

days). This can be much better appreciated in the graphical display of the bar chart in Figure 13-7 (above). Note that the critical path for the network has been shortened by two days in this example.

With the retained logic option, a partially progressed out-of-sequence activity (D) splits with the completed part residing behind time now and the incomplete part still adheres to its original predecessor (B).

Progress Override

The next example demonstrates how the network would be calculated using the progress override option in the same example. When the progress override option is used, the network calculation assumes that the previous logic was in error and the predecessor(s) to the out-of-sequence activity can be rescheduled to minimize the impacts.

The starting point is, once again, the network shown in Figure 13-5 and the bar chart in Figure 13-6. Using the same status as in the retained logic example, the situation now looks like what is displayed in Figure 13-9 and Figure 13-10.

As indicated in the example, the late finish of the predecessor to activity D will be set equal to the latest early finish date of the entire network (i.e.

the last activity). Activity D no longer depends on activity B.

This approach essentially takes the predecessor out of the near term scheduling calculations. Here again, the float and critical path will probably change because of the out-of-sequence activity.

The calculation process is this: Start with Activity A and indicate the actual start date. Update Activity D and calculate the early dates for Activity E. Complete the backward pass for all activities except B. Change the late finish date for B to equal the new early finish date from E.

Activity D still is shown with a late finish of Day 8 and the total network again finishes on Day 10, two days early. But now the late finish for B = 10, the same as for E. Thus the late start for B = 8.

With the progress override option, the predecessor activity (B) of an out-of-sequence progressed activity (D) acts as if it has no successor and its late dates slide to the end of the project causing the float value to become very large.

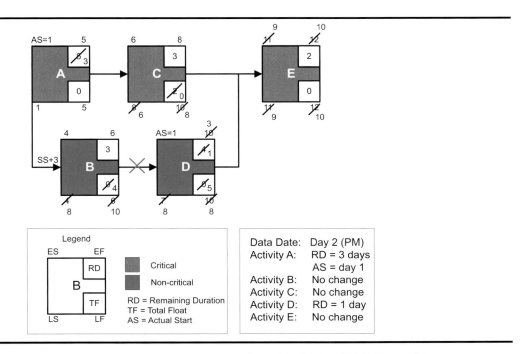

Figure 13-9 Out-of-Sequence Progress - Progress Override Option (PDM Network)

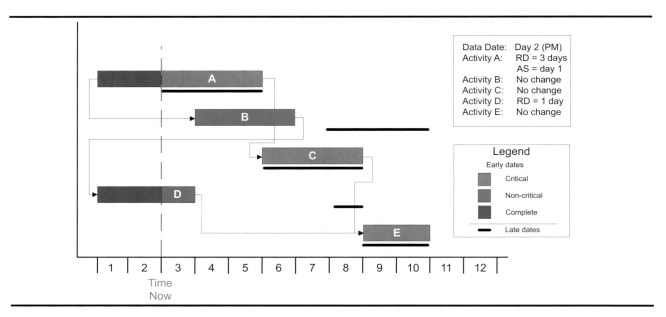

Figure 13-10 Out of Sequence Progress - Progress Override Option (Bar Chart)

Impact on Total Float

There can be significant differences in calculations of total float between these two methods. The next example uses each of the two software system options to illustrate how the total float varies. Figure 13-11 shows two parallel paths. Path A-B-C is critical and D-E-F has 8 days of total float.

Time now has advanced to day 9, the end of the day. Activities A and B started and finished on time. Activity D has not started but activity E has been reported as complete. The software, using the retained logic option, assumes that although Activity D was not a true prerequisite for beginning Activity E, it must still be required for the start of the next activity (Activity F).

The total float is now revised as follows for path D-E-F: initially 8 days, activity D was not started and therefore lost 9 days (the length of time that passed until the status date); activity E was completed and thus added 6 days. The revised total float is now 8 − 9 + 6 = 5 days. This is indicated in Figure 13-12.

Given the same network conditions, some scheduling software programs, using the progress override approach, would tie Activity D to the completion of the network as shown in Figure 13-

13. As can be seen, there is a substantial difference in the float for Activity D, from 5 days to 353 days using this approach, than there was using the retained logic. The impact is the same as if activity D were a dangling activity, that is, it did not have a successor.

This is not a hypothetical example. Many years ago, uproar developed in one company regarding incorrect scheduling calculations within the software. As is common, more than one scheduling software package was being used on the project. There had been an update and one system output said there were a few days of float on a particular activity, while the other scheduling software indicated there were over 350 days of total float for the same activity. Both sides concluded that their answer was correct.

Surprisingly enough, they were both right. The difference was tracked to this very subject: out-of-sequence logic status. One program had a default for the progress override option while the other used retained logic. It was not a matter of miscalculation at all, but a case of differing defaults within the software. Today, using more modern analysis techniques, many schedulers will run schedule health metrics each week. As a matter of course, the metrics would have identified this situation as out of sequence progressing.

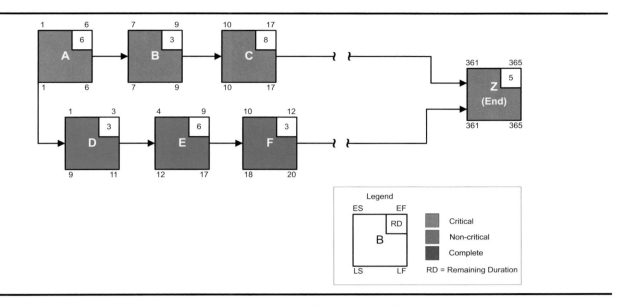

Figure 13-11 Impact on Total Float - Sample Network

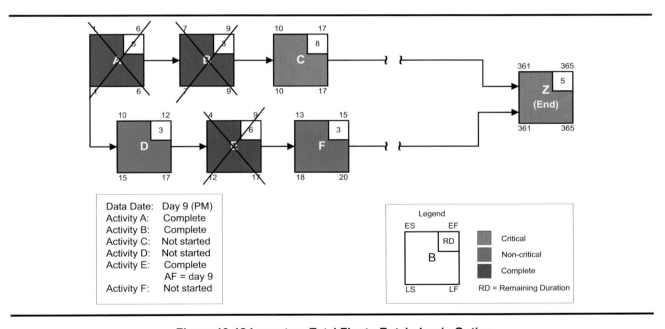

Figure 13-12 Impact on Total Float - Retain Logic Option

As seen in this example, substantial impacts can occur in network calculations that greatly affect analysis. It should be apparent that the defaults of scheduling software should be planned, known and understood. If more than one scheduling package were used on a single project, which is becoming more common, confusion can easily result merely because of differing defaults in the software.

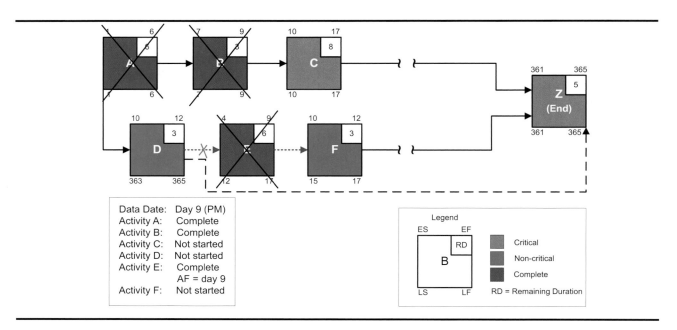

Figure 13-13 Impact on Total Float - Progress Override Option

Conclusion

The process of updating the project schedule will result in changes to activity float. Also, activities may not always be performed in sequence. The importance of knowing the default settings of the scheduling software is especially apparent in the schedule update process. Progress will not always go exactly according to plan. Activities performed out of sequence may be calculated using either retained logic or progress override options. There will be major differences in total float values for some activities, depending on which of these options is used. It is important to recognize what process is being used before attempts at analysis are made or false conclusions could result.

Chapter 13 Review Questions

13-1.   List four key inputs needed on a schedule update to allow accurate current status reporting.

13-2.   A schedule has been updated to reflect current project status. One particular activity was reported as starting 5 days late, but its total duration has been shortened by 2 days. Before the update, this activity had 11 days of total float. How much float does it have now?

13-3.   What happens when activities have status reported that indicates they were performed out of sequence?

13-4.   Explain the "retained logic" method for addressing activities worked out of sequence.

13-5.   Explain the "progress override" method for addressing activities worked out of sequence.

13-6.   Does it matter which of the two options (progress override or retained logic) is used within a scheduling software program? What are the implications for schedule analysis?

13-7.   Why does remaining duration provide better information regarding schedule status than percent complete?

True or False

13-8.   Reported schedule status is always as of the "time now" date.

13-9.   For forecasting purposes, for an activity in progress as of the "time now" date, the actual start date is more important than the remaining duration.

13-10.   Once an actual date has been reported, the previously calculated early dates and late dates lose their significance.

13-11.   An actual start date can be chronologically later than "time now".

13-12.   With the "retained logic" option for handling activity status reported out of sequence, the out-of-sequence activity cannot be completed until the predecessor has been completed.

13-13.   The main reason for needing to know the software default for out-of-sequence status is its impact on schedule analysis.

The answers to these questions can be found in Section 6, Solutions.

Case Study

13.1 ANALYZING THE SCHEDULE

A critical path method scheduling system is being used to control a manufacturing application. The area of greatest interest is contained in the schedule fragnet shown below that depicts the key activities in the manufacture of 200 identical electronic assemblies.

Activity	Description	Duration	Total Float
A	Design assemblies	80	12
B	Assemble	32	12
C	Wire	32	12
D	Install assemblies in frames	40	12
E	Checkout	30	12
F	Ship	2	12

Activity A is complete and was completed on schedule.

Answer the following questions:

1. Activity B was completed in 40 days. What is the revised total float for activities C through F?

2. On the next schedule update, activity C is 50% complete and has required 9,000 hours to date by using 50 people working 8 hours per day. It is determined that any benefits from the learning curve have already been realized.

    a. What are the forecast total hours for this activity?

    b. If staffing for activity C were maintained at 50, what is the forecast duration?

    c. What will this do to the total float?

    d. The baseline schedule for activity C was based on an estimate of 64 man hours per unit, but the experience from the first 50% has indicated 90 hours per unit is required to complete wiring. The supervisor in charge of wiring has indicated that similar performance can be expected for the remaining duration of the activity. Should the schedule be statused using the baseline estimate of the actual experience to date? Why?

    e. How much would staffing need to be on activity C to complete it within its allowed 32 days, assuming additional staff would not affect productivity rates?

    f. What other alternatives could be employed rather than increasing staffing for wiring?

The solution to this case study can be found on the Humphreys & Associates, Inc. web site.
www.humphreys-assoc.com

Chapter 14

Schedule Changes

Objectives of this Chapter:

1. Discuss reasons for schedule changes.
2. Describe the difference between routine updates and baseline changes.
3. Discuss considerations in determining whether schedule changes are "significant".
4. Define "work-around" plans and what might be changed in a project to implement one.

As discussed in the last chapter, the very act of incorporating actual progress to the schedule results in variances to the original plan. These variances do not mean that the plan must be changed, since the update is just a snapshot of where the project is versus where it should be according to the baseline plan. This updated information can then be used to better manage the effort. Some of the questions to be asked are: will more or fewer resources be required? Has a risk event occurred? Is a strategy change warranted? What specific project components are varying and why? However, other changes occur besides update status. Project scope, for example, has a tendency to change over time, even in the best-defined and managed projects. Regulatory requirements change, economic conditions change, and even technical objectives may change because of advances in technology during the life of the project. One of the biggest problems on long term design projects is that the hardware and software planned for use may become obsolete before they are installed. This condition can be aggravated when a project is extended or delayed, allowing more time for technological breakthroughs.

There are other reasons for change: the owner/customer may decide to revise the completion date based on changing need for the product,

cash flow considerations, or because of revised corporate strategy. Any of these reasons should result in an approved change to the original schedule and cost baseline since the original plan is no longer valid. Also, scope changes may occur as detailed items, perhaps overlooked during the early project definition, are included. That is why, in the first step of the entire project management process, the need for careful work definition was stressed.

This chapter only addresses schedule changes and how they need to be included in the analysis and management process. A more comprehensive view of the entire change control process is covered in Chapter 34, "Baseline Revisions and Change Control."

No matter how skillful a project manager may be, the project will be impacted by changes. There are generally a minimum of two schedules that are actively being maintained during the life of a project. They are most commonly referred to as the 'current' and 'baseline' schedules.

Not all changes to the schedule are handled the same way since some are just a result of the normal update process and are applied regularly to the current schedule. Others are revisions to the approved plan and are made, with the required approvals, against the baseline schedule.

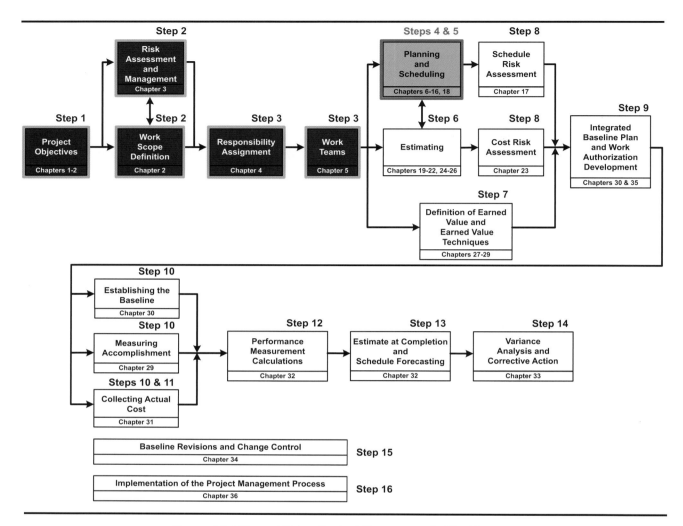

Figure 14-1 Earned Value Project Management: The Process

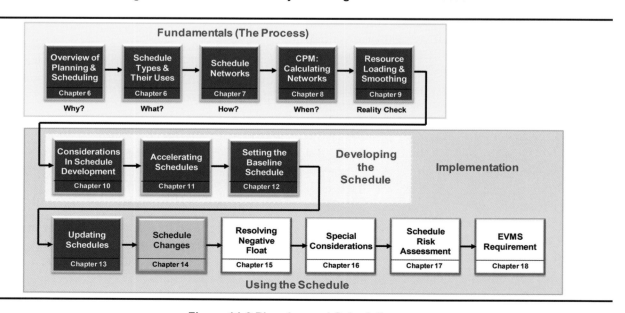

Figure 14-2 Planning and Scheduling

Routine updates to the current schedule result from recognition of status, progress, and forecast information. Examples are the reporting of completed activities, reported status of partially completed activities, and new estimated start or finish dates for those activities not yet begun. Other changes might result from schedule optimization and may involve activity resequencing resulting in changes to the Estimate at Completion (EAC) or changes to coding classifications. These changes might also necessitate similar modifications to the baseline schedule.

There are certain circumstances when the baseline will be modified. If the project scope were changed and activities added, deleted, or modified; when rolling wave planning takes place and future planning packages are converted to detailed work packages; and when Management Reserve or Undistributed Budget is applied to the schedule, then the baseline schedule will be changed. All of these situations require formal authorization and change management. Any changes to the baseline are duplicated and updated in the current schedule. The two schedules must remain synchronized to allow the measurement of the current against the baseline schedule.

The schedule data base generally contains schedules other than the current and baseline. These are usually historical versions of schedules archived at the end of a week, month or some significant time in the life of the project and stored for reference or backup. Additionally, 'what-if' schedules that explore alternate schedule strategies may also become part of the stored schedules in the data base. These schedules are usually stored in another area of the server commonly referred to as a "sandbox". Experimental or "what if" schedules have solved significant execution problems and/or have incorporated such extensive scope changes that they have replaced all or part of baseline schedules following review and approval.

Duration Changes

There are two categories of duration changes: duration changes for activities in progress and changes for future activities. Each has different considerations. For activities in progress, duration changes are a part of the normal update process and are represented by changing the remaining duration of the activity. However, changes to durations for future (not yet started) activities should not be made unless a valid reason can be demonstrated. These types of changes may be legitimate updates to the network or they may be unauthorized attempts at hiding true schedule status. The circumstances surrounding the future change are the key to the decision whether to change a future duration. Duration changes in the future caused by scope of work changes or other owner/customer approved direction represent baseline changes.

Adjusting duration for currently active tasks is simply a reflection of experience to date. A serious judgment error occurs when the two, current and future durations, are used in tandem to cancel each other out. This occurrence is easy to see for two activities on the critical path. If an activity with zero float were extended by two weeks, the total float on the critical path would decrease to a negative 2 weeks. If a future activity along the same path were shortened by two weeks, the effect would be to return the total path length to the original value and the float would now be zero weeks again. This practice is a flagrant misuse of the CPM scheduling technique and can discredit and invalidate the effort spent to create and maintain the schedule.

Consider this example. A very large network, consisting of approximately 30,000 activities, was being updated monthly. It was apparent that current activities were slipping, yet somehow the total float always remained zero. That the float was exactly zero made it seem more than a little suspicious, so the schedule was investigated by the owner/customer. Closer inspection revealed that when an update was made, the total float became negative. So the scheduler would find an activity on the critical path six years in the future and shorten it by the exact amount of the critical path slip. This action by the scheduler would adjust the report back to zero total float, and who was going to notice it in that giant schedule? When confronted on this topic, the contractor replied, "Who is to say that we can't shorten that activity by 4.2 weeks? We will expedite it to the best of our ability. Besides, it isn't hurting anything now." It was at that moment that the owner/customer realized the value of having a network change report, one that would compare the activities in the current schedule with the previous one and identify the activity durations that were changed. This exception report could then be used to verify legitimate changes and isolate the suspicious ones. Maybe the future activity could be shortened, but the contractor was not performing any meaningful analysis to justify the actions taken. All that was happening was a loss of visibility resulting in a loss of credibility.

Network change reports can be generated using different techniques in the major schedule software packages. One technique involves saving the current schedule prior status/progress/forecast update and then using an internal or external process to compare the newly updated current schedule against the saved schedule. Results can be produced in tabular or graphical form clearly exposing, on an exception basis, activities that have their major attributes modified, such as dates, durations, resources, etc.

Measuring Schedule Status

How is schedule status determined? The most obvious answer is by managing total float and its variances; how much did float change and why? However, there are other factors to consider. For example, total float is an excellent measure of the activities that are influencing the completion date of the project and how well they are progressing. It is not a good measure of overall activity completion. But there needs to be some other quantifiable measure of that status. This topic will be addressed later in the chapters on performance measurement when some additional measures of schedule status that do a precise job of measuring schedule performance are defined and explained. The point to be made now is that total float is a very important measure of schedule status, but it is not the only one, nor does it give the best picture of overall schedule performance.

Defining Significant Changes

"Significant" is a relative term. A two day schedule slip is significant if there are only two days of float available. On the other hand, a four-week

slip may not be significant if there are 50 weeks of float available and the activity is intentionally being delayed to smooth the resource profile. Thresholds need to be set during the schedule planning process to define "significant" so that management can be alerted whenever that threshold is crossed.

An absolute statement is that the frequency of the update cycle has a bearing on what is considered significant. An activity will lose as much float as the passage of time if there were no reported progress; i.e. an activity with no progress during a four-week month will lose four weeks of float. Therefore any activity that has less total float than the frequency of the update cycle must be considered significant. The activity would have negative float on the next update if no progress were recorded. Attention must be paid to its progress now; that example sums up what "significant" is. Other definitions of significant schedule delay are possible as related to earned value status; these are discussed in Section 4.

Recording the Changes

From a record-keeping standpoint, all changes are significant. This is true at least until the project has been completed, any claims resolved, and the contract is closed. Documentation of changes can be the single most critical factor for success in a legal proceeding. Having documentation that identifies what changes occurred, when they were made, what their impacts were , and even who made them, is often the crucial factor in determining who or what was at fault for delays and the associated costs.

Schedulers should avail themselves of the 'notes' fields that are available for each activity in contemporary scheduling software. The 'notes' field will contain an audit trail of explanations related to the use of directed dates, lags, modified activities and the reasons, dates and the names of the individuals that authorized the changes. Standards for inserting notes should be developed in the schedule planning document since the notes fields are generally unformatted text fields. Project managers should ensure that the standards are followed from project commencement, since there is discipline required to record the information in the level of detail required to make it useful.

Similar to the real estate mantra of location, location, location, the project management mantra should be document, document, document. Humans have short memories, scheduling software when properly maintained, has a much longer, and more reliable one.

Work-Around Plans

When changes to the project schedule begin to threaten established contractual milestones, a "work-around" plan becomes necessary. The plan consists of finding a different way of accomplishing the same objectives whenever the current schedule begins to vary too much from the baseline. There are three generally recognized work-around plan strategies:

1. Relax the technical specifications.
2. Reallocate resources.
3. Change the network logic.

Reallocation of resources could mean shifting resources from the future to the present to accelerate progress, or adding additional resources.

Of the three approaches listed above, the third is the least painful. Changes to the logic are schedule/sequencing changes rather than real project scope changes. In many cases, a logic change is possible because the original logic developed was too conservative for execution. The most common example, frequently occurring in engineering and design projects, is to wait for all information about preceding activities to be complete before beginning any work on succeeding activities. It may be possible, however, to begin some of the successor activities with only partial information. Doing so allows those activities to be executed in parallel, or at least overlapped, with their former predecessors. This strategy shortens the associated activity paths and saves project time. However, there is a potential for prematurely starting successor activities before their predecessors are complete, thus raising the risk of re-work or an "out of sequence" message from the scheduling software. In this example, modifying the network to reflect a start to start

relationship instead would eliminate the "out of sequence" warning.

Work-around plans to resolve scheduling problems sometimes are ingenious. One electric power cogeneration project had such a tight schedule that it was all but impossible to find an engine (diesel generator) in the total time allotted for design and construction of the project. The project was schedule-driven, meaning that schedule considerations were the driving force in decisions between schedule and cost. Since the only manufacturer who could support the schedule was overseas, and the delivery time by barge made it impossible to meet the schedule, the plan was revised to construct the generator on the barge as it was in transit. The remainder of the construction would proceed in parallel and the barge was transformed into a floating electric generating plant. This approach significantly shortened the schedule from what it would have been for a land-based operation.

Another example of a work-around plan occurred during the construction of a church near Jacksonville, Florida. The foundation had been completed and the parking lot was in place. When the contractor began to dig the trenches to allow for drainage for the new parking lot, an Indian burial ground was discovered. This meant a minimum of a five-week delay while artifacts were recovered and relocated. Rather than delay completion of the project by five weeks, the decision was made to redesign the parking lot so that it would slope in a different direction. This allowed the drainage trenches to be located elsewhere and the Indian burial ground to remain undisturbed.

Work-around plans are generally developed using 'what-if' schedules. A what-if schedule is usually a copy of the current schedule modified with the proposed activities, resources and logic to mitigate a technical problem or a schedule slip. Various scenarios can be played out with data transfer to the project cost system to gauge the impact to cost that the schedule changes will incur. Once management has approved the changed schedule, the changes can be rolled into the current schedule or the entire what-if schedule can replace the current schedule as long as the current schedule was 'frozen' during that process. Depending on the nature of the changes, the baseline schedule may have to be modified also.

Baseline Changes

It is important to distinguish between routine schedule changes and baseline changes. Routine changes are applied against the current schedule, and the scheduling software automatically calculates revised start and finish dates and float values. However, as identified in Chapter 12, the baseline schedule will not change unless one of the following six conditions exists:

1. The schedule is impacted by approved scope changes.

2. The project is delayed or accelerated or other owner/customer direction is received.

3. Rolling wave planning takes place where planning packages are converted to detailed work packages.

4. Management Reserve or Undistributed Budget is applied to the project and scheduling adjustments result.

5. When the schedule is replanned within the existing budget based on updated knowledge of the scope, project conditions, new ideas, etc.

6. When unrecoverable slippage has occurred, with owner/customer approval.

The first five reasons make perfect sense when the owner/customer authorizes approved changes to the scope or if the project dates are changed by direction of the project manager or owner/customer. The last reason is the difficult one: when unrecoverable slippage has occurred. To prevent abuse, this last option must be tightly controlled. The control prevents changing the schedule simply because the project is late. In some circumstances, replanning the schedule to a new completion date will make the schedule data meaningful again and the schedule a more useful management tool. The project manager and the owner/customer must approve this schedule change.

Changes to the baseline must also be reflected in the current schedule since that is where the work in process is statused. Generally, the order of schedule changes is that the current schedule is changed first and then the changes are copied to the baseline, after approval. In any event, a complete record of all changes must be retained, generally until contract close, and an electronic history of all baselines and key current schedules should be maintained on or off line.

Conclusion

Many sources and types of changes occur during the life of a project. One of the main challenges, besides controlling the number and size of the changes, is to distinguish between those that are revisions to the original approved plan, scope changes, and those that are merely part of the normal update process. Approved changes in scope are reflected in both the baseline and the current schedules. Routine updates are made to the current schedule. Routine updates may result in a forecast slippage in the project completion date, with the resultant need to implement "work-around" plans to recover the indicated delay. The intent is never to revise the plan to match performance, but only to revise it to reflect the actual scope and execution of the project. A record of these changes must be kept, since they may be a critical part of future analysis.

Chapter 14 Review Questions

14-1.   Differentiate between current schedule updates and baseline changes.

14-2.   Why should baseline changes be treated differently than current schedule updates?

14-3.   Should activity duration changes for activities in progress be handled differently than duration changes for activities not yet started? Why?

14-4.   Why does the frequency of the schedule update cycle have an impact on the definition of "significant" as it applies to total float?

14-5.   What are the three most common approaches for "work-around" plans that must be implemented when contractual milestone dates cannot be met?

14-6.   List the 5 conditions that could initiate a schedule baseline change.

True or False

14-7.   Routine updates result from scope changes.

14-8.   Shortening future activities can eliminate negative float on the critical path.

14-9.   Adding or deleting activities is always considered a baseline change.

14-10. Total float is one of the best measures of schedule status.

The answers to these questions can be found in Section 6, Solutions.

Case Study

14.1 ANALYZING SCHEDULE CHANGES

A network schedule was prepared for a small project. Figure 1 shows the network logic as well as the activity names, durations, current schedule starts, and current schedule completions. This case concerns time analysis only.

In the normal course of business, additions were made to the original scope of work. As scope was being added, the project was also progressing. Reported status is shown in Figure 2.

1. Based on the combination of reported status and additional scope/activities, the overall project completion date has been delayed from August 15th to December 5th based on the latest forecast dates.

    Your assignment is to determine how much of this forecasted 80-day slippage is because of additional scope and how much resulted from delay in completion of activities.

2. The analysis required to answer question 1 above will result in identifying only a portion of the 80-day slippage. There is another impact besides the two contributors listed in question 1 above that will account for the balance of the 80-day slippage. What caused this additional slippage?

Essential information to address these questions is contained in Figure 3, which is a comparison report between the original baseline schedule and the current schedule.

The variances between baseline and actual start dates and finish dates have been calculated and appear in the two rightmost columns. As an example, the start variance for Activity A is displayed as zero days. That is because the baseline start and actual start were the same (May 5). The finish variance is 5 days, which means that there was a slip of 5 working days (one calendar week). For activities that were added as new scope, an "n/a" appears in the baseline columns since they were not part of the original baseline schedule. The revised network logic is also included in Figure 3.

The solution to this case study can be found on the Humphreys & Associates, Inc. web site.
www.humphreys-assoc.com

Figure 1 Part 1 of 2

Activity ID	Duration (Days)	Current Start (mm/dd)	Current Finish (mm/dd)
A	1	05/05	05/05
B	5	05/08	05/12
C	3	05/15	05/17
D	6	05/18	05/25
E	12	05/18	06/02
F	2	05/26	05/29
G	9	06/05	06/15
H	3	05/08	05/10
I	4	05/11	05/16
J	7	05/05	05/15
K	5	05/16	05/22
L	5	05/23	05/29
M	3	06/16	06/20
N	35	06/21	08/08
O	5	06/16	06/22
P	5	06/16	06/22
Q	5	06/16	06/22
R	5	06/16	06/22
S	5	06/16	06/22
T	8	06/23	07/04
U	3	08/04	08/08
V	5	08/09	08/15

Figure 1 Part 2 of 2

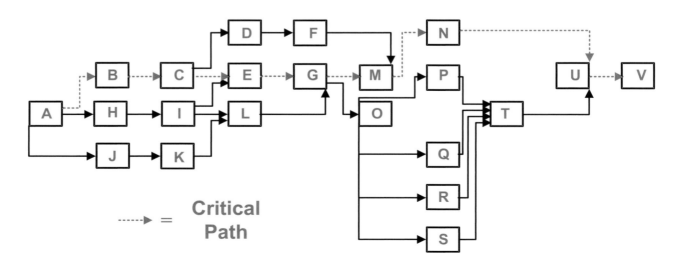

------▶ = Critical Path

Figure 2

Name	Actual Start (mm/dd)	Actual Finish (mm/dd)	% Complete	Actual Duration (days)	Remaining Duration (days)
A	05/05	05/12	100%	6	0
B	05/15	05/26	100%	10	0
C	05/29	06/01	100%	4	0
D	06/02	06/13	100%	8	0
E	06/02	07/07	100%	26	0
F	n/a	n/a	0%	0	2
G	07/10	n/a	33%	5	10
H	05/18	05/18	100%	4	0
I	n/a	n/a	0%	0	4
J	05/05	05/11	100%	5	0
K	n/a	n/a	0%	0	5
L	n/a	n/a	0%	0	5
L1	n/a	n/a	0%	0	4
L2	n/a	n/a	0%	0	2
M	n/a	n/a	0%	0	3
N	n/a	n/a	0%	0	35
N1	n/a	n/a	0%	0	18
N2	n/a	n/a	0%	0	12
N3	n/a	n/a	0%	0	10
O	n/a	n/a	0%	0	5
P	n/a	n/a	0%	0	5
Q	n/a	n/a	0%	0	5
R	n/a	n/a	0%	0	5
S	n/a	n/a	0%	0	5
T	n/a	n/a	0%	0	8
U	n/a	n/a	0%	0	3
V	n/a	n/a	0%	0	5
V1	n/a	n/a	0%	0	6

Figure 3 Part 1 of 2

Name	Current Start (mm/dd)	Current Finish (mm/dd)	Baseline Start (mm/dd)	Baseline Finish (mm/dd)	Start Variance	Finish Variance
A	05/05	05/12	05/05	05/05	0	5
B	05/15	05/26	05/08	05/12	5	10
C	05/29	06/01	05/15	05/17	10	11
D	06/02	06/13	05/18	05/25	11	13
E	06/02	07/07	05/18	06/02	11	25
F	06/14	06/15	05/26	05/29	13	13
G	07/10	07/28	06/05	06/15	25	31
H	05/15	05/18	05/08	05/10	5	6
I	05/19	05/24	05/11	05/16	6	6
J	05/05	05/11	05/05	05/15	0	-2
K	05/12	05/18	05/16	05/22	-2	-2
L	05/25	05/31	05/23	05/29	2	2
L1	06/01	06/06	n/a	n/a	0	0
L2	06/07	06/08	n/a	n/a	0	0
M	07/31	08/02	06/16	06/20	31	31
N	08/03	09/20	06/21	08/08	31	31
N1	09/21	10/16	n/a	n/a	0	0
N2	10/17	11/01	n/a	n/a	0	0
N3	11/02	11/15	n/a	n/a	0	0
O	07/31	08/04	06/16	06/22	31	31
P	07/31	08/04	06/16	06/22	31	31
Q	07/31	08/04	06/16	06/22	31	31
R	07/31	08/04	06/16	06/22	31	31
S	07/31	08/04	06/16	06/22	31	31
T	08/07	08/16	06/23	07/04	31	31
U	11/16	11/16	08/04	08/08	74	74
V	11/21	11/21	08/09	08/15	74	74
V1	11/28	12/05	n/a	n/a	0	0

Figure 3 Part 2 of 2

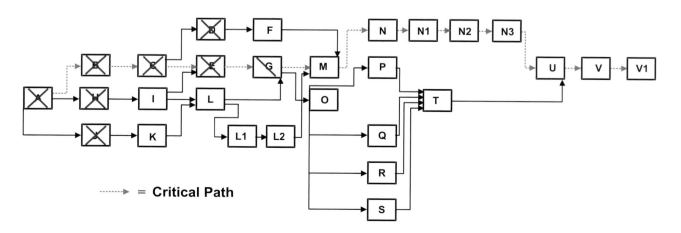

------▶ = Critical Path

Chapter 15

RESOLVING NEGATIVE FLOAT

Objectives of this Chapter:

1. Introduce exception reporting for schedule data.

2. Discuss how to analyze total float.

3. Learn the approach to resolving negative float in CPM: isolating the causes of float deterioration, assessing the impact, and determining resolution alternatives.

4. Consider multiple formats for monitoring the trend of total float and overall schedule status.

Many textbooks and courses address the subject of CPM networks and how they are calculated. That, of course, is the most fundamental need for new schedulers. However, other topics become much more important once a scheduler starts working with actual projects. None of these is more important than the question of how to resolve negative float. Once negative float appears in a network, which usually happens even as the initial baseline schedule is being developed, there is an issue to resolve.

Negative float means that the project end date or major milestones cannot be met based on the current plan for accomplishing the work. If the project end date or milestone dates are important (and they always are if a schedule were being used), that requires the scheduler to identify the cause of the negative float, note its impact, and recommend possible solutions.

The resolution of negative float is such a key activity that it is cost effective to spend as much effort as possible avoiding the condition in the first place. Consequently, analysis of float trends while they are still positive takes on importance. This chapter will address that topic and then explain how to analyze the condition when negative float occurs in spite of best efforts being made on a project.

Before the main topic of this chapter is examined, it is first necessary to consider how float is reported and analyzed. It is better to avoid the negative float condition in the first place than to be adept at resolving the problem. By regularly employing schedule health checks, as discussed in Chapter 10, Considerations for Developing a Useful, Quality Schedule, schedulers will be able to recognize and even mitigate negative float conditions early.

Float Analysis at Status Update

As each new update occurs, there are reams of possible report data that could be produced. Producing the right information to be distributed to the relevant members of the project team and management requires understanding of their roles and the data. Always remember that a schedule is primarily a communication tool. It is also important to note that scheduling does not end with production of reports. Schedulers are in one of the best positions to analyze facts to a conclusion and to present recommendations to take advantage of favorable variances as well as to mitigate unfavorable ones.

Questions need to be asked about what is happening to total float each time there is an update,

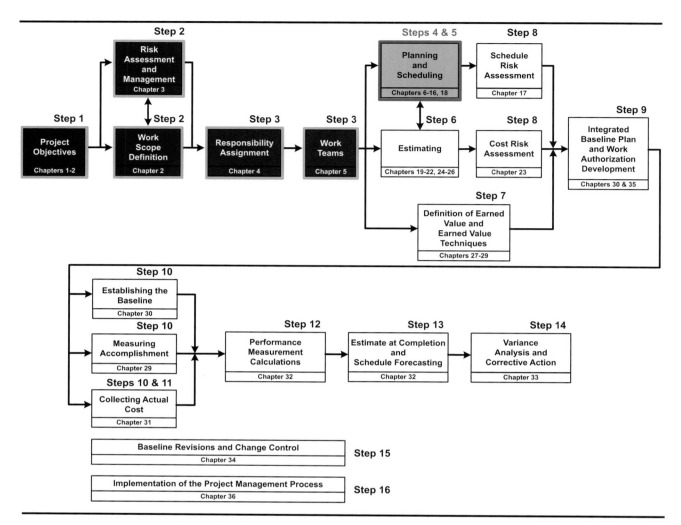

Figure 15-1 Earned Value Project Management: The Process

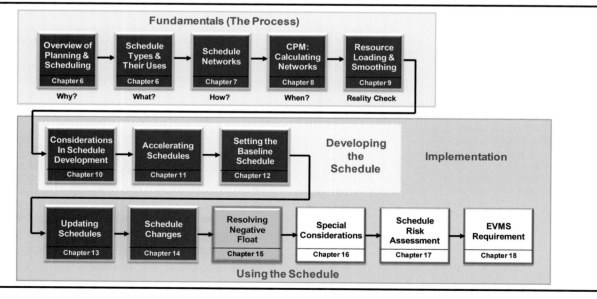

Figure 15-2 Planning and Scheduling

since total float gives the quickest picture of critical changes on an exception basis. The following questions should be routinely investigated each time:

1. What are the activity paths with the lowest float?

2. Is the trend improving or deteriorating on these paths?

3. Which activities are causing the problem?

4. Why are those activities in trouble?

5. What can be done to resolve the problem?

The first place to look is in the total float report. This standard report is available in any automated scheduling system, and it should be sorted by total float listing the most critical activities first. Although it may take some additional effort, it is worthwhile to maintain the results over the previous six update periods in another file to be able to see the trends in float. The length of each period will vary depending on whether the company policy is to update the schedule weekly, semimonthly or monthly. These two types of reports are discussed on the following pages.

A Total Float Report typically contains much more information than just the total float, but that is the key column of information and the basis for any numerical sorts. Both float value extremes on this report should be checked. The lowest float activities are important for obvious reasons, but what about the high float values? Activities with high float are also important to check because they reflect conditions that may not be correct in the network file.

If there were an incorrect logic tie, or no tie, or a logic tie is made to the end of the project rather than developing the intermediate logic, the result will likely be a very high float value. In many instances, float reports with activities that show hundreds of weeks of supposed total float, the real story has been found to be that the logic is incomplete or incorrect. This warrants just as much attention as critical activities. After all, these dangling activities may be critical, but that is unknown since they are not properly tied in the logic.

Figure 15-3 illustrates the type of information that will help analysis of network status. This is a variation of the Total Float Report that would contain only the first column of information shown here. This Figure illustrates the float for the current month (July). The additional columns allow trend analysis by observing what has happened over the past five months.

With this additional input, it can be seen that activity path B, while carrying a -3.1 weeks float, has actually improved slightly over the past four months. Path E, on the other hand, has +2.1 weeks of float but has steadily deteriorated over the pictured interval and is likely to become negative soon if the cause of the slip is not identified and addressed.

Path	Current Month July (weeks)	June (weeks)	May (weeks)	April (weeks)	March (weeks)
A	-4.2	-3.1	-2.7	-0.5	0.0
B	-3.1	-2.0	-2.5	-4.0	-4.0
C	-1.7	+1.7	+1.7	-1.0	-0.5
D	+0.2	+1.9	+1.5	+1.9	+1.9
E	+2.1	+3.0	+3.5	+3.8	+4.0

Figure 15-3 Trend in Float by Path

Isolating the Cause of Float Deterioration

Once it has been determined that certain activity paths are slipping and using up their available float, further analysis should be conducted. The initial review should be conducted by the scheduler. However, the scheduling group alone should not do the analysis of float, because the problems might be strictly technical in nature. The overall project team needs to participate in the review, with the scheduler/team preparing the initial analysis. The scheduler takes initial responsibility because it is possible to catch items such as an inaccurate update, a data entry error, or an incomplete update in which some of the status may have gone unreported. These types of systemic errors are best caught and corrected before they are exposed to the entire project team.

Note that this discussion directs attention to analyzing an activity path rather than each activity. That is because total float is shared along a path and a reduction in float in one of the activities will result in an equal reduction for every other activity along the path. What needs to be compared when trying to isolate the cause of float loss? At a minimum the following must be compared:

- Baseline vs. current start date (Start Variance).

- Baseline vs. current duration (Duration Variance).

- Baseline vs. current completion date (Finish Variance).

All of these facts should be considered because a variance in any one of these comparisons will change the float value, reducing it if project activities are slipping. A sample of a report that provides this type of information is shown in Figure 15-4. In some schedule software, 'traffic light' indicators can be set to adhere to user-set thresholds to allow rapid determination of issues requiring further analysis and correction. In this example, a red flag indicates a current schedule slip from the baseline, green means the current is ahead of schedule, and yellow a user-defined warning of the current approaching baseline values.

The report shown in Figure 15-4 can be a very useful format. Each update of the schedule causes the start and finish dates to move within the current plan, but the real question is how is progress compared with the approved baseline plan?

This report immediately provides that information. It compares the start and completion dates (actual or forecast) with the baseline start and completion dates. This analysis also allows the actual duration to be compared with the baseline duration. Ordinarily, this information can be better presented in a graphical format, with the baseline dates drawn on a bar chart in one color and the current file dates drawn immediately above it in another color. This provides an instant picture of how many activities have slipped or advanced versus the original plan. So why use a chart like the one shown here? The answer is that it is easier to deal with when there are thousands of activities to compare.

Activity	Baseline Start	Current Start	Start Variance	SV Ind	Baseline Finish	Current Finish	Finish Variance	FV Ind	Baseline Duration	Current Duration	Duration Variance	DV Ind
A4000	Jan 28	Apr 04	49 days		Mar 21	Jun 26	68 days		39 days	59 days	19 days	
A4200	Apr 07	Mar 26	-8 days		Jul 31	Aug 19	12 days		82 days	81 days	-1 day	
A4400	Apr 04	Apr 08	2 days		Jul 01	Jul 29	18 days		62 days	66 days	4 days	
A4600	Apr 04	Apr 15	7 days		Oct 30	Aug 01	-63 days		147 days	75 days	-72 days	
A4800	Mar 10	Mar 26	12 days		Oct 29	Jul 14	-76 days		165 days	57 days	-108 days	
A5000	Mar 03	Apr 23	37 days		Jan 30	Sep 26	-82 days		228 days	110 days	-118 days	
A5200	Oct 31	Oct 31	0 days		Nov 06	Nov 06	0 days		5 days	5 days	0 days	
A5400	Nov 07	Nov 07	0 days		Jan 14	Dec 05	-21 days		40 days	20 days	-20 days	
A5600	Feb 04	Dec 08	-36 days		Feb 27	Jan 07	-37 days		18 days	17 days	-1 day	

Figure 15-4 Baseline vs. Current - Date and Duration Variances

It is not enough to pinpoint the activity slip that caused the float reduction. Questions need to be asked, and answered, such as: What caused the activity to slip? Did it take longer than planned, and if so, why? Were there sufficient resources? Was there a technical problem that delayed the activity regardless of the priority assigned to the activity?

Float will decrease or may even be entirely eliminated if critical activities are delayed. However, it is not always that simple. Sometimes a delay would not have had major impact if the logic had been more accurate. A common problem is that the initial logic, and maybe even the baseline plan, uses "nice to have" logic rather than "need to have" logic.

It would be nice if everyone had everything they could possibly need before starting an activity, but it is almost always possible to begin with just partial information. This converts finish-to-start activities to finish-to-finish activities and start-to-start activities. This also shortens the total schedule. Negative float may be caused simply because of the network structure. There may be "hard" logic ties that are not necessary. This becomes obvious when the network updates start revealing examples of activities completed out of sequence. If a successor activity were completed while a prior restraint was not, then the previous activity was not a requirement and the logic is wrong. Or, one might conclude that a successor activity completed out of sequence introduces risk to its predecessor. Why? Because an activity completed out of sequence creates a potential for rework.

Another possible cause of schedule delay is changed market conditions. If the economy suddenly accelerates, there may be a shortage of labor and/or material that could cause competition for resources and/or elongate lead times. Another common source of delay is difficulty in resolving comments on vendor drawings, impacting release for fabrication. This can delay the start of integrated design. Design changes also may occur, which result in new activities not in the original schedule logic. These changes can result in a confusion of priorities if the critical path changes as a result of the design changes.

Late receipt of information among contractors or between a supplier and an engineering firm may have schedule impacts. This is especially difficult to resolve, since it shifts blame among contractors or among departments within a single organization. Without careful coordination and expediting, a project can deteriorate to a finger-pointing exercise among different companies.

Another reason that float may become negative is from any fixed date that is imposed on the network. This may be an intermediate milestone, an interface point between organizations, or a contract required date. It may also be an arbitrary date imposed by management to force a schedule to be an aggressive schedule. In each of these cases, negative float does not necessarily indicate a project end date slippage. If the date has been arbitrarily imposed, it is probably advisable to allow the negative float to exist rather than expend additional resources unnecessarily to "resolve" the condition.

Sometimes the cause of the float problem is simply a matter of errors in input. This is one good reason why the scheduler should make the first pass through the network reports to determine as much background as possible before meeting with the various project disciplines. This not only eliminates trivia such as errors in update from the discussions, but also allows the scheduler to determine possible alternatives to recommend for technical consideration. Meeting time can then be used productively to discuss acceptable resolution alternatives rather than investigating a data dump of reports.

Impact of the Delay

After the root cause of the schedule delay has been ascertained, an identification of the impact and an assessment of it are needed. This is accomplished by identifying the specific items that will be delayed. This is information readily retrievable from any CPM system and will allow a conclusion as to whether or not these items are truly needed. Some input will probably not be ready for a succeeding milestone or activity. The consequences of not having the complete information needed can then be evaluated.

It may be that the identified impact, per the schedule reports, can be avoided altogether by redoing the logic to more accurately reflect the actual project conditions. This refers back to the earlier discussion of "nice to have" logic versus "need to have" logic. If the float problems are because of input errors, there may be no impact to the schedule once the errors are corrected.

Resolution Alternatives for Negative Float

There is no single approach to resolving negative float that will work universally. Each case must be analyzed on an individual basis, since the alternative resolutions will be dependent upon the cause of the slip. Some possible solutions include:

1. Expedite critical activities.

   This choice is the most obvious one. This solution can be accomplished by adding staff or by expediting the source of the delay. Examples are assigning additional people to problematic activities or assigning an expeditor to a vendor that is not meeting schedule promise dates. Both of these actions will increase project cost, so implementing either or both must be a carefully evaluated. It is not always necessary, or even preferable, to resolve a schedule slip through use of additional resources, since other recovery options exist. Reference Chapter 11, Crashing the Network, for further information.

2. Revise the schedule logic.

   While the last option was the most obvious, this is the one that should be investigated first. Why expend additional resources if a logic change will solve the problem? Check the logic for "soft" ties, ties that are not really required but are there because an activity needs to be tied somewhere. All activities in a logic network will usually be tied somewhere so that activity paths can more easily be analyzed. If a product were not needed to support any additional activities, it should be tied to the project completion. How-

ever, this may result in large positive float values.

The second instance of logic revision involves a check of sequential activities to see if they could be completed in parallel, either partially or fully. This is not meant to be a random overlapping of activities that should have been performed in sequence, but rather a close look at the logic to see what the actual needs are and if any acceleration in downstream activities can logically take place.

3. Redefine procurement packages.

   This is a creative solution used when the interface between engineering and construction becomes a problem. In the second chapter of this book (relating to work scope definition), the interface problem that occurs at the design/construction interface was discussed. "Product User Mapping" was recommended to improve this interface definition (see Figure 2-18). This mapping identifies all of the work products needed for a particular contract. When negative float occurs, it could be because one of the work products will not be available when needed for its associated contract.

   One alternative solution is to remove that work product from the contract in question and plan a supplemental issue to the bid package for later drawings. This allows more time (i.e. float) for completion of the drawings. A more drastic solution is to change the scope of the contract, removing the offending work product from the scope of work for that contract and placing it in a later contract. Any contract change must be negotiated with the owner/customer; however, these issues should be brought to the attention of the owner/customer early as other potential solutions may be ascertained.

4. Reschedule or use the built in schedule margin.

   The schedule margin was discussed in detail in Chapter 10, Considerations for Developing a Useful, Quality Schedule.

As a reminder, the schedule margin is a buffer of time usually built into a schedule and is under the control of the project manager. If the delay exceeds the schedule margin and the completion date cannot be met, one alternative is to slip the completion date. This is the easiest solution in all cases, but also the least desirable. In some instances, slipping the completion date may be the only choice. An example would be when a slippage occurs early in the project and a proposed resolution is developed, but the cost of the revised plan is greater than the cost impact of the slipped date. In that case, the preferred solution is to delay completion.

5. Consider an Over Target Schedule (OTS).

If all other options have been considered without relieving the negative float problem, the only option remaining would be to implement the Over Target Schedule (OTS). The OTS is an established baseline schedule that extends beyond the contract completion date. An OTS requires the prior coordination or approval (as applicable) of the owner/customer. Care should be taken to identify the specific negative float causes and jointly developed remedies to provide confidence in a new plan and schedule.

6. No action.

Another possibility is to leave the condition as is. The impact may be minor enough that replanning is not needed, and it is possible that future progress will recover the slip.

In any event, each month (or each larger or smaller reporting period update), variances will need to be tracked. One way of reporting the status and following it is shown in Figure 15-5.

The report shown in Figure 15-5 can be a very powerful report format to use for effectively monitoring project status in a monthly report or similar information vehicle. It can be used to address all negative float paths. Remember, total float is shared among all activities on an activity path, so it is not necessary to analyze each individual activity with negative float. In this report, the negative float item is described as well as the float value. The cause of the float problem is then documented concisely in the next column, and its impact listed in the following column. Most importantly, a column is provided for resolution of the item. This can also allow documentation of follow-up on prior months' negative float items by maintaining them on this report until resolution.

A report such as the one illustrated in Figure 15-5 can be used very effectively to close the loop between old variances and their current status and resolution. The key is the last column on the right. If every variance were addressed with a statement such as "engineering to resolve" with no subsequent follow-up, all that would be accomplished is the development of a well documented set of project problems for an auditor to find.

This scenario actually happened on a project. Everyone on the project team had scrupulously analyzed each month's reports and the variances indicated on them to document what was occurring on the project. Unfortunately, the engineering department put a great deal of effort into identification of the impact but paid little attention to the "Resolution" column. Over time, the list of problems that said "Engineering to resolve"

Item	Negative Float Items	Float (weeks)	Cause	Impact	Resolution
1	ABC2365- Conduit Layout Plan of Auxiliary Building	-4.5	Last Issue of Flue Gas Instrument Piping Diagram delayed	ABC2365 will not be available for Bid Package Issue	Issue ABC2365 as part of a supplemental Bid Package subsequent to issue for bids

Figure 15-5 Resolution Alternatives

became formidable. At about that time, an external agency audited the project. The auditors were very impressed with the project control systems and how well things were organized and documented. They were far less impressed with all of the unresolved problems.

When the auditors launched a series of questions at engineering, engineering suddenly realized it was time to "shoot the messenger". While there were other factors involved, it was not long after that the report was discontinued. Of course, this is not a recommended solution since the problems and engineering's inability to solve them were simply removed from view. The project schedule continued to deteriorate as the unresolved problems mounted.

Float Analysis by Project Team

There are many ways to evaluate schedule status and whether it is improving over time or not. Besides the indicator of total float, there are other trends that can be reviewed. Among these are the following:

- Most critical activity or activities based on lowest float.
- Number of critical activities.
- Trend of total float.
- Average total float.
- Number of activities on/behind schedule.
- Product counts.

Figure 15-6 shows only the most critical activity's total float on the project for that particular month's update. It can be seen that between February 1 and March 1, there was an acceleration of 1.8 weeks accomplished on the most critical activity (31712). However, while this activity was being expedited, another activity (29788) was being ignored. It lost at least 2.5 weeks of float during March, since it was at -4.2 weeks as of April 1 and was -1.7 weeks or better as of March 1. This is known since the worst activity on March 1 was only -1.8 weeks. During May, this activity recovered all of its slippage and the project had no activities with negative float.

Month	Activity No.	Description	Total Float (weeks)
Feb 1	31712	-----	-3.6
Mar 1	31712	-----	-1.8
Apr 1	29788	-----	-4.2
May 1	34311	-----	+0.2
Jun 1	34311	-----	+1.5

Figure 15-6 Analysis - Most Critical Activities

The status of the critical activities improved further still during June, as the worst activity gained 1.3 weeks during the month. A whole story of project status emerges from this small chart.

Another trend is shown in Figure 15-7. This graph tracks the number of critical activities from one month to the next, with "critical" defined by the user. The definition of critical must remain the same from month to month for the trend to have any meaning.

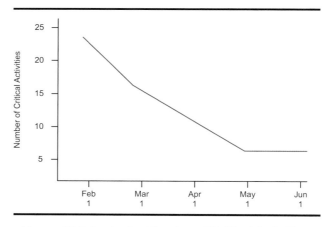

Figure 15-7 Analysis - Number of Critical Activities

However, the project may be nearing completion, so the number of critical activities could be reduced by the reduction in the remaining work. At the end of the project the number of critical activities will be 0.

Total product counts, while primitive in their simplicity, do provide a look at what is occurring in the total network file rather than just with the critical activities. These statistics can be tracked as shown in Figure 15-8.

Date	Cum. Schedule	Cum. Actual Complete	Variance Complete
Feb 1	168	2	-166
Mar 1	352	155	-197
Apr 1	505	397	-108
May 1	712	656	-56
Jun 1	886	893	+7

Figure 15-8 Analysis - Number of Activities On or Behind Schedule

An easier way is through schedule variance (SV) or schedule performance index (SPI) that will be discussed in Chapter 32. The type of information expressed by product counts can be more completely represented if totals are kept as shown below.

Total Drawings	762
Scheduled to Date	485
Completed to Date	470
Quantity Early	20
Quantity Late	35

To make the information more useful, product counts may be grouped by engineering discipline (i.e. mechanical drawings, electrical drawings, civil drawings, etc.). The objective of counting items such as drawings (or specifications or tests performed) is to allow an overall measure of schedule status that supplements the critical path information. This presupposes that each product is of approximately equal value in terms of labor hours required to complete.

These types of counts are unnecessary when earned value reporting (see Chapter 27, Earned Value) is used. However, in the absence of earned value, this approach at least supplies additional information to provide a more clear understanding of status. For example, if 318 drawings have been completed but only 273 were scheduled to be complete, the project is 45 drawings ahead of schedule. But if the critical path shows -6.2 weeks of total float, a great deal of work has been done on the wrong drawings. The measurement of scheduled versus completed activities is one of the schedule health checks discussed in Chapter 10, Considerations for Developing a Useful, Quality Schedule. The Baseline Execution Index could be grouped by discipline to provide this information.

Conclusion

The intent of a baseline schedule is to have a defined plan to follow for management of the project. An automated scheduling system produces a significant amount of data, so it is helpful to prepare and distribute exception reports that allow rapid identification of variances. As deviations occur and if actual progress falls behind the plan, the correct response is to find ways to change the trend in order to support the plan. The best way is to first isolate the cause of float deterioration, which means identification of the root cause of any schedule slip. After the cause has been determined, the impact of the slip should be described. Next it is crucial to uncover as many resolution alternatives as possible, limited only by the creativity of the project team. It is possible that the cost of the best solution is higher than the cost of the impact of the schedule slip. Circumstances such as this suggest that no action be taken and the slip be allowed to occur.

Preventive action is still preferred to the crisis management that often occurs after negative float appears. Therefore, it is always a recommended course of action to address decreasing float conditions while they are still positive. Trends should be closely watched and activity paths with low values of float analyzed and addressed with the same care as negative float paths.

Chapter 15 Review Questions

15-1.   List at least three considerations that should be evaluated when schedule total float reports are issued. Specifically, what should be investigated?

15-2.   Why should activities with very high values of positive float be investigated at all?

15-3.   Should every activity with low/negative float be investigated, or just every activity path? Why?

15-4.   In determining the cause of lost total float, baselines should be compared against what three pieces of information in the current network file?

15-5.   Provide five methods that can be used to eliminate negative total float.

15-6.   Once the cause of float deterioration has been confirmed, what are the next steps to be taken?

15-7.   Identify one way to determine overall schedule performance that can be combined with the total float information to get a more accurate picture of overall status.

True or False

15-8.   Float analysis should be conducted by the scheduling group alone.

15-9.   A comparison of baseline total duration versus current duration will provide information about changing values of total float.

15-10.   If the duration of an activity on the critical path were reduced by one week, the project end date will be forecast to be one week earlier (assuming no other changes).

15-11.   Total product counts, scheduled versus actual, provide a form of schedule performance.

15-12.   Since the critical path method is a form of management by exception, there should be no real concern until after activities have total float values that are negative.

15-13.   One approach to resolving negative float conditions is to see if the logic can be restructured so that more sequential activities are converted to parallel activities.

The answers to these questions can be found in Section 6, Solutions.

Case Study

15. 1 RESOLVING NEGATIVE FLOAT

In the schedule activity path in the figure below, the total float (that is shared among the activities) has dropped to -4 work days during the current update cycle. The full logic of the network is not shown, only part of it.

Activity D ties into activity E (not shown) and the path continues to the end of the project. Activity path A-B-C-D is the only path for which you are responsible that is currently negative. You are the lead scheduler and you must come up with recommendations as to how this negative condition can be solved.

Answer the following questions:

1. What does the negative total float for this path indicate?

2. What options do you have to return this path to zero float? Explain how your recommendations will solve the negative float condition.

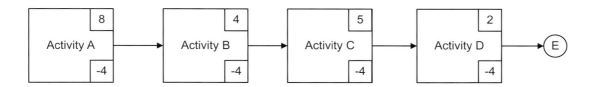

Legend

All durations are in work-days.

The solution to this case study can be found on the Humphreys & Associates, Inc. web site.
www.humphreys-assoc.com

SPECIAL NETWORKING CONSIDERATIONS

Objectives of this Chapter:

1. Describe the impact of Not-Earlier-Than and Not-Later-Than constraints and Imposed directed dates applied to both activity starts and finishes in a critical path network.

2. Define 'soft' and 'hard' constraints and explain the implications of both on the schedule.

3. Explain the concept of secondary float and how it relates to total float.

4. Calculate critical path in a network of parallel, start-to-start and finish-to-finish relationships.

5. Explain the "hidden opportunity" often contained in a network of SS-FF relationships.

6. Define approaches for addressing network activities for support functions (such as supervision, administration, etc.) within a CPM.

7. Explain schedule considerations involved with the working calendar.

Many scheduling fundamentals have been presented and explained in the preceding chapters. There are, however, a number of special conditions that need to be understood before CPM analysis is complete. This chapter presents conditions that alter the normal interpretation of CPM output. It also considers cases that may provide problems for some scheduling software packages.

A thorough discussion of network calculations is not complete without recognition of several special calculation considerations. If these problems are ignored, analysis is affected and potential solutions to problems may be missed. More importantly, opportunities for improvement to the quality of the schedule may be overlooked. These considerations include the topics of directed dates, secondary float, and the effect of parallel start-to-start and finish-to-finish relationships in the network. However, there are some schedule software programs that cannot calculate the last factor of dual overlapping activity relationships.

Other concerns relate to the treatment of level of effort activities in a network. These are ongoing support tasks such as supervision, coordination, and contract administration that extend over the entire duration of the project or just selected phases of the project.

Directed Dates

Directed dates refer to any date limitations imposed on the calculation of the critical path network. Specifically, these refer to the following restrictions:

- Not Earlier Than (NET) dates impact the forward pass calculation only.

- Not Later Than (NLT) dates impact the backward pass calculation only.

- Imposed dates (ON) supersede network calculations.

Directed dates are sometimes called by other names such as "constraints", "target dates", or "required dates". By whatever name, their func-

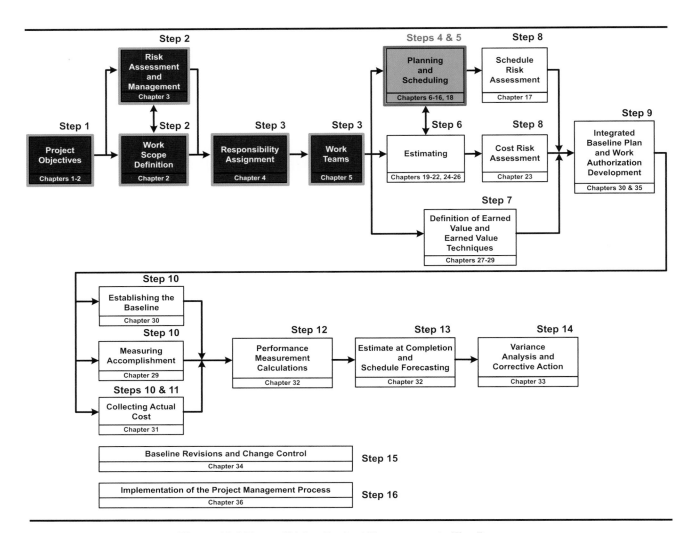

Figure 16-1 Earned Value Project Management: The Process

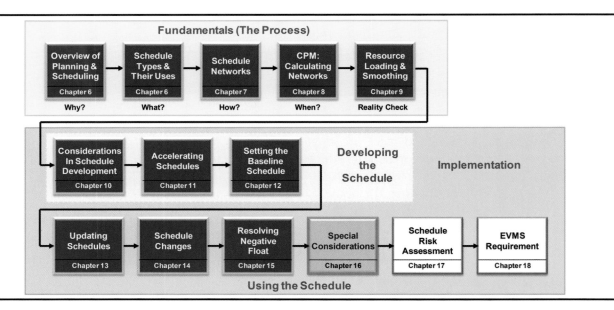

Figure 16-2 Planning and Scheduling

tion is the same. They put artificial limitations on when certain activities can start or finish. These limits can be placed on the beginning or end of any activity.

Not-earlier-than (NET) dates mean that an activity cannot start or finish any earlier than a specified date, no matter what the previous calculations indicate. These constraints are usually used to show availability of critical personnel or material to the project, such as Customer/Government Furnished Equipment (CFE/GFE), software drops, material deliveries or availability of key personnel. In-bound actions to the project that are to occur at a planned time are candidates for this constraint. As will be seen, these dates only affect the forward pass calculation that determines early start and early finish dates.

Other types of constraints, collectively referred to as Not-Later-Than (NLT) constraints, assign dates to the schedule showing when an activity cannot start or finish later than a specified date. These dates affect the backward pass that develops the late finish and late start dates. Example uses of these date constraints include contractual delivery dates, program reviews and other major program events. In general, NET constraints help the schedule show what is possible in the schedule, and NLT dates help the schedule show what is necessary.

These classes of date constraint are usually referred to as 'soft' constraints, because they help inject reality into the schedule without causing the network logic to break to achieve the goals of the constraints. Used in moderation, soft constraints provide the realistic finishing touches to a schedule with specific possibilities and necessities. For example, where negative float exists, a conflict exists between what is possible and what is necessary. This conflict must be addressed before the schedule can be considered a realistic plan.

A third general type of date constraint is grouped under the classification of imposed date (ON) constraints. These constraints are used in both the forward and backward pass of the schedule calculations and can completely supersede network calculations and distort the true critical path. These constraints are usually referred to as 'hard' constraints.

Before reviewing some of the more common directed dates, it is essential to draw attention to the following: this discussion should be considered to be one of a general nature. The treatment of some constraints may vary from one scheduling product to another. Further, it is possible (but not likely) that the constraints definitions or their operation may be modified in a new software release by a vendor. It is essential to fully understand the operation of the software being used to be able to accurately gauge the impact of any directed date on the schedule. It is also important to know that some directed dates directly impact the critical path by forcing the network logic to break the honoring of the constraint date.

Some software allows the imposition of deadline dates that are not listed as constraints but may well act as constraints. It is important to understand how the software tool in use handles the various constraints and deadlines imposed. Date constraints that may cause this condition are referred to as 'hard' constraints because they have the ability to modify the logic and thus reduce flexibility of the schedule to accurate portray the critical path. The use of 'hard' constraints is considered bad practice and thus restricted by most prime contractors and government oversight agencies such as the Defense Contract Management Agency (DCMA).

To illustrate how date constraints affect the scheduling calculations, begin with the Start Not Earlier Than constraint. Figure 16-3 shows an example of the impact of a Start Not Earlier Than date. Activity A is a build and is followed by two activities, both have finish-to-start relationships with the first. However, activity B is a test activity and will have to be delayed until the arrival of test equipment. Thus, the test will be prevented from starting by a Start Not Earlier date.

There is an alternative to a directed date in this example. A milestone, "deliver test equipment", could be inserted in lieu of a directed date. Using the milestone to position the remaining logic could be preferable to a constrained date. It would contain a directed date constraint, but the reasoning for the constraint would be obvious, as shown in Figure 16-4.

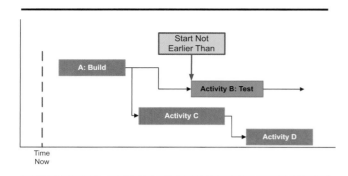

Figure 16-3 Start Not Earlier Than Constraint

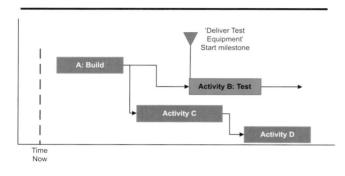

Figure 16-4 Delayed Activity Using a Milestone

Regardless of how the Start Not Earlier Than constraint is applied, it will only affect the early dates and will have no further impact if activity A's finish extends beyond activity B's delayed start date, as shown in Figure 16-5. This is why it is considered a soft constraint. It will not break the logic of the schedule, but will be ignored once its usefulness has expired.

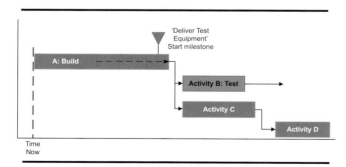

Figure 16-5 Start Not Earlier Than Constraint Bypassed

Another alternative to provide a delay in a schedule would be the use of a Schedule Visibility Task (SVT). An SVT is non-contract, outside work required to be performed before contractual work

can be performed such as a facility conversion, team partner effort, government review of documents, etc. In this example, an activity is assigned to represent the development and delivery of test equipment. Because the activity represents outside effort, it could be an example of a Schedule Visibility Task (SVT). However, if an SVT or a delivery milestone were used to show the reason for the delay, as in Figure 16-6, it must be statused as any other activity with the latest forecast to the anticipated delivery date, or with actual start and finish dates to show the completion of the delivery.

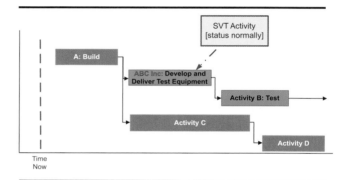

Figure 16-6 Delay Using a Schedule Visibility Task

What calculations are made in the scheduling program to determine the total float as a result of the use of date constraints? Figure 16-7 displays a bar chart for a small project and will be used to illustrate the process. The bar chart is a time-based representation of a network where 6 activities (A through G) have been planned in series and one activity (Activity C) is planned to start after activity A and conclude before activity G. Focus on Activity C because it is the least critical activity. Not only does it have 15 days of total float, but it is all free float.

The start and finish dates in the following examples are represented by day numbers rather than calendar dates, therefore weekends, holidays, and other calendar specifics are not considered. Critical activities are colored red and the non-critical activity is green. These are the early date bars. The black bars represent the late dates and are shown immediately below the early date bars.

Without any directed dates, Activity C can begin no sooner than day 6, but could start as late as

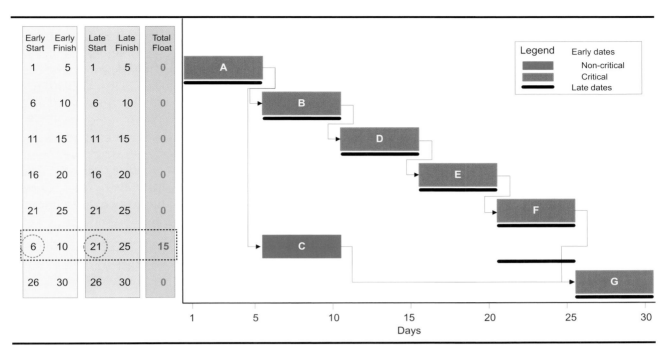

Figure 16-7 Small Project Bar Chart

day 21 and still support the finish date. This is why the total float value equals 15 days. What happens when some arbitrary constraints are imposed on Activity C?

As proposed above, the desire is to delay the start of an activity until an external event, such as the delivery of materials, can occur. In Figure 16-8, Activity C must be delayed until day 10 when the materials are expected to arrive. A Start Not Earlier Than date of day 10 is placed on the start of C. The early start date is moved from day 6 to day 10, and the early finish from day 10 to day 14. The late dates stay the same. This has the effect of lowering the total float from 15 days to 11 days.

In another case, Activity C represents the completion of essential documentation that must be delivered to a contractor (link not shown) and the 'drop dead' date is day 21. The work must be complete by the end of day 21 but it can be completed earlier. By placing a Finish Not Later Than constraint on the activity, it can be seen that the late dates have been affected so that the late finish is day 21 and, thus, the late start is now day 17. The early dates remain the same. This results in a diminished total float for the path from 15 days to 11 days. A similar result could be obtained by placing a Start Not Later Than constraint on the late start instead. See Figure 16-9.

If the project calls for an activity to take place on a specific date, such as a non-moveable visit by the president of the corporation, then an imposed date could be used. If the visit activity is Activity C, observe what happens if a must start date of day 10 is imposed on it, as shown in Figure 16-10. Both the early and late start dates become day 10. But based on the way that total float is calculated, late start minus early start, that means TF = 0. Activity C, the least critical activity in the network, now shows as a critical path item. Of course there really are 11 days of float available to C, but because of the directed date, the software now treats it as a critical item.

What would happen if another hard constraint, Must Finish On, is applied on an already critical activity? Figure 16-11 shows the result of the imposition of a must finish date of day 18 on activity E, two days earlier than originally forecast. Without constraints, the early and late finish dates for activity E were day 20. The result was a projected earlier finish for the project but a -2 day total float for all activities prior to E. This date constraint also had a far more serious impact.

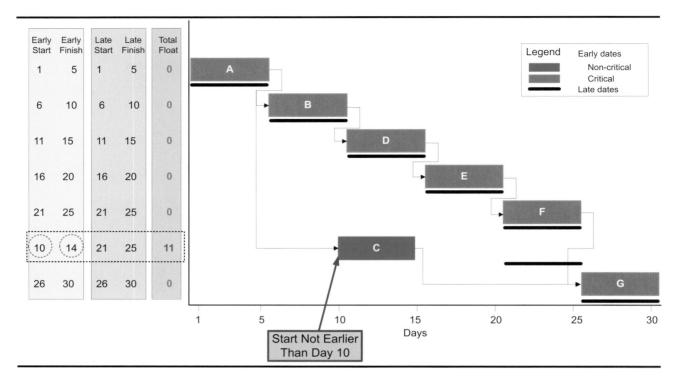

Figure 16-8 Start Not Earlier Than Constraint

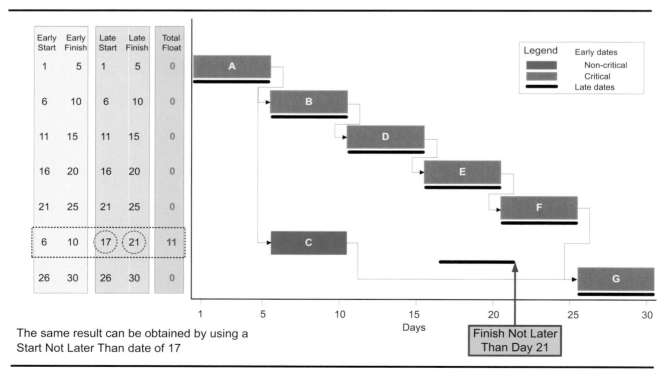

The same result can be obtained by using a
Start Not Later Than date of 17

Figure 16-9 Finish Not Later Than Constraint

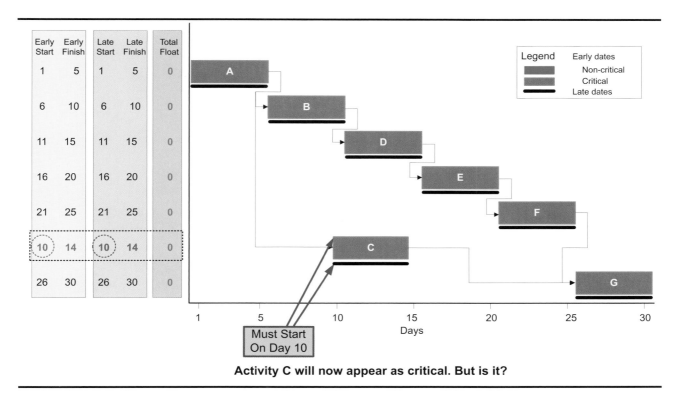

Early Start	Early Finish	Late Start	Late Finish	Total Float
1	5	1	5	0
6	10	6	10	0
11	15	11	15	0
16	20	16	20	0
21	25	21	25	0
10	14	10	14	0
26	30	26	30	0

Must Start On Day 10

Activity C will now appear as critical. But is it?

Figure 16-10 Must Start On Constraint

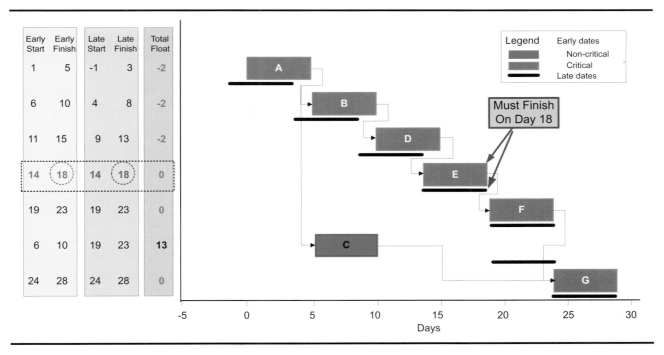

Early Start	Early Finish	Late Start	Late Finish	Total Float
1	5	-1	3	-2
6	10	4	8	-2
11	15	9	13	-2
14	18	14	18	0
19	23	19	23	0
6	10	19	23	**13**
24	28	24	28	0

Must Finish On Day 18

Figure 16-11 Must Finish On Constraint

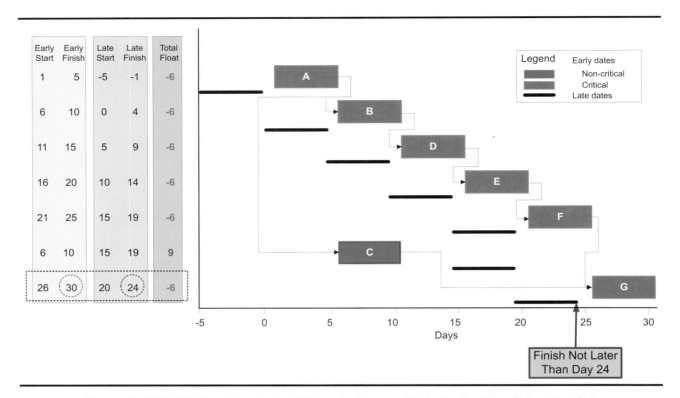

Early Start	Early Finish	Late Start	Late Finish	Total Float
1	5	-5	-1	-6
6	10	0	4	-6
11	15	5	9	-6
16	20	10	14	-6
21	25	15	19	-6
6	10	15	19	9
26	30	20	24	-6

Finish Not Later Than Day 24

Figure 16-12 Finish Date Constrained Network - Imposed Date Earlier Than Calculated Date

The logic flow on the critical path was interrupted at activity E breaking the integrity of the network; Activity E now overlaps its predecessor, activity D. The possibility of resolving the schedule delay would be further diminished if the same resource were assigned to both activities since the resource would be overloaded by the parallel tasks.

Under certain circumstances, a target date may be set on the project. The project manager may have been given a customer required date for the project delivery. The initial project bar chart shown in Figure 16-7 shows a projected completion of day 30.

But when the customer demanded a delivery by day 24, the impact was that the float on all the activities was reduced by 6 days. Figure 16-12 shows that the critical path TF became negative. This means that the desired earlier completion will only become feasible if drastic action is taken, everyone has to work faster, possibly work overtime or otherwise expedite their activities. Replanning must occur to determine how or whether the new goal can be achieved.

Logic might have to be changed to either overlap work or to perform the work in parallel and that would only be possible if permitted by the nature of the work. However, only those activities on the critical path are candidates for replanning and subsequent schedule modification. No other activities contribute to the late condition because of the flexibility.

What about positive critical path float? Can there be this condition? Of course, setting the finish date for the project after the early finish date, this condition is created. Now all activities and paths have positive float, thus increasing the flexibility.

Figure 16-13 displays a generalized spectrum of constraints. It is ordered in the preferred use of the constraints, their impact to the flexibility of the schedule, from soft to hard constraints and many other key variables including total float. The constraints shown in the figure are not contained in every scheduling product; they may work similarly but be differently named. Hard constraints are those where the fixed dates have been included as a result of events that are mandated, such as government reviews.

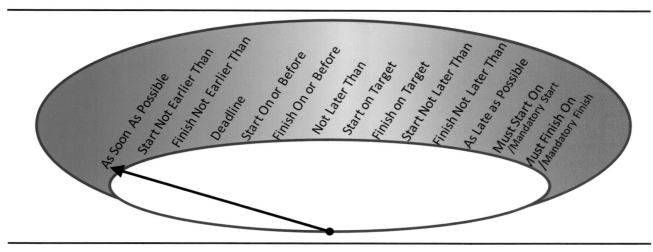

Figure 16-13 Constraint Date Spectrum

There are different degrees of 'hardness' that become increasingly more restrictive on the schedule as the gauge moves into the red zone. Hard constraints will impact the calculation of the total float and reduce the schedule's ability to correctly forecast a feasible finish date.

Some scheduling programs support the deadline constraint. This constraint is preferred by the DCMA over some of the hard constraints such as Finish Not Later Than or Must Finish On. Through the careful setting of some of the schedule program's parameters, the Finish Not Later Than constraint can be made to perform like the deadline constraint and thus be in compliance with the DCMA's practices by maintaining schedule logic. [Note: As of the date of this publication, the National Defense Industrial Association (NDIA) is in the process of developing an IMS Scheduling Guide that will define best practices for schedulers and schedules. The information contained in this figure may vary slightly from that publication.]

Directed dates should not be applied until the initial network is developed. It is important to develop the initial baseline without constraints to test its realism and to ensure that the constraints will be able to be met. Once constrained, if negative float were created, the logic may have to be re-visited, durations reduced or the project descoped (with owner/customer concurrence and contract modification) in order to honor the commitments. An abuse of directed dates is to use them as an anchor or to fix dates instead of using proper logic.

The conclusion is that directed dates can be used to make any activity in the network look critical. This manipulation of the real status means that directed dates should be strictly limited to important milestones. Excessive use of directed dates would greatly distort the status picture and confuse decision making. Because of their importance to analysis, a separate list of directed dates should be maintained, and all activities with a directed date identified as such within the file. Information on the origin and reason for the insertion or change of each directed date should be recorded in the 'notes' field of the schedule to assist in tracing the critical path.

Why have directed dates at all? Certain key events are fixed in time and that should be reflected in the schedule. These dates include the overall start and completion dates for the project. Contract milestones, such as major design review dates, are also valid uses of the directed date. Major contractor interface points can also be assigned a directed date since coordination may be a challenge. That one contractor is delayed because another is not complete becomes a matter of concern and could become the subject of a claim. For outdoor construction projects, seasonal considerations may merit use of a directed date. An example would be that excavation work must be completed before the rainy season.

Ambient temperature becomes a factor as well in extreme climates. One construction project in northern Ontario, Canada, had a directed date that the main buildings had to be enclosed by December 1. That was necessary since there was much concrete work to do, and it would have been impossible to place and cure concrete cost effectively with ambient air temperatures as low as minus 40 degrees. If the building were not enclosed by December 1 (allowing temporary heating), the project would have been closed down until spring. This proved to be quite an accurate date, since severe weather set in on December 3 and did not improve for months.

Secondary Float

Total float and free float have already been defined, but now a third type of float enters the picture. Secondary float is similar to total float, but it is calculated from an intermediate event rather than from the project finish date. Directed dates can cause secondary float to become an important consideration. The project end date is not affected, but intermediate dates are. Figure 16-14 offers another sample network that will be used to clarify the difference between total float and secondary float. The total float values are

illustrated for each activity. There is no secondary float, because there are no directed dates.

But now in Figure 16-15 an incentive finish date of day 15 has been placed in the network as shown. The "incentive" finish date may have been entered by the project manager to encourage completion of certain activities deemed to be technically high risk thus leaving some cushion to rectify any issues. A Finish Not Later Than date of 15 entered as the late finish changes the calculated dates for the activities shown in the dashed line box. The area of impact is strictly limited to those activities contained within the outlined box.

Comparing Figure 16-14 versus Figure 16-15 demonstrates how the total float and secondary float values compare for the same activities before and after the imposition of the incentive finish date. The comparative results are shown in Figure 16-16. Interpreting these dual floats is straightforward. When an activity in the path has a total float of 17 days and a secondary float of 3 days, it means that this particular activity may be delayed (or stretched) by a maximum of 17 days before it impacts the overall project completion date. However, it may only slip by 3 days before impacting the incentive finish date.

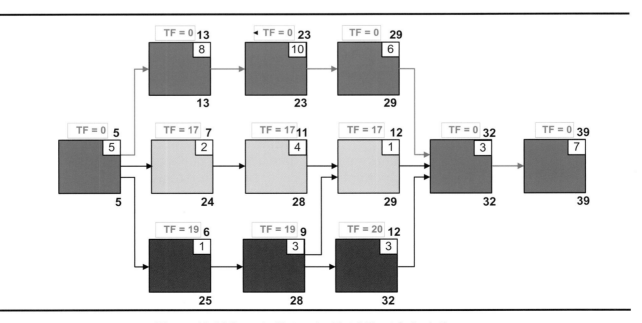

Figure 16-14 Sample Network - Total Float Calculations

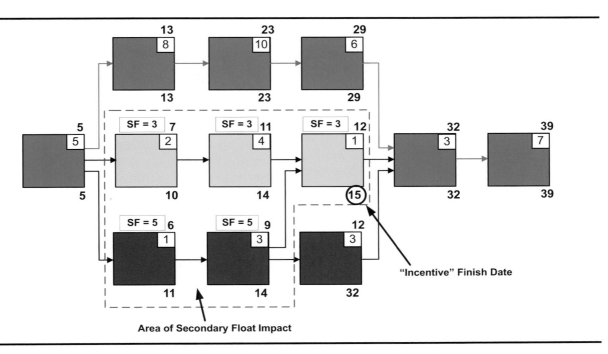

Figure 16-15 Comparing Total and Secondary Float

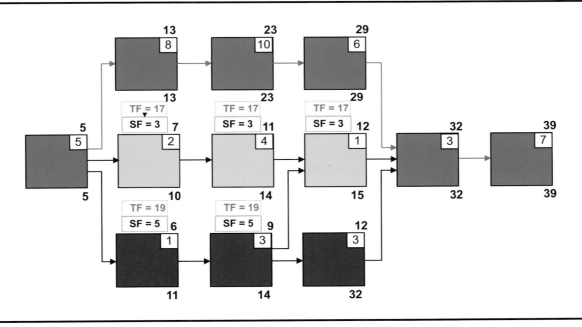

Figure 16-16 Total Float vs. Secondary Float

Most software packages are only able to calculate and retain two types of float, although three types (total, free, and secondary) are addressed in this text. If intermediate dates are inserted, such as the incentive milestone in the example, the secondary float will replace the value of the total float while still being called total float. In effect, the program treats it as a new project finish date for that activity.

Parallel SS/FF Relationships

The mechanics of how leads and lags are processed in CPM was discussed in Chapter 10. It was also noted that some scheduling software does not permit multiple relationships between activity pairs and thus these parallel relationships cannot be applied.

Parallel start-to-start and finish-to-finish relationships between the same two activities introduce confusion. An example demonstrates how confusion can manifest itself. A simple three activity network is used with some fairly elaborate relationships, as shown in Figure 16-17. Activity B is start-to-start with Activity A, but with a two day lag. That translates into B cannot start until two days after A starts. This does not mean that B does start two days after A, just that it cannot start any earlier than that. The finish-to-finish relationship between A and B features a three day lag, meaning, B cannot finish until at least three days after A finishes. These lags, or lag factors, are used for offsetting parallel activities that do not start and finish together.

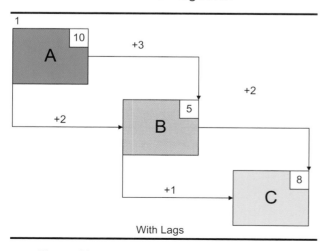

With Lags

Figure 16-17 Parallel, SS/FF Relationships 1

To calculate the early dates, the forward pass is performed for this network. If A starts on day 1, B cannot start until day 3. Since the duration for B is 5 days, the early finish (EF) for B is day 7 (end of day). That addressed the start-to-start path between A and B, but what about the finish-to-finish path between A and B?

Looking at the other part of the relationship, it is known that Activity A will not finish until day 10 because of its 10 day duration. The 3-day lag between the finish of A and finish of B states that B cannot finish until at least day 13 (three days after day 10). Since B is five days long, the ES for B becomes day 9. The problem is that these calculated dates conflict with those calculated from the start-to-start relationship. Which one rules? The situation is depicted in Figure 16-18.

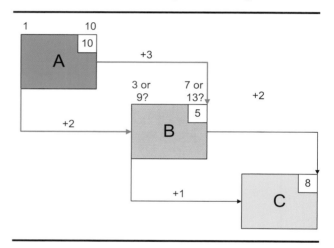

Figure 16-18 Parallel, SS/FF Relationships 2

The solution is a simple one, but many schedule programs will not allow multiple relationships between the same two activities for this very reason. The solution is the same as seen in earlier chapters for the forward pass calculation. When two paths converge on a single activity, the later date is always selected on the forward pass. Once again, the rule makes sense in this application according to the logic. While B may start as early as day 3, it cannot finish before day 13. If the duration is to be maintained as 5 days, the later dates must be chosen so that the finish date will not be before day 13.

The same situation arises with the second part of the network; there is inconsistency, and once

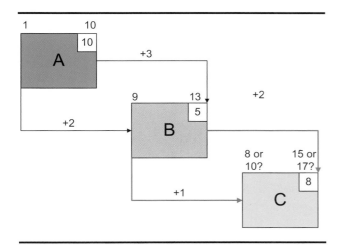

Figure 16-19 Parallel, SS/FF Relationships 3

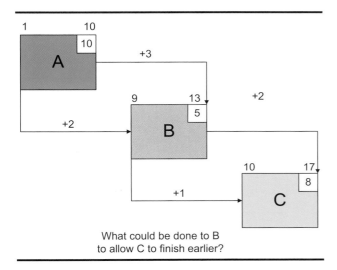

What could be done to B
to allow C to finish earlier?

Figure 16-20 Parallel, SS/FF Relationships 4

again the late date must be selected. This scenario is pictured in Figure 16-19.

This creates a situation where the software produces an inferior result from a project standpoint. The late dates must be chosen over the early dates for the reasons explained, but there is an opportunity to complete this mini-project earlier without changing the logic. The situation is pictured in Figure 16-20. This is a trick question, but it has a valid solution. Look at the figure to find the opportunity.

Actually, something odd has to be done to accomplish this feat of CPM trickery. If Activity B is lengthened by two days, the total project is shortened by two days. This happens because

the dates for Activity B are driven by the finish-to-finish relationship from Activity A. If B is lengthened by two days, B can start two days earlier (the end date is fixed). Starting B two days earlier allows C to start two days earlier because of its start-to-start relationship. Activity C, unlike B, has its dates driven by the start-to-start relationship because that link yields the later dates. So starting C two days earlier also means finishing C (and the project) two days earlier. In this unusual case, lengthening one of the activities shortens the project.

There is also a point to be made about this example: avoid applying too much logic to any series of activities. Imagine trying to explain this logic to a non-scheduler. In addition, someone attempting to use the schedule may become disillusioned as well as confused. Then, the use of a schedule as a communication tool is defeated.

Level of Effort

Level of effort (LOE) activities are those that do not result in a specific end product or deliverable item. Examples of LOE activities include administration, coordination activities, supervision, and so forth. These activities, when included in CPM networks, are likely to confuse the analysis by creating additional critical paths besides the "real" critical path. This result is inevitable since most LOE tasks continue for the total duration of the project, and some beyond the final deliverable. Since the critical path is defined as the longest path, all or many of the LOE activities will suddenly appear as separate critical paths. The situation is depicted in Figure 16-21.

One possible resolution is to leave LOE activities completely out of the network file, and many companies do just that. However, if a resource loaded schedule is used (as is required for a valid baseline), an important part of the budget is missing. This may amount to as much as 25-30% on some complex design projects.

Another solution being adopted by some companies is to detach LOE task(s) from the network by adding independent start and completion activities as shown in Figure 16-22. A positive aspect of this method ensures that the LOE activity will never become part of the critical path since it is

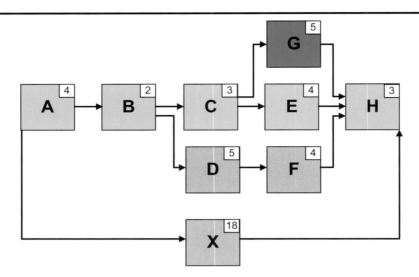

Activity X is Project Management

Figure 16-21 LOE Example

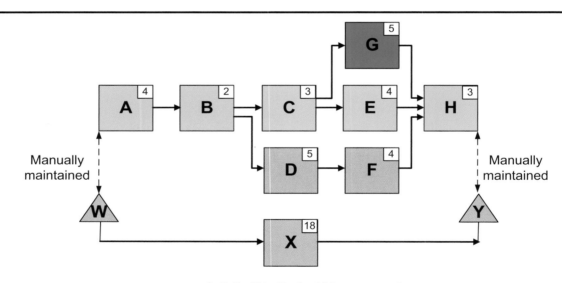

Activity X is Project Management

Figure 16-22 Alternate LOE Solution

not attached to the network. However, it should be noted that the one activity start and one activity end network rule would be broken and that network delays or advances would necessarily demand manual adjustments to the independent LOE path.

Recommended Solution

Because LOE activities continue for the duration of the project, some adjustments must be made to save continual warnings of false critical paths.

There are two possible recommendations: (1) designate the activity with a special code that isolates it as an LOE activity and then exclude all LOE activities from float reports, or (2) shorten the duration of all LOE activities by one day so that they will no longer be recognized as "critical path". The latter solution may require more maintenance if the project lengthens or shortens as a result of bad or good progress.

Because of the need to include all of the resources in a network schedule, one of these solutions is suggested rather than deleting all LOE activities. Solution 1 is better because all entries that are coded as LOE can be ignored in analysis. Even if LOE activities are shortened by one day (solution 2), they will still appear as near critical paths that demand attention.

In either solution, do not connect the LOE tasks to any discrete project milestone or event to avoid the possibility that the LOE task could accidentally drive the critical path of the project.

Calendar Considerations

Calculations of activity durations and float paths are affected by the chosen calendar. If multiple calendars are specified, which is common, network calculations are further complicated. The first question relates to defining activity durations. How many hours are there in the standard day? Is there more than a single shift? How many work days are there in a week? Current creative work schedules are arising; such as 4-ten hour days; 5-nine hour days one week and 4-nine hour days the next week with Friday off; or schedules with workday lengths of 9,9,9,9,9,9,9,9,8,0 each two weeks. As the number of variations increases, the difficulty of duplicating them in the schedule also increases.

An additional complication is that different organizations may be working according to differing calendars. Engineering, testing, and manufacturing will likely have varying working hours or perhaps even days. Thus two parallel, five working day duration activities that start together may not be scheduled to finish together.

However, that is not the end of the questions. Early schedule software packages assumed an 8:00 A.M. start time and a completion time of 8:00 A.M. on a subsequent day. This made network calculations simple since a 1-day duration would always show as day 64 - day 63 = 1 day elapsed. But this did not fit most people's idea of what a completion date meant. If something were due on March 16, how many people would assume that meant at start of business on March 16? A March 16 due date will always be assumed to mean at the end of that calendar day. Consider the April 15 deadline for filing IRS returns and all of the near midnight postmarks. Schedule packages began to reflect that reality and show a 1-day duration as beginning at 8:00 A.M. and finishing at 5:00 P.M. that same day. Essentially all popular scheduling packages now use this latter approach, referred to as the "AM-PM convention." This was discussed previously in Chapter 8, "Critical Path Method Fundamentals," and has been used throughout this text.

Conclusion

Analysis of CPM is not complete until factors that effectively "trick" CPM are evaluated for impact. The use of directed dates, for example, will redefine the critical activities. This may or may not reflect the true project condition. Schedule software limitations may also restrict certain uses of combined start-to-start and finish-to-finish relationships, making it difficult to represent the true logic. Other limitations may make it impossible to calculate secondary float and total float separately, resulting in unintended outcomes.

Special considerations may also be required for handling support activities that last for the duration of the project. The conclusion to be drawn is that the defaults and limitations of scheduling software should be tested and known in advance of application to specific projects, and procedures are needed to prevent human error that limits or invalidates the use of the schedule.

Chapter 16 Review Questions

16-1.   Define the "Not-Earlier-Than" (NET) directed date and discuss how it impacts the network calculation.

16-2.   Discuss how secondary float differs from total float.

16-3.   What relationships cause some scheduling software to fail when handling multiple relationships between the same two activities?

16-4.   What is the problem introduced with "Level of Effort" activities when they are included in a schedule network?

16-5.   What is the "AM-PM" convention used by many scheduling software packages?

True or False

16-6.   Use of any directed date will supersede the normal network calculation.

16-7.   Use of directed dates can make activities that are not critical appear to be critical.

16-8.   There are no valid reasons to use a directed date.

16-9.   It may be possible to shorten the total project duration by lengthening one of the activities.

16-10.   The use of a "Not-Later-Than" (NLT) directed date will affect the backward pass calculation through the network, typically reducing the float value of that activity.

The answers to these questions can be found in Section 6, Solutions.

Case Study

16.1 A MORE COMPLEX NETWORK

A. Arrange these activities in logical sequence using PDM.

1. Activity A initiates the project.

2. Activity B can start 1 day after activity A finishes.

3. Activity A precedes activity C.

4. Activity D can start after B finishes, but cannot finish until 2 days after C finishes.

5. Activity E can start 1 day after activity C starts.

6. Activity F is preceded by activities D and E.

7. Activity X runs the life of the project.

Activity Durations

$$A = 5$$
$$B = 2$$
$$C = 3$$
$$D = 4$$
$$E = 3$$
$$F = 2$$

B. Perform the forward and backward path calculations to determine the critical path.

The solution to this case study can be found on the Humphreys & Associates, Inc. web site.
www.humphreys-assoc.com

Chapter **17**

SCHEDULE RISK ASSESSMENT

Objectives of this Chapter:

1. Explain that schedule risk is a characteristic of all schedules.
2. Identify the steps involved in performing a risk assessment.
3. Explain the difference between the critical path and the highest risk path in a network.
4. Discuss the considerations involved in developing realistic activity duration estimates.
5. Introduce rules for combining distributions along a network logic path.
6. Explain the relationship between cumulative likelihood curves and risk mitigation strategy development evaluation.
7. Learn how to test the validity of CPM results with risk analysis.
8. Explain how multiple risk paths are combined to determine the likely project completion date.
9. Address increased risk at points of path convergence.
10. Address concerns when implementing risk analysis.
11. Discuss different approaches to risk measurement tools: PERT and Monte Carlo simulation.

This chapter[1] concerns a topic that is being required on capital intensive projects with increasing frequency. Within the U. S. Department of Defense, for example, Schedule Risk Assessment (SRA) has become a part of the Integrated Master Schedule (IMS) Data Item Description [DI-MGMT-81650 (latest revision)] requirements. Conducting an SRA is also number eight in the GAO's best practices. Projects without this requirement that consider schedule risk in their analyses are considered forward-thinking. While the importance of evaluating schedule risk is universal, many project applications do not yet consider it in their analyses. The reason is basic: most people still are unaware of the statistical technology available for evaluating schedule uncertainty. And like all process refinements, many others have operated for years or decades without it and see no reason to change their way of doing business now.

On the other hand, the conduct of a statistical based SRA was, in the past, a cost intensive effort involving specialized expertise and software. Today, robust software applications are significantly more transparent and easy to use and are much more cost effective than their predecessors. This development puts the SRA process within the means of the even the most modest of projects.

The central concern is that there is uncertainty in virtually everything that occurs on a project, and ignoring risk does not make it go away. All calculated CPM results are based on durations that are considered absolute values when in fact the

---

1. Dr. David T. Hulett contributed information for this chapter.

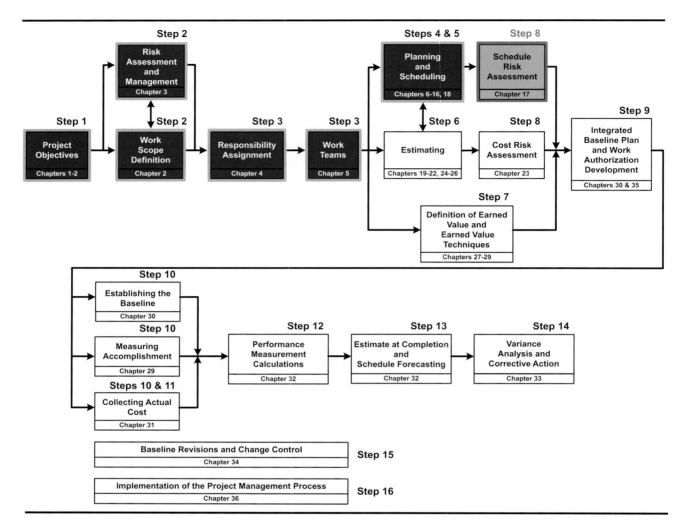

Figure 17-1 Earned Value Project Management: The Process

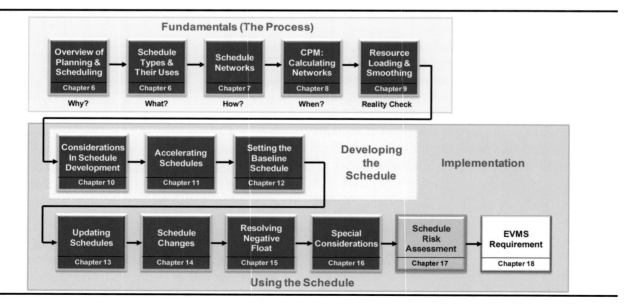

Figure 17-2 Planning and Scheduling

durations are quite uncertain. There is both theory and available computer software to address schedule risk. That theory is addressed in this chapter. Also covered is how schedule analysis, which incorporates the reality of uncertainty, differs from traditional CPM analysis and supplements it with additional information.

Schedule risk is part of an overall risk assessment program (reference Chapter 3). As such, it is represented twice in the flowcharts. It is shown on the Planning and Scheduling flowchart as part of the process of using a schedule, and it is also displayed in the Project Management flowchart as part of a complete risk assessment program that also includes consideration of technical and cost risk.

Commuters who drive their own cars to work in every major metropolitan area practice schedule risk assessment each morning. There are many variables to consider: weather conditions, time of day, road construction, season of the year, traffic flow patterns, etc. Everyone knows traffic will be heavier and slower moving if it were raining. It will be even slower if there were a major storm. Because everyone knows this, many people will leave earlier to "beat the crowd", or leave even earlier to be ahead of the rush. If there were a major university along the route, the status of the current school year is important because of the greatly increased number of commuters. Meanwhile, road construction further impedes the commuter. All of these factors must be considered when evaluating what time it will be necessary to leave for work in order to arrive there on time. This is a practical form of schedule risk assessment practiced by nearly everyone on a continuing basis. Those who give no consideration to factors such as these will frequently arrive late. There is a reward for schedule risk assessment and a penalty if it were ignored.

Schedule risk exists in every project. The risk can be quantified, analyzed, and mitigated, or it can be ignored. Unfortunately, ignoring it does not make it go away. In this chapter, methods are discussed to check the boundaries of the risks faced on every project. Up to this point a number of good practices based on CPM have been presented. However, the results are not always reliable. A risk analysis provides information that

CPM cannot. The accuracy of the schedule depends on its logic, the degree of participation in its development by those who will execute it, and the accuracy of the estimator. Even if the logic reflects how the work will be done, the estimates (or duration) may be inaccurate.

An example of this is shown in Figure 17-3. This simple logic includes durations that are estimates that include contingency believed to be "adequate" to deal with schedule slip risk. The CPM approach simply adds up estimates along the various paths and compares them at the finish. Thus, the schedule estimated completion date includes the contingencies. The critical path has the longest duration and least total float. In this example, it is Path A that has a total duration of 24 months compared with Path B's 15 months. But how long will this project have actually taken when complete?

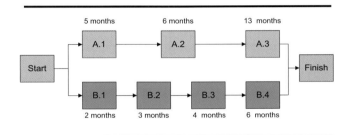

Figure 17-3 Risk Assessment with CPM

Figure 17-4 shows one possibility.

Path A	Months	Path B	Months
Activity A.1	4	Actiivty B.1	2
Activity A.2	7	Activity B.2	3
Activity A.3	14	Activity B.3	15
		Activity B.4	8
Total	**25**	**Total**	**28**

Figure 17-4 Risk Assessment with CPM Network

Path A, the path identified as "critical", received all the management attention. It was well managed and slipped by only one month. As completed, Path B took longer, mostly because Activity B.3 was predicted to be high risk by a team participant because its specification included stringent fabrication quality measures and took 15 months. Since Path B was not initially identified as "critical", it did not receive the attention it deserved until a team member pointed out the potential risk.

Risk analysis of this project, as planned, should have concluded:

Path A, the critical path, is tightly managed and the probability is high that a schedule slip, if any, would not exceed one month.

Path B, the highest risk path, has a good chance of exceeding its 22 month schedule by several months. It could easily end up taking longer than Path A and jeopardize the whole project schedule.

The situation is shown in Figure 17-5. Comparing CPM and risk analysis, CPM missed the potential of Path B's impact on the project. Risk analysis correctly warned that Path B was a potential problem, but it gave the ultimate result, 28 months, only about a 5% likelihood of occurring. However, with risk analysis, management might have paid more attention to Path B, perhaps by establishing risk mitigation measures, and thus avoiding this 4 month extension of the project. Highest risk paths are generally long and challenging, but may not be the critical path. The critical path should be receiving management attention and be relatively certain. A near-critical path should also be managed as there is still a great deal of schedule extension risk. Identifying high risk paths, therefore, provides management information not explicitly available with single-point estimates.

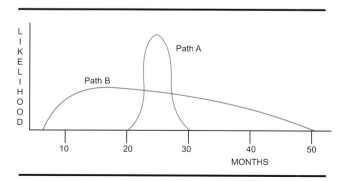

Figure 17-5 Risk Analysis of the Project

Reasons for Risk Analysis

Results can be serious when the potential impacts of high risk schedule paths are ignored. Contractors may incur penalties, such as liquidated damages, for late completion of a project. Also, incentive fee may be lost. Additional costs may be incurred in the rush at the end of the project to accelerate efforts in an attempt to meet the completion date. Worst of all, a reputation for being late can be a major hurdle to overcome in highly competitive environments.

Not all of the exposure is on the side of the contractor either. The owner/customer may lose revenue and profits on a daily basis because of the unavailability of the product. Late schedules also lead to overruns that are just as difficult to justify on the owner's/customer's side as on the contractor's side. Thus it is incumbent upon the owner/customer to either conduct its own risk analysis and/or to participate in the overall project Schedule Risk Assessment.

The inescapable fact is that even standard projects are risky. Site conditions vary. There was an instance of several months schedule delay because of underground pipe and live electrical duct banks not included on drawings. But one-of-a-kind or first-of-a-kind projects are particularly risky because:

- Technology may be unproven.

- Design readiness is more difficult to achieve; unanticipated problems may occur with no ready solutions.

- Little or no historical data are available.

- Objectives may be redefined in mid-project.

- Contractors, suppliers, and labor are less familiar with what is required to get the job done.

In all types of projects, there is additional uncertainty associated with regulatory and permit requirements, funding limitations, unpredictable weather, unexpected geological conditions, and communication problems between contractors and the owner/customer. Challenges escalate and schedule risk increases as more contractors and subcontractors become involved with a project.

A Schedule Risk Assessment (SRA) involves a number of goals. They include estimating the likelihood of exceeding the baseline schedule and identifying paths that are potential problem areas so that they can receive increased management attention. In effect, a risk assessment provides an early warning of threats to the schedule. It allows integration of risk concerns into project planning and management.

Those responsible for a risk assessment should adhere to standards of honesty and provide unbiased estimates of the potential risk because these estimates lead to the best risk mitigation strategies. It is quite common for people to avoid exposing risk on their projects or even downplay the risk that exists. Those doing the risk estimating tend to be the most knowledgeable about forecasting the overall project risk exposure; they are the best sources of information. Finally, those who lead projects should become competent in risk analysis, which usually requires training in techniques.

Risk Definition and Use of a Risk Assessment

The term "risk" is used broadly to include both of the classical concepts: uncertainty, where probabilities of possible future events are unknown; and risk, where those probabilities are known and given, also called "measurable uncertainty." Risk of a schedule slippage is driven by many factors, some known and some unknown. All risks are in the future. In practice, these risk exposure factors need to be quantified, using expert judgment when data are not available. Use of qualitative terms such as "moderate" or "high" is not adequate, because what is considered moderate to one may be high to someone else. Quantification helps to focus the debate.

Among the important benefits of schedule risk assessments are the following:

- Facilitates better bid/no bid proposal decisions based on an assessment of the potential for schedule slippage that is quantified and explicit.

- Provides an estimate of the schedule reserve requirements to specifically limit risk to an acceptable level.

- Provides advance warning for project management so that attention can be focused on high risk areas and their timing. Thus extra resources can be allocated to those areas if necessary, risk mitigation strategies can be activated, and the owner/customer can be warned in advance so that other plans can be made in the event of a schedule slippage.

A risk analysis improves the participants' understanding of their projects by providing a focus on the weak points of the planning assumptions. Communication about project risk may be difficult because of differing positions between contractor and owner/customer. In the long run, talking about schedule risk is better than concealing it, since it is real and will not go away even if it were ignored.

There are other considerations as well. The company might have other strategic goals that are more important than reducing schedule risk. The company might need a particular contract to expand into a new line of business or just need the work to maintain staff, and might bid an aggressive schedule knowing there is greater risk. Even good risk analysis does not ensure good management decisions. The solutions that reduce risk may be costly, and cost overrun may be a more serious concern of the contractor and the owner/customer.

Even with a well-disciplined risk analysis, management may make bad decisions with good information. Risk is not the only strategic factor in decisions. The other problem is that, unfortunately, bad results can happen even from good decisions. There is a very low possibility that a major problem may still occur.

Cost overrun is another reason to closely review schedule risk. Remember that anytime the schedule changes, the cost will most likely change also. Schedule delays may be caused by the same factors that force increased costs. Often the risk of overrunning cost and schedule objectives derives from technical uncertainties. Attempting a new and/or challenging technical or performance task often takes more time and resources than estimated. Integrated risk analysis (integrated technical, schedule, and cost risk analysis), is being discussed by some forward-thinking companies, but there is no agreement yet on how to undertake it.

The CPM Approach to Schedule Risk

The CPM encourages attention on the critical path as the most vulnerable area of the schedule. Experienced schedulers will also watch near-critical paths (those with low total float) because even small slips can delay the project and/or can change the critical path. A trend of declining total float may indicate lack of attention to developing problems or inadequate resources being applied to difficult tasks. Identifying and tracking near-critical paths still does not quantify the risk of exceeding the estimated completion date.

The basic shortcoming is the single point estimates of work to be performed in the future. These are frequently inaccurate, but CPM does not explore the likelihood of other durations occurring. Management does not know whether the activity durations along the critical path are conservative or optimistic. While the critical and near-critical paths are known, CPM does not identify the highest risk paths.

Many schedules are driven by directed end dates and milestones. Negative float on the critical path is a simple indicator of the extent of trouble from such fixed dates. In this context, it is difficult to provide meaningful schedule risk assessments along with mitigation strategies.

Probabilistic Approach to Schedule Risk

The steps involved in assessing the risk of a schedule are as follows:

1. Create a complete and quality-checked CPM network.

2. Develop three duration estimates (optimistic, pessimistic, and most likely) for each activity.

3. Identify a duration distribution method for all activities.

4. Compute the path distribution.

5. Evaluate the results:

   a. Estimated completion date certainty.

   b. Identify high risk paths.

6. Initiate status monitoring.

A CPM/PDM network representing the project's schedule and logic is a requirement before any computations can be made. The baseline duration estimates will be used as a central point in developing a probability, so they should be "best guess" (most likely) or "expected" (average) durations. If project managers do not give direction to provide "expected" durations, allowances of unknown duration could be built in to each baseline estimate, and this will make risk analysis more difficult.

The next step is to identify a distribution representing possible durations for each activity using data or, more likely, expert judgment. The computations will be done with computer software. These programs also help set up the assumption distributions that cannot be done feasibly by hand. The resulting Critical Path lengths distribution will lend itself to finding the schedule reserve recommendation that represents an acceptable level of risk for the contractor or the owner/customer. High risk paths are identified so that management attention can be focused on them.

Example: Building Foundation Activity

The shortest duration represents how fast the activity could be completed, assuming good luck with everything going well and no unpleasant surprises. For example, experience with similar projects may indicate that the foundation of a building can be completed in as little as three weeks. The longest or pessimistic estimate may be ten weeks. In the past, bad weather, labor or material unavailability, site conditions or equipment failure have caused significant delays in completing the foundation on similar projects. Are the durations between three weeks and ten weeks equally likely? Is so little really known about the project? The answer should be no. Experience probably offers a good idea of how long this type of foundation typically takes. This is the "most likely" or "best guess" estimate and is often the estimate used in CPM analysis. If the foundation were to be constructed many times, it would average five weeks. Unfortunately, the actual foundation is only constructed once, so this must be an estimate of the future.

Sometimes a time frame can be estimated "on average" if the project were done many times. This "average" duration may be different from the "most likely" or "best guess" estimate. This concept has no direct corollary in CPM, although it was central to PERT (which will be discussed later in this chapter).

The digging and placing the foundation activity may be estimated as the stated range that the experts provided.

Low = 3 weeks.

Most likely = 5 weeks.

High = 10 weeks.

A triangular distribution puts most of the likely completion dates within plus or minus one week of the most likely 5 weeks. This is pictured in Figure 17-6.

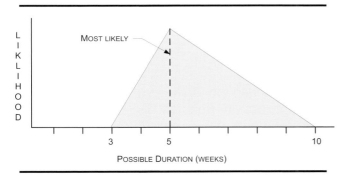

Figure 17-6 Building Foundation Activity

This distribution is not symmetrical. There is more likelihood of outcomes above five weeks than below it. Expressed another way, it is more likely to exceed a five week estimate than to improve upon it. The degree to which a duration will be improved or exceeded is a fundamental risk analysis concept. Uncertainty is quantified, expressing the risk in the estimates. With the

assumption range of three to ten weeks, what is the "expected" duration? The "expected" duration is the average length of time the activity would take if it were performed many times. This is different from the most likely duration, or mode of the distribution. The mode is the single length of time it would most frequently take. These durations are illustrated in Figure 17-7.

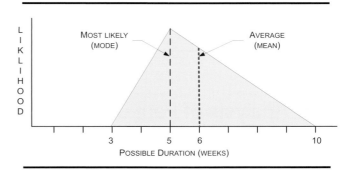

Figure 17-7 Most Likely and Average Durations

With an asymmetrical distribution, when the high and low durations are not equally distant from the mode or most likely, the mean or average is different from the mode. With the triangular distribution, the expected duration is calculated:

(Low + Most Likely + High) / 3

In this example, that calculates as (3 + 5 + 10) / 3 = 6 weeks. That means there is an expected schedule slip of one week over the most likely estimate of five weeks.

Example: CPM Path Duration

For this example, assume a simple two activity path, finish-to-start, as follows:

Activity	Duration
Activity A101	50 days
Activity A102	80 days
CPM most likely duration	130 days

The question to be explored is, "Is 130 days adequate for this path?" CPM assumes that the duration estimates are accurate and provides a single point estimate of path duration. In reality, the estimates may not be accurate. What more can be done?

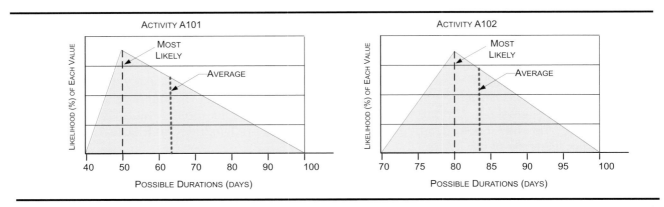

Figure 17-8 Low and High Possible Durations

Risk Analysis of Path Duration

On further investigation, the activities can take fewer or more days than the most likely estimate. In particular, there is a small likelihood that A101 will take 100 days, twice the most likely estimate, and Activity A102 may take as much as 20 extra days, a 25% slippage. While these extremes are possible, they are not very likely. The most likely and the average estimates for these two activities are shown in Figure 17-8.

A triangular distribution portrays this information. In general, this is a good assumption and it is an easy distribution to use. Note the difference between the most likely and average duration for each.

Activity	Low Range	Most Likely	High Range	Average Duration
A101	40	50	100	63.3
A102	70	80	100	83.4
Total Path		130		146.7

This table summarizes the information from the CPM and preliminary risk analysis approach to the duration of Path A. The most likely estimate is 130 days. The risk assessment shows that the average duration is 146.7 days, an "expected" or average schedule slippage of 16.7 days.

If the path were done many times, it would exceed the most likely estimate by an average of 16.7 days. It is not appropriate to add up the lows and highs of the activity distributions.

If it is only 1% likely that A101 will take 100 days and 1% likely that A102 will take 100 days, then it is only 0.01% likely that Path A will take 200 days. The only exception to this rule is if some factor, common to determining the durations of A101 and A102, causes their durations to be correlated.

It should be noticed that each of these CPM estimates is more likely to exceed the initial duration estimate, that is, they are "skewed right." Schedule estimates are often optimistic, either because those who provide duration estimates truly believe things will go well or because owners/customers require certain schedule deadlines. Conducting a risk assessment is a way of examining these assumptions and the validity of the resulting schedule without necessarily changing the CPM estimates. Ultimately, however, it may result in a new CPM estimate.

Continuing with the example, a risk analysis combines the activity duration distributions to calculate a total path duration distribution as shown in Figure 17-9. The technique most commonly used is Monte Carlo simulation, to be described later. It would be natural to assume that adding the most likely estimates of 50 days and 80 days would at least give the most likely path duration estimate. This is not the case, however, with estimates that are optimistic (or aggressive, "success-oriented"), as they often are on a project.

Only risk analysis provides this information. That is why CPM is the beginning of a complete scheduling exercise, not its end result.

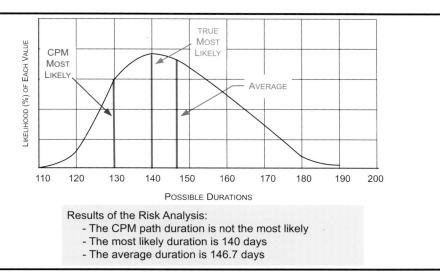

Results of the Risk Analysis:
- The CPM path duration is not the most likely
- The most likely duration is 140 days
- The average duration is 146.7 days

Figure 17-9 Risk Analysis of Path Duration Example

Cumulative Likelihood Curves (S-Curves)

Cumulative likelihood is just another way to portray a distribution. It is constructed by adding up all of the probabilities (in percent) in a cumulative fashion from low to high range values. Since all possible likelihoods are included, the total accumulates to 100%. Below the "low" estimate, there is no likelihood (0%). Below the "high" estimate, there are all of the possible durations (100%). The curve often results in an "S" shape, and is called an "S-curve."

A main purpose of the S-curve is to discern how likely it may be to expect variations in a particular estimated duration. Reading off the curve for any duration yields the likelihood in percentage terms of durations occurring with less than that value.

Subtracting that likelihood percent from 100% gives the likelihood of durations longer than the estimate.

Potential outcomes can be calculated to provide an acceptable risk of schedule slippage. For some companies, a 50% risk of schedule slippage might be acceptable, while for others a 30% risk may be the worst that is acceptable. For very conservative industries, such as the electric utility industry, a 5% chance of slippage may be deemed too high to be acceptable.

The S-curve is a graph of cumulative probabilities, so no values are possible below the low estimate or above the high estimate as shown in Figure 17-10. At all intermediate points along the curve, there is a varying probability of those values occurring.

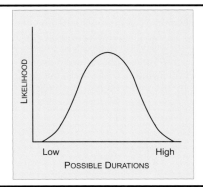
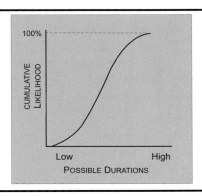

Figure 17-10 Constructing the S-Curve

If an estimate of a project's duration is A days, the S-curve says that 35% of the likely durations are below that level. This is shown in Figure 17-11. By subtraction, there is a 65% likelihood of exceeding the schedule by A days.

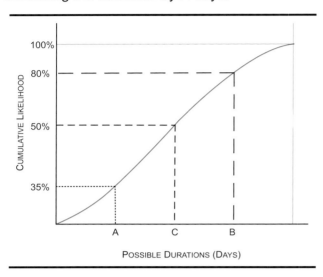

Figure 17-11 Likelihood of Slippages and Contingencies

Conversely, suppose the company wanted to bid a schedule with only a 20% chance of exceeding the schedule. This confidence requires a bid of B days. The difference between B and A is the schedule reserve that is added to the estimate of A days to achieve an acceptable level of risk. The reserve for 50% success is C-A days. The value 50% is a common level of risk aversion.

The project team may have to manage to A days, while the project manager has C-A days of schedule reserve to control. The company might control B-C days. Suppose B days represents a "disastrous" delay. Then there is a 20% likelihood of disaster, or worse.

Now look at the cumulative probability curve, or S-curve, for the Path Duration example. The S-curve is an easier way to get the results from a risk analysis. It shows in Figure 17-12 that the CPM estimate for Path A of 130 days appears on the curve at the 14% level. This means that there is only a 14% likelihood of Path A actually being accomplished within the 130 day duration. Conversely, there is an 86% probability of this path requiring more than 130 days to complete. The CPM estimates in this case were very optimistic. A project manager would want to add some additional schedule reserve, probably at least 15 days, to bring the likelihood of success up to 50-50. A conservative project manager could decide on an even longer duration to further reduce the risk of potential schedule slip.

There are two caveats to be aware of:

1. The S-curve assumes that no further risk management actions will be taken. This is the best that can be done with activities on path A. In fact, risk management may narrow the ranges on the activity durations and straighten the S-curve.

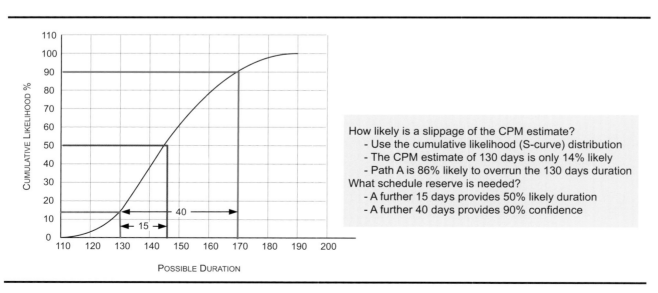

Figure 17-12 Cumulative Distribution for Path A

2. Discussion of where on the cumulative probability curve the manager wants to be must consider other factors. These include the place of this project in the company's strategic plan, the contractor/ owner/customer relationship, the state of other business and the profitability of the company, the competition for this project, and other factors that may be unique to the specific industry or corporation. Risk of slipping the schedule is not the only factor. Accepting a level of risk is the rule, not the exception.

Validity of CPM Estimates

The only way to know whether a CPM estimate is more or less valid is to perform a well-disciplined, quantitative risk analysis. A less valid estimate is one that is more likely to be exceeded, or one that has a significant chance of slippage. In Figure 17-13, estimate B is more "valid" than estimate A. It may, however, be unnecessarily long and safe from risk.

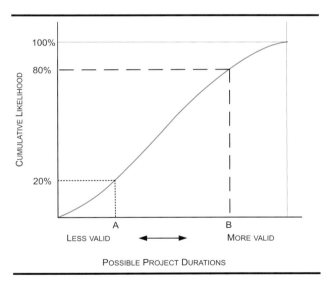

Figure 17-13 Validity of CPM Estimates

The CPM is just the beginning of a complete analysis. A risk analysis uses more information about the activity duration estimates and so is able to provide more information about the path duration. Since optimistic estimating is quite common, the example discussed shows that the CPM is usually optimistic. This is not a reflection of equivocation on the part of the scheduler, but

more a recognition of the fact that there is always an absolute minimum duration for any activity, but the absolute maximum can be very long and hard to pinpoint. This tends to make most distributions skew right, with all that entails. Because of these factors, every schedule should be accompanied by a quantified risk analysis, so the owner/customer or project manager understands the risks and challenges of managing to that schedule.

Highest Risk Path

High risk paths to project completion should be identified for the project manager and owner/customer, as well as to intermediate milestones for those who have responsibility for those events. With CPM, the critical path is identified. With risk analysis, the distribution of the various paths at a path convergence point or at the end of the project can be compared explicitly. The highest risk path can be identified by comparing path distributions' S-curves to see which has the longest potential duration. Reference Figure 17-14.

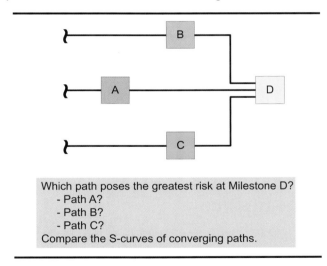

Figure 17-14 Identifying the Highest Risk Path

The highest risk path to the project finish (Activity D) is determined by comparing S-curves. The S-curve posing the greatest risk to the scheduled finish date identifies the highest risk path. The amount of risk in the CPM estimate depends on the shape of the S-curve and its position relative to the other curves. This is illustrated in Figure 17-15. Path B might be identified as the critical path by a CPM analysis. It is being tightly managed to reduce risk. Its S-curve is far to the right but quite vertical. Path C was not identified as the critical path, but other factors must be considered. It is near critical (toward the right of the graph) and risky (gradually sloped S-curve), so it greatly jeopardizes the CPM schedule. Path A may have the most risk because its S-curve is even more gradual than path C.

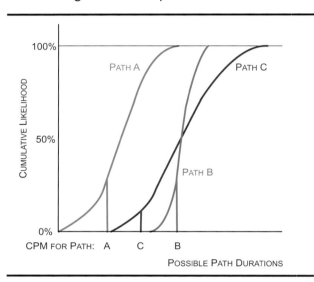

Figure 17-15 Identify the Highest Risk Path

But since path A is a slack path (toward the left of the graph), it does not greatly endanger the CPM schedule. Its S-curve is to the left of both B and C paths. Considering all of the factors, path C may be called the highest risk path.

Schedule Risk at Path Convergence

With CPM, the completion date of converging paths is supposedly known with certainty. With an early start strategy, beginning all activities as close as possible to the early start dates calculated in the forward pass of the network, the float indicates a margin for successful completion at a path convergence. Even with late starts, CPM shows that each path is completed "just-in-time" at each convergence point. A risk analysis does not accept the duration estimates as accurate. Path durations are distributions. It is natural to use these distributions at path convergence (or merge) points to determine the likelihood of com-

pleting a milestone or starting the next activity, e.g. integration and testing.

Schedule Bias

The bias in a schedule is the difference between the average duration and the nominal duration. The average duration is computed from risk analysis, while the nominal is calculated from the CPM. The bias is defined as the average minus the nominal, so that the bias is usually positive with optimistic CPM estimates of duration. In effect, the bias is a measure of the realism or lack thereof of the CPM estimate. If activity duration estimates are optimistic, the bias will grow along any path as shown in the example just completed. The bias of path A = 146.7 - 130 = 16.7 days; reference Figure 17-9.

Merge Bias at Path Convergence

Something new happens to schedule bias at merge points; places where two or more activities combine at a single event. Instead of building up gradually along a path, it may jump dramatically as each of several paths' risks interacts. The slippage risk increases significantly if the next schedule event or activity relies on the completion of more than one path.

As in real projects, the computer schedule indicates that the points of risk are greatest when:

- There is more risk on the converging paths.

- The CPM estimates are more aggressive.

- There is little flexibility or margin for error because float has been used early in the project. The schedule is pushed toward the late starts, producing "just-in-time" scheduling.

Each of these factors increases the likelihood that at least one path will not be complete by any particular date. This is a critical point in the understanding of what a risk analysis does.

As Figure 17-16 shows, path A is a slack path and may have followed an early start strategy. Its S-curve does not overlap those for path B and path C. The date for completing milestone D, which requires completion of paths A, B, and C, is a distribution derived from path B and path C. If a specific date is chosen, the S-curves can be read to determine probability.

For example, at 150 days, the probability that these two paths are both complete is about 52% (80% x 65% = 52%). At any date, if the paths overlap, the likelihood that milestone D is complete is the product of the two paths' completion, read off of their S-curves.

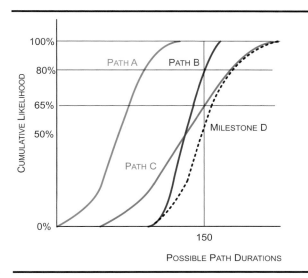

Figure 17-16 Merge Bias at Convergence

Completion Possibilities	Path B and C Likelihood	MIlestone D Likelihood
B and C	.80 x .65	.52
B but not C	.80 x.35	.28
C but not B	.20 x .65	.13
Not C, Not B	.20 x .35	.07
Total Likelihood		**1.00**

Four combinations are possible at 150 days, but only one permits completion of milestone D. These likelihoods are read off the S-curves where they overlap and then are multiplied together. If there were even more overlapping S-curves, only one of many cases would imply successful completion of the milestone. This is why the presence of more converging paths reduces the probability of completion by any given date. Milestone D's cumulative likelihood curve is shifted to the right from even the path curve that

is farthest to the right (if the converging paths' S-curves overlap), indicating the presence of the merge bias.

In complex network structures, the chance for risk build-up is substantial. With a single path network, there is no path convergence. With many path convergences, chances exist for build-up of expected schedule slippage and needed risk mitigation strategies. Parallel and cross-connected project network structures have more chances for risk build-up than a simple, one path network. There is more chance that a near-critical path will turn out to be high risk. Finding the high risk paths becomes more complicated.

Directed Dates

Directed dates can be imposed to make a schedule look as if it achieves the requirements of the owner/customer. If the logic and durations are realistic, the CPM may not indicate negative float. Even if no negative float results, risk assessment may show that schedule slippages are possible. If directed dates are imposed, however, slippages that are technically and logically possible are not permitted by the software and the risk analysis is thwarted. This is illustrated in Figure 17-17.

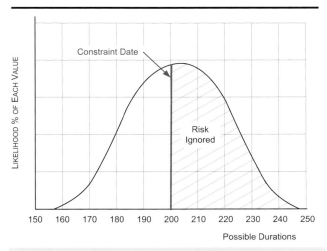

Constraint date and risk analysis not-later-than date of 200 working days.

Figure 17-17 Direct Dates

In this figure, a Not-Later-Than constraint date has been placed at 200 days. This is common for important milestones or at the project completion.

The risk analysis is unable to show dates beyond 200 days, even though the bulk of the likelihood exceeds 200 days, unless the constraint is removed before the analysis is conducted. The constraint at 200 days gives the project manager the false impression of impending success rather than a realistic impression of the likelihood of schedule slippage.

Reducing Durations to Fit the Schedule

Often contractors are under pressure to produce schedules their internal data show are not feasible. If they produce schedules with unreasonably short durations, all that remains is a "feel good" picture of success instead of a useful tool for project management. This is an abuse of scheduling technology that is, unfortunately, too common. A risk analysis can help explore this situation.

The project manager or the owner/customer may explore the duration estimates if overly optimistic scheduling were suspected. In one case, the CPM may be accepted as the low estimate, but all of the risk suggests schedule slippage. More realistic distributions may show the mode, or most likely, value of the distribution shifted to the right as shown in Figure 17-18. Exploring uncertainty ranges is a good way to validate the CPM schedule.

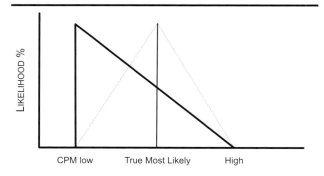

A risk analysis can help assess the impact of unrealistic durations.
- The CPM is the low estimate
- The most likely estimate may be shifted to the true most likely for the risk analysis

Figure 17-18 Reducing Durations to Fit the Schedule

Fast Track Impacts

Fast tracking may be an appropriate response to scheduling pressures, but it is a risky strategy. It increases the likelihood that something will go wrong and have to be redone. It may delay the project, exactly the opposite result intended. Fast track should not to be confused with concurrent engineering. With concurrent engineering, the requirements of later project participants are solicited in earlier stages. For instance, manufacturing, logistics and field support may all contribute during the engineering phase of an aircraft's development. Concurrent engineering and its concept of integrated product teams are designed to reduce risk.

Late Start Scheduling

Intentionally delaying the start of activities until their latest possible start date delays expenditures and improves near-term cash flow. If this practice were employed consistently throughout the network, the CPM would show all paths becoming critical but still will indicate that the schedule is achievable, as long as float does not become negative.

However, in this scenario, the CPM schedule will not reveal the true extent of the risk. A risk analysis calculates the merge bias at path convergence points. Merge bias becomes more severe as more and more path S-curves start to overlap. Consider a two-path example with paths A and B leading to milestone C as shown in Figure 17-19.

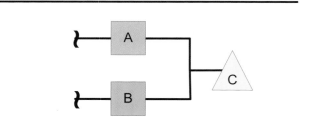

Figure 17-19 Two Path Example

The identity of the highest risk path may change with late starts. The curve in Figure 17-20 shows that the durations computed by CPM for path A and path B are the same. Unfortunately, path B is a risky path and becomes the highest risk path because of late status. The S-curve for milestone C is shifted to the right, and the merge bias is significant.

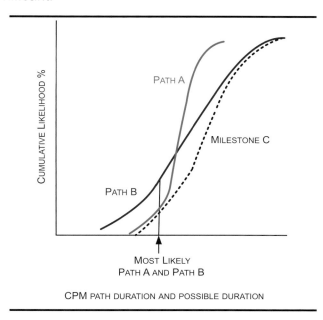

Figure 17-20 Late Starts on Path B

Early Start Scheduling

Early starts on path B might remove it from the calculation of risk at milestone C. In Figure 17-21 float is enough to shift path B's S-curve far to the left so that it barely overlaps that of path A. In this case, there is hardly any merge bias at all at milestone C.

Risk Analysis Pitfalls

There are some pitfalls to developing accurate input assumptions. These tend to be people problems rather than technical theory problems. Estimators may be too confident in their own initial estimate. They may be reluctant to admit that there are any ranges, or that the ranges may be substantial even with the best estimating technique. This is a failure to realize that risk may be inherent in the scope definition and may not reflect a weakness in the estimate.

Meetings are often convened to resolve scope definition differences. This does not work well in a risk analysis context, because the differences

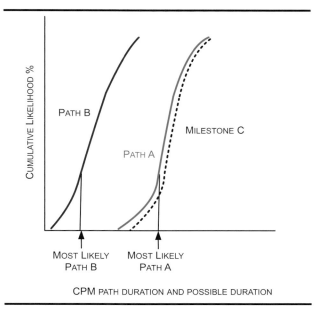

Figure 17-21 Early Starts on Path B

in range may stem from legitimate concerns. Reaching a consensus will tend to cause the true ranges to be narrowed and extreme risks eliminated. This hides the true risk.

A recent or dramatic event may blind estimators to the underlying range supported by perfectly valid data. Even dramatic events sometimes occur at the extremes of duration changes. Estimators experiencing one bad delay may revise their ranges to reflect that experience rather than to fit the event into historical context. There should be a determination if the dramatic experience warrants a revision of the historical range, but it does not mean that the prior experience should be voided.

Risk assessment frequently is ignored or not conducted in a quantified way for various reasons:

- The Owner/Customer has not asked for it.
- The project manager has "more important" things to do.
- There is a fear of bad news.
- Risk-scoring or risk-ranking in a qualified way that has been acceptable in the past.
- It is difficult.

Some owners/customers are asking for risk analysis at regularly scheduled intervals. There are companies that routinely perform schedule risk assessments before every bid and during execution as part of the ongoing management of the project. This is especially true in high risk projects, specifically those with a fixed price and/or very tight schedules that incorporate penalties into the contract for being late. This type of analysis has also been used as part of the bidding process and contract negotiation process. Detailed evaluations show when activities are actually expected to occur in comparison with the proposed target schedule. This structured process helps support negotiation objectives, as penalties/bonuses for late/early completion can be better evaluated and weighed against anticipated costs for accelerating schedules.

The project management profession is emphasizing risk management, and all indications are that quantifying risk will continue to become more important in all industries.

Risk Implementation

Sometimes companies are required by the Request for Proposal (RFP) to identify high-risk portions of the contract when submitting a bid. Usually the risks are ranked or grouped ("A" risks, "B" risks) and the company must identify what they plan to do about the risk. This approach does not quantify risk; it merely identifies the risk and requests potential risk mitigation strategies without the additional discipline of defining the magnitude of potential risk. Oftentimes, even if a quantified risk assessment were done, it is never reviewed or revised again during the life of a project. The problem is that risks change over time. Management action is surely being taken to address problem areas as the project progresses, and this action will affect the risk and may even change which activities involve the most risk.

The risk assessment should be reviewed and/or updated as part of the monthly or quarterly status report. Some activities will have been completed, leaving no remaining risk. Some will be partially complete, so risk is limited to the remaining portion of the work. There may even be new information on future activities that affects their risk. This could include items such as changed market conditions, developing labor shortages in certain crafts or skill areas, or the emergence of new technology. It is not necessary to do an equally detailed risk report with each status update, but rather identify those items that are changing. This management by exception approach can focus on high risk paths, new risk paths, and the impact of past management actions on risky paths. An updated assessment of project risk should become a routine part of all status reviews.

What else is needed when implementing a risk assessment approach? Risk analysis needs to become part of the corporate culture. Software needs to be acquired that is compatible with in-house scheduling software tools. Training on risk assessment techniques and explanation of how to properly interpret results is also important. Review of the changing risk conditions should become a regular part of status review meetings. One of the biggest challenges may still be to get people to think in terms of a range of possible outcomes rather than a single point value. In solving problems, often there is only a single "right" answer, and in order to find out what it is, the most effective solution is to perform a risk assessment and find out what the boundaries really are.

With all of the considerations and possibilities for error, how successful can a schedule risk implementation be? A major cogeneration project incorporated schedule risk as part of the weekly update of the CPM. Its success was measurable. Approximately eight months before the scheduled completion of this three year project, the schedule risk assessment revealed a slippage in the completion date that was likely to be about three months. This was in spite of the fact that the official schedules continued to show that the project would be on time. When the last milestone was finally achieved, it fell exactly at the midway point between "earliest most likely date" and "latest most likely date" for completion of that event. The projected range had been one week between early dates and late dates on its S-curve, with nearly all of the projected dates falling within a five week window.

Chapter 17 Schedule Risk Assessment   341

Schedule Risk Analysis Output

The type of output information produced for evaluating schedule risk varies somewhat in format between risk tools. An example of output generated by a widely used Monte Carlo simulation risk analysis tool is shown in Figure 17-22. The calculation shows the probability of completing an activity, or the entire project, on or before a specific date.

The program generated this distribution by selecting possible durations for all the activities driving this deliverable. The tool then recorded the completion dates and constructed the graph and the histogram. What this means is the samples used for the durations are plugged into the duration field of the network activities and the watched activity (ID 666) is recalculated for the finish date. This iteration was done 1,000 times using a random number sampling process. The result is the Schedule Risk Histogram.

The histogram shows that the earliest completion for this activity is 2/13/13, the latest completion is 4/16/14, and the expected completion date is 8/29/13. These dates can be read directly from the x-axis of the histogram. The Completion Probability Table is a summary of the probability of completing on or before a specific date.   The results of this simulation indicate that there is only

a 50% - 55% chance of meeting or improving upon the scheduled delivery date of 8/20/13.

If the project team wants higher confidence in the probability of meeting its date for Hardware Delivery, then the scheduled date should be moved later or the appropriate amount of schedule margin should be added to the schedule.

Cost Risk Analysis Output

With a resource loaded schedule and the associated costs for those resources, a cumulative distribution function of the probability of the effort costing some value or less can be modeled. Figure 17-23 displays the probabilities of achieving the budgeted cost for the project. The planned budget of $2.496 million has only a 25% - 30% chance of being met with the expected cost being $2.508 million.

Other Scheduling Issues

Another limitation of CPM is that it cannot handle probabilistic branching easily. Different scenarios with different networks are required.   These results could be presented with their probabilities. Risk analysis can handle probabilistic branching in one run. The result would change as the probability of an event occurring changes. This allows the project manager to see the result and evalu-

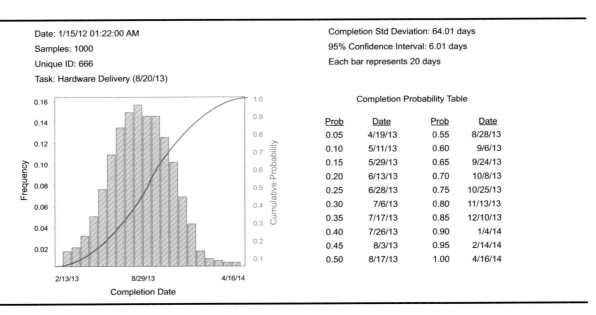

Date: 1/15/12 01:22:00 AM

Samples: 1000

Unique ID: 666

Task: Hardware Delivery (8/20/13)

Completion Std Deviation: 64.01 days

95% Confidence Interval: 6.01 days

Each bar represents 20 days

Completion Probability Table

Prob	Date	Prob	Date
0.05	4/19/13	0.55	8/28/13
0.10	5/11/13	0.60	9/6/13
0.15	5/29/13	0.65	9/24/13
0.20	6/13/13	0.70	10/8/13
0.25	6/28/13	0.75	10/25/13
0.30	7/6/13	0.80	11/13/13
0.35	7/17/13	0.85	12/10/13
0.40	7/26/13	0.90	1/4/14
0.45	8/3/13	0.95	2/14/14
0.50	8/17/13	1.00	4/16/14

Figure 17-22 Schedule Risk Histogram

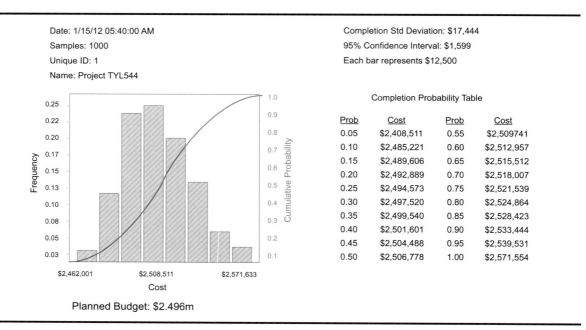

Date: 1/15/12 05:40:00 AM

Samples: 1000

Unique ID: 1

Name: Project TYL544

Completion Std Deviation: $17,444

95% Confidence Interval: $1,599

Each bar represents $12,500

Completion Probability Table

Prob	Cost	Prob	Cost
0.05	$2,408,511	0.55	$2,509741
0.10	$2,485,221	0.60	$2,512,957
0.15	$2,489,606	0.65	$2,515,512
0.20	$2,492,889	0.70	$2,518,007
0.25	$2,494,573	0.75	$2,521,539
0.30	$2,497,520	0.80	$2,524,864
0.35	$2,499,540	0.85	$2,528,423
0.40	$2,501,601	0.90	$2,533,444
0.45	$2,504,488	0.95	$2,539,531
0.50	$2,506,778	1.00	$2,571,554

Planned Budget: $2.496m

Figure 17-23 Cost Risk Histogram

ate the alternatives. Possibly resources can be reallocated to make a product more reliable (if the concern is getting the product to pass a test), or more attention can be focused on a testing or permitting agency's requirements.

Risk Assessment Tools

There are two different approaches that have been used to assess the risk inherent in all schedules. These are the Program Evaluation and Review Technique (PERT) and Monte Carlo simulation. PERT was the first to be used, while the most widely used of these currently is the Monte Carlo simulation.

PERT

PERT was developed as a formal technique for the U.S. Navy Polaris submarine program in 1958. While it was similar in many respects to CPM, the basic purposes were somewhat different. CPM was developed for commercial scheduling and project management and remains in common use today. PERT was used to forecast probabilities associated with project duration and cost. The underlying concepts of PERT were basically twofold: a project can be modeled as a network of events (not necessarily activities) and

the time between events is a probabilistic function (not deterministic as in CPM).

PERT relies on simple equations to combine distributions described by their mean and standard deviation, a measure of dispersion. Means can be added under some general conditions and standard deviations of activities can be combined by a simple formula to derive the standard deviation of a path completion.

PERT was intended not so much to manage a project better, but to determine the mean (average) and standard deviation (variability around the mean) of the completion time of the project. Later, the same applied to cost. The basic concept is the PERT critical path uses average durations based on the ranges of possible durations. PERT recalculates activity durations to incorporate the full range of possible durations. However, the fundamental critical path is calculated without recognizing the presence of the merge bias. This means that even PERT underestimates schedule risk.

The average duration computed weighs the most likely value four times as heavily as the low and high ranges. This Beta Distribution is not as risky as the triangular, which would weigh all three values equally.

Average in PERT = (Low + 4 x Most Likely + High) / 6

Average (triangular) = (Low + Most Likely + High) / 3

For PERT, the average is unlikely to be too far from the most likely duration. It is calculated based on the rule that average activity durations along an uninterrupted path can be added to get the average path duration.

Some statistical concepts must be addressed in order to understand PERT fully. Any statistics book can be consulted for further definition and information beyond the rudimentary discussion presented here.

One important concept is that of the standard deviation. While two activities may have the same average duration estimate, one will be riskier than the other based on their associated standard deviations. Refer to Figure 17-24. The distribution for Activity B has more risk than that for Activity A because its duration may lie further from the average. Said another way, the standard deviation for B is greater than that for A. In PERT, the Standard Deviation for an activity is calculated as:

$$\sigma = (\text{High} - \text{Low}) / 6$$

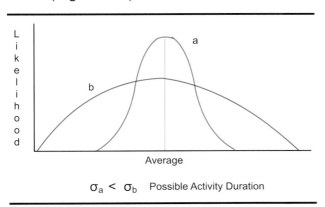

Figure 17-24 Standard Deviation

Another point to note is that the standard deviation of the path is smaller than the sum of the activities' sigmas (or standard deviations). This is shown in Figure 17-22. To calculate the standard deviation of the path it is necessary to calculate the variance. The variance is the square of the standard deviation. The standard deviation of the path cannot be calculated by adding the activity

standard deviations but it can be calculated by taking the square root of the sum of the variances of the activities.

Figure 17-25 shows how these computations are made based on some given information for a 6 activity network with two paths. Shown are the best case, worst case, and most likely estimates for the activities. The expected time for each activity is calculated using the PERT formula. The PERT formulas for standard deviation and variance are also used.

In a deterministic calculation, the most likely duration would be used exclusively and the two paths would be identical at 28 weeks. However, the Path U-V-X-Z has an expected duration of 30 weeks and a standard deviation of 3.6 weeks. The other path, U-W-Y-Z has an expected duration of 26 weeks and a standard deviation of 2.4 weeks. Shown are the best case, worst case, and most likely estimates for the activities. The expected time for each activity is calculated using the PERT formula. Notice that if paths were being calculated in a deterministic model, the most likely estimates would be used and the critical path would be 23 weeks.

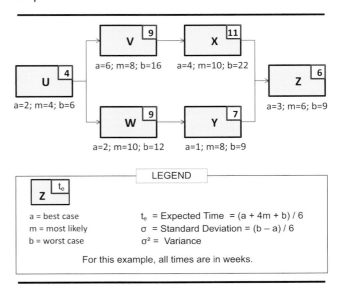

Figure 17-25 Six Activity Network Example

PERT assumes that the activity durations are independent of each other, but this assumption may be inaccurate. If some activities take longer than their average duration, will other activities

Activity	a (Best Case)	m (Most Likely)	b (Worst Case)	t_e (Expected Time)	σ (Standard Deviation)	σ^2 (Variance)
U	2	4	6	4	0.67	0.44
V	6	8	16	9	1.67	2.78
W	2	10	12	9	1.67	2.78
X	4	10	22	11	3.00	9.00
Y	1	8	9	7	1.33	1.78
Z	3	6	9	6	1.00	1.00

Figure 17-26 PERT Calculations

take longer too? If so, the equation will underestimate the path's standard deviation.

Figure 17-26 shows all of the PERT activity calculations from which the expected durations and standard deviations for the two paths were calculated.

For Path U-V-X-Z, the standard deviation (ó) is the square root of the sum of the variances for the activities in the path. The values for the path can be seen in Figure 17-26.

$$\sigma \sqrt{(0.44 + 2.78 + 9.00 + 1.00)} = 3.62$$

To keep the example simple, the standard deviation has been rounded up to a value of 4.0. Figure 17-27 shows this same information presented as a normal distribution curve. One standard deviation plus or minus from the mean is .68 or 68% of the area under the curve. This means that the probability for this path is 68% that the project will take between 26 and 34 weeks. It also means that it is 84% likely (50% + 34%) that this path will be completed within 34 weeks and 97.5% likely (50% + 34% + 13.5%) that it will be completed within 38 weeks.

For Path U-W-Y-Z, the standard deviation (ó) is the square root of the sum of the variances for the activities in this path. The values for the path can be referenced in Figure 17-26.

$$\sigma \sqrt{(0.44 + 2.78 + 1.78 + 1.00)} = 2.45$$

To keep the example simple, the standard deviation has been rounded up to a value of 2.5. Figure 17-28 shows the normal distribution curve for

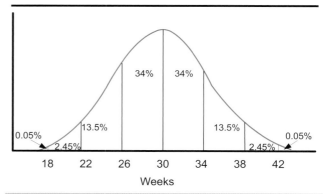

Path U-V-X-Z	t_e = 30	σ = 4.0

84% probability that the path finishes in 34 weeks or less

Figure 17-27 Distribution Curve for Path U-V-X-Z

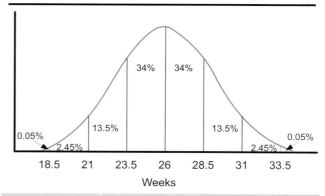

Path U-W-Y-Z	t_e = 26	σ = 2.5

84% probability that the path finishes in 28.5 weeks or less

Figure 17-28 Distribution Curve for Path U-W-Y-Z

Path U-W-Y-Z. This means that the probability for this path shows that it is 68% likely that the project will take between 23.5 and 28.5 weeks. It also means that it is 84% likely (50% + 34%) that this path will be completed within 28.5 weeks and 97.5% likely (50% + 34% + 13.5%) that it will be completed within 31 weeks.

Monte Carlo Approach

The Monte Carlo approach is calculated based on user-specified distributions. These distributions are then combined to produce a range of project completion dates. This is done using any of a number of available software packages. The Monte Carlo approach requires the existence of a CPM network and user specified distributions of activity durations. Projected schedule estimated completion dates are then computed based on multiple iterations, with random selection of activity durations for each iteration.

Each activity distribution can be specified with a formula for the particular distribution desired or the activity owner can select the "best fit" picture (graph) of the distribution from a set of possible distributions. Users familiar with the particular software application being used for the simulation can assist the activity owners in their selection or simply elicit a response as to the optimistic case, the pessimistic case, or most likely case for each activity. Some popular distributions include the triangular distribution, the beta distribution, and the chi-square distribution. Again, any statistics book can be consulted for further definition and information on the distributions and their characteristics.

The Monte Carlo simulation consists of a specified number of iterations performed to calculate activity and project completions. The final output is a distribution of possible completion dates. Risky activities are identified by the number of times they are calculated to be on the critical path. More iterations mean longer computer run time resulting in greater accuracy.

Cost Effective Implementation

One of the greatest challenges faced when implementing a Schedule Risk Assessment is the mental hurdle of performing the additional analytical work. After all, many organizations barely have adequate staff to develop and maintain a CPM schedule using single point estimates. The prerequisite of having a CPM logic and developing probability distributions for durations of all activities in a 10,000 activity network appears intimidating. That this is not just a onetime effort makes the challenge even more daunting. Just as the critical path will change based on recorded progress and delays, the highest risk path may also change over time. This means repeated efforts in defining the new risks encountered as the project progresses.

A successfully used short cut is to categorize all of the activities in the network file into defined risk categories. This approach recognizes the fact that there are not 10,000 different risk distributions in a 10,000 activity network. Virtually all activities fall into a few general categories and distributions of risk. The number of defined risk categories will vary from project to project, but the principle is the same. All activities can be classified by some terminology (high risk, medium risk, low risk, etc.). Standard distributions can then be developed for each risk category. The triangular distribution may be selected as the standard for most or all categories, with subsets of risk that are skewed left, skewed right, or normal distributions. The task is then to identify a risk category for each activity one time, specify a standard distribution, and maintain it throughout the life of the project until conditions change. Once a category has been applied to each activity, then all of the steps described in this chapter can be quickly implemented.

Successful schedule risk implementation is not only possible, it is necessary to identify the highest risks to successful project completion and completion on time.

Conclusion

Inclusion of the consideration of uncertainty will greatly enhance the available information from a CPM network. By using existing schedule risk software and accepted theory, it is possible to evaluate a schedule network to determine its paths of greatest risk. These risk paths may differ substantially from the defined critical path in a CPM network. While the critical path is the longest defined path through the network logic, the highest risk path has the potential of requiring even more time. This reality could result in a further delay to the completion date of the project. This does not mean CPM should be eliminated or replaced, since a valid CPM network is needed as a starting point for performing a schedule risk assessment. Rather, a risk assessment is a supplement that provides additional information to help ensure successful, on time, project completion.

Risk management uses the results of a risk assessment to work for the best outcome, but even the correct decisions may be accompanied by unfavorable results that have a low probability of occurrence. Nevertheless, the results of the risk assessment will indicate the most likely strategies for success.

When performing a schedule risk assessment, there must first be a valid CPM network for analysis. Then activity duration estimates are reviewed and a duration distribution for activities is determined. These distributions must then be combined to determine activity path distributions. The results should then be evaluated to identify high risk paths and recommend possible schedule contingency provisions. Finally, results should be monitored and updated as the project progresses and risks change.

Implementation considerations include the need for trained personnel to solicit the information on activity duration distributions. Many people have the tendency to provide unrealistic, narrow distribution bands or to be unduly influenced by recent dramatic (but unlikely) events. Valid CPM logic is especially important since there is a dramatic increase in risk at points of activity path convergence. This is known as "merge bias". If the logic includes many "nice to have" prerequisites, the result will be an exaggerated risk buildup at path convergences. The use of risk categories, assigned to each activity, will speed the process of implementation.

Two techniques have been employed for determining schedule risk: the Program Evaluation and Review Technique (PERT) and Monte Carlo simulation. The PERT technique is largely historical. Monte Carlo is understood best and is most frequently used. The biggest challenge remains, which is collecting the best data to use for any of these techniques.

Chapter 17 Review Questions

17-1.   Can the highest risk path for a logic network be different from the critical path? Explain.

17-2.   Discuss the difference between the terms "uncertainty" and "risk".

17-3.   Identify three important uses of schedule risk assessment.

17-4.   Identify the proper sequence of activities in a risk assessment by sequentially numbering the following steps in the order that they must occur:

_____   Compute the activity path distribution.

_____   Initiate status monitoring.

_____   Create a CPM/PDM network.

_____   Calculate a duration distribution for activities.

_____   Develop activity duration estimates.

_____   Evaluate the results.

17-5.   Calculate the expected duration of the following activity, using a triangular distribution: minimum duration = 6 weeks, most likely duration = 8 weeks, maximum duration = 16 weeks.

17-6.   Explain how a cumulative probability curve of project durations can be used to recommend a value of schedule slippage reserve.

17-7.   How is schedule risk affected by the convergence of multiple activity paths in a network at a single point?

17-8.   Activity paths A, B, and C converge as common predecessors to milestone D. Paths A, B, and C have been analyzed using risk techniques. The cumulative percent likelihood curves for possible path durations of path A and B overlap, while path C does not. Path A has a 50% likelihood of completing within its assigned duration, while path B has a 60% chance and path C has a 95% chance. What is the likelihood that milestone D will be achieved on time?

True or False

17-9.   The highest risk path may be the one that actually determines the project duration, rather than the critical path.

17-10. An advantage of a schedule risk assessment is that it allows the determination of a single point duration estimate for each activity.

17-11. In most distributions, the expected duration and most likely duration are the same value.

17-12. A cumulative likelihood curve (S-curve) of a schedule risk assessment portrays the likelihood of each duration occurring.

17-13. The bias in a schedule is the difference between the average duration and the nominal duration.

17-14. Merge bias describes the tendency of schedulers to estimate short durations so that when the activity slips, it may still support the project completion date.

17-15. The risk associated with completing an activity or total network may be greatly changed when directed dates are used.

17-16. The use of late start scheduling greatly increases the risk in a project schedule.

17-17. PERT is an early risk assessment tool that heavily weights the most likely duration in the computation of average duration.

17-18. "Expected duration" is another way of describing the average duration.

17-19. High risk activities are identified in schedule risk studies, using the Monte Carlo approach, by the number of times they are determined to be on the critical path.

The answers to these questions can be found in Section 6, Solutions.

Case Study

17.1 MAKING ACTIVITY DURATION DISTRIBUTIONS

Joe and Nancy Drive to Work

Joe and Nancy work downtown at the Better Late Than Never Construction Company. They have just moved to the west side of town and commute to work on the freeway. Getting to work on time poses a problem because the freeway can back up, causing significant delays.

Nancy wants to try out her project schedule management skills on this problem. She knows that good data is important in developing a project schedule. In the four weeks they have been commuting, she has collected the following data:

Driving Activity

Minutes Range	Minutes Midrange	Frequency
16 - 25	20	0
26 - 35	30	1
36 - 45	40	5
46 - 55	50	4
56 - 65	60	3
66 - 75	70	2
76 - 85	80	2
86 - 95	90	1
96 - 105	100	1
106 - 115	110	1
116 - 125	120	0
	Total	20

1. What is the most likely or "best guess" duration of the driving activity?

2. Assuming the best guess duration is the estimated duration, when should the "getting to work" project start (when should they leave home to arrive at 8:30AM)?

3. What is the average or "expected" driving duration? Is the average the same as the best guess?

The solution to this case study can be found on the Humphreys & Associates, Inc. web site.
www.humphreys-assoc.com

4. Draw the frequency distribution represented by the data above. What geometrical shape does it look like? Is it symmetrical? Is the "best guess" duration a good planning number?

5. Even with these data, is it possible to be 100% sure of getting to work on time? Why and Why not?

Suppose Joe and Nancy want to get to work on time, but they are not rigid about it. They have found that "the traffic" is a pretty good excuse for being a few minutes late if it were not used too often.

6. Convert the frequency distribution to a cumulative likelihood curve (S-curve) for which the cumulative percentage likelihood equals 100%.

7. When should Joe and Nancy leave for work? Using the S-curve, what is the likelihood of being late, given your estimated start time? How rigid are they about on-time arrival at Better Late Than Never Construction Company?

8. Given the S-curve, how likely is it to slip beyond the best guess estimate of duration?

9. How much time allowance would you add to the Drive Activity's best guess estimate to achieve:

    •   A 50% likelihood of slippage?

    •   A 20% likelihood of slippage?

10. Suppose the boss Mr. Bigg will "have your job" if he catches you coming in late. When might Joe and Nancy start their trip now?

Case Study

17.2 COMBINING DISTRIBUTIONS ALONG A PATH

Joe and Nancy Drive, Park, and Walk to Work

Joe noticed that Nancy's CPM network was incomplete. It did not include parking and walking from the parking lot to the office (the Park and Walk activity). Since they had not kept track of how long that took, they had to use their 'expert judgment'.

They concluded that it usually took only 15 minutes to find a spot and walk to the office. One day it took 25 minutes, and on another day it took only 5 minutes. From this information, Joe constructed the following distribution:

Park and Walk Activity

Minutes Range	Minutes Midrange	Frequency
2.5-7.5	5	1
7.6-12.5	10	5
12.6-17.5	15	8
17.6-22.5	20	5
22.6-27.5	25	1
	Total	20

1. Draw this frequency distribution. Convert it to a cumulative likelihood curve (S-curve).

2. Identify the best guess duration and calculate the average duration for the Park and Walk Activity. Are they Different? Why or why not?

3. Adding the best guess estimates for the two activities, Drive and Park & Walk, how long does it take to get to work?

4. Replace the best guess estimates with the average estimates. Now, how long does it take?

5. Replace the estimates for the two activities with their 90th percentile duration estimates. Now how long does it take to get to work?

The solution to this case study can be found on the Humphreys & Associates, Inc. web site.
www.humphreys-assoc.com

Using Software to Combine Distributions Along a Path

Joe and Nancy realize that combining distributions of in-line activities is not as simple as adding up the low, most likely, and high estimates. They know that the only values from the activity distributions that can be added to get an equivalent value on the distribution representing the path duration are the averages.

They know that computer software will do the work of combining the activity distributions. Nancy uses available software at Better Late Than Never to combine the activity distribution assumptions. Shown below are the assumptions and results for the Drive, Park, and Walk Project.

- Driving Activity triangular distribution.

- Park & Walk Activity triangular distribution.

- Drive, Park & Walk Path result distribution:

  - 'Bell-Curve'.

  - 'S-Curve'.

- Tables of S-curve results for the path showing:

  - Minutes (on the X-axis) corresponding to points of cumulative likelihood (on the Y-axis).

  - Cumulative likelihood (Y-axis) corresponding to minutes of time (on the X-axis).

Driving Activity

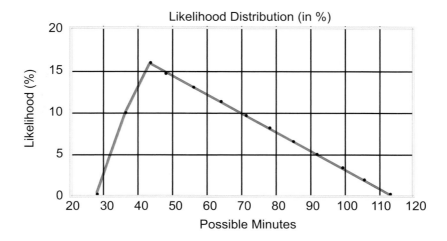

Likelihood Distribution (in %)

Park and Walk Activity

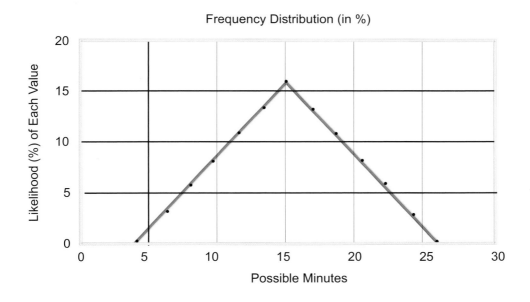

Frequency Distribution (in %)

Drive, Park, and Walk Path

Frequency Distribution (in %)

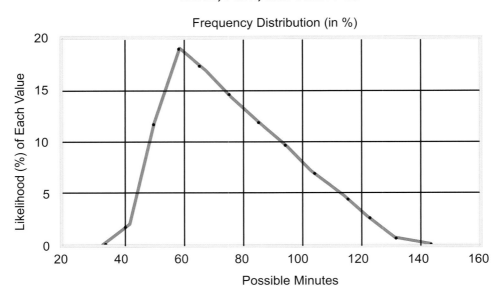

Drive, Park, and Walk Path .

Cumulative Likelihood (S-Curve)

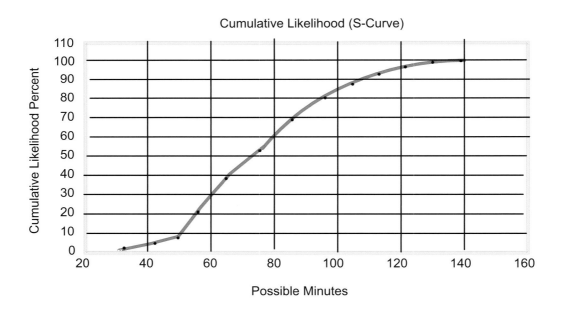

Path Result Distribution
S-Curve Results in Tables

Drive Activity, Park and Walk Acitivty Path		Drive, Park, and Walk Activity Path	
Cumulative Likelihood	Minutes	Minutes	Cumulative Likelihood
10	52	35	1
20	57	40	1
30	62	45	3
40	67	50	8
50	73	55	15
60	79	60	25
70	86	65	36
80	94	70	45
90	104	75	54
95	112	80	62
		85	69
		90	76
		95	81
		100	86
		105	90
		110	94
		115	96
		120	98
		125	99
		130	99
		135	99

6. Using the S-curve results for the Drive, Park & Walk path, how likely is it to get to work in 35 minutes, the sum of the two low estimates? Circle the number representing the answer on the appropriate table and find it on the S-curve graph.

7. How likely is it to take 2 hours and 15 minutes, the sum of the two high estimates? Circle the number representing the answer on the appropriate table and find it on the S-curve graph.

8. What is the 90th percentile of the path distribution? Is it the same as the sum of the 90th percentile durations of the two activities? Why or why not?

9. What is the 'most likely' estimate of the project, approximately? Is it the sum of the two activity best guesses?

10. How likely is the project to slip beyond the sum of the most likely activity estimates?

11. Using these answers, list some for the pitfalls in relying on a CPM single-point estimate based on the best guesses of activity durations?

Getting to the Wednesday Meeting

Nancy has an important meeting on Wednesday at 8:30 sharp. Because of the meeting, it is more important than usual for Nancy and Joe to be on time.

12. Using the cumulative likelihood function for the project, when should they leave home on Wednesday morning to be only 20% likely to arrive late?

13. Suppose Nancy is giving the presentation at the meeting and Mr. Bigg will be there. How might her starting time change because of this fact?

Parking and Walking Activity

Cumulative % Likelihood Graph

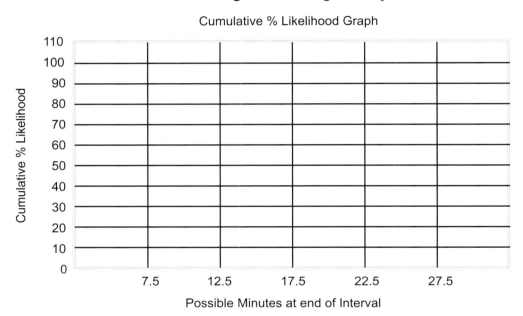

Possible Minutes at end of Interval

Parking and Walking Activity

Frequency Graph

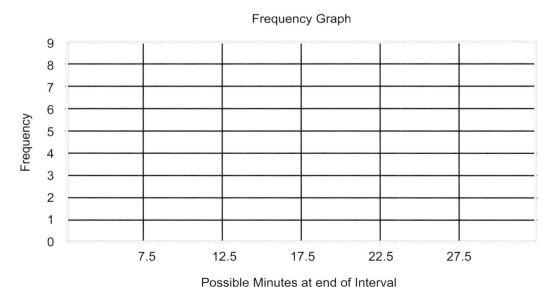

Possible Minutes at end of Interval

Case Study

17.3 SCHEDULE EAC AND PATH CONVERGENCE

Mike Commutes by Train

Mike also works at Better Late Than Never Construction. He lives south of the city and takes the train but walks the last 3 blocks from the station to the office. It takes him 1 hour and 10 minutes to get to work. (For this case study, assume that his trip duration is certain.)

Mr. Bigg also wants Mike at the 8:30 meeting. He asks his executive assistant, Bob, to make sure that both Nancy and Mike arrive on time.

Bob is not a sophisticated scheduler. He simply asks Nancy for her best guess on how long it will take to drive, park, and walk. She says "It is most likely to take 40 minutes to drive and 15 minutes to park and walk." He asks Mike who says "70 minutes".

1. Draw the two-path CPM network for the project "Getting Nancy and Mike to the meeting".

2. Assuming Nancy and Mike start at the same time, identify the critical path using the best guess estimates from Mike and Nancy.

3. Assuming that early starts is the only risk management approach open to Bob and using the best guess CPM estimates Mike and Nancy provided him:

   • Who should he contact first to make sure the meeting will start on time?

   • When should he call?

Identify the critical path using the average duration estimates for Mike and Nancy. Based on the average durations, when and who should Bob call first?

Nancy shows Bob the cumulative likelihood distribution she calculated in the previous problem set and tells him what it means. Now Bob has the information at his disposal to do an analysis of the risk of starting Mr. Bigg's meeting late.

**S-Curve for Nancy's Path to Work
Drive, Park, and Walk Path**

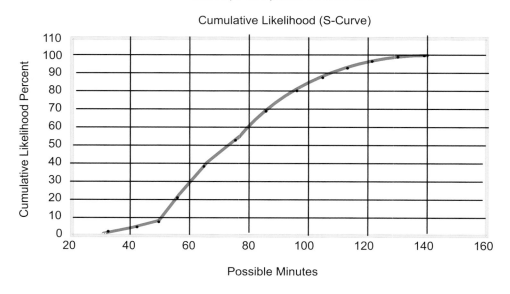

4. Assuming that Mike and Nancy start at the same time, compare their project schedule estimate at complete cumulative likelihood distributions for the project "Getting Nancy and Mike to the Meeting". (Hint: Overlay Mike's 'S-curve' on the graph above.)

5. Which person's trip poses the most risk of slipping the meeting? Is this the critical path? The highest risk path?

6. Now, who should Bob call first on Wednesday and when should he call to make sure there is a 90% likelihood that Nancy and Mike get to the 8:30 meeting on time? Why so early?

7. Add a curve to the graph above to represent the EAC distribution for 'risk management with early starts' for Nancy as required in question number 6.

The Alternate Plan

Joe and Nancy experiment with other routes and find out that driving on surface streets always takes 70 minutes. The Park & Walk activity distribution still has the same distribution as before.

8. Draw a cumulative likelihood curve for the 2-activity path including the surface street alternate. (Hint: Change the X-axis values on the Park & Walk S-Curve below).

Park and Walk Path

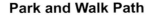

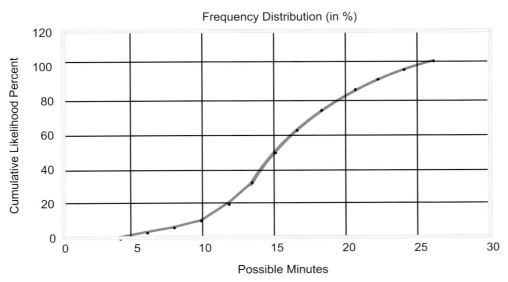

9. For Joe and Nancy's trip to work, superimpose the cumulative likelihood S-curve for the alternate plan's EAC on that of the original plan on the graph below. Why is one more vertical than the other?

Drive, Park, and Walk Path

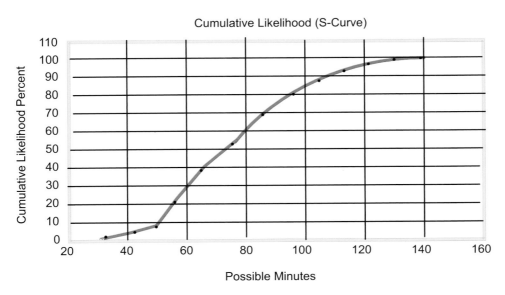

10. Often alternate plans will reduce risk but at an increase in cost. Is that true of the 'surface street' plan, and if so, why?

Data Problems

Often past data are not entirely accurate or, if accurate, are not current or relevant to the project being scheduled.

How would your answers change if you found out that Joe's and Nancy's data were taken from the last 4 weeks of August when everyone on the west side goes on vacation? (Notice that the meeting is scheduled for the Wednesday after Labor Day.)

Drive, Park, and Walk Path

Cumulative Likelihood S-Curve

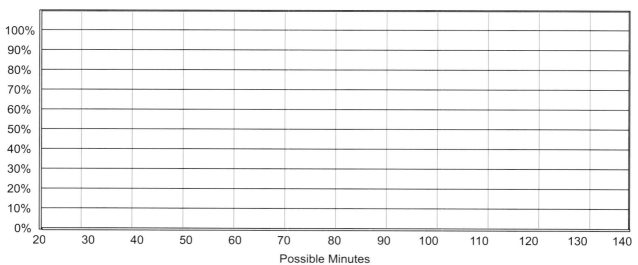

Drive, Park, and Walk Path

Cumulative Likelihood S-Curve

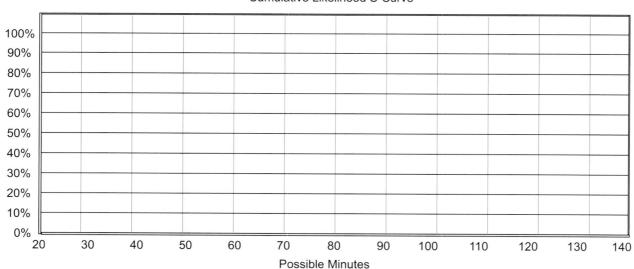

Drive, Park, and Walk Path

Cumulative Likelihood S-Curve

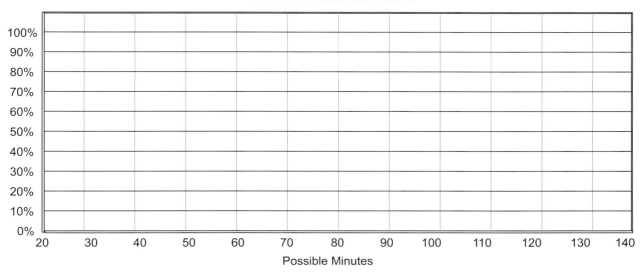

Possible Minutes

Drive Surface Streets, Park, and Walk Path

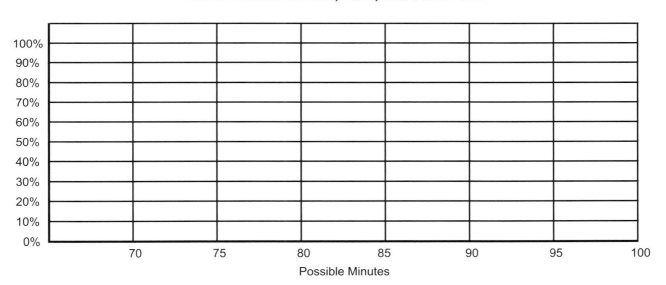

Possible Minutes

Chapter 18

SCHEDULING IN A PERFORMANCE MEASUREMENT ENVIRONMENT

Objectives of this Chapter:

1. Identify the specific scheduling requirements for a project or contract that includes application of the ANSI/EIA-748 (latest revision) EVMS Guidelines.

2. Stress the importance of horizontal and vertical schedule traceability when scheduling in a performance measurement environment and adhering to the ANSI/EIA-748 (latest revision) EVMS Guidelines.

This chapter addresses the scheduling application and its use with the Earned Value Management System Guidelines (EVMSG) contained in the ANSI/EIA-748 (latest revision). No attempt is made here to explain all the guidelines and their application. However, in this chapter the discussion centers upon specific requirements imposed on scheduling systems with contracts subject to the EVMSG.

The EVMS approach can be summed up as a three step process; schedule short measurable tasks, budget the tasks, measure accomplishment of the tasks, which is quite compatible with the approach of development and maintenance of a project schedule.

The specific requirements for an EVMS scheduling application are typical of capabilities that any effective scheduling system must possess if it were to be integrated with the scope of work and cost system.

Not all projects require scheduling and cost systems to be electronically integrated; however, scheduling and cost must interface for project information to be consistent, especially when time/cost tradeoffs must be made.

System Description

An Earned Value Management System Description, or system description for short, defines and depicts how all subsystems, including the scheduling system, are integrated. It is used to demonstrate the processes, information flow, and to identify standard symbology and reporting requirements. It defines the number of schedule levels used to manage the project, as well as how consistency will be assured among these levels.

Companies sometimes make the mistake of over-specifying their scheduling approach here. Once a commitment is made in the system description, it becomes a requirement for system operation and is also required by contracts with EVMS application. If the system description does not contain specific detail, it should be supported by procedures.

Schedule Traceability

The requirements for schedule traceability were discussed in Chapter 12; a brief summary is included here. Vertical traceability ensures that work package start and complete dates are consistent with the schedule dates of the control

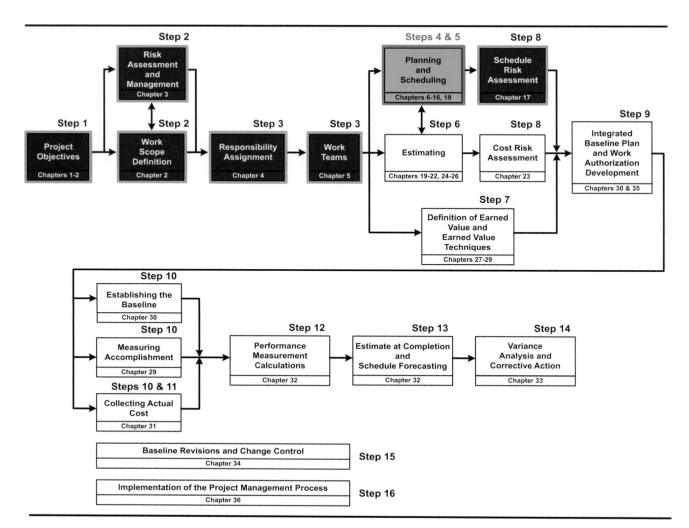

Figure 18-1 Earned Value Project Management: The Process

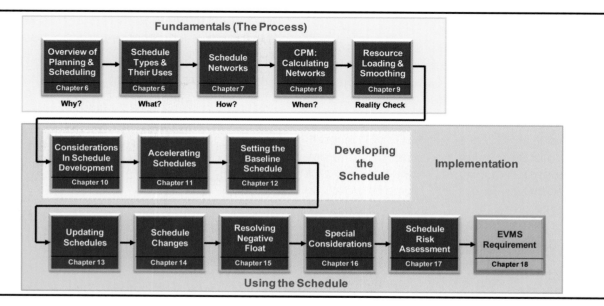

Figure 18-2 Planning and Scheduling

account or project. Traceability also ensures that control account schedules will support the Master Schedule, particularly major milestones. It should be emphasized that this does not prevent the company from managing the schedule. Vertical traceability is still satisfied if work package schedules require completion ahead of the Master Schedule requirements. As outlined in the Data Item Description DI-MGMT-81650, this allows the contractor some additional flexibility (schedule margin) to increase the chances of making the project required dates.

Horizontal traceability requires that all project interfaces among organizations internally and externally are identified clearly and consistently. The availability of milestone tables assist in the confirmation of both vertical and horizontal traceability.

Achieving horizontal traceability is not easy in a large project environment; but it is critical to having a complete and useful schedule. One method used to help achieve horizontal linkage is to build a matrix of all responsible control account managers (CAM). The CAMs are listed on the horizontal and vertical axes of the matrix. In a series of meetings, each CAM is asked to identify the CAMs from whom input is needed and the CAMs to whom output is owed. When completed, the matrix defines the input and output needs. The matrix is then refined to define the exact inputs and outputs owed so the logic in the network schedule can be built with the appropriate links. This integration process can take a number of weeks on a large project.

While horizontal and vertical traceability are important within the schedule, the IMS also has other traceability requirements. One major requirement is scope traceability. As defined by the Generally Accepted Scheduling Principles (GASP) referenced in Chapter 6, Principle #1 (Completeness) of a valid schedule requires the IMS to include all "Authorized discreet effort for the entire contract, with essential subcontracted or other external work or milestones integrated yet distinguishable from internal work". GASP Principle #2 (Traceable) also requires that tasks "are coded to relate tasks or milestones to source or dependent documents, tools and responsible organizations". Finally, while not a GASP princi-

ple, schedules should be historically traceable displaying the evolution of the schedule from the initial baseline development, through authorized changes, until current configuration.

Reconciliation to Time-Phased Budgets

All activities must be clearly associated with WBS elements. This requirement is essential if scope were to be tied to schedule (and budget). There are some additional aspects to this requirement:

1. The baseline and forecast information contained within the integrated master schedule must coincide with the cost system.

2. Schedule status (i.e. reported progress) must be the same within the integrated schedule and cost system.

3. Control account milestones must be incorporated within all other schedules (where applicable).

These requirements relate to the underlying concept of integrated project management; the EVMSG that cost and schedule must be integrated at the control account level. A problem occurs when resource loaded schedules do not agree with cash flow projections, time phased budget baselines, and estimates developed in other parts of the organization. Even the totals may not be consistent among the estimate, the resource loaded schedule, and the cash flow projections. While this anomaly may happen on commercial contracts, on contracts with the federal government subject to EVMSG application, schedule and budget baselines must be traceable. Obviously, any well-managed project management system must guard against these types of inconsistencies and have processes in place to ensure integration.

Reconciliation of Progress and Performance

When the schedule progress information and the earned value information exist in two different tools, there is the possibility that they will provide different pictures of the current condition unless they are reconciled. Schedule progress in terms of actual starts, actual completions, and percent complete inputs should depict the same status as earned value inputs to the cost system that generates performance information. This is best achieved in resource loaded schedules where schedule and work progress are reported together from the schedule.

Short of integrating the schedule and performance inputs into the schedule, a process for reconciliation must be established. Often these processes are supported by electronic validation and audit tools.

Contract Requirements

While the contract will define the specific deliverable documents and due dates, the following items are required for all contracts with EVMSG and PASEG applications. The schedule must be:

- Complete: The schedule captures the entire discrete, authorized project effort from start through completion.

- Traceable: The schedule logic is horizontally and vertically integrated with cross-references to key documents, tools and responsible organizations.

- Transparent: The schedule provides visibility to assure it is complete, traceable, has documented assumptions, and provides full disclosure of project status and forecasts.

- Statused: The schedule has accurate progress through the status date.

- Predictive: The schedule provides meaningful critical paths and accurate forecasts for remaining work through project completion.

- Usable: The schedule is an indispensable tool for timely and effective management decisions and actions.

- Resourced: The schedule aligns with actual and projected resource availability.

- Controlled: The schedule is built, baselined, and maintained using a stable, repeatable, and documented process.

Control account and work package milestones are developed during the planning process consistent with higher level scheduled events. Typically, different schedule levels are maintained in various formats (see Figure 18-3). Some may be manually prepared while others are automated. Ideally, it is less demanding on the scheduling organization if the most detailed schedule is maintained within a CPM format and summary level schedules are produced automatically from the same database.

The level of detail within the WBS and that of the schedule level are comparable as demonstrated in Figure 18-4. The Master Milestone Schedule corresponds to the highest level of the WBS, since both refer to overall project scope. The Intermediate Schedules typically correspond to the next level of the WBS, the major system or end product level. Detailed schedules reflect the detailed WBS elements at a correspondingly lower level.

A schedule is required to support an earned value requirement. This can result in the schedule needing to be created to support progress measurement for the earned value system. Each measurable work element, usually the individual activity in the schedule, is assigned an earned value technique; this technique must be the same for all activities within the work package. This places restrictions and expectations on the schedule.

For example, an activity that has been assigned the earned value technique of 50/50 cannot have a baseline plan that allows the start and completion of the activity to be in more than two contiguous months. An activity with the milestone earned value technique assigned would have measurable milestones associated with it that are used to earn value based in completion of the milestones.

These are certainly not pure scheduling requirements; they flow into the schedule from its association with the earned value requirements and the earned value engine.

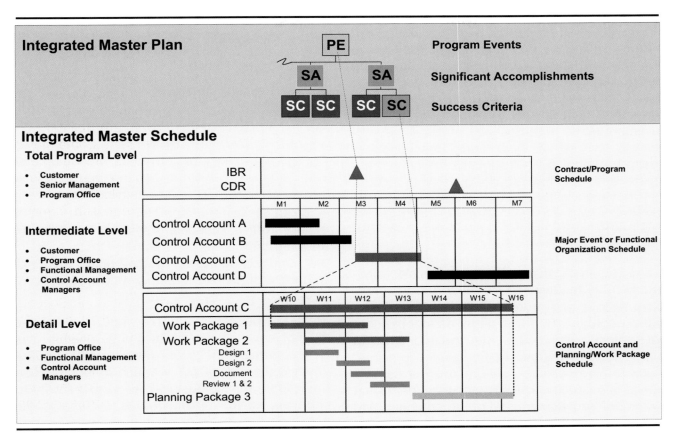

Figure 18-3 Schedule Integration - Schedules Must Tier

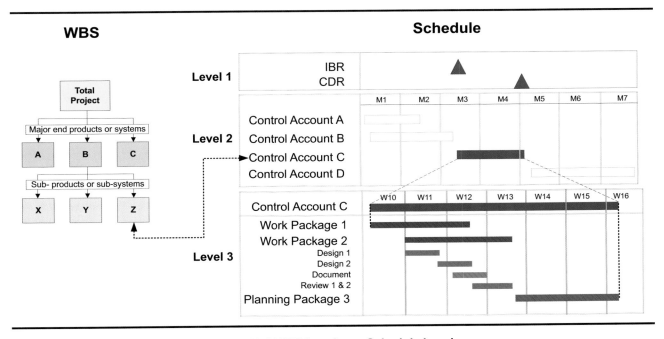

Figure 18-4 WBS Levels vs. Schedule Levels

Special Requirements

Careful reading of contractual requirements is basic to developing a compliant schedule. The current version of DI-MGMT-81650, Integrated Master Schedule, has over 70 individual requirements that must be met to achieve compliance. Development of a compliance matrix is recommended when this Data Item Description is required by contract. The matrix should list the requirements and their source along with a statement of how the requirements will be met. An example could be the requirement that the schedule be accessible by "product, process, and organization."

In this requirement, the word accessible translates to "able to be grouped and sorted by" product, process, and organization. A compliance matrix would list the three items as independent requirements and explain the method used to satisfy the requirement. In the case of "process" the explanation used by several top line companies is: a process code is established identifying the various processes used in the company and each activity and milestone in the schedule must be coded with the appropriate code (e.g. software testing, system engineering, or qualification testing).

Meeting all contractual and company requirements, as well as all requirements of tool interfaces, could easily require 20 different codes to be applied to each activity when in the earned value environment. A partial list of the codes used in one application is shown below. The schedule may be filtered, grouped, and sorted by any or combinations of these to provide the answers to customer and management questions.

1. Product.
2. Process.
3. Performing Organization.
4. Responsible Organization.
5. Contract Line Item (CLIN).
6. Recurring/Non-recurring.
7. Integrated Master Plan reference.
8. Statement of Work Reference.
9. Manager.
10. Scheduler.
11. Project Phase.
12. Drawing number.
13. Lot number.
14. Earned Value Technique.
15. Charge Number.
16. Work Breakdown Structure ID.

None of these requirements is unreasonable to expect from a scheduling system that supports an integrated project management approach. If cost and schedule are not properly integrated with each other, extraordinary problems will soon develop.

Many horror stories are told about projects that did not have integrated cost and schedule systems. Since the two are interrelated, artificially keeping them separate is bound to result in contradictions and confusion. An aerospace hardware application maintained a resource loaded schedule and a separate cost baseline. While separation would not be a problem if the two were carefully interfaced and verified with each other, this was not being done on this project. As schedule slippage occurred, various explanations were given.

However, the real reason for the schedule slippage was that the resources required to complete the scheduled work were far more than that budgeted and authorized for the fiscal year. As a result, it was impossible to complete all of the scheduled work with the authorized budget. Since the cost and schedule groups were not coordinating with each other, the cost baseline did not match the schedule baseline. This difficulty had gone undetected in the planning phase and was not even apparent until the variances appeared.

A similar situation occurred in an electric utility application with a large number of small projects in each calendar year. Projects were not being completed as planned. Because the cost and schedule information were not integrated, it became quite a challenge to find the sources of the slippage. As it turned out, the many small projects scheduled did not always match the many small projects budgeted. As a result, there were instances in a fiscal year where no budget had been authorized for a project that had been scheduled.

This problem generally happens with large projects, but can also happen with smaller projects if cost and schedule are not part of an integrated planning process. For this reason, the project management process is just as necessary on numerous small projects as on individual large projects.

A strong project management process is particularly significant today when large capital projects are deferred and small maintenance projects on older facilities take their place as life extension projects.

Conclusion

Four key implementation considerations must be included in the schedule portion of a performance measurement system when the contract requires the application of the Earned Value Management System Guidelines:

1. System description.

2. Schedule traceability.

3. Reconciliation to time-phased budgets.

4. Contract requirements.

These requirements, when successfully applied, ensure that the scheduling portion of the project management system supports the objective of an integrated cost and schedule system.

Chapter 18 Review Questions

18-1.   Describe the purpose of the System Description as it applies to the scheduling subsystem of an overall project management system.

18-2.   How do resource loaded schedules sometimes raise problems within an EVMSG (Earned Value Management System Guidelines) system application?

True or False

18-3.   Reported schedule status must be the same within the integrated schedule and the cost system.

18-4.   If a detailed schedule milestone were scheduled earlier than the same milestone shown on a summary schedule, this is a violation of the requirement for vertical traceability.

18-5.   It is advantageous for a contractor to describe its best possible system in the System Description, since it can always be changed in the implementation phase of the contract.

The answers to these questions can be found in Section 6, Solutions.

Case Study

18.1 SCHEDULE TRACEABILITY

The CANDU Company has produced three items to illustrate how its scheduling system functions:

1. A computer-generated Master Schedule showing major WBS elements.

2. A computer-generated Intermediate Schedule for WBS 1010000 Console Subsystem.

3. A Control Account Plan (CAP) for control account 1040ADC within WBS element 1010500 showing work packages schedules, the 'detail schedule' in this package of reports.

Attached are representations of those schedules.

Case Study Requirements

Review the schedules and answer the following questions.

1. Are milestones and time spans traceable?

2. Are the milestones meaningful?

3. Can work progress be traced?

4. Can the cumulative BCWP through October be determined from the information in the CAP, i.e. statused milestones and percents complete?

5. Name at least three things that could be done to this scheduling system and its reports that would dramatically improve its effectiveness.

Note:

SRR stands for Systems Requirements Review.

IBR stands for Integrated Baseline Review.

PDR stands for Preliminary Design Review.

EPA stands for Engineering Prototype Available.

SSR stands for Systems Software Review.

The solution to this case study can be found on the Humphreys & Associates, Inc. web site.
www.humphreys-assoc.com

Master Schedule

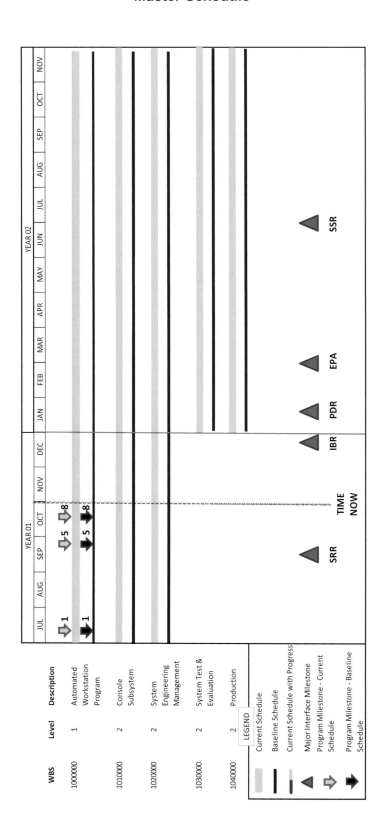

Intermediate Schedule: Console Subsystem

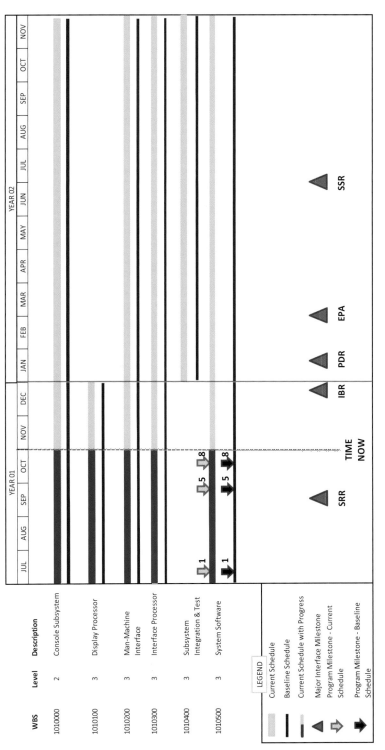

Control Account Plan Detail Schedule

CONTROL ACCOUNT PLAN

WBS REFERENCE: 1010201
SCHEDULE REFERENCE: ADA LVL 1 001 R0
Element of Cost (EOC): L-Labor, M-Mat'l, S-SubKtr, O-ODC
REFERENCE MILESTONES:
PROGRAM: Engineering Data Integration System
CONTROL ACCOUNT TITLE/NO.: PRE-SRR DOC MGMT SOFTWARE DEVELOPMENT / 1040ADC
CAM: THAD BAKER
PROGRAM MGR: BROAD STEARMAN
DATE: 7/15/Yr1
REV NO.: Orig.
PAGE: 1 OF 1
TOTAL: 12 MOS

WORK TASK NO./EOC	WORK TASK DESCRIPTION	CWA NO	EV METHOD		JUL	AUG	SEP	OCT	NOV	DEC	JAN	FEB	MAR	APR	MAY	JUN	TOTAL 12 MOS
				MILESTONES	System Requirements Review			Integrated Baseline Review		Preliminary Design Review			Engineering Prototype Available		System Software Review	
1	Management/administration of developing system software	A3G01	1 LOE	BCWS-HRS	23	30	35	20	20	20	20	20	20	20	20	35	283
				BCWS-$	$1,650	$2,153	$2,511	$1,435	$1,435	$1,435	$1,435	$1,435	$1,435	$1,435	$1,435	$2,511	$20,305
				BCWP-HRS													0
				BCWP-$													$0
2	Requirements Definition & Analysis to support SRR	A3G01	5 % Complete	BCWS-HRS	57	80	50										187
				BCWS-$	$4,090	$5,740	$3,588										$13,418
				BCWP-HRS	31% WS / 31% WP	43% WS / 43% WP	26% WS / 26% WP										0
				BCWP-$													$0
3	Support Risk Identification & Assessment (1 thru 5 = 20 hrs per milestone; 6 thru 9 = 10 hrs per milestone)	A3G01	2 Milestone	BCWS-HRS	20	40	40	10	10	10	10						140
				BCWS-$	$1,435	$2,870	$2,870	$718	$718	$718	$718						$10,047
				BCWP-HRS													0
				BCWP-$													$0
4	Software Integration Testing & Software/Hardware Interface Testing	A3G01	5 % Complete	BCWS-HRS							50	160	250	260			720
				BCWS-$							$3,588	$11,480	$17,938	$18,655			$51,661
				BCWP-HRS					7% WS / 5% WP	22% WS / 15% WP	35% WS / 20% WP	36% WS / 20% WP					0
				BCWP-$													$0
5	Test Planning 150 Requirements (5 hrs per requirement)	A3G01	6 Units	BCWS-HRS			10	100	100	100	190	150	100				750
				BCWS-$			$718	$5,740	$7,175	$7,175	$13,633	$10,763	$7,175	$1,435			$53,814
				BCWP-HRS	Units WS		2 / 0	16 / 12	20 / 15	20 / 22	38 / 40	30 / 25	20 / 20	4 / 10	0 / 6		0
				BCWP-$	Units WP												$0
6	Design, Code & Unit Test	A3G01	5 % Complete	BCWS-HRS			59	173	336	336	709	709	664	664	550		4800
				BCWS-$			$4,233	$12,413	$24,108	$24,108	$50,871	$50,871	$47,642	$47,642	$39,463		$344,401
				BCWP-HRS			1% WS / 1% WP	4% WS / 2% WP	7% WS / 5% WP	7% WS / 6% WP	15% WS / 10% WP	15% WS / 14% WP	14% WS / 14% WP	14% WS / 14% WP	11% WS / 10% WP		0
				BCWP-$													$0
7	Software Input - Preliminary Documentation & Release	A3G01	3 50/50	BCWS-HRS										70	70		140
				BCWS-$										$5,023	$5,023		$10,046
				BCWP-HRS													0
				BCWP-$													$0
8	Interpret, analyze & coordinate document management software design with System Engineering & other subsystems (10% of WP #6)	A3G01	7 Apportioned	BCWS-HRS				17	34	34	71	71	66	66	55		480
				BCWS-$				$1,220	$2,440	$2,440	$5,094	$5,094	$4,736	$4,736	$3,946		$34,442
				BCWP-HRS													0
				BCWP-$													$0
9	Purchase of compilers, research materials, DNA specialists, etc. supporting design	A3G01	5 % Complete	BCWS-HRS					$2,500	$5,000	$5,000	$5,000	$3,000				$20,500
				BCWS-$					12% WS / 12% WP	24% WS / 24% WP	24% WS / 24% WP	24% WS / 24% WP	16% WS / 16% WP				0
				BCWP-HRS													$0

PAGE TOTALS					JUL	AUG	SEP	OCT	NOV	DEC	JAN	FEB	MAR	APR	MAY	JUN	TOTAL
MONTHLY BCWS				HOURS	100	150	200	300	500	500	1000	950	900	1000	1000	900	7500
				DOLLARS	$7,175	$10,763	$14,351	$21,526	$38,376	$40,876	$76,751	$73,163	$67,576	$71,751	$71,751	$64,575	$558,634
CUM BCWS				HOURS	100	250	450	750	1250	1750	2750	3700	4600	5600	6600	7500	
				DOLLARS	$7,175	$17,938	$32,289	$53,815	$92,191	$133,067	$209,818	$282,981	$350,557	$422,308	$494,059	$558,634	
MONTHLY BCWP				HOURS	0	0	0	0	0	0	0	0	0	0	0	0	0
				DOLLARS	$0	$0	$0	$0	$0	$0	$0	$0	$0	$0	$0	$0	$0
CUM BCWP				HOURS	0	0	0	0	0	0	0	0	0	0	0	0	
				DOLLARS	$0	$0	$0	$0	$0	$0	$0	$0	$0	$0	$0	$0	
MONTHLY ACWP				HOURS													0
				DOLLARS													$0

Time Now

LEGEND:
△ = Start Activity
☐ = Complete Activity - Plan
▽ = Delayed Activity - Revised Plan
◇ Filled in symbol indicates completed activity - actual

Earned Value (EV) Codes:
1. Level of Effort
2. Milestone
3. 50/50
4. 0/100
5. % Complete
6. Units Complete
7. Apportioned

APPROVALS:
CAM: _____ DATE: _____
PROGRAM MGR: _____ DATE: _____

Review

SECTION 2 QUIZ

Note: There may be more than one answer to a question.

1.   A good schedule provides multiple benefits for the program. Which of the following is not true?
A. Provides management by exception.
B. Becomes a common basis for communication.
C. Facilitates forecasting manpower requirements.
D. Provides no project completion date.

2.   The Gantt Chart was the first computerized schedule system.
A. True.
B. False.

3.   Milestone charts are the most efficient tools to use to forecast schedule problems.
A. True.
A. False.

4.   Which of the following do not define the critical path?
A. The longest path through the schedule.
B. The minimum amount of time to complete the project.
C. The total float values are less than zero.
D. The path with the highest technical risk.

5.   Which calculation is used to determine total float?
A. LF - EF.
B. LS - ES.
C. start + duration.
D. finish - duration.

6.   Which set of dates is calculated from the forward pass?
A. Early Start, Early Finish.
B. Late Start, Late Finish.
C. Leveled Start, Leveled Finish.
D. Early Start, Late Start.
E. None of the above.

7.   Which set of dates is calculated from the backward pass?
A. Early Start, Late Start.
B. Late Start, Leveled Start.
C. Leveled Start, Leveled Finish.

    D. Leveled Finish, Late Finish.

    E. None of the above.

8.   What is the total float value for an activity that has the late finish equal to the early finish?

    A. Zero.

    B. Cannot be calculated.

9.   What are resources?

    A. People.

    B. Materials.

    C. Equipment.

    D. Laboratories.

    E. All of the above.

10.   Resources must be loaded into a CPM schedule.

    A. True.

    B. False.

11.   When using resource scheduling, what kinds of constraints are possible?

    A. Time constraints.

    B. Resource constraints.

    C. Technical constraints.

    D. None of the above.

12.   Can the resource leveling priority rules be changed during the life of the project?

    A. Yes.

    B. No.

13.   Which of the following are not used in resource leveling?

    A. Total float.

    B. Free float.

    C. Duration.

    D. Time constraints.

    E. Activity number.

    F. Level 3 WBS.

    G. Technical risk.

    H. Sick time.

14.   What happens to the CPM schedule dates after a resource schedule is calculated?

    A. The early dates are replaced by the resource dates.

    B. The late dates are replaced by the resource dates.

    C. Both early and late dates are replaced by the resource dates.

    D. None of the above.

15.   What is the bottom line result after accelerating (crashing) the schedule?

    A. Increased cost.

    B. Reduced time.

    C. Increased technical risk.

    D. All of the above.

    E. Only A and B.

16. Why does the project need a baseline schedule?
    A. Provides a saved set of planned dates.
    B. Allows for schedule variance analysis.
    C. Provides a convenient place to record actual status.
    D. Is part of the Performance Measurement Baseline.

17. The baseline schedule changes each time a CPM calculation is performed.
    A. True.
    B. False.

18. You are reviewing a baseline schedule and find actual status for some activities. Is this a problem?
    A. Yes.
    B. No.

19. Vertical traceability is more important than horizontal traceability.
    A. True.
    B. False.

20. Free float can be larger than total float.
    A. True.
    B. False.

21. Which of the following are network development techniques?
    A. Top-Down.
    B. Logic.
    C. Bottom-Up.
    D. Line of Balance.

22. Top-Down schedule development typically over-estimates durations.
    A. True.
    B. False.

23. When should date constraints (if needed) be applied to a network?
    A. Never.
    B. During initial baseline development.
    C. After the initial network is developed.

24. Aggressive schedules can become unrealistic early in the project.
    A. True.
    B. False.

25. Organizational schedules do not provide sufficient visibility for total program impacts.
    A. True.
    B. False.

26. What methods are available for statusing networks with out-of-sequence progress?
    A. Retained logic.
    B. Critical Path Method.
    C. LOB.
    D. Free Float.

E. Progress override.

27.   Which of the following are good practices to handle cyclic funding (e.g. annual) in a schedule?
A. Increase duration of activities.
B. Stop and resume activities.
C. Split activities.
D. Delete activities.

28.   Schedule status should be on the baseline schedule.
A. True.
B. False.

29.   Sources of project risk include:
A. Outside the project influences.
B. Previous similar projects.
C. One-of-a-kind projects.
D. All of the above.

30.   Performing a risk assessment ensures good decisions.
A. True.
B. False.

31.   To combine distributions on a schedule network path, add:
A. Most likely durations.
B. Average durations.
C. Probability distributions.
D. Standard deviations.

32.   Which of the following are risk assessment tools?
A. PERT.
B. Monte Carlo.
C. CPM.

33.   In a performance measurement environment, activities do not need to be identified to a WBS element.
A. True.
B. False.

Questions 34 to 39 relate to Activity ABC which has the following pertinent information:

Early Start   = Day 83.
Early Finish = Day 90.
Late Start   = Day 86.
Late Finish = Day 93.

Use the "AM-PM" convention to answer the questions (i.e. a 2-day duration activity beginning on day 3 ends on day 4).

34.   What is the total float?

35.   What is the activity's duration?

36.   Which of the following describes the free float:
A. 7 days.
B. 4 days.
C. 3 days.
D. Cannot be determined from this information.

The schedule is updated to include progress and the actual start of Activity ABC is reported as Day 85.

37.   What is the revised total float?

38.   What is the planned duration?

39.   Can the project end date still be supported?

40.   What five types of information are needed to develop a baseline schedule?
A. _____
B. _____
C. _____
D. _____
E. _____

41.   Name at least six uses of a scheduling system.
A. _____
B. _____
C. _____
D. _____
E. _____
F. _____

42.   Which of the following statements are true about hammocks?
A. There is a single start date and end date for each hammock.
B. It must be at least three months in duration.
C. It can be useful in "what-if" analysis.
D. It has more than one set of detailed activities supporting it.

43.   Templates are only useful in projects that contain more than 1,000 activities.
A. True.
B. False.

44.   Which of the following statements are true about templates?
A. They represent standard activity sequences repeatedly used in a large network diagram.
B. They allow faster logic preparation time through the use of standard activity sequences.
C. They must be less than two months in total duration.
D. All of the above.

45.   There is more than one hammock for an associated group of detailed activities.
A. True.
B. False.

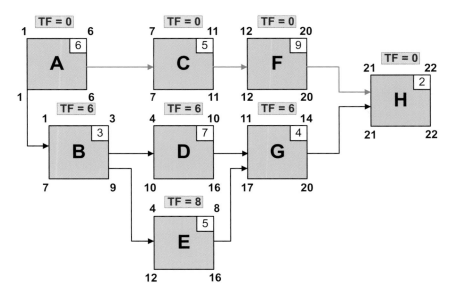

Figure 1

Using Figure 1, answer questions 46 to 52.

Activity D has a "Start Not Earlier Than" directed date of day 7 applied to its start date.

Given this condition,

46.   What is the total float of Activity D?

47.   What is the total float of Activity G?

48.   What is the total float of Activity F?

49.   When is the expected finish of Activity D?

50.   When is the expected start of Activity G?

51.   What is Activity E's total float?

52.   What is Activity E's free float?

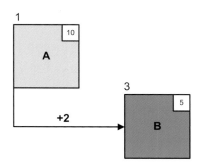

Figure 2

53.   Based on Figure 2, Activity B CAN start:
        A. On Day 1.

B. On Day 2.

C. On Day 3.

D. On Day 4.

E. It cannot be determined.

54. The schedule baseline should be changed:

A. When there is an approved scope change.

B. When the project is officially accelerated or delayed.

C. If unrecoverable slippage has occurred, with owner approval.

D. All of the above.

55. The requirement that schedule dates at interface points between contractors or organizations must be consistent is known as vertical traceability.

A. True.

B. False.

56. For recording schedule status, the choice of remaining duration versus activity percent complete for updating the schedule will always result in the same schedule position.

A. True.

B. False.

57. A revised forecast completion date for an activity is a routine update and should not be considered a baseline change.

A. True.

B. False.

58. Shortening durations for future activities is an accepted way of resolving negative float.

A. True.

B. False.

59. A "Not-Earlier-Than" directed date impacts:

A. The forward pass only.

B. The backward pass only.

C. Both the forward and backward pass.

60. All directed dates affect the total float calculation.

A. True.

B. False.

61. A lag between activities may be positive or negative.

A. True.

B. False.

62. Which of the following statements are true about secondary float?

A. It measures status against an intermediate milestone rather than against the project completion date.

B. It is always greater than free float for the same activity.

C. It is another name for free float.

D. It cannot be calculated without the assistance of a computer.

63. A non-critical activity may be made to appear critical by inserting an imposed date.

A. True.

B. False.

64.   The highest risk path in a schedule network is always the critical path.
A. True.
B. False.

65.   A CPM network is a prerequisite for quantifying schedule risk.
A. True.
B. False.

66.   The advantages of the Bar Chart display include:
A. It is easy to prepare.
B. It is easy to understand.
C. It provides early warning of schedule slips.
D. It is an effective analytical tool.
E. All of the above.

67.   Fill in the meaning of the following common scheduling notations:
A. ES   _____
B. DU   _____
C. FF   _____
D. LF   _____
E. NET   _____
F. CPM   _____
G. NLT   _____
H. AS   _____
I. FS   _____
J. EF   _____
K. SS   _____
L. RD   _____
M. PDM   _____
N. TF   _____
O. AF   _____
P. LS   _____
Q. SF   _____

The answers to these questions can be found in Section 6, Solutions.

ESTIMATING

SECTION 3

ESTIMATING

Once schedules have been established, resources can be loaded on the individual schedule activities. The amount of resources to be loaded typically emanates from estimates, and then the schedule serves as the basis for cash flow development and the total estimate. This iterative process leads to the creation of an overall baseline plan, which becomes the basis for measuring a project's success.

The discussion now turns from resource loaded schedules to the cost discipline. Once an estimate is integrated with the planning schedule, it is submitted for review and approval. Upon approval, it becomes the target time-phased budget for accomplishing the project scope of work. This makes even preliminary estimate numbers important. Once a number has been "locked in" as a budget, it is too late to say that it does not reflect the project's needs. Because of the importance of developing a realistic baseline plan, it is not surprising that most estimating and scheduling groups have very experienced people involved.

Estimating begins with the definition and purpose of an estimate. Prerequisites for estimate development are considered next. This is followed by a presentation of the various types of estimates and their particular characteristics (objectives, detail, quality, anticipated accuracy, and format). The next topic is estimate development. This includes definition of the steps included in the overall estimating process, as well as specifics regarding estimating methods, sources of estimate inputs, estimating guidelines, and methods for calculating indirect costs and cash flow requirements. Learning curves and their application to estimate development will be investigated. Estimates always include an element of uncertainty, and this will be discussed in cost risk assessment. Cost risk will be evaluated for presentation to reviewers and management during the approval process.

Once an estimate is prepared, the next step is a team review before submittal to management for approval. Management will make a decision as to how much cost risk it is willing to assume, the estimate will be adjusted to bring the cost risk to the level desired, and the adjusted estimate will become the approved estimate. Once the estimate is approved, it becomes the budget or the bid, as appropriate, for the project. The effort then shifts from development of the estimate to maintenance and improvement in future estimates. This includes the topic of traceability, which ensures consistency of data between levels of detail within an estimate as well as consistency over time among the various estimates produced during the life of a project. Adjustments to the estimate based on changes to the definition of the project scope must be reflected. This ensures fair comparisons can be made between estimated and actual costs, so that this information can be used to produce more accurate future estimates. This information can be retained in databases. Lastly, the application of automated estimating systems in the production of estimates is considered.

Chapter 19

THE ESTIMATING PROCESS

Objectives of this Chapter:

1. Define "estimate" and describe its purpose.

2. Identify the impacts of poor estimating.

3. Identify the prerequisites for estimate development.

4. Explain why the Work Breakdown Structure (WBS) is needed.

5. Discuss the level of detail at which estimates are developed.

6. Explain why the WBS Dictionary is needed for estimate development.

7. Explain why standard formats/templates for estimate presentation must be established at the summary and detail level.

The estimating process defines an estimate and explains how it can have a profound impact on an organization's financial status. The estimate is a key ingredient leading to development of an approved plan that can be used for comparisons with actual progress. The estimate plays a key role in developing a plan that is achievable. A poor quality estimate will lead to an unrealistic plan that is very difficult to overcome. The best management systems will actually serve to highlight over/underruns early in the process.

The "Estimating" block of the master flowchart for the project management process (Figure 19-1) has been expanded for the series of estimating topics (Figure 19-2). These more detailed steps will be followed as the subject of estimating is addressed. Consideration of learning curves and cost risk assessment will be part of an iterative process of estimate development.

Of all project management professionals, one could argue effectively that estimators lead the most precarious existence. If their estimates are too high, they may cost the company new jobs. If their estimates are too low, the company may lose money. This is especially a concern with Firm Fixed Price contracts for large projects. If the estimator hits the final cost exactly, then he or she would be lucky.

Whenever there is a big disparity between estimated and final actual cost, the first explanation offered is rarely that the project was not managed well. The answer on everyone's lips is, "It was a bad estimate." Automation helps most areas of the Critical Path Method (CPM) process, but estimate development is still one of the most challenging applications for a computer in project management. Considering these facts, why would anyone want to be an estimator?

Estimating is an important and challenging position requiring a great deal of technical expertise. While it is essential that scheduling personnel be familiar with the technical scope of their projects, engineers must provide assistance in the definition of how they will perform the work. Estimators are often required to be more independent. This has been carried to extremes in some organizations. For an automobile manufacturing project,

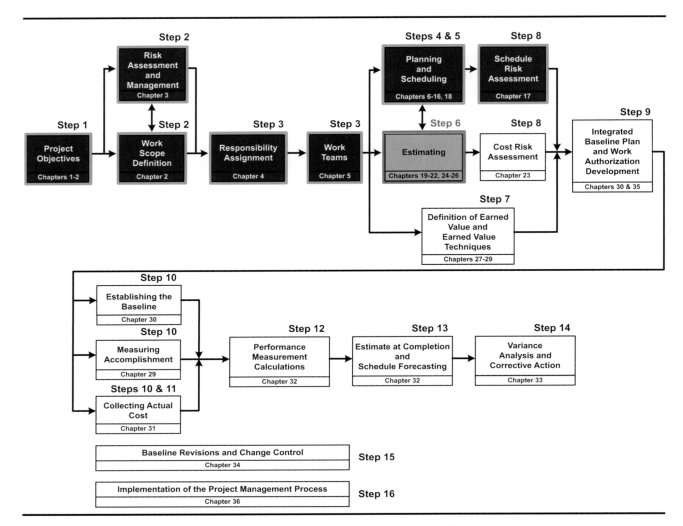

Figure 19-1 Earned Value Project Management: The Process

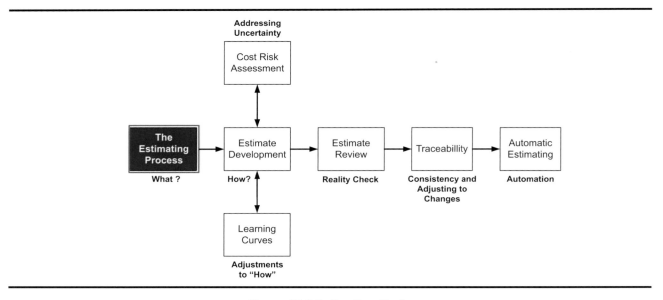

Figure 19-2 Estimating Topics

the estimators were actually redoing the conceptual engineering to make it more cost effective.

This chapter does not deal with developing specific estimates, because the focus would become too narrow in scope and would need volumes of associated source material as references. Besides, development of an estimate depends entirely on the design maturity information available at the time of estimate generation. Covered in some detail is the definition of the boundaries of what estimating is and the important characteristics of a successful estimating application.

For some experienced estimators, these chapters will be a review. For others, much of the material will be new. In either case, the material will provide a fresh perspective on the estimating process. Few organizations have a well-defined systems approach to estimating. Actually, organizations frequently rely on an individual's personal experience without written guidance. This reliance often results in unnecessary disruption when a senior estimator retires or is on vacation.

Impact of the Estimate

Every project starts with an estimate. The estimate may be a decisive factor in whether a project is initiated. While a low estimate may win a project or result in project authorization (for internal projects), there are usually repercussions later.

The estimate will frequently be a deciding input to go/no go decisions on whether to proceed with a project. While accuracy is important, deadlines are equally important in estimate production. A late estimate can be as useless as an inaccurate one.

What is an estimate? An estimate is an anticipated cost that reflects a scope of work performed within a specified time frame with defined assumptions. The larger and more complex a project, the more assumptions will be needed to define the estimate conditions.

The objective of an estimate is viewed differently depending on whether the organization produc-

ing it is the contractor or the owner/customer. In a competitive bidding situation, the contractor wants to win the contract award, but not at the expense of financial stability. Winning the contract is not enough; expectation of a reasonable profit is also necessary. The owner/customer wants to get the lowest price with an acceptable quality of work. However, awarding a contract with a price that is too low in a firm fixed price arrangement can be counterproductive as the contractor may go bankrupt before project completion. The owner/customer must then either convert the contract to cost plus or re-compete the effort. The former approach means cost overruns to the original budget and probably schedule delays. The latter approach means cost overruns (probably greater than contract conversion), virtually certain schedule delays, and, most probably, litigation.

Impacts of Poor Estimating

The impacts of poor estimating are varied and serious. A contractor that cannot win contracts will soon be out of business. Almost as damaging as no contracts are canceled contracts. Tight budgets are required, and when those budgets overrun, it does not take long before the project becomes a candidate for elimination.

Another concern that occurs in regulated industries is that incurred costs may be disallowed when rates are set. Spending the money no longer automatically assures that it will be passed on to the consumer. The responsibility is now frequently on an organization to prove that the money was spent prudently. That effort becomes more difficult when major cost overruns become exaggerated because of unrealistically low original estimates.

The ultimate price for poor estimating is business failure. In a firm fixed price environment, this is a very real threat. The reverse side of this is also true: an accurately estimated, carefully managed fixed price contract can yield higher profits than a "cost plus" type contract with a variable percentage of return.

Prerequisites for Estimate Development

Before an estimator responds to a request for an estimate, there are certain prerequisites to be established. These include the following:

1. A set of guidelines for estimate development need to be in place. These guidelines provide the framework for the estimating process.

2. A structure, against which estimates are organized, must be established. This should be the project Work Breakdown Structure (WBS). Because companies generally produce similar products for different contracts, the project WBSs will be similar. That means actual costs will be collected in similar buckets. Consistent WBSs organized by product lines result in the ability to update estimating databases/templates, which, in turn, improves the accuracy of future estimates.

3. A WBS dictionary that defines the boundaries of scope for each element must be prepared because it is essential to understanding what is included in the estimate as well as for assuring that charges are correctly reported later.

4. Standard estimate formats/templates should be defined. A summary page format should exist for estimate review at the highest levels, but additional formats should be available for more detailed analysis during the review phase.

Guidelines

Guidelines to fulfill the first requirement must be developed, if they do not already exist within the organization. This addresses at least the following items:

A. A procedure for initiating estimates.

B. A definition of estimate types, their objectives, accuracy, level of detail, methods of development, and time required for preparation.

C. A procedure for developing contingency recommendations.

D. A procedure for applying escalation to estimates.

E. A procedure for estimate development.

F. A procedure for estimate review, including a list of items required as part of the estimate package for the estimate to be considered complete.

G. The role of software/templates in the estimating process, if any.

H. The role of risk analysis in development of a final estimate.

I. A definition of estimate traceability (both vertical and historical) and how it is to be achieved.

J. A listing of estimating "rules of thumb" or specific guidelines used in the preparation of conceptual estimates.

K. An approach for comparing actual costs and estimates, so that actual project experience will be used to guide the development of more accurate estimates in the future.

L. A procedure for developing cash flows and termination liability, which are necessary to determine funding requirements.

Without this type of guidance, the estimating process is neither consistent nor reliable. These items do not have to be addressed in voluminous detail, but could be adequately covered in less than ten pages. Defining each small step in the process may not be productive because it may eliminate better approaches that might otherwise be developed. It may also discourage anyone from using the procedures.

The overall objective is to produce estimates that reflect the best information available and are developed within an organized and formalized process. Item A implies far more guidance than just what form must be completed to request an estimate. It should also include identification of who is responsible for securing which information. Types and formats of estimates (see Item B above) are identified so that a requester knows what to expect when an estimate is needed and how long it should take to produce. Nearly all of the remaining topics listed here will be covered in more depth in the succeeding chapters.

Work Breakdown Structure (WBS)

The Work Breakdown Structure (WBS) and templates are the framework for all cost estimating; they should also be the basis for all subsequent actual cost collection. A WBS and templates serve cost estimating for three primary reasons:

1. To provide consistency between estimates, thereby facilitating estimate comparisons.

2. To provide a summarization structure that guarantees vertical traceability from detailed accounts to summary accounts, thereby, defining the interrelationships between various account levels.

3. To provide a basis for establishing standard estimate formats/templates.

If the same structure does not support estimate development and actual cost collection, it will never be possible to confirm that the estimated costs were accurate. Without such verification, an inaccurate set of costs may be used in the development of new (and inaccurate) estimates. The entire process is much simpler if the same Work Breakdown Structure is used during the entire project life cycle. The only change will be the level of detail needed, thereby requiring lower levels of the WBS to satisfy customer and/or contractor needs. Additional discussion regarding WBS development is contained in Chapter 2.

Templates

It is important to coordinate the WBS and the use of templates. The WBS is used for control of significant project elements while the templates are used to capture all cost elements, no matter how small.

By using a translation table to map templates against the WBS elements they support, it is possible to coordinate the templates. Note that a variable number of templates may support a single WBS element.

Another factor in creation of templates is that material and labor costs must be segregated at the lowest level. This is important, because they are each subject to different escalation factors, differing market availability, and differing treatment in an Earned Value Management (EVM) System. Combining these cost elements in a single template may be logical, but consideration for visibility into separate elements of cost must exist.

The lowest level of a template for construction contracts is typically the commodity level at which unit productivity rates are maintained by the company. Therefore, it is the level at which a detailed estimate is actually generated. If the template were maintained at a more summary level, the unit rates would not be applicable to all entries. The appropriate lowest level of a template must relate to the place at which unit rates are maintained within the company. For example, in a construction project the contractor subdivided pipe to each individual size. However, unit rates were accumulated in groups such as 2" and under pipe, 4"-12" pipe, and over 12" pipe. For estimating purposes, it would be wasted effort to estimate the quantity of 1" pipe versus the quantity of 2" pipe.

Individual commodity codes for the project were maintained for entries like:

- Carbon steel pipe, schedule 40, < 2"

- Carbon steel pipe, schedule 40, 4" - 12"

- Carbon steel pipe, schedule 40, over 12".

Related items were also estimated to the same level of detail (note the size is the same):

- Carbon steel pipe, schedule 40, 4" -12"

- Valves, 4" -12"

- Pipe supports & hangers, 4" -12" pipe

- Welding, carbon steel pipe, schedule 40, 4" -12".

Since this was the lowest level to be estimated, some thought was given to how tasks could be grouped. For example, all of the items shown above could be included within the category of Pipe Installation, carbon steel, 4"-12", rather than broken out individually. The advantages of preparing the estimate by individual component are that each of these categories has very different unit productivity rates, and it is easier to find standard rates at this level than to have a composite rate for the activity "Pipe Installation, all inclusive."

An all-inclusive rate is useful if the historical records are available for the specific type of application being estimated. What are the advantages of maintaining the elements at the more summary level? Estimate development is more timely because there are fewer cost isolations to estimate, and there is also less detail to track during the project. Even with more detail, there is no improved visibility unless actual costs are tracked at the same level of detail. This becomes the determining criteria: how detailed will actual costs be tracked? Detailed estimating followed by summary tracking simply does not provide meaningful data.

Other guidelines in the WBS definition and template creation include not mixing incompatible items in a single WBS and keeping equivalent dollar value items at the same level of the WBS. One example of an incompatible item is a large overhead crane (major mechanical equipment) as part of the dollars per square foot cost of constructing a building. Of course it is part of the building, but analysis is skewed when there are ten buildings to compare and only one has an overhead crane. It makes more sense to separately evaluate the crane cost and the building structure cost, both of which can be found in various estimating tables.

WBS Dictionary and Code of Accounts

Equally important as the WBS dictionary is the template structure that defines what cost elements are included within each control account. The basic direct cost elements in an EVMS are labor, material, subcontracts, and other direct costs (ODCs). Most organizations have a standard "Code of Accounts" that further defines each direct cost element category into lower levels of detail that becomes the basis for the template creation and usage. The purpose of the dictionary is to define boundaries to work content. The purpose of the templates is to assist an estimator in cost element delineation within or beneath the WBS dictionary work content boundaries.

A motor scooter engine account might be entered into a dictionary to read, "Includes all labor and material associated with the engine's manufacture and installation. This includes the engine block, lubrication system, the fuel-air system, ignition system, and associated instrumentation. Design and testing of the engine are excluded, as are all supervision/management activities."

The template might further delineate the direct cost elements by dividing labor into manufacturing and assembly, material into parts and equipment, subcontracts into the subcontracted items, and ODCs into travel and miscellaneous.

As discussed in Chapter 2, it is important to list both inclusions and closely related work that is excluded. A helpful hint is to identify the WBS in which the excluded work belongs.

Estimates and cost collection in the production/manufacturing environment are routinely performed at extremely low levels of detail. Unit standards of 0.1 labor hour are not uncommon. This is appropriate because even small work activities become significant when they are repeated 10,000 times. Historical records are usually available to support this type of detail in well documented templates.

Estimate Formats/Templates

Definition of an acceptable template format that all users can agree upon can be a difficult process. However, once established, it should be maintained as-is to facilitate comparisons of estimates for different projects. All forms should be consistent through the automatic summarization capability.

The same formats should be maintained throughout the history of the project. When estimates are updated as more accurate information becomes available, it will be possible to trace the changes in the estimate by category or element of cost.

The type of information presented in a summary format should include something similar to Figure 19-3.

Material, equipment, ODCs, subcontract costs and labor cost should be listed separately because they are analyzed independently. For example, the number of labor hours is needed for comparison with other projects without the impact of varying labor rates.

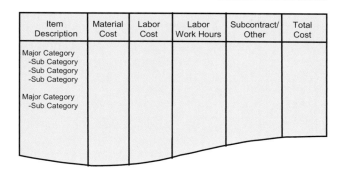

Figure 19-3 Levels of Estimate Detail 1

	Unit	Qty.	Work Hrs.	Labor Unit Rate	Labor $	Material $	Equip. $	Freight $	Taxes $	Total $
Detailed Items										

Figure 19-4 Levels of Estimate Detail 2

A total cost is required for bottom line analysis. These cost items are a must for all of the major categories and subcategories of the estimate for each WBS element.

Considerably more information would be required in a detailed reporting format, such as that shown in Figure 19-4.

Labor dollars have little meaning unless their source can be determined. The dollars result from the number of labor hours, which in turn results from the quantities and labor installation unit productivity rates. All of these columns are therefore included on the form.

Conclusion

The role of estimating in any organization is a very important one, one that can make or break the company financially. Estimates end up on the front pages of newspapers when projects are announced, and end up in bold print when project costs exceed estimates. With this kind of visibility, estimate preparation merits the same intense scrutiny applied to political issues.

The estimating process functions properly only when specific factors are in place. Before any estimates are prepared, a set of guidelines or procedures for developing estimates is needed. A template structure provides the framework for the estimate details while an accompanying dictionary defines the scope included within each individual account. Standard formats for presentation of the estimate should also be established, with varying levels of detail tailored to its intended use. Once all of these are available, an understanding exists between the requester and the developer regarding estimate expectations.

Chapter 19 Review Questions

19-1.   Discuss the problems associated with estimates which are (1) too low or (2) too high.

19-2.   Discuss the difference in the owner/customer view and the contractor view of the bidding process.

19-3.   How does shifting from a Firm Fixed Price contract to a Cost Plus contract shift the emphasis on cost between contractor and owner/customer?

19-4.   List four important prerequisites that should be in place before an estimate is produced.

19-5.   Why is it important to assure consistency of the templates with the WBS?

19-6.   What are the three primary reasons for developing a WBS and using it with a template structure?

19-7.   Discuss the tradeoffs between visibility and accuracy in template structure detail.

True or False

19-8.   It is critically important that actual costs be collected in a way that they can be compared with estimated costs.

19-9.   The lowest level of construction cost estimating is typically the commodity level.

19-10. Since the amount of available detail varies throughout the life of a project, estimates should be prepared in different formats depending on when in the project life cycle they were prepared.

19-11. It is always in the best interests of the customer/owner to award contracts at the lowest price offered.

19-12. Labor, equipment, subcontracts, ODCs and material costs typically are combined in a single cost element and cannot be separately identified.

19-13. Estimating procedures are not important since each project is a little different than the last one and the amount of available information for preparing the estimate varies on a case-by-case basis.

The answers to these questions can be found in Section 6, Solutions.

Chapter 20

TYPES OF ESTIMATES

Objectives of this Chapter:

1. Explain that different types of estimates have different objectives, methods, accuracies, and levels of detail.

2. Identify the characteristics of a typical Conceptual Estimate, Preliminary Estimate, Detailed Estimate, and Definitive Estimate.

3. Discuss when in a project's life cycle each type of the estimate is produced.

4. Understand the relationship between project definition and estimate accuracy.

This is introductory material for defining and understanding estimates. Too often, a request goes out for an estimate without proper definition of the type of estimate. The detail, quality, accuracy, and format vary greatly according to the type of estimate. An understanding of the characteristics of the different types of estimates is essential before they can be produced and reviewed. Most of the remaining chapters on this topic are affected by the type of estimate.

Various names are used for the different types of estimates. Unfortunately, standard terminology does not exist. The names vary somewhat from industry to industry; even to the extent that the number of different types of estimates produced during a project varies. The Department of Energy, for example, recognizes seven types of estimates. Computer software engineering and development firms typically use three methods. Because of the unique nature and estimating methodologies used for software, these are discussed in some depth in Chapter 21, "Estimate Development."

Most industries typically use three or four types of estimates. In this text, four types of estimates will be addressed:

- Conceptual
- Preliminary
- Detailed
- Definitive

The quality of any estimate depends not only on the ability of the estimator, but also on the available information. Without an accurate definition of scope, the estimator is forced to make assumptions that may not come true. The time available for preparing the estimate will also be a major contributing factor to the quality of the output. If there were insufficient time allowed to review the drawings, an estimator may be forced to use rough guidelines and "rules of thumb", even when detailed drawings and designs are available. If other similar projects have recently been estimated, the estimator's job is much easier. The existing estimate can be used as a template with adjustments made to reflect the differences between the two projects.

The following sections look at the differing objectives, methods, accuracy, and detail of each of the four types of estimates listed above.

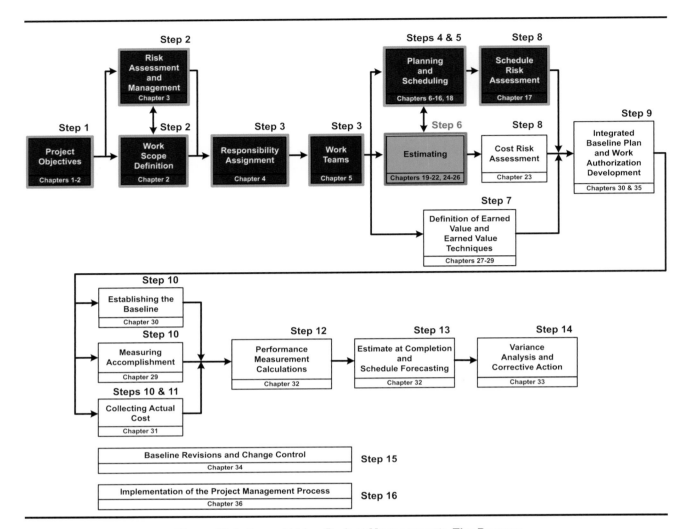

Figure 20-1 Earned Value Project Management: The Process

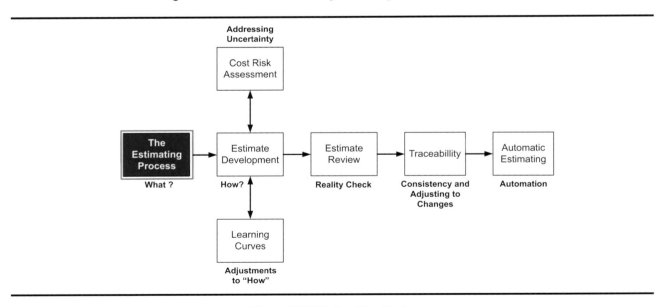

Figure 20-2 Estimating Topics

Conceptual Estimates

The first type of estimate produced on any project is called the conceptual estimate. It is also called "order of magnitude," "round table," "screening," "blue sky," "study," "back of the envelope," and "expert." The objective of a conceptual estimate is to produce an estimate for study or planning purposes and to produce that estimate in one to two days. It is typically used for studying alternatives and for making "go/no go" decisions on possible future projects. It also may be used for "what if?" studies.

Because the project is only a possibility at this time, the owner/customer organization typically prepares this estimate to determine whether to pursue a project.

Methods used for development of a conceptual estimate are quick and approximate, reflecting the very short time available. The general procedure is to use a parametric guideline developed from historical records and modify it as appropriate to reflect any specific information known. A parametric guideline relates a "cost driver," such as horsepower of an engine, units/day on an assembly line, engineering/manufacturing complexity, lines of code for software programs, or electrical output of a power plant to total cost. There is insufficient time to develop a detailed schedule; so generic schedules of similar projects are used. Of course, that implies that these must be ready in advance as reference tools.

Certain general characteristics that define the overall parameters of a project are needed as a starting point. The type of project is not enough. Size also has a direct bearing on cost. There are exponential sizing rules for projects of similar type available in the literature for many industries. For example, subsonic airframe costs for a specified number of units tend to fit an exponential formula in the form of Cost = $a(Wb)$ where a and b are constants derived from a regression analysis of actual subsonic airframe cost data normalized to the same number of units, and W is the weight of the airframe to be estimated. These can be used as a quick basis for an estimate or as a rough check of an estimate prepared in a more detailed manner.

Location of the project can be especially important if it were an international construction project. Differences in currency, productivity, and infrastructure will be substantial and will have a significant impact on cost. For example, constructing an industrial project in a remote location may mean building roads, railroads, docks for unloading ships, housing for workers, installing power lines for many miles, providing a source of drinking water, and figuring out the logistics of providing food and other supplies to workers. Such costs can be substantial.

A conceptual estimate is the least accurate of all estimates and should never be used as a basis for awarding contracts. A conceptual estimate, by its very nature, is the riskiest of all types because of the considerable uncertainty, which results in a very wide spread of possible outcomes. The format of a conceptual estimate will be summary in nature and limited in detail to total cost and the cost of major categories. There is an underlying assumption here. In order to be able to produce quick and relatively accurate conceptual estimates, guidelines must already be established and understood.

Preliminary Estimates

The next type of estimate is the preliminary estimate. It is also known as a "budgetary estimate" or "appropriations estimate." The objective of this estimate is to reflect project specific information to provide a number tailored to the particular project at hand. As such, it usually does not make use of the parametric guidelines (except for software) that the conceptual estimate uses. The preliminary estimate will be used for development of the initial project budget. Another of its functions is the documentation of schedule activity (summary) durations. Just as schedule affects cost, the resource assumptions will affect schedule. Since the preliminary estimate is only prepared after major systems engineering decisions have already been made, it can be used for variance analysis of the early design portion of the work.

The methods used for developing this type of estimate are more precise. While historical guidelines may still be used as a starting point, they are refined based on available systems engineering documents. Engineering is usually 10-20% complete at the time this estimate is prepared, and information is on file. This would include major equipment costs, (via either verbal or written quotes) since purchasing may have been initiated. On production and manufacturing projects, identification of major material items is available.

The expected accuracy of this estimate is better than the conceptual estimate because specific project information is now incorporated. This increased confidence level reflects itself in a reduced cost risk. Greater detail should be available in the estimate output as well. The major categories of the conceptual estimate are broken down to the next level of detail because the data is now available.

Because of the greater availability of information and more attention to detail, the preliminary estimate will generally require 2-4 weeks to prepare. The cost estimating template intended for the more detailed estimates that come later should be used for this estimate to expedite comparisons with the later estimates.

Detailed Estimates

The third type of estimate is the detailed estimate. It serves as the basis for evaluating development, production, or construction bids and awarding contracts. The owner/customer has defined the project work scope to a level of detail that is sufficient for potential contractors to develop detailed estimates to support their bids. The detailed estimates of the bidders are evaluated by the owner/customer to determine which bid provides the best value to the owner/customer. That decision results in a contract award and the winning bid serves as the basis for project baselining and control.

Accuracy should now have improved to +20%, -10% and any cost risk not included in the bid/negotiated cost becomes an amount retained by the owner/customer (an amount not within the awarded target price). The amount retained by the owner/customer covers overruns of the negotiated cost for which the owner/customer is responsible (the part of an overrun that is not a

reduction of the company's profit), unknowns outside of the contracted work scope (e.g., natural disasters), and potential future additions to the contracted work scope.

The detailed estimate, as its name suggests, should be prepared at the lowest level of detail of the full account structure. The improved accuracy and detail comes with a price: preparation time is now 5-8 weeks for a large, multi-year project with complex development, construction, and/or manufacturing processes.

Definitive Estimate

The final, most detailed type of estimate prepared is the definitive estimate. Any additional cost for work performed later is more properly classified as cost engineering. The objective of the definitive estimate is to establish a detailed baseline for the monitoring and control during the execution phases of the project. It will be used for variance reporting, productivity analysis, cost trend analysis, and Estimate at Completion (EAC) development.

The methods used for developing the definitive estimate are more exact than for the earlier ones. The previously prepared detailed estimate provides a foundation for the definitive estimate. Engineering drawings and other design documents are nearly complete now, allowing exact quantity takeoffs. Equipment and material prices are known because firm bids have been received. Much of the effort associated with this estimate is cost reconciliation more than it is cost estimating.

Accuracy should be within 10%. Many argue for a +/- 5% accuracy, but there still are some potential costly unknowns: within contract scope changes, supplements to purchase orders, redesign, and rework. The smallest of these are the supplements to existing purchase orders, which by this point should primarily be for missing, damaged, or otherwise unacceptable material and equipment items. This is the cost risk assumed by the company in the cost estimate that was approved for bidding purposes. Usually, this cost risk is identified as Management Reserve (MR) by the company's project manager once a contract has been awarded.

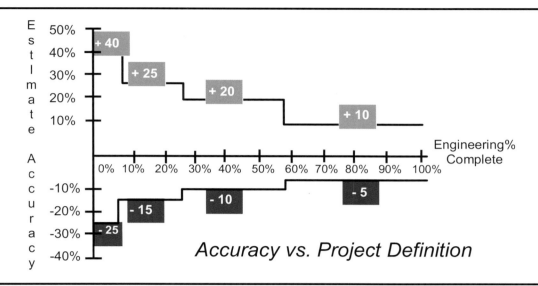

Figure 20-3 Types of Estimates

The size and complexity of the project being estimated determines the amount of time needed for a comprehensive estimate preparation. However, this estimate will generally take more total workdays to complete than the others because of the amount of information that needs to be reviewed.

Figure 20-3 summarizes pictorially much of what has been said in this chapter. Estimate accuracy improves over time. As mentioned earlier, stated accuracies of +/- 20% can be misleading because the typical variation is greater on the high side than the low side. And as demonstrated in Figure 20-3, the reason for improved accuracy is advanced engineering/design completion. The four different types of estimates are all pictured here, represented by the various "steps" in the figure.

Impact of "Fast Track" Projects on Estimating

On a fast track project, the phases of the project overlap to a great extent rather than following each other in sequence. The most common examples are on design/construction and development/production projects, when construction/production begins well before engineering is completed.

There are implications of this approach that affect cost (such as a much higher risk that scope changes will involve a lot more than just revising a line on a design drawing), and these implications must be considered. The impact is that estimates need to be produced earlier, with less information, than is usually available. This requires greater use of guidelines and standardization.

Conclusion

While the exact number varies between organizations, four types of estimates are generally used: conceptual, preliminary, detailed, and definitive. Each of these estimate types has a different objective and varies in accuracy and amount of detail. This is important to understand when an estimate is requested, developed, or reviewed. The primary differentiating features that separate these estimate types are the amount of information and time available to develop them and the point in the life cycle where the estimate is performed. The amount of available information and time available, in turn, affects the expected accuracy of the recommended estimate number.

Chapter 20 Review Questions

20-1.   List four types of estimates.

20-2.   Why is the Conceptual Estimate typically prepared by the owner/customer?

20-3.   Explain why it is important for the different types of estimates to be defined in each company.

True or False

20-4.   Parametric guidelines are most likely to be used in the development of detailed estimates.

20-5.   A Preliminary Estimate reflects project specific information.

20-6.   There should be reduced amounts of management reserve (cost risk) associated with each subsequent estimate.

20-7.   In an engineering/construction or development/production project, the Detailed Estimate is typically prepared during the bid/award process.

20-8.   Even for very large projects, a Conceptual Estimate is short in duration.

20-9.   An accurate definition of scope is an essential contributor to an accurate estimate.

The answers to these questions can be found in Section 6, Solutions.

Chapter 21

ESTIMATE DEVELOPMENT

Objectives of this Chapter:

1. Explain the general process of developing a complex estimate.

2. Identify three different methods of developing an estimate.

3. Identify sources of information for developing estimates.

4. Understand the role of defaults in estimate preparation and their limitations.

5. Explain the use of parametric guidelines in estimate development and review.

6. Explain indirect costs and their calculation.

7. Explain the procedure for developing a cost flow, with an example.

8. Discuss escalation calculations in estimate development.

9. Present techniques for comparing costs between different size projects of the same type completed in different years and of differing capacities.

10. Explain accepted techniques for developing estimates for software development projects.

This is the heart of the estimating topic. Indeed, this could easily be a separate book. The presentation emphasizes the approach to developing an estimate and the large amount of input that must go into it for it to reflect the best available information. As represented on the estimating sub-flowchart, this is the "how" of estimating. Only key calculations will be performed. In the next chapter, we will show how estimates should be modified when repetitive operations are involved.

There are many approaches to developing estimates. That is because the approach must be specifically based on what is being estimated. Accordingly, this chapter will focus on the important factors in the development process. We will look at standard estimating methods, sources of estimating information (both who and what), level of detail, guidelines for quick results, and methods of developing cost flows. We will also explain how to make fair comparisons between costs of projects completed in different time frames and how to adjust for varying output capacities of operational industrial plants and production facilities.

The Estimating Process

The steps involved in the process of estimating are addressed at a summary level. These steps are shown pictorially on the flowchart, "The Estimating Process," Figure 21-3. Each of the flowchart blocks will be discussed in turn.

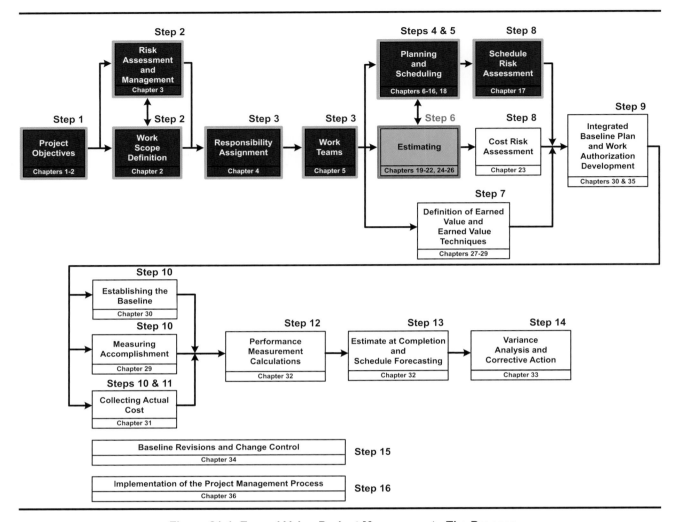

Figure 21-1 Earned Value Project Management: The Process

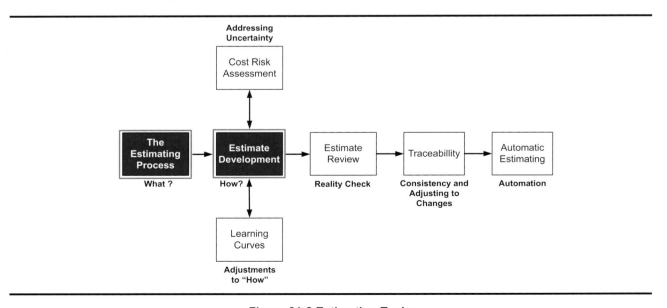

Figure 21-2 Estimating Topics

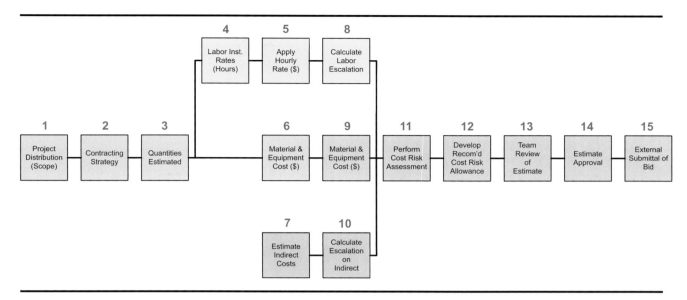

Figure 21-3 The Estimating Process

1. **Project Definition (Scope)** - The starting point of any estimate is a description of the project. On studies and early budget requests, the scope may be very general. If there were not enough information available to allow exact scope definition, there must be enough to at least allow comparison with other similar projects.

2. **Contracting Strategy** - A basic understanding of how the work is going to be accomplished contractually is necessary because that will affect the way the estimate is prepared. Subcontracts, for example, are usually prepared as a lump sum number, while the main contract is developed in detail. The estimated number of labor work hours may or may not be developed for subcontracts, with less likelihood of being separately listed for firm fixed price work. Cost plus work will certainly list labor hours as a separate estimate column entry because an estimate of the labor to accomplish the subcontracted effort is necessary to be able to effectively negotiate with potential subcontractors.

3. **Quantities Estimated** - This is information that will have to be developed in order to price labor and material because both cost elements are directly related to the quantity of work to be performed. This is part of the scope definition on all projects.

4. **Labor Installation Rates (Hours/Unit)** - These totals are derived directly from the previous block (Quantities Estimated). Unit rates are applied to those quantities (hours required to install or produce a single unit multiplied by the total number of units) to determine how many labor hours will be required for installation (or production).

There are many possible sources of this data, including a number of commercially available databases that list estimated costs in detail for all types of project work. The best source of information for these calculations is internal company records from previous similar jobs. Note, however, that the variation from one project to another for what initially appears to be exactly the same kind of work may be significant. Variances of 300% or more are not unusual between industries or companies for similar work.

Because the unit rates used have a direct bearing on what the final estimated cost will be, companies are very secretive about the rates they use for preparing estimates in competitive environments. Most organizations are continually trying to "fine tune" unit rates because this will have a direct bearing on whether bids are successful and whether the organization makes money.

Another factor used in calculating labor installation and assembly rates in manufacturing applications (or any other application where there are multiple identical units) is the learning curve. The concept of learning curves will be explained in Chapter 24. Basically, it is an adjustment made to the standard rates for single units. The estimator will also need to consider any differences in skill levels between previous work and the current effort.

5. **Apply Hourly Rates ($)** - Once the number of labor hours required to do the work is estimated, it is a simple matter to convert this to dollars using labor rate tables available for the type of work. Owners/customers must rely on generic wrap rates (rates that combine all direct and indirect rates into one composite rate) while contractors can use their proprietary rate tables, which include skill levels, to convert hours to dollars.

6. **Material & Equipment Cost ($)** - The quantity being produced or services being ordered are also used to directly calculate the material and equipment costs. The unit cost is derived from pricing books or catalogs, or from up-to-date files in purchasing of recent bids received by the company or purchase orders placed. If equipment were rented, the period of rental becomes important.

7. **Estimate Indirect Costs** - Indirect costs are not directly identified with any single final cost objective, but relate to two or more cost objectives. As such, indirect costs are usually estimated and collected separately from all direct costs and applied as rates. The labor, material, and equipment costs discussed above are all direct costs and must be combined with the indirect costs to produce the total estimate.

8. **Calculate Labor Escalation** - Once a base labor cost is estimated, it must be modified by the expected escalation in labor costs. Union agreements, historical salary increase data, inflation rates, and other considerations will cause the estimator to need to adjust the base labor cost. To calculate the amount of labor escalation, the expenditures must be time-phased over the life of the project. The project schedule (or a generic schedule if the specific project has not yet been scheduled) will permit an estimate for the distribution of labor hours. For estimates prepared early in the project such as the Conceptual Estimate, historical information on staffing will be used as the basis for time-phasing labor hours. Once a project plan is established, specific staffing curves by type of labor category should be available for more exact calculations.

Escalation is accomplished individually for labor, material, and indirect costs because each are driven by different factors and will likely have different escalation rates.

9. **Calculate Material & Equipment Escalation** - This is accomplished very differently depending on the amount of project information that has been defined. Initially, material and equipment escalation is based on historical profiles of similar projects. Then, as a detailed schedule becomes available, escalation will be based on projected delivery dates. This is because nearly all orders have provisions for payment due on delivery with a 30-day grace period. Finally, once the orders are placed, escalation can be projected based on the terms and conditions of the purchase orders or contracts. If the project were short in duration, there will be no escalation provisions and no calculation is required.

10. **Calculate Escalation on Indirects** - Indirect costs are applied to projects as rates based on the estimated direct business base of the contractor. A company's

Accounting Department routinely forecasts indirect rates into the future for use in project cost estimates using its estimate of indirect cost escalation. When available, these forecasted rates should be used to calculate the indirect costs to be applied to the project's direct cost estimate. Otherwise, the estimator will have to justify why rates different from that determined by the Accounting Department were used. When indirect rates are being applied, the estimator must not make the mistake of applying escalation to both direct and indirect costs. That would be double-counting the effect of escalation.

11. **Perform Cost Risk Assessment** - Once the escalation has been combined with the base costs for labor, material, and indirect costs, an initial total estimate value results from the combination of these numbers. However, the estimate is still not complete. Any estimate can be accomplished to this point based on facts, but now the subjective is evaluated. What amount for cost risk should be added to the preliminary total to allow for the unknowns that plague every project? During the proposal phase, contractors will estimate the cost risk associated with its estimated cost. For bidding purposes, the cost estimate will be adjusted to encompass that part of the cost risk the company is willing to take upon itself and will identify the remaining cost risk in its bid, assuming the owner/customer requested such information. After award, if in an earned value environment, the risk taken by the contractor is a major factor in determining management reserve (see Chapter 30 for a discussion on management reserve). The remaining cost risk is taken on by the owner/customer.

For many years, cost risk was evaluated subjectively by considering how "hard" or "soft" each entry was and then recommending an allowance on that basis. For example, a "hard" number may need only a 5% allowance, while a "soft" number may need a 15%-25% allowance based on the type of estimate being prepared. In recent years, however, software programs have become available that allow cost risk to be evaluated using statistical methods applied to uncertainty. This will be covered in detail in Chapter 23, "Cost Risk Assessment."

12. **Develop Recommended Cost Risk Allowance** - Based on a formal cost risk assessment or by more primitive means if one were not performed, a cost risk allowance is determined for later recommendation to management for approval. Contractors with awarded contracts should share this assessment with their owner/customers because often the owner/customer is able to assist with mitigation of the risk.

13. **Team Review of Estimate** - The accuracy of an estimate depends on the quality of project scope definition. The objective is to include the best available information in the estimate development process. The internal team review of the estimate documentation is to ensure the best information has been included. The same group of people who provided input to the estimate should be allowed the opportunity to review it prior to formal submission for approval. This will verify their input was understood and correctly incorporated.

14. **Estimate Approval** - This is the formal executive management review and approval of the estimate. In this step, the cost risk allowance (if any) will be established as well as any allowance for profit or other adjustments made. The estimate should be presented in standard formats agreed upon in advance. Only at this point is the final estimate total defined.

15. **External Submittal of Bid** - A standard transmittal letter, usually by the contracting office for executive approval, should be prepared for submission of the bid to the requesting authority. Usually, any cost risk allowance included in the bid is not identified separately, but is distributed across the base estimate. However, if

requested by the owner/customer, the cost risk not absorbed in the bid will be identified separately in the bid as the cost risk to the bid amount that, if realized, would result in a cost overrun to the definitized contract cost. If the estimate were only being developed for internal use, it could be officially included in any corporate documents as the approved budget.

Estimating Methods

In March 2009, the U.S. Government Accountability Office (GAO) published a Cost Estimating and Analysis Guide.[1] In Chapter 11 of the Guide, Developing a Point Estimate, three commonly used estimating methods are identified – engineering build-up, analogy, and parametric. Each of these methods is discussed below.

The **Engineering Build-up Method** consists of identifying all of the detailed items at the lowest levels of the WBS and then summing them up to arrive at the total project cost. This is certainly the most time consuming method of the three described here. It is also the most accurate. In many instances, this cannot be used because of a lack of information. The detailed information must exist to allow the takeoffs and summation of line items, and this is frequently not the case. This technique would never be used for a conceptual estimate.

The **Analogy Method** makes use of known costs from prior projects of similar type. These costs are then adjusted (if necessary) to reflect specific differences between projects. The adjustment allows development of quick and accurate estimates using detailed historical data from the base project. This method requires that applicable and accurate historical records are available for similar work. This technique can be used on breakthrough technologies as well by using data from a small pilot project as a basis for the project estimate.

---

1.   U.S. Government Accountability Office. *GAO-09-3SP, GAO Cost Estimating and Assessment Guide.* Washington, D.C., March 2009.

With the **Parametric Method**, a total cost is derived based on specific factors that have a high correlation to total cost. This could be the number of lines of code programmed for a software development project, engineering/manufacturing complexity, square feet of floor space for an office building, weight of an airframe, electrical output for an electric generating station, capacity of a refinery, or power output of an engine. This estimating method also requires a comprehensive historical data base of similar projects.

Inputs for Estimate Development

Figure 21-4 provides an indication of the many different types of inputs needed for developing an estimate.

The list that follows is fairly comprehensive. Some of these inputs apply to preliminary type estimates or later. These include "equipment and material lists," "up-to-date equipment and material costs," and "historical unit rates for labor (work hours)." Other inputs would be restricted to conceptual estimates. These include "rules of thumb," "estimating guidelines," and "defaults." The remainder of the items listed should apply to all estimates.

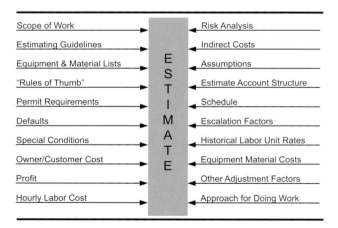

Figure 21-4 Inputs for Estimate Development

Figure 21-5 lists typical estimating system outputs. While fewer in number, they define the principal elements of an estimate. There should be a total recommended cost, a list of all documented assumptions, a cost flow, and results of a risk analysis that indicate the degree of comfort (or discomfort) in the estimate numbers. The total estimated cost is not final until the cost risk results are evaluated and a cost risk allowance is determined and included in the total. The estimate itself should be presented in formats agreed upon in advance, probably in multiple levels of detail. This allows various levels of management to review the estimate at a level of detail consistent with their knowledge and interest.

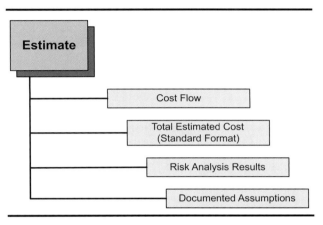

Figure 21-5 Estimate Outputs

Sources of Estimate Inputs

Inputs for development of an estimate originate with virtually every member of the project team. Management provides the start and completion dates, as well as the contracting philosophy and priorities in the time versus cost equation. Engineering provides the technical scope of work. Purchasing provides the lead times for material and equipment, as well as information on recent purchases of similar items. Construction provides input on the construction schedule and the installation hours required to do the work. Manufacturing/production provides input on the manufacturing/production process, schedule and unit rates. Scheduling provides the overall integrated schedule within the constraints of management dictates and functional (e.g., engineering, construction, production) input. Contract administration provides supporting information on later estimates. Accounting provides indirect rates to be applied to direct costs. Corporate policy on such items as union versus non-union labor and escalation are incorporated into the development of the estimate.

Since all estimates depend on the technical scope of work, those responsible for design/engineering will always have the most input to the estimate. This will include some form of statement of work, engineering drawings and specifications, equipment lists, engineering bill of material, and input regarding services to be supplied by others. If the estimate were for a construction project, information on bulk commodity quantities would also be essential. This may include items such as concrete, structural steel, electrical cable, piping, valves, printed circuit cards, titanium, etc. If it were a manufacturing/production estimate, technical description of the product and the quantity to be manufactured would be important pieces of information. An estimate for ongoing operations would require input on process flow requirements, e.g., number of gallons per hour of product produced or number of waste drums handled.

An estimate input that must be available is the schedule. An accurate estimate cannot be developed without a cost flow, and a cost flow cannot be developed without a schedule. Besides task durations, scheduled delivery dates for major cost items are also required since payment is tied to delivery.

The Use of Defaults in Estimate Preparation

A default is an assumed input to be used when exact information is unknown. It reflects a reasonable condition that is typical of most efforts and, therefore, may be used until better data is available. Earlier in a project, more of these inputs will be used in place of the definitive inputs. It is worth taking a closer look at defaults because of their possible value in saving estimate review time as well as development time.

When adequate information is not available to prepare an estimate, other tools must be used. This is particularly true in the case of conceptual estimates. These tools include estimates for similar projects, factored estimates, industry data, estimating "rules of thumb," and general estimating factors. These are classified as defaults.

Defaults are not applicable for all estimate inputs. For example, there can be no default for plant type or vehicle size. The number of defaults will vary based on the type of estimate. Many defaults are permissible in the conceptual estimate; a few are allowed in the preliminary estimate; and no defaults are allowed in the detailed or definitive estimates.

The list of potential defaults that can be used to assist the preparation of quick conceptual estimates is extensive, but are also generally project specific. Some defaults are little more than documented assumptions, such as permit requirements, water quality, fuel availability and type, waste water discharge requirements (temperature and water quality), and type of cooling system. Other defaults can be defined through corporate guidelines. Projected escalation rates would be an example of that. Corporate philosophy may also dictate whether to have permanent on-site buildings, whether union or non-union labor will be used, or how reliable the electric power source has to be.

Standard summary schedules should be available for new project studies or consideration of alternatives. Such schedules can be prepared for an entire family of similar projects using differing assumptions and the estimator can pick and choose which one applies best in the next scenario. The schedule selected is then used for escalation and cost flow computations. They also provide a starting point for "level of effort" support staffing (see Chapter 29) and provide standard lead times for assumed equipment deliveries. Their main purpose is to be used for the generation of conceptual estimates. Later estimate types should be based on specific project schedules.

Estimating Guidelines

In this section, guidelines are referred to as support tools for generating estimates based on summary type information. Guidelines are aids to quick calculations, using some predetermined relationship between cost and various variables ("cost drivers") that have a high correlation to cost. An example of a parametric approach to estimating is the curve shown in Figure 21-6.

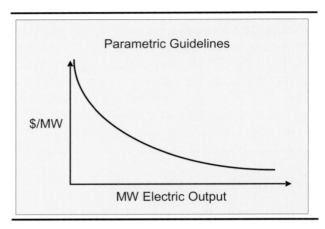

Figure 21-6 Estimate Development Example 1

As an electric plant gets larger (i.e., more megawatts produced), the cost per megawatt of electricity generated decreases. This is an example of economy of scale. No curve like this stands on its own. It must be modified based on the known parameters for the particular project being estimated. Site conditions may vary widely from one site to the next. If the project is planned as an accelerated project, there may be cost increases caused by decreased productivity and increased overtime. This may be offset by reduced escalation and the shorter duration for support services.

Other factors may enter as well. If the sample curve for electricity, reflected in Figure 21-6, was for a cogeneration plant, another factor to consider is volume of steam sales. It takes dollars to generate steam to produce electricity (in a thermal plant).

If there are significant steam sales, money is recovered from those sales but there is less electricity to sell. Thus the cost per unit produced (kilowatt or megawatt) appears high. This is an example of a curve correction that would have to be considered. See Figure 21-7.

Guidelines that develop cost based on some physical characteristic of equipment or technical parameter may be found in many places – vendor catalogs, engineering handbooks, and technical society publications. An illustration of this is presented in Figure 21-8. Once again, these types of guidelines are intended for quick and approximate estimate generation.

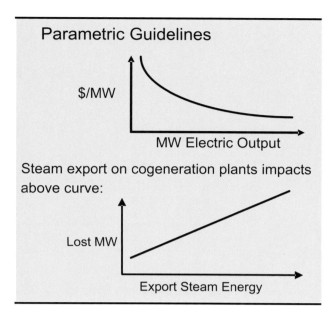

Figure 21-7 Estimate Development Example 2

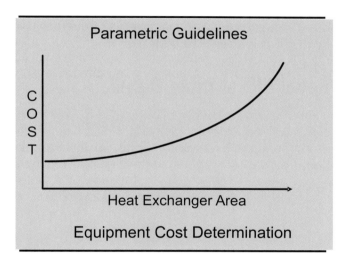

Figure 21-8 Estimate Development Example 3

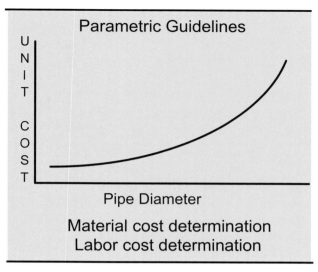

Figure 21-9 Estimate Development Example 4

ment items are willing to sell at actual cost in order to keep shops open and stay in business. During periods of vigorous economic expansion, those same suppliers collect hefty premiums for that same equipment to expedite orders in shops with major backlogs. Geographic location can also be especially important in international markets.

Environmental permitting has become a significant variable in developing schedule lead times, which, in turn, impact estimates, especially cost flows. If the estimate being developed were not a conceptual one (i.e., there is more than one to two days' time required for estimate development), vendor quotations will be solicited. Whether they are verbal or written depends on the amount of time available.

Approximate ranges provide a quick check of the credibility of the bottom line numbers for a detailed estimate as well. Historical records may indicate that a typical construction project cost breakdown has the following split by major cost category:

50%   Equipment and material cost.

25%   Construction labor cost.

10%   Owner's cost (for management/ review).

10%   Field purchases.

5%   Engineering cost.

As an example, both labor costs and material costs increase with the size of pipe installed. This is shown in Figure 21-9.

While curves like those discussed in the previous examples are easy to use, they must be modified because of a variety of factors. This is where the estimator's experience comes into play. Installation difficulty may vary by 300% between an easy, open installation and one that is crowded with complications of physical clearances and live power lines in an operating plant. Market anomalies can also be substantial. During depressed markets, many manufacturers of heavy equip-

If an estimate reflects engineering as 15% of the total cost, there is an immediate reason for checking these costs more closely. What might cause the project to vary so much from the expected norm? Most likely, there is an incorrect assumption or error somewhere in the detail. This is not the definitive way to review an estimate, but it is a way to get some feel for the credibility of the numbers before plunging into detailed review.

Other guidelines, which are really "rules of thumb," can be used to develop quicker estimates. In one organization, much time was spent each year on estimating new platforms needed in operating plants to improve access to key equipment or valves. Each piece of steel was estimated based on detailed drawing takeoffs of the dimensions and the exact weight of steel. At some point it was realized that there would be no real loss in accuracy if an average figure of so many dollars per square foot of platform space were used instead of exact takeoffs. Guidelines like this can be used to produce quicker estimates in many applications, without a significant loss in accuracy. The following are example guidelines that can be used for estimating:

- New software program development (lines of code developed per hour for various software program types).

- Design drawings (average number of hours required to produce each size of drawing).

- Testing and inspections (percent of direct hours associated with the test or inspection).

- Commercial buildings and residential housing (dollars per square foot).

- Operating plants (hours or dollars per waste drum handled or per unit produced).

Similarly, operating and maintenance costs can be developed for any size industrial plant based on historical records and age of the unit. All of these have a common objective: quick development of an acceptably accurate estimate assisted by historical records or experience.

Level of Estimate Detail

It is not always a matter of choice as to how much detail will be created for each type of estimate. For conceptual estimates, it is not possible to produce extensive reports detailing the estimate

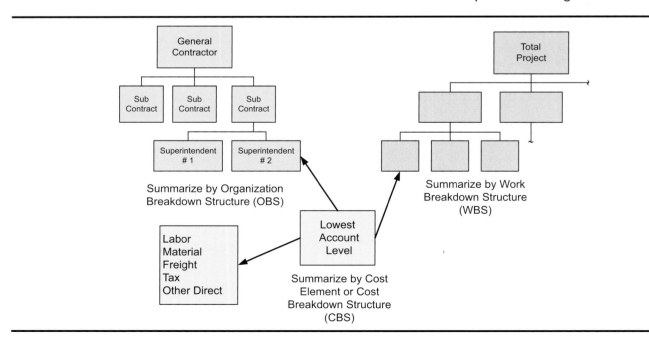

Figure 21-10 Level of Detail Summarization

because such information simply is not available. Conversely, virtually all project variables have been defined before the detailed and definitive estimates are produced. This allows far greater definition in these latter documents. There is a correlation between the type of estimate and the detail to which it should be prepared within the Work Breakdown Structure (WBS).

Depending on the number of levels of detail used within the WBS, the estimates might look something like this:

Conceptual	Level 3 (or 4)
Preliminary	Level 5
Detailed	Level 6.
Definitive	Commodity Code Level or schedule activity (task) level

Whatever the lowest account level used, the level of detail of the estimate must serve many functions. Figure 21-10 depicts these functions. The level used must allow summarization by organizational element, by cost element, and by the WBS.

Calculation of Indirect Costs

Indirect cost is associated with several different definitions. This section will review various uses of the term.

The U.S. Government, in its Federal Acquisition Regulations, defines indirect cost as:

> *Any cost not directly identified with a single final cost objective, but identified with two or more final cost objectives or with at least one intermediate cost objective.*[2]

The ANSI/EIA Standard 748-B, Earned Value Management Systems, defines indirect cost as:

> *The cost for common or joint objectives that cannot be identified specifically with a particular program or activity. Also referred to as overhead cost or burden.*[3]

Finally, Robert Kemps, in his book Fundamentals of Project Performance Measurement, defines indirect costs as:

> *The cost incurred by an organization for common or joint objectives which cannot be identified specifically with a particular project or activity. Also referred to as overhead costs.*[4]

While there are some variations between these definitions, the underlying principle in all of them is that indirect costs are not assigned to a single cost objective, project, or activity, but are collected separately and later allocated to direct costs to get the total cost for a project or contract.

Typically, the determination of indirect costs and their application to direct costs is contained in a company's Cost Accounting Standards (CAS) Disclosure Statement, which is the defining document as to what is an indirect cost versus a direct cost and which indirect costs are applied to which direct costs. Companies estimate their indirect costs as defined in the Disclosure Statement. They also estimate the direct cost business base to which the indirect costs will be applied. The Accounting Department uses these estimates to determine the indirect rates to be applied to direct costs. Throughout the company's fiscal year, both the indirect budgets and the direct cost base are evaluated to determine whether the rates being applied represent actuality. If not, the rates are adjusted for the purpose of minimizing year end adjustments.

Developing a Cost Flow

At this point, the calculations are not complete because escalation has not yet been considered. The normal next step in the process of developing the labor and non-labor costs would be to time phase the labor and non-labor costs over the schedule for the project. Escalation would then be applied based on what year the costs were planned to occur.

2. Federal Acquisition Regulations. *Part 2, Definition of Words and Terms.*
3. *GEIA Standard, Earned Value Management Systems, EIA-748-B.* July 2007.
4. Kemps, Robert R. *Fundamentals of Project Performance Measurement, Sixth Edition.* Orange, CA: Humphreys & Associates, Inc., 2011.

For example, using labor only, the hours were to be expended in the following profile at a cost of $27.31 per hour (all-inclusive rate):

Year	Hours	Cost
Current	10,000	$273,100
Current + 1	70,000	$1,911,700
Current + 2	150,000	$4,096,500
Current + 3	300,000	$8,193,000
Current + 4	225,000	$6,144,750
Current + 5	40,000	$1,092,400
Total Labor	795,000	$21,711,450

The result would be a labor cost of $21,711,450 (current year dollars). Now the escalated cost must be calculated. Assume that the escalation rate forecast is 5.00%, compounded annually.

The easiest first step is to calculate a table of what the escalation factors would be for each year. This would normally be done on a computer, with databases established for detailed escalation rates for many different categories of cost items. This example is simpler since we have only one cost category and a single escalation rate.

The formula used is: $E = (1 + i)^x$

Where:

E = escalation factor (compounded)

i = escalation per year (e.g., i = 0.05 for 5% escalation rate)

x = number of years escalation rate is applied (if the rate for every year were equal)

Current year   1.0000 multiplier

Current year + 1   1.0500 multiplier

Current year + 2   1.1025 multiplier

Current year + 3   1.1576 multiplier

Current year + 4   1.2155 multiplier

Current year + 5   1.2763 multiplier

Because of the compounding, "current year + 5" uses a 1.2763 factor rather than a 1.25. These factors are then applied to the labor hours planned for each of the project years:

Current	$273,100 x 1.0000 = $273,100
Current + 1	$1,911,700 x 1.0500 = $2,007,285
Current + 2	$4,096,500 x 1.1025 = $4,516,391
Current + 3	$8,193,000 x 1.1576 = $9,484,217
Current + 4	$6,144,750 x 1.2155 = $7,468,944
Current + 5	$1,092,400 x 1.2763 = $1,394,230
Total Estimated Labor Cost	**$25,144,167**

This is an increase of $3,432,717 compared with the current, unescalated dollars (i.e., "base" dollars). This is why the estimate must include among its assumptions the current date for the estimate and all assumed escalation provisions.

However, there is still something wrong with this example, although all of the calculations and numbers are correct. If an estimate were submitted exactly like this example, it would be ridiculed or at least recognized as coming from an inexperienced estimator. The key word here is "estimate". Why is a cost of $1,394,230 forecast for the final year? How was that number derived? It came from an estimate (the number of labor hours to be spent in that year) modified by another estimate (the escalation rate), without any adjustment for the fact that some parts of the labor dollar "all-inclusive" rate will be changing at different rates than other parts. Each of those estimates has a percentage of uncertainty associated with it that increases in magnitude as we start multiplying all of these numbers together. The only things we can be sure of are that there will not be exactly 40,000 labor hours spent in the final year and each hour will not cost exactly $34.86 ($27.31/HR X 1.2763). To expect seven digit accuracy five years in the future is totally unrealistic.

A more likely cost flow presentation and estimate would probably look like this:

Estimate for Project ABC ($ x 1000)	
Current year	$273
Current year + 1	$2,007
Current year + 2	$4,516
Current year + 3	$9,484

Estimate for Project ABC ($ x 1000)	
Current year + 4	$7,469
Current year + 5	$1,394
Total Estimate	**$25,143**

All dollars are "as spent" dollars (escalated dollars).

Corporate escalation guidelines of 5.0% have been used, with compounding annually.

Even this presentation may be too exact depending on the type of estimate being prepared. The above example would apply to a detailed or definitive estimate, but not necessarily to a conceptual estimate. A conceptual estimate would be presented even less precisely, with a projected cost flow and project total like this:

Estimate for Project ABC ($ x 1000)	
Current year	$273
Current year + 1	$2,000
Current year + 2	$4,500
Current year + 3	$9,500
Current year + 4	$7,500
Current year + 5	$1,227
Total Estimate	**$25,000**

Now the project cost has been rounded to the nearest million dollars, with individual years limited to $100,000 accuracy. The exceptions are the first and final years of the project. The initial year of a project will have much lower costs than later years (especially in a long duration project) and will need to be expressed more exactly since it will be the basis for a budget in the short term. The last year is then used as a balancing number to allow the total to be an even $25 million. Alternatively, the current year could have been listed as $300,000 and the final year as $1,200,000.

When presented this way, it is easy to understand why the numbers should be rounded. When decisions about whether or not to proceed with a project are being made, this project will be evaluated as a $25 million project regardless of whether the estimate is presented as $25 million, $25,143,000 or even $25,144,167. It can be argued that a proposed number with unwarranted

accuracy (such as the $25,144,167) is even misleading, since it implies a degree of confidence in the information source that simply is not there.

The detailed example just presented is still too simplified for most projects that are beyond the Conceptual Estimate stage. This example was for a contract that included labor only, with material furnished by others.

If labor and material will be required, as well as some type of Other Direct Costs (ODC), each has to be considered separately. Escalation projections will vary by year and by each category. A table of escalation guidelines might look like this:

Escalation Guidelines Table			
Period	Labor	Material	ODC
Current year	5.00%	4.75%	4.50%
Current year + 1	5.50%	5.25%	4.50%
Current year + 2	5.50%	5.50%	4.75%
Current year + 3	5.75%	5.50%	5.00%
Current year + 4	6.00%	5.50%	5.00%
Current year + 5	6.00%	5.50%	5.00%

Escalation factors would then be determined the same as shown earlier in the labor cost example, except now there would be three sets of factors applied to three different cost flows.

Escalation Guidelines Table			
Period	Labor	Material	ODC
Current year	1.000	1.000	1.000
Current year + 1	1.050	1.048	1.045
Current year + 2	1.108	1.102	1.092
Current year + 3	1.169	1.163	1.144
Current year + 4	1.246	1.227	1.201
Current year + 5	1.310	1.294	1.261

The labor cost flow would be determined the same as before, from a time-phased labor hour spread. Other Direct Costs (ODC) are usually divided into travel and miscellaneous for the purposes of cash flow Travel cash flow is dependent on work scope involving travel and when it happens. The other ODCs are minor in nature and usually can be time-phased proportional to labor.

That only leaves the material component. As with the labor component of the total estimate and cost flow, this depends on the quality and availability of information. For the Detailed Estimate and the Definitive Estimate, the material cost flow should be derived from the following five documents:

1. A summary project schedule.

2. Planned material delivery dates.

3. Projected milestone payments (identified in contracts and high dollar, long term purchase orders).

4. Planned commodity installation curves (provided by the contractor performing the installation).

5. Escalation tables.

A base cost flow can now be established. The base cost flow is the planned rate of expenditures for each of the three listed categories by year in current year dollars. The escalation factors would next be applied from an escalation table like the one shown above.

For the Conceptual Estimate, simplified approaches are used. A composite escalation rate will be used that factors in each of the individual escalation rates weighted according to the makeup of the anticipated total project cost; e.g., 55% material, 35% labor, and 10% ODCs. This single escalation factor is then applied to the overall base cost flow without escalation derived from historical or other information.

For "Current year + 3," the relative weights of the three component factors would be calculated as follows:

Escalation = (0.55 x 1.163) + (0.35 x 1.169) + (0.10 x 1.144) = 1.163

This composite factor would then be applied against the total projected cost for "Current year + 3".

Use of Other Escalation Factors

Short cuts for calculating escalation are sometimes used instead of the tedious approach described above, which requires a large amount of information to be available. This is especially the case for Conceptual Estimates prepared to evaluate various alternatives quickly.

The short cut most frequently used is to find the median of project expenditures, that is, the point where half of the costs occur before that date and half occur afterwards, and escalate the total project cost estimate at that point rather than escalating each year's expenditures individually. While this is not as precise as the detailed method, it allows quicker answers and in some cases is the only approach that can be used because of incomplete project information. This can be used with escalation tables to compare projects with different completion dates.

There are many tables of comparative costs over time available from the federal government and from various trade journals. Some of these take the form of a base year cost with an arbitrarily assigned value of 100 for that year. The base year may vary and may even change over time. Using indices like this requires a slightly different approach towards escalation calculations than those presented so far. The next example uses this type of index. The values presented are not based on any published index.

Cost of Widgets 2010 = 100			
Year	Cost	Year	Cost
2010	100	2017	169
2011	112	2018	175
2012	126	2019	177
2013	136	2020	176
2014	143	2021	182
2015	151	2022	188
2016	159	2023	193

Say that the last widget project had a midpoint expenditure date of June 30, 2010 and cost of $148 million. A new widget project, with the same scope of work and the exact same project schedule, has a midpoint expenditure date of June 30, 2023. Because it has the same schedule, the assumption is that the project durations are the same and the shape of the cost flow is the same. What would the expected cost be for the new project on a comparable basis?

This is as easy as figuring the ratio of costs now to then and applying that factor to the original project cost.

$$\frac{2023 \text{ index}}{2010 \text{ index}} = \frac{193}{100} \times \$148 \text{ million}$$

$$= 1.93 \times \$148 \text{ million}$$

$$= \$285 \text{ million}$$

If the estimated cost for the new project is more than $285 million, it is expected to be more expensive to complete than the 2010 project on a comparable basis. Analysis like this is frequently used when comparing costs of similar projects completed at different points in time to see which projects were most economical to finish. The crux of the analysis is having similar projects to compare. If the 2010 project had a capacity of producing 2 million widgets per year and the 2023 plant will have an output of 3 million widgets per year, a comparison like this will be of little value. Even in that circumstance, however, the first step would be the same as shown here. That answer would then have to be modified based on an adjustment factor for the difference in output.

One adjustment that is made in such comparisons is an exponential relationship of the following:

$$\left(\frac{3 \text{ million}}{2 \text{ million}}\right)^{0.7} \times \$148 \text{ million} = 1.328 \times \$148 \text{ million}$$

$$= \$196.5 \text{ million}$$

The 0.7 exponent reflects the fact that a production plant's cost will not increase linearly with the output. The value of the exponent is empirically derived based on a company's past experience. When a plant doubles in size, as measured by output, it does not quite double in cost. Many of the onetime costs associated with acquiring and preparing the site are virtually the same regardless of the fact that one plant has a greater capacity. This has long been recognized when comparing similar projects with differing production rate capabilities.

Combining these two adjustments, we can now compare the differing outputs and the differing escalation impacts.

$148 million x 1.328 x 1.93 = $379.3 million (rounded to $379 million)

Thus on a comparable basis, a 2 million widget plant completed in 2010 for $148 million would be approximately the same as a 3 million widget output plant completed in 2023 for $379 million. These types of comparisons are frequently made in industry for cost justification or simply to compare projects.

Estimating Operating and Manufacturing Costs

It is necessary to categorize estimated costs. This is certainly true in operations or manufacturing environments when analyzing operations at less than full capacity. The estimator needs to understand how much of the operation is recurring cost and how much of the operation is nonrecurring cost. The U.S. Department of Defense, in its Data Item Description (DID) for the reporting of functional hour and cost data, requires the separation of recurring and nonrecurring cost. The DID provides a definition of those costs as follows:

Recurring Costs - *Repetitive elements of development and investment costs that may vary with the quantity being produced, irrespective of system life cycle phase and appropriation. Recurring cost categories include procurement and production activities; acceptance testing; maintenance and support equipment, training, and data; test articles built to an operational configuration; and certain elements of Systems Engineering and Program Management (SE/PM).*

Nonrecurring Costs - *Nonrepetitive elements of development and investment costs that generally do not vary with the quantity being produced, irrespective of system life cycle phase and the appropriation. Nonrecurring cost categories include Product Design and Development (PD&D) activities; System Test and Evaluation (ST&E); tooling; pre-production activities; design and development of support equipment, training, and data;*

and certain elements of Systems Engineering and Program Management (SE/PM).[5]

One possible application of this categorization of costs would relate to a reduction in output/throughput of 50% for a particular facility for the following fiscal year. The initial reaction might be that the estimate for the next year's operation should also be reduced by 50%, but this is not the case. The first step required would be to categorize the annual costs based on the categories above (recurring and nonrecurring). Let us assume that the split of total cost by these categories is as follows:

Recurring Costs: 75% of total estimate

Nonrecurring Costs: 25% of total estimate

There is no reduction in fixed costs as a result of reduced output/throughput by definition. Variable costs will decrease by 75% (the same as output/throughput), again by definition.

The next step is to determine the revised estimate requirements based on cost category to reflect the revised output. This will be easier to follow with sample numbers, so the assumption is that the previous annual estimate was for $1,000,000. Calculation of the next year's estimate will then be calculated as follows:

Type of Cost	Fiscal Year 1	Fiscal Year 2	Notes
Recurring Costs	$750,000	$375,000	1
Nonrecurring Costs	$250,000	$250,000	2
Total Budget	$1,000,000	$625,000	

Note 1.   Seventy-five percent of the $1,000,000 estimate ($750,000) is Recurring Cost and therefore reduces linearly with reduction in output/throughput. Therefore, a 50% reduction in output/throughput means a 50% reduction in this portion of the estimate (50% of $750,000 = $375,000).

Note 2.   Twenty-five percent of the $1,000,000 estimate ($250,000) is Fixed Cost. It does not

5.   U.S. Department of Defense, OSD/PA&E/CAIG. *Functional Cost-Hour Report, DI-FNCL-81566B.* Washington, D.C., April 2007, 13.

change despite the reduction in output/throughput.

Total revised cost estimate for reduced output of 50%: $625,000.

In the example, a 50% reduction in output/throughput results in only a 37.5% reduction in estimated costs. The correct categorization of costs into recurring and nonrecurring components is the key element in successful cost estimate projections of this type. The same type of analysis would apply to operating a production line at less than full capacity.

Software Estimating

Engineering and construction/production projects have relied heavily on thorough and accurate estimating techniques for many years. But how is this applied in completely different work efforts, such as a development project for new computer software? Software is a specialized application that has received attention because of the increasing importance (and budgets) associated with this dynamic industry. While it is easy to measure progress on a production line or a physical installation, what is the best approach for measuring output on intellectual effort like software development?

In the past, the generally used estimating method was to quantify the effort based on the number of software lines of code developed or the number of function points. This worked well when a single waterfall life cycle was used and when most applications were developed using second or third generation languages. The 1981 publication of Software Engineering Economics by Dr. Barry Boehm included the definition of the Constructive Cost Model (COCOMO). This model used lines of code as a basis for developing estimates of cost for software and adjusted the calculations based on a number of factors. COCOMO quickly became the most widely used software estimating process and automated versions were available from a number of software tools providers.

Earlier, in 1979, Allen Albrecht of IBM developed an approach to software estimating based on what he called "function points". Albrecht considered five items as function points: the number of inputs, number of outputs, number of inquiries by users, the number of data files that would be updated by the program, and the interfaces to other applications.

Other software-estimating practitioners have evolved variations of these models or created other models to estimate cost. With the evolution and maturing of the software industry, these earlier approaches have evolved as well. Multiple Government-approved software life cycles exist and development languages vary from Java to Computer Aided Software Engineering (CASE) generated executable code. Extensive use of Commercial-Off-The-Shelf (COTS) products and processes significantly alter the cost of software intensive efforts. They also require the use of much more comprehensive estimating tools.

Both lines of code and function point estimating have evolved since their origination. More information on function points can be obtained from the International Function Point Users Group (IFPUG). The IFPUG provides data and information about the use of function points. In 2010, IFPUG produced Release 4.3 of its Counting Practices Manual.

COCOMO evolved into COCOMO II and remains the longest and most widely used method of estimating software efforts. Several variations of COCOMO reflect estimates for particular programming languages or the use of COTS.

Like any application, the availability of historical data improves the accuracy of a software estimate regardless of the method used to evaluate its status. Another important consideration is that the competence of the estimator is more significant than the estimating approach.

Conclusion

The estimate development process is a logical one. There are three methods commonly used for developing estimates. Their application depends on the amount of available detail for project scope. The Engineering Build-up Method is employed for a detailed or definitive type estimate, because it relies on the availability of detailed design and scope information. The Analogy and Parametric Methods are used for conceptual estimates because they do not require detailed information. A preliminary estimate may use any or all of the three methods depending on the amount of specific information that is available.

The key objective is to have the estimate reflect all of the best available information on the project. As such, it should include inputs from all knowledgeable team members as well as any design documents. A considerable amount of information must be standardized before an estimate is prepared. This includes the determination of any estimating guidelines and defaults to be used when project-specific information is lacking.

Special considerations in estimate development include the definition of indirect costs and the development of a cost flow. If the project being estimated is of long duration, then escalation will also be factored into the final numbers.

While most estimates involving extensive labor, material, and equipment are prepared with a similar approach, there are special applications that require other techniques. Specific models for developing estimates are available for specialized applications, such as the COCOMO II model and the Function Point Counting method used for estimating software development costs. With any model, however, there needs to be some calibration of the generic model or rates to the specific application through the use of current or historical data for similar projects.

Chapter 21 Review Questions

21-1.   What is the first essential step in the estimating process?

21-2.   Explain how material quantities are important for developing a cost estimate.

21-3.   Identify and explain the three methods commonly used for developing estimates.

21-4.   A final bottom line cost does not constitute an estimate by itself. What additional information must be provided, at a minimum, so that the estimate can be evaluated?

21-5.   Why is the schedule important for developing the cost estimate?

21-6.   What is a default, as applied to estimate development, and what is its role in estimate preparation?

21-7.   Provide an example, from the text or from personal experience, of a parametric guideline.

21-8.   Which type of estimate, Preliminary or Definitive, would be prepared in more detail? Why?

21-9.   Provide a general definition of indirect costs.

21-10. Why is it imperative that the "base date" of the estimate be identified, i.e. the date on which costs are based?

21-11. What are the five main sources of information needed for developing a cash flow for project material?

21-12. What are the two principle parameters that are used when estimating software costs?

True or False

21-13. A composite labor rate is a rate that combines the direct labor rate with the indirect rates that apply to labor into one overall rate.

21-14. Accuracy in estimates is very important, so numbers should always be expressed in exact dollars.

21-15. One reason that it is important to isolate the labor and material components of a cost estimate is that they are each subject to separate escalation rates.

21-16. There is no straightforward way to compare the relative costs of two projects that were built in different years with different capacities.

21-17. "Rules of thumb" may be used for developing faster estimates and for quick summary review of an estimate.

The answers to these questions can be found in Section 6, Solutions.

Case Study

21.1 DEVELOPING AN ESTIMATE

A 10-mile long, 10" pipeline is being installed cross-country between two existing lines. All that is required is installation of the pipe and a control valve at each end. Assume 5% allowance of total direct costs for construction indirect cost for a project of this type. The new construction will be in Arizona.

1. Using the attached estimating guidelines, develop a quick conceptual estimate of what the cost of the project will be.

2. The Right-of-Way has not yet been acquired, nor has the route for the pipeline been surveyed. There are no apparent problems with the terrain. How should your estimate be adjusted, if at all, when considering these factors?

Hint: Make sure to state your assumption.

The solution to this case study can be found on the Humphreys & Associates, Inc. web site.
www.humphreys-assoc.com

ESTIMATING GUIDELINES
Cross Country Pipelines

Cost per Mile	3" Pipe	4" Pipe	6" Pipe	8" Pipe	10" Pipe
Labor	$25,000	$30,000	$40,000	$60,000	$65,000
Material	$19,000	$25,000	$40,000	$65,000	$73,000
Subtotal L&M	**$44,000**	**$55,000**	**$80,000**	**$125,000**	**$138,000**
Freight and Taxes	$2,000	$3,000	$5,000	$8,000	$10,000
Engineering	$1,000	$3,000	$4,000	$4,000	$4,000
Environmental	$1,000	$2,000	2,000	$2,000	$2,000
Right-of-Way	$10,000	$15,000	$20,000	$20,000	$20,000
Subtotal Add-Ons	**$14,000**	**$23,000**	**$31,000**	**$34,000**	**$36,000**

Above costs are based on New Mexico Installation. Adjustments for nearby areas are as follows:

Texas:	-5%
Oklahoma:	0%
Arizona:	+10%
California:	+20%

Cost for hydrostatic testing of pipe:

$5,000 for less than 8"

$10,000 for pipe between 8" and 16"

	3" Pipe	4" Pipe	6" Pipe	8" Pipe	10" Pipe
Control Values	$10,000	$13,000	$20,000	$30,000	$40,000
Control Valve with Isolation Valve	$18,000	$25,000	$45,000	$70,000	$100,000

Case Study

21.2 ESTIMATE MODIFICATION

The attached estimate was developed for the YR2 for receiving and disposing of low-level wastes at a western site. A review by waste management staff revealed a false assumption: the amount of waste to be processed would be the same as in YR1. However, half of the waste will now be processed at a different location. An estimate reviewer has asked the question, "Doesn't that mean we should cut the estimate in half?" Your assignment is to address that comment in an upcoming meeting.

As part of the preparation for that meeting, accomplish the following:

1. Identify each cost category as either a fixed cost, a variable cost, or as a semi-variable cost.

2. Develop a total of the costs for each category.

3. Provide an approximation of how much the estimate should actually be reduced for a 50% reduction in waste handled (total dollar reduction and percentage reduction).

Be prepared to explain your answer and the reason why each cost was categorized in the particular category chosen.

The solution to this case study can be found on the Humphreys & Associates, Inc. web site.
www.humphreys-assoc.com

FIGURE 1 Year 2 Estimate		
	Hours	**Cost**
ONGOING SUPPORT	**26,300**	**3,552K**
Support Services		
Training, emergency response	4,500	695K
Regulatory compliance		
Records management		
Project Controls		
Clerical support		
Information management		
Quality assurance		
Waste Acceptance	5,700	645K
Waste acceptance		
Equipment		
Transportation	2,400	365K
Facilities Management	13,700	1847K
Facility inspections & maintenance		
Facility development & coordination		
Environmental surveillance		
ADMINISTRATIVE MANAGEMENT	**4,000**	**391K**
Administrative Management Support	900	134K
Prepare budget requests		
Hire personnel, attend meetings		
Perform long range planning		
Respond to action items		
Issue RFP's and select contractors		
Prepare & respond to results from ES&H		
Questionnaire and site disposal areas		
Technical Management Support	3,000	249K
Implement conduct of operations		
Implement QA/QC		
Develop/review SOP's and DOP's		
Manage projects		
Participate in conferences and meetings		
Provide technical contractor support		
Site tours and visits	100	8K
TRAINING	**500**	**23K**
AUDITS	**450**	**25K**
Audits	170	10K
Audit Corrective Actions	280	15K

FIGURE 1 Year 2 Estimate (Continued)	Hours	Cost
NON-CONFORMANCE ACTION	**80**	**5K**
PIT AND SHAFT EXCAVATION	**950**	**2,336K**
Pit and Shaft Excavation in Old Area	320	243K
Manage the design and excavation of shafts in the old area		
Excavate pit 38 in old area		
Pit and Shaft Excavation in Expansion Area	630	2,093K
Engineering design cost of new pits		
Manage the design and excavation of pits and shafts in the expansion area		
Remedy Indian ruins in the expansion area; excavate three ruins		
WASTE RECEIPT	**520**	**19K**
Weigh Vehicle	60	3K
Compare with weight reported by the generator		
Re-inspection of Manifest	230	8K
Comparison of Load to Manifest	230	8K
Ensure manifest correctly describes package		
WASTE PLACEMENT	**230**	**9K**
Waste Placement	230	9K
Place LLW (including PCB's) into pits & shafts		
Place LLW (asbestos) into pits		
WASTE BURIAL	**210**	**8K**
Waste Burial (Low Level Pit and Shafts)	210	8K
INSPECTIONS	**20**	**2K**
Daily/Weekly Inspections & Record Maintenance	20	2K
CAPITAL EQUIPMENT/WORK ORDERS	**800**	**112K**
Capital Equipment (O.E.)	800	38K
Procure and Develop Work Orders		
Capital Equipment (C.E.)	0	74K
CERTIFICATION/ASSESSMENT	**20**	**1K**
MATERIALS AND SUPPLIES	**0**	**168K**

Chapter 22

LEARNING CURVES

Objectives of this Chapter:

1. Explain the concept of learning curves and their application.

2. Define and present examples of Unit Learning Curves.

3. Define and present examples of Cumulative Average Learning Curves.

4. Provide typical learning curve values for various types of operations.

5. Discuss factors that limit the applicability of learning curves.

Learning curves are applied rigidly in some industries, especially those with high rate production, and completely ignored in others. The basic underlying reason for establishing learning curves is that repetitive tasks should result in improved productivity as the number of repetitions continues to increase. This improvement is typically quantified as a rate of improvement. When the estimated improvement rate for completing a task is plotted versus the number of units produced, the display is a curve, which decreases to the right as the number of units increases.

Put into the simplest terms, the cost of manufacturing or installing a unit should decrease as the number of units involved increases. This is generically pictured in Figure 22-3. The concept of learning curves is not a new idea. It originated in the mid-1930's with T.P. Wright in the Journal of Aeronautical Sciences.[1] The original application related to the manufacture and assembly of aircraft in the aerospace industry.

Wright observed that as the number of units doubled, the unit value or cumulative average value

tended to be a constant percent of the value of the unit number that was doubled. The constant percent reduction is called the slope. For example, assuming the slope is 80%, if unit 10 had a value of 100, unit 20 would have a value of 80 and unit 40 would have a value of 64. This relationship is represented by the following equation:

$$Y_x = T_1 \times (X)^b$$

Where:

T1 is the theoretical or estimated value of the first unit,

X is the unit being calculated,

b is the exponential value associated with the slope,

The value of b is calculated by the equation (ln S) / (ln 2), where S is the slope as a decimal,

Y_x is the calculated value of unit X given a first unit value and a slope.

When the above equation is plotted on log-log paper, it plots as a straight line.

Figure 22-3 shows an 80% unit learning curve plotted in normal coordinates. Note the steep-

---

1. Wright, T.P. *Factors Affecting the Cost of Airplanes.* Journal of Aeronautics Sciences, Vol. 3, No. 4, 1936, 122-128.

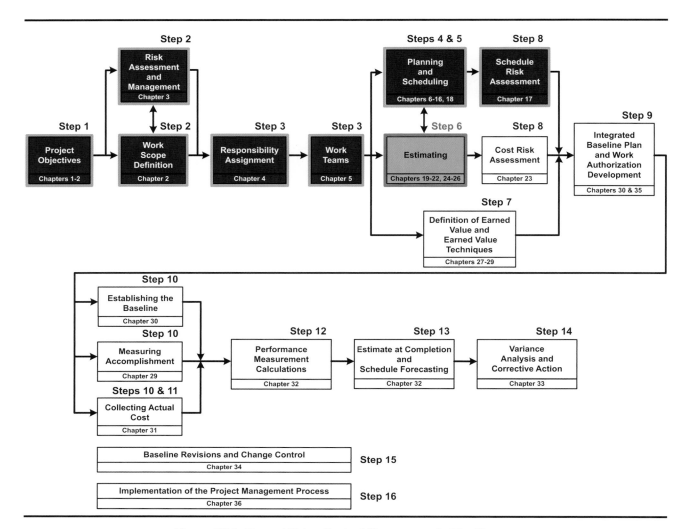

Figure 22-1 Earned Value Project Management: The Process

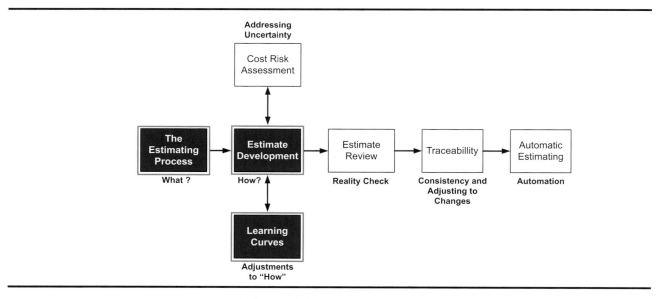

Figure 22-2 Estimating Topics

ness of the slope at first and the almost flat slope at unit 200.

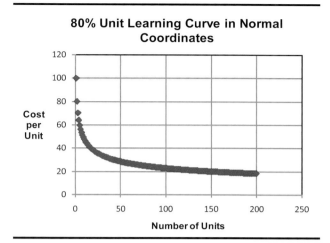

Figure 22-3 Learning Curve - Normal Coordinates

Figure 22-4 shows an 80% unit learning curve plotted in log – log coordinates. Note that the data plots in a straight line, which is why the constant percent reduction is called the slope. Also note that the ordinates of a log – log graph will never begin with zero.

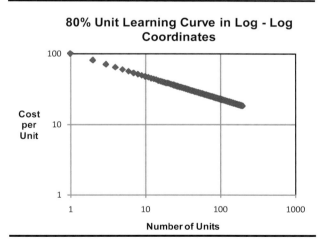

Figure 22-4 Learning Curve - Log-Log Coordinates

As time went on, learning curves were applied in many other situations as well where highly repetitive operations occur. Two types of learning curves are typically referred to: the Unit Learning Curve and the Cumulative Average Learning Curve. Each will be explained fully, including how the curve is calculated.

Unit Learning Curve

Unit Learning theory states that the value of each unit follows the constant rate rule. Thus, if unit 10 is expected to take 100 hours to manufacture, unit 20 is estimated to take 80 hours and unit 40 is estimated to take 64 hours, assuming an 80% learning curve slope.

Cumulative Average Learning Curve

Cumulative Average Learning theory states that the cumulative average value through a unit follows the constant rate rule. Thus, if, as of unit 10, the average cost for the first 10 units were expected to be 100 hours per unit, the average cost for the first 20 units would be estimated to be 80 hours and the average cost for the first 40 units estimated to be 64 hours, again assuming an 80% learning curve slope.

If the y-axis of Figures 22-3 and 22-4 were re-labeled to be Cumulative Average Cost per Unit, the figures would represent the plots of a Cumulative Average Learning Curve of 80%. The math is the same, only the parameter being measured changes.

The Difference between Unit Linear and Cumulative Average Linear

So what is the real difference between the two methods? The answer lies in the computation of the total cost of a lot or a production run. Taking the example of a first unit value of 100 (would be the same for both methods) and an 80% slope, we assume the total production run of 200 units in divided into two lots of 100 each.

Remember that for Unit Linear, the total cost will be the sum of the unit costs, and that for Cumulative Average Linear, the total cost will be the unit value times the total number of units up to that point. The following table shows the calculation results for both methods:

Lot	Unit Linear	Cumulative Averange Lincear
First 100 Total Cost	3,265	2,271
Second 100 Total Cost	2,007	1,362
Production Run Total	5,272	3,633

The significant difference between the two methods seen in the above table is a warning that an analyst must be careful as to which method to use. It would take an 84% Cumulative Average Linear slope to arrive at the same total cost for 200 units as the Unit Linear method with an 80% slope, but the lot costs would still be different. Most analysts use the Unit Linear Method because it is the one that usually best fits actual production run data. Some analysts have chosen the Cumulative Average Method solely because it is much easier to calculate total costs. That could be a significant error because as the table shows, for the same slope, the Cumulative Average Method produced a value for the total production run that was 31% lower. The analyst should determine which method would best fit the operations being estimated before developing an estimate.

Determining the Learning Curve to Use

Based on the information provided above, there are three questions to be answered:

1. Which Learning Curve Method should be used?

2. What slope is the proper slope?

3. What is the value of the first unit?

The best way to answer questions one and two is to have access to past project data and use the analog method discussed in Chapter 21. But in the case of learning curves, use of the analog method is not as easy as using a physical characteristic that is a cost driver for the product. Regression analysis is normally used to find best fits to an equation, but the equation to be fit is an exponential equation that cannot be analyzed

using linear regression analysis. However, a simple transformation of the equation puts the formula into a form that can be analyzed using linear regression analysis as follows:

The equation to be fit to the data is:

$$Y_x = T_1 \times X^b$$

Taking the natural log of both sides of the equation yields:

$$Ln(Y_x) = Ln(T_1) + b \times Ln(X)$$

This is an equation in the form of y = a + bx, which is a linear equation, not an exponential equation, and can be analyzed using linear regression analysis. For a data set of known unit values, simply enter the Ln of each Y and the Ln of the corresponding X into the regression data base. The regression analysis will provide the best-fit values for $Ln(T_1)$ and b. Take the anti-log of $LN(T_1)$ to find the regressed value of T_1. By substituting these values back into the original equation, a Y value can be calculated for every desired value of X.

To determine which Learning Curve Method to use, accomplish the regression analysis using unit values the first time through and cumulative average values the second time through. The regression analysis process will produce statistics as to how the regressed equation fits the input data. One statistic is the Coefficient of Determination, or R^2 in mathematical notation. The closer R^2 is to 1.0, the better the fit. In most recurring operations, the unit linear method provides the best fit. An R^2 of .9 or better is considered a good fit. An R^2 less than .9 may mean the resultant equation does not adequately represent the data that are being analyzed. It is always good practice to plot the actual data points on the same graph as the regressed curve to visually analyze how well the curve fits the data. Often, outlying data points can be seen that, upon inspection, should not have been included in the data set.

Unit values are often not available to accomplish a regression analysis to determine a unit linear slope because only lot data is available. The question is: at which unit is the average lot value plotted? It is not the unit at the halfway point in the lot. The answer depends on three variables: the size of the lot, where the lot in located in the production run, and the expected learning slope. For example, assuming an 80% learning slope with the first lot being 50 units, the plot point would be about unit 17, not unit 25. For a 90% slope, the plot point would be between units 18 and 19.

Lot plot points can be calculated using the following procedure. They are dependent only upon the slope of the learning curve. Thus, to determine a plot point, simply assume a slope and a T1 (100 works fine, but the value does not matter), calculate the unit values for the lot size (number of units) and location within the production run, sum the unit values, find the average, and then find where that average value fits within the unit values calculated for the lot. That becomes your plot point. For lot sizes of 20 or more, it is only the first lot in a production run that will require a plot point adjustment. The following lot plot points, while not being exactly the lot midpoint, will be close enough to result in a reasonably accurate unit learning curve slope for the data being analyzed. Run your lot average cost data through linear regression using the estimated plot points. If the regressed slope were significantly different from the slope assumed for plot point determination, the plot point calculations should be rerun using the regressed slope and then lot data re-entered. The resulting curve fit (R^2) should be much better.

How the value of the first unit is determined varies from company to company. If there were a prototype, it may be used as the first unit value, but should be adjusted for known differences between the prototype and production (e.g., hard tooling versus soft tooling, engineering changes to fix issues discovered in the prototype, and time break between prototype and production). If there were not a prototype, some companies would directly estimate the value of the first unit by incorporating all the inefficiencies they expect to occur. Others will estimate a value for a unit that they expect to come close to meeting standards. Unit 200 is commonly used as the "standard unit" because the learning is close to being flat at that point (see Figure 22-3). Once the

"standard unit" value is determined, the first unit value is calculated by "backing-up" to the first unit using the learning slope to be used for the estimate.

Be careful when using the "standard unit" method. One company tried to convince a customer that it used a steeper than normal learning curve for use in its proposal in order to reduce the cost and described how they would achieve that steeper curve. Upon questioning, it was found that the estimate was derived by estimating a value at unit 200 and backing up the steeper learning curve. The actual production run was to be 150 units, so the steeper curve actually produced a higher estimate, not a lower estimate. Needless to say, the ensuing discussion between the contractor and the customer was very interesting.

Typical Learning Curve Values

The value of expected learning curves varies according to the proportion of how much the operation is machine-controlled versus manually controlled. Obviously, there is a much shallower learning curve (the percentage value of the slope is higher) associated with operations that are mostly machine-controlled. Typical learning curve values for manufacturing operations correspond to the following values:

95% learning curve: mostly machine-controlled (e.g., when manual effort is mostly setup time).

90% learning curve: machine-controlled with some manual (e.g., requires manual effort to position parts during manufacture).

85% learning curve: mostly manually controlled with some machine assistance (e.g., subassembly of more than one part using tooling to assist with positioning the parts).

80% learning curve: manually controlled (e.g., effort in a final assembly line).

Impacts to Learning Curves

Learning curves gradually spread from the aerospace industry to manufacturing in general. Although learning curves have been observed and used in many manufacturing operations, there are many factors that can result in the expected learning curve not actually being realized. Some of these have been documented by Synan and Larson.[2] Among the major contributors to unrealized learning curves are the following:

1. Operator turnover rate (new employees do not meet the expected standards immediately).

2. Production reworks (however, if real data were used to establish the estimated learning slope, it probably already has some rework built in).

3. Material handling and downtime (learning curve calculations typically assume that material will be available when needed).

4. Engineering changes.

5. Rework of vendor supplied parts.

Another consideration is the continuity of the production cycle. If there were a break in continuity, there would be some loss of learning improvement.

Because of these factors, preparing a bid that assumes a perfect learning curve may result in cost overrun. An example of a typical misapplication was a company that was bidding on an aerospace manufacturing contract and historical records indicated that a learning curve of 80% could be expected. The bidding was expected to be very competitive, so the company decided to bid assuming a 70% learning curve. This added optimism had no basis in fact, but did lower the bid cost as desired. When the bid was successful in attracting a contract, the company found that they could not meet the estimated learning curve. The result was a significant cost overrun and loss of credibility.

2. Synan, John F. and Larson, Frederick K. *Development and Application of Learning Curves.* American Association of Cost Engineers, 1989 Transactions, 33rd Annual Meeting, G.2.4.

A phenomenon has been observed as a project nears completion. Because of several factors such as scarcity of parts, delaying difficult work to the end, and worker inefficiency that naturally occurs when the end of a project is in sight, the learning slope flattens and even starts to go upwards. This phenomenon is often referred to as "toe-up" because of what it looks like on a graph. Figure 22-5 illustrates this.

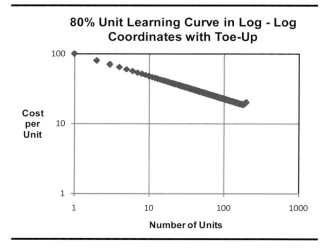

Figure 22-5 Learning Curve Showing End of Production Inefficiencies

Conclusion

The cost of manufacturing or installing one unit decreases when the number of units involved increases. This phenomenon has been recognized in certain industries for decades and is called the learning curve. There are two defined learning curves - the Unit Learning Curve and the Cumulative Average Learning Curve. Both reflect in different ways how the slope of the unit rate improvement is calculated. Learning curves are always represented for a doubling of the number of units being estimated. While this is a useful concept, there are many factors that can negate the learning curve or cause it to be less than anticipated. These must be considered when applying learning curves to the estimating process.

Chapter 22 Review Questions

22-1.   What are the two types of learning curves?

22-2.   Explain the concept of a learning curve.

22-3.   Unit 50 took 20 hours to complete and the average cost for the first 50 was 28 hours. Unit 100 required 16 hours to complete and the average cost for the first 100 was 23 hours. Calculate the learning curve slope for both types of learning curve.

22-4.   What is the biggest contributor to the expected slope of the learning curve?

22-5.   What are some of the factors (list at least 3) that must remain constant for learning curves to be meaningfully applied?

True or False

22-6.   Learning curves can be applied to any repetitive task or project for which conditions remain the same.

22-7.   Typical learning curve values for aircraft manufacturing are in the 75%-80% range.

22-8.   The standard definition of learning curves applies only to the doubling of the number of units in question.

22-9.   Learning curves were introduced in the 1960's and have been widely applied since that time.

The answers to these questions can be found in Section 6, Solutions.

Case Study

22.1 ESTIMATING COST SAVINGS

The 10-mile pipeline in Case Problem 21.1 is actually the first of a series of 8 similar tie-ins to be made. The same work crew, same equipment, and same supervision will be applied to all of these mini-projects. You are to prepare a quick estimate of the anticipated cost savings to be realized from learning curves on this series of repetitive activities. Assume there are no significant variations in terrain that will impact cost.

1. Using the solution for Case Problem 21.1, which item (s) are likely candidates for application of a learning curve?

2. Assuming a 90% unit learning curve, how much will the eight (8) installations cost for the tasks experiencing this improvement? Calculate costs only for the tasks experiencing productivity improvement. What is the difference in the estimate in dollars?

Hint: Make sure to state your assumptions.

The solution to this case study can be found on the Humphreys & Associates, Inc. web site.
www.humphreys-assoc.com

COST RISK ASSESSMENT

Objectives of this Chapter:

1. Explain the difference between Monte Carlo and Latin Hypercube sampling techniques.

2. Define the relationship between number of iterations (trials) in a Monte Carlo simulation and result accuracy.

3. Present examples of probability distribution shapes and explain their application.

4. Identify typical results and formats of risk simulation outputs and explain how to use them.

5. Learn to interpret risk assessment output statistics.

6. Learn how to use risk assessment to establish recommended cost risk allocations.

7. Explain how to apply risk analysis to "what if?" studies.

8. Provide implementation tips for successful application of risk analysis results to decision-making.

Technical risk and schedule risk were introduced earlier as separate topics. This chapter introduces cost risk which, as its name suggests, attempts to evaluate the uncertainty within a cost estimate. Of all of the types of risk assessment, this is the one that has been applied on the most projects and for the longest period of time. It is appropriate that this form of risk is covered last because both technical risk and schedule risk are inputs that greatly affect cost risk. Therefore, cost risk includes the cost impact of technical and schedule risks. An estimate should not be considered complete until a cost risk assessment has been accomplished.

The bulk of this discussion addresses cost risk assessment and how it can and should be applied to a project environment. For more detailed information on the statistical aspects of cost risk assessment, refer to the statistics references in the bibliography. The documentation manuals that are provided with reputable cost risk software packages will serve as a valuable background reference to this important and involved topic.

The subject of risk assessment is important to the entire estimating process. Although the final estimate will be a single value, there is an entire range of values within which the actual cost may finally occur. Risk assessment attempts to determine what that range is and how likely individual values are within that range. Risk analysis is qualitative and/or quantitative. A quantitative approach is emphasized in support of estimate development. The qualitative approach, ranking various cost categories as "high," "medium," or "low," provides data that is more difficult to apply to the process of selecting a bid value or project budget.

Risk Model Definition

The first question to be evaluated is whether a value is deterministic, i.e., a single value. The deterministic condition rarely occurs on a project,

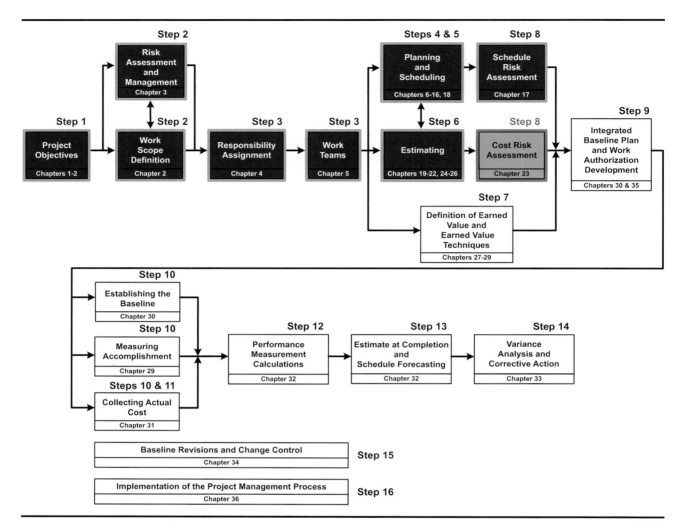

Figure 23-1 Earned Value Project Management: The Process

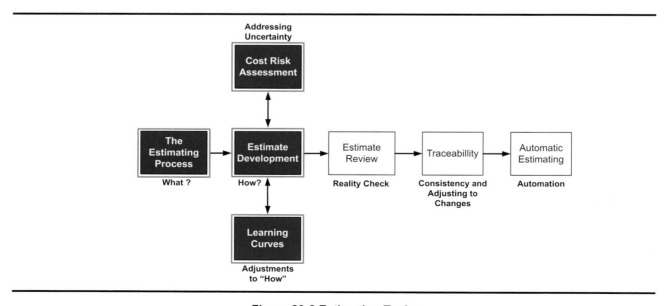

Figure 23-2 Estimating Topics

and is a trivial subject in the risk assessment process. The typical case is a probabilistic value that may have a range of values. Determining what the range is and the associated probability of each individual value will be much of the effort involved in risk assessment. Even with a known purchase order or signed contract on a Firm Fixed Price contract, the final value is not deterministic. Options may be deleted or added and scope changes may occur. Even in project cost items with a high degree of certainty, there will be the possibility of variation.

A more significant question is whether a given variable is dependent or independent. A dependent variable involves other variables; an independent one does not. The assumptions used through most of the discussion in this chapter relate to independent variables. When there are dependencies between variables, the analysis becomes more complex. Refer to the bibliography for published papers or other sources that address this topic.

Risk Analysis Sampling Techniques

Rather than make the presentation in this chapter redundant to that contained in Chapter 17, "Schedule Risk Assessment," the discussion will be limited to the Monte Carlo technique and a variation of it known as the Latin Hypercube. Monte Carlo is the most common technique used for generating probabilities through random sampling. While the uncertainty is described in a probability distribution modeled by the user, the generation of statistics requires a random sampling of all possible values.

Both the Monte Carlo and Latin Hypercube methods accomplish this, but in slightly different ways. Monte Carlo is truly random sampling, but it requires a large number of samples before the input distribution is truly representative. This is particularly true of distributions that have extreme values of very low probability.

Latin Hypercube, however, forces "random" numbers to come from all areas of the probability curve. Thus, while iterations may cluster near the midpoint value for Monte Carlo, the iterations will immediately represent all areas of the distribution in Latin Hypercube. This means that a representative distribution can be achieved in fewer iterations using Latin Hypercube. Some software programs provide for choosing either of these techniques. If thousands of iterations are used, the two methods will yield similar results.

Output accuracy is dependent on the number of trials or iterations. Since accuracy varies with the reciprocal of the square root of the number of iterations, there is no real advantage in conducting enormous numbers of trials. Going beyond a few thousand iterations is not warranted from an accuracy standpoint. This is illustrated as follows:

Iterations	Accuracy Percentage
100	+/- 10%
1000	+/- 3%
10,000	+/- 1%

It quickly becomes a case of diminishing returns. While a greater number of iterations increases accuracy, it also increases computer run time. This is especially true if a large number of output distributions are being analyzed.

Probability Distributions

A probability distribution can be specified to help define the range of values that a variable may assume. Expert opinion is the best source for identifying the likely shape. Although there are many possible forms for distribution shape, a project risk analysis is typically better served by avoiding exotic distribution forms. In the daily business world, a small number of distribution shapes are all that are needed to provide reasonable output. This discussion will be limited to the three most common distributions. Other sources such as risk evaluation software documentation or a statistics text will provide a plethora of additional possible curve shapes.

The first type of distribution is the normal distribution, shown in Figure 23-3.

The normal distribution is used frequently and represents those situations where there is no greater likelihood of an overrun than an underrun.

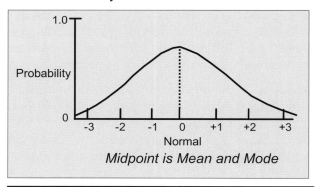

Figure 23-3 Other Considerations

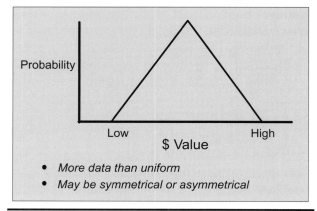

Figure 23-5 Triangular Distribution

A uniform probability distribution (Figure 23-4) can be used instead when a range is known with some certainty but there is no idea of what the relative likelihood would be for any particular value within that range. This would most likely apply to a conceptual estimate.

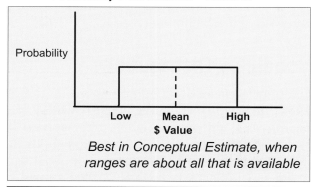

Figure 23-4 Uniform Probability Distribution

The most frequently used of all distributions in project risk assessments is the triangular distribution. Triangular distributions need not be symmetrical such as the one shown in Figure 23-5, and they allow for differing probabilities for each value. This means they contain more information than the uniform distribution. There are many more possible distribution shapes, but these three will likely allow an accurate assessment of most risk situations.

Risk Assessment Outputs

Once the distribution shapes and input extremes have been specified by the risk assessment team, it is up to the software to generate the probability distributions for each variable analyzed. The example figures shown here are outputs from actual risk simulations on the software program @RISK™. Figure 23-6, depicts the results from a simulation that included only 100 iterations. Because of the limited number of trials, the Latin Hypercube technique was a must. The arrow indicating "Expected Result" is the value at which there is a 50% chance of an underrun and a 50% chance of an overrun.

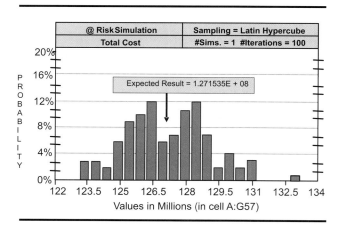

Figure 23-6 Actual Risk Simulation Results

Note that in this example the expected result is not the most probable result. There are considerably more likely values both above and below the expected result. This is not a flaw in the diagram; it is a characteristic of this particular distribution.

The number of simulations is indicated as one ("# Sims.=1"), which means that the results are the result of a single test, conducted 100 times (100 iterations). Therefore, a single probability distribution has been generated. If multiple simulations had been performed, a series of distributions would have been produced. Each distribution would vary slightly from the others, since they would each be generated by the selection of random numbers.

The horizontal axis also contains a somewhat obscure reference to "In Cell A:G57". The risk software used in these examples receives its input from other software spreadsheet programs, and this reference refers to the address in the spreadsheet in which this number resides. This allows verification that the distribution generated is, in fact, for the correct numerical value being evaluated.

The same information can be expressed in a different format using a cumulative probability curve, like the one contained in Figure 23-7. This is the common industry presentation format. This format has been used in the electric utility industry since the 1980s. This curve presents the probability of the estimate being underrun for each value on the X-axis. The "Expected Result" will be at the 50% confidence level. An 80% confidence level indicates that there is an 80% probability that the associated cost value will be underrun. Note that this graph is also the result of a 100-iteration simulation using the Monte Carlo technique.

If the number of iterations were increased, say to 1,000, the curve becomes much smoother as illustrated in Figure 23-8.

Risk Assessment Output Statistics

The computer run is completed in minutes or hours, depending on the number of outputs being analyzed and the capability of the hardware on

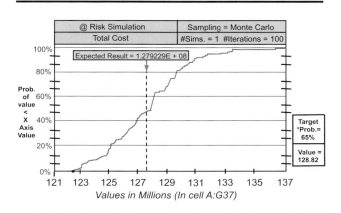

Figure 23-7 Cumulative Probability Curve 1

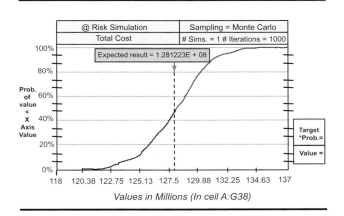

Figure 23-8 Increased Iterations

which it is run. The computer calculation produces certain statistics. Some of these have already been seen in the previous figures. These include the expected result and the range of possible results. Tables of output data make some of the outputs more specific, such as the maximum expected result and the minimum expected result. The number of simulations is listed. While this will ordinarily be "one" in the project environment, it could be more than that, particularly if multiple alternatives are being evaluated. The number of iterations is recorded, which provides information on the expected accuracy as explained earlier. The standard deviation will be calculated and reported, providing information about the dispersion of the set of data around the mean.

Two other outputs, skew and kurtosis, require further explanation. Both of these outputs provide further information on the shape of the distribution curve. Skew indicates the degree of asymmetry, with a higher value indicating more asymmetry. A skewed curve may be right-skewed or left-skewed, although project applications will virtually always be right-skewed. This is shown in Figure 23-9. The reason for the preponderance of right-skewed curves is that there is almost always an absolute minimum that cannot realistically ever be exceeded. However, there is much more exposure on the high end of the distribution (the right side). In fact, the maximum cost may be nearly open-ended. It is because so many distributions have a right-skewed shape that risk assessment is so important in the first place.

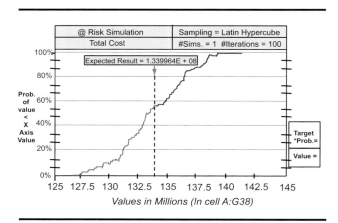

Figure 23-9 Right Skewed Example

Kurtosis is a measure of how "flat" or "peaked" a distribution is. The higher the value of kurtosis, the more peaked the distribution is. This is illustrated in Figure 23-10, which also demonstrates why kurtosis is used to evaluate distributions.

A high value of kurtosis means that there is a greater likelihood that a given value will be near the mean. Said another way, most of the values tend to cluster near the expected value. In a way, this may be a red flag at the distribution itself, since a very high kurtosis may very well indicate a false optimism on the part of those who provided input to the distribution. False optimism is a common problem with developing distributions.

Besides the graphical distributions drawn, such as that shown in Figure 23-8, charts are generated with detailed information relating output values to probabilities determined from the Monte

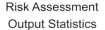
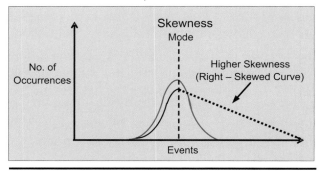

Figure 23-10 Kurtosis Example

Carlo simulation. These can be presented two ways: by value or by probability. The intervals of the value can be specified.

Cumulative Percentage Values ($ x millions)	Probability
2.0	53%
2.5	86%
3.0	98%

Or

Cumulative Percentage	Probability Value ($ x millions)
0%	1.0
10%	1.1
20%	1.3
30%	1.5
40%	1.7
50%	1.82
Etc.	Etc.

A major reason for performing cost risk analysis in the estimating process is to determine the degree of variability in the numbers presented to management in order to assist them in evaluating the organization's risk in using those numbers. If there were a small likelihood of an underrun, there is a large likelihood of an overrun. That should suggest to the review team that the final number should be increased to allow for these concerns and the likely upward pressure on the cost. A further review of the details of the risk analysis will identify the specific high cost risk items that are driving the high risk at the project level. The choice at this point is to determine if the high cost risk items can be mitigated without increasing the bid or to increase the cost estimates of the high risk items, which, in turn, will increase the bid. The risk assessment process allows quantification of the likely and possible increases in cost, which can be very valuable in a Firm Fixed Price contracting environment.

How is this quantification accomplished? The curve in Figure 23-8 provides the cumulative distribution of the probability of an underrun. Thus a 10% value means that there is a 10% chance of underrun, but a 90% chance of overrun. This would not be a comforting situation to an executive about to submit that number as a bid. This output would suggest that the executive should only be 10% confident that the project team will underrun that cost estimate. By increasing the bid to deal with the obvious exposure to cost increase, the percent likelihood of underrunning the submitted estimate can be increased.

An example of how this can be applied is based on the data presented in Figure 23-11. An estimate value of $220 million will have a 60% likelihood of underrunning. This translates into a 60% confidence level of an underrun. Depending on the project, the market conditions, and how this project fits in the corporate strategy, that 60% may be seen as an acceptable level or an unacceptable level of risk. In very conservative industries, a 40% chance of overrun would certainly be seen as intolerable. In higher risk-taking industries, such a risk would probably be viewed as acceptable. For the purpose of this example, assume that executive management has reviewed the output results and has concluded that a 90% chance of underrun is desired. In other words, they are unwilling to accept greater than a 10% probability of overrun.

This same output curve can be used to quantify what that means in terms of the estimate to be submitted. As shown in Figure 23-12, it would take an estimate of $230 million in order to have a 90% likelihood of underrun. Other values could be selected and read off the curve just as easily.

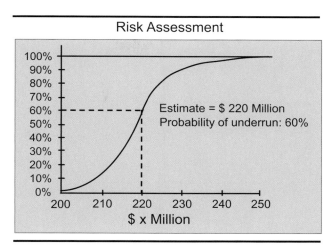

Figure 23-11 Other Considerations Example 1

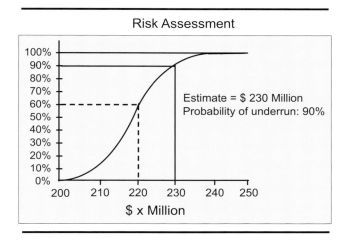

Figure 23-12 Other Considerations Example 2

The shaded area in Figure 23-13 corresponds to the bid increase that would have to be added to the base estimate of $220 million to raise the confidence level to that desired by management. So, $10 million would be required in this example to satisfy the parameters set by management. Conversely, lowering the estimate by $10 million would virtually guarantee a cost overrun. This process can be taken a step further by having the estimator recommend a bid increase or decrease value based on the shape of the cumulative probability curve and past practice within the organization.

Of course, even with a 90% level of confidence, there is a chance of overrun. According to the distribution presented in this example, it would require a bid increase of $30 million and a final estimate value of $250 million to virtually elimi-

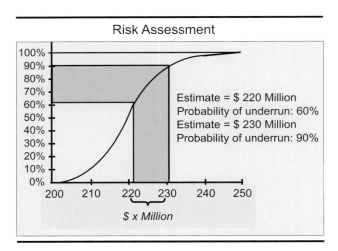

Figure 23-13 Other Considerations Example 3

nate any possibility of overrun. This amounts to a 13.6% bid increase.

Very high risk projects could require a 40 or 50 percent bid increase allowance before all risk of overrun could be considered to be removed. This simply may not be tenable. Allowing that much increase on the bidder's side may assure that some other bidder would get the contract. Allowing that much cost risk coverage on the owner/customer side will likely result in cancellation of the project because the costs are not feasible.

So it comes back to a matter of tradeoff - trying to keep the price as low as possible while still having a reasonable chance of performing the work for the estimated/budgeted amount. What risk analysis brings to the table is a strong numerical basis for making those hard decisions.

One guideline that must be remembered is that the estimate being evaluated for cost risk must include identification of the cost risk of the basic estimated cost. Recognize that the estimate is not complete until a risk assessment has been performed, an evaluation of the results has been made, and a determination has been made by management as to how much of the risk should be reduced by an increase in the estimate that will be used for the proposal bid price.

Conducting a Risk Assessment

With computer-based software readily available, it is a simple process to evaluate risk and compare the impact of certain changes. Of course,

the bigger challenge is getting accurate input data from knowledgeable sources to allow an accurate risk assessment to be simulated. There is one other question: If risk assessment were to be used for evaluating alternatives in "What if" studies, how could results be compared when each scenario is based on random number selection? Even the same scenario will generate slightly different results every time another simulation is conducted.

This problem has been addressed in some software programs through the use of a "seed." An option exists within the program that allows a seed value to be turned on and off. If it is "off," each new simulation uses a completely new set of random numbers. If it were "on," all simulations use the same set of random numbers generated for the first simulation. This allows the alternatives in question to be analyzed consistently. Graphical comparisons can then be made between various scenarios. The choice with the highest expected value may not be the riskiest choice, depending on the shape of the distribution.

From an implementation standpoint, it should be remembered that these sophisticated computer calculations are only as good as the information input and those interpreting the results. The quickest way to discredit a risk analysis approach is to have a project overrun when management was previously told that there was a 99% chance of underrun. The output accuracy is limited by the expertise of the evaluation team. If the team does not properly grasp what it means to be 99% sure of an underrun, the results will not reflect reality.

Fortunately, there are ways to improve accuracy. First of all, the people most knowledgeable of the project variables are the ones who must be interviewed. Multiple inputs should be obtained so that there is less of a chance risk conditions are overlooked. It is easy to combine and assign various weighted values for each of the multiple inputs within a risk analysis program. A risk analysis expert should be used to orient the team toward the objectives, methods to be used, and the meaning of the input they will be providing. Emphasis should be placed on avoiding the common tendency to provide unrealistically narrow bands of values.

Probably the two biggest pitfalls of conducting a risk assessment are unrealistic (narrow) bands of values and an inability to come to terms with true minimum and maximum values. Typically, people tend to overlook factors that could drive costs outside of expected ranges. It takes a risk analysis expert to point out these factors.

Another factor to note is that it is better to focus on the 5% and 95% values rather than the 0% and 100% values. To use an example from schedule risk assessment, a commuter may know with 95% certainty that her commuting time to work will not exceed one hour. But to guarantee a number that could never be overrun, the true answer may be many orders of magnitude larger. She could be in a car wreck and not get back to work for months, much longer than the realistic maximum time of one hour. And, of course, the absolute maximum time is infinity in this example. These extreme considerations add little to the risk assessment process.

Implementation Examples

Risk analysis for cost is not a new concept. The Program Evaluation Review Technique (PERT) was an attempt at this in the early 1960s, and cost risk analyses have been used as a project management tool for decades. Since that time, its use has spread to much smaller projects. It can even be applied to small cost, short duration, capital improvement projects. However, it is another classic example of something that works, but is frequently misunderstood and misapplied.

A problem sometimes encountered with cost risk assessments is the age old problem of internal politics. A risk analysis went awry because the outcome was practically dictated before the assessment was even begun. The 95% confidence level of underrun had nothing to do with reality, and the absolute 100% confidence level was still severely overrun. Again there was nothing wrong with risk analysis theory, but the implementation was flawed.

Conclusion

The theory and technology exist for performing cost risk assessments. Since all projects contain significant uncertainty, it is not advisable to deny the existence of uncertainty and present an estimate as a single point value. It is far better to provide a value and then analyze its likelihood of being exceeded. This information can then be used by executive management to settle on a value for which the risk of overrun is acceptable. The estimate is then no longer "$25 million," but "$25 million with a 35% likelihood of being overrun." This provides better information for management's use, especially when a decision is being made as to whether to pursue a project.

Various data sampling techniques exist, with most cost risk assessments using the Monte Carlo approach. This technique requires a large number of iterations to provide a sampling of possible outcomes with improved accuracy inherent in larger samples. Standard output results allow an objective evaluation of the level of risk and the likelihood of specific results. This information can then be used in a program of risk management. A cost risk assessment should be conducted by someone familiar with the theory because there are many incorrect assumptions people make when providing input on likely cost outcomes.

Chapter 23 Review Questions

23-1.　Describe the difference between the Monte Carlo approach and the Latin Hypercube approach to risk assessment.

23-2.　What is the expected accuracy of a Monte Carlo simulation with 25 iterations?

23-3.　Explain what is meant by the "expected result" in the output distribution from a risk simulation.

23-4.　How can alternatives be compared in risk simulations when all numbers are randomly generated and even the same set of conditions would result in slightly different answers?

23-5.　Describe what is meant by "skewness" of a distribution.

23-6.　What is the best distribution curve form to use when the range of values is known, but there is no information concerning the relative likelihood of values within the range?

23-7.　Why is a cost risk assessment used in estimate development?

23-8.　What are some reasons that risk assessments can go awry?

23-9.　In soliciting input for a risk distribution, how should the interviewer explain what is intended by the limits for minimum and maximum values?

True or False

23-10.　There is not much difference in accuracy between a ten thousand iteration and a one million iteration risk simulation.

23-11.　For most business applications, the normal distribution, uniform distribution, and triangular distribution will be sufficient for modeling the risk profile.

23-12.　Most real life project applications, if asymmetrical, will be skewed left.

23-13.　Kurtosis is a measure of the shape of the probability distribution curve that measures how close the likely values congregate near the mean.

23-14.　When a risk assessment of an estimate is accomplished, it does not matter whether it includes hedges against an overrun since that is what is being evaluated.

The answers to these questions can be found in Section 6, Solutions.

Chapter **24**

ESTIMATE REVIEW

Objectives of this Chapter:

1. Discuss the major items to consider in an estimate review.

2. Explain the critical impact of assumptions on the estimate results.

3. Discuss the importance of having a defined scope and documented technical basis for the estimate.

4. Define "check estimates" and explain their use in the estimate review process.

5. Emphasize the importance of conducting team estimate reviews prior to executive review and approval.

Every estimate needs a reality check. Assumptions are made in an estimate that may significantly impact the bottom line number, and those assumptions should be verified as being reasonable. More often than not, a "bad" estimate is simply an estimate for a different job than the one that was completed. Estimate reviews can be very political. Mid-managers may have already advised senior managers of their estimate and may defend their number to keep from losing face. Senior managers may have given an informal number to the client, and they may be committed to that number. Nevertheless, it is not productive for an analyst to make the estimate artificially match the "right" number. An estimate should be the result of a team effort, with the lead estimator acting as the coordinator of that effort. All those with input to the estimate should review their portion before it is submitted to executive management for approval.

An important element in producing an accurate estimate is the estimate review. In all reviews, the reviewers should have a copy of the basis of estimate and the assumptions made in producing the estimate. The review activities will depend on the type of estimate. For example, a conceptual estimate has no detailed information that needs reviewing because project definition has not yet occurred. Only the most general guidelines may apply, such as the size and type of project, expected duration, definition of major cost drivers, and assumptions. A detailed estimate would require review of considerably more information, including the project design that has occurred to date, plus any services, material, or equipment that may be required to accomplish the work.

If there are any special conditions that make the project different from most related projects, they should be identified for the reviewers. In all cases, the estimate reviewers should make use of whatever historical data are available to compare with the estimate at hand. It is far easier to start from a prior estimate with known conditions and delineate the differences than to try to confirm the estimate on a line item by line item basis.

Depending on the type of project, the duration (including scheduled start and completion dates) may be critically important. For example, in construction the start date could mean changing labor rates because of collective labor agreements expiring, could have an escalation impact for material purchased, and certainly affects the

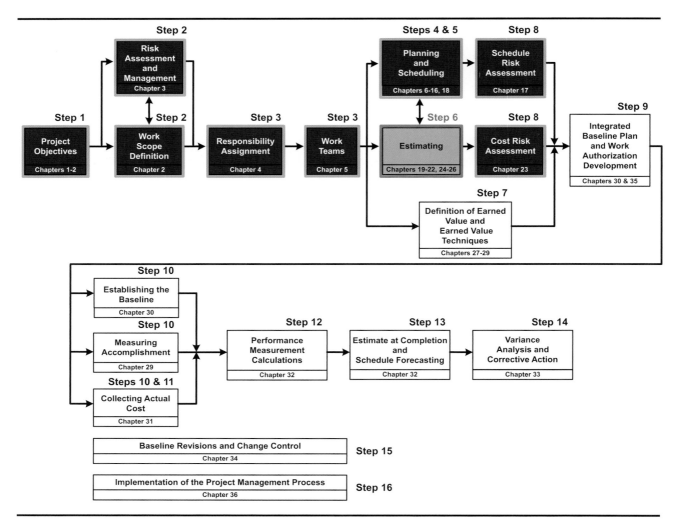

Figure 24-1 Earned Value Project Management: The Process

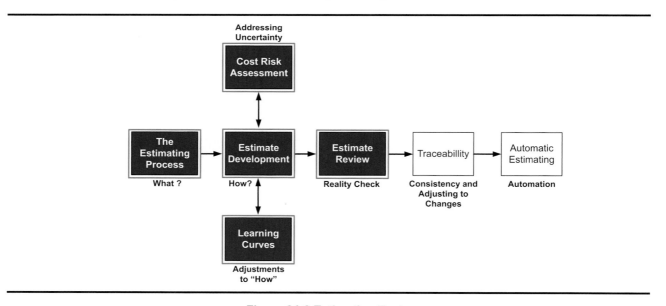

Figure 24-2 Estimating Topics

length of time (and cost) for supporting services on job sites or in engineering/design offices. A compressed schedule for software may result in significant increase in staff loading over exactly the same work for a project with a more extended schedule.

What are the minimum assumptions that should be identified? Again, this depends on the nature of the project, but certain items would be required for any estimate. These include the start and completion dates; major milestones and their planned dates of completion; escalation assumptions, environmental conditions; the desired products, services, or project output, which are the project objectives; major equipment or material needs; any adjustments to productivity and the reasons for them; and acceptable risk. This list could be greatly expanded if individual items for specific types of projects were included as well.

It is hard to overemphasize the importance of documenting assumptions as part of the estimate package. Many companies rightly do not consider the estimate complete unless it is accompanied by a complete list of assumptions. This is true even more so for international projects. The challenges associated with international estimating are complex at best, not only because of the difficulty of predicting productivity rates, but also because of currency fluctuations and lack of infrastructure. This makes listing assumptions even more critical.

Other factors needing definition in the assumptions are items that may be included or excluded within the numbers on a case-by-case basis. Some examples are profit, cost of money, fuel costs, allowance for risk, and consulting/startup help from suppliers of hardware, software, or equipment.

External Reviews

Most of what has been presented so far has related to reviews of estimates generated within the organization. Estimates are also submitted by external organizations, either as bids for work, as estimates of scope change cost impacts, or in response to specific requests to develop a "check estimate." A check estimate, sometimes called a "fair value estimate," may be requested when a

second opinion is needed to evaluate an estimate or series of bids. While most estimators are not anxious to have their work checked by independent third parties, the primary purpose of a check estimate is not to discredit the original estimate. Its purpose is usually to verify scope and assumptions.

Check estimates are also used for checking bids. In this role, it is referred to as a "fair value estimate" and is prepared by the organization that has requested the bids. The estimating group is given the identical information that the bidders receive and the same amount of time to respond. A number of benefits are derived from this approach. First, the internal estimators will identify areas that are unclear or contradictory, allowing clarification to the bidders before bids are submitted. Second, this provides the customer/owner with an approximate estimate figure. While bidder collusion is an unlikely event, it is possible that all bidders will miss an item of scope or consistently misunderstand some portion of the scope. Third, it provides the in-house estimators the chance to fine-tune their estimates. Input from another source may provide better information than is available for some aspect of the project.

Fair value estimates have been used to successfully identify many inadequate estimates. On one project, the bidder had actually prepared an estimate for one main product when two were intended. On another two-unit project, portions of the initial estimate had been prepared for two units but submitted to a third group who assumed the numbers were for a single unit and doubled them!

In tight economic times, there is the ever present danger of the "low ball bid," an estimate too low to realistically perform the work, but one for which the bidder plans to compensate with overpriced scope changes later. The numbers and names have been modified to protect the guilty in this example. For the project being bid upon, Bidder A submitted $500,000, Bidder B submitted $250,000, and Bidder C submitted $300,000. The fair value estimate was $475,000. When Bidder A was asked if he were comfortable with the bid, he responded, "That is what it will take to do the job." Discussion suggested that both Bidder B and Bidder C had underbid the project to get the work. Since it was a low evaluated bid situation, eliminating the other two bids required some justification. The bidders were asked if they, too, were comfortable with their bids. They indicated that they were. At that point, it was demonstrated to them that it was impossible to do the work for that amount of money. Still they held their ground. The bids were evaluated on the basis of the number of hours in the fair value estimate of $475,000 and priced according to the various bidder billing schedules and a winner was selected. The final actual cost (with changes) was $600,000. Without the fair value estimate, the assumption would have been that Bidder A was the one who missed the bid.

It also helps to understand the work scope when reviewing the estimate. In a project management organization, there was a small section that did nothing but computer software programming. No one outside of that section understood the details of the processes they were involved in. When the supervisor of the group was given an ultimatum to define what was required to complete the project control system software development effort, he took the task seriously. After a few weeks of long nights and weekend work, he emerged with THE BOOK which had an enormous amount of detail that could withstand any scrutiny. His general manager finally shrugged his shoulders and could do nothing but accept it if he wanted the work done. What had started as an attempt to limit the size of a four-person group had now been justified to be increased to 30 people!

A postscript to this story is that the group never got bigger than six or eight people, and was later absorbed by the Computer Services Department when it became aware of the emerging (and competing) empire outside of their corporate walls. The product of that group was never seen in project management. The bottom line is that great documentation carried the day, even when the conclusions were absurd. This should make it apparent that detailed backup can justify any estimate, if no one can find a loophole in it.

Conversely, lack of documentation makes any estimate seem suspicious. An estimating group that was producing useful estimates in a trying environment was under constant attack because they would not release any of the detailed basis and assumptions for their numbers. It was an approach of, "Here are the numbers. Take it or leave it." Any questions or challenges were met with the response, "It's included." The net result was that virtually no one trusted or accepted the group's output.

Other Factors in Estimate Reviews

One of the difficulties with estimates, and a primary reason for addressing cost risk assessment, is that everyone has a different comfort level that they want in an estimate. In one organization doing electrical design and drafting work, the scope of responsibility was split between two individuals. Neither of them was an estimator, but they were technical people providing estimates for technical work. Every time either was asked for an estimate, the response was very different. One, a very conscientious worker who always hoped for the best, would always present an estimate that had only a slim chance of being met. The other individual was the opposite extreme. Every estimate had a 100% certainty of underrun. Some projects could have been and were completed in 2-3 hours, despite an estimate of 20 hours. The two individual estimates were always combined before being presented to management, so the extremes canceled each other out. The average of the two estimates would invariably be a fairly good estimate.

While few people ever approach either of these extremes when developing an estimate, there are still varying degrees of uncertainty that have to be addressed. It is necessary to be familiar with an estimator's track record to get a better idea of what the current numbers might mean in terms of risk. This, too, is part of the estimate review process.

Team Reviews

If a team review of the estimate were planned (a strongly suggested approach), it would be essential to have an "up front" understanding of what each team member's responsibility entails. The engineering or design group should confirm the scope used by estimating as well as checking the validity of any technical assumption. Estimating should be responsible for the unit rates. Purchasing should verify lead times for ordering any materials or equipment. Since they are in daily contact with vendors, the purchasing group should maintain updated files reflecting current prices and order backlogs. Guidelines that restrict comments to their respective areas of expertise will reduce arguments among the reviewers.

Once a team review has been completed, the estimate is ready for submission for executive review. An estimate submitted should include a cost risk assessment. Once an estimate has received final review and approval, including an adjustment for the cost risk being included within the estimate, it becomes either the budget for an in-house project or a bid on a Request for Proposal (RFP).

Conclusion

The challenge to an effective estimate is that even non-estimators produce estimates, sometimes without an adequate database of information. Without careful review of scope and assumptions, as well as of unit rates, quantities, labor rates, escalation rates, and all of the other contributing factors that go into the preparation of the estimate, the best estimate product will not be produced. Because a good estimate should include input from numerous team members within their specific areas of expertise, those same team members should have the opportunity to verify that their input was properly incorporated. The objective is to produce the best possible estimate. Anything less is not acceptable. Once approved, the estimate becomes the official budget for the project or the bid.

Chapter 24 Review Questions

24-1. Besides the estimate numbers and cash flow, what critical element of any estimate should always be carefully reviewed?

24-2. What is a "Check Estimate" and what is its function?

24-3. What is a "Fair Value Estimate" and what is its function?

24-4. Why is a team review of the estimate important?

True or False

24-5. All estimates should be reviewed in the same manner.

24-6. One important reason for engineers to review the estimate is to verify the validity of the technical assumptions.

24-7. An advantage of limiting reviewers to their area of expertise is the reduction in battles over responsibility boundaries.

24-8. The value of an estimate is dependent in some part on the accuracy of its assumptions.

The answers to these questions can be found in Section 6, Solutions.

Case Study

24. 1 ASSESSING THE ESTIMATE

Review the attached estimate summary sheet for completeness. Is enough information provided to assess the estimate? Additional detailed sheets are available to support this summary but are not included with the Case Problem because they provide no additional type of information. The detailed sheets include further definition of these categories only. Items to consider include the following:

1. What is the basis of the estimate?

2. What type of estimate is it and what is the expected accuracy?

3. Are the major categories and subdivisions logical?

4. Most importantly, what additional information would you demand as a Project Manager in order to be able to evaluate this estimate?

5. Will it be difficult to collect actual costs in this same account format?

The solution to this case study can be found on the Humphreys & Associates, Inc. web site.
www.humphreys-assoc.com

Low Bid Corporation, Inc.
Project "Y" Estimate Summary
June 22, Year 1

Code	Description	Estimate ($)
Labor		
1000	Civil/Structural	355
2000	Mechanical	803
3000	Electrical	695
4000	Instrumentation	802
5000	Systems	197
6000	Field	848
7000	Project Management	280
8000	Accounting	0
9000	Administration	110
10000	Procurement	337
	Total Labor	**4,427**
Equipment		
11000	Mechanical	48,099
12000	Electrical	3,175
13000	Instrumentation	1,652
	Total Equipment	**52,926**
Overhead		
15000	Total Home Office	797
20000	Geotechnical	71
25000	Sales Tax	3,039
30000	Field Expenses	22,117
	Total Overhead	**26,024**
Total Cost		**83,877**

Chapter **25**

TRACKING THE ESTIMATE

Objectives of this Chapter:

1. Explain why it is difficult to make accurate comparisons between estimates and final actual cost data.

2. Define estimate traceability (vertical and historical).

3. Define major categories of variance analysis, which must be considered in estimate versus actual comparisons for completed work.

4. Define an approach to tracking the estimate over time with variance analysis.

5. Present procedural approaches to improving estimate traceability.

Following the completion of a project, the final actual cost is almost always compared to the estimate. It is important, therefore, that changes to the original estimate are tracked. The biggest problem with reconciling the estimate to the actual cost is that there is frequently a complete disconnection between those two numbers. This results when changes to the basis for the original estimate are not tracked. Being able to explain any variances is more than just a way of keeping score or an act of self-preservation. It is often needed to justify the differences to organizations that are external to the one performing the work. Understanding the differences allows an organization to prepare more accurate estimates in the future. If the assumptions that were used or the productivity rates were invalid, the quickest way to determine that is to compare the standards against the actual costs. Surprisingly, many estimating organizations do not do this.

Estimate Traceability: Tracking the Estimate

One of the biggest challenges in analyzing the accuracy of estimates is that the project and its conditions change after the final original estimate was prepared. Actual costs may not be comparable with estimated costs until adjustments are made. This is not a result of poor project control because many of these changes are inevitable during the life of a project. Purchase orders for material will be supplemented after order placement. In many projects, orders must be placed before final exact totals are known because of long lead times. Even the final design quantities will vary from the final actual quantities ordered because of waste, failed inspections, damage, or loss. The exact final quantity is not known when estimates are prepared, so a built-in variance is virtually guaranteed. In addition, contracts may be revised. Scope changes are inherent to projects and significant enough that a separate chapter is devoted just to that subject.

Other sources of variance include escalation on long term projects. The only certainty with escalation is that the actual rate will be different than the estimated rate. On ten year, billion dollar projects, even slight changes in escalation can mean $50-100 million impacts over the life of the project. Interface problems with suppliers, designers, or other contractors are another

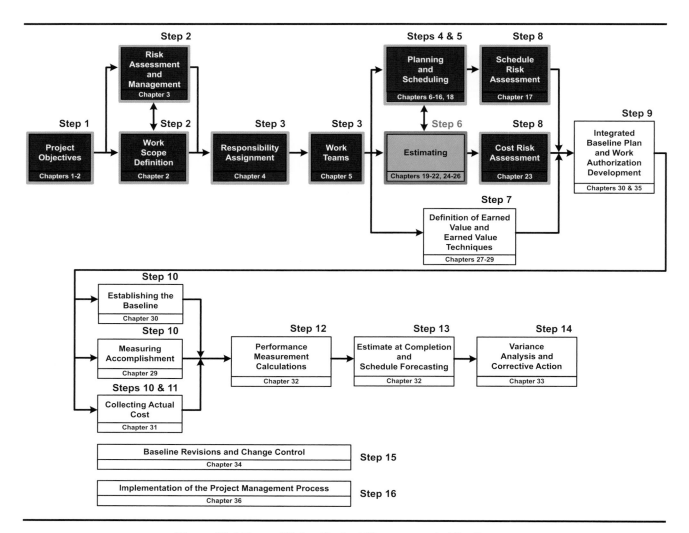

Figure 25-1 Earned Value Project Management: The Process

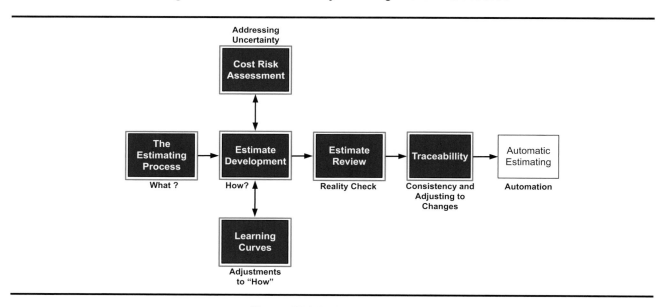

Figure 25-2 Estimating Topics

source of potential change not considered in the conditions and assumptions used to originally develop the estimate. Heavy outdoor construction has more than its share of upsets, including unpredictable weather, lack of access to work areas, "surprises" underground such as undetected underground ducts, and even overcrowding within a structure once it is erected. All of these will impact the cost.

Other hazards can cause actual project conditions to deviate from what was expected in the original estimate. Unit installation rates may be negatively impacted by material or equipment delays, inadequate training, schedule changes, scope changes, or poor supervision. On the surface, it would not seem that scope changes would have significant effect on unit rates. But as staffing needs increase significantly, there may be overcrowding, inadequate time for proper training or supervision, or increased overtime to make up for the staffing shortage.

The purpose of this discussion is to highlight the need for a mechanism to track estimates over time. This ensures that the estimate reflects the project that was completed.

The situation will look something like this for any estimate item:

Estimate Item 1234	
Conceptual Estimate	$1,000,000
Preliminary Estimate	$ 930,000
Detailed Estimate	$ 955,000
Definitive Estimate	$1,008,500

This is not a problem as long as detailed variance analysis is performed:

Estimate Item 1234	
Conceptual Estimate	$1,000,000
Preliminary Estimate	$ 930,000
Variance	$ 70,000

Explanation of variance:

1. Escalation saved (firm price) $30,000
2. Deleted Option #1 $25,000
3. Reduced piping outlet $15,000

Using this example, the variance from the conceptual to the preliminary estimate should be explained in this type of detail. It not only explains the changes, but allows the changes to be categorized and combined. Similar variance analysis would be necessary for the changes from the preliminary to the detailed estimate and from the detailed to the definitive estimate.

For the variance analysis to be useful, it must be performed for more than just the total project cost. To assist future analysis, it should also be performed for all major estimate components. A common failure of many estimating systems is that actual costs are not tracked consistently with the original estimate. The result is that no feedback is possible. The differences may be subtle. For example, electrical cable tray installation may or may not include the support hangers. If the estimate were prepared one way and the actuals collected on a different basis, an incorrect variance would be reported. This often happens when the cost engineering function of a project is handled by a different group of people than those who do the estimating.

Another common failure is that the original estimate is ignored after production of the final estimate and award of the contract. Subsequently, the scope, the materials used, or the schedule may change. If these changes are not tracked, the actual costs will not match the scope or the conditions of the final estimate. In a majority of situations where estimating is under fire because of inaccurate estimates, investigation revealed that the estimates were not inaccurate at all once they were adjusted to be on a comparable basis with the actual costs. What happens far too often is that the project that was estimated is not the one that was delivered, and no one was making comparisons and tracking the changes as the project unfolded.

Estimate traceability, refers to two distinct considerations:

1. **Vertical traceability** - the ability to accurately summarize data with no exclusions, no double counting, and correct summation totals.

2. **Historical traceability** - the ability to accurately track changes to the estimate

over time so that all estimates can be related when project scope and estimate scope are consistent.

Historical traceability is also an important consideration because justification may be needed for changes. In addition, an objective of any successful estimating system is to improve accuracy over time. This occurs when there is a continuing feedback of actual costs consistent with the estimated costs, allowing estimating standards to be revised when necessary. If conditions or the scope are not the same, any comparison between the two will be tainted. This renders comparisons of estimated versus actual costs useless unless adjustments for changed scope and conditions are made. Vertical and historical traceability are both shown pictorially in Figure 25-3.

Figure 25-4, provides a comprehensive form that can be used to document changes for variance explanation. The left hand column lists the typi-

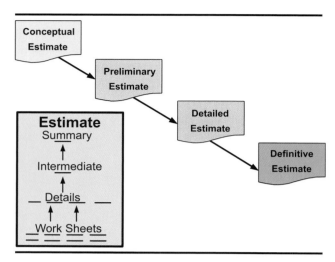

Figure 25-3 Estimate Traceability

cal major categories of the estimate. These categories may vary from organization to organization, but should not vary from project to project within a single organization.

Category	Original Estimate (1)	Revised Estimate (2)	Total Variance (3)	Schedule Changes (4)	Escalation Rate Changes (5)	Scope Changes (6)	Estimate Refinement (7)	Estimate Versus Actuals (7)	Estimate Omission or Duplication (7)	Cost Risk Reevaluation
Major Equipment	100000	113950	13950	5000	---	0	3750	5200	0	---
Material & Other Equipment	20000	15950	(4050)	200	---	0	(250)	(2000)	(2000)	---
Construction/ Production	60000	68700	8700	5000	---	1200	(700)	3200	0	---
Engineering	10000	13850	3850	850	---	3000	0	0	0	---
Owner's Cost	10000	10850	850	850	---	0	0	0	0	---
Escalation	20000	24850	4850	4500	350	0	0	---	---	---
Cost Risk	25000	21420	(3580)	2000	---	420	---	---	---	(600)
Grand Total	245000	269570	24570	18400	350	4620	2800	6400	(2000)	(600)

Notes:
(1) Original estimate dated December 16, Year 1.
(2) Reflects May 18, Year 1 Estimate Update.
(3) Column (2) – Column (1).
(4) Project Schedule Extended 10 Months at Customer/Owner Direction.
(5) Reflects revised Corporate Guidelines dated March 1, Year 1.
(6) Includes all scope changes processed through April 30, Year 2.
(7) See attached sheets for additional detail.

Figure 25-4 Estimate History Form ($ x 1000)

The columns should include the following information:

Original Estimate - The estimated cost provided in the Conceptual Estimate

Revised Estimate - The current estimate

Total Variance - The total cost difference between the Conceptual Estimate and the current estimate

Schedule Changes - Costs resulting from acceleration or delay of baseline schedules

Escalation Rate Changes - Costs from all categories associated with revised escalation criteria (increase or decrease).

Some clarification is in order here. A schedule change will have an escalation impact as well, but these should be tracked separately. The increased escalation caused by a change in schedule belongs in the "schedule change" impact column. Increased (or decreased) escalation caused by rate changes belongs in the escalation impact column.

Scope Changes - Any changes to contracts on the project related to additional (or decreased) costs concerning scope of services. These are not just changed products, but modifications to services provided as well. Providing a field engineer for a year with no change to the technical scope of the project itself is still a scope change, assuming that no budget was provided for such an individual in the original contract. This category also includes the obvious: project design changes, changes because of unknown site conditions, and owner-directed changes. It excludes labor productivity and rate (direct and indirect) changes.

Note: Rate changes sometimes are classified as scope changes because, in EVMS, it is optional whether budgets can be changed as a result of rate changes. However, for estimate tracking purposes, it is a best practice not to include rate changes in the scope change category regardless of how rate changes are treated in the company's EVM System.

Estimate Refinement - Includes estimate revisions that are not scope changes, e.g. revised productivity values, revised direct and indirect rates, quantity variations (estimated versus final

design), changed market conditions, and invalid estimate assumptions. This is probably the hardest to categorize of all of the columns. These are not estimating errors, although they may appear so. Revised productivity values may be necessary for a variety of reasons, including assumptions that were not valid.

Estimate versus Actuals - This includes incorporation of actual project costs so they can be used to adjust the revised estimate. Examples are estimated versus actual purchase order values, estimated versus actual contract values, and quantity variations between drawing quantities and actual installation. It does not include schedule changes or escalation rate changes, which have their own columns.

Estimate Omission or Duplication - This is reflected from the estimator not understanding the intended scope. It includes items like missed component redundancy, overlooked items, or inadvertent double budgeting. It excludes scope changes.

Cost Risk Reevaluation - Includes costs from adjustments to the cost risk from project evolution. In effect, this is a balancing column. As all of the other categories increase or decrease, they will be offset by cost risk mitigation or occurrence unless the bottom line total is also changing. Of course, cost risk should be decreasing with each succeeding estimate over the life of the project as actual costs and better definition of scope occur.

While each of the categories of estimate changes has been explained, further discussion is needed to explain how the form is used. This is provided in a column by column basis for the sample completed Estimate History Form shown in Figure 25-4. Again, each column is explained here.

Category - The sample categories listed may not apply to every possible project. What should be included in this column is a breakdown of total estimated cost into standard sub-categories typically used by the organization. Indirect costs may be included or listed separately.

Original Estimate - This shows the total project estimate of $245,000,000 divided into the major cost categories.

Revised Estimate - The current estimate has increased to $269,570,000. Note that all dollars on this sample form are expressed in thousands of dollars. It is evident which categories have increased or decreased, and by how much.

Total Variance - This is column (2) minus column (1).

Schedule Changes - Note that all of the categories have increased because of a schedule change. This is explained in the footnote (note 4). Each of the major categories was evaluated to determine the specific cost impact of the extended schedule.

Escalation Rate Changes - All of the impact of escalation, $350,000, has been entered in the escalation rate changes column. This is a summation of the net changes on each of the categories caused by escalation rate variation. Some may have increased while others decreased, but the net change is shown as a single line entry. In this example, the specific changes by category in thousands of dollars were:

Major Equipment	$1200
Material & Other Equipment	$ 300
Construction/Production	$(800)
Engineering	$(150)
Owner's Cost	$(200)

Another option would have been to list each of the category cost changes caused by escalation rate variations individually. However, the significant information is the net change. Just because three of the categories experienced a decrease in escalation does not mean that there was a negative escalation rate. It means that the revised escalation projections are based on better information.

Scope Changes - Approved scope changes have impacted three of the cost categories. An additional cost risk amount of $420,000 was added for the additional scope of work. This amounted to 10% of the $4,200,000 in changes in the engineering and construction/production categories.

Estimate Refinement - An additional $3,750,000 has been added to the Major Equipment category

because an option in the original quotation from the bidder was missed in the original estimate. Material quantity variations from plan have resulted in a decrease of $250,000 to Material & Other Equipment. Improved productivity rates have resulted in a reduction in construction/production costs.

Estimate versus Actuals - A major increase of $5,200,000 resulted from supplements to existing purchase orders that had not been anticipated. Material & Other Equipment was reduced by $2,000,000 because of discounts realized from quantity purchases. A major construction contract was placed for $3,200,000 more than was budgeted.

Estimate Omission or Duplication - A decrease of $2,000,000 was recorded in the Material & Other Equipment category because of the inadvertent double budgeting of a $2,000,000 item.

Cost Risk Reevaluation - As a project progresses towards completion, there is better definition of the scope and estimates become reality. Uncertainty also decreases as purchase orders are placed and contracts are awarded. Typically, this results in a reduction in the project cost risk over time. On this estimate update, a $600,000 reduction was recorded as a single line entry. As with the escalation rate changes discussed previously, cost risk could have been reduced by category if tracked that way. However, most organizations argue that when cost risk is well defined by individual categories, the cost risk allocation should be eliminated and placed within the allotted estimate/budget for those categories.

Vertical traceability is assisted by automation, but so is historical traceability. This is especially true if the software keeps an automatic record of changes to the files. The surest path to accurate historical traceability is to strengthen the interface between those preparing the estimates and those analyzing the actual costs. This can be assisted organizationally by having the two responsibilities in the same organizational unit. If there were no formal change control process, it would be almost impossible to accomplish accurate variance analysis from one estimate to the next. Change control is needed for many other reasons besides estimating and is addressed in detail later.

Conclusion

There are two types of estimate traceability: vertical and historical. Vertical traceability means that the various pieces and parts of an estimate must all add up accurately at the subtotal and grand total levels. Vertical traceability should be automatic in an automated system if the programming was correctly implemented.

Historical traceability is more difficult. It refers to the necessity of maintaining a measure of how the project has changed over time and how that has impacted the numbers presented in the original estimate. There are many other reasons besides changed scope that can cause the estimate value to change. A form presented in this chapter has been used to analyze and explain estimate changes over time.

Chapter 25 Review Questions

25-1. What is the biggest challenge in comparing the final cost of a project to its original estimate?

25-2. What are the two main reasons for comparing a project's actual cost with the estimate?

25-3. Exact calculations from engineering design drawings of required material will still vary from the actual quantities that need to be bought. Why?

25-4. What is meant by vertical traceability in an estimate?

25-5. What is meant by historical traceability in an estimate?

25-6. List at least 5 reasons why estimate totals change over time.

25-7. Discuss what is meant by "estimate refinement."

25-8. Explain the advantages of keeping escalation as a separate item.

25-9. Explain the advantages of including escalation within the individual estimate accounts.

True or False

25-10. Variance analysis of changes from one estimate to the next is important for achieving historical traceability.

25-11. All possibilities for disaster should be included within an estimate to ensure that nothing is excluded.

25-12. Creating a document with a standard format for tracking costs is logical for supporting a database for future projects.

The answers to these questions can be found in Section 6, Solutions.

Case Study

25.1 ESTIMATE HISTORY

A recently completed project that was Firm Fixed Price and had been very tightly bid, has an overrun in cost. The original price estimate was for $142 million. The profit was $15 million. The final actual cost was $158.8 million. The charge has been made that Estimating "blew the estimate" and that is the reason for the overrun and the loss of profit. You must evaluate the cost history to evaluate the causes of the overrun and determine if this were primarily an estimating problem. The following information is known about the causes of cost overrun:

1. The project was completed six months late, resulting in a $3 million increase in escalation, an increase of $1 million in extended owner's cost, and an increase of $600,000 in increased production related costs.

2. Actual escalation rates were 1.5% higher than forecasted in the corporate escalation guidelines. This resulted in a $1.7 million increase.

   Note: Estimating does not provide these forecasts. They merely use the forecasts provided by the organization in developing the estimate.

3. Internally approved scope changes resulted in increases to various categories as follows:

Major Equipment:	$ 4.5 million
Material/Other Equipment:	$ 2.3 million
Production:	$ 8.0 million
Engineering:	$ 1.2 million
TOTAL:	$16.0 million

4. Problems in manufacturing (it was a new process) resulted in productivity rates lower than estimated. This led to a $7.9 million overrun in production costs.

5. Estimating failed to realize that a new piece of equipment, which should have been included in the "material & other equipment" category, would have to be built to support the new process. This $2.1 million item was inadvertently left out of the estimate.

6. Purchase orders placed for major equipment totaled $2 million less than budgeted. Material and other equipment, on the other hand, cost $1.5 million more than estimated.

The solution to this case study can be found on the Humphreys & Associates, Inc. web site.
www.humphreys-assoc.com

The breakdown of the original estimate into major categories was as follows:

Major Equipment:	$ 60.0 million
Material & Other Equipment:	$ 12.0 million
Production:	$ 36.0 million
Engineering:	$ 6.0 million
Owner's Cost:	$ 5.0 million
Escalation:	$ 8.0 million
Profit:	$ 15.0 million
TOTAL	$142.0 million

Assumptions:

1. Project duration is 24 months

2. Escalation impact estimated to be 5.6% of the total project cost.

Your assignment consists of the following:

1. Complete Figure 1 (Estimate History Form) to categorize the causes of cost overrun.

2. What percentage of the cost overrun was because of estimating inaccuracy?

3. On a fair comparison basis, how accurate was the estimate? Consider the scope basis for the initial project versus the actual scope encountered. Next consider the assumptions which were part of the original estimate. When these are considered, was the estimate underrun or overrun?

4. What recommendations might be made to improve the accuracy of the next estimate.

FIGURE 1
Project ABC
Estimate History Form ($ x 1000)

Category	Original Estimate (1)	Revised Estimate (2)	Total Variance (3)	Schedule Changes (4)	Escalation Rate Changes (5)	Scope Changes (6)	Estimate Refinement	Estimate Versus Actuals	Estimate Omission or Duplication	Profit
Major Equipment										
Material & Other Equipment										
Construction Production										
Engineering										
Owner's Cost										
Escalation										
Profit										
Grand Total										

Notes:

(1) Original estimate dated January 5, Year 1

(2) Reflects July 31, Year 1 estimate update

(3) Column (2) - Column (1)

(4) Completion date slipped 6 months on planned 2-year project

(5) Reflects revised corporate guidelines dated March 15, Year 1

(6) Includes all scope changes processed through August 15, Year 1

Chapter 26

AUTOMATING THE ESTIMATING FUNCTION

Objectives of this Chapter:

1. Explain the difficulties with automating the estimating function compared with automating other project management functions.

2. Discuss potential advantages of advanced automation implementations for estimating.

3. Define estimating software evaluation considerations.

4. Discuss the pitfalls of implementation, which may prevent benefits of estimate automation from being realized.

The last step in the estimating process is automation. Many organizations do not yet employ automation for estimate generation except for the use of spreadsheet programs. The challenge is that each estimate tends to be so unique that, automated or not, the estimator has to virtually define every entry. Successful automation applications for estimate generation have been employed in companies that do a lot of similar estimates. All other aspects of the project management process have long since been universally automated, and estimating will eventually join them.

Estimating has been the last area of project management to be effectively automated. Whereas automated scheduling and cost engineering software programs were widely used by 1980, estimating continued to be performed for years afterwards without automated assistance. Even now, estimating is performed in many organizations with nothing more advanced than standard spreadsheet programs. Nevertheless, the interest level in automating the estimating process has been very high. On a survey of potential project management automation opportunities among electric utilities, over 90% of all respondents indicated that automating the estimating process was a priority area.

Some advanced implementations have reverted to spreadsheet application after high-powered automation programs were purchased. What is the problem or challenge associated with estimating that makes it more difficult than earlier project management discipline implementations?

One big challenge is that no two estimates are ever the same. Any estimator must make a determination of which of the historical standards usually used will apply in a given situation. In industrial applications especially, the standards may have to be adjusted by 200-300% or more before they can be used for a given application. Detailed estimating requires looking up specific unit rates from tables, and for most automated programs this takes just as long as if the material were looked up in a reference handbook manually. The bottom line is that much of estimating demands careful attention and judgment calls, neither of which is easily automated.

In spite of the difficulties, there are excellent estimating packages available that can facilitate preparation of quicker, more accurate, and more consistent estimates. This chapter discusses some of the considerations for an organization that is automating the estimating function. It is not an exhaustive list of all possible factors, but

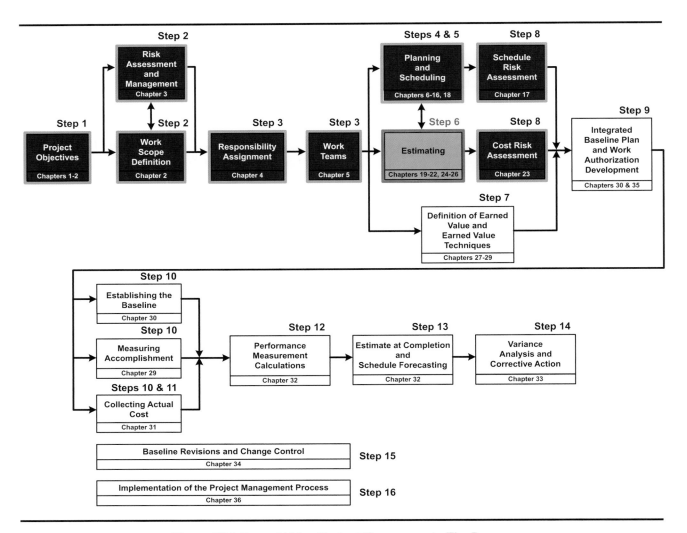

Figure 26-1 Earned Value Project Management: The Process

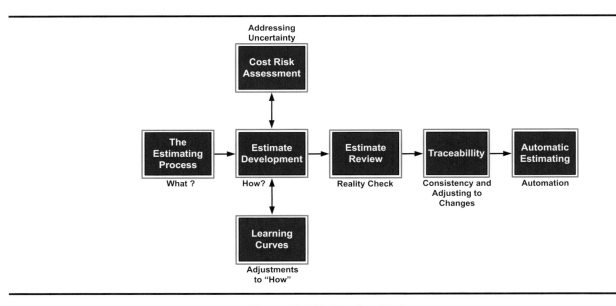

Figure 26-2 Estimating Topics

rather highlights some of the more important considerations.

The most basic question is "why automate?" What advantage is there to incurring the extra expense and effort associated with the initial automation implementation effort? The answer lies in the time saved in preparing future estimates and the organized record keeping. Databases can be organized and easily retrieved by anyone. Global changes are much quicker, and most estimates experience the need for global changes on an almost continuous basis. Changed escalation rates, a new labor union contract, a new tax ruling - all impact many or all of the accounts in an estimate. Automated estimates allow repetitious computations to be entered once and not repeated. All of these factors result in quicker estimates from an automated process.

There are other advantages as well. The accuracy of the calculation is built in one time and thereafter is automatic, as is the generation of standard output formats. Defaults can be defined one time and accessed whenever needed. The information can be re-sorted quickly. The advantages increase if the estimating software can interface with other project control applications, such as the scheduling or cost modules. Many programs allow for additional time saving through quantity takeoffs with a light pen. This is especially prevalent in all types of construction projects. If transactions are automatically recorded, it is easier later to understand where and how the estimate changed.

An advanced capability is one which, in effect, allows for the use of artificial intelligence. All of the "right questions" can be identified once by experts and programmed into the estimating process. This allows future estimators to merely answer questions and allow the computer to do the preprogrammed calculations, rather than having to remember each of the pertinent questions in subsequent estimates.

Possibly the biggest advantage with using an automated estimating approach is consistency. The difficulty with achieving consistency in estimates is expressed by the wise old saying:

The same work under the same conditions will be estimated differently by ten different estimators, or by one estimator at ten different times.

Anonymous

Of course, even consistency can have its limitations. In one company, which specialized in firm fixed price contracts, the estimate summaries had been programmed on a spreadsheet. When the system was converted to a new estimating package, the two systems were run in parallel for awhile. Discrepancies in the totals immediately began to appear between the two systems. When analyzed, it became evident that the manually programmed spreadsheet had a formula entered incorrectly so that one of the cells of data was being excluded from all of the totals. The original system had been producing incorrect estimates for a long time. Why was it never caught? The estimating organization had refused to allow team reviews, and management had supported them in that position. This is an actual case history that supports the importance of team estimate reviews.

A number of estimating systems is available, and that number increases on a regular basis. This reflects the great need of industry for effective estimating tools. While some systems are clearly better than others, no comparison will be made here because software is continually being upgraded and the information would be out of date before publication.

Commercial data bases exist that contain standard estimating data. This data can be linked to estimating software. Nevertheless, the existence of such information is not a panacea for estimators. Great care must be taken when applying commercially available unit rates for installation to a given application. Rates will vary widely based on the industry, location, and specific project conditions. It is always preferable to develop an in-house database suited to a company's particular history. The commercial data may be used as a starting point in the absence of accurate corporate historical records. New rates developed over time from historical records as they are created will supplement, and probably replace, the commercial data.

Software Evaluation Considerations

The following criteria should be used in evaluating estimating software:

1. Ease of use.

2. Flexibility.

3. Available databases.

4. Software capabilities.

5. Market considerations.

6. Computer requirements.

7. Security.

Ease of use has multiple aspects. While menu-driven data entry is very helpful for a beginner, a more experienced user will find this slows down the operation. Ideally, it should allow for both methods with the user making the choice. Another key question is, "How much is user defined?" While it is convenient to have a library of standard selections in the software, most applications will have some unique aspects requiring special handling. Many data tables will be needed. How easy is it to create them? Are there provisions for listing assumptions associated with the estimate development process? Is there a mechanism for recording the date of the entry, so later users will know if it may be necessary to update the pricing information?

Flexibility is one of the most important factors in software, especially in relation to report options. How easily can reports be specified or standard reports modified? Most companies have specific needs concerning the layout of its reports. They also have specific report formats and the software should be able to produce those formats. The ability of the user to easily define formulas to manipulate the data can also be a big plus. Sort capability is another criterion, which permits the user to put the data in the format most useful to the project. Reference data in the database will need to be changed to reflect the unique conditions of the project being estimated, but the reference data must remain the same for the next estimate.

While it is always best to have a personalized database, one is not always available. In that case, the **available databases** containing standard information can be a starting point for personalizing data over time. A built-in capability to develop and incorporate a personalized database is a significant advantage. A further bonus would be factors based on geographic location.

Software capabilities are one of the most dominant evaluation factors. Will it interface with other scheduling or cost software packages? Is automated quantity takeoff available? This was one of the capabilities that initially provided popularity for automated estimating systems. Are there provisions for performing "What If" analyses? Another key factor is the ability to do risk analysis or to interface with a program that does risk analysis. Other key software capabilities would include: an option for rounding estimates, ability to make global estimate changes, variance reporting, category and sub-category totals, the presence of an audit trail (the entry date for changes), and the ability to handle different estimate types.

Obviously, one size does not fit all when it comes to the estimating software. Many can only produce estimates at the lowest (most detailed) level. This is a major problem because only a small minority of all estimates is produced at this level. Too many of the commercially available packages only allow development at a very detailed level where each nut and bolt must be counted, estimated, and totaled together. Yet some of the most important estimates are the conceptual estimates to decide whether a project is pursued. Specifics at the detail level may not be known. A conceptual estimate should not be developed by adding up nuts and bolts. Many more conceptual estimates are produced by some organizations than detailed estimates.

The ability to round answers is useful to avoid producing reports that show estimated cost to an unrealistic degree of accuracy. Few would accept an "estimate" of $1,110,123.61 for a project. Such accuracy simply is not believable except in the final accounting reports.

Market considerations are important because one of the difficulties with so many estimating packages on the market is that it may be hard to assess the stability of each one. Some are new and not well established, and this can affect technical support and training. Price is always one of the first points of consideration in many evaluations, but it may not be the most valid (especially with estimating software). The accuracy and ease-of-use of the product documentation is a critical factor to be evaluated. This becomes very important if the company marketing the product cannot provide full technical support (hot lines, user groups, etc.). When selecting an estimating package, the evaluators should check references of others who are using the estimating software. Questions should be answered on use of the software itself, the documentation, and the responsiveness of the vendor when problems were experienced.

It is important to consider the **computer requirements** for any software package. What are the memory requirements for the package (including RAM requirements)? What type of computer model is required for optimum or even satisfactory performance? If memory or run time requirements mean that all of the department or project hardware will have to be upgraded to use the product, a company will want to consider whether this is the right package. Will the software perform equally well in a multi-user environment? Can it be licensed for use in a Local Area Network and/or Wide Area Network? What is the price?

Security is certainly an important factor. Outsiders should never be able to "hack" into the system and adequate security needs to be built into the system. Certain people may need to access the estimate for review purposes, but should not be allowed to change it. Some estimators will be authorized to revise the estimating standards when that becomes necessary. Others will be restricted to making changes only in the current project file. An audit trail should be maintained to document when the estimating standards are changed, and by whom. The date of changes is also important so that it is possible to quickly tell how long a given value has been resident in the database without revision.

Implementation Concerns

A key concern in all software applications is that the software should support the system requirements, not define them. The software must support an organization's system, not define it. If a particular package does not support what is needed, an organization should continue researching other packages. Requirements must be defined before the software is evaluated. Another misapplication that occurs is an inappropriate level of detail. As discussed earlier, conceptual estimates require different system characteristics than detailed estimating, and the software must reflect this reality. Ease of use must remain a consideration. Nevertheless, there is little doubt that real time savings are possible through use of an automated system. The proliferation of available packages indicates that many companies believe there is a true gain to be achieved.

Conclusion

Estimating is the most difficult of the project management functions to successfully automate. This is apparent from the fact that schedule and cost control functions were automated widely long before estimating software was used in many industries. The challenge stems from the large measure of experienced judgment that goes into the development of any estimate. This judgment is not readily automated. As with other project management functions, the way to properly select an automated estimating program is to first define what it is that must be accomplished. Once the objectives are known, it is possible to intelligently address the many choices available in estimating software. Consistency of output and documentation will justify automation in most applications.

Chapter 26 Review Questions

26-1.   Describe some of the advantages of automating the estimating function.

26-2.   Describe some of the problems with automating estimating.

26-3.   Briefly describe five evaluation considerations for automating estimating.

True or False

26-4.   Automation of estimating occurred on a widespread basis before scheduling was automated.

26-5.   The availability of standard estimating databases commercially available makes estimating a "cook book" exercise.

26-6.   Estimating standards may have to be modified by as much as 200-300% when applying them in different industries or applications.

26-7.   A shortcoming of some estimating software packages is an inability to produce conceptual estimates because of a requirement to build the estimate from detailed tables and then total the entries.

26-8.   The requirements of the estimating process should be defined and understood before automation is considered.

The answers to these questions can be found in Section 6, Solutions.

Review

SECTION 3 QUIZ

Note: There may be more than one answer to a question.

1.   Labor and material costs must be maintained separately because:
   A. That is the historical approach.
   B. They must be calculated and analyzed individually.
   C. Different people in the organization are responsible for labor and material.
   D. All of the above.

2.   Which of the following are general requirements for estimate development?
   A. A Template Structure and Dictionary.
   B. Defined estimate formats.
   C. Historical records from previous projects.
   D. A and C.

3.   The overall project management process will be facilitated if there is a separate Cost Estimate Template Structure and Work Breakdown Structure
   A. True.
   B. False.

4.   Summary estimate formats will usually include information on quantities to be installed by category.
   A. True.
   B. False.

5.   List 4 types of estimates:
   A. _____
   B. _____
   C. _____
   D. _____

6.   Which of the following is not used as a common estimating technique?
   A. Bottom-Up.
   B. Top-Down.
   C. Parametric.
   D. Expert Opinion.

7.   Which of the following is the most important input to the development of an estimate?
   A. Scope of work.
   B. Escalation factors.
   C. Schedule.

    D. Profit objective.

    E. Assumptions.

8.   Indirect costs are:

    A. Costs that cannot be escalated.

    B. Costs that cannot be estimated.

    C. Costs that cannot be identified to a single project.

    D. Costs that cover scope of work changes.

9.   Which of the following would you accept as a conceptual estimate?

    A. $327,943,311.

    B. $327,943,000.

    C. $327,900,000.

    D. $328,000,000.

    E. $300,000,000.

10.   For estimating software development costs, which of the following techniques are used?

    A. Parametric.

    B. Grassroots.

    C. Trend Analysis.

    D. Monte Carlo.

11.   A 90% Unit Learning Curve means:

    A. It will take 90% as many labor hours for each successive doubling of the unit number being produced.

    B. It will take 90% as many labor hours for producing 200 units compared with 100 units.

    C. It will cost 90% as much in total dollars for each successive doubling of the number of units produced.

    D. 90% of the time there is a reduction in total labor hours when the number of units produced doubles.

12.   Using the Monte Carlo approach for cost risk assessment, which of the following increases in the number of iterations will result in the greatest improvement in accuracy?

    A. 100 to 1,000.

    B. 1,000 to 10,000.

    C. 10,000 to 100,000.

    D. 1,000,000 to 10,000,000.

13.   In a cost risk assessment, which of the following probability distributions should be used when the most likely value is known but it is equally likely to be underrun or overrun?

    A. Uniform distribution.

    B. Normal distribution.

    C. Triangular distribution.

    D. Beta distribution.

14.   Which of the following output statistics from a risk evaluation measures the degree of asymmetry of a probability distribution?

    A. Standard deviation.

    B. Mean.

    C. Kurtosis.

D. Skewness.

15. A triangular distribution may be symmetrical or asymmetrical.
    A. True.
    B. False.

The following output table resulted from a risk assessment. Answer questions 16 to 18 based on this information.

Cumulative % Probability	Value
0%	$100,000
10%	$150,000
20%	$175,000
30%	$200,000
40%	$215,000
50%	$225,000
60%	$235,000
70%	$250,000
80%	$270,000
90%	$295,000
100%	$400,000

16. What is the likelihood of overrunning a budget of $175,000?

17. What is the most likely value of the probability distribution?
    A. $225,000.
    B. $400,000.
    C. Cannot be determined from this data format.

18. The estimate is $250,000 for this project. If management wants an 80% confidence level that the project will be completed within budget, how much should the budget be increased over the estimate?

19. A "check estimate" is:
    A. A verification of all the estimate numbers by a supervisor.
    B. A separate estimate developed independently by a third party to be compared with the original estimate.
    C. A review of engineering assumptions by an estimator.
    D. A review of estimating assumptions by engineering.

20. Estimate traceability includes which of the following concepts?
    A. The ability to track estimates from one project to the next.
    B. The ability to tally estimates from the detail to the summary totals accurately.
    C. The ability to track a project from one estimate to the next on a comparable basis.
    D. The ability to reconcile estimates produced by different organizations.
    E. All of the above.

21.   Estimating is more difficult to automate than scheduling.
    A. True.
    B. False.

22.   Two of the main advantages of automating estimating include:
    A. Consistency of results.
    B. Ability to maintain a single database.
    C. More accurate estimates.
    D. Quicker results.

23.   COCOMO, the Constructive Cost Model, is:
    A. A parametric estimating technique used for preparing estimates for software development.
    B. A wide-band delphi approach to estimating.
    C. An expert group method used for preparing estimates for software development.
    D. An automated program used for producing quicker escalation calculations.

24.   It is possible to make fair cost comparisons between different size construction projects completed in different years.
    A. True.
    B. False.

25.   The schedule is a critical input to estimate development for a construction project. Name three pieces of information related to the schedule used for cash flow development that are derived from the schedule.
    A. _____
    B. _____
    C. _____

The answers to these questions can be found in Section 6, Solutions.

EARNED VALUE

SECTION 4

EARNED VALUE

The first three segments of this text introduced work definition, risk assessment, contracting and organizational considerations, scheduling requirements, and factors that contribute to a successful estimating system. Now an explanation is added to show how progress is measured as a project follows the path from initiation to completion. This allows consistent comparisons to be made between planned and actual progress. Variances can then be determined and used on an exception basis to identify primary causes of variances and the need for corrective action. Proper visibility into status will allow management to make the course adjustments needed to successfully complete the project within technical, schedule and budget goals.

Section 4 begins with an explanation of "earned value" and describes its use for determining accurate project status. An example of the use of earned value methods for monitoring progress is presented in Chapter 28 in the brick wall case study. In Chapter 29, a review of accepted techniques for determining earned value is presented for directly measurable effort as well as for work that has no defined end product. These techniques are used in the establishment of the performance measurement Baseline (PMB) that incorporates all of the technical scope, schedule, estimating, and earned value techniques into a single integrated project plan. Once the plan has been established, the work is authorized. Actual costs are collected and progress is reported based on the selected earned value techniques. The comparison of these three data elements: planned accomplishment or budget, actual accomplishment (earned value), and actual cost, allows performance variances to be determined. This permits corrective action to be initiated in a timely manner.

The three data elements cited above are usually referred to as Budgeted Cost for Work Scheduled (BCWS), the planned accomplishment; Budgeted Cost for Work Performed (BCWP), the actual accomplishment; and Actual Cost of Work Performed (ACWP), the actual cost. These elements are also known as Planned Value (PV), Earned Value (EV), and Actual Cost (AC). Where applicable, especially in the performance measurement calculations, both abbreviations for each element will be shown.

The data produced by an earned value management and reporting system allows numerous indices and performance measures to be calculated. It will be shown how these can be used to develop accurate estimates of anticipated costs at completion, providing early warning of schedule and cost performance problems. The use of this information in the status reporting process will be demonstrated with an integrated performance report. Further analytical approaches will be developed for combining the information derived from a CPM scheduling system with the schedule information available from an earned value reporting system.

Changes are a part of every project. Suggestions for formalizing the change control process, as well as tips on how to limit the number of changes, will be presented later in a Section 4 chapter.

Chapter 27

EARNED VALUE

Objectives of this Chapter:

1. Define the concept of earned value and explain its use as a measure of the work accomplished.

2. Identify the shortcomings of an approach that only compares planned costs with actual costs.

3. Introduce the concepts of cost variance and schedule variance.

4. Explain how the use of a performance oriented approach provides early warning of potential problems.

Having completed the discussions of scheduling and estimating, the discussion turns to earned value, the third related aspect that is a data element for analysis. This topic was introduced in the first chapter when the need for a measure of actual accomplishment was explained. This chapter continues that initial introduction; development and application of earned value techniques will be covered in Chapter 29, "Measuring Accomplishment".

One of the fundamental requirements of any useful project management system is the ability to determine accurate status of a project. Otherwise, development of a plan loses its value, since there is no way to accurately assess how closely the plan is being followed or to monitor results of corrective action. Earned value is an effective way to do so. Once the earned value is determined, it can be compared with the actual cost of doing that work and the planned performance for that work. This provides much better visibility than the examples in the first chapter that compared only planned and actual costs.

While some may think of earned value as merely a contractual requirement to be followed on large contracts, this is far from the case. Earned value has been used in industry as well as on government contracts for decades because it provides needed project visibility. It has been applied in the petrochemical industry, the electric utility industry, aerospace industry, transportation, automobile industry, and various space programs. It has been successfully applied on environmental cleanup projects, software development applications, engineering and design, construction, maintenance, manufacturing, and in start-up and testing applications. It has been used on firm fixed price contracts, cost plus contracts, and all of the various hybrids in between these two extremes. It has also been applied on billion dollar projects and on $10,000 projects, the main difference being the degree of detail in the implementation. It is hard to find an industry or application that has not used earned value. In some industries it is a way of life.

Its success has been apparent. On an international project decades ago, the instrumentation subcontractor was able to control its work so well with earned value that it literally got too far ahead of all the other contractors and had to be slowed down. On a project where everything seemed to be behind schedule, it alone had control of the work scope, schedule and cost performance. Even well before that, the concept was applied on industrial projects before the term had even been invented. Upon hearing an explanation of the

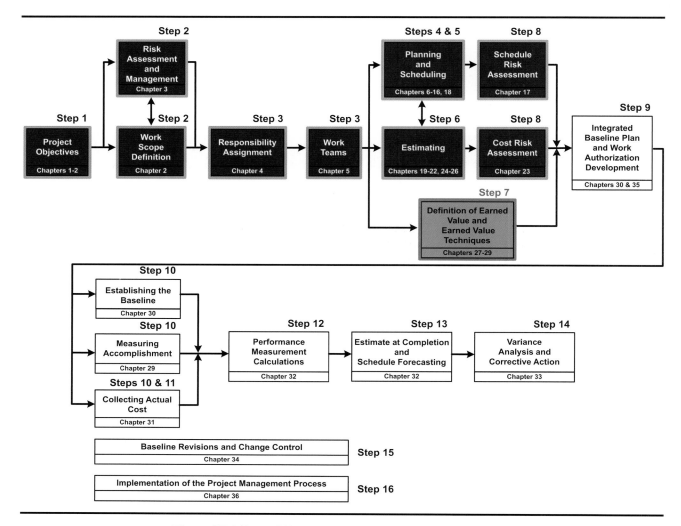

Figure 27-1 Earned Value Project Management: The Process

"new" concept of earned value, a senior manager once said "Now I understand what you're talking about. That is the approach used long ago, but it was called 'accomplishment value.'"

Application of the concept swept through many industries because of schedule slippages, cost overruns, and difficulty in accurately determining current status. Determination of percent complete became an issue of contention because of inaccurate estimated costs at completion. How could final costs be accurately forecast if there were no objective methods used for assessing how much of the project was completed? In a few years, organizations also realized that earned value would provide an excellent mechanism for progress payments.

Many of the requirements for successful earned value applications were already in place when customers/owners began placing demands on contractors for earned value reporting. Contractors, however, were frequently not eager to have this visibility of status in the hands of the customer/owner. This was a reflection of the power of the tool more than a concern for additional cost. One company had a sophisticated earned value reporting system in place in an industrial application on an engineering contract in 1972. It was a standard application used for internal control and applied on other contracts with other clients. However, the owners/customers were never aware of its existence. Years later, capabilities such as these became selling points when bidding new projects. As should be the case, some contracts are awarded based on the project management capabilities of the organization selected.

The need for earned value may never be more apparent than after reviewing a typical monthly project report for a project that does not use it. The reader would find summaries of status in words (qualitative more than quantitative), tables of actual cost to date subdivided by various categories, charts showing quantities of material installed, lists of delinquent items, expediting status of critical delivery items, staffing levels, data on construction equipment usage, and cash flow forecasts. Even with all that data, it would be impossible to make an informed evaluation of what the status of the project really was. That was because of conflicting information and virtually no way to develop an informed overall picture of accurate project status. As Dan Goldin, former NASA Administrator, once said, "If you cannot measure it, you cannot manage it."

The concept of earned value has now been applied so widely to so many different types of applications that it is an assumed capability of most successful organizations. This chapter will explain in more detail why this concept was developed and how it can be used to better understand project status.

The Concept

The fundamental concept in the application of cost and schedule controls is that of earned value. Earned value is the budgeted value for an element of work that has been completed, with that value determined from what had initially been planned for accomplishing that element of work. For example, if a mock-up unit for $300,000 were planned, when that mock-up unit is complete then $300,000 worth of budget is earned. Time of accomplishment and true costs of that unit have no effect on what is earned for it, but these will be measured against the earned value to determine the cost and schedule variances. Earned value has other names and abbreviations, such as EV, performance, accomplishment, work done, and Budgeted Cost for Work Performed (BCWP).

A chart such as the one shown in Figure 27-2 is often used to show cost performance on a proj-

ect. At first glance, it would appear that the contract is overrunning; however, this may not really be the case. Is the project ahead of schedule because it is now beyond "time now" with the planned budget position? Or is there an overrun because the actual costs have exceeded the planned budget? Which is the true story: ahead of schedule or cost overrun?

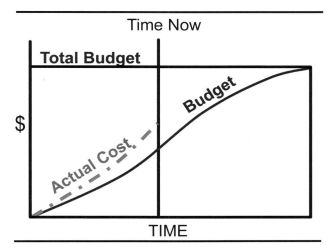

Figure 27-2 Budget Plan vs. Actuals

What is missing in this example, illustrated in Figure 27-3, is an indicator of how much work has been accomplished.

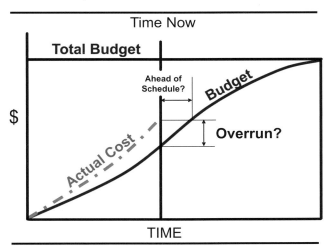

Figure 27-3 Overrun or Ahead of Schedule?

Measurement of how much work is complete may take many forms. Some examples of measurable increments of work could include tests performed, design reviews performed, lines of software code, drawings completed, reports delivered, units delivered, units designed, or units integrated and tested. A dollar value can be associated with such elements based on labor and materials required to do the work. When defined properly, earned value provides a very close approximation of the value of the work accomplished. The objective of an earned value approach is to find the most accurate way of evaluating the value of work performed.

Work accomplishment over time can be planned and the estimate of costs becomes the budget when it has been authorized. This is illustrated by the "budget" line in Figure 27-4. The budget value spread over time reflects the value of work based on cost estimates/budgets, integrated with schedules, for the authorized work.

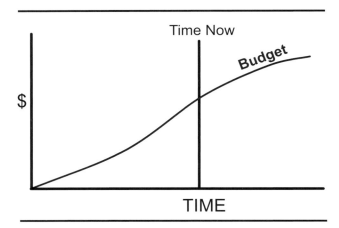

Figure 27-4 Planned Accomplishment

In Figure 27-5 three tasks (or work packages) are shown with start and finish dates. Task 1 and Task 2 are easy to evaluate in terms of the budgeted value they should earn. Task 1 has been completed, so all of its budget would be earned. Since Task 2 has not begun, it earns zero credit. The challenge of earned value measurement is reflected by the status shown for Task 3: the work has begun but it has not been completed. Clearly some of the budget should be earned, but how much? Solving the "work in process" measurement problem is the crux of performance measurement and will be addressed extensively in Chapter 29.

How is it possible to know if a project were ahead of schedule or over budget (or both)? When cost has exceeded plan?

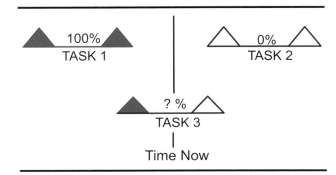

Figure 27-5 Earned Value of a Task

Two views, one in Figure 27-6 and one in 27-7 offer a starting point. In Figure 27-6, earned value is compared with budget (or the planned accomplishment) to provide an indication of schedule status. In this case, the position is unfavorable. The indication is that the project is behind schedule because less work has been completed than was scheduled to be accomplished at this point in time.

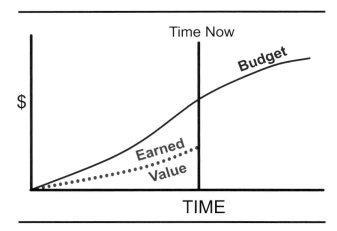

Figure 27-6 Planned vs. Actual Accomplishment

In Figure 27-7, actual cost is compared with earned value to assess the cost position of the project. This figure shows that the cost expended exceeds the value of the work completed, or an unfavorable position. This graph indicates that the project is indeed overrunning.

The project status can be portrayed even more concisely by combining all three curves on a single graph, shown in Figure 27-8.

This type of graph presents a much more complete picture of cost and schedule position in a single view.

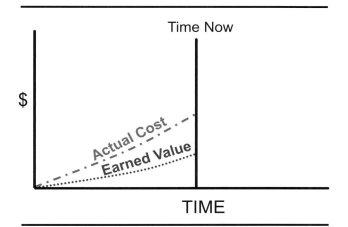

Figure 27-7 What's Been Accomplished? What did it Cost?

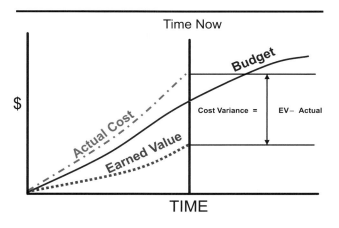

Figure 27-9 Cost Variance

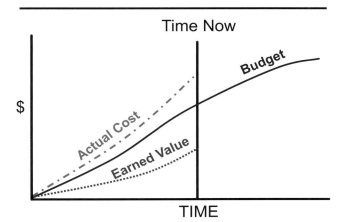

Figure 27-8 Earned Value is a Good Approximation

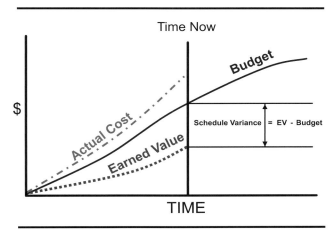

Figure 27-10 Schedule Variance

It does not merely compare planned and actual costs; it also allows consideration of what work has been performed for that cost. By using the same units of measure for all three lines on our curve (usually work hours or dollars), the budgeted cost, actual cost, and earned value can all be easily compared. If only the two lines in Figure 27-2 were considered, the conclusion would be that the budget were overrun. However, the addition of the earned value line allows a more accurate assessment that less work than planned is being completed. Also, the work that is being completed is costing more than it should according to the budget. By adding the third line, a cost concern is visible, whereas with just the traditional comparison of planned versus actual costs, it would not have been evident.

There are two comparisons of special interest: the cost variance and schedule variance. These are defined in a standard way that is presented in Figures 27-9 and 27-10 respectively.

The standard representation of the cost variance is to subtract actual cost from earned value, so the cost variance shown in Figure 27-9 is a negative number and represents an unfavorable condition. A graphical picture of schedule variance appears in Figure 27-10 and an unfavorable status is presented here as well. Far less work has been completed than was scheduled to be completed.

While these are standard definitions, the last one needs a little more explanation. A schedule variance measured in dollars is difficult to comprehend. It is easy to see that if $500,000 worth of work has been accomplished while $600,000 was intended to be completed, consequently $100,000 less work was accomplished than planned. However, this does not translate well into "We are $100,000 behind schedule." That type of statement seems to imply that if another $100,000 were spent, the project would be back on schedule.

That, of course, is not the case. It is the accomplishment of work that is the key, not the expenditure of money. Still, to those unfamiliar with the concept, it sounds like nonsense when schedule variance is measured in dollars. An attempt is sometimes made to convert this dollar variance to a time variance. This is discussed in detail in Chapter 32. The bottom line is that schedule variance is just an indicator. The true indication of being ahead of or behind schedule will come from the CPM scheduling system rather than from a numerical schedule variance.

The two most important characteristics of earned value are that it is an OBJECTIVE measure of work accomplished and that it is based on the BUDGETED value. That it provides an objective measure of work accomplished is valuable when assessing percent complete. Without earned value, it becomes a guessing game and a point of contention regarding a project's exact percent complete.

This can be a real problem if contract payment includes progress payments based on percent complete. On a tour of a construction project, two of the company's personnel got into a heated argument over the percent complete of the project. One argued that it must be "at least 40% complete" while the other maintained that it was "30% complete at best." This argument took place a quarter of a mile away from the project site and neither of them had even seen the inside of the buildings. Their assumptions of progress were based on the exterior appearance of the buildings and their own experience of where a project would have to be to have reached that status. The project was later converted to an earned value approach and it turned out that the actual progress on that day was less than 20% complete. The key point is that once the basis for earned value is defined and agreed upon, there can be no argument. It is possible to pull out a

report and learn that the project is exactly 19.47% complete and everyone inside and outside of the organization will get the same answer.

It is tough to figure out where you are going if you don't know where you are. Earned value helps focus where you are.

The Earned Value Process

To develop an earned value system, effort is further broken down into smaller segments called tasks. Each task is assigned a scope of work, scheduled start/finish dates, and a budget. It is important that tasks are short in duration and meaningful subdivisions of the work. Short tasks will facilitate earned value assessment for work in process.

Measurement of a task in process involves quantifying (in hours/dollars) actual technical accomplishment at the present time. In Figure 27-11 the actual accomplishment is visible, as is the actual cost of the work. Based upon these measurements, it is evident that not as much was accomplished as was planned. In other words, the project is behind schedule and way over budget. With this earned value data, it is possible to project schedule slippage and cost at completion.

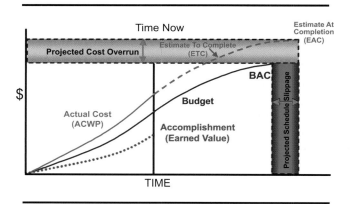

Figure 27-11 Cost and Schedule Impacts

This early warning capability is one of the most valuable outputs of a properly implemented earned value management and reporting system. It allows trends to be identified and corrective actions to be taken before the potential problems become fact. Without the earned value component, it is not possible to know that a project will overrun in cost until the actual costs exceed the Budget at Completion (BAC); that allows no room for corrective action.

Earned value does not always show that a project is behind schedule and overrun on costs. It predicts cost underruns and the potential of an earlier completion date just as effectively as it predicts potential problems. Its main value is the early indication of true status, allowing corrective action to be taken at a time when it can have a positive impact on the outcome of the project.

The Value of Earned Value

Earned value provides better visibility. In turn, better visibility supports timely management decisions. It cannot guarantee that the information will be used or that better decisions will be made. Management can still choose to ignore or discount the input. Although it should be obvious that having more accurate information provided earlier in the project is valuable to the project manager, this is often difficult to quantify. Having a well defined scheduling system, combined with earned value information, provides the opportunity to shorten the schedule which is worth a quantifiable amount on a daily basis. This can either be figured on the basis of additional profit (because of an earlier entry into a market) or cost savings associated with a shorter duration (reduced overhead and level of effort expenses).

In some instances, it is possible to point to a particular condition that would have been overlooked without the regimen and structure of an earned value management and reporting system. A senior manager of one company once challenged a young project controls engineer to demonstrate where any resources had been saved through the use of the recently implemented earned value management and reporting system. It just so happened there was a recent and dramatic example. The variance analysis reporting had been indicating one account that had been grossly overrunning for some time. After repeated investigations, it was finally revealed that charges were being included in that account for some related work no longer in the scope of the project. However, the company in question found the effort useful and had continued the work while charging it to the related account with no explicit definition for the completion of that work. Part of the problem was that there was no WBS Dictionary that captured the true scope of work to be performed. Of course upon discovery, the work was immediately stopped. If that work had continued, an extra $1 million would have been charged to the project.

Conclusion

The earned value process allows the planning and measurement of work accomplishment. This information, when combined with the actual costs for performing the work and the planned accomplishment, provides a picture of integrated cost and schedule status. This has been one of the project management system objectives of this entire text. How can you know where you are going to finish in time and cost if you don't know where you are? Earned value effectively quantifies the current position. This information enables one to more readily predict a more realistic Estimate at Completion (EAC), using techniques that will be discussed in greater detail later.

Chapter 27 Review Questions

27-1.   What is earned value?

27-2.   Why is earned value an important part of the project management process?

27-3.   What two other cost/schedule status measures is earned value typically compared against?

27-4.   What is the earned value of a completed task? Of a task that has not begun? Of a partially completed task?

27-5.   If earned value were higher than actual cost, what does that signify? What is likely to happen to the forecasted cost at completion compared to the approved budget?

27-6.   If earned value were below the budget at a point in time, what does that mean in terms of status?

27-7.   Define cost variance and schedule variance.

27-8.   What are the two most important characteristics of earned value?

27-9.   From an earned value standpoint why is it important that tasks be kept relatively short in duration?

27-10.   Explain how earned value can be used to provide early indication of final cost and schedule position on the project.

27-11.   A control account has just been completed. Budget and actual costs were measured in labor hours. The budget for the account was 250 hours, the actual reported charges were 350 hours, and the account finished one month late on a three month schedule. What is the earned value?

True or False

27-12.   Earned value is also sometimes called Budgeted Cost for Work Performed, or BCWP.

27-13.   The concept of earned value was applied in industry even before the term "earned value" was invented.

27-14.   Earned value can provide an accurate basis for assessing percent complete for a project.

The answers to these questions can be found in Section 6, Solutions.

Case Study

27.1 The Importance of Earned Value

You have just been assigned as Project Manager to a project that is already in progress. Your predecessor has apparently managed this project successfully and is being rewarded with a larger project assignment. She tells you that the project is underrunning, and provides a status report, that provides the following information:

Planned Expenditures to Date: $28,500,000

Actual Expenditures to Date: $22,749,000

Approved Budget: $57,000,000

She states that the project is about half done and many of the problems from the early stages of the project are now resolved. You are a little uneasy because this particular project manager has had a string of successful projects that later end in disaster, after she has moved on to other work. She freely admits that she is far better in the early stages of a project than in the later stages. "All those details at the completion of a project bore me," she states. You ask how she has determined that the project is half done and she responds, "When you've managed as many projects as I have, you have a feel for these things." This raises your level of concern rather than easing it. You ask for more information on the details of the project's budget and scope, and you are provided with the information in Figure 1.

There is a status meeting planned for two weeks from now, and the former project manager will be out of the country for an important meeting on her new assignment. You must be prepared to address the status of the project as you assume control of the managerial responsibilities. Be prepared to address the following questions:

1. Based on the information in Figure 1, address the following questions:

    (a) What is the real percent complete?

    (b) What is the percent spent?

    (c) According to the plan, what should the percent complete be now?

2. At the upcoming meeting, what should your general assessment of the project's status be?

3. Based on your findings, what recommendations might you make?

Hint: Determine the budgeted value of work that was scheduled to be performed and the budgeted value of work actually accomplished.

The solution to this case study can be found on the Humphreys & Associates, Inc. web site.
www.humphreys-assoc.com

FIGURE 1
Project Budget Information & Status

The $57 million budget is subdivided as follows:

System Design:	$ 5,000,000
Product Manufacturing:	$16,000,000
Product Assembly & Test:	$12,000,000
Administrative Support:	$ 6,000,000
Material Costs:	$18,000,000
TOTAL:	**$57,000,000**

STATUS

System Design:	Complete
Product Manufacturing:	200 units out of 1,000 units complete. Each unit requires $16,000 to manufacture.
Product Assembly & Test:	150 units out of 1,000 completed. Each unit requires $12,000 to assemble and test.
Administrative Support:	A total of $2,400,000 has been spent to date, which is according to plan.
Material:	Material costs are not charged to the project account until that material is used. To date, $3,500,000 has been charged to the project. While this is less than was planned, the status report states: "While the project is behind on material expenditures, the material is available and so there is no problem. It is normal on this type of project for material usage to be a little behind and the difference is traditionally recovered towards project completion."

PLANNED ACCOMPLISHMENT AS OF THE REPORT DATE:

System Design:	Complete
Product Manufacturing:	500 units were to be completed.
Product Assembly & Test:	300 units were to be complete.
Administrative Support:	$2.4 million scheduled to be spent.
Material:	$9.5 million of material should have been used.

Chapter 28

THE BRICK WALL

Objectives of this Chapter:

1. Explain, with an example, the differences between the budgets versus actuals approach and the earned value approach.

2. Demonstrate the importance of improved planning.

3. Demonstrate that earned value provides improved visibility of likely project outcome much earlier in the project.

4. Demonstrate that earned value provides lessons learned to be applied to future projects.

This chapter offers a simple example of how earned value can be used. The illustration will help clarify the concept and solidify understanding.

The Brick Wall Example

I'm going to have a brick wall built in my backyard. It will be six feet high, two feet wide, and six feet long (technical scope of work). I get a couple of estimates from contractors and find that they all say it will cost about $10,000. The contractor plan is a simple one: it will take four workers a total of four days (schedule) and they will each cost $250 per day (cost). It will take $6,000 worth of material as well (cost). The resources required are therefore:

Four workers, $250 each for 4 days	$4,000
Materials	$6,000
Total Planned Cost	$10,000

That sounds pretty good, but I am going to be out of town and will not be able to monitor the work progress. I therefore ask for more details from the contractor concerning his plan. The contractor provides the plan shown in Figure 28-1.

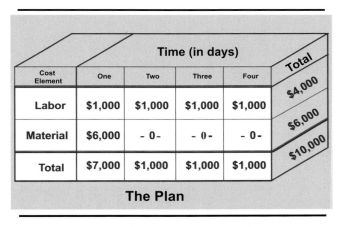

Cost Element	Time (in days)				Total
	One	Two	Three	Four	
Labor	$1,000	$1,000	$1,000	$1,000	$4,000
Material	$6,000	- 0-	- 0-	- 0-	$6,000
Total	$7,000	$1,000	$1,000	$1,000	$10,000

The Plan

Figure 28-1 Budget vs. Actuals

The plan shows that the material will all be on site the first day, so the entire $6,000 material budget is planned for that day as well as the first $1,000 for labor.

The total budget for day one is, therefore, $7,000. The only remaining expenses will be the $1,000 of labor for each additional day. I accept the contractor's plan, but inform him that I will be out of town and want a daily progress report. My contractor responds, "Sure, just leave your phone number and I'll call you." So I contract the job with him and leave town.

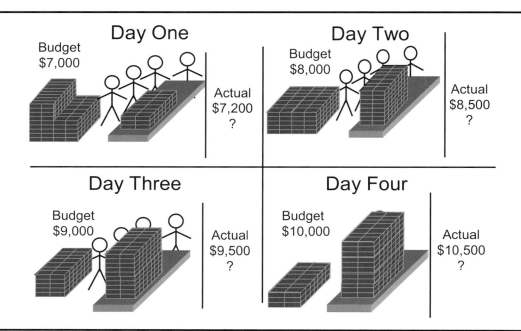

Figure 28-2 Four Days of Bricking

In his phone call the first night, he states, "The bill for day 1 is $7,200." That is just about on plan as far as cash flow is concerned, but I have no idea what has been accomplished. Hence, there is a question mark. The next day he calls to say, "The bill through day 2 is $8,500." The budget was $8,000 through day 2, but it doesn't sound too bad as far as cash flow. However, once again I do not know what was accomplished. He may have finished the job with a $1,500 underrun and two days ahead of schedule, or just be getting the foundation in place. I need to know the status so that I am not unpleasantly surprised later on. The developing status is shown in Figure 28-2.

On the fourth day, he proclaims, "The bill is $10,500." I'm not very happy about the price, but at least the wall is done and I will have it for the day I need it. But then he adds, "Wait a minute. I didn't say I was done. There is still some more work to do." At the end of day 5, I get the bill: $11,000. My final status appears in Figure 28-3. Not only is it a day late, but I have a $1,000 overrun in cost.

I'm angry because I have no idea what happened to drive the cost up or do I know why the project had its completion delayed by one day. I had a party planned for the fifth day so the workers were finishing the wall with my guests partying

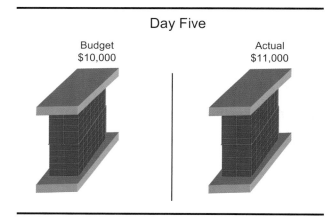

Figure 28-3 Budget vs. Actual Day Five

nearby. I call the contractor to find out what happened. I get no answer because he has gone on to building other brick walls and does not even remember mine. Besides that, his office wants to know when my check will arrive. "We've built your project, but we have no interest in financing it." Where do I go now? One of the things that performance measurement would have done for me is to build a data trail so that I would have had a better idea how I was progressing and I would have known at the end what happened.

Realizing there must have been a better way to do this project, I ask my neighbor about his experience with his own brick wall. He replied, "Why, I used the performance measurement approach and I can tell you to this day what happened on each of the days when the wall was being built. This is how you should have done it."

Earned Value Brick Wall

Here's how my project would have turned out using the earned value approach instead of the "budget versus actuals" approach. The objective and the resources to accomplish that objective are the same as before. The only difference is that now I will use performance measurement (earned value) concepts to budget, schedule, measure progress, and make projections for my wall.

First of all, this time I want a plan from the contractor that is better defined. I also want better control over schedule and cost. So this time I say, "Listen, I know you have to buy your material up front but I don't want to know about it until you actually use the materials, just like you planned labor costs at the point of use."

The material is:

$6,000 / 6 feet = $1,000 per foot

This is easy math, so the contractor time phases the material at point of usage/installation just as the labor resource is planned.

This is not the only level of detail that could have been selected. The contractor could have planned and measured the status for every brick for very specific accuracy, but such a measurement system would have cost too much compared with the benefit of increased visibility. This is one of the criteria to be considered: design the performance measurement system according to the complexity, magnitude and risk of the project. If these were gold bricks using a new state of the art bonding technique, it may very well have been warranted to measure at the individual brick level.

To split up the material line to better represent progress, he says, "On the first day I'll get one half foot of wall constructed, on the second and third day it will be two feet each day, and I'll erect 1-1/2 feet on the final day. That works out to $1,000 per foot for materials." The rest of the plan looks about the same as before, because

the labor was planned at the point of use, except that now we have a planned accomplishment rate of actual work. So the plan that is submitted by the contractor now looks like Figure 28-4.

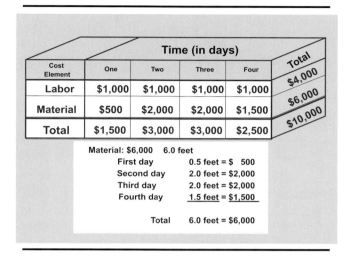

Cost Element	Time (in days)				Total
	One	Two	Three	Four	
Labor	$1,000	$1,000	$1,000	$1,000	$4,000
Material	$500	$2,000	$2,000	$1,500	$6,000
Total	$1,500	$3,000	$3,000	$2,500	$10,000

Material: $6,000   6.0 feet

First day	0.5 feet =	$ 500
Second day	2.0 feet =	$2,000
Third day	2.0 feet =	$2,000
Fourth day	1.5 feet =	$1,500
Total	6.0 feet =	$6,000

Figure 28-4 Planning Using Earned Value

Now this looks like a better plan, but I ask the contractor for his specific work plan for the first day of the job. The details for day 1 are provided in even greater detail in accordance with my request (see Figure 28-5).

Task	Schedule
Excavate footing Labor 1/4 day	△ 250 △
Form work and supports Labor 1/4 day Material $50	△ 300 △
Place foundation Labor 1/4 day Material $150	△ 400 △
Construct 0.5 feet of brick wall Labor 1/4 day Material $300	△ 550 △

Total planned value	Labor	$1,000
	Material	$ 500
		$1,500

Figure 28-5 Detailed Planning for Day One Using Earned Value

The workers will arrive at 7:30 A.M. and will work eight hours. The first thing they will do is excavate for the footings which should take 1/4 of a day. All four workers will be working for that 1/4 of a day, a cost of $250. Next they must erect the forms and supports and that is another 1/4 of a day, or another $250. They need some material to support the work such as lumber, nails, reinforcing rods, etc. and the estimate for that material is $50. Cumulatively, the estimate is $500 for labor and $50 for materials.

The next planned activity is to place the foundation for another 1/4 of a day ($250) and they will use about $150 of concrete. The last thing they will do on day 1 is to put up the 1/2 foot of brick wall for which they will use another 1/4 of a day ($250) and the materials for this will cost $300.

The contractor says, "That's how I plan to build this wall. I have $1,000 worth of labor and $500 of materials, or $1,500 total for the day." I say, "It sounds good. Call me tomorrow and let me know how it's going."

The contractor calls the next day and says, "I said I would do the footings and they're done as planned. Well, they cost a little more than expected ($300 versus $250 planned) but they are done. Also, we finished the forms and supports right on schedule and budget. Next we placed the foundation, but we had a little problem. I had one of my people draw up the original plan and there was an oversight I didn't catch. The concrete in the foundation has to harden before we can start laying bricks, so we didn't get any bricks laid. The problem is my crew is to be paid based on hours rather than tasks completed and they have a rule that says we have to pay them for a full day, even if no work is available. So the foundation cost 1/4 day more than planned, or an extra $250."

The status for day 1 is shown in Figure 28-6.

So the progress of my wall at the end of day one is this: I first planned to excavate and this was completed, so I earn the full $250 budget that was planned for this work even though I consumed $300 in actual costs to accomplish the excavation task.

Next I planned to complete the forms and supports at a value of $300. This was also completed, so my earned value for form work is $300, and I consumed $300 in actual cost to accomplish the forms and support task. I completed the foundation that was budgeted at $400, so I also earn $400 for that task despite $250 extra cost for labor for the last two hours of the day (in which no effort was performed). This brought the actual cost to $650 for that task. However, I

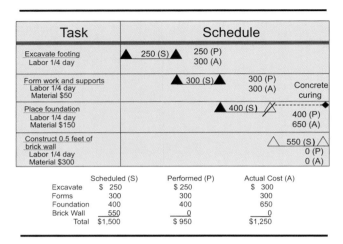

Task	Schedule		
Excavate footing Labor 1/4 day	▲ 250 (S) ▲	250 (P) 300 (A)	
Form work and supports Labor 1/4 day Material $50	▲ 300 (S) ▲	300 (P) 300 (A)	Concrete curing
Place foundation Labor 1/4 day Material $150	▲ 400 (S)	400 (P) 650 (A)	
Construct 0.5 feet of brick wall Labor 1/4 day Material $300	△ 550 (S) △	0 (P) 0 (A)	

	Scheduled (S)	Performed (P)	Actual Cost (A)
Excavate	$ 250	$ 250	$ 300
Forms	300	300	300
Foundation	400	400	650
Brick Wall	550	0	0
Total	$1,500	$ 950	$1,250

Figure 28-6 Earned Value after Day One

didn't get any bricks laid, so there is no earned value for that task. The planned value for that last task was $550, so I am behind schedule by $550. What was the cost for the first day? The actual cost was $1,250 for the first day, versus a plan to do $1,500 of work and an earned value of $950. The wall is behind schedule and it is costing me more than planned. Most of the problem is because of the oversight concerning the concrete hardening time. Status is shown pictorially in Figure 28-7.

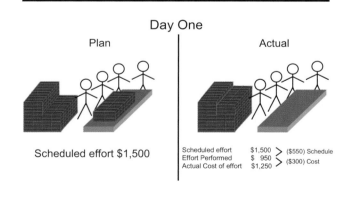

Day One

| Plan | Actual |

Scheduled effort $1,500

Scheduled effort	$1,500	> ($550) Schedule
Effort Performed	$ 950	
Actual Cost of effort	$1,250	> ($300) Cost

Figure 28-7 Earned Value Status Day One

The schedule variance, as shown, is ($550) and the cost variance is ($300). Both of these represent unfavorable status. Had I used the traditional approach of budget versus actual cost ($1,500 versus $1,250), I would not have been concerned because it was so early in the project that there would have been adequate time to recover. I realize that I am, on a percentage basis, significantly behind schedule and over cost.

After those first day results, that night I gave my contractor an earful of complaints.

This must have been a successful motivational speech, because the news was much better when he called the next day. The workers erected 2.5 feet of wall on that second day. Not only had the crew caught up to the schedule, but they had worked efficiently and eliminated the unfavorable cost variance as well. So at the end of day two, my plan, earned value, and actual cost were all equal to $4,500. This is shown in Figure 28-8. At this point, I am back on schedule and within budget.

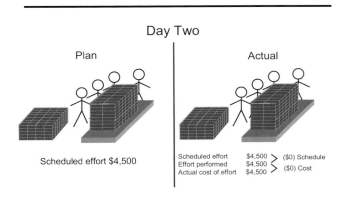

Figure 28-8 Earned Value Status Day Two

Disaster struck on the third day - it rained. The rain prevented the workers from laying any bricks but my contract required full pay since they all showed up for work. Although $3,000 worth of work was planned for day three, that brought the total plan to $7,500, none was accomplished. The actual costs incurred, however, were the full amount of labor ($1,000). So my day three status (displayed in Figure 28-9) is $3,000 behind schedule and $1,000 over cost.

The sun is out on day four and my contractor's workers are back to work laying bricks. They actually completed the work scheduled through day three and earned $3,000 (earned value), while adding $3,000 of actual costs. The crew is working efficiently now at the original planned

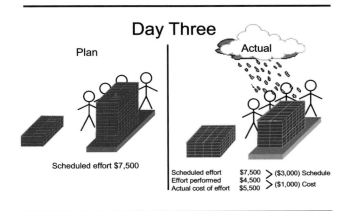

Figure 28-9 Earned Value Status Day Three

rate, just a day late because of the rain. However, they remain behind schedule and over cost on a cumulative basis. We have not completed the wall as planned through the end of day four. The planned value of work was $10,000 (the total budget for the project), while the earned value is $7,500 and the actual costs are $8,500. While some of the unfavorable schedule variance has been reduced, the cost variance remains at ($1,000). Remember, the schedule variance at job completion will be zero regardless of how late the project is completed. This is true by definition since we will always earn the entire planned budget at completion when the project is finished. The status through day four is displayed in Figure 28-10.

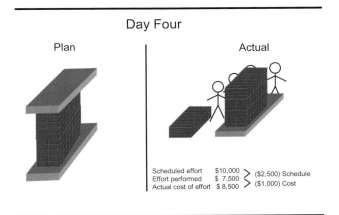

Figure 28-10 Earned Value Status Day Four

Finally, the wall is completed on day five at a final cost of $11,000 (see Figure 28-11).

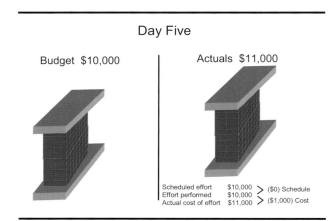

Day Five

Budget $10,000   Actuals $11,000

Scheduled effort	$10,000	> ($0) Schedule
Effort performed	$10,000	
Actual cost of effort	$11,000	> ($1,000) Cost

Figure 28-11 Earned Value Status Day Five

It is finished one day late and $1,000 over cost. Not only was I able to see that end result in advance, I can explain exactly what happened.

Figure 28-12 displays the full life of the brick wall example.

Note that the Budget at Completion remains the same at all times. Budget only changes with scope changes, and there were no scope changes on this job. Graphical presentations can often make it possible to determine trends in performance measurement. This is an important feature of performance: trying to get information early enough to allow management to make deci-

sions based on an accurate assessment of status. For example, it can be seen that from day one earned value was lagging behind. The best accomplishment achieved was even with the plan. The same can be seen with actual costs. With the schedule and cost variance trends being negative, it was a fairly safe bet that the end date would slip at some additional cost. Then the questions become "How far?" and "How much?"

Notice a few things about this example. The use of an earned value system does not guarantee a problem-free project. This sample project still cost $11,000 to complete and took a day longer than scheduled. However, compared with the "budget versus actual" approach, that is where the similarities end. With the performance measurement approach, an early indicator showed what was about to happen. An accurate status was available so that trade-off decisions could be made earlier in the schedule, saving cost or at least credibility. For example, if I needed to have the wall finished by the end of day four because of the party, I could have requested a fifth or even sixth worker to ensure a timely schedule completion. I could have balanced my technical versus cost versus schedule priorities. If it were top priority to finish the wall, additional cost could have expedited completion. Another option would have been to change the technical specifications.

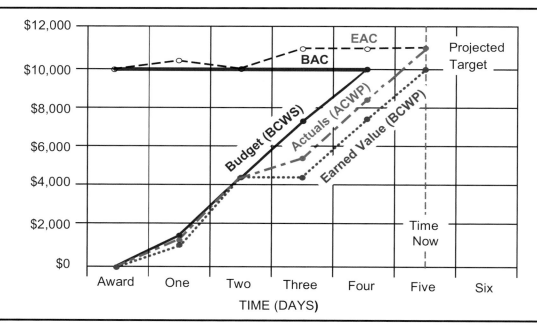

Figure 28-12 Earned Value Graphics

Lowering the requirement for the wall from six feet to five feet in height would have saved time and cost, and I may have had the wall completed on time with cost savings. The key consideration is that the availability of true status information that was timely would have allowed me the option to consider trade-offs and choose whatever course of action that I believed was most appropriate.

It is also apparent at the end of the project exactly what went wrong. While it may not have saved this brick wall's schedule or budget, on the next one I can be smarter. For example, I will know to ensure that the contractor's plan has allowed time for the concrete to cure. I will also have a better idea what productivity rate to expect from the actual wall construction. This will allow the contractor and me to better assess the planned schedule based on the scope of work and planned resources.

Conclusion

An earned value approach is a significant improvement over a budget versus actual approach because it provides a cost effective common denominator for status. Planning to the extent practicable with available information is crucial to the eventual success of any project. An earned value approach allows an early warning system that should result in schedule and/or cost savings. It also allows trade-offs to be made between technical requirements and cost and schedule objectives. Lessons learned from a system that provides for an historical data base will benefit future projects.

Chapter 28 Review Questions

True or False

28-1. Earned value visibility can prevent schedule slippage and cost overruns as long as there is a stable statement of work.

28-2. Budget versus actual cost data and detailed schedules are just as accurate for managing a project as the earned value approach but more time consuming, the cost is higher, and there is no common denominator.

The answers to these questions can be found in Section 6, Solutions.

Case Study

28.1 THE BRICK WALL

It is now time to reexamine the brick wall example from this chapter. That example must be referred to while addressing this case study. It is now the end of day 3, the day of rain that caused the effort to fall behind schedule and to indicate cost overrun. Decisions must be made as to whether to accelerate the project to ensure that it finishes on schedule or possible to intentionally delay it to try to recover some of the cost overrun by using only the most efficient workers. The key to this decision will be accurate forecasts of what the cost and schedule will be for each of these scenarios. In other words, an Estimate at Completion (EAC) must be developed for each case. Your assignment then is to generate an EAC for each alternative (actually a pair of "what if?" scenarios) based on the following information:

Case A   To finish on day 4, the remaining work may need to be done on overtime. The pay rate for overtime is time and a half, i.e. 50% higher than for straight time. Choosing this alternative would be appropriate if this is a schedule critical project (i.e. it is imperative that the project finish on time, even if costs increase as a result).

Case B   Consider the alternative of delaying completion of the project to day 6. Because of the cost overrun to date, a decision could be made to stretch the completion while using only the most efficient workers. Our assumption is that elimination of the two least productive workers will improve productivity by 15%. Choosing this alternative would make more sense if this is a cost critical project (i.e. cost impact is more important even if it means a schedule delay).

1. What is the most likely EAC if no corrective action is implemented?
2. Develop an EAC for Case A.
3. Develop an EAC for Case B.

Note: It is important to evaluate what future performance is likely to be when developing an EAC. Thus the circumstances that produced the current conditions (as described in Chapter 28) must be considered in determination of projected final costs.

The solution to this case study can be found on the Humphreys & Associates, Inc. web site.
www.humphreys-assoc.com

Chapter **29**

MEASURING ACCOMPLISHMENT

Objectives of this Chapter:

1. Define work packages and their distinguishing characteristics.
2. Present examples of work packages.
3. Define types of work measurement.
4. Describe and explain the most commonly used earned value techniques.
5. Explain the application and limitations of each earned value technique.
6. Discuss the application of earned value and contract considerations.
7. Discuss when earned value is credited for labor and material.

The various options for calculating earned value for work in progress will be presented in this chapter. In addition, some important concept definitions will be introduced and explained. This is a detailed discussion of how earned value is applied.

On the Figure 29-1 flowchart, there are two interface considerations: one with baseline development and one with variance analysis. This reflects the point that the earned value techniques have two functions: planning work accomplishment and measuring actual work accomplishment. The earned value techniques selected will be used in the planning process to support development of the performance measurement baseline (PMB). The same techniques must be used when measuring accomplishment. The actual status will then be compared with actual cost and planned progress to support the variance analysis process.

The earned value concept provides an orderly, systematic, timely and accurate means of determining the budgeted value of the work that has been accomplished. These means are addressed in more detail in this chapter. Work packages are the most detailed element of an earned value approach where plan, accomplishment, and actual cost are compared.

Work Packages

A key to an effective performance measurement system is the selection and definition of work packages. The control account scope and budget are divided into lower level detail called work packages and planning packages. The use of work packages allows definition of the total scope of a project at the lowest level. A work package consists of detailed short duration tasks, including material and other direct cost (equipment, travel, computer time, etc.) that are part of the identified scope of work. The important characteristics of a work package include:

1. Represents work at levels where it is performed.
2. Clearly distinguished from all other work packages.

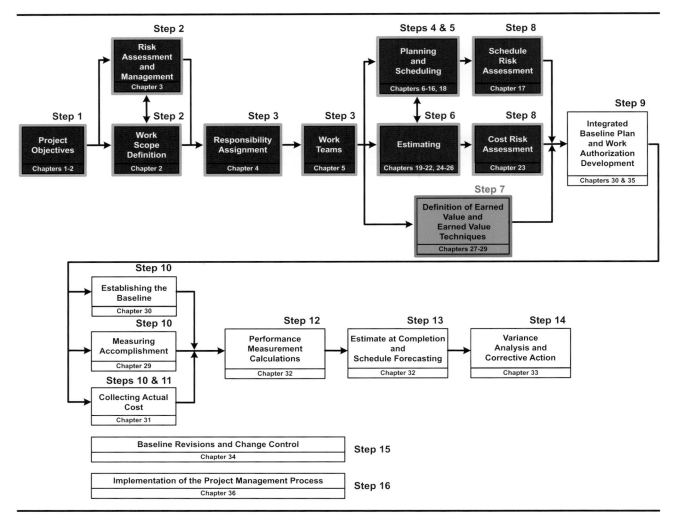

Figure 29-1 Earned Value Project Management: The Process

3. Responsibility assigned to a single organizational unit and control account.

4. Scheduled start and completion dates.

5. Budget expressed in terms of dollars, labor hours, or other measurable units.

6. Duration is limited to a relatively short span of time or it is subdivided by individual milestones to facilitate the objective measurement of work performed.

Work packages are the basic building blocks used for detailed planning, responsibility assignment, and control of contract performance. For effective management, a work package should be clearly identified, scheduled, budgeted, and assigned to a single organization responsible for its completion. The sum of all the work package budgets, plus any planning package budgets, must equal the control account budget.

Work packages presuppose that the detailed work scope is known. Since it may not be possible to define the detailed scope for a multi-year project well in advance of the actual work performance, it typically is not possible to develop work packages for all of the work in a long term project at the time of contract initiation. In those cases, "planning packages" are developed for future work. These are elements of work scope, schedule and budget that will be defined into work packages as scope becomes better defined. This transition from future planning packages to near-term work packages is often referred to as "rolling wave" planning.

Typical Work Packages

Regardless of the application, each work package consists of a logical aggregation of work that will take a few weeks to a few months of effort. Examples of work packages for different types of applications include the following:

Software Program Development

- Module(s)/Unit(s) Requirements Analysis.
- Module(s)/Unit(s) Design.
- Module(s)/Unit(s) Code and Test.
- Module(s)/Unit(s) Integration and Test.
- Problem Change Report Resolution.
- Module(s)/Unit(s) Hardware & Software Integration.
- Software Specification Segments.
- Design Reviews.

Engineering

- Stress Analysis Study.
- Power Supply Design.
- Transmitter Specification.
- Develop Test Plan.
- Build Logic Brassboard.
- Analyze Circuit Design.

Manufacturing

- Build 25 Units of Assembly 237596F.
- Fabricate Jig Fixture for Welding Subassembly 1611FG45.
- Test 40 Units of Assembly TR6385-X.
- Fabricate 250 Cable and Harnesses for System P3-17.
- Kit Components for 5,000 Transmitter Antennas.

Quality Assurance

- Calibrate Test Stands for Final Assembly.
- Inspect Lot Sample 17 for the AN/SSQ-41.
- Prepare a Quality Assurance Plan.
- Inspect Incoming Units.

Construction

- Forms Completed.
- Concrete Placement Completed.
- Valves Installed.
- Insulation Installed.

It is within the control account at the work package level that work measurement occurs.

The three types of work measurement are:

1. Discrete effort.
2. Apportioned effort.
3. Level of Effort (LOE).

Each of these will be discussed, with examples given, for the initial planning process and for the earned value determination during the status process.

Discrete Effort

The examples for discrete effort are the most numerous because there are many different ways of assessing status for work that is objectively measurable with defined work products. Discrete effort methods that have been extensively used over the years are the following:

- Incremental Milestones.
- 50/50 Method.
- 0/100 Method.
- Equivalent Units.
- Units Complete.
- Percent Complete.
- Combination of the above.

Each of these work measurement or earned value techniques is useful in different applications, depending on the duration of the work package and the nature of the work to be accomplished.

Milestone Definition

All of the work measurement or earned value techniques to be presented rely directly or indirectly on milestones. A milestone is a key event in a project based on planned work accomplishment rather than a fixed time interval. The milestones discussed in this chapter must be the same milestones selected for the scheduling system. A "good" milestone includes certain characteristics:

- It is a product or event.

- It is within the authority of the performer.

- It has clear, objective criteria for measuring accomplishment, quantified whenever possible.

- It is directly related to the work package scope of work.

- It is weighted in relationship to the time-phased budget.

- It is expressed with a scheduled calendar date that can be identified to control account and summary schedules.

Some of these characteristics merit further explanation. As suggested in the first item on the list, a milestone is an event or product. The distinction between activities and events is important here. An event does not consume time or resources. It is a point in time that corresponds to the initiation or completion of some activity. "Prepare drawing" is not an event and can never be selected as a milestone. "Issue drawing," on the other hand, is an event that occurs at a single point in time and could be selected as a milestone. Many milestones will correspond to the completion of some product.

Milestones are used to gauge progress at a work package level. This status is then summarized at the control account level and used to evaluate performance. It therefore follows that any milestone selected for measuring performance within a control account must be within the authority of the control account manager responsible for that account.

While a milestone is an event, there must be a clear definition of when that event is considered to have occurred. Using the earlier example, when is a drawing issued? Is it considered issued when it goes to design drafting for final check? Or is it considered "issued" when it has received approval? Does "issued" mean that the drawing transmittal letter has been prepared, or even that the drawing has been received at its intended location? No one should have to guess which of these points actually refers to drawing issue, since it must be defined at the time of milestone selection. This is the "objective criteria" referred to in the list of milestone characteristics. Another example might be that "cabinet design verified" means that Quality Assurance has signed the completion report and issued it to the project manager. This is an objective criterion for completion that can be verified by anyone, even someone unfamiliar with the technical requirements.

The requirement that a milestone be "weighted in relationship to the time-phased budget" needs clarification, because this is a common problem. The objective is to plan the work the way it is anticipated to be performed.

In a four month work package, with planned values of 25 resources per month (i.e. 25+25+25+25 = 100 total budget), milestones should be selected that correspond to this plan. The goal is to have a milestone worth the resources required to achieve it. Selecting milestones in each month that are worth 10-10-10-70, when the resource plan does not fit that profile, will still yield the total budget of 100, but then there is a built-in variance within the system. Even before the work effort is initiated, it is obvious that reports will indicate that the effort is overrunning in cost for the first three months.

If work were performed as anticipated but the plan does not reflect this (i.e. 25 per month), only 10 will be earned while 25 will be expended in actual cost. This results in a fictitious variance of (15) for each of the first three months. At the end of three months, if everything went as anticipated but not planned, the cumulative earned value would be 30 while the cumulative actual cost would be 75. This unfavorable cost variance of (45) would initiate a need for variance analysis that is not warranted. Effective planning should minimize fictitious variances as much as possible. The plan should reflect how the work is anticipated to be performed.

Some companies are creative in their earned value techniques. One engineering/software firm developed a new approach that factored in technical criticality. If an activity were especially critical technically, it would earn more than its budgeted value upon completion. If it were not so critical, it might earn less than its budgeted value upon completion. This is not accepted earned value methodology. The earned value must always be equal to its budgeted value when the work is complete. In this example, the engineers on the project felt they knew more than the project management staff and so they would "correct" a perceived shortcoming. This is one of the reasons why it is important to have a specialized functional group that maintains the validity of the project management function so that procedures can be applied correctly and consistently.

A milestone always has a scheduled calendar date for its accomplishment, and this date appears at the work package level, on the control account schedule, and on any summary schedules. If a network CPM schedule were used on the project, the dates for these milestone events must be the same on the network and the control account schedule forecast dates. All schedule baseline dates must be consistent. This is the requirement of schedule traceability previously addressed. The goal is integration of all the project management information so that there is consistent reporting. Milestones are in the project schedule, resources are applied to the project schedule (in control account plans and/or in CPM networks), and these are consistent with the time-phased budget plan. With an integrated system, changes in any portion will be accurately reflected in all other system documents.

Examples of typical milestones from various industries include:

- System specifications approved.
- Preliminary design released.
- Prototype material list issued.
- Brassboard tested.
- Printed circuit card design released.
- Mechanical cabinet design verified.
- Wire list released.
- Test specifications completed and submitted.

- System integration drawings issued.
- Unit requirements defined.
- Unit coding completed.
- Unit released.
- Unit's integration completed.

A common characteristic of all earned value techniques, whether for discrete effort, apportioned effort, or for level of effort, is that earned value must be calculated consistent with the method selected during baseline establishment. The various rules discussed so far are not some arbitrary requirements, but relate to the need to avoid false variances. Work must be planned and earned consistently. The intent is to be able to identify true variances that require management attention, which allows early corrective action so that no significant problems occur. If the explanation for variances were frequent, "it is a system glitch", it will not take long before the system loses its credibility.

There are many possible examples of inconsistent earned value technique application. If a work package were planned using the 0/100 technique, but earned value is credited using the 50/50 technique, a false indication of status is reported. There will be earned value when the activity starts (using the 50/50), but no credit was planned until completion (using the 0/100 technique). That means status will appear to be favorable. In other words, the work will appear to be ahead of schedule when all that happened was a misapplication of an earned value technique.

In the discussion of each earned value technique, note that actual costs are not included in the calculations. It is not necessary to know what has been expended in order to assess or calculate earned value.

Incremental Milestone Technique

This earned value technique is generally used when discrete work packages exceed two months in duration. At least one milestone per month is desirable, but a single month may have more than one milestone. As before, each milestone is well defined and has a budget that is a portion of the whole work package budget. Milestones must be objective and product-oriented as opposed to arbitrary points in time. An example of incremental milestones is shown in Figure 29-2. Each of the four milestones is assigned a value corresponding to the budget associated with accomplishment of that milestone.

Milestone	Budget
1	300
2	1,200
3	1,200
4	600
Totals	3,300

Figure 29-2 Incremental Milestone - Planning

Claiming earned value with this technique is shown in Figure 29-3. The darkened triangles indicate accomplishment of milestones 1 and 2 which allows earning the budget for those milestones. Milestone #1 (300 budget) and milestone #2 (1,200 budget) equals the earned value for completed work of 1,500. The budget assigned to the milestone is earned when it is accomplished. With this technique, there is no partial credit for being "almost" done. Budget values for each milestone are planned in the period they are to be accomplished and earned value is recorded in the period they are actually accomplished.

Milestone	Budget	Earned Value
1	300	300
2	1,200	1,200
3	1,200	0
4	600	0
Totals	3,300	1,500

Figure 29-3 Incremental Milestone - Status

Milestones should represent verifiable events. Since completion criteria are established in advance, there should be no question whether a milestone is complete or not. The milestones should be in sequential order of how the work is to be accomplished.

Examples of incremental milestones for constructing a concrete wall might be "forms completed," "concrete placement completed," and "forms stripped." Incremental milestones for pipe installation might be "pipe delivered on site," "pipe placed," "welding completed," "hangers and supports completed," "valves installed," "insulation installed," and "hydrostatic testing completed." For software development, incremental milestones could include "200 lines of code written," "code tested," and "integration of code with project."

Incremental milestones can be readily applied to engineering projects as well. Progress on activities such as specification preparation will usually be tracked by events like "specification completed and approved," "issued for review and comment," "comments incorporated," and "final specification approved and issued." The same type of milestones can be defined for engineering design drawings or studies. Since these events typically are tracked anyway, putting a weighted value on completion of each of these milestones allows the application of incremental milestones to engineering.

There are other factors to consider as well. On one engineering project, all of the milestones seemed to be scheduled, with regularity, for the last working day of the month. When this is done consistently, there is a strong possibility of distortions in earned value reporting. If the person who had to approve a large drawing package before it was issued was on vacation or otherwise indisposed, it could slip from one month to the next, along with all of its earned value credit. What usually happened was that there would be a month of very substandard performance followed by a month of extraordinary performance. The next month would once again be a similar cycle. When the monthly trend line for project status began to look like a sawtooth curve, it became apparent that the way the milestones were scheduled resulted in two months of progress followed by a month of almost no progress, followed once again by double progress. While it was true that drawings were periodically being issued late, being a day or two late on a ten year project had little or no consequence. But, this was causing such distortion that reporting was changed so that only cumulative performance was reviewed.

50/50 Technique

This earned value technique is used when work packages are two consecutive accounting months or less in duration. The 50/50 technique is typically used when the work package begins in one reporting period and completes in the next one. There are two milestones: start and complete. Each of these events has criteria to define its accomplishment. This technique is best used when the effort consists of several short operations and calculation can be accomplished cost effectively.

Figure 29-4 illustrates a planning example. The total budget for this work package is 1,000.

Milestone	Budget
1	500
2	500
Total	1,000

Start — Complete

Figure 29-4 50% / 50% - Planning

A start and completion milestone have been indicated, with each milestone valued at one half (50%) of the total budget, or 500.

The 50/50 technique resembles the incremental milestone technique, except that there are only two milestones, they are always start and completion events and they have equally weighted values. The actual start results in 50% of the budget being earned while the remaining 50% is earned at completion. This is shown in Figure 29-5.

Earned value, as required, is credited the same way in which it is planned. There is no way of accumulating credit between the start and finish dates, and that is why it should be limited to tasks planned to take place over no more than two consecutive reporting periods.

Milestone	Budget	Earned Value
1	500	500
2	500	0
Total	1,000	500

Start — Complete

Figure 29-5 50% / 50% - Status

For software development, the starting event might be "initiate programming of one screen of code" and the completion event might be "one screen of code ready for test." For engineering, it might include a short engineering study. The start and completion dates of the study would initiate the earned value credit.

One of the major problems with 50/50 planning is to control inappropriate use. Frequently, the 50/50 approach has been selected as the earned value technique for an effort that is a minimum of two months long. The effort starts, 50% of the total budget is credited as earned value, and then progress halts. If no work progress were made and the completion date slips for another five months, there is still 50% earned value credit in the system. If other tasks are initiated in the next reporting period that earned value credit will obscure the fact that the first task did not complete as planned. From an earned value standpoint, everything is still on schedule. The problem is obvious: start enough tasks and nothing need be finished for many months and there will be no early warning of potential schedule impact from the system reports.

In order to minimize problems with the 50/50 technique, variants of that technique such as 25/75 or 40/60 can be used. All of these choices would be a result of the planning process and their application is the same. All would span two months but the division of budget would be based on the budget plan for the start and finish milestone. If approximately 25 percent of the budget were estimated for the first milestone, it would be more accurate to use a 25/75 technique.

0/100 Technique

Unlike the 50/50 technique, the 0/100 earned value technique allows no earned value until the task is actually complete. This prevents the problem described in the previous paragraphs. This planning technique would be strictly limited to work packages that are planned to start and complete within the same reporting period. No earned value credit is recognized until the work package is complete, and then it is all earned. Once again, the completion criteria must be clearly identified. Examples would include receipt of small valves or hydrostatic testing of tanks or pipe.

Hydrostatic testing is a perfect application of the 0/100 technique. This is true not only because of the short duration of such a task, but also because it makes sense from a work accomplishment standpoint. With a 24-hour hydrostatic test, for example, the work is not really 96% complete if there are no leaks after the first 23 hours. If a leak develops in that last hour, the test must be redone from the beginning after necessary repairs are completed. In other words, the work is 0% complete until it is 100% complete.

The same could be applied to testing new software programming. Until the test has been satisfactorily performed, there is no end product. Remember that one of the important considerations when selecting earned value techniques is to evaluate what best reflects the nature of the work and its accomplishment.

An example of 0/100 planning is illustrated in Figure 29-6. A statused 0/100 work package is shown in Figure 29-7.

Milestone	Budget
1	0
2	500
Total	500

Figure 29-6 0% / 100% - Planning

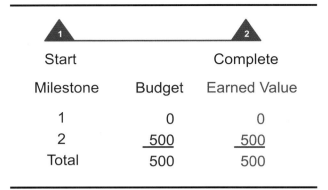

Milestone	Budget	Earned Value
1	0	0
2	500	500
Total	500	500

Figure 29-7 0% / 100% - Status

Units Complete Technique

This technique is used when physical counts of products or completed output are the usual status measurement. This includes feet of cable installed, feet of pipe installed, cubic yards of concrete poured, cubic yards of earth moved, tons of steel erected, square feet of platform erected, number of electrical terminations made, etc. All of those examples are from the construction industry where this technique is most frequently used. It also applies equally well in the manufacturing industry, where numbers of units completed, brassboards installed, tests performed, etc. are normal accounting of status.

It can just as readily be applied in the software development industry with number of lines of code programmed or function points completed used as a measure. Quantities planned to be completed by reporting period must first be determined. A monthly reporting period is assumed in this example. Planned accomplishment need not be linear, and usually will not be linear. Next, a relationship between quantity installed and budgeted value must be established. In this case, it has been determined that the budgeted value to complete a foot of installation is $100. This unit value is then applied against the number of units planned for each month. January, with a planned accomplishment of 1,500 feet, will thus have a budget of 1,500 feet X $100/foot = $150,000 for that month.

In a similar manner, the budget for each month can be determined. The total amount of work to be completed (6,700 feet in this example) and the total budget ($670,000) must be related by the per unit value of work (i.e. $100 per foot). The planning for this technique is exhibited in Figure 29-8.

Month	January	February	March	April	Total
Budget Feet	1,500	2,000	2,200	1,000	6,700
Budget @ $100 per foot	$150,000	$200,000	$220,000	$100,000	$670,000

Figure 29-8 Units Complete - Planning

An example of how credit is earned using the "units complete" technique is displayed in Figure 29-9. Note that the earned value is always based on the quantity completed times the budgeted rate per unit, and not based on the planned quantity to be completed. So when 1,000 feet were completed in January, the earned value was based on $100/foot X 1,000 feet = $100,000. That 1,500 feet were planned to be accomplished does not figure in the calculation of earned value. Remember, the budgeted value of each unit is used and not the actual cost. Whether the 1,000 feet completed in January actually cost $87.50 per foot or $175 per foot has no bearing on the determination of earned value.

Month	January	February	March	April	Total
Budget Feet	1,500	2,000	2,200	1,000	6,700
Budget @ $100 per foot	$150,000	$200,000	$220,000	$100,000	$670,000
Quantity Installed	1,000	2,000	2,000	1,700	6,700
Earned @ $100 per foot	$100,000	$200,000	$200,000	$170,000	$670,000

Figure 29-9 Units Complete - Status

Units complete is a natural application of earned value to any project that results in the production or installation of a quantity of homogeneous products. These products may be PC boards, Computer Software Configuration Item (CSCI), automobiles, CD players, audio cassettes, engines, or design drawing counts. It is also a natural application in the construction industry for

a number of reasons. For one, installation of large quantities requires many months to accomplish and the earned value techniques presented so far do not apply well. Secondly, construction projects have always tracked quantities installed versus quantities scheduled on quantity installation curves. It is a simple matter to define a budgeted value for each unit installed and then multiply that by the quantities completed. For activities that have significant time consuming preparatory tasks, such as pipe installation, a better method is to use the Equivalent Units Technique described next. Both of these techniques are frequently used for earned value determination on construction or manufacturing projects.

Equivalent Units Technique

This method is used for work packages that contain a series of like units with repetitive operations, with planning based on unit standards, standard hours and pay points. It is the most detailed method for earned value determination. The plan is based on planned completions; the earned value is based on actual completions.

There is a fine difference between equivalent units and units complete. Five equivalent units may be complete but there may not be five finished units. Five equivalent units may relate to 10 part As, 10 part Bs, 7 part Cs, and 2 part Ds. On units complete, there are physically five finished products when five units are reported complete.

The equivalent units method is frequently used in a manufacturing environment and is based on the operations that go into making up one unit of a product. It is also used in construction for work activities that include many different steps as part of the installation. It applies best on any project that consists of many repetitive operations.

The key to this earned value technique is to divide the process into small component steps that occur between milestones. Milestones are typically considered to be major events. As events are subdivided ever smaller between the milestones, it is possible to identify "yard-stones," "foot-stones," and even "inch-stones."

When the equivalent units earned value technique is used in manufacturing, it is operating on the "inch-stone" level. The following example illustrates how this technique could be applied in the production environment. The sample project consists of the manufacture and delivery of a large number of sealed electronic component units. The number of completed units would be counted if the "units complete" earned value technique were used. However, with the "equivalent units" technique, the manufacture of a single unit is divided into its component processes ("inch-stones") and the relative value of each of these steps determined. An example of the weighted values for each step in the process might look like:

Step	Weight
1. Fabricate brassboard	30%
2. Complete wiring	30%
3. Test electrical circuit	15%
4. Install cover	15%
5. Seal unit	10%
Total Weight	**100%**

These percentages are based on industrial engineering standards which indicate that historical studies have shown that installing the unit cover, for example, requires 15% of the total cost of the unit. For developing the plan, the next step is to determine how many units, per month, would be in each step of the process.

Quantity	Jan	Feb	Mar	Apr	May
@ step 1	600	700	800	1000	1000
@ step 2	500	600	750	1000	1000
@ step 3	300	500	600	900	1000
@ step 4	100	300	400	700	1000
@ step 5	0	100	200	600	1000

Next, the planned value of each monthly reporting period would be determined. A sample calculation for the month of January follows.

January Planned Accomplishment

600 units @ step 1 X 30% credit =
180 equivalent units complete

500 units @ step 2 X 30% credit =
150 equivalent units complete

300 units @ step 3 X 15% credit =
45 equivalent units complete

100 units @ step 4 x 15% credit =
15 equivalent units complete

0 units @ step 5 X 10% credit =
0 equivalent units complete

Total planned accomplishment in January:
390 equivalent units complete

There are several points to note about this plan. At the end of January, the plan is to actually have zero units physically complete and ready to ship. Nevertheless, much time and effort will have been expended in preparing 600 of the units for eventual shipment. From a budget standpoint, effort equivalent to finishing 390 units will be expended, according to the plan, in January. The same type of calculations would then be performed for each of the succeeding months. When it is time to calculate May, the situation looks like this:

1,000 units @ step (1) x 30% credit =
300 equivalent units complete

1,000 units @ step (2) x 30% credit =
300 equivalent units complete

1,000 units @ step (3) x 15% credit =
150 equivalent units complete

1,000 units @ step (4) x 15% credit =
150 equivalent units complete

1,000 units @ step (5) x 10% credit =
100 equivalent units complete

The plan is to have 1,000 equivalent units complete at the end of May. At the end of May, 1,000 units are physically complete. This must always be true: equivalent units complete and actual units complete are equal at the completion of the associated work effort.

A budgeted value for each unit is needed before we are complete. Assume that the total budget for producing these 1,000 units is $200,000. That means each unit has a budgeted value of $200. This value would then be applied to the equivalent units calculation. So the planned budget accomplishment for January is 390 X $200/unit = $78,000.

When it is time to determine status for earned value reporting at the end of January, it is important to count how many units are actually at each step in the process. For example, at the end of January, 705 units are at step (1), 450 are at step (2), 128 are at step (3), 75 are at step (4), and 16 are at step (5). The earned value status would be calculated as follows:

705 units @ step (1) x 30% credit =
211.5 equivalent units complete

450 units @ step (2) x 30% credit =
135 equivalent units complete

128 units @ step (3) x 15% credit =
19.2 equivalent units complete

75 units @ step (4) x 15% credit =
11.3 equivalent units complete

16 units @ step (5) x 10% credit =
1.6 equivalent units complete

Total equivalent units complete:
378.6

The earned value for this work accomplishment expressed in dollars would be 378.6 x $200 = $75,720. Note that some units were actually completed ahead of the plan in January (16 completed versus 0 planned).

A similar approach could be applied to software coding by counting lines of code completed and assigning a complexity factor to the lines. A software program consisting of 1,000 lines of code may be categorized by degree of difficulty:

500 lines "easy" x 0.8 =
400 equivalent lines of code

400 lines "moderate" x 1.0 =
400 equivalent lines of code

100 lines "difficult" x 2.0 =
200 equivalent lines of code

While the total lines of code is fixed (1,000), the budgeted value for different categories of difficulty may vary. If coding classified as "moderate" is valued at $100 per line, then the example states a budgeted value of $80 per line for "easy" code and $200 per line for "difficult" code. However, one equivalent line of code is worth $100, and we can value the lines as they are planned and completed much like the manufacturing example above. The completion of 100 lines of "easy" coding would be valued as 80 equivalent lines @ $100 per line = $80 earned value.

Equivalent units has also been used in construction for cases such as pipe installation, because there are many steps of partial completion before a pipe is considered finished. As many as ten steps of partial budget credit have been used for pipe installation.

Percent Complete Technique

The least desirable of the discrete earned value techniques is the Percent Complete method. The reason that this is the least desirable is that it is a subjective measure of status and objective status measures provide more definitive assessment. With this method, the plan is developed by forecasting what the percent complete will be at the end of each month and then applying that percentage against the approved Budget at Completion to determine the planned accomplishment. It works like this on a cumulative basis for a control account with an approved budget of 5,000 labor hours:

Month	Cumulative % Complete Planned	Planned Accomplishment
January	10%	500 hours
February	30%	1,500 hours
March	50%	2,500 hours
April	65%	3,250 hours
May	90%	4,500 hours
June	100%	5,000 hours

The problem with this can be seen by referring to the examples in Figure 29-10 and Figure 29-11. Figure 29-10 shows the plan for the Percent Complete earned value technique while Figure 29-11 also depicts the earned value through the status date.

In Figure 29-10, there are two milestones, the start (January 3) and completion (April 25), and a total budget at completion 785. The spread of budget between those two milestones has no apparent basis. There is no objective way of verifying the validity of the plan or the accuracy of the reported status shown in Figure 29-11.

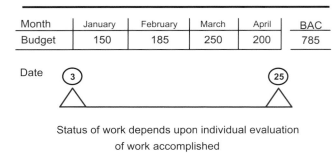

Month	January	February	March	April	BAC
Budget	150	185	250	200	785

Date ③   ㉕

Status of work depends upon individual evaluation of work accomplished

Figure 29-10 Percent Complete - Planning

Month	January	February	March	April	BAC
Budget	150	185	250	200	785
Earned Value	150	150			

Status Date

Date ③   ㉕

Status of work evaluated as a percentage of the budget. As of the status date 335 was planned while 300 was earned.

Figure 29-11 Percent Complete - Status

In both Figure 29-10 and in the example of the time-phased distribution of labor hour budget shown above, there should be a number of questions before accepting this plan. These might include:

1. What is the basis for the percentages planned over time? Are they based on historical records? Do the same conditions apply on this project?

2. How will status be determined? What objective criteria will there be to support the reported completion percentages?

3. Can this work be tied to some form of product counts (such as drawings, specifications, electrical terminations, lines of code)?

Each month, the person providing status for the work package makes an assessment of progress by estimating what percent of the total job has been completed. This percent is applied to the budget at completion to arrive at the current earned value, just as is shown above for the planning stage. This method is not encouraged because it is subjective and one of the goals of

earned value is to keep measurement objective. The selection of this technique is limited to situations when the following conditions exist:

1. Long duration (3 months or more) work package.

2. No possible milestones to measure progress.

3. No quantities to count.

An example may be a long engineering study, when there are no intermediate products and the amount of work to be performed depends on intermediate findings.

The potential problems with the use of this earned value technique are many. Besides the concern about a lack of objectivity, it tends to be applied on long term, high budget tasks. This means the cost and schedule exposure is greater than with most other tasks using the previously described techniques. People are not trained to fail, and so there is a natural tendency to report status "on schedule" during most of the task regardless of the real progress or lack thereof. This prevents potential concerns from surfacing early, when they can most easily be rectified.

A related concern is that the person reporting status also is typically aware of how much cost has been applied to the task. This increases the temptation to report progress equivalent to the expenditures to date. This quickly becomes the "budget versus actual cost" approach that was previously discredited.

In order to mitigate problems with this method, there are generally requirements that the control account manager responsible for the work prepare objective criteria, referred to as quantifiable backup data (QBD) or metrics, that define the detail of the work and the budget associated with each detail. The QBD are kept by the CAM and used to provide the monthly earned value. These quantifiable backup data can be informal and are maintained by the CAM; however, they are part of the plan and under change control.

The number of earned value techniques used varies in every organization. Some will claim they use far more than the six discrete techniques described here, but other techniques are variations of these techniques.

Apportioned Effort

Other methods are used for work packages that do not lend themselves to the discrete techniques. The first of these is "apportioned effort." The apportioned effort method is used when certain activities are performed in direct support of other direct activities. Inspection is the most typical example of this method. The amount of items to be inspected is directly dependent on the number of items that are produced. Because of this, inspection is estimated and planned as a percentage of the production effort. Planned and actual accomplishment is calculated as a percent of the planned and actual accomplishment earned by the prime work package(s).

Other examples of apportioned effort include final assembly testing, reliability testing, and subcontract liaison. To use this method, there must be a way to establish the percent of inspection to production. In the example shown in Figure 29-12, 10% of production cost is planned for inspection each month.

Inspection estimated as 10% of related production Control Account

	Budget		Earned	
	Production Control Account	Inspection Control Account	Production Control Account	Inspection Control Account
June	200	20	150	15
July	500	50	450	45
Aug	100	10	150	15
Total	800	80	750	75

Figure 29-12 Apportioned Effort - Planning and Status

In June, the production control account has a budget of 200. The associated apportioned effort account, the inspection control account, is therefore calculated as 10% of 200, or 20. Computing the earned value is also straightforward. The same percentage (10%) is applied to what actually happens in the production control account. Therefore, when 150 earned value is credited in the production control account for June, the earned value for the apportioned effort account is determined as 10% of 150, or 15. There must be

some historical basis for the allocation, whether it be 10% or some other value.

Once the percentage allocation is determined and entered into the project management software program, there is no requirement for further planning or status reporting by the person responsible for that control account. This is true because the plan is developed, even time-phased, by automatic calculation from the direct account on which it is based. System software can easily be programmed to apply the predetermined percentage allocation based on the direct control account to calculate the associated apportioned effort control account plan. The same is true for status reporting. As the base direct account is statused, the associated earned value credit for the apportioned effort account can be automatically calculated.

Level of Effort

Certain tasks are difficult to quantify in terms of work accomplished. These tasks are referred to as Level of Effort (LOE) and have the following characteristics:

1. General or supportive activities.

2. No definite or deliverable product.

3. Budget is scheduled over the period of performance.

4. Earned value is based on the passage of time.

5. By definition, earned value equals planned accomplishment.

Level of Effort activities are those that typically have no associated technical end product. These include project management, contract administration, field support engineers, supervision of any type, and clerical support (if not included in the overhead rate).

There are some unusual characteristics from an earned value standpoint. Because earnings, by definition, always equal budget, there will never be any schedule variance. However, there could be a cost variance. Figure 29-13 shows that the time phased budget does not have to be linear. Figure 29-14 shows monthly status; this is always the same as the budget and depicts an on schedule condition.

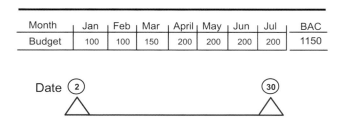

Month	Jan	Feb	Mar	April	May	Jun	Jul	BAC
Budget	100	100	150	200	200	200	200	1150

Date ②   ㉚

Figure 29-13 Level of Effort (LOE) - Planning

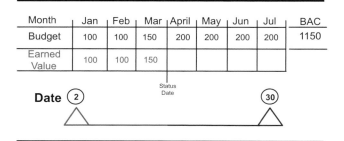

Month	Jan	Feb	Mar	April	May	Jun	Jul	BAC
Budget	100	100	150	200	200	200	200	1150
Earned Value	100	100	150					

Status Date

Date ②   ㉚

Figure 29-14 Level of Effort (LOE) - Status

The earned value for each month will be these same as the monthly budget, but the actual cost will be whatever is charged to the LOE account. If staffing buildup occurred faster than anticipated, with 200 in March instead of the 150 planned, there would be an unfavorable cost variance of (50).

Because of some of the features of LOE, it has been the source of more than a little "game playing", or masking of data, over the years. If LOE were combined with technical products in a control account, true cost variances in the "real" work can be masked or partially offset by the LOE component. If LOE and discrete are mixed within a control account, actual cost should be collected at the work package level in order that separate variance analysis can be performed for both earned value components. If LOE were a large portion of the control account budget, a separate control account may be warranted.

Other Earned Value Techniques

The combining of the percent complete method with the incremental milestone method has become popular and is referred to as the "percent complete of milestone" or "milestone percent complete" method. This method allows taking partial credit for a milestone when the activity toward the milestone has started but has not been completed. The budget could also be spread over several months.

It is critical that the same assumptions used in planning for earned value also be used in its subsequent determination. Otherwise there are built-in system variances that have nothing to do with the real variances occurring on the project. This causes a management reporting system to be discredited before it can demonstrate its worth. This includes the creation and documentation of objective criteria for use in measuring performance when using the percent complete and "milestone percent complete" earned value techniques. This objective criteria defines what is planned to be accomplished each month and assigns a budget value to that planned accomplishment. The objective criteria defined during the planning process becomes a part of the baseline plan and is used each month to determine the earned value.

When is Earned Value Credited?

Establishing when earned value credit should be claimed for labor is simple: it is simply done when the work is accomplished. However, there are many options when it comes to claiming earned value for material, equipment, and purchased services. There are several different points in time that material, equipment, purchased services, and any other element that may be paid in a different accounting period can be meaningfully measured. For major items, such as for large pieces of manufactured equipment, one of the best methods is to take credit as progress payments are made. If the contract were correctly defined, the payments will be based on actual physical progress. Milestones are developed based on planned progress, and then payments (and earned value) are awarded as they are accomplished. Refer to Chapter 31, "Collecting Actual Cost," for more information regarding recording actual cost in the same accounting period as earned value is claimed.

For large items that do not have a long fabrication process, a typical place to take earned value is at time of material receipt. "Material receipt" implies more than just the physical presence of the material; it assumes it has been received, inspected and accepted. An additional point in time for taking credit for material is at time of installation or usage. This is especially appropriate for items that are to be fabricated and erected on site after receipt. Examples would be cooling towers, precipitators, and large chimneys. Using this approach, the material receives earned value credit at the same time as the labor for installing the material does.

Bulk items can be measured at two different points: receipt or usage. Point of receipt is a good measurement point if it were used within a short period of time and does not sit in inventory. Point of usage makes more sense as the credit point if the item will be kept in inventory longer than one accounting period; some argue that 60 days should be the limit for holding in inventory. Some material systems award credit when material is removed from inventory rather than when it is received or used. In these situations, the assumption is that the material will be used soon after withdrawal from inventory.

One of the reasons that there may be a large time frame between material delivery and usage is management's desire to provide comfortable lead times for manufacturing or construction. There is an associated trade-off involved with building in schedule float between when material is required at the facility and when it is actually intended to be used. In the case of manufacturing, it may mean the need for a larger warehouse to store excess material. In construction, it will mean the need for a larger "laydown" area for material/equipment storage. This may be judged a small expense for the insurance of having supplies when they are needed so that work is not delayed.

Other Comments

The question is sometimes asked, "Why bother with earned value for material?" The value of objectively determining progress for labor is obvious: the accomplishment of the work is an ongoing process and it is possible to affect the outcome of the project by taking appropriate management steps early in the performance of the work. Whether these steps were successful or not can also be evaluated based on the measurable outcome of the change in direction. However, the control of material costs actually occurs at the time of the bidding process. Once the specification requirements have been determined, the cost control consists of soliciting multiple bids and evaluating those bids for the lowest cost alternative. Subsequent actions are record keeping only, since the material/equipment cost control actions have already been taken.

It is important to be able to forecast final costs of a contract and of a project, and material and equipment costs may constitute as much as 65% of the total project cost. There needs to be some measure of how material costs are faring against the budget and how much of any variance is because of quantity variations versus unit cost variations. The methodology of earned value provides a scorekeeping capability for the material costs as well as the labor costs and allows a better forecasting of final costs. The isolation of each of these components can be calculated as discussed in Chapter 32, "Performance Measurement Calculations and Estimates at Completion."

Conclusion

Control accounts are composed of work packages which is the level at which performance is planned and earned value is credited. A work package has specific defining characteristics. The way that earned value is planned and credited depends on whether the work is directly measurable ("discrete"), based on the amount of effort in some other direct account ("apportioned effort"), or whether it is a function of project duration ("level of effort"). There is one option for applying earned value to apportioned effort or level of effort activities, but there is a wide range of choices for measuring discrete activities. The method selected depends on the duration of the activity, the nature of the work, and whether or not there is a quantity of like work products. Earned value techniques are applied to labor, material and other direct costs.

Chapter 29 Review Questions

29-1.   What is a work package?

29-2.   Where does the work package fit within the framework of the Work Breakdown Structure?

29-3.   What are the important characteristics of a work package?

29-4.   Give an example of a work package.

29-5.   Identify the three types of work measurement.

29-6.   Name the six earned value methods used for measuring discrete effort.

29-7.   Which earned value methods used for measuring discrete effort should not be used for work packages that are three months long or longer?

29-8.   For work packages such as inspection or testing that directly relate to the number of items being produced or inspected, what earned value technique would be an appropriate application?

29-9.   When is earned value credit taken for labor?

29-10.   When is earned value credit taken for material, equipment, and/or purchased services?

True or False

29-11.   It is at the work package level that cost and schedule should be formally tied together.

29-12.   A work package contains a series of control accounts.

29-13.   Actual costs must be captured at the work package level so that meaningful variance analysis can be performed.

29-14.   The Equivalent Units earned value technique is a further refinement of the Units Complete technique.

29-15.   Because the earned value for a Level of Effort control account, by definition, always equals budget, there will never be any cost variance or schedule variance.

29-16.   When the Apportioned Effort earned value technique is used, it will always reflect a negative schedule variance if the direct account it is related to also has a negative schedule variance.

29-17.   Variations of the earned value techniques described in this chapter are possible by allowing partial percent complete between incremental milestones or by varying the start and completion values of the 50/50 technique.

The answers to these questions can be found in Section 6, Solutions.

Case Study

29.1 CONTROL ACCOUNT PLAN EXERCISE 1

Scenario

Thadeus Kowolski is a project engineer on the MOR-DED Project. One of the tasks he has been assigned is the development of the transmission for the motor scooter. While Thad is renowned throughout Cushperson for his engineering ability, he is not too sharp at what he calls "bean counting." You have been assigned to assist Thad in developing his control account plan.

Thad has identified eight tasks or work packages involved in developing the transmission. He has estimated the time phased resources for each work package and described particular events that take place in the work packages in exhibit 1. He would like you to establish the proper work in process (WIP) earned value technique and record them in exhibit 2. The system used at Cushperson allows the following types of earned value methods:

1. Level of Effort
2. Milestone
3. 50/50
4. 0/100
5. Percent Complete
6. Units Complete
7. Apportioned Effort

EXHIBIT 1 - TASK PLANNING SHEET

TASK DESCRIPTION	Total Resources	A	M	J	J	A	S	O	N	D	J	F	M
1. Engineering Management for the total effort (Mr. Kowolski)	3,800	Start ▽ 500	500	500	500	500	500	200	200	200	Complete ▽ 200		
2. Design Transmission	20,000	Start Conceptual Design ▽ 4,000	Initial Concept Complete ▽ 5,000	Initial Draft Complete ▽ 6,000	Final Approval ▽ 5,000								
3. Draft 18 Drawings, roughly 6 released per month	9,000			Start First Drawing ▽ 3,000	3,000	Final Release ▽ 3,000							
4. Tooling Fabrication	4,000					Start ▽ 2,000	Complete ▽ 2,000						
5. Engineering Liaison with Tooling & Manufacturing	6,000					Start ▽ 1,000	1,000	2,000	Complete ▽ 2,000				
6. Manufacture Model 1	34,000							Start ▽ 17,000	Complete ▽ 17,000				
7. Quality Inspection of Model 1	3,000							Start ▽ 1,500	Complete ▽ 1,500				
8. Conduct Developmental Test on Model 1	5,000										Start ▽ Complete ▽ 5,000		
Total Resources	**84,800**	4,500	5,500	9,500	8,500	6,500	3,500	20,700	20,700	200	5,200		

Transmission Design Control Account Plan

Exhibit 2 – Transmission Design Control Account Plan

(1) Work Package	(2) WIP	(3) Value		A	M	J	J	A	S	O	N	D	J	F	M
1. Engineering Management		3,800	BCWS	▷									▷		
			BCWP												
			ACWP												
2. Design Transmission		20,000	BCWS	▷	▷	▷	▷								
			BCWP												
			ACWP												
3. Draft 18 Drawings		9,000	BCWS				▷	▷							
			BCWP												
			ACWP												
4. Tooling		4,000	BCWS					▷	▷						
			BCWP												
			ACWP												
5. Engineering Liaison		6,000	BCWS					▷			▷				
			BCWP												
			ACWP												
6. Manufacture Model 1		34,000	BCWS						▷		▷				
			BCWP												
			ACWP												
7. Quality Inspection of Model 1		3,000	BCWS						▷		▷				
			BCWP												
			ACWP												
8. Conduct Developmental Test		5,000	BCWS									▷	▷		
			BCWP												
			ACWP												
Incremental			BCWS												
			BCWP												
			ACWP												
Cumulative			BCWS												
			BCWP												
			ACWP												

WIP Types 1) Level Of Effort 2) Milestone 3) 50/50 4) 0/100 5) Percent Complete 6) Units Complete 7) Apportioned Effort

Chapter **30**

Establishing the Performance Measurement Baseline

Objectives of this Chapter:

1. Define what a performance measurement baseline (PMB) is and explain its function.

2. Describe the summary steps involved in establishment of a PMB.

3. Explain the concept of "rolling wave" planning and how this is applied to long duration projects.

4. Illustrate how total project budget is categorized for project management purposes.

5. Explain that the budgeting process is more than just development of a single value - it must be a time-phased dollar value.

The steps involved in establishing a schedule baseline were presented in prior chapters. At that point, they were presented as part of the Planning and Scheduling portion of the overall project management flowchart. It was mentioned at that time that the schedule baseline serves as the basis for development of the cost baseline as well. Now it is time to incorporate the cost portion of the plan into a single comprehensive baseline, called the "performance measurement baseline" (PMB). This is the integrated plan that has been the goal since the first chapter of this book. Its aim is to unify technical scope, schedule, and budget into an overall plan that will be used to monitor and control all aspects of the project. Use of the term "baseline" in this chapter refers to the PMB.

Performance Measurement Baseline Development

A performance-oriented approach requires that baseline plans be developed from the scheduling, estimating and budgeting efforts, and perfor-

mance measured against the plan. This plan is known as the performance measurement baseline, or PMB. Figure 30-2 depicts the PMB as the planned expenditures over time to perform the authorized scope of work.

The process of establishing a schedule baseline was presented earlier in the text. Since it was a resource loaded and leveled schedule, that baseline becomes the primary input to the establishment of the overall project performance plan.

This plan is formally known as the **performance measurement baseline**. In his book, Fundamentals of Project Performance Measurement, Robert R. Kemps defines PMB as follows:

"The time-phased budget plan against which contract performance is measured. It is formed by the budgets assigned to control accounts and the applicable indirect budgets. For future effort, not planned to the control account level, the performance measurement baseline also includes budgets assigned to higher level CWBS elements and

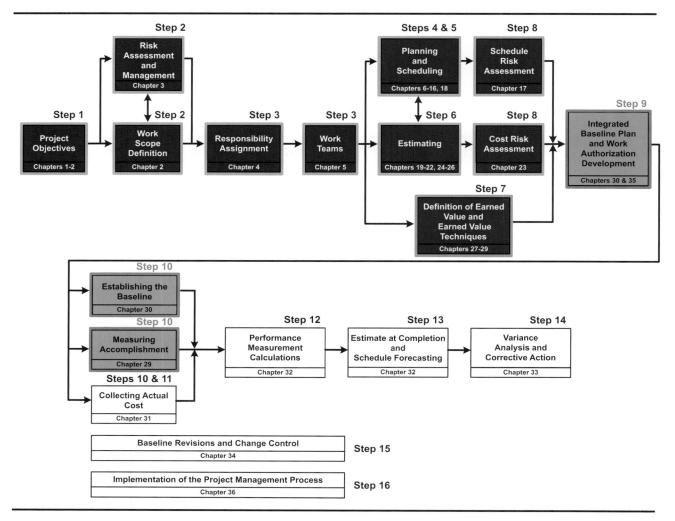

Figure 30-1 Earned Value Project Management: The Process

undistributed budgets. It equals the total allocated budget less management reserve."[1]

A summary explanation of the steps involved in overall baseline establishment includes:

1. Definition of the work scope. This is accomplished within the Work Breakdown Structure and associated WBS Dictionary.

2. Establishment of a high level schedule for accomplishing the same work. This includes the primary schedule objectives of the project and a summary level schedule of activities and events required to support those objectives.

3. Estimation of the resources required to accomplish the work.

4. Incorporation of the information from the scope of work and estimate into a detailed schedule (plan). The resources in the estimate should be used as a basis for the activity durations in the schedule.

5. Once the resources for accomplishing the work have been identified and time-phased, dollars can be assigned to determine the total project baseline. This includes all costs: labor, material, equipment, subcontracts, other direct costs, overhead and indirect costs, and expenses.

1. Kemps, Robert R. *Fundamentals of Project Performance Measurement, Sixth Edition*. Orange, CA: Humphreys & Associates, Inc., 2011.

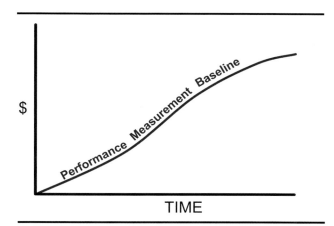

Figure 30-2 Performance Measurement Baseline

Many iterations are involved in baseline establishment. The schedule is needed for development of the escalation costs and duration of Level of Effort costs in the estimate, but the estimate is needed for determining the durations for schedule activities. Both schedule and estimate rely heavily on an exact definition of the technical scope of work. Constant cross-checking between scope, schedule, and budget is required to ensure that all components of the baseline are consistent. Since the schedule is typically developed at a lower level of detail than the scope of work, the likelihood exists that information will also flow backwards from the schedule to the scope document as work is further defined during the iterative planning process. Questions will arise during schedule preparation regarding detailed work products that were not considered in the statement of work. The entire task of baseline (PMB) establishment could be a vehicle for improved project team communication regarding project objectives and details for accomplishing those objectives.

One of the difficulties of establishing a baseline for a long duration effort is that exact work details for many years in the future cannot possibly be known at the time of initial baseline establishment. There is no option to wait for such minutiae to establish a baseline since progress cannot be assessed and managed until one is established. The other problem is that it takes a significant amount of time to establish a large project's baseline. One of the greatest challenges occurs when there is a lack of adequate detail in the statement of work.

Rolling Wave Planning

The "rolling wave" concept recognizes that at the time of initial planning that there may be a lack of detail in the statement of work for future activities. Rolling wave integrates two approaches to developing a plan: top-down and bottom-up. Bottom-up consists of developing all of the specific requirements at the lowest possible level and then summarizing that information upwards for use in the total project plan and budget. This would be used for near term activities and would be described in specific work packages within the control account. Top-down planning, as its name suggests, would be used for higher level planning for far term activities that presently lack specific detailed scope. These would also be defined within the control account but not in specific work packages. Instead, this scope and budget would be allocated to planning packages that are scheduled in the future. As more information becomes available with the passage of time, the planning packages would be converted to one or more detailed work packages. This merging of the top-down with the bottom-up approach is called rolling wave. Conceptually, this would look like Figure 30-3.

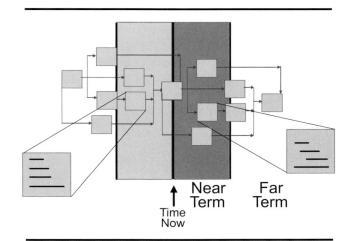

Figure 30-3 Rolling Wave Example 1

Another concept that may be used, especially on larger projects, is the summary level planning package (SLPP). These are elements of scope and budget that are assigned to higher level WBS or OBS levels but are not yet identifiable to a specific control account. The scope of work and budget for these SLPPs are time phased and the

Estimate at Completion is periodically assessed. At the earliest opportunity, at least prior to their start or in accordance with the defined "freeze period", SLPPs are assigned to control accounts to be detail planned. This can be done as a part of the rolling wave process. Summary Level Planning Packages are a part of the performance measurement baseline as shown in another Rolling Wave example in Figure 30-4.

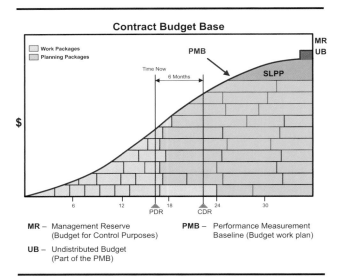

Figure 30-4 Rolling Wave Example 2

It is good practice to always have the detailed information available for at least six months in advance. This is frequently accomplished by planning nine months into the future and then expanding detail on future activities each quarter. Thus there is always expanded information for the next six to nine months. This is an effective approach to avoid unpleasant future surprises, such as the realization that material or labor resources are needed but are not available because they have not been arranged in advance.

There are other factors that go into determining the time frame for detail planning using the rolling wave concept. A major milestone, such as Preliminary Design Review (PDR) or Critical Design Review (CDR) may define the future duration of expanded detail. There may be revisions to design philosophy at these critical milestones suggesting that detailed planning beyond that point is not recommended. An inadequately defined statement of work may limit the amount of detailed planning that could occur. Another consideration relates to planning packages. When the start of a planning package moves into the window of detailed planning, near term work packages should be developed from the scope of work and budget defined in the planning package.

If establishment of a performance measurement baseline (PMB) is an extended effort because of the particular characteristics of the project, then another approach may be considered. An interim baseline could be used for the initial project work since early project work tends to be conceptual in nature, and lends itself well to independent planning. This involves establishing a near term baseline against which progress can be measured and then planning the remainder of the project.

In some cases on larger projects, baseline schedules have been developed for establishing the project baseline. This is like scheduling the activity of developing the schedule. If the process is complicated enough and takes sufficient time, this is a worthwhile effort.

Performance Measurement Baseline Structure

The distributed budget portion of the performance measurement baseline, and actual cost, is assigned to control accounts consistent with how the work was planned, with enough charge number detail to support three reporting structures. This is pictured in Figure 30-5. Every cost charge collected must be able to be assigned to a WBS element, an OBS element, and an element of cost defined within the accounting system.

This provides enough information for analysis of project costs. It is then possible to interpret costs for work products, for organizations supporting the performance of the work, and for element of cost.

The total project cost is subdivided logically, as shown in Figure 30-6 and Figure 30-7. The total contract value is divided between profit/fee and the base contract cost, or Contract Budget Base (CBB). The CBB is further subdivided between the performance measurement baseline (PMB)

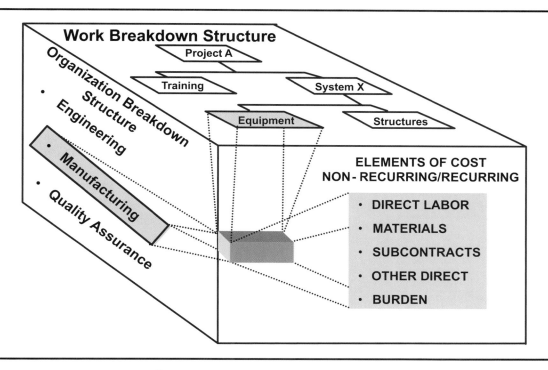

Figure 30-5 Reporting Structure Data Matrix

for known effort and the Management Reserve (MR) that is withheld for unknowns. During the life of the project, management reserve decreases as it is identified for specific in-scope applications while the PMB increases by a corresponding amount. At all times the sum of the budget in the PMB and MR equals the value defined as the Contract Budget Base (CBB). The PMB is further subdivided into distributed budget (the budget assigned for specific control accounts) and undistributed budget. Undistributed budget (UB) is budget applicable to project or contract effort that has not yet been identified to lower level WBS or OBS elements. In effect, UB is a temporary holding account. One common usage of UB occurs when an approved scope change is received late in a reporting period when there is insufficient time to allocate the scope, schedule, and budget to control accounts. Note that UB has scope defined, while Management Reserve does not.

Distributed budget is divided into control accounts as discrete effort, apportioned effort, and level of effort work packages. This is pictured in Figure 30-7. All of these work package measurement techniques were previously defined during the detailed planning process.

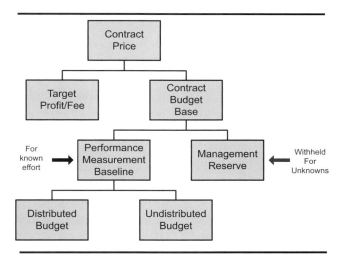

Figure 30-6 Total Project Cost Distribution

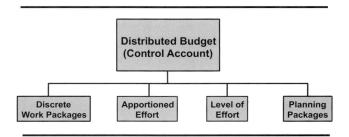

Figure 30-7 Elements of the Base and the Baseline

The remainder of distributed budget in control accounts may be assigned to planning packages that will later be converted to work packages in accordance with the rolling wave process.

Over time, Management Reserve will decrease as it is authorized to individual control accounts for additional internal scope. This is shown in Figure 30-8.

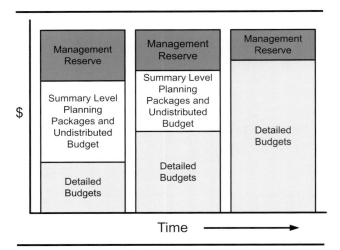

Figure 30-8 Management Reserve

Logs typically will be maintained to record the transfers of Management Reserve to the PMB, as well as the allocation of Undistributed Budget and the incorporation of contractually approved scope changes. These logs are described in Chapter 34, "Baseline Revisions and Change Control."

Some discussion about Management Reserve is needed. While some companies may use the term "project reserves" or other terminology, the concept is the same. A project reserve is not intended to cover contractual changes in scope. Nor is it part of the "undistributed budget" mentioned in the PMB definition presented earlier. Most importantly, it is not a "slush fund" to cover project management mistakes. Management Reserve is an amount of the total allocated budget withheld for management control purposes rather than designated for the accomplishment of a specific task or set of tasks. Put another way, it is part of the total project budget intended to be used to budget anticipated but not currently known or defined in-scope work. Management

reserve is essential for providing the project manager some flexibility to manage the project.

One additional point of clarification concerns the term "total allocated budget." The Total Allocated Budget, or (TAB), will always equal the Contract Budget Base (CBB) except if there were an over target baseline (OTB). An over target baseline results when a formal reprogramming of the PMB is performed because it is no longer valid for measuring performance. This condition may arise when initial approved budgets were too tight or conditions, not scope, have changed in the accomplishment of the project objectives. An OTB redefines what 100% of the project is equal to, and the Budget at Completion (BAC) is increased. This should not be confused with funding. The BAC may be revised but the funds may still be limited to the original negotiated contract amount. There must be funding for all in-scope actual cost that is invoiced by the company and approved by the customer. An OTB does not change the contract value, but actual cost still needs to be supported by funding. In this case only, the TAB does not equal the CBB. The CBB continues to be the amount for authorized work while the TAB is used for the purposes of performance measurement.

All of the budgets are entered in the Responsibility Assignment Matrix that depicts the intersection of the WBS and organization structure. This provides a detailed breakdown of the budget that can be summarized by work product or by organization. Project reserves are maintained separately, as shown in Figure 30-9.

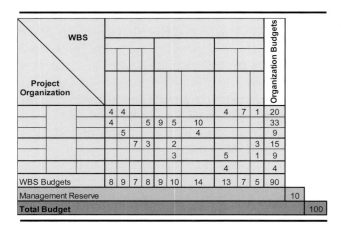

Figure 30-9 Budget Summary

Timing of the Baseline Establishment

The correct time to develop a baseline is immediately after contract award. Some bid requirements within the defense industry have gone a step further, requiring so much detailed information from the bidders that it virtually forces them to produce a baseline as part of the bidding process. While some contractors may grumble about this, since it does significantly increase the cost of bidding, a number of them have been doing just that as a form of self-preservation. On firm fixed price contracts, for example, it is too late to develop plans after contract award. A surprising, costly finding then could mean financial ruin.

Typically, there is little freedom as to when to establish the baseline as contract requirements will define those requirements. The requirement will usually direct a formal baseline submittal to the client/owner within 60-90 days after contract award. Requiring times shorter than that does a disservice to the quality of the baseline; conversely, requiring more time than 60-90 days results in other project priorities interfering with baseline development. After submittal, there is a review and approval of the baseline. A careful review of the proposed baseline by the owner assures that the client/owner and contractor mutually understand the project scope and how to best complete that scope. Points of contention should be identified and resolved at this point, before they become scope changes or claims later.

Early baseline development is also crucial because it is one of the best mechanisms for communication among project team members in the early stages of a project. It allows all of the project personnel to become more familiar with the project objectives and how they can best be accomplished. Potential difficulties and risks can be identified and addressed at this time. The baseline then serves as a formal document of the plan to accomplish the work and will be used throughout the project to measure comparative performance.

Work Authorization

Once the planning process has been completed, the work scope has been carefully defined and scheduled, budgets have been allocated, and performance measurement methods have been identified, the work must be formally authorized. On the highest level, every organization has some form of work authorization. A project must be authorized before work can be performed and actual costs charged against that project. If it were an internally managed project, then the top level work authorization may be as simple as a memorandum from executive management. If it were an external project, the process would become more formalized. The client/owner/customer organization must formally authorize the contractor to proceed. The contractor must then authorize a project manager to define and initiate the project.

At this point, it no longer matters whether it is an internally or externally managed project. The person responsible for the accomplishment of project objectives, either a project manager or a person acting in the role of project manager, will next authorize personnel to start charging time to a project work order as they pursue the accomplishment of baseline establishment, technical, schedule, and budget project objectives. Some organizations go no further than this in the work authorization process, while others continue the authorization process to a much more detailed level.

In some organizations, a project manager will issue work authorization documents to functional managers, IPT Leaders (Work Teams), or control account managers who support the performance of a project. These documents are the vehicle for the project manager to delegate the responsibility for accomplishing specific project tasks, with associated budgets and schedules, to these supporting organizations. Formal signatures may be required to indicate mutual agreement that the specific scope of work defined within the authorizing document can be accomplished within the schedule and budget objectives.

A further step that may be required is that the functional managers, who are in receipt of work authorization documents from the project man-

WORK AUTHORIZATION DOCUMENT						PAGE / OF 1 / 1		
CONTROL ACCOUNT TITLE System Test Plan/Procedures					WBS NO. 1.3.3.2		CONTROL ACCT NO. 33-8	
CONTROL ACCT MGR Peder Pederson				ORGN NO. 4000			DATE 15 May Year1	
PROGRAM NAME XYZ PILOT PRODUCTION II							REV. NO. 1	
PROGRAM NUMBER. 86-1900		CONTRACT NO. 19987563		TYPE CPIF			REV. DATE 10 Apr Year2	

SCHEDULE	REFERENCE SCHEDULE		CA BASELINE SCHEDULE		Work Authorization Status		INTERIM	
	NO. EEL-LVL1-001-R0	DATED 2 Feb Yr02	START 1 May Yr02	COMPLETE 30 Sept Yr02			FIRM	X

BUDGET (Excludes Overhead and G&A)			
HOURS AND ELEMENTS OF COST	AMOUNT AUTHORIZED		
	THIS AUTHORIZATION	PRIOR AUTHORIZATION	TOTAL AUTHORIZATION
DIRECT LABOR HOURS	900	2500	3400
CONTRACT LABOR HOURS			
TOTAL HOURS	900	2500	3400
DIRECT LABOR $	$ 51,300	$ 142,500	$ 193,800
CONTRACT LABOR $			
MATERIAL $			
SUBCONTRACT $			
OTHER DIRECT COST $			
TOTAL $	$ 51,300	$ 142,500	$ 193,800

WORK PKG CHARGE NO.	WORK STATEMENT (Include applicable reference documents/schedule dates for each item unless noted above.)
33-8101 33-8102 33-8103	Develop LP/PP test plans and procedures for test equipment, simulation equipment, system design and testing methods (IAW CDRL Item AOOB and AOOC). Develop system test plans 1000 hrs Develop system test procedures 1500 hrs Total 2500 hrs **Revision 1** Update LP/PP test plans and procedures to reflect changes in system design and testing. 900 hrs

PERFORMANCE COMMITMENT		DATE	RELEASE AUTHORITY		DATE
Control Acct Mgr	*Peder Pederson*	4/10/Year2	Cost Control	*Lars Larson*	4/12/Year2
FM/IPT Leader	*Hans Hanson*	4/10/Year2	Contract Admin	*Inga Ingabretson*	4/12/Year2
Program Functional/WBS Mgr	*Johan Johanson*	4/11/Year2	Program Mgr	*Pauline Paulson*	4/13/Year2

Figure 30-10 Work Authorization Document

ager, will issue an even lower level authorization to designated individuals who are responsible for accomplishing the work in particular control accounts. This becomes the final authority for project personnel to actually begin the detailed work. Figure 30-10 is an example of a Work Authorization Document. It contains the technical scope of work, scheduled start and completion dates of that work, and the authorized budget to perform the work.

There is symmetry to the entire project management process, one that insists that work scope, schedule, and associated budget all be consistent and integrated. If they are not, the systems will not provide the information necessary to manage the project. This is true for work authorization as well as it is for work definition, planning and budgeting, and the other project management processes.

The work authorization process assumes the availability of certain prerequisite information. Before a meaningful authorization document can be prepared, there must be a structure for a project scope of work. This is the WBS, a mechanism for identifying the project scope and relating it to the schedule, as well as for developing initial estimates and budgets, for authorizing the work and for later collection of actual costs. The WBS is accompanied by a two part document known as the WBS Dictionary. It includes a WBS Index that lists all of the WBS elements and the dictionary portion with the corresponding element descriptions. The Organization Breakdown Structure (OBS) identifies the responsibility for accomplishing the scope of work. A summary schedule is also needed with key milestones identified. Budgets are identified by WBS element and authorized accordingly. Charge numbers recognized by the accounting system are then assigned to each control account. The preparation of work authorization documents may result in revision to any of these items. These items are needed because the information for the work authorization is used as follows:

1. Work Breakdown Structure (WBS).

   The WBS defines how the work is organized. Since it serves as the framework for the integration of all project management activities, it is an essential ingredient for a work order reference.

2. Responsibility assignment from the Organization Breakdown Structure (OBS).

   The work authorization document requires a reference to the OBS for identification of who is responsible for the work. This will also allow identification of reporting relationships.

3. Scope of work.

   Reference to the WBS Dictionary will allow visibility into the specific work being authorized.

4. Schedule assignment (period of performance).

   As part of an integrated management system, the schedule must be integrated with the scope of work to be performed. This means that the schedule must be identified on the authorizing document and/or the baseline period of performance entered.

5. Budget assignment.

   When work is authorized, the associated budget for accomplishing that work must be known. This budget value must correspond with the previously referenced scope of work and schedule for completing the work.

6. Charge number assignment.

   Identifying the charge number (or numbers) for the scope of work assists in the correct collection of actual costs.

Once the work has been formally authorized (to whatever level of detail), it requires a formal change order to modify the scope of work, the schedule, and/or the budget. The change order is processed to the same level of detail as the original authorization document. This is discussed further in subsequent chapters.

Conclusion

Because of its central importance to the concept of project control, establishment of the integrated technical, schedule and budget performance measurement baseline (PMB) justifies significant time and effort in its development. Much of the processes described in this text ultimately support creation of the baseline. Each control account has its own time-phased baseline. When all of these are summed together, the time-phased baseline for the project has been established.

The performance measurement baseline consists of the work scope definition, the schedule and the budget. The schedule defines the period of performance of each work element defined in the scope and the budgets are time-phased consistent with the schedule. The scope, schedule and budget are formally authorized in a work authorization between the project manager and the person assigned responsibility for performing the work.

Chapter 30 Review Questions

30-1. Explain the purpose of the Performance Measurement Baseline (PMB).

30-2. Work packages present the work scope in detail, so how can they be used to control very long duration projects when details are not known for work to be performed years in the future?

30-3. How far into the future should detailed planning extend?

30-4. Explain the need for, and use of management reserve.

30-5. When should the performance measurement baseline be established?

True or False

30-6. The time-phased PMB is the dollar value of work that is planned to be accomplished over time.

30-7. The first step in the baseline establishment process is to develop the schedule.

30-8. A primary distinguishing characteristic between undistributed budget and management reserve is that UB has an associated scope of work, while MR does not.

30-9. The schedule baseline is a primary input to the establishment of the performance measurement baseline (PMB).

30-10. A major benefit of the work authorization document within a project is that it serves as an in-house contract between the project manager and the Control Account Manager (CAM).

The answers to these questions can be found in Section 6, Solutions.

Case Study

30.1 CONTROL ACCOUNT PLAN EXERCISE 2

Scenario

Karen was surprised when one of her group leaders on the Automated Interdiction System (AIS) Work-station Project, a Control Account Manager (CAM), called to ask her about performance measurement. All of the CAMs had been trained, and, consulting her list, she realized that Thad had missed the training. Because the program was in the front end planning stages, not much had been done with detailed planning and status. This was a perfect opportunity to get to know Thad better and to practice her EVMS class work.

Thad walked in with his Control Account Plan (CAP) in hand. Karen sat down and they began to review the plan.

Exercise

1. Using Thad's Control Account Plan (Exhibit 1), assign earned value methods to each.

2. Consider how to do an update status of milestones and how to assess earned value.

The solution to this case study can be found on the Humphreys & Associates, Inc. web site.
www.humphreys-assoc.com

CONTROL ACCOUNT PLAN

WBS REFERENCE: 1010201
SCHEDULE REFERENCE: ADA LVL 1 001 R0

Element of Cost (EOC): L-Labor, S-SubKtr, M-Mat'l, O-ODC

PROGRAM: Engineering Data Integration System
DATE: 7/15/Yr1
REV NO.: Orig.
CONTROL ACCOUNT TITLE/NO.: 1040ADC — PRE-SRR DOC MGMT SOFTWARE DEVELOPMENT
CAM: THAD BAKER
PROGRAM MGR: BROUD STEARMAN
PAGE: 1 OF 1

Reference Milestones (YEAR 01): JUL — System Requirements Review; NOV — Integrated Baseline Review
Reference Milestones (YEAR 02): JAN — Preliminary Design Review; APR — Engineering Prototype Available; JUN — System Software Review

Work Task	EV Method / CWA	Metric	JUL	AUG	SEP	OCT	NOV	DEC	JAN	FEB	MAR	APR	MAY	JUN	TOTAL 12 MOS.
1. Management/administration of developing system software (EOC: L)	A3G01	BCWS-HRS	23	30	35	20	20	20	20	20	20	20	20	35	283
		BCWS-$	$1,650	$2,153	$2,511	$1,435	$1,435	$1,435	$1,435	$1,435	$1,435	$1,435	$1,435	$2,511	$20,305
		BCWP-HRS													0
		BCWP-$													$0
2. Requirements Definition & Analysis to support SRR (EOC: L)	A3G01	BCWS-HRS	57	80	50										187
		BCWS-$	$4,090	$5,740	$3,588										$13,418
		BCWP-HRS													0
		BCWP-$													$0
3. Support Risk Identification & Assessment. 1 thru 5 = 20 hrs per milestone; 6 thru 9 = 10 hrs per milestone (EOC: L)	A3G01	BCWS-HRS	20	40	40	10	10	10	10						140
		BCWS-$	$1,435	$2,870	$2,870	$718	$718	$718	$718						$10,047
		BCWP-HRS													0
		BCWP-$													$0
(milestones)			[1][2][3]	[3]	[4][5]	[6]	[7]	[8]	[9]						
4. Software Integration Testing & Software/Hardware Interface Testing (EOC: L)	A3G01	BCWS-HRS									50	160	250	260	720
		BCWS-$									$3,588	$11,480	$17,938	$18,655	$51,661
		BCWP-HRS													0
		BCWP-$													$0
5. Test Planning 150 Requirements (5 hrs per requirement) (EOC: L)	A3G01	BCWS-HRS			10	80	100	100	190	150	100	20			750
		BCWS-$			$718	$5,740	$7,175	$7,175	$13,633	$10,763	$7,175	$1,435			$53,814
		BCWP-HRS													0
		BCWP-$													$0
6. Design, Code & Unit Test (EOC: L)	A3G01	BCWS-HRS			59	173	336	336	709	709	664	664	600	550	4800
		BCWS-$			$4,233	$12,413	$24,108	$24,108	$50,871	$50,871	$47,642	$47,642	$43,050	$39,463	$344,401
		BCWP-HRS													0
		BCWP-$													$0
7. Software Input - Preliminary Documentation & Release (EOC: L)	A3G01	BCWS-HRS										70	70		140
		BCWS-$										$5,023	$5,023		$10,046
		BCWP-HRS													0
		BCWP-$													$0
8. Interpret, analyze, & coordinate document management software design with System Engineering & other subsystems (10% of WP #6)	A3G01	BCWS-HRS			6	17	34	34	71	71	66	66	60	55	480
		BCWS-$			$431	$1,220	$2,440	$2,440	$5,094	$5,094	$4,736	$4,736	$4,305	$3,946	$34,442
		BCWP-HRS													0
		BCWP-$													$0
9. Purchase of compilers, research materials, DNA specialists, etc. supporting design (EOC: M)	A3G01	BCWS-HRS													0
		BCWS-$					$2,500	$5,000	$5,000	$5,000	$3,000				$20,500
		BCWP-HRS													0
		BCWP-$													$0

PAGE TOTALS

	Metric	JUL	AUG	SEP	OCT	NOV	DEC	JAN	FEB	MAR	APR	MAY	JUN	TOTAL 12 MOS.
MONTHLY BCWS	HOURS	100	150	200	300	500	500	1000	950	900	1000	1000	900	7500
	DOLLARS	$7,175	$10,763	$14,351	$21,526	$38,376	$40,876	$76,751	$73,163	$67,576	$71,751	$71,751	$64,575	$558,634
CUM BCWS	HOURS	100	250	450	750	1250	1750	2750	3700	4600	5600	6600	7500	7500
	DOLLARS	$7,175	$17,938	$32,289	$53,815	$92,191	$133,067	$209,818	$282,981	$350,557	$422,308	$494,059	$558,634	$558,634
MONTHLY BCWP	HOURS	0	0	0	0	0	0	0	0	0	0	0	0	0
	DOLLARS	$0	$0	$0	$0	$0	$0	$0	$0	$0	$0	$0	$0	$0
CUM BCWP	HOURS	0	0	0	0	0	0	0	0	0	0	0	0	0
	DOLLARS	$0	$0	$0	$0	$0	$0	$0	$0	$0	$0	$0	$0	$0
MONTHLY ACWP	HOURS													
	DOLLARS													

LEGEND:
△ = Start Activity
⇧ = Complete Activity - Plan
◇ = Delayed Activity - Revised Plan
Filled in symbol indicates completed activity - actual

Earned Value (EV) Codes:
1. Level of Effort 4. 0/100 7. Apportioned
2. Milestone 5. % Complete
3. 50/50 6. Units Complete

APPROVALS:
CAM: _____ DATE: _____
PROGRAM MGR: _____

Chapter 31

COLLECTING ACTUAL COST

Objectives of this Chapter:

1. Identify the types of actual cost information needed to support project management.

2. Discuss the interface between the accounting organization and project management.

3. Discuss considerations involved in cash flow management.

4. Describe a mechanism for expediting receipt of actual cost data for analysis.

5. Identify procedures for minimizing inaccurate charges.

An essential input needed for determining the cost position of a project is the actual cost associated with performing the work. Of the three components discussed for determining project status (planned accomplishment, actual accomplishment, and actual cost), actual cost is the one that every organization must have available. Surprisingly, it may not be easy to incorporate. In an organization that does not have an integrated approach to project management, this component will be a challenge. This is because long-existing accounting approaches may need to be modified to match how the work is performed and posting of actual costs will need to be in the same accounting period as earned value is reported. It may be difficult to enhance older systems.

As shown in the flowchart, the actual cost will be compared with the project plan and earned value.

Actual Cost Components

Actual cost consists of two primary components: direct costs and indirect costs. Direct costs are costs incurred specifically for an end objective such as a contract or project. Examples of direct costs include the cost of an engineer's hours while working on a project and the material to build a production unit of a weapons system.

Indirect costs are costs incurred for a broader cost objective and are allocated across all contracts or projects within the company. Indirect costs are also termed overhead costs or burdens. Examples of indirect costs include the cost of the accounting department and the rent on the company's buildings. Indirect costs are typically accumulated in "pools" which are allocated to each contract based on the direct costs. While most project management actions address direct costs, it is important not to lose sight of indirect costs because these overhead costs often make up 50% or more of the costs of a contract or project.

Each company defines direct and indirect costs to suit its business needs. Frequently, these definitions evolved from government contract requirements or accounting requirements customary to an industry segment. The Controller's organization is typically responsible for the definition of direct and indirect costs as this information is critical to operating the accounting system.

Companies that perform government contracts often are required to comply with the Cost Accounting Standards (CAS) promulgated by the Cost Accounting Standards Board (CASB). Compliance with the CAS requires the submittal of a Cost Accounting Disclosure Statement. Among

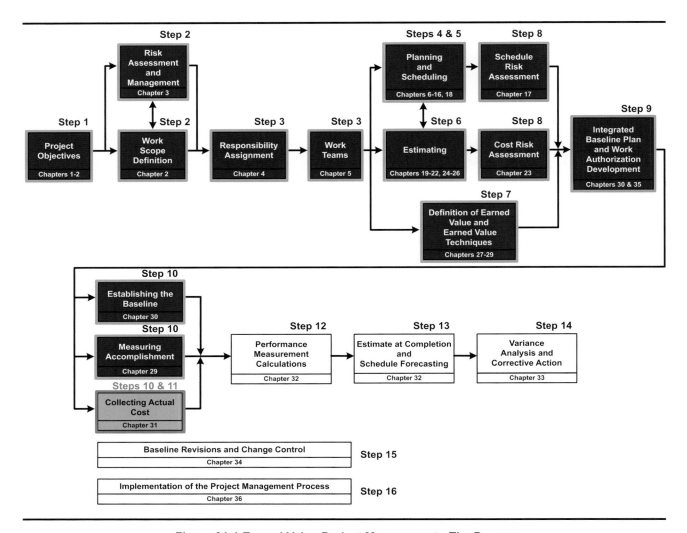

Figure 31-1 Earned Value Project Management: The Process

	Direct Cost Samples	**Indirect Cost Samples**
Labor	• Engineers time for designing subsystem • Craft hours to assemble subsystem	• Accounting Department's hours • Human Resources Department hours
Material	• Computer system that is part of the end product • Piping for end product	• Software applications for the company's accounting system • Office furniture
Other Direct Costs	• Travel costs to install end product	• Registration and travel costs to attend an industry conference
Subcontract	• Specialty company's cost to design module of a subsystem in the end product	• Facility maintenance cost to cut lawn and maintain landscaping at company's offices

Figure 31-2 Cost Element Examples

other things, this document describes which costs are categorized as direct costs and indirect costs and how the indirect costs are allocated.

Direct and indirect costs contain four generic cost elements: labor, material, other direct costs, and subcontracts. The accounting system must be able to identify actual costs by cost element. Figure 31-2 illustrates examples of each of the cost elements.

Data Element Sources

Actual costs are an important component of a complete project management system, but this data does not stand alone. It must be compared with other data and integrated into a useful information format. During system design, use of a "data source matrix" will help prevent overlooking an important aspect of the system. Data for each

cost element must be summarized through the WBS and OBS, and actual cost collection methods must integrate with the accounting system's chart of accounts. Figure 31-3 shows the data sources for the four cost elements.

The source of actual labor cost data is the employee time report that shows the number of hours worked and the specific accounts those hours supported. Material costs may be gathered from material invoices and/or other material usage documentation. This documentation includes warehouse records identifying when material has been withdrawn from inventory along with its actual value. The source of actual costs for Other Direct Costs (ODC) depends on the item. Source data for travel costs is the travel and expense report that details expenses associated with each trip. Source data for other ODCs typically are invoices or accounting accruals. Subcontracts are treated by some companies as

Data Element	Cost Element					
	Labor	Material	Other Direct Costs			Subcontract
		Low Value/ High Value	Travel	Data Processing	Other	Fixed Price/ Cost Reimbursable
Actuals (ACWP or AC)	Electronic Labor Reporting	Material Transfer	Travel and Expense report	Inter-Departmental Transfer	Invoice/ Accounts Payable/ Accrual	Invoice/ Subcontractor CPR
Budget (BCWS or PV)	Control Account Plan	Control Account Plan	Control Account Plan	Control Account Plan	Control Account Plan	Progress Report/ Subcontractor CPR
Earned Value (BCWP or EV)	Work Status Report	Statused shop order schedule/ Control Account Plan	Work Status Report	Work Status Report	Work Status Report	Progress Report/ Subcontractor CPR
EAC	VAR	VAR	VAR	VAR	VAR	Progress Report/ Subcontractor CPR
BAC	Work Authorizing Document	Work Authorizing Document	Work Authorizing Document	Work Authorizing Document	Work Authorizing Document	Subcontract/ Subcontractor CPR

Figure 31-3 Data Source Matrix

material and by other companies as Other Direct Costs; the different treatment usually relates to how overhead costs are allocated to subcontracts. Regardless of the treatment, subcontractor actual costs enter the accounting system via an invoice.

Each earned value management system data element has a data source. Budget information comes from both the work authorization document (for total budget) and from the control account plan (for the time-phasing of the total budget). Earned value is determined from a work status report, the project schedule, or other source that identifies tasks completed. Regular variance analysis reporting reveals the latest trends for the estimate at completion that may be greater or less than the approved budget.

Accounting Interface with Project Management

An earned value project management system must be based on accurate information. Therefore, the accounting system, which provides the official actual costs for a company, is critically important to the project management system. The two systems address different company objectives. The accounting system ultimately must provide accurate reports to management concerning revenue, profitability, net worth, and cash flow. The project management system must provide management and customers the status and projections for the cost and schedule objectives of a particular project. The key interfaces between the two systems include accounting pol-

icies and procedures and the data collection software subsystem.

Accounting policies and procedures define how a company collects costs. Through these policies and procedures, the company defines what tools or subsystems will collect costs, how costs are classified or grouped, how costs map into a "chart of accounts," and when the accounting cycles start and end. The infrastructure formed by these accounting policies and procedures forms the data set with which the project management system must interface. Figure 31-4 shows the typical accounting subsystems that interface with the cost elements in a project management system.

Key accounting policies and procedure items that must be clearly understood in order to develop the appropriate interfaces with the project management system include:

- **Definitions of direct and indirect costs** – Some companies define positions such as Contracting Officer as an indirect position. While rationale can be reasonable defining certain positions as direct or indirect, the project management system must align with the definitions in the accounting policies and procedures.

- **Definitions of indirect pools** – Most high technology companies are organized into multiple pools such as Engineering, Manufacturing, Logistics, and Field Support. The reason for organizing into different pools is to allocate the common company costs on an appropriate basis that best represents usage. The project management system must accommodate the indi-

Accounting Subsystem	Direct Cost Element				Indirect Costs
	Labor	Material	Other Direct Costs	Subcontracts	
Timekeeping	X				X
Payroll	X				X
Purchasing		X	X	X	X
Accounts Payable		X	X	X	X

Figure 31-4 Accounting Subsystem Interfaces with Project Management

rect pools defined by the accounting system.

- **Classification of subcontracts** – Some companies treat subcontracts as Material while other companies treat subcontracts as Other Direct Costs. The difference is that Material usually carries an indirect charge that is applied to the subcontractor's costs while Other Direct Costs do not.

- **Definition of accounting calendar** – Companies operate on different fiscal year calendars and define an accounting month differently. Since a calendar year contains 52 weeks and 13 weeks in a quarter, companies can use various schemes to define an accounting month. A common scheme called the 4-4-5 approach defines each quarter with 4 weeks in the first month, 4 weeks in the second month, and 5 weeks in the third month. Each quarter then contains 13 weeks. Using this approach means that accounting period end dates will not necessarily occur in the named month. For example, consider a company that starts its accounting cycle on a Sunday. The first Sunday in the month could be January 3 which would make the end of the accounting period January 30. The February accounting month would therefore start on January 31. Regardless of the scheme used to define the accounting periods, the project management system must align with the accounting calendar to ensure data consistency.

Obviously, the above list is not exhaustive, and many other accounting policy and procedure items could affect interfaces with the project management system.

The other significant interface mentioned at the beginning of this section is the data collection software subsystem. The accounting system requires information from the data collection software to feed the general ledger chart of accounts. The project management system requires the data collection software to segregate costs by element of cost, summarize data through a Work Breakdown Structure, and summarize data through the Organization Breakdown Structure. Regardless of the software used, the key interface between the data collection system and all other subsystems is a code field entered on all source documents. Companies call this code field various names including charge code, charge number, activity code, case number, and charge ID. For this text, this field is referred to as the charge code.

During the early days of project management systems, software systems placed a great premium on minimizing characters in the charge code. As software advanced and data storage costs diminished, companies built "intelligence" into the charge code to facilitate data sorting. This intelligence in the charge code included fields such as contract number, control account, work package, organization, WBS, element of cost, direct/indirect, chart of accounts code, recurring/non-recurring, funding source, contract line item number, and type of task. An important consideration in developing the charge code is the practical reality of employees using the correct number on source documents such as electronic time reports, expense reports, purchase orders, and material requisitions. Shorter charge codes are easier to remember and typically lead to fewer errors. The approach most often employed for charge codes is to use whatever field already is used by the accounting system supplemented by a look-up table that includes all other relevant fields. The charge code must define a unique field that captures the costs at the source.

A key consideration in defining the charge code relates to the level at which actual costs are collected in the project management system. The best practice, and the approach used by most companies today, is to collect actual costs at the work package level. Collecting actual costs at the work package level aligns BCWS, BCWP, and ACWP at the same level and enables effective variance analysis and consistency of cost element data. To minimize the proliferation of charge codes, some organizations collect costs at the control account level rather than at the work package level. Other organizations go to the opposite extreme and collect costs at the individual activity or task level below the work package. Neither of these approaches is incorrect;

however, the collecting costs at work package level yields the best trade-off of the cost to collect and evaluate actual cost data.

Cash Flow Considerations

In an ideal project management environment, funds would be available to support whatever level of resources are required to successfully achieve the project plan. The reality is that most large projects are subject to incremental funding or funding limitations at various points in the project life cycle. Because of these funding limitations, project managers must address two issues: Does the plan fit within the funding profile? Does the current situation fit within the available funds? Before discussing how project managers address these issues, it is critical to understand the difference between budgets and funds.

Budgets are simply a written plan. In an earned value project management system, the total budget is the Budget at Completion (BAC). The time phased increments of the BAC are termed the Budgeted Cost for Work Scheduled (BCWS). The actual accomplishment of work is represented by the Budgeted Cost for Work Performed (BCWP). All of these values are no more than numbers written on a piece of paper or contained in a database. Goods or services cannot be bought with a budget; although having the budget authorized enables a manager to initiate the activities to commit the company's funds. On the other hand, Actual Costs of Work Performed (ACWP) represent funds expended by the company to obtain goods or services. Whether the invoice has been paid or not, the company will ultimately authorize the transfer of funds to the provider of the services. The Estimate to Complete (ETC) is a time phased estimate of future funds required, and the Estimate at Completion (EAC) represents the estimate of the total funds required. BCWS, BCWP, and BAC are budget values. ACWP, ETC, and EAC represent funds. Be careful not to confuse them.

An objective of the planning process should be to develop a budget plan (BCWS) that fits within the customer's funding profile. Typically, the customer will include a funding profile as part of the contract or will convey it to the contractor by let-

ter. A budget plan that does not fit within the initial funding constraints is unrealistic. Therefore, the budget process is iterated until the initial plan fits within the funding profile. Remember, if the company signed the contract for the specific funding profile, it is the company's responsibility to perform the contract within that funding profile. Conversely, if the customer changes the funding profile from what was agreed to in the contract, the contractor should be entitled to a constructive change if a new funding profile is inadequate to achieve the schedule objectives.

Once the project plan is in place and contract performance is underway, the project manager must monitor the funds committed and expended. Funds expended in excess of the available contract funds are incurred at the company's risk. Company executives are very careful regarding decisions about putting company funds at risk and rely on project managers to inform them prior to putting the company in this situation. Therefore, project managers should routinely evaluate the ACWP, ETC, and EAC with the funding profile.

A complete funding analysis must also include commitments. Commitments are orders that have been placed, but the goods or services have not been invoiced by the provider or the funds have not yet been paid. Any goods or services that require a purchase order can have outstanding commitments, so commitments could apply to material, subcontracts, or Other Direct Costs. Outstanding commitments are tracked closely for material because the time lag between purchase order and receipt is often significant. Figure 31-5 illustrates the time delays for material from order to payment.

Material Costs

When earned value is computed for material, equipment, and purchased services, it is essential that the actual cost be recorded in the same time period as the earned value. This can be accomplished at several different points in time, as illustrated in Figure 31-6. There is cost exposure from the time that an order is placed until the material is used ("final disposition"). Taking earned value credit is usually done at one of five

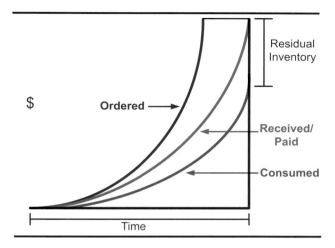

Figure 31-5 Material Accounting

points in the process. This is indicated by the diamond figures.

One of the most popular points to take earned value credit for material is at the point of receipt, because it is normally the point at which the liability is recognized within the accounting system. This approach simplifies the interface with accounting, but this convenience should be weighed against the greater utility of crediting earned value at the point of usage. Material that is sitting in inventory or storage does not really reflect progress of the project. Point of usage is where the material is actually employed on the project and indicates actual progress.

If material earned value is taken at time of usage, it may be necessary to collect actual costs in a holding account. The recording of actual cost (ACWP) is delayed until the time the material is used and cost is then transferred to the specific control account for the material. For example, when 10% of the material is pulled out of a bin of bulk material, then 10% of the actual cost, as well as 10% of the earned value for that material, would be transferred to the project. Taking earned value at this point will also provide more accurate usage variance analysis since it will reflect the actual consumption of material.

Indirect Costs

Most of the discussion so far has centered on direct costs, or those costs that are associated with the direct accomplishment of project work. Another category of cost is the indirect cost, also known as "burden" or overhead cost, and this can be a substantial portion of the total cost. The definition of indirect costs varies from one organization to the next. There is no standard definition for what should be included. In general, indirect costs are costs that are not exclusive to any single contract or program, but that apply to all contracts. All organizations have indirect costs, unless that organization exists for only a single project. As soon as a second project is initiated,

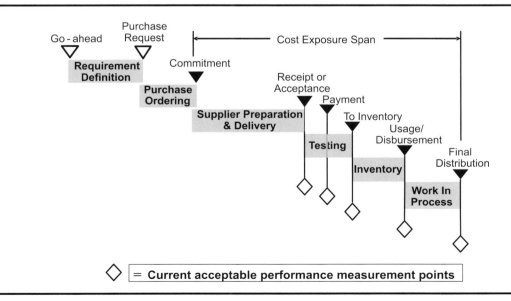

Figure 31-6 Material Measurement

or marketing is performed to find a second project, it is no longer appropriate to charge all of the company's expenses to the single charge code/project. Expenses are then collected in an overhead account and later prorated to direct costs on individual projects or subsets of projects.

Certain indirect costs are fixed, such as the cost of an office building, its depreciation, as well as top executive costs. Even if the number of projects and number of employees vary, there will still be a company president and a building required to house employees. Other indirect costs are variable, such as fringe benefits, office furniture, company vehicles, supplies, computers, fringe benefits, vacations, sick pay, and telephone costs. Even these definitions will vary. In the case of employee reduction, there may be a requirement for reduced office space if the cut were large enough. In that case, it is no longer a "fixed" indirect cost. Fringe benefits may not be truly variable, i.e. varying in direct proportion to the direct costs or number of employees, if there were a disproportionate number of senior employees retained or terminated. This is because vacation and sick time are typically a function of longevity with the company.

Indirect cost rates for example, may be 100% meaning that there are as many indirect costs as direct costs. They may be expressed as a multiplier to the base of direct costs using a 2.00 multiplier to arrive at total cost. Some organizations have higher rates which translate into an even larger impact on total cost.

One factor to keep in mind about indirect cost is that it is commonly driven by factors outside of the project's control. It is therefore somewhat of a confusion factor in the management of a project and does not require the same type of detailed analysis on a monthly basis that is accorded the direct cost. Indirect cost, and the components that contribute to its makeup, must be analyzed in detail but that can be done monthly, quarterly, or at year end, according to company practice. At that point, planned versus actual values for each component of an indirect rate should be identified and explained. This indirect cost analysis will generally be performed by the accounting function and the impact of that analysis provided to the project office.

Normally, different overhead rates are developed for each major functional organization within a facility. These rates are developed based upon the indirect costs expected to be incurred. A matrix showing the kinds of indirect costs that can be generated by the different functional organizations is shown in Figure 31-7.

	Executive	Marketing	Operations
Indirect Salaries and Wages	$	$	$
Payroll Fringe	$	$	$
Incentive Compensation	$	$	$
Advertising		$	
Business Conferences	$	$	$
Travel	$	$	$
Overhead Transfers between Divisions, etc.	$	$	$

Figure 31-7 Matrix of Indirect Cost

The complexity of this matrix will depend largely on the type of industry and the nature of the business involved. For burden or overhead rate development, a formula such as the following is used:

$$\frac{\text{Overhead Pool}}{\text{Direct Cost Base}} = \text{Rate}$$

This rate is then calculated for each overhead pool. A typical direct cost base for engineering might consist of labor dollars. For manufacturing, the direct cost base might be equipment cost, equipment hours, or even floor space. A good base has a strong correlation to the indirect costs being consumed. If the overhead pool totals $119,750 while the direct cost is $95,800, then the overhead burden rate would be:

$$\frac{\$119,750}{\$95,800} = 125\% \text{ Burden Rate}$$

The 125% overhead, or "burden rate," for the fiscal year is a planned ratio of the cost of elements to support the base. The 125% indicates that for every $1.00 of direct cost used, $1.25 of other indirect cost elements is needed to support it.

The rate used for budget and earned value must be the same. The rates used for actual costs will be based on actual experience and may vary from the budget rate. Incorporating overhead rates into a Performance Measurement System is a matter of developing planning rates and identifying actual rates. The planning rates are applied to the direct cost budget to determine the indirect cost budget. Since earned value is based on budgeted costs, the planning rate is also applied to the direct cost earned value to determine the indirect cost earned value. The third data component, actual indirect cost, must be based on the actual or "estimated actual" rate. An "estimated actual" may be necessary when an audited actual rate is not available in a timely manner.

Indirect costs must be analyzed in the same manner as the direct costs. An example of indirect cost analysis is displayed in Figure 31-8.

	Direct $ x Indirect Rate = Indirect $			Total $
Budget	100	110% (BID)	110	100 + 110 = 210
Earned Value	80	110% (BID)	88	80 + 88 = 168
Actual Costs	130	120% (Price)	156	130 + 156 = 286

(42)
(118)

Impact of indirect on Schedule Variance = (22)

Impact of indirect on Cost Variance = (68)

Figure 31-8 Indirect Analysis - An Example

Figure 31-8 shows the method used to separate the direct and indirect variances and individually calculate their impacts. The bid rate for overhead was 110%, so 110% of the direct cost base is added as indirect cost. In the example, a direct cost of $100 results in for a total cost of $210. When the direct earned value was lower than anticipated ($80 versus $100), the same indirect rate of 110% is applied against the $80 to determine the earned value with indirect cost included. This results in a value of $168. The actual direct costs were reported as $130, with an actual indirect rate of 120%. Applying this higher indirect rate to the higher actual direct costs results in an actual cost of $286.

Further analysis of this information shows that the direct cost variance was ($50) calculated as $80 - $130. However, the total cost variance was ($118), or $168 - $286. Out of the total cost variance of ($118), therefore, ($50) was because of direct costs and ($68) was because of indirect costs.

The same type of analysis can be performed for the schedule variance as illustrated in Figure 31-8. In this example, there was a much larger impact from the indirect costs on the cost variance than on the schedule variance.

It is not possible in all cases to segregate the impact of direct cost and indirect rates on the total variance. Frequently, the control account manager or another individual responsible for performing the variance analysis does not even know the indirect cost and is not held responsible for that analysis. Indirect rates may be applied at a summary WBS level rather than at individual control accounts or applied to control accounts after control account manager direct analysis has been performed. In these cases, a summary level manager, accounting, or the project office provides the indirect analysis.

Late Reporting of Actual Costs

When presenting seminars or workshops on the topic of project management, a recurring statement of objection is something like, "The theory is great, but it won't work here. And the reason it won't work is that our accounting system is so messed up that it takes us weeks after close of books to get our actuals." This excuse is not valid for preventing implementation of an effective project management system. One hundred percent accurate accounting results are not needed to run the system, as it is more important to get timely data than exact data. An effective approach that has been used in many organizations to speed up the data analysis process is to use the preliminary, unaudited accounting results for beginning the analysis. If numbers change, it is normally a minor correction. The exact figures can be included in the next month's analysis. This guarantees that all cumulative to date data will be accurate except for the current month, which will likely be 99% accurate or better. This approach will reduce turnaround time for monthly accounting information.

Accuracy of Reported Actual Costs

All of the project performance data and actual costs will be used on an exception basis to identify areas of project concern and therefore must be accurate. This means it is a key concern that the labor, material, equipment, purchased services, and other direct costs be charged to the correct account in the WBS and accounting structure. This is a legitimate problem and experience shows that total labor hours worked and dollars charged to a project are normally very accurate, but the distribution of that total to all of the appropriate accounts can be where problems occur.

On one engineering contract, the last three digits of the base charge code for general services was 000. During the life of this very long term project, there were well over 100 accounts established to collect actual costs to the specific tasks involved. However, this large project had many part time experts who were consulted on an as needed basis only. These people were familiar with the 000 charge code and not much else. When the client complained about the excessive charges to this one account, attempts were made via internal memorandums to discontinue the charges. However, peripheral staff to the project were the ones least likely to see such a memo and the charges continued. Were the project personnel being obstinate? Actually, they were more interested in doing their job than worrying about the "bean counting" efforts associated with their time charges. In many cases, they did not know the exact rules and used the easy solution of charging to the general account. The solution that was finally implemented was to close the general account, forcing all project personnel to charge to the specific accounts.

There are two points to this story. First, technical personnel are more interested in doing their job in their area of expertise than in recording hours worked to specific charge numbers and processing time reports. Second, some type of formal

control needs to exist to determine who can charge what control accounts. What this really suggests is that there needs to be some type of work authorization that determines allowable cost charges. On the highest level, every organization has some form of work authorization whereby a client must authorize a contractor to begin work and the contractor's project manager must have a mechanism for authorizing the project personnel to charge the project. This includes definition of a project work order. Few problems can occur at this point. The situation becomes more interesting when specific control account charge codes are included.

Earlier, control accounts were defined as well as how they represent the intersection of the detailed work to be done (WBS) and the organizational elements responsible for performing the work. This can serve as a source for improving cost reporting accuracy. With most cost reporting now automated, it is a simple matter to define a filter that will disallow any charges to an account unless it has been defined as acceptable in advance. The responsibility matrix can be the basis for the filter that defines acceptable charges. This needs to be done using the individual employee identification number to be successful for labor. An individual charge account can be officially closed until a project manager or designee authorizes it to be opened to charges. Any attempted charges to the account prior to authorization will be rejected by the system. This would include labor charges, but must also include all material charges and other direct or indirect costs. This presupposes the existence of an accurate charge code list that indicates which accounts are open to charges at any given time. An open charge code list must be created and maintained for each project to assist in the determination of proper charges. The cost accounting organization may be the one to maintain these records.

This approach may still not resolve all concerns, but it will guarantee that unauthorized personnel will not be charging the project or any specific accounts. It also ensures that material costs and no other inappropriate direct/indirect costs are charged.

Do incorrect costs still occur and how widespread can they be? An unusual opportunity occurred that allowed a glimpse into that question. In one instance, the person responsible for cost collection and reporting in a contractor organization was released. He had been highly regarded by the client/owner/customer organization and so he was immediately hired by the client/owner. Suspecting that some of the charges to detailed accounts looked inaccurate, he was asked about the accuracy of the charges. The response was that there had been a lot of inaccurate reporting to certain control accounts, but that the totals were always correct. His initial assignment was to correct the known errors. This took him a month, but from that point on at least there was a higher comfort level that accurate productivity data were being used for analysis. Because of the past problems, however, the somewhat extreme precaution was taken that surveys were continually done to assess what areas the contractor's personnel were working in, how many people were assigned, and how long they took to perform the work. These surveys were used as a check against reported time. The accounting department also conducted audits to ensure that the individual time reports matched the time reported on the monthly invoices. Similar reviews were performed for all material costs and other direct costs.

How much effort is justified in the quest for accurate detailed cost reporting? Labor charges have been discussed, but material cost collection can be even more difficult. The biggest challenge relates to collecting material costs in the same time frame as the planned accomplishment (or budget) and the earned value. If all three components, budget, earned value and actual cost, are not reported in the same reporting period, then misleading variances will occur. Since this information is being used to manage the project on a continuing basis, it is very important that the data be comparable. Planned and actual accomplishment for material may be logically taken at point of receipt or at point of usage, but the receipt of invoices, payment if those invoices and the recording of actual cost in the accounting system frequently occur independently of the receipt or usage of the associated material. This can result in the need for determining "estimated ACWP".

Estimated ACWP is a projection of actual costs to be recorded in the analysis and reporting system before they are actually included in the accounting records. The reason for this approach is to ensure an actual cost is included in the time period consistent with the planned and actual accomplishment. This eliminates false variances and allows the data to be useful and timely for project management purposes. Records of "estimated ACWP" are also maintained so that once the actual cost is recorded in the accounting system the estimate is reversed.

An additional challenge may occur in high rate production or use of material. Numerous quantities of low cost material items will typically be purchased on a single bill of material and then used wherever needed. This frequently results in a single bill of material being applied to multiple WBS elements. If this occurs without a detailed material system tracking capability, then it may be difficult or impossible to determine how many units were applied to each WBS element. This is an area that should be addressed in advance so that detailed tracking is possible.

Precautions that should be taken to minimize incorrect charges include the following:

1. Define a filter within the automated time/cost collection program that will only accept pre-approved charges. This means if an employee's ID number were not authorized for account ABCXYZ, then no charges would be accepted from that employee in that account. It also means that material cost and other direct costs will not be accepted if the account has not been approved to receive charges.

2. Provide pre-coded electronic lists with all standard prefixes for program, project, contract, and organization already completed. The employee then must only complete the charge for the specific account worked.

3. Keep charge codes as simple as possible. It will be much easier to get correct charges if people can remember them.

4. Limit the number of possible charge accounts to a reasonable number. Of course there is always a tradeoff between

visibility and number of accounts, but remember the objective. It is far better to have accurate charges to 50 accounts than inaccurate charges to 1,000 accounts.

5. Do spot checking. Those responsible for analyzing the numbers should have some idea of what charges are anticipated as well as what problems are being encountered. This will help ensure accurate time charging as well as better analysis of what the real project status is.

6. Maintain historical records so that there is some idea of what the numbers should be. If actual costs are deviating significantly from the expected costs, the first question to ask is, "Are the charges being reported correctly?" Besides improving accuracy, this can save a lot of unnecessary finger-pointing because of false variances.

7. Clearly define what belongs in each account. Even the most motivated employee cannot correctly guess where a charge belongs each time if the WBS dictionary does not precisely define what work scope is included within the account.

8. Implement a detailed material tracking system if high quantity, low value items are to be handled as bulk commodities.

Reporting Labor Hours versus Labor Dollars

Another consideration in the reporting of actual costs is the "labor hours versus dollars" question. It has been a long-standing debate as to which approach is preferable. The argument to control the project in hours reflects several considerations:

- Most engineers, production, and construction people think in terms of hours. This includes labor unit rates expressed in hours, historical "rules of thumb" using hours, and progress reporting in hours.

- The manager for a control account may have no control over who is assigned to the work or what their dollar rates are. In that case, hours can still be managed but dollars may not be controlled at this level of the organization.

Conversely, those who argue in favor of controlling by dollars point to the following considerations:

- Material and other direct costs cannot be expressed in hours. Therefore, labor hours must be converted to dollars in order to describe the overall status of the project in one common denominator (dollars).

- The contract is negotiated in dollars, and customer reporting is in dollars. Control account managers should be responsible for managing, analyzing, and reporting their portion of the contract cost including all costs from direct through total cost.

There are additional considerations if dollars are used for control. One of these is the time value of money. A dollar today is not the same as a dollar ten years ago or ten years from now.

International projects bring special challenges when managed on a currency basis. With multiple currencies involved on a single project, it is not as simple as converting from one currency to another. Since currencies could fluctuate relative to each other on a daily basis, the date on which the conversion is made will impact the number of dollars booked to the project. When considering the earlier discussion of when to charge material costs to the project, the difficulty is magnified if multiple currencies are involved. Recognizing the cost at point of usage may differ substantially from the cost that would have been reported if the currency conversion had been made at the point of receipt or payment. This must be recognized as a possibility that is part of Cost Variance (CV).

There is no absolute answer to the question of whether it is better to control a project in hours or dollars at the detailed working level, since the considerations identified for both sides of the argument are true. Each organization, and possibly each project, must decide for itself how labor costs will be managed on a project. Either approach can be made to work, but dollars must be forecast for the Estimate at Completion (EAC).

Therefore, even if labor hours are used for managing at the control account level, someone in the project office or in accounting must price these hours for forecasting purposes (and probably for reporting purposes as well). The trend in industry has been moving to control account managers being authorized budgets at least at the direct dollar level.

Conclusion

Collecting actual costs accurately is an important component of a successful integrated project management system. While companies have collected actual costs since the beginning of trade, there are additional factors relating to the use of actual costs in a performance oriented project management system. One of these is timeliness since stale information can be of little use in the day-to-day control of a project. This may necessitate procedures to use unaudited data, prior to its official release, for analysis purposes. Another factor demanding attention is consistency of information which means that actual cost reporting must be consistent with how budgets were planned and accomplishment measured. There are special considerations in tracking material costs, especially if large quantities of similar items are used in multiple WBS elements.

While accounting will be concerned about exact total project costs, project management needs actual costs by control account to allow integration of this information with the planned budget and earned value. It is imperative that there be an agreeable interface between the accounting and project management departments so that this data will meet the needs of both groups. If actual charges are recorded to incorrect control accounts, the information derived for management of the project will be tainted. It is very important that specific precautions be taken to minimize incorrect cost charges.

Many basic decisions must be made in the use of an accounting system on a particular project. These decisions include: the level at which costs are to be collected (work package or control account), the method of addressing indirect costs (including the level of detail at which such analysis will occur), the point at which material, equipment, and purchased services costs will be allocated to the project, and whether control of the project at the detailed working level will be based on labor hours, direct dollars, or total dollars (including overhead).

Chapter 31 Review Questions

31-1.   With an earned value reporting system in place, why would a fundamental piece of data such as actual cost still be required?

31-2.   How does the accounting view of cost differ from the project management view?

31-3.   Most accounting systems provide actual cost information too late to be useful in the project management process. Assuming accounting cannot provide its reports as needed by the project, what is a possible solution?

31-4.   Discuss the ways available to guard against incorrect labor time charges (i.e. correct totals but coded to the wrong individual accounts).

True or False

31-5.   When cash flow analyses are developed, they should consider material commitments.

31-6.   The total labor cost of a project may be twice what the direct labor charges are because of indirect costs.

31-7.   Estimated ACWP is used when earned value has been credited for a product or service while no actual costs have yet been incurred.

31-8.   Careful coding of time reporting into the accounting system will ensure that charges have been collected to correct accounts.

The answers to these questions can be found in Section 6, Solutions.

Chapter 32

PERFORMANCE MEASUREMENT CALCULATIONS AND ESTIMATES AT COMPLETION

Objectives of this Chapter:

1. Explain how to use the information from an earned value reporting system to evaluate project status.

2. Discuss the limitations of schedule variance as an indicator of schedule status.

3. Explain how to develop the Estimate at Completion (EAC).

4. Define the Cost Performance Index (CPI) and its use.

5. Define the Schedule Performance Index (SPI) and its use.

6. Define the To Complete Performance Index (TCPI) and its use.

7. Provide formulas for the calculation of independent estimates at completion (IEAC) used to validate reported EACs.

8. Explain how performance metrics can be used in combination to analyze earned value and schedule data.

9. Introduce a performance report format that integrates cost and schedule status reporting.

10. Explain how labor, material, and ODC cost variances can be analyzed by evaluating the cost components that produced the total cost variance.

Analysis of data is another important project management activity. The information from the integrated project management system assists in identification of areas for further management attention and action. These data are used to mathematically evaluate how performance is progressing and to develop accurate forecasts of where the project is headed. This is another key benefit (and objective) of the system: early indication of expected final costs and schedule completion. The performance measurement calculations defined in this chapter will be used when preparing the Variance Analysis Report discussed in Chapter 33. An integrated report format for presenting system output is also presented in this chapter.

Performance Measurement Calculations

In this chapter, the information derived from an earned value reporting system will be used to show how it helps to evaluate project status. When comparing planned performance with actual performance, variances are inevitable. So attention should be focused only on those variances that might have a significant impact on the project. Analysis of these variances will allow

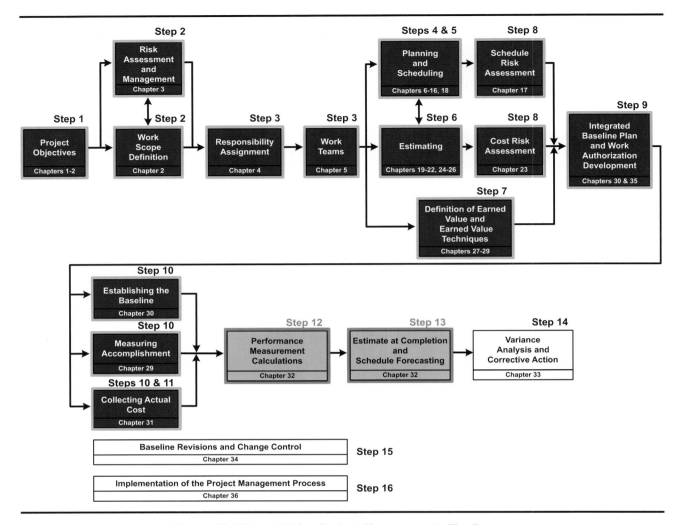

Figure 32-1 Earned Value Project Management: The Process

early warning of future cost and schedule impacts.

Calculations to support project analysis will be introduced. Many of these will be shown two different ways. Some in industry are using nomenclature different from the traditional BCWS (Budgeted Cost for Work Scheduled, BCWP (Budgeted Cost for Work Performed), and ACWP (Actual Cost of Work Performed). These same data elements are also know as PV (Planned Value), EV (Earned Value), and AC (Actual Cost). Where applicable, both will be shown.

Remember the traditional approach that was presented in the very first chapter of this text? All it did was compare planned spending with actual spending, with no measure of what work had been accomplished for the money spent. It told

very little about cost or schedule progress. For a more meaningful comparison, earned value is compared with budget (planned accomplishment) and with actual cost to allow determination of a schedule variance and cost variance, respectively. A positive value indicates favorable performance and a negative value indicates unfavorable performance.

Something else to remember is that cost variance and schedule variance do not mix with each other or cancel each other out. A poor cost variance combined with a good schedule variance does not mean that everything is all right. This is shown in Figure 32-2.

Costs at completion can also be compared to get a projected variance at completion. The Variance at Completion (VAC) is calculated as BAC - EAC,

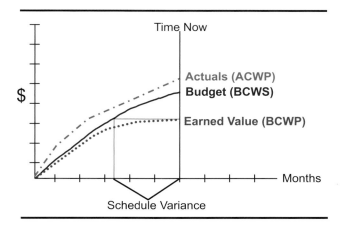

DO NOT ADD Cost Variance (CV) to Schedule Variance (SV)

Budget = $ 225 ⟩ 50 Favorable SV

Earned Value = $ 275 ⟩ (50) unfavorable CV

Actual Cost = $ 325 ⟩ 0 = ?

Schedule Variance is a subjective indicator.
Cost Variance is an objective indicator.

Variance Calculations: SV = Earned Value (BCWP) – Budget (BCWS)
CV = Earned Value (BCWP) – Actual Cost (ACWP)

Figure 32-2 Mixing Variances

or the budget minus the estimated final cost. Once again, a positive number indicates a favorable condition (projected cost underrun).

Schedule variance is sometimes converted to a time variance. These conversion techniques are approximations but can provide some picture of how serious a schedule variance is becoming. Two formulas that are frequently used are:

1. $SV\text{ (months)} = \dfrac{SV_{cum}}{EV_{(Monthly\ Average)^*}}$

    $Also = \dfrac{SV_{cum}}{BCWP_{(Monthly\ Average)^*}}$

2. $SV\text{ (months)} = \dfrac{SV_{cum}}{PV_{(Monthly\ Average)^*}}$

    $Also = \dfrac{SV_{cum}}{BCWS_{(Monthly\ Average)^*}}$

*Monthly average can be the cumulative monthly average, current month, or a recent month average (e.g., last 3 month average).

For illustration purposes using formula 1, assume that a cumulative schedule variance of +80 is being analyzed. One approach to convert this dollar schedule variance to a time variance is to look at the rate at which earned value is being accomplished. This can be done by dividing the total earned value to date by the number of months since contract initiation. This gives an average earned value per month. The cumulative schedule variance is then divided by that result. In this example, the cumulative earned value is 200 and the contract has been active for

three months. With a rate of 66.7 earned value per month, the favorable schedule variance of 80 represents about 1.2 months' worth of work.

This is calculated as: 80/66.7 = 1.2 months ahead of schedule

A different answer will result if average monthly budget is used in place of average monthly earned value as in formula 2. Continuing with the previous example, the plan was to accomplish 40 units per month, so 80 ahead corresponds to two months ahead. It is considered more accurate to use a rate of earned value rather than a planning rate because the rate at which work is being accomplished would certainly seem to be a more accurate indicator than the rate at which work was supposed to be accomplished.

These are not the only calculations that might be used. Instead of the cumulative average rate, performance could be limited to the current month or the average of the last three or six months. This type of rolling average helps to eliminate the effect of a non-linear monthly budget and earned value curves.

Another way of viewing status is to look at the horizontal distance along the graph instead of the vertical distance (see Figure 32-3).

Figure 32-3 Graphical Schedule Conversion

This is a much simpler approach than the calculations described previously and it eliminates the problem addressing non-linear curves. This figure shows that this month's cumulative earned value should have been earned almost 3 months earlier.

Using only performance measurement data to try to establish schedule position is risky. Since performance measurement data is usually reviewed at a higher, more summary, level than where the schedule was developed, the delay of critical items that could impact the completion of the control account may not be visible.

Schedule and cost status may also be represented in a performance measurement system as a percentage. The schedule and cost variance percentages are calculated as follows:

$$SV\% = \frac{SV}{PV} \times 100 = \frac{SV}{BCWS} \times 100$$

$$CV\% = \frac{CV}{EV} \times 100 = \frac{CV}{BCWP} \times 100$$

The denominator for the schedule variance percentage is the cumulative budget because this is the plan against which one is ahead or behind. The denominator for the cost variance is the cumulative earned value, because this is the value of the work accomplished to date against which there is either an underrun or overrun.

A plot of the cost and schedule variances provides valuable trend information for management evaluation. One example is shown in Figure 32-4.

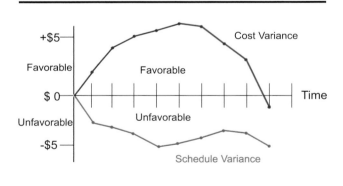

Figure 32-4 Trend Analysis

In this plot, we only know whether the variances are favorable or unfavorable, but we do not know the significance with respect to the total budget for the data plotted. This plot would have a different shape if it were a plot of the percentages rather than the dollar variances; however, we still would not have a perspective of the magnitude of the variances. A way to address this is to draw 10% threshold variance lines on the dollar chart. In this manner, both the magnitude and the seriousness of the variance are shown on the same chart. This is shown in Figure 32-5.

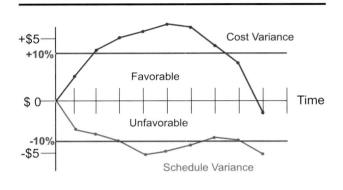

Figure 32-5 Trend Analysis with Percentage Threshold

The trends shown in this plot are typical because project budgets tend to be more than adequate in initial months. Also projects tend to be optimistically scheduled. Most cannot staff up to the projected resources as quickly as they plan to, so the end result is positive cost and negative schedule variances in the beginning stages of a project. As you can see here, they trend negatively in later phases.

Developing the Estimate at Completion (EAC)

The chart in Figure 32-6 provides a representation of how the Estimate at Completion (EAC) could be reported.

The EAC is shown as a dollar value at a specified point in time and is composed of actual costs to date plus the estimated costs to complete the authorized work. It also illustrates another feature of the EAC: it should be a time phased forecast of future costs, not just a single point of reference. The Estimate to Complete (ETC) will be developed at the same level of detail as the original budget that was prepared.

The principle questions to be answered in developing an Estimate at Completion (EAC) are when will the project be completed and how much will it cost?

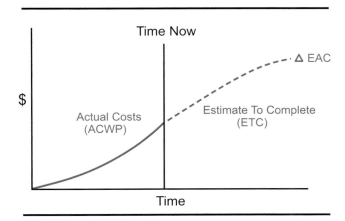

Figure 32-6 Estimate at Completion

The EAC is also known as the Latest Revised Estimate, Final Indicated Cost, Cost at Completion, and Estimated Cost at Completion. Whatever it is called, all of these terms refer to the projected cost at project completion. The general formula for developing an EAC is:

$$EAC = \text{Cumulative Actual Costs} + ETC$$

with ETC equal to the Estimated Cost to Complete the project. The ETC considers only the costs expected to be spent from "time now" to the end of the project. The ETC should be developed based on all available information at the time the forecast is prepared.

When developing an EAC or ETC the following should be considered:

1. The "as of" date of the estimate.

2. The current (not baseline) schedule to completion.

3. Performance to date (compared with the budget).

4. Remaining work and its anticipated performance.

5. Rates (direct and indirect).

6. Commitment values for material, equipment, and purchased services that have not yet been recorded as actual costs.

7. Scope changes that are approved but not yet incorporated in the baseline.

8. Pending scope changes or known change requests.

9. Funding constraints (for time-phasing future costs).

Preparation of a detailed EAC is time consuming. Because of this, there are typically two types of Estimates at Completion (EAC) prepared on a project. The first and more frequent of these is part of the monthly variance analysis cycle discussed previously. Whenever Variance Analysis Reports (VARs) are prepared for a control account exceeding established reporting thresholds, the EAC must be evaluated for impact. In this manner, significant happenings on a project are incorporated on a month-by-month basis into the projected final cost of the project. This is not all-inclusive, however, because a revised forecast may not be prepared for control accounts not requiring a VAR. However, if a control account does not require a VAR, but the CAM determines that the schedule and/or cost variance trend indicates a future impact, the EAC may be updated.

The second type of EAC generated is the comprehensive EAC, which consists of a reevaluation of all control accounts with remaining authorized work. This type of EAC is a "bottoms-up" or grass roots effort, starting with the most detailed information on the project and progressively summarizing it to higher levels. The comprehensive EAC is a major undertaking and therefore is not done on a monthly basis. Most organizations prefer to prepare a comprehensive EAC on an annual or semiannual basis, depending on other business planning activities. The eight factors listed above are evaluated for every control account on the project and then combined into an overall assessment of the projected final cost of the project. This becomes the revised EAC. Even control accounts in which no work has been performed will be evaluated to reflect latest available knowledge. Work that has been completed in an active control account may provide an insight into a future control account in regards to problem areas.

Certain considerations should be included in any comprehensive EAC effort. Most importantly, the development of the EAC should focus on what work has been accomplished rather than just what money has been spent. In order to accurately forecast remaining cost, a firm understanding of work remaining is necessary. This presupposes a solid understanding of what work has been completed.

Another important consideration, which is sometimes overlooked, is determination of the expected completion date, which is item 2 above. This will directly affect the EAC because of a direct relationship between total project duration and cost for support services such as schedule maintenance, administration, and supervision. There is also the potential for increased escalation as a project's completion date extends into the future.

The EAC also provides useful information to the organization. The EAC can be used for identifying the need for new hires as well as for projecting layoffs. It is needed for planning and revising the base for overhead forecasts. It will be used for cash flow analysis and forecasts of profit. It may be reported to an external customer and can serve as the basis for decisions of project deferral or cancellation. There will be an increased level of credibility in the estimate number if its generation can be traced to an established and logical procedure.

Performance Indices

Schedule variances and cost variances have already been discussed. This data can also be represented as a ratio that provides a measure of cost efficiency known as the Cost Performance Index (CPI) or schedule efficiency called the Schedule Performance Index (SPI).

Cost Performance Index (CPI)

Under the efficiency concept, the purpose of the Cost Performance Index (CPI_E) is to indicate the efficiency with which work has been accomplished. Thus, the CPI is most frequently defined as:

$$CPI_E = \frac{EV}{AC} = \frac{BCWP}{ACWP}$$

Under the performance concept, the purpose of the Cost Performance Index (CPI_P) is to indicate the actual cost of each planned dollar of work

accomplished. The formula for this CPI_P is merely the inverse of the one shown above or:

$$CPI_P = \frac{AC}{EV} = \frac{ACWP}{BCWP}$$

The CPI_P formula is also used for developing independent statistical Estimates at Completion (IEACs). The CPI_E as defined above displays an efficiency percentage for the work completed. For example, a CPI_E of 0.89 would mean that operations are at an 89% efficiency level, with 100% defined as the budgeted level. Expressed another way, for every dollar spent, $0.89 worth of work has been accomplished. This is, of course, unfavorable.

There are some interesting phenomena regarding the CPI. Some contractors will not use CPI_E as a predictor of performance until the project is at least 25% or 30% complete. This conflicts with research studies[1, 2] on hundreds of contracts that conclude that CPI_E essentially never improves after a contract is only 15% to 20% complete. This is even earlier than many contractors think it has any predictive value.

Some reasons why this occurs may be that contractors are "front end loading" their budgets (and therefore earned value), meaning the budgets will be too lean for work performed in the later part of the contract. So if a project starts poorly, it has little chance of recovering since the later budgets will be even more challenging than the early ones. Other contributing factors may be depletion of management reserve in the early phases of the contract. On production and construction contracts, the receipt of firm fixed price material can initially give artificially high contract Cost Performance Index results. On research and development efforts, costs accelerate after early contract stages when testing problems occur and the pressure of behind schedule delivery situations start to impact costs.

1.   Christensen, David and Heise, Scott. *Cost Performance Index Stability.* Paper, www.suu.edu/faculty/christensend/evms/CPIstabilityNCMJ.pdf, 1993.
2.   Christensen, David and Rees, David. *Is the CPI-Based EAC a Lower Bound to the Final Cost of Post A-12 Contracts?* Paper, Journal of Cost Analysis and Management, 2002.

Schedule Performance Index (SPI)

Schedule Performance Index is defined as:

$$SPI = \frac{EV}{PV} = \frac{BCWP}{BCWS}$$

The SPI is merely another measure of schedule performance, providing a picture of the relative rate at which work is being completed compared to the planned rate. An SPI value of 0.50 would indicate that half as much work has been accomplished as was planned to be accomplished (at time now). This is only an indicator of total work accomplished without regard to whether it was actually the work that was scheduled or whether it was critical work.

The implication is that the "wrong" work can be accomplished early in order to achieve enough earned value credit to make the SPI look acceptable. While this type of game-playing is more trouble than just doing the work, it can happen unintentionally. So while an SPI of 1.00 means that the same total value of work was completed as the total value of the work that was scheduled, there is no guarantee that the project schedule is trouble free. The SPI should never be used for schedule status without supplementing it with information from the CPM schedule.

To Complete Performance Index (TCPI)

While the CPI_E looks at performance in the past, the TCPI represents projected performance in the future based on the EAC. It compares the budget for remaining work with the estimate for remaining work, allowing a measure of required performance to achieve the estimate at completion. The formula, with some sample numbers, is contained in Figure 32-7.

$$TCPI_{EAC} = \frac{\text{Budget for work remaining}}{\text{Estimate for work remaining}} = \frac{BAC - BCWP_{Cum}}{EAC - ACWP_{Cum}}$$

$$TCPI_{EAC} = \frac{210{,}000 - 70{,}000}{230{,}000 - 80{,}000} = \frac{140{,}000}{150{,}000} = .93$$

Figure 32-7 "To Complete" Performance Index (TCPI)$_{EAC}$

The obvious use of the $TCPI_{EAC}$ is to compare it with the CPI_E, since this comparison provides an immediate indication of whether or not the EAC is realistic or not.

One case, shown in Figure 32-8, illustrates the interpretation of the data. Is the EAC realistic in the example given in Figure 32-7 considering that the contract is 33% complete? By dividing the budget for the remaining work by the estimate for the remaining work, the efficiency required to achieve the EAC is calculated. Based on the earlier referenced studies of contracts and CPI_E performance, one would have to conclude that the organization projecting the EAC used in the TCPI calculation was being too optimistic since the projected performance efficiency is greater than that experienced in the past.

CPI_E	$TCPI_{EAC}$
Performance to date	Projected Performance
0.875	.93
For every $1.00 of actual cost we earned $0.875 worth of planned work	For every $1.00 of actual cost, we estimate to earn $ .93 worth of planned work to finish on EAC

Figure 32-8 Performance Indices Comparison

Independent Estimates at Completion (IEAC)

Independent EAC calculations have become almost standard and may be used to predict the final cost of a project. This result can then be compared with the reported estimate at completion (EAC).

Typically, an independent EAC (or IEAC) is derived by adding cumulative actual cost to the budget of the work remaining, which is modified by a performance factor such as the Cost Performance Index (CPI_E).

$$IEAC = \left(\text{Actual Cost to Date} + \frac{\text{Budget of Work Remaining}}{\text{Performance Factor}} \right)$$

The term "budget of work remaining" is defined as Budget at Completion (BAC) minus cumulative earned value (EV), or the Budgeted Cost of Work

Remaining (BCWR). Different answers will result depending on what method is used to predict the future performance factor. Some measure of performance to date will be used, but that may be a 3-month rolling average, 6-month rolling average, or cumulative to date performance.

There are many ways of developing Independent Estimates at Completion (IEAC). One Department of Defense Request For Proposal required the IEAC to be calculated seven different ways supplemented by a subjective EAC. Three useful calculations are as follows:

1. $\text{IEAC} = \left(AC_{cum} + \dfrac{BAC - EV_{cum}}{(EV_{cum}/AC_{cum})} \right)$

   $\text{Also} = \left(ACWP_{cum} + \dfrac{BAC - BCWP_{cum}}{(BCWP_{cum}/ACWP_{cum})} \right)$

   Since earned value divided by actual cost is the CPI_E and the calculation assumes the same cost performance in the future as in the past, the calculation can be simplified to the following unless an Over Target Baseline has been implemented:

   $$\text{IEAC} = \frac{BAC}{CPI_E}$$

2. $\text{IEAC} = \left(AC_{cum} + \dfrac{(BAC - EV_{cum})}{(80\% \times CPI_E) + (20\% \times SPI)} \right)$

   $\text{Also} = \left(ACWP_{cum} + \dfrac{(BAC - BCWP_{cum})}{(80\% \times CPI_E) + (20\% \times SPI)} \right)$

3. $\text{IEAC} = \left(AC_{cum} + \dfrac{(BAC - EV_{cum})}{(CPI_E \times SPI)} \right)$

   $\text{Also} = \left(ACWP_{cum} + \dfrac{(BAC - BCWP_{cum})}{(CPI_E \times SPI)} \right)$

The first IEAC assumes that future work will be accomplished at exactly the same cost performance efficiency that has been experienced to date. This method does not include any regard for CPM schedule status, technical progress or difficulty, or future changing conditions. This may not be an appropriate conclusion if applied at the completion of the design phase of a project as production is starting. An entirely different set of conditions may be in operation at that point. All of these calculations are a guide more than a definitive answer. They are, however, much more accurate when applied at the control account level rather than at a summary level where various factors cancel each other out.

While the first IEAC considers only cost performance, the second IEAC takes into account schedule performance and uses weights for the CPI and SPI. These weights can be modified depending in the importance determined for each.

The third IEAC is similar to the second except that the CPI and SPI efficiency rates are equal and are multiplied by each other. This calculation can provide a wider variance range than the first two. The SPI and CPI should be cumulative to date. The idea behind this is that a behind schedule condition as indicated by the SPI usually leads to additional cost overruns. This is true for at least two reasons: it typically requires additional resources to recover schedule position, and a poor SPI is an indicator of possible delay in completion which will directly increase cost. If SPI > 1.0, however, the addition of SPI to the equation would lessen the impact on the final EAC compared with using the CPI only.

There is another reason why these IEAC formulas are of interest. If the project were experiencing an overrun to date, these analyses provide a check against the reasonableness or achievability of the manager's projection. This may be of interest when reporting thresholds are considered. One of the key difficulties in implementing a performance measurement system is to set the thresholds correctly. The intent is to make it a tool for management by exception, which requires a definition of the boundary of what is acceptable and what constitutes a significant variance. Depending on how close the project is tracking to plan and how tight the thresholds have been set, there can be an overwhelming number of variances to address. An effective system will limit itself to a reasonable number of variances to analyze each month. This can be done by requiring analysis of only the worst five or ten accounts. The IEACs help to focus attention on the higher risk control accounts.

One approach prioritizes attention on the accounts that have the biggest potential for improvement if the performance could be brought back to plan from its current level. That can be objectively determined by comparing the range of IEACs with the manager's projection and with other indicie data. The magnitude of this answer indicates how much potential improvement there is. It considers all of the following factors:

1. How large the accounts are

2. How much performance is varying from plan

3. How much work is remaining

These are all important considerations. If one control account is off by 20% and another is off by 15%, the size of the control account will be an important factor. However, no matter how far a control account is varying from plan, there is little if any opportunity to recover costs if the control account were already 95% complete.

An example will clarify the situation. Assume that there are five control accounts with the following cumulative data:

	Control Account				
	CA 1	CA 2	CA 3	CA 4	CA 5
BCWS	500	150	200	10,000	3,500
BCWP	500	200	200	9,500	1,500
ACWP	500	400	100	14,500	2,500
BAC	1,000	1,000	1,000	10,000	6,000
CAM EAC	1,000	1,100	800	15,000	7,000
BCWR (work remaining BAC-BCWP)	500	800	800	500	4,500
FUNDS REMAINING (EAC-ACWP)	500	700	700	500	4,500
CPI_E	1.00	0.50	2.00	0.66	0.60
SPI	1.00	1.33	1.00	0.95	0.43
TCPI	1.00	1.14	1.14	1.00	1.00
IEAC 1	1,000	2,000	500	15,263	10,000
IEAC 2	1,000	1,600	544	15,200	10,454
IEAC 3	1,000	1,600	500	15,303	20,000

Control Account #5 clearly is the top priority for management attention. Comparing the IEACs and other statistical data, the "potential improvement" is greater than the other control accounts. This results from the data indicating that it is a very large control account, has considerable work scope remaining, and has significant cost and schedule problems. All of the IEACs are greater than the CAM's projection with the third being extreme. Since the BCWR and the ETC are equal, the TCPI is 1.00. But, the historical performance shown with the CPI_E of .6 and the SPI of .43 does not indicate that the remaining work can be completed for the CAM's EAC of $7,000, which indicates that the CAM's EAC should be revised. However, what the indicie analysis does not include is an evaluation of the remaining

work. There is the possibility that the work performed to date, while costing more and having a negative schedule position, will result in much lower future costs. The indicie data will show areas to target for further analysis and improvement, but should always include an analysis of the content of the remaining work scope.

Control Account #2 is next in line for attention. While it is not a large account, the variance from plan is significant and there is also considerable work scope remaining.

Control Account #4 is by far the largest, but it is almost done and there is little difference whether it completes at a CPI of 1.00 or its historical 0.66. With only 5% of the work remaining, this account's performance is already largely determined.

Control Account #1 has performed at budgeted levels so there is no action required.

Control Account #3 is performing efficiently and is a candidate for reduction of the CAMs EAC; again however, the remaining work must be analyzed.

By using this approach, it is possible to print out a list of those accounts needing immediate attention by sorting the results of the analysis. This approach has been used successfully on some large projects to focus attention on a limited number of variances. However, this is just one approach. Many should be examined for best applicability to any given project.

Preparing a Range of Estimates at Completion

By going a step further, it is possible to produce a whole family of Estimates at Completion (see Figure 32-9).

The BAC is the currently approved budget (including all approved scope changes). Based on an analysis of project status, potential risk in the remaining work and the likelihood of various scenarios occurring, projections can be developed to represent a range of possible outcomes. The best case EAC projection assumes ideal conditions for the remainder of the project. A worst case EAC scenario can be projected by

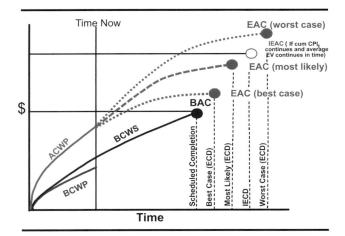

Figure 32-9 Range of Estimates at Completion

recognizing any negative trends and possible future disruptions to project completion. The most likely EAC should be developed based on recognition of performance to date and the probable future conditions to be encountered, which may be different than those experienced to date. The important element here is to use judgment. The projections should always be compared with the EAC which will result if current performance continues until the end of the project. The Independent Estimate at Completion calculations can be used as a tool to aid in forecasting the best, worst, and most likely EAC projections.

Percent Complete

Notice that the EACs exhibited in Figure 32-9 are dependent on the projected completion dates. The value for the EAC does not stand alone; it must be accompanied by the projected completion date as extension of that date usually has a negative cost impact.

One of the advantages of an earned value management and reporting system is the ability to precisely and objectively determine the percent complete of a project in a budget sense. The definition is:

$$\text{Percent Complete} = \frac{\text{Work Complete}}{\text{Total Work}} \times 100$$

$$\text{or} = \frac{EV_{cum}}{BAC} \times 100 = \frac{BCWP_{cum}}{BAC} \times 100$$

In order to accurately portray the project percent complete, the Budget at Completion (BAC) should include any management reserve.

Most organizations like to compare this value with the percent spent of a project in a funding sense. The definition is:

$$\text{Percent Spent} = \frac{AC_{cum}}{EAC} \times 100 = \frac{ACWP_{cum}}{EAC} \times 100$$

The denominator reflects whatever the best projection of final cost is, or the Estimate at Completion. The comparison of these two percentages reveals how fast money is being spent compared with how fast work is being completed.

Estimated Completion Date (ECD)

In calculating an Estimate at Completion (EAC), the date on which it is believed that the work will be completed must also be estimated. There are several methods available to calculate the number of Months to Complete (MTC) the work remaining. The calculation may be based on (1) the current Budget value, (2) an average Budget value, (3) the current Earned Value or, (4) an average Earned value.

1. $MTC = \dfrac{BAC - EV_{cum}}{PV_{cur}} = \dfrac{BAC - BCWP_{cum}}{BCWS_{cur}}$

2. $MTC = \dfrac{BAC - EV_{cum}}{PV_{avg}} = \dfrac{BAC - BCWP_{cum}}{BCWS_{avg}}$

3. $MTC = \dfrac{BAC - EV_{cum}}{EV_{cur}} = \dfrac{BAC - BCWP_{cum}}{BCWP_{cur}}$

4. $MTC = \dfrac{BAC - EV_{cum}}{EV_{avg}} = \dfrac{BAC - BCWP_{cum}}{BCWP_{avg}}$

The Estimated Completion Date (ECD) is determined by adding the estimated number of Months to Complete (MTC) the remaining work to the time now date.

ECD = Time Now Date + MTC

Average Performance Rate Required to Achieve ECD

Just as the TCPI formula can be used to evaluate the cost performance required to achieve the

EAC, the average rate or performance required to achieve the estimated completion date can be calculated:

$$\text{Average Performance to Complete} = \frac{BAC - EV_{cum}}{MTC}$$

$$\text{Also} = \frac{BAC - BCWP_{cum}}{MTC}$$

Subsequent to this calculation a comparison can then be made to further evaluate future performance by analyzing past performance:

$$\text{Past Average Performance} = \frac{EV_{cum}}{MTD} = \frac{BCWP_{cum}}{MTD}$$

Where MTD = Months to Date

Combining SPI with CPM Information

So far CPM scheduling and earned value status have been discussed separately. Now CPM and earned value data will be combined with the result that much better assessments can be made about project status and performance. Either set of data alone is helpful, but only when the data are combined is a complete picture of the project possible.

The situation exhibited in Figure 32-10 shows a schedule variance equal to zero, indicating things are precisely on schedule. But look at the network status within. If the critical path goes through the top path, then the project is behind schedule. If the lower path were critical, the project is ahead of schedule.

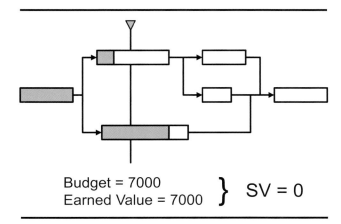

Budget = 7000
Earned Value = 7000 } SV = 0

Figure 32-10 Performance Measurement Data Concern

If total float (TF) on the critical path were a negative value, the CPM schedule indicates a slippage in the final completion date. If the total float were positive, more slippage can take place without any impact to the project completion date. A Schedule Performance Index (SPI) status of less than one indicates that less total work was accomplished than scheduled. If the SPI were greater than one, then more total work has been completed than planned. Combining SPI and total float data from a CPM schedule can yield more information than either piece of data alone as seen in Figure 32-11.

SPI	TF	
>1	>0	Ahead of schedule
<1	<0	Behind schedule
>1	<0	Critical activities behind, but total work ahead (priority problem)
<1	>0	Critical activities ahead, but total work behind (future trouble)

Figure 32-11 Combining SPI and TF Data

It is easy to see that if positive float were available and the Schedule Performance Index (SPI) were greater than one, the project is ahead of schedule. When total float is negative and SPI is less than one, then the project is clearly behind schedule.

Unfortunately, practical experience typically shows mixed indicators like the last two cases in Figure 32-11. A situation where SPI is greater than one and the critical path total float is negative indicates more total work has been accomplished than planned, and yet, the project end date is slipping. The simplest explanation for this situation could be that management has not placed appropriate priority on the critical path tasks. Another explanation could be that a critical path activity cannot be accomplished for reasons such as lack of customer furnished information, delay of materials from suppliers, or technical design flaws, and the organization is performing other work out of sequence to keep the work force productively engaged. A situation where

SPI is less than one and the critical path total float is positive indicates less total work has been accomplished than planned, but the project can finish ahead of the planned completion date. A possible explanation for this condition is that management has held off starting portions of the work because information or material is not available, but the affected work is not on the critical path. Another possible explanation is that the CPM schedule was poorly constructed and the critical path does not reflect the true plan to accomplish the work. The bottom line in these situations where the earned value data conflicts with the CPM schedule data is that the systems are providing red flags to investigate root causes. The valuable information is often found in the determination of the root cause rather than simply the comparison of the system metrics.

Combining SPI with CPI (Labor Only)

If a control account under review contains only labor charges, it is possible to isolate the impacts of overstaffing/understaffing versus labor productivity. Material costs will mask this effect if included within the same account, because material cost variances cannot be related to staffing or productivity variances.

Combining SPI and CPI information implies underlying causes as illustrated in Figure 32-12. A CPI greater than one indicates that the work was done efficiently or less expensively. So when that condition occurs in combination with an SPI of less than one, which indicates not enough total work was accomplished relative to the approved plan, conclusions could be drawn that not enough resources have been allocated to the control account, less complex work is being performed and the more complex has been deferred, the skill mix being used is different from plan, or that the actual rates applied are less than plan.

A condition where CPI is less than one and SPI is greater than one could indicate that there may have been overstaffing relative to the approved plan, paid overtime was worked, more costly personnel were used, or the planned costs have

been understated. Often, of course, there is a combination of these factors.

SPI	CPI	
<1	>1	Understaffing? Less expensive resources?
>1	<1	Overstaffing? Overtime worked? Planned costs understated?

Figure 32-12 Combining SPI and CPI (Labor Accounts)

Reporting

Do people actually use all of these calculations? Yes. These calculations are a tool to focus attention on problem areas in order to implement earlier corrective action. The calculations also aid in identification of risk items that can become unfavorable cost and schedule drivers. By reviewing the data, management attention can be devoted to the highest priority items.

Report Formats

There are many ways to report project status, but one of the most concise reports that includes a significant amount of information is the Contract Performance Report (CPR). It can be formatted to summarize information by work product via the Work Breakdown Structure (excerpt shown in Figure 32-13) and/ or by organization (excerpt shown in Figure 32-14). The data included in the report includes: the budget, the earned value, and the actual cost. There are also columns for the cost variance and schedule variance as well as the BAC, EAC, and the at completion variance. This information is reported for the current month and cumulative to date.

The examples contained herein are limited to cumulative to date information. The last columns on the right reflect the impact to the cost at completion, comparing the current forecast against the approved budget. Any variances in the completion cost are also identified here on a WBS basis and at the bottom line total.

WBS Elements	Cumulative to Date					At Completion		
	Budget	Earned Value	Actual Cost	Schedule Variance	Cost Variance	Budget	Estimate	Variance
(1)	(2)	(3)	(4)	(5)	(6)	(7)	(8)	(9)
Fossil Unit								
Structures & Improvements	20,000	22,000	18,000	2,000	4,000	50,000	46,000	4,000
Boiler plant equipment	40,000	37,000	39,000	(3,000)	(2,000)	200,000	210,000	(10,000)
Turbine generator equipment	10,000	10,000	12,000	0	(2,000)	50,000	50,000	0
Accessory electrical equipment	3,500	3,000	2,800	(500)	200	35,000	35,000	0
Misc. power plant equipment	500	700	600	200	100	5,000	5,000	0
Project Services	29,000	27,000	31,000	(2,000)	(4,000)	70,000	75,000	(5,000)
Perf. Meas. Baseline	103,000	99,700	103,400	(3,300)	(3,700)	410,000	421,000	(11,000)
Management Reserve						30,000		
TOTAL	103,000	99,700	103,400	(3,300)	(3,700)	440,000		

Figure 32-13 Performance Report - Work Breakdown Structure

Project Organization	Cumulative to Date					At Completion		
	Budget	Earned Value	Actual Cost	Schedule Variance	Cost Variance	Budget	Estimate	Variance
(1)	(2)	(3)	(4)	(5)	(6)	(7)	(8)	(9)
Program Management	10,000	10,000	9,000	0	1,000	40,000	40,000	0
Engineering	25,000	23,000	25,000	(2,000)	(2,000)	60,000	64,000	(4,000)
AJAX Excavation	26,000	25,000	24,900	(1,000)	100	112,000	112,000	0
ACE Site Services	4,000	4,000	3,700	0	300	16,000	16,000	0
Airborne Surveyors	12,000	11,500	11,800	(500)	(300)	22,000	22,000	0
ACME Hauling	15,000	14,700	16,300	(300)	(1,600)	80,000	84,000	(4,000)
Testing	7,200	7,700	9,000	500	(1,300)	50,000	53,000	(3,000)
Special Support	3,800	3,800	3,700	0	100	30,000	30,000	0
Perf. Meas. Baseline	103,000	99,700	103,400	(3,300)	(3,700)	410,000	421,000	(11,000)
Management Reserve						30,000		
TOTAL	103,000	99,700	103,400	(3,300)	(3,700)	440,000		

Figure 32-14 Performance Report - Project Organization

Reviewing the top line of data, Structures & Improvements, in Figure 32-13, reveals that the cumulative earned value of 22,000 (column 3) exceeds both the cumulative budget of 20,000 (column 2) and the cumulative actual cost of 18,000 (column 4).

This indicates that, at this point, this part of the project is in a favorable condition with regard to both cost and schedule. This is confirmed by the positive value of 2,000 for the schedule variance and 4,000 for the cost variance. Based on this information, it might be expected that the EAC would show an underrun in "At Completion" cost.

That is what is reported, since the EAC shown in column 8 is 46,000.

This is 4,000 less than the approved budget of 50,000 shown in column 7. This means that future costs are predicted to be as budgeted, but the cost underrun to date has been reflected in the forecast. No additional underrun (beyond that which has occurred) is foreseen.

Analyzing Material Cost Variances

When forecasting final costs, one of the key inputs is material cost and the associated cost variances. Remember that the cost variance is defined as:

CV = Earned Value - Actual Cost

Once the cost variance is known, the next step is to isolate its components. These are the price variance (PV), the variation in price for each unit purchased, and the usage variance (UV), the variation in the number of units earned. These are defined and calculated as follows:

$$PV = (EV\ Unit\ Price - AC\ Unit\ Price) \times AC\ Quantity$$

$$Also = (BCWP\ Unit\ Price - ACWP\ Unit\ Price) \times ACWP\ Quantity$$

$$UV = (EV\ Quantity - AC\ Quantity) \times EV\ Unit\ Price$$

$$Also = (BCWP\ Quantity - ACWP\ Quantity) \times BCWP\ Unit\ Price$$

Both of these components need to be analyzed separately for the material variance analysis process. The results should be reflected in any EAC projections as well as used as further explanation in the "problem analysis" section of the Variance Analysis Report.

An example of a control account follows:

Budget: 10 units @ $5/unit = $50 total

Earned: 10 units @ $5/unit = $50 total

Actual: 12 units @ $6/unit = $72 total

The cost variance is: CV = $50 - $72 = ($22)

The components of this variance would be determined like this:

Price Variance = ($5 - $6) x 12 units = ($12)

Usage Variance = (10-12) x $5/unit = ($10)

Notice that the price variance and usage variance, when added together, always equal the total cost variance:

($12) + ($10) = ($22)

In this example, the price variance and quantity (i.e. usage) variance both contributed nearly equally to the overall cost variance.

In other cases, one of the components may actually offset the other. These variances are shown pictorially in Figure 32-15.

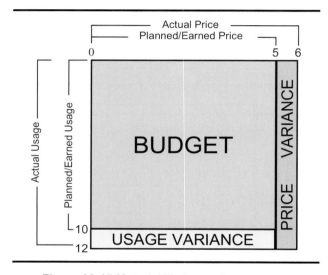

Figure 32-15 Material Variance Components

Analyzing Labor Cost Variances

The same discussion that was used for material variances also applies to labor variances. Once again, a labor cost variance can be broken into its components: a rate variance (RV) and a usage variance (UV).

These are defined and calculated as follows:

$$RV = (EV\ Rate - AC\ Rate) \times AC\ Labor\ Hours$$

$$Also = (BCWP\ Rate - ACWP\ Rate) \times ACWP\ Labor\ Hours$$

$$UV = (EV\ Hours - AC\ Hours) \times EV\ Hourly\ Rate$$

$$Also = (BCWP\ Hours - ACWP\ Hours) \times BCWP\ Hourly\ Rate$$

These results should similarly be considered in the "problem analysis" section of the Variance Analysis Report and in any projections of revised Estimates at Completion (EAC).

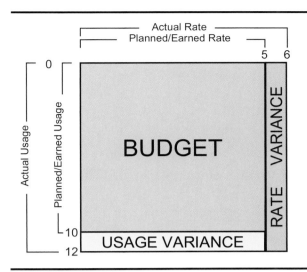

Figure 32-16 Labor Cost Variance Components

An illustration of the labor cost variance components is contained in Figure 32-16.

Earned Value and Cost/Schedule Impact Identification

While earned value may not be the solution to all management problems, it gives a far more accurate picture of status than comparing planned and actual expenditures. One of its biggest advantages is the capability of projecting cost overruns and schedule slippages early in the project as shown in Figure 32-17. Please remember, without knowing where a project is (Earned Value), how can a realistic Estimate to Complete be generated?

Conclusion

In this chapter, the standard calculations performed to interpret and analyze data from an inte-

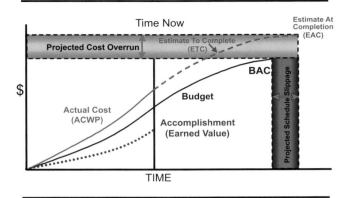

Figure 32-17 Cost and Schedule Impacts

grated cost/schedule system were discussed. The use of these formulas to forecast project status at completion is an important capability of an effective project management system. Estimates at completion, which are developed from the best available project status information, can be checked for reasonableness statistically. This provides an objective review of a subjective process.

Software exists that will quickly detect likely data errors, while also indicating which areas merit closer attention. The data can be presented in trend format for easier analysis. This allows more time and attention to be devoted to the analysis of variances and follow-up to previous action plans rather than digesting, reviewing, and formatting data.

The ability to integrate cost and schedule information into a single, concise report is one of the advantages of earned value reporting. The Contract Performance Report (CPR) with both WBS and organizational formats is the typical format used to report earned value data both internally and externally.

Chapter 32 Review Questions

32-1.   Explain how a graphical picture of trend analysis can be manipulated by switching between cost variance or schedule variance (numerical value) versus cost variance percent or schedule variance percent.

32-2.   Explain what is meant by a CPI_E of 1.20.

32-3.   What different information content is included in the CPI_E and $TCPI_{EAC}$?

32-4.   What information is indicated by a SPI of 0.80?

32-5.   Describe generally how statistical Independent Estimates at Completion (IEACs) are generated to assess the validity of the reported EAC.

32-6.   Discuss the difference in information content of the total float in CPM and schedule variance.

32-7.   Explain why being far ahead of schedule may not be desirable in some cases.

32-8.   What does it mean when total float is negative and SPI > 1.0?

32-9.   What does it mean when total float is positive and SPI < 1.0?

32-10. What is the formula for calculating percent complete using earned value data?

32-11. Discuss the meaning of price variance and usage variance as applied to material cost variances.

32-12. A control account has been completed with an actual cost of $500,000. The approved budget was $450,000 and the earned value is $450,000. The control account was supposed to take 6 months to complete but actually required 8 months. What is the schedule variance?

32-13. Identify the factors that are to be considered in the development of an Estimate to Complete (ETC) and Estimate at Completion (EAC).

True or False

32-14. Acceptable project status may be achieved many ways, including a favorable cost variance that is larger than an unfavorable schedule variance.

32-15. There are defined analytical approaches used to approximate the schedule variance in time instead of in dollars.

32-16. Precise schedule status may be determined by dividing the cumulative schedule variance by the average earned value per month.

32-17. When using schedule variance conversion techniques to predict time variances, it is more accurate to use cumulative schedule variance divided by average planned accomplishment per month then to use cumulative schedule variance divided by average earned value per month.

32-18. An approach sometimes used to interpret data is a rolling 3-month or 6-month average, because it is more stable than current period performance and more responsive to trends than cumulative to date performance.

32-19. Cost variance percent is defined as CV/Earned Value X 100.

32-20. A CPI_E of 0.7 would mean that work is being accomplished in 70% of the time defined in the CPM schedule.

32-21. The Estimate at Completion is a single point value of projected cost.

32-22. The Estimate at Completion is calculated by adding actual cost to date to the estimated cost to complete the work scope remaining.

32-23. A comparison of CPI_E with $TCPI_{EAC}$ provides an insight into the validity of the Estimate at Completion.

32-24. The Schedule Performance Index (SPI) and CPM analysis provide different views of schedule status which complement each other.

32-25. An SPI of 1 means that the project is on schedule.

32-26. If SPI > 1.00, that means that SV > 0.

32-27. A Contract Performance Report can be prepared for summary information by organization or by Work Breakdown Structure.

32-28. The following formula is always true for material cost variances: CV = PV + UV, where PV = price variance and UV = usage variance.

32-29. There is no equivalent concept to material price variance and usage variance for labor analysis.

32-30. There are two types of Estimates at Completion commonly prepared on a project: a monthly forecast which is part of the variance analysis process and a comprehensive EAC performed once or twice per year.

The answers to these questions can be found in Section 6, Solutions.

Case Study

32.1 PROJECT PERFORMANCE ANALYSIS

Highway Project

Task:

Build 60 miles of highway over a period of one year.

Budget Data:

5 miles per month at $500,000 per mile.

Assumptions:

1. Planned linear accomplishment of work.

2. All work is measurable except Program Management/Support, which is LOE.

3. No work in process at end of month.

Latest Performance Reports:

See the Monthly Performance Data Table and Contract Performance Report (CPR) for Month 7 that follow this page.

Calculate the:

*   Schedule Variance Percentage (SV%)

*   Cost Variance Percentage (CV%)

*   Cost Performance Index-Efficiency (CPI$_E$)

*   Cost Performance Index-Performance (CPI$_P$)

*   Schedule Performance Index (SPI)

*   Month ahead or behind schedule

*   Percent Complete

*   Percent Spent

*   To Complete Performance Index (TCPI)

*   Independent Estimate at Completion (IEAC)

*   Estimated Completion Date (in months) (ECD)

*   Average Performance Rate Required to achieve ECD

The solution to this case study can be found on the Humphreys & Associates, Inc. web site.
www.humphreys-assoc.com

Note 1: Reference the Earned Value Analysis Formulas section in Section 6 for details on how to calculate the items listed above.

Note 2: Where multiple formulas are provided to calculate a selected statistic, select what you consider to be the most likely outcome or most accurate indicator and be prepared to support your selection.

In addition:

1. Based on the CPR data, what type of subcontract is used for the materials (cement, steel rods, etc.)? Cost Plus, Time and Materials, or Firm Fixed Price?

2. Where multiple formulas are provided to calculate a selected statistic, select what you consider to be the most likely outcome or most accurate indicator and be prepared to suppport your selection.

3. Using the CPR for month 7 and the Contract Performance Report Data Item Description extract, be prepared to discuss the contractor's best, worst, and most likely estimated cost at completion. Use your analysis to support your position.

Highway CPR Progress Months 1 Through 7

(In millions of dollars)

Month	Current			Cum to date			Average	
	Budget	Earned Value	Actuals	Budget	Earned Value	Actuals	Budget	Earned Value
1	2.5	1.0	1.0	2.5	1.0	1.0	2.5	1.0
2	2.5	1.5	1.5	5.0	2.5	2.5	2.5	1.3
3	2.5	2.0	2.25	7.5	4.5	4.75	2.5	1.5
4	2.5	1.5	1.25	10.0	6.0	6.0	2.5	1.5
5	2.5	1.5	1.75	12.5	7.5	7.75	2.5	1.5
6	2.5	2.0	2.25	15.0	9.5	10.0	2.5	1.6
7	2.5	4.0	4.5	17.5	13.5	14.5	2.5	1.93

Budget At Completion = $30M
Estimate At Completion = $30.5M
Estimated Completion Date = Month 15 (3 months late)
Note: Budget is based on a plan of 5 miles per month at $500,000 per mile.
       5 miles X $500,000 per mile = $2,500,000 (Budget)

Status is based on the number of miles completed times the budget value of $500,000 per mile.

Example: In month seven, 8 miles were completed.
          8 miles X $500,000 per mile = $4,000,000 (Earned Value)

Classification (when filled in) _____

Contract Performance Report
Format 1 - Work Breakdown Structure

Dollars In _____ $000

1. Contractor
a. Name Wippity Bipp Construction Co.
b. Location (Address & Zip Code)
1 Briarpatch Lane
Thumperville, CA 90633

2. Contract
a. Name CALTRANS 20
b. Number XX-0763
c. Type CPFF
d. Share Ratio N/A

3. Program
a. Name Highway 73 Extension
b. Phase RDT&E
c. EVMS Acceptance No (Yes) (2001/05/06)

4. Report Period
a. From (YYYY/MM/DD) _____
b. To (YYYY/MM/DD) Month 7
i. Date of OTB/OTS (YYYY/MM/DD) _____

5. Contract Data
a. Quantity 1
b. Negotiated Cost $30,000,000
c. Est. Cost of Auth. Unpriced Work 0
d. Target Profit/Fee $3,000,000
e. Target Price $33,000,000
f. Estimated Price $33,500,000
g. Contract Ceiling N/A
h. Estimated Contract Ceiling N/A

7. Authorized Contractor Representative
a. Name (Last, First, Middle Initial) Quick, I.M.
b. Title Program Manager
c. Signature I.M. Quick
d. Date Signed (YYYY/MM/DD) Month 8, 10th.

6. Estimated Cost at Completion

	Management Estimate at Completion (1)	Contract Budget Base (2)	Variance (3)
a. Best Case	30,000		
b. Worst Case	36,000		
c. Most Likely	30,500	30,000	-500

8. Performance Data

Item (1)	Current Period Budgeted Cost Work Scheduled (2)	Budgeted Cost Work Performed (3)	Actual Cost Work Performed (4)	Variance Schedule (5)	Variance Cost (6)	Cumulative Budgeted Cost Work Scheduled (7)	Budgeted Cost Work Performed (8)	Actual Cost Work Performed (9)	Variance Schedule (10)	Variance Cost (11)	Reprog. Cost Variance (12a)	Reprog. Schedule Variance (12b)	Budget (13)	At Completion Budgeted (14)	Estimated (15)	Variance (16)
a. WBS																
Program Mgmt./ Support	160	160	110	0	50	1,150	1,150	650	0	500				1,950	1,350	600
Excavation Base	650	1,000	1,225	350	-225	4,500	3,200	3,727	-1,300	-527				8,000	8,403	-403
Hauling	340	600	825	260	-225	2,100	963	1,713	-1,137	-750				3,600	4,190	-590
Materials	850	1,390	1,390	540	0	6,125	5,325	5,325	-800	0				10,500	10,500	0
Testing/Inspection	67	157	170	90	-13	592	522	572	-70	-50				750	770	-20
b. Cost of Money	0	0	0	0	0	0	0	0	0	0				0	0	0
c. Gen. & Admin.	433	693	780	260	-87	3,033	2,340	2,513	-693	-173				5,200	5,287	-87
d. Undistributed Budget																
e. Subtotal (Performance Measurement Baseline)	2,500	4,000	4,500	1,500	-500	17,500	13,500	14,500	-4,000	-1,000				30,000	30,500	-500
f. Management Reserve																
g. TOTAL	2,500	4,000	4,500	1,500	-500	17,500	13,500	14,500	-4,000	-1,000				30,000		

9. Reconciliation To Contract Budget Base
a. Variance Adjustment
b. Total Contract Variance

Classification (when filled in)

CONTRACT PERFORMANCE REPORT (CPR)
DI-MGMT-81466
DATA ITEM DESCRIPTION (DID) EXTRACT

10.2.2.2.1 Management Estimate at Completion - Best Case. Enter in Block 6.a.1 the contractor's best case estimate at completion. The best case estimate is the one that results in the lowest cost to the Government. This estimate should be based on the outcome of the most favorable set of circumstances. If this estimate is different from the most likely estimate at completion (Block 6.c.1), the assumptions and conditions underlying this estimate should be explained briefly in Format 5. This estimate is for informational purposes only; it is not an official company estimate. There is no requirement for the contractor to prepare and maintain backup data beyond the explanation provided in Format 5.

10.2.2.2.2 Management Estimate at Completion - Worst Case. Enter in Block 6.b.1 the contractor's worst case estimate at completion. The worst case estimate is the one that results in the highest cost to the Government. This estimate should be based on the outcome of the least favorable set of circumstances. If this estimate is different from the most likely estimate at completion (Block 6.c.1.), the assumptions and conditions underlying this estimate should be explained briefly in Format 5. This estimate is for informational purposes only; it is not an official company estimate. There is no requirement for the contractor to prepare and maintain backup data beyond the explanation provided in Format 5.

10.2.2.2.3 Management Estimate at Completion - Most Likely. Enter in Block 6.c.1 the contractor's most likely estimate at completion. This estimate is the contractor's official contract EAC and, as such, takes precedence over the estimates presented in Column (15) of Formats 1 and 2 and Blocks 6.a.1 and 6.b.1. This EAC is the value that the contractor's management believes is the most likely outcome based on a knowledgeable estimate of all authorized work, known risks and probable future conditions. This value need not agree with the total of Column (15) (Block 8.e). However, any difference should be explained in Format 5 in such terms as risk, use of management reserve, or higher management knowledge of current or future contract conditions. This EAC need not agree with EACs contained in the contractor's internal data, but must be reconcilable to them. The most likely EAC also will be reconcilable to the contractor's latest statement of funds required as reported in the Contract Funds Status Report (DI-MGMT-81468), or its equivalent, if this report is a contractual requirement.

Case Study

32.2 CONTROL ACCOUNT ANALYSIS

Previously, you evaluated ten activity paths using Total Float data. In this case, we have added two additional items of information to each path: the Schedule Performance Index (SPI) and the Cost Performance Index (CPI). Review the combination of TF, SPI, and CPI for each path and answer the following question:

Which Control Accounts now deserve more management attention each month? On what basis did you make your decision?

Note: Control Accounts (CA) normally contain more than one activity path. For example, CA 32 contains two paths but path 32-2 is the most critical. See the diagram below.

Control Account 32

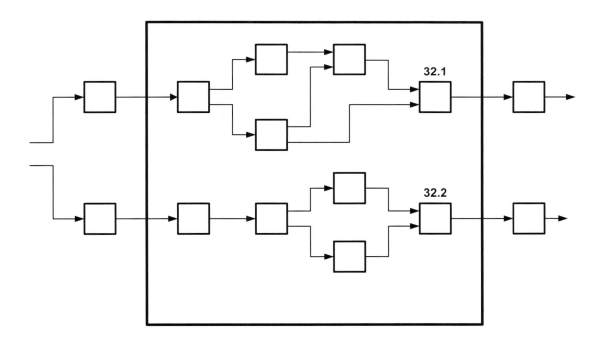

The solution to this case study can be found on the Humphreys & Associates, Inc. web site.
www.humphreys-assoc.com

SCHEDULE AND COST PERFORMANCE INDICES

ControlAccount		August	September	October	November
11	SPI	0.62	0.55	0.48	0.48
	CPI	0.32	0.28	0.29	0.33
26	SPI	1.06	1.09	1.04	1.09
	CPI	0.72	0.68	0.68	0.67
27	SPI	0.77	0.82	0.81	0.78
	CPI	0.73	0.72	0.69	0.66
29	SPI	1.00	1.00	1.00	1.00
	CPI	1.03	1.01	0.97	1.02
32	SPI	0.78	0.75	0.76	0.72
	CPI	0.78	0.76	0.70	0.67
35	SPI	1.00	FIN	FIN	FIN
	CPI	0.65			
43	SPI	0.45	0.44	0.43	0.41
	CPI	0.52	0.50	0.49	0.46
53	SPI	0.49	0.47	0.47	0.48
	CPI	0.73	0.64	0.65	0.65
55	SPI	0.62	0.68	0.59	0.57
	CPI	1.04	0.98	1.03	1.02
87	SPI	1.23	1.26	1.19	1.21
	CPI	0.57	0.56	0.58	0.55
92	SPI	0.72	0.68	0.64	0.59
	CPI	1.11	1.07	1.03	1.05
94	SPI	1.00	1.00	1.00	1.00
	CPI	2.16	2.23	2.55	2.61

All indices are cumulative through the end of the month.

SPI = BCWP/BCWS   CPI = BCWP/ACWP

>1 favorable   <1 unfavorable

PATH FLOAT

Activity Path	August	September	October	November
11-1	5	8	3	-2
11-2	4	2	3	-4
26-1	3	5	5	5
27-1	7	5	4	16
29-1	5	8	7	3
32-1	4	30	30	31
32-2	6	7	8	2
35-1	6	Finished	Finished	Finished
43-1	7	7	7	2
43-2	4	18	4	-4

Total Float (in days) as of the end of the month.

Chapter 33

VARIANCE ANALYSIS AND CORRECTIVE ACTION

Objectives of this Chapter:

1. Identify variances from plan as a starting point for analysis and corrective action.
2. Discuss the considerations that determine a "significant" variance.
3. Discuss the use of a Variance Analysis Report for identifying and addressing variances.

A sustained effort is required to get the project to this point and enable its day-to-day management. All of the necessary foundation work has been completed and there should be an integrated, detailed plan in place, as well as good visibility into current status. Accounting contributes the actual cost component, and it is now possible to calculate the cost and schedule position at any level of detail within the Work Breakdown Structure and the Organization Breakdown Structure.

Now the benefits of the carefully developed plan are realized, and the plan can be used for effective management of the project.

Variance Analysis

The entire process of developing an approved baseline plan and then determining status against that plan has one primary purpose: to identify significant variances. Once significant variances are identified, causes can be analyzed and corrective actions determined and implemented.

The Work Breakdown Structure (WBS) and Organization Breakdown Structure (OBS) are integral to "management by exception" because these tools enable variance identification from summary to detail levels. Earned value data, including variances, can be reported both internally and externally using the levels of the WBS and OBS.

Accordingly, variance analysis should be tailored to the appropriate management level or external reporting level. Ultimately, the control account at the intersection of these two structures represents the key point for variance identification and analysis. A picture of how the variances can be traced is shown in Figure 33-2.

If the highest summary level in the WBS were reviewed, an unfavorable variance of (100) is found. The data reveals that the major component contributing to this variance is the (280) variance from the Turbine Generator Equipment. It is then possible to look at the next lower level of detail within or beneath the Turbine Generator Equipment element of the WBS and find the source of this variance. The Condensing System, with its variance of (460), is the source of this unfavorable condition. Lastly, the variance can be isolated to a specific control account for the condensing system and the specific cause of the variance located. The condenser itself has experienced a (600) variance to date and is the source of the unfavorable variance at the summary level of the WBS. At the summary levels, offsetting positive variances reduced the significant variances.

This control account variance also manifests itself in the organization summary. A variance in the Cooling System Superintendent's area of (410) traces to the Superintendent-Condenser

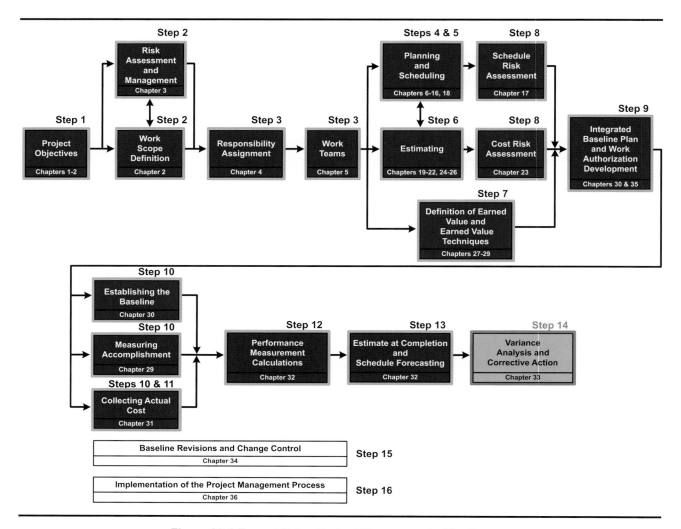

Figure 33-1 Earned Value Project Management: The Process

with its (460) variance. The source of this performance variance could similarly trace to the control account for the condensing system.

Variance Thresholds

Since variances will always occur, significant variances must be defined. The objective is to determine a threshold that, if exceeded, requires some type of analysis, corrective action, and documentation. For variances less than the threshold, no action is required. If set correctly, thresholds support an effective management by exception process.

Many different thresholds are used. Typically, thresholds exist for external reporting to customers and for internal management purposes.

External thresholds usually are associated with specific levels of the WBS, usually the reporting level, and are either defined in the contract or negotiated with the customer. Internal thresholds usually are established at the control account level. The same project could have multiple thresholds depending on size and risk of its control accounts. Variance thresholds may also change over the life of a project. Over time and as work is performed and actual cost collected, a percentage threshold may be difficult to breach. A problem could become very large before it is addressed. For these reasons, management could choose to tighten the variance thresholds later in the project. Conversely, management could choose to set looser variance thresholds for low risk WBS elements or control accounts.

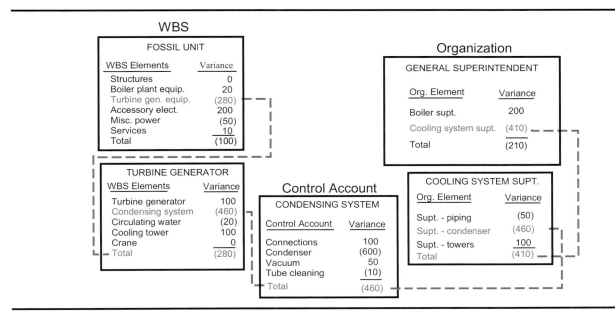

Figure 33-2 Data Traceability

Guidance that may be used in determining the definition of significant variance includes:

Absolute Amount - This is the simplest approach, stating that if a certain value is exceeded, then a variance analysis must be performed. This approach could be used when a company identifies a value (such as $10,000) that is large enough that it must always be explained regardless of the size of the control account. The advantage to this approach is that it is simple to use, and variances exceeding the chosen threshold can be quickly identified. The drawback is that it does not take into effect the size of the control account or whether the project is 5% complete or 95% complete. It will result in needless variances being explained, in some cases, while others that deserve attention are overlooked. This threshold may also be established in labor hours or any other logical measurable unit.

Percentage Threshold - With this approach, the emphasis is placed on percentages rather than absolute numbers. The threshold might be ± 15%. If a variance exceeds $15,000 for a control account that has $100,000 in cumulative earned value (or planned expenses to date), then a variance analysis must be performed. A percentage threshold is also a fairly simple approach, but has the same disadvantages as

the Absolute Amount approach. For a very large control account, such as $10,000,000, a variance of $1,490,000 would require no explanation with a 15% threshold. Meanwhile, a very small account of $10,000 would need explanation whenever the variance exceeded $1,500. The Percentage Threshold may also be established in labor hours or any other logical measurable unit.

Combination Absolute Amount and Percent of Budget/Earned Value - This approach combines the previous two techniques to eliminate some of the problems encountered with their individual use. An example of a variance threshold using this technique would be: ± $10,000 and ± 15% variance. While this approach requires slightly more complicated calculations than the previous two approaches, it also yields better results because is eliminates variance analysis of small dollar value variances. Managers will not be saddled with explaining $1,500 and/or 15 hour variances regardless of the percent variation. It should be noted that large control accounts can still incur relatively large variances before the percent threshold is breached. Different thresholds could be established for those large control accounts to mitigate this disadvantage.

Other Considerations in Setting Thresholds - Regardless of how the thresholds are set, effective thresholds should also be tailored to different types of data. The most common types of data for threshold tailoring include: cumulative versus current period data, favorable versus unfavorable variances, and the WBS or organizational levels.

With respect to current period and cumulative data, a higher tolerance is generally appropriate for the current period data. An example of typical percent thresholds applied differently would be 10% for cumulative data and 20% for current period data. The cumulative variance is typically more meaningful than the current period variance. The cumulative variance indicates the overall status of the reporting element whereas the current period only indicates the magnitude and direction of one data point. The purpose of reporting current period variances is to identify significant items that will likely lead to a significant cumulative variance. Relaxed current period thresholds prevent burdening the variance analysis process with transient and insignificant variances.

So far variances have been discussed as if they are all created equal, but they are not. A favorable variance and an unfavorable variance deserve different treatment. Whereas a -15% variance may be considered significant, it may take a +25% variance or more before action is required. Some even question why positive variances be investigated at all. What is wrong with doing better than planned? Should we do worse because we are doing too well? A very large positive variance may be a reflection of poor planning or incorrect time charges more than it is an indication of incredible performance. In the case of incorrect time charges, a very favorable performance may tip off the project office to procedural problems in the charging or coding of time to individual control accounts.

The WBS and organization structure should be considered when developing and tailoring variance thresholds. While a cumulative variance threshold of 20% may adequately identify variances at the control account level, a tighter variance threshold such as 10% at level 3 and 5% or less at level 2 may be necessary to ensure that appropriate variances are addressed.

Technical criticality and risk are also considerations when defining variance thresholds. A tighter (i.e. smaller) threshold on a control

account for particularly significant technical work that has a high degree of risk could be used. A likely candidate for this type of special treatment would be any control account that, if delayed or unsuccessful, could cause the ultimate failure or major delay of the overall project.

To summarize what has been said so far, defining variance thresholds is not a casual process. After all, once this definition is set, it may be used for the remainder of the project for identifying areas for management attention and corrective action. There are so many factors to consider that usually a table will be required to describe all of the possible cases. Such a table is shown below. The variance thresholds include cost variances, schedule variances, and variances at complete (VAC). To simplify, the thresholds are limited to those at the control account (lowest) level.

	Current Period Data	Cumulative to Date Data	Variance At Completion
Favorable Variance	+30% and $25,000	+20% and $100,000	+ 15% and $200,000
Unfavorable Variance	-20% and $10,000	-10% and $75,000	-10% and $150,000

With all of the factors covered previously, there may still be a surprise in the sample values for significant thresholds in the table. Even though incremental data has "looser" standards than cumulative data on a percentage basis, it still must have tighter ones on the absolute dollar value amount. This is because data are being compared that was collected for just one month rather than data that have been accumulating since the beginning of the project.

Are there any other alternatives for defining what "significant" means? Yes. No matter which option is chosen and no matter how tight or loose the thresholds are set, there is the possibility that the system will choke on its own action item list. No one can intelligently address that many variances on a continuing basis month to month. Recognize that each month brings a new set of additional variances. The system breaks down if it reaches the point where it is barely possible to process the new month's variances before the next month's data appears.

In this scenario, all that is happening is documentation of all the problems with little time to do anything about them and absolutely no time to follow up on last month's problems. Was the action taken effective in resolving the condition? It will never be known if it takes everyone's attention to address the new variances.

What is the answer? One approach that has been used successfully on projects is the Top 5 Approach. A variation of this is the Top 10 Approach or the "Dirty Dozen". What is suggested by this method is that there are a limited number of variances that can be properly investigated, documented, and addressed in any reporting period. Whatever that number is (five, ten, or otherwise), the number of monthly variances analyzed should not exceed that number. In effect, it is a threshold for the thresholds. The underlying concept is that it is better to address the most significant concerns well than to try to address a lot of variances poorly. Remember, the process is supposed to be a tool to assist management of the project, not a burden to the progress of the project. This approach may be especially useful for external reporting of variances. The purpose is to reduce the quantity of variances being analyzed and increase the quality of that analysis, including more real time corrective action planning and implementation of those plans.

How does one determine what the worst five variances are? The best option is the one that is most comfortable to the project manager. What if there were no standard? There is a way to criticality define control account variances that has been used successfully. It is included in the discussion of calculating independent estimates at completion, contained in Chapter 32, that projects the final estimated costs.

If there were an external reporting requirement that includes variance analysis reporting, a typical approach would be to analyze variances internally but only report the five or ten worst to the owner/customer. There may also be contractual requirements that determine at what level of the WBS and/or OBS variances are reported. These requirements will generally be at a higher level than variances that are analyzed internally; con-

sequently, the customer reporting may be a summary of the internal analysis.

In any event, there are significant, streamlined, intelligent approaches to variance analysis such as conducting analysis on cumulative data only. Because the current period data is a subset of the cumulative data, what occurred in the current period is in the cumulative analysis.

Variance Analysis Reports

After a variance has been identified and determined to be significant, the next step is the initiation of a Variance Analysis Report (VAR). The VAR is a living, working document to communicate causes, impacts and corrective action. A sample form is shown in Figure 33-3.

At the top of the form are headings that identify the account name, number, and the reporting period. The data should also be presented to allow a quick assessment of the account's current status. All of the information described so far can and should be automatically produced by the system. There are certain hints that facilitate the variance analysis process. For example, the variance analysis form shown in Figure 33-3 should be created and electronically transmitted when the variance analysis threshold has been exceeded. Only those Variance Analysis Reports requiring explanation should be prepared. The major sections of this Variance Analysis Report are addressed in more detail in the following sections.

Heading Information/Earned Value Data

The current and cumulative data are presented at the top of the form. This format should be printed on an exception basis only for those accounts that exceed pre-defined thresholds. This report shows that a total of $300,000 has been earned versus a planned accomplishment or budget of $380,000 to date, resulting in an unfavorable schedule variance of ($80,000) or (21%). The cost variance is not as large, ($30,000) to date or (10%). However, both variances became worse during the current month, July. The report also indicates that the EAC is $1,300,000, which results in a projected variance at completion of ($100,000). These variances are to be analyzed

Variance Analysis Report

Title: Condensing System
Number: 62-091-1.82-6   Report Period: July

($000)	Budget	Earned Value	Actual Cost	Schedule Variance	VAR %	Cost Variance	VAR %
Current	30	20	22	(10)	(33)	(2)	(10)
Cumulative	380	300	330	(80)	(21)	(30)	(10)

1,200	1,300	(100)
Budget At Completion	Estimate At Completion	Variance At Completion

Problem Analysis

Impact

Corrective Action Plan

Estimate At Completion Justification

Control Account Manager   Approvals

_____   _____   _____   _____
      Signature   Date   Signature   Date
_____   _____
        Title   Title

Figure 33-3 Variance Analysis Report

and addressed within the Variance Analysis Report.

Problem Analysis

The first challenge is to identify the cause of the problem, which requires isolation of significant variances and the reason for each. Cost variances must be discussed separately from schedule variances. Some of the entries that have been found in this section of the form have little constructive value. The cause of the problem was once explained, "The control account is currently behind schedule because less work was accomplished than planned." Another notable explanation, "We are experiencing a negative cost condition because it is costing us more than we expected when we developed the budget." There are also the vindictive statements: "This control account is experiencing an overrun because our estimating group is incompetent and we never believed we could complete the work with this unrealistic budget anyway", and, "The reason this control account is behind is because

we are spending all of our time filling out these forms."

While many of the above statements may be true, what should be contained in this section of the form should read more like:

"The transmission design has not met the specification (Revision C, dated July 15, Year 1) relative to fuel economy. Specifically, test conditions have shown a performance of 16% less than that required. The specification can be met in the current configuration, but it has required some additional redesign. This has caused an overrun of 100 labor hours or ($5,000). In addition, the problem demanded the attention of our most senior engineers (not budgeted) and resulted in a labor rate variance of ($7,000). These same factors have lead to the schedule variance of ($10,000). Critical path analysis reveals that there are 4 additional weeks of float available,

by that time the problem should be resolved."

A few descriptions such as the one above are worth far more than dozens of reports restating the obvious. Notice that the explanation of the variance has been broken into its components - how much was because of quantity variation (more labor hours) and how much was because of rate variation (cost per labor hour). This is the complete and correct method for analyzing labor cost variances. The same approach could be used for interpreting material cost variances. This was previously discussed in Chapter 32, "Performance Measurement Calculations and Estimates at Completion."

Some companies must be very secretive about labor rates, so it may not be possible to conduct analysis on an employee-by-employee basis, as implied by the example above. The approach still could be used in the following manner. At the beginning of a project, an estimated rate is developed for the costs of a given control account and is used for the budget (example, $50/hour). As progress occurs on the control account, the total number of hours and total labor cost should both be known. This allows calculation of an average cost per hour incurred to date that could then be compared with the planned average rate. In this way, labor rate costs can be compared even if individual rates are unknown.

Impact

After the cause of the problem has been determined and clearly stated, the next section to complete on the Variance Analysis Report addresses the impact of the variance on the control account or project. This requires identification of the cost and schedule impact, as well as the technical impact (if any). Since analysis is performed on a control account basis, it is also useful to determine if the variance in the account affects any other control accounts.

One of the impacts that must be investigated is the impact on the estimate at completion. Is the variance experienced to date a temporary one, or will it persist to project completion? This returns to the basic visibility question described in the first chapter. There is a place at the bottom of the sample form to justify the change to the EAC or explain why no revision is needed.

For schedule variances that exceed reporting thresholds, impact discussion should focus on the next significant project milestone. The impact analysis should address whether or not the variance will cause a change to the next significant project milestone, any critical path milestones, and/or the ultimate project milestone such as Initial Operational Capability.

It is possible that a variance has no impact. This could occur because of how the control account was planned. One example would be that milestones were planned for the last day of the reporting period. If the milestone were not complete on that last day, but will be complete on the first day of the next accounting period, no earned value can be claimed. In that case, large monthly variances may have no significance to final cost because it is just a shift of dollars by a day or two to another reporting period.

Corrective Action Plan

If there were a real impact, then a corrective action plan should be developed and documented. This will allow future monitoring to see if the condition has been corrected. Actions described should be specific. The plan should include not only specific actions to be taken, but also identification of who is responsible for implementing those actions and by what date they should be effective. If no corrective action were possible, explain why. An example of no corrective action is inadequate initial budget because of a poor estimate. If an estimate were too low and becomes the budget, it will be very unlikely that any actions will correct a negative cost variance. Schedule variances can almost always be recovered by putting more resources on the project (i.e. higher staffing levels) or by expediting missing information, but productivity cannot artificially be increased to unreasonably high levels by decree.

It is possible that the same control account being addressed in the Variance Analysis Report has required prior explanation as well. If so, results of previous corrective action plans should be included to confirm whether or not they have been effective.

Item #	WBS	Description of Action	Date Identified	Assigned To	Status	Status Date	Closure Date
1	AR555.01.01	Refine the design of Tail Pylon Main to incorporate Design Revision	4/12/Yr 1	J. Smith	In work	5/15/Yr 1	6/15/Yr 1
2	AR555.01.02	Revision to teardown coupling for stabilizer.	5/1/Yr 1	T. Jones	In work	5/15/Yr 1	9/25/Yr 1
3	AR555.01.03	Redesign of main section 06201-06007-109	5/1/Yr 1	F.Carboni	In work	5/15/Yr 1	6/24/Yr 1
4	AR555.01.04	Overtime to complete design on schedule	5/12/Yr 1	C. Johns	In work	5/15/Yr 1	5/30/Yr 1

Figure 33-4 Corrective Action Log

Corrective Action Logs are often used to document identified corrective action plans and manage them to their conclusion. The log will generally contain a description of the planned action, the control account, an estimated completion date, and the name of the person responsible for completing the action. The log is used to ensure that plans are statused and that results of plans are included in the succeeding months VARs and if necessary, reported to the customer. A sample Corrective Action Log is shown in Figure 33-4.

Estimate at Completion Justification

If a significant cost variance has occurred, then the Estimate at Completion (EAC) should be reevaluated. This does not mean that the assumption must be made that the rate of overrun will continue as is until completion, but it should be analyzed for final impact. The EAC should also be reviewed if a significant schedule variance has occurred since it frequently requires additional resources to recover schedule variance. If the cost or schedule variance that has already occurred to date were not resulting in an increased EAC, an explanation is required that defines how the variance will be recovered.

Approvals

Requiring approval of the VAR is a safeguard against the types of poor entries used previously as bad examples, but it is much more than that.

The corrective action plan expressed on the VAR form will likely require some change in the status quo of how the project is operating. It may mean more staff, different staff, additional expediting services, or other action plans that will have a cost impact to the project. It may also mean re-prioritizing the work, with staff released from other activities to address the more pressing concerns identified in the impact to the project section. It demands the attention of someone with the authority to authorize the expenditure of any needed additional funds now, with the intent of producing better results in the future, as a result of the actions to be taken.

Conclusion

The project team invests much time and effort into the development of the baseline plan for accomplishing the project objectives, and even more time accumulating status of progress against that plan. Much of that effort is ineffective if the output were not compared with the input and deviations from plan scrutinized. By comparing the performance against the plan, it is possible to make mid-course corrections that assist completion of the project on time and within the approved budget. The Variance Analysis Report (VAR) is the vehicle for responding to significant variances. The definition of "significant" is decided in advance by the selection of defined variance analysis thresholds. If these thresholds are exceeded, a formal process of variance analysis should be initiated.

Chapter 33 Review Questions

33-1. What is being compared through variance analysis?

33-2. What is referred to by the term "data traceability"?

33-3. How is a "significant" variance defined?

33-4. Which of the following requires tighter thresholds:

    A. Cumulative data or current month data?

    B. Favorable or unfavorable variances?

    C. High WBS levels or low WBS levels?

33-5. Why bother to analyze very positive variances?

33-6. Explain the Top 5 approach for reporting variances.

33-7. A Variance Analysis Report (VAR) contains cost and schedule performance data. What type of information do the four sections on the VAR requiring narrative analysis need?

True or False

33-8. Variance thresholds may be set by considering the absolute value of a variance and/or the variance percent.

33-9. The Estimate at Completion may require review if a significant schedule variance has occurred.

33-10. In the "problem analysis" section of the VAR, a general description of the problem should be provided.

33-11. In some instances, it may be appropriate to put a tighter threshold on a control account that is especially technically critical.

The answers to these questions can be found in Section 6, Solutions.

Case Study

33.1 CALCULATION OF COST AND SCHEDULE VARIANCES

Attached is a recap of the data from the transmission design control account.

Using the equations:

SV = Earned Value - Planned Value (EV - PV) or (BCWP - BCWS)

CV = Earned Value - Actual Costs (EV - AC) or (BCWP - ACWP)

Calculate the SV and CV for both incremental and cumulative data.

Transmission Control Account Variance Worksheet

		A	M	J	J	A	S	O	N	D	J	F	M
Incremental	BCWS (or PV)	4,500	5,500	9,500	8,500	6,500	3,500	20,700	20,700	200	5,200		
	BCWP (or EV)	4,500	500	5,500	6,500	7,000	5,000	9,200	20,700	2,200	18,700		5,000
	ACWP (or AC)	4,500	4,600	7,600	7,600	6,800	6,000	8,800	13,900	22,900	16,400	3,400	1,400
	SV												
	CV												
Cumulative	BCWS (or PV)	4,500	10,000	19,500	28,000	34,500	38,000	58,700	79,400	79,600	84,800	84,800	84,800
	BCWP (or EV)	4,500	5,000	10,500	17,000	24,000	29,000	38,200	58,900	61,100	79,800	79,800	84,800
	ACWP (or AC)	4,500	9,100	16,700	24,300	31,100	37,100	45,900	59,800	82,700	99,100	102,500	103,900
	SV												
	CV												

The solution to this case study can be found on the Humphreys & Associates, Inc. web site.
www.humphreys-assoc.com

Interpreting and Calculating Cost and Schedule Variances

Interpreting Cost/Schedule Conditons:

The objective of this exercise is merely to get you familiar with interpreting cost and schedule variances.

The following table includes the nine different cost and schedule conditions that can exist in an Earned Value Management System. In the blanks provided, indicate the meaning of each condition.

	Compare			Meaning						
	Schedule/Cost Performance			Schedule			Cost			
	BCWS (or PV)	BCWP (or EV)	ACWP (or AC)	On	Ahead	Behind	On	Under	Over	
1.	$100	100	100							
2.	100	150	150							
3.	150	100	100							
4.	100	100	150							
5.	100	150	200							
6.	150	100	150							
7.	150	150	100							
8.	100	150	100							
9.	200	150	100							

Chapter 34

BASELINE REVISIONS AND CHANGE CONTROL

Objectives of this Chapter:

1. Identify types and causes of changes that occur on projects.

2. Describe the elements of a change control program.

3. List specific actions that can be taken to minimize changes.

4. Explain how changes are incorporated into the approved baseline.

5. Define and discuss internal replanning.

6. Describe what is meant by a "rubber baseline" and explain why this is an unacceptable approach for effective project management.

In Chapter 30 "Establishing the Performance Measurement Baseline," the concept of developing the schedule baseline was extended to completion of the total integrated performance measurement baseline (PMB). Previously schedule changes were addressed, but that topic is now broadened to include technical and budget changes to the performance measurement baseline. This topic is as important as the original task of producing the baseline. Widespread changes, if not incorporated properly and quickly, will negate the value of the performance measurement baseline.

Change Control

It takes a dedicated effort to establish the initial technical/schedule/budget baseline against which actual performance will be measured. Once an approved baseline is in place and status is being measured, management control efforts are just beginning. Variances that must be addressed will inevitably occur. Unanticipated changes to the plan will also occur. These changes may affect the technical scope, schedule, and/or budget of the project, and may require

revisions to the baseline. If changes are not documented and controlled, the danger exists that the baseline against which the project is being measured may no longer reflect that project scope. In order to have a firm basis for project control, the baseline must incorporate approved changes as they occur.

Types and Causes of Changes

Changes to the performance measurement baseline are typically defined as externally driven or internally driven. Externally driven changes consist of contract modifications from the customer. Externally driven changes should be reflected in the baseline once the change has been authorized by the customer's contracting representative, regardless of whether the contract change has been definitized (i.e., issued in a formal, signed contract modification). Externally driven changes should be incorporated into the performance measurement baseline in a timely manner, typically within two accounting cycles after authorization by the customer. Externally driven changes could result in the addition of new work

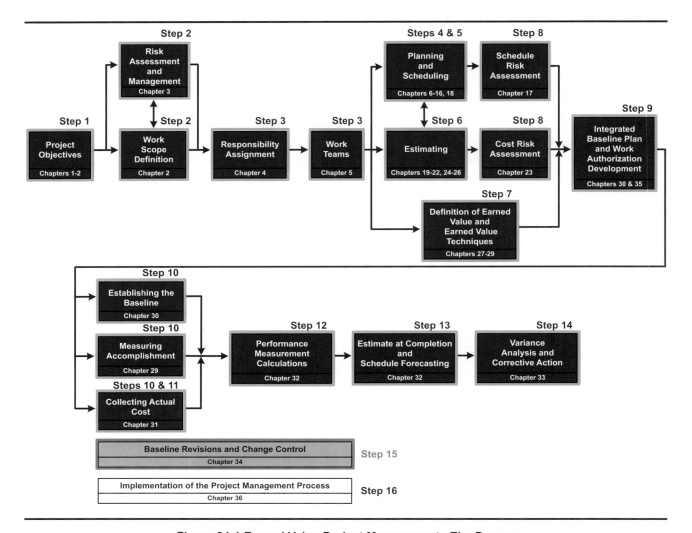

Figure 34-1 Earned Value Project Management: The Process

to the contract, changes to existing work scope, or deletion of work scope.

Internally driven changes consist of actions directed or approved by the contractor's project manager. Examples of internally driven changes include application of management reserve to control accounts, conversion of planning packages to work packages, and replanning of the future effort in existing control accounts. A common cause of internal changes results from significant differences between the basis of estimate and the actual execution plan. For example, an organization responsible for producing drawings based its estimate on a given number of design modules and standards which resulted in an estimate of 100 drawings. After contract award, the design organization changed its approach to

meet the contract scope, and the revised technical approach resulted in an additional 50 drawings required by the drawing organization. The drawing organization agreed on a budget with the project manager based on 100 drawings, yet they now have to produce 150 drawings for the same budget because of the design organization's new approach. This situation provides a legitimate request to the project manager for the application of management reserve. Assuming adequate management reserve exists, the project manager must decide whether to use management reserve to provide additional budget to the control account. If the project manager applies management reserve in this example, the control account manager's baseline will provide the most realistic basis for evaluating performance. If the project manager decides not to apply management reserve, the control account manager should increase the Estimate at Completion and report a projected overrun for the cost of the effort for the 50 additional drawings. In either situation, the actual cost and the EAC will likely be the same; however, application of management reserve enhances the insight into the progress of the revised work scope because a budget will be in place for accurate comparison of cost and schedule variances. Other situations that may result in application of management reserve include contract work scope requirements that were overlooked in the estimate, estimating errors, and significant direct or indirect rate changes. Other internally driven changes, such as conversion of planning packages to work packages and replanning of the future effort within existing work packages, potentially result in changes to the time phasing of budgets or internal schedule milestones. Accordingly, these changes must be formally documented to ensure proactive control of the performance measurement baseline.

Implementation of both externally and internally driven changes to the performance measurement baseline must include formal documentation that identifies the changes to the budget, schedule, and work scope.   This formal documentation must also include the requisite approval from the project manager as well as concurrence of the control account manager as was done with the initial work authorization. A key tenet of baseline control, just like work authorization, is that the baseline changes should be documented and approved prior to work commencing on the changed scope, schedule, or budget.

Elements of a Change Control Program

An effective change control program must provide for early identification of changes, thorough evaluation of them, and documented procedures for resolving and incorporating them. Key elements of a change control program include policies addressing how changes will be identified, documented, and submitted for approval; management participation in review of changes; timely reporting of changes, their description, and cost and schedule impact; timely incorporation of

changes into the project baseline plan; formal training of the requirements for change control for team members; and effective planning, negotiation and administration of contracts.

How to Control Changes

Although project changes cannot be eliminated, the following guidelines help minimize changes:

1. **Define the scope.** The clearer the scope of work, whether at the contract level or at the control account level, the lower the likelihood that changes will be necessary. If this were not done, the door is wide open to continuous changes.

2. **Formally identify who is authorized to initiate and approve changes.** In most cases, approval is limited to the project manager even though the change is often conceived at lower levels of the project organization. If approval were not limited to the project manager, there is the strong possibility that every phone call between owner/customer and contractor parties may unintentionally initiate a change. Engineers are notorious for discussing technical options on how to accomplish a design objective that one party assumes is a verbal authorization to proceed with a design change.   Once the change is incorporated on drawings, disapproval of the change by the owner/customer means yet another cost: changing the drawings back to their original condition.

3. **Analyze change patterns.** Is there a characteristic of the information flow that results in more changes than would normally be expected? There may be historical patterns that can be incorporated in the planning process. If historical records indicate that eighty percent of the changes typically occur within the first six months, then staffing profiles should consider this condition. If changes occur consistently throughout the project duration, then that should be considered in the plan. Patterns may vary based on the type of contract. Engineering changes may be concentrated in the late stages of

design while manufacturing and construction encounter most of their changes in the early stages. These types of patterns can be anticipated in both the planning and the staffing processes.

4. **Set a dollar threshold for changes.** Many changes are so small that the cost of processing them may almost equal the cost of performing the revised work. It is not uncommon for there to be an agreement in advance that no change requests will be submitted below a defined dollar value. If there are many small changes of a similar type, these may be submitted all at once. This should never be done without prior agreement, and the owner/customer should always be made aware of the status of these changes. Additionally, care must be exercised to determine how accumulated changes are implemented in the change control process. Budgets should not be changed retroactively.

5. **Document change history and costs.** A tracking mechanism ensures that changes are incorporated into the project baseline and serves as a valuable source of information if disputes arise over costs at the end of the project.

6. **Provide budget reserves for changes.** A management reserve should be established to budget known unknowns. There will be internal changes in scope that will need to be budgeted and this will be allocated from the management reserve controlled by the project manager. The amount of management reserve initially established may be based on the contract value, historical project performance, project risk, and other factors.

7. **Evaluate all impacts of changes.** Cost impacts are quickly identified on change request forms, but there is a strong tendency to claim that there is no schedule impact. In most cases, this is true. It is possible to add some small amount of work to the project and still complete the main project work on time as a result of additional staffing authorized by the budget received for the change. However, as these minor changes accumulate, eventually a complete revamping of the project plan may be required. One small change may not affect technical or even schedule but a hundred small changes surely do.

One of the strategies sometimes used to help control changes is to assign a full time contract administrator(s) to the project team. This person acts as a focal point for all of the contractual activity, including changes. This allows the other team members to pursue the work that is their main responsibility.

Change Control and the Baseline

Changes to the approved baseline plan must be as formal as the initial baseline establishment. This baseline plan, formally known as the performance measurement baseline (PMB), is made up of the summation of all of the time-phased control account budgets. One premise is that the baseline must be changed specifically at the level where the additional work scope will occur. That means the impact of the change must be identified at the individual control account level. The effects of a change order flowing down through the Work Breakdown Structure to the individual control accounts is displayed in Figure 34-2.

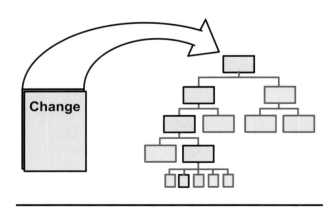

Figure 34-2 Change Control

Figure 34-3 indicates, in an exaggerated example, how changes will cause the project baseline to change over time. The objective is that the performance measurement baseline always reflects the integrated technical/schedule/budget baseline.

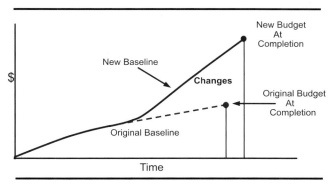

Figure 34-3 Effect of Changes

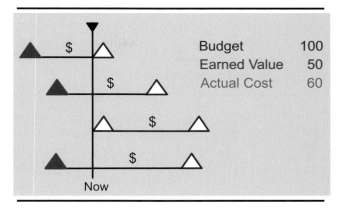

Figure 34-4 Control Account 1

Baseline Changes at the Control Account Level

The next series of examples shows what happens at the control account level when a change is executed. The simplest case is when a change occurs to a control account that has not yet begun. Since no performance has been measured to date, all that is required is that the control account be increased by the amount of additional budget and the schedule changed, if required, for the approved additional scope of work. The additional budget must then be spread over time, which may include extending schedules from the original baseline schedule because of the additional work scope.

The next case, identified as Control Account 1, demonstrates what happens when progress has already been recorded in a control account. In this case, changes to the budget may obscure performance to date that could mask potential problems and make the data from the account unreliable for forecasts. Control Account 1 contains four work packages and the status is shown in Figure 34-4.

To avoid losing the historical performance of the control account, the account impacted by the change should be closed and a revised control account opened. The current budget should be made equal to the earned value because that represents the portion of the work that is actually complete. Consequently, this erases any schedule variance that existed at the time of the change, which is a logical step since the schedule must be reevaluated as a result of the

approved change. The original schedule may no longer be a realistic basis for determining schedule performance.

An important point to remember, however, is that the actual cost is maintained. Actual costs can never be changed, no matter what revisions are made to the scope of work or baseline, because they represent factual history. This means that any cost variance at the time of account closeout will be maintained and will continue to provide a basis for accurately forecasting future costs. The closeout of Control Account 1 is pictured in Figure 34-5.

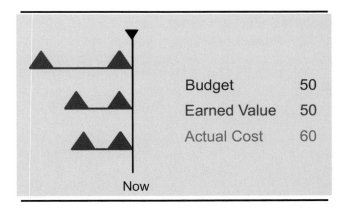

Figure 34-5 Control Account 1 Closeout

The revised control account is identified as Control Account 1A, and its status is pictured in Figure 34-6. It contains the revised budget for the remaining work, including any budget impact identified by the change. The budget corresponds to the revised scope of work, now provides a valid basis for measuring performance on the revised work, and historical records have not been lost.

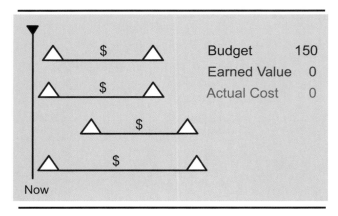

Figure 34-6 Control Account 1A

In systems that do not follow "good practice" for project control processes, a common error is that the budget and earned value will be set equal to the actual costs to date. This eliminates all variances at the time of the change and does not accurately reflect the work performed at closeout. The appeal of this approach is that past cost/schedule variances are eliminated. However, this also invalidates productivity measures such as the Cost Performance Index (CPI) used in evaluating revised estimates at completion. A major weakness in this practice is apparent: one of executive management's greatest needs concerning the project is to get early, accurate forecasts of the project's final costs.

Incorporating Changes into the PMB

As with the establishment of the original performance measurement baseline (PMB), three aspects should be considered when incorporating changes: the technical scope, the schedule for accomplishing that scope, and the associated budget. The original scope for the project/contract is defined in the contract and then organized within the Work Breakdown Structure (WBS). The WBS Dictionary defines the technical boundaries of each element and identifies the work products. At a more detailed level, the scope is identified in the control account plan. The work scope is subdivided into the individual work packages or tasks that form the control account. Whenever a change is initiated and approved, the change must flow down through the WBS to the control account plan and the affected work

packages. A change may result in additional work packages, or existing work packages may be modified or deleted.

The schedule is also likely to be impacted by any changes to the technical scope. There will be additional activities to perform (or fewer in the case of deleted scope), and these activities may or may not impact the project's critical path. An analysis of the project's schedule must be performed after incorporation of the changes to determine whether or not there has been any impact to the project's completion date or any other key milestones. The change incorporation may require a "work around" plan to be initiated as discussed in Chapter 14, "Schedule Changes."

The cost component of the PMB was initiated with the estimate, which became the budget once it was approved. The distribution of the authorized budget should be tracked in logs that specify the allocation of the budgets and their intended use (see "Detailed Tracking of Changes"). When changes occur, it is essential that the impact be identified to the control account/work package level. This will make it possible to know at all times exactly what has been authorized for each account. Revised Work Authorization Documents are also issued that reflect the revision of scope, schedule and budget and these revised documents will always trace to the logs.

Detailed Tracking of Changes

Incorporating changes at the control account level, as discussed previously, requires careful documentation to identify the current technical scope of work/schedule/budget integrated into the performance measurement baseline (PMB). This is usually accomplished through a WBS dictionary, schedules and budget logs that are maintained by the Project Controls group as part of the project management office. Examples of logs that may be used to document the distribution of the original contract budget as well as changes to it include a Contract Budget Base Log, an Undistributed Budget Log, and a Management Reserve Log. Figure 34-7 is an example of a Contract Budget Base Log.

Date	Change	Contract Target Cost (1)	Authorized Unpriced Work (2)	Contract Budget Base (3)	Management Reserve (4)	PMB (5)	Undistri- buted Budget (6)	Direct Budget (7)	Overhead Budget (8)	G&A Budget (9)
1/2	ABC Contract 1	120	-	120	10	110	10	40	40	20
1/25	Contract Change 001	20	-	20	2	18	-	8	8	2
1/31	**January Summary**	140	-	140	12	128	10	48	48	22
2/5	Contract Change 002	-	45	45	0	45	20	11	11	3
2/15	Contract Change 003	-	30	30	0	30	19	5	5	1
2/23	Contract Change 004	30	-	30	2	28	-	12	12	4
2/28	**February Summary**	170	75	245	14	231	49	76	76	30
3/6	Changes 002 and 003 Negotiated	70	-	(5)	3	(8)	(39)	14	14	3
3/31	**March Summary**	240	-	240	17	223	10	90	90	33

Figure 34-7 Contract Budget Base Log

This log records the original authorized value of the contract (less fee or profit) and all subsequent changes. Changes are totaled by month to allow tracking of the authorized technical/schedule/budget baseline from project initiation through the current month. The changes may be priced or unpriced at the time of their inclusion on the log. Unpriced changes could occur when work has been authorized but the exact value of the change has not been negotiated.

The Contract Budget Base Log would identify the project, the contract number, the project manager, and the name of the person responsible for maintaining its update in addition to the budget data pictured. It provides a complete history of the cost portion of the PMB from the time of contract award throughout the life of the project. The information listed includes:

Date - Identifies the date of the reported change.

Change - A brief description of the change.

Contract Target Cost - The initial entry of $120 defines the starting value of the contract. Subsequent changes are listed by contract change number. The dollars may be expressed in whatever unit is appropriate (whole dollars, thousands of dollars, millions of dollars, etc.).

Authorized Unpriced Work - Contract change orders number 002 and 003 have been authorized but the exact value of the change has not been negotiated; therefore, the Contract Target Cost column has not been increased. The antici-pated costs (45 and 30, respectively) are listed in this column. On March 6, when the changes have been negotiated, this column reverts to a zero budget value. At the same time, changes 002 and 003 have been approved for a total value of 70, not 75, and that means that 70 is added to the Contract Target Cost.

Contract Budget Base - The current budget value of the total contract. Note that contract changes 002 and 003, while not included in the Contract Target Cost column initially, are included in the Contract Budget Base. On March 6 when the changes are negotiated for 70 instead of the estimated value of 75, a negative adjustment of (5) is made in this column.

Management Reserve - An amount of the total allocated budget withheld for management con-trol purposes rather than designated for the accomplishment of a specific task or set of tasks. As internal changes are identified and approved, management reserve is allocated to control accounts. It is not a part of the performance measurement baseline. Management Reserve (MR) should be established for the base contract. Each approved and negotiated change may also have a portion withheld for management reserve.

Performance Measurement Baseline - The value of the PMB. It will always equal the Con-tract Budget Base less the management reserve.

Undistributed Budget - Budget applicable to project or contract effort that has not yet been identified to specific lower level WBS or OBS elements. Undistributed Budget (UB) is in effect a temporary holding account with statement of work and budget and will be reduced when budget is allocated to the WBS/OBS elements. The budget held in undistributed budget must always have a corresponding scope of work. It is similar to a checking account. Budget that is initially in the checking account is reassigned to other accounts as it and the appropriate statement of work are distributed. This is also shown in Figure 34-7 as occurring on March 6.

Direct Budget - The value of direct labor, material, and other direct costs. Some organizations may choose to break this into three individual columns to reflect each of the component costs. Some organizations may also choose to include budgets at the control account level in the baseline log.

Overhead Budget - The associated overhead costs for the previous column (Direct Budgets). In this sample, overhead costs are 100% of direct costs.

General and Administrative Budget - A budget for the General and Administrative (G & A) costs of doing business. A percent allocation is decided in the contract (and for each subsequent approved change) that is added to the total direct and overhead cost.

These various columns in Figure 34-7 are related to each other. "Contract Target Cost" (column 1) plus "Authorized Unpriced Work" (column 2) equals "Contract Budget Base" (column 3). The "Contract Budget Base" equals "Management Reserve" (column 4) plus the "PMB" (column 5). The "PMB" entry equals the sum of "Undistributed Budget" (column 6), "Direct Budget" (column 7), "overhead budget", (column 8), and "G and A Budget" (General and Administrative budget, (column 9). One other variation that is used in some organizations is that labor hours may be listed in addition to the direct cost. This would be a useful entry in organizations that emphasize the management of labor hours, in addition to labor dollars, at the control account level.

The first row entry in Figure 34-7 identifies the budget status at contract initiation. The Contract Target Cost of $120 is listed in the Contract Budget Base (CBB) column since there is no authorized unpriced work at this point. The CBB is divided into $110 in the PMB and $10 allocated to Management Reserve. The PMB is further subdivided into its component parts: $10 for Undistributed Budget, $40 for direct budget, $40 for overhead budget, and $20 for G & A budget. Subtotals are included for the end of each month so there is always a trace of the initial contract to the current contract status.

The budgets allocated to control accounts are documented in the Management Reserve and Undistributed Budget Logs and may also be entered into the Contract Budget Base Log. The budget log or logs do not stand alone. They need to be accompanied by more detailed documentation that displays the specific impact on individual control account plans. A change request form, shown in Figure 34-8, will be needed. This form allows a more definitive description of the change than is possible on a log. It also provides a reason for the change and shows specific schedule and budget impact. A revised control account plan should be electronically attached to the change request form. WBS dictionary, authorization documents, and schedule changes are also documented consistently with the budget log.

Internal Replanning

A key tenet of an effective project management system is that the performance measurement baseline should reflect the plan to execute the work. Often, the execution plan changes and the performance measurement baseline no longer synchronizes with the schedule and/or the approach to accomplish the scope of work. One important approach to keep the baseline synchronized is active use of the Rolling Wave concept described in Chapter 30. Another approach is to replan open work packages, which is termed internal replanning. Internal replanning should not change budget history; therefore, the most desirable approach for internal replanning is to close open work packages at existing earned value amounts and open new work packages to replan the remaining budget. This approach is

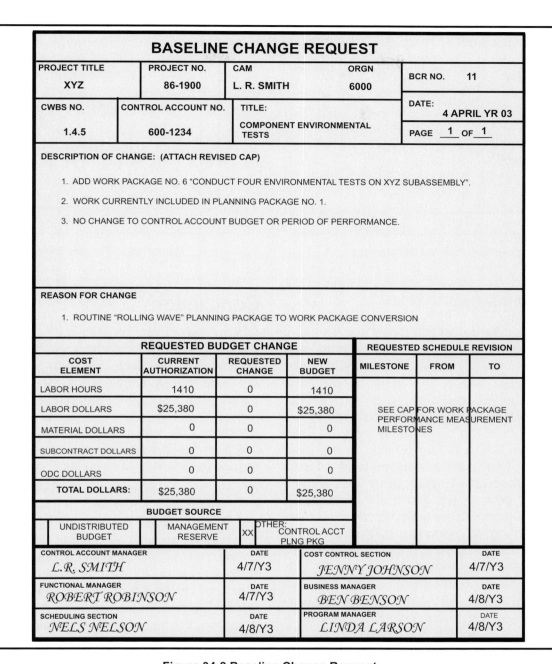

BASELINE CHANGE REQUEST

PROJECT TITLE	PROJECT NO.	CAM	ORGN	BCR NO. 11
XYZ	86-1900	L. R. SMITH	6000	

CWBS NO.	CONTROL ACCOUNT NO.	TITLE:	DATE: 4 APRIL YR 03
1.4.5	600-1234	COMPONENT ENVIRONMENTAL TESTS	PAGE __1__ OF __1__

DESCRIPTION OF CHANGE: (ATTACH REVISED CAP)

1. ADD WORK PACKAGE NO. 6 "CONDUCT FOUR ENVIRONMENTAL TESTS ON XYZ SUBASSEMBLY".

2. WORK CURRENTLY INCLUDED IN PLANNING PACKAGE NO. 1.

3. NO CHANGE TO CONTROL ACCOUNT BUDGET OR PERIOD OF PERFORMANCE.

REASON FOR CHANGE

1. ROUTINE "ROLLING WAVE" PLANNING PACKAGE TO WORK PACKAGE CONVERSION

REQUESTED BUDGET CHANGE				REQUESTED SCHEDULE REVISION		
COST ELEMENT	CURRENT AUTHORIZATION	REQUESTED CHANGE	NEW BUDGET	MILESTONE	FROM	TO
LABOR HOURS	1410	0	1410	SEE CAP FOR WORK PACKAGE PERFORMANCE MEASUREMENT MILESTONES		
LABOR DOLLARS	$25,380	0	$25,380			
MATERIAL DOLLARS	0	0	0			
SUBCONTRACT DOLLARS	0	0	0			
ODC DOLLARS	0	0	0			
TOTAL DOLLARS:	$25,380	0	$25,380			

BUDGET SOURCE			
UNDISTRIBUTED BUDGET	MANAGEMENT RESERVE	XX	OTHER: CONTROL ACCT PLNG PKG

CONTROL ACCOUNT MANAGER	DATE	COST CONTROL SECTION	DATE
L. R. SMITH	4/7/Y3	*JENNY JOHNSON*	4/7/Y3
FUNCTIONAL MANAGER	DATE	BUSINESS MANAGER	DATE
ROBERT ROBINSON	4/7/Y3	*BEN BENSON*	4/8/Y3
SCHEDULING SECTION	DATE	PROGRAM MANAGER	DATE
NELS NELSON	4/8/Y3	*LINDA LARSON*	4/8/Y3

Figure 34-8 Baseline Change Request

consistent with the example shown in Figures 34-5, 34-6, and 34-7. Figure 34-9 shows the effect of internal replanning.

In internal replanning, schedule and budget should only be moved with associated technical work scope. Otherwise, budget may be "front loaded," a practice characterized by having most of the budget early in the project while most of the work is later in the project. The impact of this practice is to earn an overstated budget value

early in the project, masking variances (and problems) until later when little can be done to recover. Front loading defeats the purpose of earned value by obscuring the early visibility intended. Why would this be done? It may allow a contractor to get earlier payment for the work if progress payments are tied to earned value resulting in increased time value of money. It also allows potential problems to remain hidden, negating the need for variance explanations.

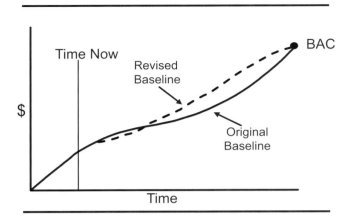

Figure 34-9 Internal Replanning

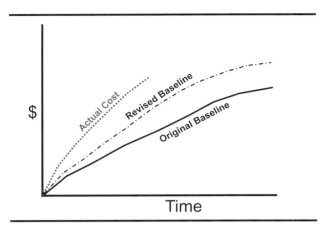

Figure 34-10 Rubber Baseline

Rubber Baseline

A notorious challenge for all project management tools is a rubber baseline, the practice of modifying the project plan to closely match the cumulative actual cost line. The work to be done remains in the future while the budget for the work is moved into the near term so as to match the cumulative actual cost being incurred. An example is shown in Figure 34-10. In essence, an example of separating scope of work from its time-phased budget. This approach defeats one of the major advantages of an effective project management system: the ability to receive timely advance warning of impending overruns. Performance appears to be better than it is because budget for future work has been "stolen" for current work. The inevitable result is that there will be insufficient budget for the future work and, ultimately, there will be cost overruns that were initially hidden.

The inherent problem from a project management standpoint with the rubber baseline is that it reflects an approach of adjusting the plan to match performance, rather than attempting to adjust performance to match the plan. This is counter to the intent of the entire project management process. The baseline change control process is intended to preclude the use of rubber baselines.

Conclusion

Changes are a way of life on any project. Since they will occur, a formal change control program is essential. While changes are inevitable, there are definite preventive steps that can minimize them, and there are other steps that will help keep the change control process organized. All efforts in this area help maintain the integrity of the technical/schedule/budget integrated performance measurement baseline.

Changes to the baseline must be identified to the specific control accounts, the work packages affected, and even the schedule activities. Since the control account is the key level for project efforts, the control account scope, schedule and budget must be formally adjusted in accordance with any approved change control documentation. For control accounts that are already in progress, this may be accomplished by closing it and reopening a new one that contains any remaining scope as well as any additional scope identified in the change. However, changes to scope, schedule, and budget may be made to future (next month and forward) open work packages without closing the work packages or the control accounts. The key is to not change the current month or the past. Two general rules are that budget is always moved with its specific scope and cost variances are not eliminated when either a work package or a control account is closed.

One technique that is used to provide traceability from the point of contract initiation through current month budget status is to maintain a comprehensive log that documents changes including when those changes occurred.

Internal replanning may sometimes be necessary. In this case, the planned schedule end date and budget remain the same but the time-phasing is revised. This is not the same as a "rubber baseline," in which the time-phasing of the planned progress curve is changed without a corresponding adjustment of the associated work.

Chapter 34 Review Questions

34-1.   What is the difference between externally driven and internally driven changes? Which is a greater challenge to project management?

34-2.   List three generic requirements for all change control systems.

34-3.   What is one of the best ways to control scope changes?

34-4.   Discuss at least four ways of controlling changes.

34-5.   Describe what is meant by an "internal replanning."

34-6.   What is a "rubber baseline?" Is this an accepted technique for project management?

34-7.   Discuss the proper procedure for closing a control account in progress and replacing it with a new control account.

True or False

34-8.   The baseline plan, or PMB, is made up of all the time-phased control account budgets.

34-9.   The performance measurement baseline (PMB) must always reflect the technical schedule and budget integrated baseline.

34-10. Changes to the PMB must be identified to their lowest level of impact.

34-11. Change control is an important element in the project management process.

The answers to these questions can be found in Section 6, Solutions.

Case Study

34.1 CONTRACT BUDGET BASE LOG

Project Searchlight

Assignment

1. Read the following Scenario.

2. Based on the information contained in the Scenario, finish preparing the Contract Budget Base Log (CBB) that follows.

3. Be careful not to forecast any negotiation positions to the customer.

4. Do not fail to consider the Fiscal Calendar on next page.

Scenario

Project Searchlight is a $108M CPFF satellite contract with a Fixed Fee of $8M. The contract was signed on 14 January Year 01. After reviewing the proposal and changes that occurred during negotiation, the project manager (PM) established a nine percent preliminary Management Reserve. The PM expected that number to fluctuate as control accounts were detail planned.

On 28 February Year 01 the PM signed the last of the Control Account Authorization Documents (CAADs), thereby establishing the Performance Measurement Baseline (PMB). At that time the sum of all control accounts equaled $93.5M. There was no Undistributed Budget (UB) at that time, and no modifications had yet been made to the contract.

On 23 April Year 01 P0001, a $1M non-fee bearing modification to the contract was negotiated.

On 16 May the last of the control accounts affected by P0001 was completed with signatures on the CAADs. The sum of the changes to all affected control accounts was $925K. All effort was distributed and the remaining budget was set aside for future unknowns.

On 22 May a Stop Work Order (SWO) was received for the AM-to-PM Converter Fractometer. This was budgeted in the program at $1.2M. By the time the effort was shut down, 33% of the task had been done and $520K had been spent. The remaining effort was removed from the control accounts. Business Administration personnel had adjusted all documentation by 29 May, the end of the fiscal month.

On 10 June a FAX was received from the Procuring Contracting Officer (PCO) that authorized the PM to proceed with analysis of an alternative Power Source Module (PSM) design. The FAX stipulated a Not-To-Exceed (NTE) of $10M (cost only), which the PM found to be acceptable. Negotiation was expected to be completed within 90 days. The PM figured she would lose about 5% during negotiation. It was anticipated that the effort would last approximately nine months at about $1M/month. The PM authorized 90 days of initial effort to be performed.

The solution to this case study can be found on the Humphreys & Associates, Inc. web site.
www.humphreys-assoc.com

On August 20th the PM authorized additional 90 days worth of effort associated with the Power Source Module design. Negotiations with the customer were delayed awaiting a support audit to be completed.

Unfortunately, negotiations were not completed until 22 October Year 01 for the Alternative PSM Design Analysis change. At that time modification P0002 for the Alternative PSM Design Analysis change was issued for $10.1M including $600K Fixed Fee. The PM established additional MR in the amount of $400K. None of the affected control accounts was revised prior to 30 October Year 01.

All effort associated with P0002 was detail planned and authorized prior to the Thanksgiving break.

1st Qtr.

January

	Sat	Sun	Mon	Tue	Wed	Thu	Fri
WK 1	4	5	6	7	8	9	10
WK 2	11	12	13	14 (Contract Signed)	15	16	17
WK 3	18	19	20	21	22	23	24
WK 4	25	26	27	28	29	30	31

February

	Sat	Sun	Mon	Tue	Wed	Thu	Fri
WK 1	1	2	3	4	5	6	7
WK 2	8	9	10	11	12	13	14
WK 3	15	16	17	18	19	20	21
WK 4	22	23	24	25	26	27	28 (PMB Established)

March

	Sat	Sun	Mon	Tue	Wed	Thu	Fri
WK 1	29	1	2	3	4	5	6
WK 2	7	8	9	10	11	12	13
WK 3	14	15	16	17	18	19	20
WK 4	21	22	23	24	25	26	27

2nd Qtr.

April

	Sat	Sun	Mon	Tue	Wed	Thu	Fri
WK 1	4	5	6	7	8	9	10
WK 2	11	12	13	14	15	16	17
WK 3	18	19	20	21	22	23 (P0001 Received)	24
WK 4	25	26	27	28	29	30	1

May

	Sat	Sun	Mon	Tue	Wed	Thu	Fri
WK 1	2	3	4	5	6	7	8
WK 2	9	10	11	12	13	14	15
WK 3	16 (0001 CAAD Signed)	17	18	19	20	21	22 (SWO Received)
WK 4	23	24	25	26	27	28	29 (SWO Docs Adjusted)

June

	Sat	Sun	Mon	Tue	Wed	Thu	Fri
WK 1	30	31	1	2	3	4	5
WK 2	6	7	8	9	10 (AUW Fax Received)	11	12
WK 3	13	14	15	16	17	18	19
WK 4	20	21	22	23	24	25	26

3rd Qtr.

July

	Sat	Sun	Mon	Tue	Wed	Thu	Fri
WK 1	4	5	6	7	8	9	10
WK 2	11	12	13	14	15	16	17
WK 3	18	19	20	21	22	23	24
WK 4	25	26	27	28	29	30	31

August

	Sat	Sun	Mon	Tue	Wed	Thu	Fri
WK 1	1	2	3	4	5	6	7
WK 2	8	9	10	11	12	13	14
WK 3	15	16	17	18	19	20 (AUW + 90 Days)	21
WK 4	22	23	24	25	26	27	28

September

	Sat	Sun	Mon	Tue	Wed	Thu	Fri
WK 1	29	30	31	1	2	3	4
WK 2	5	6	7	8	9	10	11
WK 3	12	13	14	15	16	17	18
WK 4	19	20	21	22	23	24	25

4th Qtr.

October

	Sat	Sun	Mon	Tue	Wed	Thu	Fri
WK 1	3	4	5	6	7	8	9
WK 2	10	11	12	13	14	15	16
WK 3	17	18	19	20	21	22 (P0002 Received)	23
WK 4	24	25	26	27	28	29	30

November

	Sat	Sun	Mon	Tue	Wed	Thu	Fri
WK 1	31	1	2	3	4	5	6
WK 2	7	8	9	10	11	12	13
WK 3	14	15	16	17	18	19	20
WK 4	21	22	23	24	25 (P0002 Planned)	26	27

December

	Sat	Sun	Mon	Tue	Wed	Thu	Fri
WK 1	28	29	30	1	2	3	4
WK 2	5	6	7	8	9	10	11
WK 3	12	13	14	15	16	17	18
WK 4	19	20	21	22	23	24	25
WK 5	26	27	28	29	30	31	1

Contract Budget Base Log

1	2	3	4	5	6	7	8	9	10	11
Transaction Number	Date	Description	Contract Target Cost (CTC)	Authorized Unpriced Work (AUW)	Contract Budget Base (CBB)	Management Reserve (MR)	Performance Measurement Baseline (PMB)	Undistributed Budget (UB)	Allocated (Distributed) Budget	Remarks/Notes
N/A		January CPR								
N/A		February CPR								
N/A		March CPR								
N/A		April CPR								
N/A		May CPR								

Contract Budget Base Log

1	2	3	4	5	6	7	8	9	10	11
Transaction Number	Date	Description	Contract Target Cost (CTC)	Authorized Unpriced Work (AUW)	Contract Budget Base (CBB)	Management Reserve (MR)	Performance Measurement Baseline (PMB)	Undistributed Budget (UB)	Allocated (Distributed) Budget	Remarks/Notes
N/A		June CPR								
N/A		July CPR								
N/A		August CPR								
N/A		September CPR								
N/A		October CPR								
N/A		November CPR								

Chapter **35**

SUBCONTRACT MANAGEMENT

Objectives of this Chapter:

1. Define subcontracts and major subcontracts.

2. Discuss the establishment of the flowdown requirements.

3. Discuss Request for Proposal (RFP) requirements.

4. Discuss post-award baseline lay-in.

5. Discuss considerations for subcontracts with EVMSG requirements.

6. Discuss considerations for subcontracts without EVMSG requirements.

7. Discuss additional subcontract budgeting considerations.

8. Discuss special organizational considerations.

9. Discuss revisions.

10. Discuss subcontract EVMS reviews and surveillance.

Definition of Subcontracts

It is important to understand the differences between material (material may include equipment) and subcontracts because the EIA-748 EVMS Guidelines (EVMSG) have certain requirements that apply to materials and other requirements that apply to subcontracts. Material and equipment items are generally off-the-shelf or build-to-print items that do not require design, development, or installation on the part of the supplier. Most of material and equipment is payment upon delivery and acceptance, which fits the EVMS requirement that the first acceptable point for earning value for material is the delivery of the material. Subcontracts are not included in the material/equipment restrictions because subcontracts normally require design and development effort before delivery or significant onsite installation effort (e.g., HVAC installation throughout a building) by the supplier. In these instances, making payments and reporting earned value prior to delivery or completion of installation is required to provide timely cost and schedule variance information.

Therefore, it is important to define what a subcontract is to avoid having material requirements being applied inappropriately. Different industries have different ways to define what a subcontract is because of different circumstances. However, in all instances, the differences between the handling of material/equipment and subcontracts should be understood and recognized when determining what the definition of a subcontract is.

Major subcontracts should be differentiated from non-major subcontracts because of the EVMS flowdown requirements that will be discussed in the next topic. Also, if the Contract Performance Report (CPR) Format 2 (Organizational Categories) were required, major subcontractors must

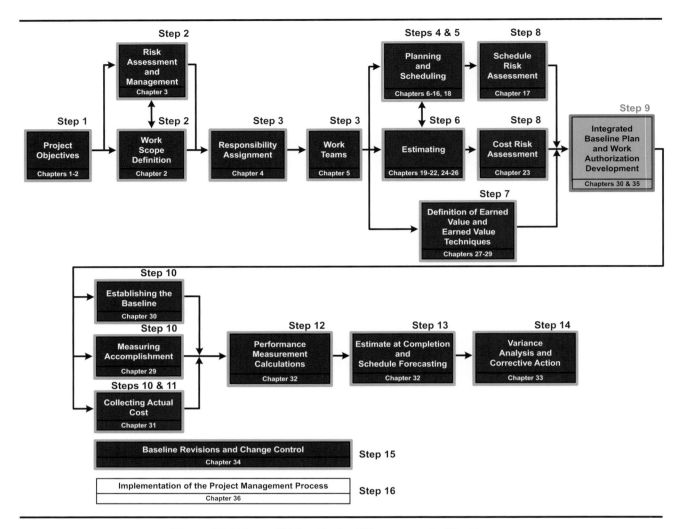

Figure 35-1 Earned Value Project Management: The Process

be included on this report Format. Thus, it is prudent to define which subcontracts are major in such a way that there is not a proliferation of subcontracts to be identified in Format 2. It is recommended that major subcontracts be defined as those for which compliance with the EIA-748 Guidelines is required. As of this printing, most federal agencies required Guideline compliance for incentive and cost reimbursable contracts with a value equal to or greater than $20M. For incentive and cost reimbursable contracts equal to or greater than $50M, the contractor's EVMS must be validated as compliant to the Guidelines by the contractor's Cognizant Federal Agency. Contracts with lesser values may also be required to be Guideline compliant if the risk were sufficient to warrant Guideline compliance. Federal agencies have required that the same thresholds

applied to prime contracts are also applied (flowed down) to subcontracts.

Note that while non-major subcontracts are not required to be compliant with the Guidelines, they should be required to provide sufficient information to allow the prime contractor to analyze and report earned value data as required by its contract. It is for this reason that non-major subcontracts are included in the following discussions.

Subcontract Flowdown Requirements

An important factor in establishing flowdown requirements to subcontractors is to evaluate the risk involved with the subcontract. The matrix in Figure 35-2 shows the risk items to be considered when deciding what level of performance management to apply to a subcontract. Contract types as well as technical, schedule and cost risk are important factors to take into consideration.

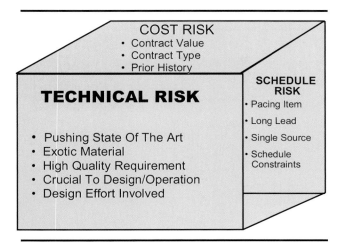

Figure 35-2 Subcontract Risk Factor

For technical risk factors, include the amount of development and design that will be required. If the deliverable or similar product has never been made before, the technical risk for the subcontract is high. If a vendor has not worked with the materials to be used or has not manufactured to the design tolerances or quality standards imposed, there may be technical risk associated with successfully producing the deliverable.

For schedule risk factors, it is important to determine if the subcontract effort were on the project critical path. Even if the subcontract effort were not on the critical path, if the performance period were extensive prior to delivery, the risk of meeting the delivery requirements or even becoming a part of the project critical path may be high.

When considering cost risk, the total price or value of the contract should be reviewed as well as the contract type. There is little cost risk associated with a Firm Fixed Price subcontract, while the risk associated with a Cost Plus subcontract can be a high risk especially if there are technical and schedule risks associated with the subcontract effort. A letter subcontract is associated with the highest cost risk as it contains the least definitive description of contract requirements.

These risk considerations should be weighed into a decision as to how much visibility and control a

prime should impose on a subcontractor. Figure 35-3 demonstrates how these factors can impact the risk for the prime contractor and the customer.

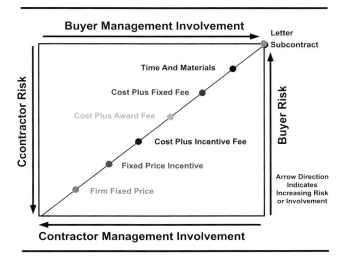

Figure 35-3 Relationship of Risk to Contract Type

The higher the risk factor the greater the visibility required of the subcontract effort. In addition to the risk factors, other factors such as value, duration, and contract type are to be considered in determining flowdown requirements. Figure 35-4 illustrates the recommended guidelines for subcontract reporting. The dollar values for mandatory compliance with the EVMS Guidelines ($50M and $20M) are used by most federal agencies as of this printing. The other values are recommendations.

Subcontract Requests for Proposals

The requirements for using and reporting earned value data are important factors to be included in the Request for Proposal (RFP) process. The requirements should be tailored to the expected value and risk of the subcontract. If a fully compliant EVMS were required, the management system and reporting requirements are well defined. However, if full compliance is not required, a tailoring of the subcontractor's data collection and reporting requirements must be clearly identified in the RFP to meet the prime contractor's requirements for reporting to its customer. How the potential subcontractor responds

TYPE OF CONTRACT	ANSI/EIA - 748 COMPLIANCE	CPR DI – MGMT - 81466A	IMS DI - 81650 - MGMT	WBS MIL - STD - 881	COST AND SOFTWARE DATA REPORTING (CSDR) [3]	INTEGRATED BASELINE REVIEW (IBR)	CONTRACT FUNDS STATUS REPORT (CFSR) DI - MGMT - 81468
COST OR INCENTIVE ≥ $50 MILLION[2]	EVM SYSTEM FORMALLY VALIDATED AND ACCEPTED	ALL FIVE FORMATS	REQUIRED	REQUIRED	REQUIRED	REQUIRED	REQUIRED
COST OR INCENTIVE ≥ $20 MILLION[2]	COMPLY, BUT NO FORMAL EVM SYSTEM VALIDATION REQUIRED	TAILORED AS APPROPRIATE [FORMATS 1,3,5]	TAILORED AS APPROPRIATE	TAILORED AS APPROPRIATE	TAILORED AS APPROPRIATE	REQUIRED	REQUIRED
COST OR INCENTIVE < $20 MILLION[2]	OPTIONAL BASED ON RISK REQUIRES PM APPROVAL & COST BENEFIT ANALYSIS	TAILORED AS REQUIRED	TAILORED AS REQUIRED	TAILORED AS APPROPRIATE	TAILORED AS APPROPRIATE	TAILORED AS APPROPRIATE	TAILORED AS APPROPRIATE
FIRM FIXED PRICE	DISCOURAGED EXCEPT FOR SEE NOTE 1	SEE NOTE 1	SEE NOTE 1	SEE NOTE 1	SEE NOTE 1	SEE NOTE 1	SEE NOTE 1

Notes:
1. For application decision, carefully consider schedule impact (Critical Path) risk, technical uncertainty, and cost (total dollar impact).
2. Applies to Then Year Dollars
3. Applies only to Department of Defense contracts

Figure 35-4 Subcontract EVM System and Reporting Requirements

to these requirements should be taken into consideration in awarding of the subcontract. The following addresses the subjects that should be covered in a Request for Proposal.

Subcontract Type

Earlier, we covered contract types and their associated risks. Several factors, including risk, affect the advisability of choosing contract types in any given situation. They affect the subcontractor's ability to provide an accurate and firm estimate of the cost of performance as well as the ease with which progress can be measured and paid. These factors include:

1. Completeness of design at time of contract bidding and award.
2. Length of the project.
3. Available sources (potential bidders).
4. Subcontractor marketplace (economic conditions).
5. Type of work involved.
6. Prime contractor's interest in participating in project activities.

A basic goal in formulating the subcontract type should be to achieve fairness to both the prime contractor and the subcontractor. Attempts to enforce one-sided agreements will inevitably result in greater problems in subcontract management. Subcontractors need an incentive to perform well, but they should not be expected to assume unreasonable risks. Similarly, the prime contractor needs protection against inefficiency and waste on the part of the subcontractor. If there were to be a continuing and successful relationship, the risks of both need to be balanced.

A mistaken belief is that the Firm Fixed Price subcontract always provides the subcontractor with the best incentive and always provides the prime contractor with the best protection. This is not necessarily true, and often, such an assumption proves to be erroneous. The factors of long term contracts, incomplete engineering, and economic uncertainties may well force subcontractors to include large cost risk reserve amounts in their Firm Fixed Price proposals to cover risks for which they cannot properly estimate the costs. As a result, the prime contractor may pay more than would have been required for a Cost Plus Award Fee or Fixed Price Incentive subcontract. Worse yet, if a subcontractor does not include a large enough cost risk reserve, a large cost overrun may result in financial insolvency or default on the subcontract. Either one is damaging for the prime contractor. On larger projects with long project durations, a more balanced sharing of risk between prime contractor and subcontractor is usually invoked.

The project management principles in this text apply to all types of contracts as discussed here, although they will be applied in differing levels of detail and with varying emphasis on technical and/or schedule and/or cost information. On Cost Plus type subcontracts, there is a need for detailed information from the subcontractor to the prime contractor to ensure that costs are properly managed. On Fixed Price type subcontracts, there is less emphasis on cost information on the part of the prime contractor because the cost risk is primarily assumed by the subcontractor. Performance measurement baseline planning and progress data, however, are still very important because of prime contractor schedule concerns and/or concerns regarding interfaces with other subcontractors.

Integrating the Subcontractor WBS

Subcontract planning begins with the prime contractor establishing a subcontract scope of work, a schedule that establishes the required dates for the major deliverables of the subcontract effort,

and a budget that is established and negotiated to measure subcontract performance.

Once these three elements of the subcontract have been determined, the prime contractor must decide on how the subcontract will be integrated into its reporting structures to the customer. The first step is to establish the Subcontract Work Breakdown Structure (SWBS).

How the prime contractor intends to integrate the SWBS will influence the way its CWBS for the prime contract is developed. The prime contractor is required to identify in its CWBS those elements that are to be subcontracted work.

There are two ways subcontract effort might be planned. All the work in single subcontract could appear as a single element on the prime contract WBS as illustrated in Figure 35-5, or the work in the subcontract could be planned in several lower level elements of the prime contract WBS as illustrated in Figure 35-6.

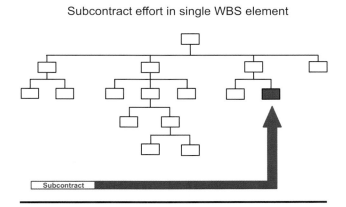

Subcontract effort in single WBS element

Figure 35-5 Prime Contract/Subcontract Integration (1 of 2)

As shown in these illustrations, the inclusion of subcontract effort in many different WBS elements has a potential for complications in managing the subcontract, which will be covered later in this chapter.

Regardless of the how the subcontract effort is integrated into the prime contract, the same principles apply as for establishing a control account for work performed. The control account is still at the intersection of the WBS and OBS, and an individual within the prime contractor's organiza-

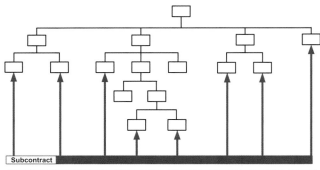

Subcontract effort allocated to multiple WBS elements
(Least desirable)

Subcontract

**Figure 35-6 Prime Contract/Subcontract Integration
(2 of 2)**

tion is assigned responsibility. This individual becomes the CAM for the subcontract effort.

In order to ensure that there is a mutual understanding of the scope of work to be performed by the subcontractor, a subcontract requirement should be the submission of a SWBS dictionary. This dictionary documents the subcontractor's understanding of the scope of work for the control account or reporting element. The prime contractor's CAM must review and approve the submitted SWBS as containing the entire work scope required by the subcontract, and that it does not contain work not required by the subcontract.

Integrating the Schedule

The second consideration in integrating subcontract reporting is how the schedule information will be reported and maintained in the prime contractor's Integrated Master Schedule (IMS). Regardless of whether EVMS flowdown is required, subcontractors should be required to have a network schedule that leads to completion of the subcontract work scope. The schedule may be a fully compliant IMS per the DID cited in Figure 35-4, a simple delivery schedule for an FFP subcontract with a short duration that does not have progress or performance based payments, or anything between the two extremes. When compliance with the IMS DID is not required, the subcontract CAM and supporting staff determine the level of tailoring required to satisfy the visibility needs of management.

Unless otherwise required, resource loading is optional, but is strongly recommended.

To comply with the prime contractor's internal schedule requirements, the subcontract CAM must verify that the RFP contains requirements to ensure the subcontractor's schedule is structured in such a way that it can easily be integrated into the prime contractor's project schedule. Therefore, the RFP and the resulting subcontract must contain specific instructions regarding the structure of the schedule [e.g., WBS and integrated master plan (IMP) requirements] and the major milestones that the subcontractor must meet. These requirements are documented in the RFP and the awarded subcontract in a Subcontract Data Requirements List (SDRL). Items included in the SDRL include the format required to integrate with the prime contractor's internal system, the frequency of submissions, the level of detail expected, the definition of the schedule content, and the control of schedule revisions.

Post Award Baseline Establishment

There are two baselines to establish, the budget baseline and the schedule baseline. The technical baseline was established with the award of the subcontract. All three baselines must be integrated. The technical work scope is contained in the IMS and in the performance measurement baseline. The IMS time phasing defines the time phasing of budget. Without ensuring the integration of the three baselines, there is very little hope that the project will be successful.

There are some aspects to baseline establishment that vary based on whether the subcontract includes the EVMS Guideline (EVMSG) requirements or does not. These will be covered after a discussion of the basics of baseline establishment.

Establishing the Schedule Baseline

With regard to the schedule baseline, interface points in addition to the major milestones in the RFP are identified as the subcontractor develops its schedule. The prime contractor's project office schedulers work directly with the subcontractor's schedulers to ensure that all interface points are identified and the subcontract schedule fully supports the prime contractor's project schedule. The interface points include hand-offs from the prime contractor to the subcontractor as well as the subcontractor's hand-offs to the prime contractor. At a minimum, the prime contractor's IMS should contain every interface point identified in the subcontractor's schedule. The prime contractor project office staff may decide to incorporate the entire subcontract schedule into the prime contractor's IMS if circumstances warrant that level of integration. The subcontractor should be required to submit its baseline schedule and any changes to the prime contractor's subcontract CAM for approval prior to implementation.

As stated before, the baseline schedule is the basis for the time phasing of the budget. It is much easier to integrate the schedule with the budget if the schedule were resource loaded. Consequently, it is recommended that the subcontract require a resource loaded schedule. The resources and their time phasing can be passed to the earned value engine for creation of a budget baseline that is automatically integrated with the schedule.

Establishing the Budget Baseline

The establishment of the budget baseline for the prime contractor's control account(s) for a subcontract falls into two phases. The initial baseline establishment is usually accomplished before the subcontract is negotiated. After the subcontract is negotiated, the budgets can be formally completed.

The initial or interim baseline may be based on the prime contractor's initial estimate of the effort, a subcontractor Rough Order of Magnitude (ROM) estimate, or subcontractor proposals prior to negotiation and award. However, in most cases the subcontractor's proposal values are usually used for the interim work plan (BCWS) values. Regardless of which of these is used, it should be noted that any of these values identified for the control account budgets will not be the

final baseline values but are established as interim values until negotiations are completed.

Sometimes the work must be started prior to completion of negotiations. When this occurs, a letter subcontract is issued, usually with a Not to Exceed (NTE) value, to allow the subcontractor to get started on high priority work while negotiations are completed. The baseline is formally established after the negotiation of the contract. The prime contractor's CAM, at this point, will plan the control account based on the negotiated value. The amount that was initially planned will generally not equal the final negotiated value. Options for bringing the initial budget in line with the negotiated value are using Management Reserve (MR) or if the use of MR were not desirable, factoring may be used. Factoring will be covered later in this chapter.

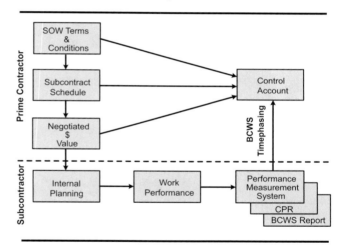

Figure 35-7 Planning the Definitized Subcontract

Figure 35-7 above depicts the example of a subcontract within a single prime contractor control account. Thus, the time-phasing of the prime contractor's control account should be easily accomplished as shown in Figure 35-8.

However, it is not always that easy. The subcontractor's price, which includes fee, is a cost to the prime contractor. Thus, the prime contractor must determine how to include the subcontractor's fee in its cost baseline. To do so requires an understanding of how fee is determined and paid. The CAM must work closely with the contracting officer during RFP development and subcontract negotiations to ensure that fee payments can be

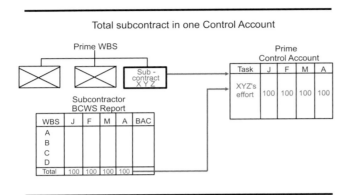

Figure 35-8 BCWS Time Phasing for Prime Control Accounts (1 of 2)

planned, earned, and costed in a consistent manner.

The question the prime contractor must ask is whether to address subcontractor fee in its EVMS or to require the subcontractor to address it in its EVMS. Most prime contractors prefer to have the subcontractor address fees in its EVMS because it passes the effort to address fee to the subcontractor. However, the subcontractor may not want to acquiesce to this solution because the CPR Data Item Description (DID) requires that the Contract Budget Base (CBB) include only cost, not fee. In order to require the subcontractor to include fee in its CBB, the prime contractor will have to include changes to the DID in the subcontract document and the subcontractor will have to agree to the changes.

Regardless of whether the prime contractor or the subcontractor tracks the fee, the prime contractor CAM must be part of the decision making process as to how fees will be paid and tracked so there is complete understanding of how subcontractor fees affect the control account variances.

If the handling of fee in a single control account appears to be difficult, consider the situation wherein a subcontract has work scope that is contained in multiple control accounts in the prime contractor's WBS. This situation is shown in Figure 35-9.

When this situation occurs, the first requirement is to ensure that the subcontractor's WBS includes WBS elements that at some level the entire work scope of a single WBS element is

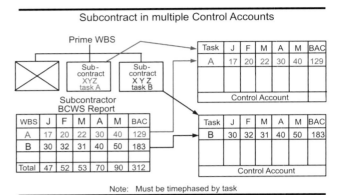

Figure 35-9 BCWS Time Phasing for Prime Control Accounts (2 of 2)

contained within a single prime contractor control account. This must be accomplished during RFP development or subcontract negotiations in the form of a required summary SWBS that identifies the relevant prime contractor control accounts. There is still the price versus cost issue, but added to that issue are the subcontractor's costs that may not be identifiable to specific SWBS elements such as G&A and Cost of Money (COM). These can be handled by having the subcontractor report data by SWBS through all indirect costs and reporting G&A and COM as non-add items in the CPR submitted to the prime contractor. But then there are the SWBS elements that are not identified to a specific product such as program management and data. These could be allocated to the prime's control accounts as shown in Figure 35-10.

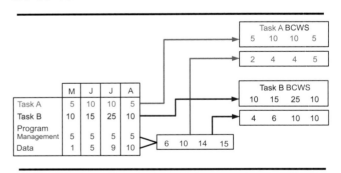

Figure 35-10 Allocation Example

What about the subcontractor's Undistributed Budget (UB) and Management Reserve (MR) as shown in Figure 35-11? These items are not time-phased and are not identified by the subcontractor to a specific WBS.

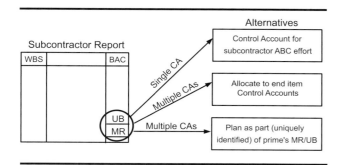

Figure 35-11 The Subcontractor's MR and UB

When the subcontract is totally within a single prime control account, the answer is simple: plan the MR and UB within the control account. It is preferred that the MR be placed in a planning package in the last month of the control account's period of performance. Because the work scope of UB is known by the prime contractor's CAM (it has been authorized by the prime contractor), it should be time-phased as best as possible in a planning package. When the subcontractor distributes the UB, convert the planning package to a work package with the proper time phasing.

When a subcontractor's work scope encompasses two or more of the prime contractor's control accounts, MR and UB can be treated in two different ways: one is to put them into the control account by either allocation of MR or assignment of the UB work scope, and the other is to include them with the prime's MR and UB accounts with a special identifier. Because it is possible that one could be assigned to the control accounts while the other could be assigned to the prime contractor's UB or MR account, both are addressed separately.

Because the subcontractor's UB has defined work scope, it should be identifiable to the prime contractor's control accounts. Thus, the prime contractor should be able to include it within control accounts. However, time phasing is still a problem. If the UB were the result of a subcontract change order that resulted from an approved Baseline Change Request (BCR) for the prime contractor control account's BAC, the baseline change should be entered as a planning package with an interim time phasing that could be re-planned as a work package when the sub-

contractor issues the budget from its UB to the control accounts within the applicable SWBS. Using this approach, the subcontractor should be directed to separately identify the change order in its BAC/BCWS so earned value and ACWP can be tracked appropriately. A change internal to the subcontractor that had to be processed temporarily through UB from subcontract control account to subcontract control account does not involve reporting to the prime because of the simultaneous UB credit and debit. This assumes that the movement is between two subcontractor control accounts, both of which feed a single prime contractor control account. However, a subcontractor's internal change that causes a movement between the prime contractor's control accounts, (e.g. a movement between SWBS levels that feed separate prime contractor control accounts) should only be made with prime contractor approval. If the UB's work scope cannot be identified to specific prime contractor control accounts, it should be included with the prime contractor's UB, but specifically identified as assigned to the subcontractor.

The subcontractor's MR is difficult to handle because it has no work scope and, therefore, cannot be specifically identified to one or more of the prime contractor's control accounts. There are two methods for this situation. The first is to put the subcontractor's MR in the prime contractor's MR account. This requires specific identification of the subcontractor's MR and a requirement that it is not available to the prime contractor for its use other than to make a distribution that replicates the subcontractor's MR distribution. The second method is to allocate the subcontractor's MR to the prime's control accounts based on their BAC ratios. The allocated MR should be time-phased in planning packages at the end of the prime contractor control accounts' periods of performance. The drawback to allocating the subcontractor's MR to the applicable prime control accounts is that the subcontractor is likely to use its MR differently than the prime allocated it to its control accounts which complicates the prime's BCR process. The first method is recommended as the preferred method.

Prime Contractor Considerations for Subcontracts without EVMSG Requirements

If a subcontractor were not required to provide Earned Value information to the prime, the prime contractor should establish procedures that provide schedule and technical plans and progress reports as needed for overall project management. The procedures must be defined during the RFP process to ensure that the subcontractor understands what the contractual requirements will be. The requirements will vary based on the type of subcontract. There are four types that will be discussed:

- Incentive or Cost Plus
- Firm Fixed Price
- Time and Materials
- Technical Support.

Incentive or Cost Plus

These subcontracts are structured similar to subcontracts with EVMSG requirements except that there is no requirement for Guideline compliance. Therefore, the subcontract must be structured such that the data provided to the prime contractor enables accurate earned value analysis and reporting. The basic requirements are shown in Figure 35-12.

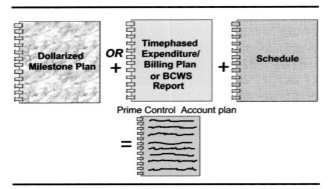

Figure 35-12 Prime Contractor Establishes BCWS Based on Subcontractor Submittals

On smaller non-major subcontracts (e.g., less than $5M and less than a year's duration), a dollarized milestone plan works well. The subcontract should be set up with payments based on the completion of milestones. The milestones are event based with a defined work scope and an assigned value (budget). The milestones are defined in a network schedule that can be used to measure progress toward the milestone. The budget is established based on the timing and value of the milestones in the prime contractor's control account plan. When a milestone is achieved, the value of the milestone is earned and the subcontractor submits an invoice for payment of actual costs incurred as allowed by the subcontract terms, which becomes the ACWP associated with the earned value.

For larger non-major subcontracts (e.g., equal to or greater than $5M and more than a year in length), billing milestones are probably not sufficient. It is preferred that, if possible, the subcontractor provides earned value data and reports from a tailored EVM System. However, if that were not possible, a time-phased expenditure/billing plan or a BCWS report tied to a resource loaded Integrated Master Schedule (IMS) is necessary to establish the prime contractor's control account plan. The prime contractor's CAM can calculate BCWP with this data based on schedule status provided by the subcontractor and verified by the CA Manager.

Firm Fixed Price (FFP)

By definition, the cost variance for a firm fixed price subcontract is always equal to zero. Consequently, the only cost data required is the payment structure of the subcontract. Federal Acquisition Regulations require that interim payments on FFP subcontracts be either performance based using a billing plan associated with milestones identified in a contractual schedule or dollarized milestones based on deliveries. In either method, the payment associated with each milestone is a negotiated fixed payment. Unlike the situation discussed under Incentive or Cost Plus contracts, the subcontractor may only invoice for the negotiated value of the milestone when the milestone is validated to have occurred. Thus, the prime contractor's control account plan is based on the timing of the events and their values. When the event occurs and is validated, earned value is taken and ACWP is set equal to the earned value.

However, while cost variance is not an issue, schedule variance is. Therefore, an IMS should be a contractual requirement for medium and high risk FFP subcontracts. Lack of progress on the schedule is not only an indicator of schedule issues, but also of technical issues because technical problems are the primary cause of schedule problems.

Time and Materials (T&M)

According to the Federal Acquisition Regulations, "time and materials contracts may be used only when it is not possible at the time of placing the contract to estimate accurately the extent or duration of the work or to anticipate costs with any reasonable degree of confidence."[1] A T&M contract "provides for acquiring supplies or services on the basis of (1) Direct labor hours at specified fixed hourly rates that include wages, overhead, general and administrative expenses, and profit; and (2) Actual cost for materials."[2]

Because the nature and duration of the work is not specifically known, T&M subcontracts are often planned as level of effort work packages with an estimated budget and budget profile. However, a T&M subcontract is sometimes a task order contract wherein individual task orders are made against the subcontract as specific work scope and durations become known. In this instance, the T&M subcontract can be planned as a planning package in the prime control account with the individual task orders becoming work packages that are conversions of part of the planning package. The resultant work packages would be planned with discrete earned value techniques.

Technical Services

Technical Services contracts are also called Labor Hour contracts. The difference between this type and T&M contracts is that there is no material involved. This type of subcontract is generally used for staff augmentation and consulting services and is planned as level of effort. As such, the BCWS is time-phased over the anticipated period of performance as established

in the subcontract. The time phasing will be based on the estimated expenditures each month.

Staff augmentation can present additional issues to be addressed. If the staff augmentation were assisting the prime contractor's staff in performing the work scope planned in work packages, there would now be two performing organizations working on the same work package. Work packages should be assigned to a specific performing organization. One solution would be to create two work packages for the effort with the staff augmentation work package apportioned to the prime contractor's work package. Also, there is the issue of labor tracking because the original budget would have been based on hours. A method should be established to record the staff augmentation's hours to allow calculation of labor efficiency versus rate variances.

Additional Considerations When Planning Subcontract Budgets

When time-phasing the subcontractor's budget in the prime contractor's control account, the prime contractor must take into consideration when subcontractor information will be available compared to when that information must be available for entry into the prime contractor's earned value database for processing.

A subcontractor requires time to process its data and analyze it before submittal to the prime. This can be mitigated somewhat by requiring the subcontractor to submit data before it is analyzed and formally reported. However, there is also the issue of the prime contractor's and the subcontractor's accounting periods not being in sync. In these circumstances, it may be appropriate to incorporate a one month delay in the prime contractor's database. Thus, the subcontractor's February data would be recorded in the prime contractor's March data. This procedure should be used only when all other possibilities have been exhausted and should be coordinated with the customer prior to implementation. The customer must understand why the procedure is necessary and how the procedure affects the data it receives.

---

1. Federal Acquisition Regulations. *Subpart 16.601, Time-and-Materials Contracts.*
2. Ibid.

Factoring Subcontract Budgets

Sometimes the final negotiated price of a subcontract is greater than the budget established for the prime contractor's control account. There are two ways this might be addressed. One is to accommodate the difference with the use of management reserve. The other is to use factoring. Factoring is generally used when management reserve is small compared to the prime contractor's remaining effort, the difference between the budget and the negotiated price is significant, and the project manager prefers to be judicious in the use of management reserve.

Factoring is the process of adjusting the subcontractor's negotiated price to match the prime contractor's control account budget (BAC). The factor is applied to the subcontractor's BCWS and BCWP, but not the ACWP or the Estimate to Complete (ETC) (all numbers are adjusted for profit, etc. as explained earlier). The factor to be used is calculated by dividing the prime contractor's control account BAC by the subcontractor's negotiated price is illustrated as follows.

$$\frac{\text{Prime BAC}}{\text{Subcontractor Price}} = \frac{\$190M}{\$200M} = .95$$

The factor is applied to budget (BCWS and BAC) and earned value (BCWP). Actuals are not factored.

If the subcontractor were supporting more than one control account, the factor is calculated by dividing the sum of the prime contractor's control account BACs by the subcontractor's negotiated price and applied to each of the control accounts.

The objectives of factoring are to ensure that the subcontractor's factored BCWS equals prime contractor's available budget, and that the subcontractor's percent complete matches the prime contractor's control account percent complete to prevent inaccurate earned value reporting. Figure 35-13 shows how inaccurate reporting could occur.

The prime contractor is always constrained to report based on the BAC and BCWS of its control account. In the situation shown in Figure 35-13, if factoring were not used, the prime contractor

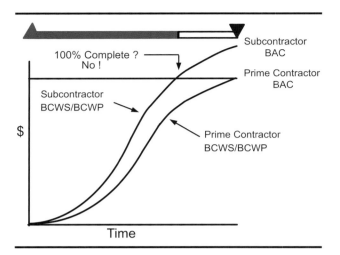

Figure 35-13 Factoring Objectives

still reports to its budgets, but must also report an earned value. If the prime contractor reports the subcontractor's BCWP as its BCWP, it will be reporting a schedule variance that is much better than reality. Additionally, because of the inflated BCWP, the cost variance is also being reported as much better than reality. Eventually, the subcontractor's BCWP will be equal to the BAC of the prime contractor. In this situation the prime contractor is reporting that the effort is complete, but is it? The subcontractor still has effort to go. The only way to avoid this situation when the BACs are not the same is to use factoring. In doing so, the percent complete of both the prime and the subcontractor will be equal. Thus, after applying the factor for both the BCWS and BCWP, the prime contractor's percent complete as calculated by the formula BCWP/BAC x 100 will be equal to the subcontractor's percent complete calculated by the same formula. This is a good check to validate that factoring is being used properly.

As noted previously, ACWP and ETC are not factored because, if they were, the ACWP and EAC reported by the prime contractor to its customer would not be correct. However, because variances will be different when reconciling the prime contractor's control account data to the subcontractor's report (a subcontractor's underrun may translate to be a prime contractor's overrun), the differences must be explained in the prime contractor's variance analyses.

Special Organizational Situations

There are two special organizational situations that need to be addressed that vary from the traditional prime contractor/subcontractor relationship. One is the Inter-Divisional Work Authorization (also known as Internal Organizational Transfer). The other is partnerships between companies that manifest themselves in what are sometimes called "badgeless organizations."

Inter-Divisional Work Authorization (IDWA)

An IDWA is work that is "awarded" to other divisions within the same company. The other division must be treated like an "arm's length" subcontractor. There is no favoritism in the "award" and the IDWA division is subject to the same flowdown requirements as to a normal subcontractor. Because of the close relationship between the prime division and the supporting division, there are items requiring special treatment that affect the prime contractor division's budget structure.

One is the application of corporate G&A assessments. Normally, corporate G&A assessment applies to all of the prime contractor's costs through overheads, which includes subcontract costs. But if the corporate assessment were applied to the supporting division and then applied to the prime division, the corporate G&A assessment would be applied to costs that already include the corporate G&A assessment. Corporations have policies for how to account for IDWA situations. When establishing budgets for the supporting division, the prime division must understand and apply the corporate policies.

Another special treatment item is the determination of the profit structure. Normal handling would result in the corporation receiving a profit twice for the same work, once for the supporting division and once for the pass through from the supporting division to the prime division to the corporation. Again, the corporation will have procedures for this situation that the prime division should incorporate into its planning.

Badgeless Organizations

This occurs when two or more companies decide to operate as partners rather than in the normal

prime contractor/subcontractor relationship, and is referred to as partnerships or teaming arrangements. The partners' personnel work as if they were all working for the same company. Often the partners will form a Limited Liability Company (LLC) to act as the single entity to which the prime contract is awarded. Figure 35-14 is a representation of what an excerpt of a Responsibility Assignment Matrix (RAM) might look like in a badgeless organization.

In Figure 35-14, two companies, Prime Aircraft (PA) and Digital Aero (DA), have entered into a partnership for the purposes of managing a contract. The figure shows an excerpt of the project's organizational structure wherein employees from both companies are spread throughout the management levels. The WBS and OBS intersections with a yellow background are control accounts. The Electrical Engineering supervisor, Mr. D. Hunt of Digital Aero has assigned Ms. S. Smith of Prime Aircraft to be the CAM responsible to perform the organization's work scope within the Cockpit WBS element. To perform the work, Ms. Smith has put together a team of three DA and two PA employees. For this totally integrated organization to work well, the following conditions should exist:

- One of the partners is selected as the "lead" (its accounting system and EVMS used for contract performance reporting).*

- All partnership personnel resources are available for planning.

- There is only one IMS for the partnership.

- Each partner's price is in the budget plan.*

- The project's statusing is entered directly in the partnership IMS.

- All labor hour charges are collected in the lead's systems.*

- All partnership personnel are typically co-located.

The items with asterisks present significant rate issues (direct and indirect) because rates are company proprietary and, in other circumstances, the partners may be competitors. The rate issue also involves the customer. The customer will

Project Organization \ WBS				Air Vehicle		
				Air Frame		
				Cockpit	Fuselage	Wing
Aircraft Project Manager P. Fisher Prime Aircraft (PA)	**Air Vehicle Engineering** L. Bucy Digital Aero (DA)	**Mechanical** B. Jones Prime Aircraft (PA)	B. Jones Prime Aircraft (PA)			
		Electrical D. Hunt Digital Aero (DA)	S. Smith Prime Aircraft (PA)	A. Edward (PA) D. Kann (DA) B. Davis (DA) V. Adams (PA) J. McHale (DA)		
		Aerodynamic M. Lucerne Prime Aircraft (PA)	K. Williams Digital Aero (DA)			

Figure 35-14 Badgeless Organization RAM

want to see the rate information that the partners are not willing to share with each other.

Another issue associated with badgeless organizations, partnerships, etc. is EVMS flowdown. The customer will sign a contract with only one organization to prevent itself from becoming a referee to adjudicate disagreements between the partners. That contract value becomes the value that defines the threshold for EVMS flowdown. If there were a designated lead partner, that partner becomes the partner responsible for receiving the contract and for complying with all contractual requirements. As the lead contractor, it will have to engage its partner (or partners) in a contractual arrangement. That creates an issue about EVMS compliance of the non-lead partner if the value of its effort requires EVMS compliance flowdown under normal circumstances. Also, if the partners elect to create a single entity as the company to be awarded the contract, strict interpretation of the flowdown requirements would mean that the newly created entity must comply with the EVMS Guidelines and may even have to be validated as having a compliant EVM System.

There is no single correct solution to the above issues as was noted by Fisher and Gasbarro in their article on Teaming Arrangements and EVMS Flowdown in the Winter 2010 issue of The Measurable News, a publication of the Project Management Institute's College of Performance Management (PMI-CPM).[3] The ultimate decision as to what is acceptable and what is not acceptable is ultimately up to the customer. Therefore, when a teaming arrangement is being considered, consultation with the customer is a must.

Revisions

In this topic we will discuss three categories of revisions to the subcontract baseline as follows:

1. Directed changes from the prime contractor to subcontractors that consist of:

3. Fisher, Doug and Gasbarro, Jim. *Teaming Arrangements and EVMS Flowdown*. The Measurable News, Winter 2010 Issue 1, www.pmi-cpm.org/pages/measurable_news/documents/MN2010Issue1Feb4.pdf.

a. Class I changes, which are out-of-scope to both prime contract and subcontract

b. Class II changes, which are in scope to prime contractor and out-of-scope to subcontractor

2. Internal re-planning - subcontractor changes to its baseline, which may consist of a time-phasing shift, allocation of MR and UB, and/or shifting of resources.

3. Formal reprogramming - changes to the subcontractor's baseline that result in a PMB in excess of the contract budget base.

Directed Changes

Both classes of directed changes need to be managed in a similar fashion, the only difference being that in Class II changes, the prime contractor must use its MR or UB to budget the change to the subcontract. The baseline must be maintained during and after all directed changes are implemented. Figure 35-15 shows the process steps for a Class I change.

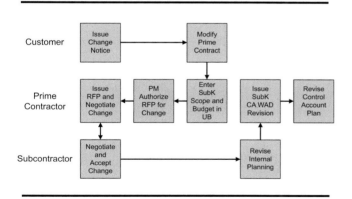

Figure 35-15 Class I Change Cycle

The process in this chart assumes that all the appropriate proposals have been made and negotiated. The steps for implementing a Class I change are:

1. Customer issues a change notice that modifies the prime contract.

2. The prime contractor enters the work scope and budget for the subcontractor in Undistributed Budget to await the results

of negotiations with the subcontractor. If there were internal effort associated with the change, the PM issues CA WADs for that work

3. The prime contractor PM authorizes release of RFP to subcontractor and complete negotiations for issuance of change order (NOTE: the subcontractor may have already submitted proposal for the effort in preparation for the prime contractor to submit the request to the customer, in which case the authorization is for final negotiations and issuance of change order).

4. Upon receipt of the RFP, the subcontractor prepares the proposal and negotiates the subcontract change with the prime contractor. If negotiations are not completed prior to a required start date, partial distribution of the subcontractor's work scope and associated budget contained in UB are made to the control account that contains the subcontracted work for partial turn-on of the subcontractor. The partial distribution is continued until negotiations are complete.

5. The subcontractor revises all internal replanning and submits to the prime contractor.

6. The prime contractor's PM distributes the negotiated budget from UB to the CAM in the form of a revised WAD. If the negotiated value were not equal to the initial budget entered in UB, the difference is either a use or replenishment of MR. If sufficient MR were not available, the factoring process described previously can be used.

7. The CAM, based on the WAD and the subcontractor's planning, revises control account budget, schedule and scope of work.

Figure 35-16 shows the process steps for a Class II change.

The process in this chart assumes the subcontractor has either identified non-authorized work

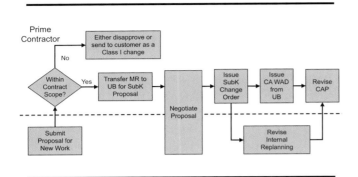

Figure 35-16 Class II Change Cycle

or has been informed by the prime contractor of work that the subcontractor believes is outside its current contract work scope. The steps for implementing a Class II change are:

1. The subcontractor submits a proposal for the "new" work to the prime contractor.

2. Assuming the prime contractor agrees the work scope is not already part of the subcontractor's current contract work scope, it determines if the work scope were within the prime contractor's contract work scope. If not, a decision is made to either disapprove the proposal or send it to the customer as a recommended Class I change.

3. If the prime agrees that the proposal were within its contracted work scope, the work scope is put in UB with a budget transfer from MR at the proposed value.

4. The prime contractor and the subcontractor negotiate the proposal and come to an agreement.

5. The prime contractor issues a change order to the subcontractor and a revised WAD to the appropriate CAM(s). Any budget difference between the UB amount and the negotiated value is accommodated by a use or replenishment of Management Reserve. If sufficient MR were not available, the factoring process described previously can be used.

6. The subcontractor incorporates the change by internal re-planning and submits to prime contractor.

7. Based on the revised WAD and the subcontractor's planning, the prime contractor's CAM revises the control account plan.

It is important to note that in a Class II change if the prime contractor decides to revise existing control account budgets, MR is used and the prime contractor's control account budget will equal the new subcontract price. If the prime contractor elects not to revise the budget, factoring must occur to prevent possible misstating of variances as shown previously in this chapter.

Internal Replanning

Although a subcontractor's internal replanning does not affect its contractual relationship with the prime contractor, it can affect the prime contractor's budget and schedule. Internal replanning can affect a subcontractor's UB, MR, and control account schedule and budget time-phasing. How much this does or does not affect the prime contractor is dependent upon how the prime contractor treated these items in its budget.

If the prime contractor planned the subcontractor's UB and/or MR as earmarked items in its UB and MR, any movement of the subcontractor's UB or MR must be mirrored by a movement of the prime contractor's UB or MR. Such a movement requires processing of a baseline change in the prime contractor's EVMS to transfer budget in the same manner as transferred by the subcontractor. It could be a transfer to one or more control accounts or a transfer between the UB and MR accounts. Of course, as required by the CPR DID, the prime contractor must discuss this movement in the CPR's Format 5.

Even if the subcontractor's UB and MR were planned within the control account, a change in the prime contract control account will still be necessary because the change will certainly change the time-phasing of the prime contract control account. This may be simple or complex depending on the prime contractor's change approval authority levels. If the prime contractor allows a CAM to approve changes to its control account (if the control account BAC does not change and any schedule change does not affect a project milestone or any other control account), the change is easy to make. It needs to be documented, however. If the CAM does not have that authority, a change must be fully processed through the prime contractor's change control system.

Formal Reprogramming

If a subcontractor requires a baseline that exceeds its Contract Budget Base (CBB), the new baseline is documented in a process called Formal Reprogramming. The new baseline, if approved by the prime contractor, is called an Over Target Baseline (OTB). If the OTB also results in a planned (baseline) schedule that exceeds contractual milestones, the new planned schedule also must be approved and is called an Over Target Schedule (OTS). It is possible for an OTS to exist without an OTB and vice versa. Figure 35-17 shows when both conditions exist.

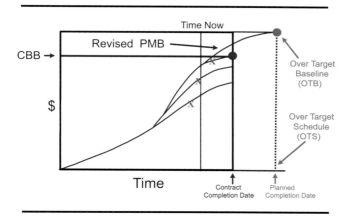

Figure 35-17 Over Target Baseline and Schedule

A subcontractor's OTB or OTS situation may or may not force the prime contractor into the same situation. It depends on whether the prime contractor can absorb the subcontractor's condition within its contractual requirements.

With regard to a subcontractor's OTB situation, a prime contractor has two methods available to absorb the subcontractor's OTB without implementing an OTB of its own, which requires the customer's approval. One is to increase the affected control account budgets to represent the subcontractor's OTB with a baseline change that uses MR to budget the change. The other is to not increase the control account budgets, but to use the factoring approach discussed earlier. Of course, with either method, the prime contractor's

customer must be notified of the condition and the method used.

If the prime contractor cannot absorb the subcontractor's OTB situation within its CBB by using either of the above two methods, the prime contractor must initiate its own Formal Reprogramming process to obtain approval of an OTB from its customer. In this situation, approval of the subcontractor's OTB request cannot be granted until the prime contractor receives prior approval from its customer.

With regard to a subcontractor OTS situation, the subcontractor's approved OTS must be reflected in the prime contractor's planned (baseline) schedule. If the subcontractor's OTS causes the prime contractor to have a planned completion date that exceeds its contractually required completion date, the prime contractor is in an OTS condition, which requires the prior approval of its customer.

Neither an OTB nor an OTS condition changes any contractual requirements. Even though the conditions are approved, the contract target cost and the contract completion date do not change.

Subcontract Data Analysis

The prime contractor conducts analysis of the subcontractor's EVM data just as the customer analyzes the prime contractor's EVM data. All of the analysis techniques, variance thresholds, and reporting requirements identified in Chapters 32 and 33 are used and will not be repeated here.

However, it is important to note that unreliable data submittals result in unreliable data analysis. The prime contractor's CAM must validate that the data provided are reliable and accurate. This is where close communication is paramount. The CAM cannot maintain an arm's length relationship. Frequent and close communication with the subcontractor is required. Schedule status must be verified by observation. Periodic project reviews should be conducted. Variance Analysis Reports (VARs) should be reviewed for adequate discussion of cause, impact, corrective action (including expected results), and EAC changes.

Another consideration is billing lag. Subcontractors report data as of the end of the accounting month. Because of the processing required for invoice submittal and because most prime contractors close the books for the accounting month within one week of accounting month end, the prime contractor's accounting system will likely not include the subcontractor's costs for the month. Thus, estimated ACWP will be required to line up with the reported earned value. When a subcontractor submits a CPR for the same reporting month as the prime contractor, the subcontractor's ACWP, even when incorporated directly into the prime contractor's CPR, is considered to be estimated ACWP. This is because the prime contractor's accounting system will not contain that month's subcontractor actual costs since it did not receive an invoice until after it had closed the books for the reporting month.

Once the prime contractor's CAM understands the subcontractor's schedule status, performance reports, variance analyses, and EAC submittals, the CAM must determine whether he/she agrees with the subcontractor's analyses. If not, communication with the subcontractor is required to discuss the areas of disagreement. Any remaining areas of disagreement are recorded by the prime contractor's CAM. That record could be the CAM's VAR if a VAR is required. Even if a VAR were not required because a threshold was not exceeded, one could be submitted to document the concern.

Subcontract EVMS Reviews and Surveillance

Whenever earned value information is required of a subcontractor, whether or not compliance with the Guidelines is required, the prime contractor must conduct reviews and surveillance. The reason for this is that the prime contractor is relying on the subcontractor's earned value data to report its earned value data to its customer. Therefore, the prime contractor must ensure that the management system being used by the subcontractor to report earned value data is set up to provide accurate and reliable earned value data if properly used.

In Figure 35-4, three levels of earned value reporting were noted including a level wherein compliance with the EVMSG is not mandatory.

The levels shown were the dollar thresholds for EVMSG compliance with validation, EVMSG compliance without validation, and EV reporting without EVMSG compliance. The review and surveillance requirements for each level will now be covered.

EVMS Guideline Compliance with Validation

This level requires that the subcontractor must be in full compliance with the EIA-748 Standard EVMS Guidelines and that its EVMS be reviewed and accepted by the Cognizant Federal Agency (CFA) as compliant with the Guidelines. If the subcontractor has received such an acceptance in the form of a Letter of Acceptance (LOA) or an Advance Agreement (AA), a CFA review is not required. If not, the prime contractor must take action with its customer to initiate the CFA review process of the subcontractor, which includes one or more Progress Assessment Visits to assess the subcontractor's readiness to undergo a validation review. The prime contractor will support the process as requested by the customer.

The prime contractor is required to conduct an Integrated Baseline Review (IBR) whether or not the subcontractor already has a CFA acceptance. If a CFA validation review were to be conducted, the IBR is usually conducted prior to the formal EVMS validation review because it demonstrates many of the Guideline requirements. Therefore, customer involvement in the IBR will likely be necessary as a prelude to the validation review.

Surveillance is the action the prime contractor takes to gain assurance that performance measurement data continues to accurately depict the status of the subcontractor's performance. Surveillance includes ensuring that the subcontractor remains in compliance with its validated system and that project data being produced continues to be valid and accurate. With regard to a subcontractor already having a CFA validation, the CFA's agent should be conducting surveillance on all of the subcontractor's contracts.

The prime contractor should coordinate surveillance on its subcontract with the subcontractor's responsible surveillance organization. Detailed guidance for conducting surveillance is contained in two documents: 1) the Defense Contract Management Agency's EVMS Standard Surveillance

Instruction (SSI) published in 2011, and 2) the National Defense Industrial Association (NDIA) Program Management Systems Committee (PMSC) Surveillance Guide.

EVMS Guideline Compliance without Validation

This level also requires that the subcontractor be in full compliance with the EIA-748 Standard EVMS Guidelines, but a CFA validation review or acceptance is not required. Instead, the subcontractor is required to certify that its EVMS is compliant with the Guidelines. The certification should include a comprehensive report on how the subcontractor's system complies with the Guidelines. The review and its report can be accomplished by the subcontractor, an independent third party, or the prime contractor. Regardless, the prime contractor should verify that the review adequately covered compliance with all of the Guidelines. Because parts of a review usually involve proprietary data, if the prime contractor were conducting the review, it may require assistance from the customer to assess the proprietary areas.

As in EVMSG compliance with validation, an IBR must be conducted by the prime contractor. Because a CFA validation is not required, customer involvement is not required, but it could be helpful. The customer should be consulted as to whether it would like to be involved.

When there is no CFA validation, the prime contractor must take the lead for conducting surveillance. In doing so, the prime contractor may be restricted to covering all aspects of a surveillance review because of a lack of access to subcontractor proprietary data. In this instance, the subcontractor's Government oversight organization must be requested to conduct the part of the surveillance review that involves proprietary data.

EV Reporting without EVMS Guideline Compliance

At this level, the subcontractor does not have to certify Guideline compliance. However, it should have or is implementing a tailored EVMS that provides valid and accurate earned value data. The primary difference between a fully compliant EVMS and a tailored EVMS is the amount of documentation required. In evaluating whether it will receive valid and accurate earned value data, the prime contractor should focus on how the schedule and cost baselines are developed, how progress is determined, and how actual costs are recorded to be in the same time period as its associated earned value. A WBS should be used with individuals assigned to be responsible for the work. The schedule should be sufficiently detailed to assess interim progress within a month and the budget should be time-phased to represent the resources required to accomplish the schedule. The reported earned value should be based on schedule progress using earned value techniques as in compliant systems.

Conclusion

Subcontracts are often a significant portion of a prime contractor's budget. Yet management of subcontractors within an EVMS environment has often been inadequate. To ensure proper management of a subcontractor, the prime contractor must manage the subcontractor in the same manner that the customer manages the prime contractor. Successful subcontract management is not difficult once the requirements, processes, and procedures presented in this chapter are understood and applied.

Chapter 35 Review Questions

35-1.   Why is it important to define subcontracts from material?

35-2.   What would be a good definition of major subcontracts?

35-3.   What contract type is the lowest risk to the customer? Why?

35-4.   What is the most important consideration when integrating a subcontract into a prime contract? Why?

35-5.   Why is it important for the prime contractor CAM to understand the fee arrangement with a subcontractor?

35-6.   When a subcontractor has work scope that is contained in more than one of the prime contractor control accounts, how are common WBS elements such as data and project management treated by the prime contractor?

35-7.   How can the subcontractor's MR and UB be included in the prime contractor's Contract Budget Base?

35-8.   If the subcontractor were not required to submit a CPR, what are the basic elements of information a prime contractor should require to be submitted in order to comply with its EVMS requirement imposed by the customer?

35-9.   When does estimated ACWP need to be used and why?

35-10. What is factoring and when is it used?

35-11. Why does an Inter-Divisional Work Authorization require special treatment?

35-12. What is the basic reason that makes a partnership (badgeless organization) difficult for satisfying EVMS reporting requirements to the customer?

35-13. What are the three categories of subcontract revisions?

35-14. What is the condition that exists when an OTB is approved?

35-15. Must a prime contractor conduct an Integrated Baseline Review on a major subcontract (a subcontract with EVMS flowdown) that already has acquired a Cognizant Federal Agency validation of its EVMS?

True or False

35-16. All contracts equal to or greater than $20M are required to be compliant with the EVMS Guidelines.

35-17. It is not required that an FFP contract establish an Integrated Master Schedule.

35-18. A subcontractor's fee is not part of the prime contractor's cost.

35-19. The CPR DID requires that all subcontracts be identified in Format 2.

35-20. A 40/60 incentive share ratio means that the subcontractor receives 60% of an underrun as an increase to its fee.

35-21. The subcontractor's UB should always be contained in the prime contractor's UB, but earmarked for use only by the subcontractor.

35-22. The cost variance for a Firm Fixed Price subcontract is always zero.

35-23. Estimated ACWP never needs to be used for subcontractors that submit CPRs.

35-24. An OTS is always the result of an OTB.

35-25. A subcontractor's OTS must be included in the baseline schedule of the prime contractor.

35-26. The prime contractor is responsible for all EVMSG compliance and surveillance activities for subcontracts that require EVMSG compliance without validation.

The answers to these questions can be found in Section 6, Solutions.

Section 4 Quiz

Note: There may be more than one answer to a question.

1.   The Schedule Variance is:
    A. Earned Value - Planned Accomplishment.
    B. Planned Accomplishment - Earned Value.
    C. Another name for total float.
    D. Planned Accomplishment - Actual Cost.

2.   The Cost Variance is:
    A. A measure of the Estimate at Completion versus the Budget at Completion.
    B. An indication of how well work is being accomplished against the budget for that work.
    C. A measure of how actual expenditures are comparing with planned expenditures.
    D. A measure of planned budget versus funds expenditure.

3.   Which of the following is not an earned value technique?
    A. Milestones.
    B. 50/50.
    C. 0/100.
    D. Manpower loading.
    E. Units complete.
    F. 25/75.

4.   Earned value differs from other cost and schedule control methods in what way?
    A. Earned value emphasizes what the contractor is doing right, while other methods focus on what contractors are doing wrong.
    B. Earned value integrates cost and schedule measures into a single value, allowing more accurate assessment of progress.
    C. Earned value allows the manager to get the work out, while "bean counters" keep the records.
    D. Earned value compares the actual staffing levels with the planned staffing levels.

5.   The Cost Performance Index (CPI) is a measure of:
    A. Cost efficiency.
    B. Schedule performance.
    C. Technical criticality.
    D. All of the above.

6.   The To Complete Performance Index (TCPI) is a formula that:
    A. Is used in calculating the award fee of a subcontractor.

B. Uses data from "time now" and calculates an efficiency for the work completed.

C. Is used as a predictor for future schedule performance.

D. Uses data from "time now" and calculates the projected efficiency required to support the reported estimate at completion.

7. Variance Analysis Reports need not include which of the following?

A. Reasons for variances.

B. Justification for reported Estimate at Completion.

C. Corrective action to address variances.

D. Contractor's profit for the reporting period.

8. The "Brick Wall" example showed that performance measurement:

A. Can prevent cost overruns.

B. Can prevent schedule problems.

C. Both A and B.

D. Can give advance warning of cost and schedule problems.

9. In June, my budget was 50, my accomplishment was 45, and my actual cost was 48. How am I doing?

A. Behind schedule, underrunning cost.

B. Ahead of schedule, underrunning cost.

C. Behind schedule, overrunning cost.

D. Ahead of schedule, overrunning cost.

10. A Schedule Variance of ($10,000) means that:

A. A behind schedule condition is occurring and it will require a $10,000 expenditure to get back on schedule.

B. A behind schedule condition is occurring and the status is that $10,000 less budgeted value of work has been completed than planned.

C. The project cost will overrun by $10,000 unless something is done to resolve the condition.

D. The project is ahead of schedule although $10,000 more has been spent than planned.

11. The CPI_E measured to date is 0.85. Calculations show that the TCPI is 1.25. What should be concluded from this information?

A. Cost performance on the project is erratic.

B. The cost/schedule system is erratic.

C. The project performance will be much better in the future.

D. The project performance will be much worse in the future.

E. None of the above.

12. The two most important characteristics of earned value are that it is an objective measure and that it is based on the _____ value for the work.

13. A work package within a control account is using the units complete technique for earned value. In March, 50 widgets were to be completed at a budgeted value of $1,000 per widget. Reported progress shows that 47 actually were completed. Which of the following is true?

A. The effort is behind schedule and the earned value for March is $50,000.

B. The effort is ahead of schedule and the earned value for March is $50,000.

C. The effort is behind schedule and the earned value for March is $47,000.

D. The effort is ahead of schedule and the earned value is $47,000.

14. Establishing a budget baseline plan is an iterative 3-step process, including: 1) defining the work, 2) scheduling the work, and 3)
    A. Accomplishing the work.
    B. Changing the work.
    C. Allocating the budgets.
    D. Estimating the completed work.

15. What are the three classifications of work measurement?
    A. Open, closed, and in-process.
    B. Discrete, Apportioned Effort, and Level of Effort.
    C. Level load, 4-4-5 calendar load, and manager's estimate.
    D. Budget, actual cost, and accomplishment.

16. One unique aspect of Level of Effort work is that:
    A. The work is not meaningful for performance measurement purposes.
    B. Earned value will always equal the scheduled budget value.
    C. It is earned on milestone accomplishment.
    D. There can never be a cost variance in an LOE task.

17. A control account is behind schedule and continues to slip further behind schedule. At completion, it had reached a status that had negatively impacted the total program schedule. What was the schedule variance (BCWP-BCWS) at completion?
    A. At a maximum.
    B. At a minimum.
    C. Zero.
    D. It cannot be determined from this information.

18. Given the information below, what is the cumulative cost variance to date for this control account?

	January	February	March
Budget	1000	1500	1000
Earned Value	800	1400	1200
Actual cost	900	1600	1100

    A. +100 (favorable).
    B. -100 (unfavorable).
    C. -200 (unfavorable).
    D. +200 (favorable).

19. Find the cumulative end of March status for the Level of Effort work package below.

	January	February	March	April
Budget	100	120	150	130
Actual cost	110	125	157	

    A. You cannot tell without earned value provided.
    B. Schedule variance is zero, cost variance is -22.
    C. Schedule variance is -7, cost variance cannot be determined.

D. Not applicable, because there is no such thing as status for LOE tasks.

20. The cost variance for material can be broken down into what two parts?
  A. Price and cost.
  B. Direct and indirect.
  C. Usage and price.
  D. Rate and usage.
  E. Cost and schedule.

21. What is wrong with the following Variance Analysis Report's explanation of the cause of the variance?

  "The cause of the May behind schedule and over cost conditions was that we were unable to meet our planned accomplishment and did not get the three Dyna-felt assembly housings built in time for delivery to the next assembly point. In addition, the tasks we did accomplish were performed at a 16% higher rate than expected."

  A. Nothing is wrong; those are pretty good explanations.
  B. This section is supposed to give the EAC impact of the problems.
  C. There is no corrective action plan provided.
  D. It only restates there are problems, but gives no real causes.

22. List the meanings of the following common project management abbreviations/acronyms:
  A. EAC _____
  B. BAC _____
  C. CPI _____
  D. VAR _____
  E. SV _____
  F. PMB _____
  G. LOE _____
  H. RAM _____
  I. WBS _____

23. What is the formula that is the basis for all other formulae that exist to derive a calculated EAC?
  A. EAC = Earned value + budget to go.
  B. EAC = Actuals (cumulative) + ETC.
  C. EAC = ETC - actuals + CPI/BAC.
  D. EAC = Earned value (cumulative) + Budget remaining.

24. The WBS includes all contract scope except LOE work.
  A. True.
  B. False.

25. The company has a problem. Tom, who was in charge of a critical control account, quit and destroyed most of his cost records. All that could be salvaged were the following bits of information:
  BAC = $120,000
  Cumulative earned value = $40,000
  Cumulative cost variance = -$10,000
  Cumulative schedule variance = +$1,000
  Estimate to Complete = $86,000

Help to reconstruct the status of Tom's control account by determining the following items. (Hint: These must be worked in the correct order.)

A. Percent complete   _____

B. Budget (cumulative)   _____

C. Actuals (cumulative)   _____

D. EAC   _____

E. Variance at Completion   _____

F. CPI_E _____

G. $TCPI_{EAC}$ _____

H. Calculate a projected EAC using the standard Independent EAC formula of EAC = Actual to date + ETC, where ETC = Work Remaining/CPI

    EAC   _____

26. Based on the $TCPI_{EAC}$ and the independent estimate at completion calculated in Question 25 G., and H., what does a brief analysis indicate?

A. Based on past performance, the control account will finish on budget.

B. Efficiency must improve a lot just to achieve the EAC, but past performance indicates the reported EAC will be exceeded.

C. The control account will finish behind schedule.

D. Nothing. The TCPI and the EAC are in no way related.

27. A control account manager identified a conceptual engineering effort as level of effort. It was not until three months after the activity should have started that the manager finally hired the engineers to start the effort. This would be revealed in the control account data as:

A. An unfavorable schedule slip.

B. A cost underrun.

C. A cost overrun.

D. Ahead of schedule condition.

28. Variations of the 0/100 and 50/50 earned value methods are not allowed (e.g. 60/40, 75/25 etc.).

A. True.

B. False.

29. Earned value credit for labor is taken when:

A. The work is planned to be done.

B. The actual costs are recorded.

C. The work is accomplished.

D. The contract says it will be taken.

30. An apportioned effort account will always be behind schedule if the direct account it supports is behind schedule.

A. True.

B. False.

31. If a significant schedule variance has occurred, which of the following should be considered as part of the total analysis?

A. CPM status and total float.

B. Impact on the Estimate at Completion.

      C. Corrective action plans.

      D. Impact on project milestones.

      E. All of the above.

32.   Variance thresholds may need to be changed during the life of a project.

      A. True.

      B. False.

33.   SPI is always greater than 1.00 when the SV is greater than 0.

      A. True.

      B. False.

34.   If total float were negative but SPI > 1.00, that indicates:

      A. There is a lack of proper prioritization.

      B. Staffing is below plan.

      C. Critical work is being expedited but overall performance is slipping.

      D. There is a mistake in the data because schedule cannot be favorable and unfavorable simultaneously.

35.   Using the Percent Complete earned value technique, a control account is reported as 50% complete. The actual cost to date is $300,000, the BAC is $500,000, and the EAC is $600,000. What is the earned value?

      A. $150,000.

      B. $250,000.

      C. $300,000.

      D. $500,000.

36.   Variance analysis thresholds are being set for a project. Which of the following choices would cause you to set your thresholds a little wider than its alternate choice? Indicate by underlining your response.

      A. Incremental data vs. Cumulative data.

      B. Favorable variance vs. Unfavorable variance.

      C. Control account vs. Summary WBS element.

37.   With the Equivalent Units earned value technique, it is possible to earn credit for completed units without any single product (unit) being completed.

      A. True.

      B. False.

38.   A work package is a subdivision of a control account. If a work package were 6 months long, which of the following earned value techniques should NOT be used?

      A. 50/50.

      B. 0/100.

      C. Incremental Milestones.

      D. Equivalent Units.

39.   A work package using the 0/100 earned value technique is reported as 95% complete. What is its earned value? _____

40.   Level of Effort planning should always be a linear spread of resources since it is only reflecting planned staffing.

      A. True.

B. False.

41.   When is a typical requirement for having the performance measurement baseline available?
       A. With the proposal.
       B. At contract award.
       C. 60-90 days after contract award.
       D. 180 days after contract award.

42.   Which of the following are NOT used as a calculation method for predicting future performance?
       A. CPI to date.
       B. CPI for previous 6 months.
       C. Staffing variance.
       D. CPM.

The answers to these questions can be found in Section 6, Solutions.

IMPLEMENTATION OF THE PROJECT MANAGEMENT PROCESS

SECTION 5

IMPLEMENTATION OF THE PROJECT MANAGEMENT PROCESS

Implementation considerations have been presented throughout this text for each subtopic of the overall process. In this chapter, the question of implementing a new way of doing business within a company will be discussed. While every large company and every successful small company will have some sort of operating management process, not all organizations understand how to best control projects. Even those who do have project management systems which have been operational for years may not have properly integrated the processes into a cohesive system. Therefore, some of the overall factors involved in implementing a change to corporate culture are addressed. A summary flowchart, Figure 36-2, is provided to highlight the main steps involved in system implementation.

Chapter 36

IMPLEMENTATION OF THE PROJECT MANAGEMENT PROCESS

Objectives of this Chapter:

1. Describe and explain the activities involved in defining, developing, and implementing an effective earned value project management system.

2. Describe the contents of the System Description and supporting procedures.

3. Describe the Storyboard and the reasons for developing it.

Background

Most organizations are resistant to change. This has become so apparent that many companies are radically re-evaluating their operations through various processes of "re-engineering," "rightsizing," "downsizing," and a host of terminology used for these processes. A key element in most of them is large change; not small adjustments that can be addressed via elimination of small activities such as training and travel. Radical change has been endorsed because organizations have learned through bitter experience that anything less results in no change at all.

Similar experiences have occurred with implementation of project management systems. There is always the possibility that change and improvement will be treated as if it were another "idea of the month" that will soon be replaced with some other fad. There is the real concern that implementation will be in name only, while employees continue to do their jobs exactly as they always have. It is not easy to initiate change, even when it includes substantial improvement. In many cases, that means it may require a dedicated task force assigned to an implementation effort to assure proper review of existing system capabilities and to identify opportunities for improvement. This can be a never-ending process because once the project management system is designed and implemented, the first question immediately becomes, "How can I do this better?" Because of the importance of timely data in the management decision process, expediting the information has a real value. Once implemented, it is useful to routinely assess where the system needs improvement or projects need help in implementing the system. This can point to process, procedure, or training deficiencies.

Many organizations have well established systems that adequately address corporate and project needs for status information. Minor procedural adjustments or incorporation of some of the ideas presented may be all that is necessary in some situations. More difficult is the situation where a change to corporate culture will be required before a successful system implementation has any chance of succeeding. Many companies have farsighted managers in the project control, project management, or financial arenas who recognize the need for much better information. More often than not, they are thwarted because the corporate culture is not ready for it.

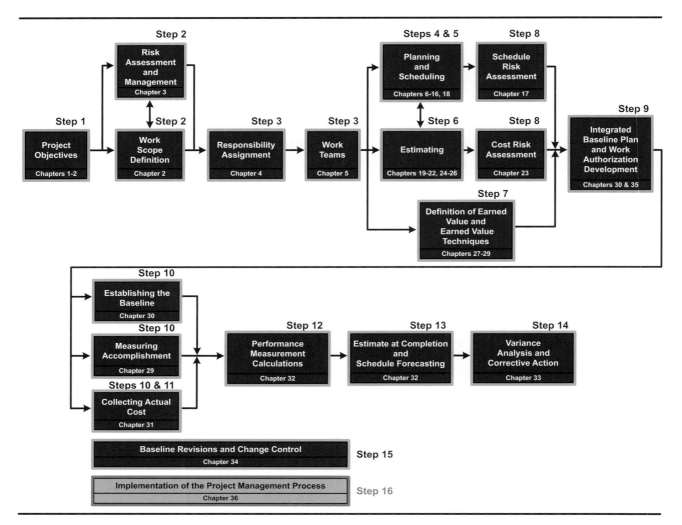

Figure 36-1 Earned Value Project Management: The Process

Consequently, there is the question where to begin when confronted with this situation?

The first requirement is top management support. The reason for this is that successful implementation must cut across many organizational lines and cannot be forced by any single functional element. This may require the assistance of an outside consultant. Why? More often than not, the answer is political. Even though there may be company individuals well grounded in the fundamentals of management systems, there is a likelihood they will be perceived as having a hidden agenda and all of the planned improvements are some sort of a "power play" to expand their power within the organization. Organizations also differ in the level of expertise in project management and they may need some expert guidance.

System Design

After management approval and support is secured for system development or enhancement, the next step is creating a development plan. This plan should include the system requirements, and who will be responsible for developing those requirements. The plan should be established with realistic completion dates.

There is a more than mere technical knowledge needed in this step of the development process. Without enlisting user support, implementation may be resisted every step of the way. The people who are expected to use the system to manage their day-to-day efforts must have a voice in its development. What can go wrong if this factor were overlooked? Some real life examples illustrate the point.

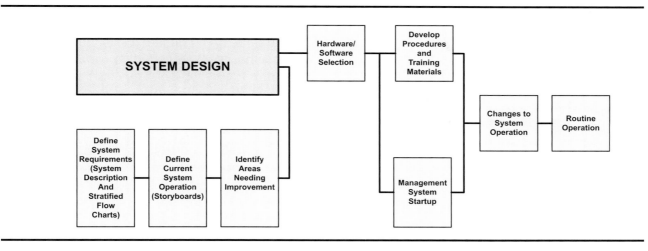

Figure 36-2 Implementation of the Project Management System

One software design organization was forced into developing systems because of almost complete lack of visibility into some very high cost projects. Top management support existed to the extent that an influential member of executive management was assigned responsibility for system development and implementation. The situation was such that no one on a project could openly defy the new mandate. A management consultant was also on board to assist in the definition of the new process.

Responsibility was delegated downward to an organization that always seemed to operate in secret. When it came time for system definition, the entire operation was veiled in secrecy. This was not just an instance of development behind closed doors; it was an example of development behind locked doors. The engineers and others who would have to use the system became increasingly concerned. What would they be required to do? Their questions were met with response such as "We have so much to do yet that we cannot even guess when we'll have enough defined to meet with you." Not very reassuring, is it?

When enough of the system was defined, it was handed down to all of the other departments. Unfortunately, there was no opportunity for comment or modification to the system that had been approved in private. The staff assigned to do the implementation had been hand picked by the consulting group. The only applicants considered were business system experts, individuals with entire careers implementing project management on government contracts. The problem was that there was no government reporting requirement on any of these projects. The situation was exacerbated by their approach, which was that of a systems "cultist."

Every question had a preordained answer and no sentence could be spoken without at least four abbreviations. Logic was not used to answer questions. The opening response to any challenge was, "The Guidelines require ____." This "we have all the answers" approach antagonized the entire project team. And while open hostility was not possible, it simmered beneath the surface awaiting a later opportunity. That opportunity came when the system implementation was nominally complete and the top managers went on to other assignments. However, the project team, having never embraced the principles and distrustful about the implementation technique, did all in their power to avoid using the system.

In effect, the same principles must be used in the overall implementation as were used in the individual parts of the project management process. No one would attempt to put together an engineering schedule without consulting engineering or a manufacturing schedule without consulting manufacturing. No one should attempt to implement a project management system without involving those who will be required to use the output from that system.

System Description

Part of the system design process includes the writing of a system description that covers the way the system is intended to operate. The system description will define the overall process without necessarily specifying all of the procedures to be used. For the purposes of this discussion, this activity is limited to the definition of the intended operation of the system.

The System Description should be the starting point for more specific documentation, such as procedures and training materials.

There are specific techniques that will assist the implementation effort by organizing and verifying all of the supporting details. These include the use of stratified flowcharts and "storyboards."

The intent of a stratified flowchart is to visually display the subprocesses associated with any of the elements of the project management process, such as the baseline schedule development process (see Figure 36-3). The chart displays all of the activities and organizations involved in developing a schedule baseline, by illustrating the sequential flow of information for each step.

Figure 36-4 is a flowchart for Baseline Schedule Development. Similar flowcharts would be prepared for all aspects of the project management process.

A typical list of such flowcharts might include the following subsystems:

- Work Scope Definition (including WBS and RAM development).

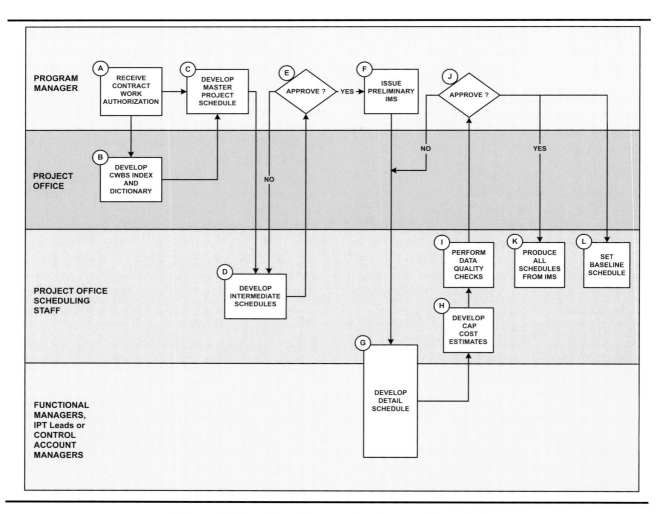

Figure 36-3 Baseline Schedule Development Flowchart

- Schedule Baseline Establishment.

- Schedule Status Reporting.

- Budgeting process.

- Project and Work Authorization.

- Performance Measurement.

- Accounting.

- Material Cost Estimating.

- Material Management.

- Subcontract Management.

- Data Analysis and External Reporting.

- Development of Estimates at Completion.

- Change Control Process.

Stratified flowcharts such as these may be used to generate procedures for each of the subprocesses described. They also make a helpful exhibit within the procedure itself. Precise definition such as this will provide a blueprint for the implementation process.

The steps in the stratified flowchart example are each identified with letters A through L. Narrative explanations that accompany each step are also helpful to define the process. An example of the narrative for Figure 36-3 follows:

A. Receive Contract Work Authorization.

   The project manager receives a contract work authorization (CWA) from contract administration. The CWA establishes the overall contract schedule and provides contract references for additional information. The CWA also authorizes the project manager to expend resources to accomplish the contract work effort.

B. Develop CWBS Index and Dictionary.

   The project office completes development of the CWBS index and dictionary.

C. Develop Master Project Schedule.

   Using the CWBS, proposal IMS, and IMP, the project manager completes development of the IMS to the master project schedule (MPS) level, modifying the proposal IMS for any changes in scope, schedule, or technical requirements. This

includes defining all IMP milestones in the IMS. This activity is carried out with the support of the project office scheduling staff by entering the data into the IMS database.

D. Develop Intermediate Schedule.

   Based on the CWBS and the master project level IMS, the project office scheduling staff begins the top-down development of the IMS to the intermediate level of schedule detail. This is usually level 3 or 4 of the CWBS.

E. Approve?

   The project manager reviews the content of the intermediate level IMS. If approved, the process moves to Step F. If not approved, the project office scheduling staff modifies the IMS as directed by the project manager (return to Step D).

F. Issue Preliminary IMS.

   The project manager issues the preliminary IMS to the functional managers or IPTs leads and CAMs.

G. Develop Detail Schedule.

   With assistance from the project office scheduling staff, the functional managers or IPT leads and CAMs, continue the development of the IMS down to the detail level. This is the basis for the control account plans (CAPs) which are composed of work packages for near term work and planning packages for downstream work. The work package activities, duration, logic, and resources are determined at this stage. All detail activities must be traceable to an IMP milestone; this ensures the detail activities are within all contractual date constraints. The project office scheduling staff assists in entering the data into the IMS based on the input from the functional managers or IPT leads and CAMs. This ensures that the scheduling staff has a good understanding of the overall schedule and is able to resolve any areas of schedule conflict or uncertainty between the various work teams. Steps G through J are an iterative process to establish the firm work authorizations.

H. Develop CAP Cost Estimates.

The project office scheduling staff prices the activity resource assignments to determine the initial cost estimate for the work effort as planned. The project office scheduling staff reviews the CAP cost estimate results with the functional managers or IPT leads and CAMs. The cost estimates are compared to the contract budget base (the performance measurement baseline plus any Management Reserve). In coordination with the functional managers or IPT leads and CAMs, the scheduling staff makes adjustments to the sequence of work and/or resource assignments as needed to ensure the CAPs are within all budget constraints. This corresponds to the budgeting process as the resource loaded schedule activities are the basis for the BCWS values.

I. Perform Data Quality Checks.

Once the detail schedule has been fully developed, the project office scheduling staff runs a set of schedule health diagnostics on the IMS. Vertical and horizontal traceability is verified. The generation of the budget baseline time phased data is also verified to correct any errors. The IMS is modified as needed to address any logic, coding, duration, resource, or other issues that are identified. If there are any major changes made to the schedule as a result of the diagnostics, the scheduling staff reviews the updated detail schedule with the applicable IPT or CAM.

J. Approve?

The project manager reviews the content of the detail level IMS (the control account plans). If approved, the process moves to Steps K and L. If not approved, the project office scheduling staff, in coordination with the functional managers or IPT leads and CAMs, modifies the IMS as directed by the project manager (return to Step G).

K. Produce All Schedules from IMS.

Following approval of the detail level IMS (CAPs), the project office scheduling staff produces the intermediate schedules and the master project schedule from the IMS database to verify the content at all levels. Both of these schedules are composed of activities summarized from the details in the IMS. This method of schedule preparation assures both vertical and horizontal traceability at all levels.

L. Set Baseline Schedule.

Also following the approval of the IMS by the project manager, the project office scheduling staff sets the schedule baseline in the schedule toolset. This establishes the master copy of the baseline IMS schedule file and all schedule baseline dates. Once approved as the baseline schedule, the IMS is subject to strict change control. Once work begins, the current status schedule reflects the current work plan for the remaining work based on the performance to date. As a result, the baseline schedule and current status schedule can be compared as needed.

Each of the preceding narratives directly relates to one of the steps in the process of schedule development shown in Figure 36-3. A similar type of narrative would accompany each step of the Performance Measurement Flowchart shown in Figure 36-4. This information could be readily transformed into detailed project procedures.

The previous example is not offered as the definitive or only way of developing schedules, but as a sample of process development. Many organizations now drive the schedule development process to a level lower than what has been described.

The Creation of Storyboards

The next step in the process of implementation is the creation of storyboards that illustrate the entire project management process. The storyboard depicts the entire information flow, including sample input and output reports and

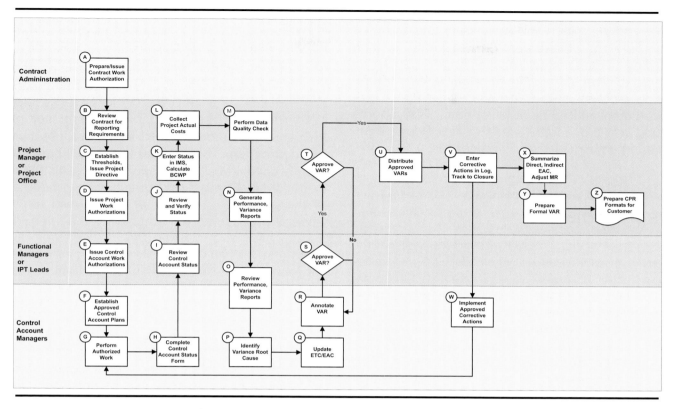

Figure 36-4 Performance Measurement Flowchart

documents. It can be developed in part by integrating all of the stratified flowcharts for all of the subsystems within the project management system. Typically, an entire conference room will be dedicated to the storyboard. It will depict everything from project authorization documents to output reports used for managing the project. The flow of data may be represented by colored tape or string that allows a trace of all data elements from the beginning of the process to the end.

The reasons for creating a storyboard include the following:

1. Represents the entire project management process at a detailed level. This allows its use as a training tool for project team members.

2. Serves as an illustration of the management process for any external customer organization.

3. Assists in procedure development.

4. Missing data elements, processes, reports/outputs, as well as ambiguity in roles and responsibilities are quickly identified.

5. Duplicate reporting systems and data sources become evident. Establishing a single source for the data improves the data integrity of the system and reduces the need for data verification and reconciliation.

6. Inefficiencies in the data collection and reporting process quickly become evident, allowing a streamlining of the process.

Improved understanding of the entire project management process by team members is facilitated by the use of storyboards. Both these and stratified flowcharts have been used with great success in numerous companies. These principles apply equally well in any industry.

A nonstandard, but likely candidate for use of storyboards, is local government. The search for innovative solutions to the financial squeeze on local governments resulting from reduced budgets and increased demand for services could benefit from this approach. This could be accomplished by applying the process to total information flow and government processes rather than limiting it to project applications. Such an approach would identify opportunities for streamlining processes so that services could be provided more efficiently at lower cost. Storyboards could also prove to be an effective tool for reengineering organizations and processes.

Identification of Areas Needing Improvement

No project management system is perfect as it is. There is always the opportunity for improvement. With a careful review of system capability, potential improvements will quickly become obvious. Once they are identified, they should be prioritized and analyzed to determine the most cost effective way of turning theory into practice. This is still part of the "system design" process.

Hardware and Software Selection

During system design and development, additional hardware and software requirements or enhancements may be necessary to support that design. It is important that the identification of the system requirements be clearly identified prior to any purchase of additional toolsets. Hardware and software are not the system; rather they provide support to the system.

Development of Procedures and Training Material

This activity is begun before actual system start-up, but does overlap it somewhat. Procedures are initially implemented on almost a trial basis, with adjustments made as necessary to keep the process manageable. The alternative is to stretch the development activity almost indefinitely while trying to define the perfect system. That approach does not work.

The challenge of producing training materials and procedures is that typically the project is already underway and the project team is consumed with managing the project technical activities. It is difficult to perform the dedicated efforts necessary to produce the system documentation and it may be handled off project, possibly with outside expertise for assistance. Once again, it is critical that project personnel be involved in the review, comment, and approval phases if the material is produced primarily by outsiders.

Procedures may be specific or general. Specific procedures can be so detailed that they will include copies of all forms and directions to fill out those forms. Some procedures have extended to 17 thick volumes of trivia that no one ever used. General procedures will emphasize the intent of the process more than the "how to complete the forms". The right approach is a compromise between these two extremes. A general guideline might be that if the procedures cannot be reviewed and understood in a few hours, no one will look at them.

Some specifics are needed, even if the general approach were chosen. For example, the frequency of reporting and the schedule update cycle should be defined in more detail. Variance analysis thresholds and procedures for analyzing and reporting variances are required to be in enough detail to be easily understood and implemented. Methods for change control need to be tightly defined, as the baseline will quickly lose its value if controls are not in place to handle changes.

Training material will be at multiple levels of detail depending on the audience. Overview training will be needed to orient management to the objectives of the new system approach and the type of information to be expected from it. Detailed system forms and procedures for their use will be appropriate for most of the key project team members. This audience is being shown what the system can produce and how it can be used for day-to-day management of the project. Even more detailed training will be needed for the end users who must handle data entry and report production. This type of training may be best handled by the supplier of the software programs in use since it should stress software commands, reports available, and data entry requirements. It should also stress any nuances of the software and provide identification of problems frequently encountered by new users. Role based training is also an effective means to combine the system process with the use of the toolsets to complete specific tasks based on a given end user's role; typical examples include training designed for a scheduler, cost analyst, or control account manager.

System Start-up

This activity refers to the testing, debugging, and initial implementation of the system. This is an important step to verify the entire system including all process steps, responsibilities, interfaces, inputs, and outputs. Procedures should be available at least in draft form by the time of start-up.

The difficulty of this phase will vary greatly from project to project. The amount of care that went into system definition (in the system description and elsewhere) will have a big effect on how easily this hurdle is overcome. The implementation team should still be "on call" throughout this stage.

Precaution should be taken to help stack the odds in favor of success. This can be done by performing the initial implementation on a small project with a supportive project team. The use of a small project will allow concerns to be identified and corrected in the Earned Value Management System Description, flowcharts, and storyboards. It is also very helpful to have the initial implementation done on a project with fairly stable technical, schedule, and cost objectives. If the statement of work were not well defined, it would put the entire implementation at unnecessary risk before the approach has been perfected.

After corrections are made to procedures, an implementation should next be attempted on a medium sized project. Only after that has been successfully accomplished should the implementation of the full project management approach be applied to a large project. It is possible to immediately apply the concepts described to a large project, but there is increased likelihood of success if new systems are implemented a step at a time. Existing systems may have to be maintained in parallel initially until confidence has been generated in the new system output.

Changes to System Operation

Several months after the first "live" project data becomes available, it will likely be time for some minor course corrections. This may include addition or deletion of inputs and outputs used on the project, changes to thresholds used for variance reporting, or even revision of analytical techniques used. Methods of improved forecasting of estimates at completion may be possible at this time. Simplified procedures should be encouraged where appropriate. Procedures should ensure some basic consistency from one project to the next without eliminating the possibility of finding more creative and better solutions. This step in the implementation process incorporates experience.

The original system development team may yet be involved, but primarily this step is the product of the members of the project implementation team. Development personnel should be kept informed as a courtesy so that similar improvements can be reflected in other development efforts.

Routine Operation

This is the final phase when a new process is implemented. There will be no development personnel involved and the project team personnel should be so comfortable with the operation that it is just another part of the management process. Reduced staffing is needed once this point is reached since all of the development and refinement activities have been completed.

Implementation Schedules

How long implementation of a new project management system may take is subject to variability. The existence of documentation does not guarantee that the implementation will be either faster or slower. In one organization, volumes of documentation were available and storyboards were quickly produced. Instead of expediting the process, warring factions spent the next three months arguing about how things should be done. It seemed that everyone had a vested interest in certain procedures and no one wanted to compromise. Other organizations have well established procedures that are simply not documented. Putting standard operating procedures on paper that already exist in practice can be accomplished quickly. Still others were novices to the field of project management, but implementation was rapid because of top management support. A rapid implementation that occurred was headed by a bright young man with lots of questions and a willingness to accept change. There was one other condition that did not hurt the effort, his father was the Chairman of the Board of the company. When authorization was needed for a critical element, there were no delays.

Records have been kept for project management system implementation efforts that included all of the basic requirements discussed in this text. The average time of implementation was 10.2 months. This includes evaluation of existing capabilities, preliminary training, system development and documentation, and start-up of the system. Remember: the software is not the system.

It is possible to evaluate, purchase and install software more quickly than that, but software evaluation should not be initiated until the information objectives of the system are well understood. There is obviously a wide range of possible durations, with five months as the approximate minimum time and the maximum almost unlimited. Some implementations are never satisfactorily completed for a variety of reasons, ranging from lack of top management support to lack of willingness to change. Figure 36-5 is an example of an Implementation Schedule.

Tailoring the System for Project Unique Requirements

Producing a project plan was briefly discussed in Chapter 1. The project plan is the set of documentation and directives that formalize the entire management approach for a given project. In particular, it describes how the System Descrip-

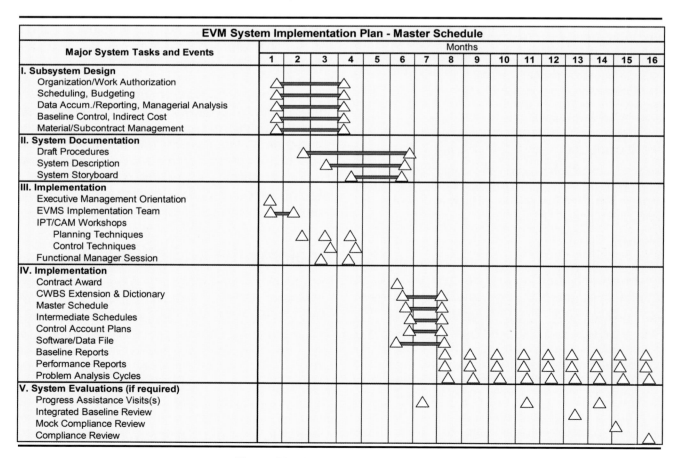

Figure 36-5 Implementation Schedule

tion and procedures will be applied to meet the project's unique internal management requirements as well as contractual requirements. This can include but is not limited to details such as the variance thresholds that apply, typical durations allowed for work packages or schedule activities, whether the schedule is resource loaded or not, specific reporting cycle requirements, specific inputs or outputs, specific earned value methods that can be used, specific data integration requirements, and other details.

Another component is to establish the data architecture for the project. The data architecture refers to the development of the approach used to organize, code, and integrate the project's schedule and cost data. Establishing this strategy is a critical up-front activity as it determines the coding requirements to be able to organize, sort, and select the schedule and cost data for a variety of reports and analyses. It determines the data import and export criteria as well as the data formats required to pull the applicable data from various application systems such as finance and accounting for use in the schedule or cost toolsets. It establishes the data content and coding required to integrate the schedule and cost data. This detail is also needed for incorporating subcontractor schedule and cost data.

Establishing these details at project start-up helps to ensure that the project's schedule and cost data include the necessary coding to be able to produce required outputs and reports from the beginning. For example, a project directive may require the detail schedule activities include the WBS, OBS, milestone reference, control account, work package, and earned value technique codes. This coding enables the ability to produce schedule views at various levels of detail using the WBS hierarchy or to trace an activity to a contractual milestone (vertical traceability). It may also provide the basis to generate the time phased cost data where the work package

reflects the start and finish dates for the underlying activities, resource assignments, and earned value method. Other coding requirements may help to select or sort the data for specific reporting needs such as by location, subcontractor, phase, or other project unique details.

Having a plan for the overall management of the project reduces the chaos and stress levels because the project team is following a game plan for managing the work effort. This plan combines the overall project control system with the project unique requirements to help ensure all project objectives are met. It demonstrates to all project stakeholders that the project is being activity managed and the approach has been well thought out. It reduces or eliminates data rework and data integrity issues that can waste valuable time.

Conclusion

Like the project management process itself, careful early definition of the system requirements will pay dividends later. Software selection should occur only after the system needs have been properly defined. This definition should include a system description and be supplemented with stratified flowcharts, procedures and training material. The entire process may be pictorially represented in a room-sized flowchart called a storyboard. It has been found that the creation of the storyboard helps project personnel understand where they fit into the overall process as well as making the process easier to visualize and comprehend. It also frequently results in streamlined processes by highlighting steps that may not be necessary, duplicate reports, or duplicate processes. The effort involved in developing a new system approach on a project will require supplemental staff that has knowledge of the implementation requirements.

Chapter 36 Review Questions

36-1.   What is the single most important reason it takes top management support to successfully implement a new project management system?

36-2.   What is the function of the system description?

36-3.   What is the value of a storyboard for a new system implementation?

True or False

36-4.   It is imperative that cost and schedule software be bought early in a project management system implementation so that procedures can be developed based on the software specific requirements.

36-5.   A project management system should never be defined and implemented without input from those who will use the system and its output.

36-6.   Procedures should be initially issued in a draft form allowing opportunity for later revision to simplify the process and eliminate steps that are found to be unnecessary or should be changed.

36-7.   Temporary staff will be required for a new system implementation, with elimination of this staff occurring once routine operation is achieved.

The answers to these questions can be found in Section 6, Solutions.

Section 6

CONCLUSION, SOLUTIONS, AND REFERENCES

SECTION 6

CONCLUSION

The process of project management is an involved one, but it is also a straightforward one that can be implemented on every project. The only difference in application from one project to another is in the level of detail. The concepts are hard to argue with. How can a project be well managed if it is not defined? The first requirement is always that the project objectives and scope be known. It is just as logical and necessary that the responsibility for accomplishing the work be defined. The work will be accomplished by a project team, so team work (encouraged by the use of work teams) will always be helpful.

Among the project objectives will always be some schedule requirement. For many projects (defined as "schedule critical"), this is a primary objective and must be supported even if the cost must increase because of extra expediting requirements. The process of scheduling must therefore be carefully implemented and understood. This is also true because the schedule directly drives the cost.

Another project objective will always be a defined budget for completing the work scope. The process of estimating takes on great importance, because the budget will be derived from the estimate.

There is one other consideration before a baseline should be established. This is the consideration of risk. An approved plan for accomplishing the project work will have little value if that plan does not reflect the realities of the project. Where are the greatest elements of risk? How can the plan be modified to mitigate the risk exposure? The plan should be achievable in order to measure against it, and the risk evaluations (technical, schedule, and cost) will assist in the evaluation of the plan.

Even with schedule and cost systems in place, a project still cannot be well managed without some objective method of determining work progress. Once earned value techniques are established, they can be used for both the development of the total baseline plan and for measuring actual progress. When earned value is compared with the actual costs and the planned budget, all of the components needed for status determination are available.

Once the plan has been established and actual progress is being tracked, it is only logical that the two would be compared to identify deviations from plan and actions taken to correct those deviations. Data analysis will also allow early warning of impending schedule slippages and cost overruns.

At this point the process is working. However, life is not a textbook. Changes to the plan are inevitable, and approved changes should be incorporated so that the plan being used to measure progress reflects the current understanding of what the project is.

As can be seen, all of these concepts make sense in any application. Which one can be eliminated and still have an effective management system? The discipline of project management has been well defined over the years and it is a time-tested process. That does not mean it cannot be improved. Improvements are occurring continuously with new automation tools to provide information in a more timely manner, expedite data analysis, and verify whether or not the input is credible.

In the increasingly competitive world market, it has never been more necessary to institute complete project management. This text has provided not only the basic tools and theory, but also some of the practical considerations that must be included in system design. As such, it can be used as a blueprint for future project system applications.

Solutions

Chapter 1 Project Management Using Earned Value

1-1.   Explain the difference between a project and a program.

Programs are collections of projects, each of whose objective must support the objective of the program. Programs share with projects the same four characteristics, an objective, a planned start date, a planned completion date and committed resources.

1-2.   What aspects of a project are managed during the controlling phase of Earned Value Management?

Project control refers to the control of project scope, and the associated schedule and budget for accomplishing that work scope.

1-3.   How is a project organized differently from a functional organization?

A project must include representatives from many different functional areas as part of a multi-disciplinary team charged with the accomplishment of the project objectives. The project organization is headed by the project manager who is assigned for the project duration. Functional organizations consist of expertise in a single technical or service area and support multiple projects over time.

1-4.   What are some frequent causes of project delays?

Project delays are often encountered because of the following reasons: scope changes (additions), delays in material delivery, changing government regulations (especially permit issuance), and lack of management coordination between the many organizations contributing to overall project success, and missing vendor design information.

1-5.   Why is a comparison of actual costs to date versus budgeted costs not adequate from an Earned Value Management standpoint?

There is no indication of what work has been accomplished. This is a serious flaw in any analysis, since there is no way of distinguishing between an over budget, ahead of schedule condition or a below budget/behind schedule condition.

1-6.   List at least three factors that will affect the level of detail appropriate for implementation of earned value on a project.

Implementation level of detail should consider the following factors:
- *Project size (cost) and duration.*
- *Technical risk.*
- *The project contracting arrangement.*
- *Desired level of management involvement.*

True or False

1-7.   The Earned Value Management process is only applicable for large projects.

False. The concepts apply to all projects. Only the level of implementation will vary.

1-8.   The fact that more money has been spent at a point in time than was planned to be spent means that an overrun in final cost is indicated.

False. It could also mean that the project is ahead of schedule and may actually underrun the budget.

1-9.   A program may be made up of multiple projects.
True.

1-10.   Performance measurement may be successfully applied in engineering, construction, manufac-turing, and software development applications, among others.
True.

1-11.   Using a measure of performance allows earlier indication of potential increases in final cost.
True. It provides a measure of cost and schedule performance against plan, allowing early vis-ibility into anticipated final cost.

1-12.   From the customer's viewpoint, a firm fixed price contract suggests the need for tight cost con-trols.
False. If it is a firm fixed price contract, the customer has no cost exposure (theoretically) and emphasis shifts to schedule performance. The contractor, on the other hand, has increased emphasis on cost control since the contract profit is at stake.

Chapter 2 Definition of Scope, Work Breakdown Structure (WBS) and WBS Dictionary

2-1.   Describe the function of a Work Breakdown Structure (WBS).
A Work Breakdown Structure is intended to assist better management of a project by providing a framework for the project scope, schedule, and budget to be integrated. It allows for the logi-cal subdivision of work scope into smaller, more manageable parcels which can more easily be defined and controlled.

2-2.   List guidelines to be considered when developing a WBS.
- *It is product oriented.*
- *It includes the entire scope of work.*
- *It reflects the manner in which the work will be performed.*
- *Each element logically aggregates those below it.*
- *It supports historical cost collection for future cost estimating purposes.*

2-3.   Explain the role of the WBS Dictionary.
The WBS Dictionary provides the definition of scope for each WBS element. This supports two objectives:
- *It ensures that estimates and scope are consistent for each cost element since the scope is defined precisely and allows comparison with defined estimate items.*
- *It assists the accurate recording of actual costs since the specifics of the control account are defined, and this can be used to verify where a particular cost should be reported.*

2-4.   Why does a WBS oriented by element of cost or organizational element cause problems when used for Earned Value Management?
A WBS oriented in this way does not allow the project visibility needed for effective manage-ment. The costs associated with producing a given end product (which is how it is estimated) are scattered throughout the WBS because a given cost element will appear in many different WBS legs. Rather than integrating the project information, this approach to a WBS scatters the information.

2-5.   Identify methods for verifying that all scope has been included within the WBS.
A number of cross-checks are possible. The work products listed in the WBS Dictionary should be verified with the schedule, the contract, and the estimate/budget as a minimum.

True or False

2-6. One approach to developing a WBS is to represent the organizations that will be performing the work.

False. This is the function of the OBS or Organization Breakdown Structure. This approach, when used in the WBS, negates its value and results in duplication of information in the summarizations of the WBS and OBS.

2-7. There is a high correlation between the level of detail within the WBS and the cost of maintaining an Earned Value Management system.

True. More detail in the WBS means more control accounts to track, which results in increased staff.

2-8. It is acceptable to have multiple Work Breakdown Structures for a single project.

False. While it is true that various legs of the WBS may correspond to different phases of the project (engineering, manufacturing, construction, etc.), all of these phases are then included within a single Work Breakdown Structure.

2-9. A WBS Dictionary will usually include enough detail to list the individual work products.

True.

2-10. All project scope must be included within a WBS, including those activities that may not be directly identified to any particular work product.

True. A primary characteristic of the WBS is that it includes all project scope.

Chapter 3 Managing Project Risks

3-1. What is the definition of a project risk?

A risk is something that, if it occurs, will impact the ability to meet the project objectives.

3-2. What is the importance of the project objectives to managing project risks?

Without knowing the project objectives the risks cannot be identified.

3-3. What is a risk threat?

A risk threat is an unfavorable impact on the project objectives.

3-4. What is a risk opportunity?

A risk opportunity has a favorable impact on the project objectives.

3-5. Who has the overall responsibility for managing project risks?

The project manager.

3-6. Who has the responsibility for identifying project risks?

Everyone on the project has the responsibility to identify project risks.

3-7. What is the purpose of the risk register?

The risk register is used to document approved risks.

3-8. What is the last activity in managing project risks?

Monitoring the approved risks.

3-9. What are the responsibilities of the risk owner?

Execute the risk action plan and monitor the risks for which he is responsible.

3-10.   What alternatives are there to managing "excessive" risks?

Take action to lower the likelihood of occurrence and/or the impact on the project, develop an action plan in case the risk occurs, and plan the project as if the risk will occur.

True or False

3-11.   The schedule impact is more important than the performance impact.
False.

3-12.   The risk owner decides whether a risk is approved.
False.

3-13.   An action plan is usually undertaken when a risk is rated "low".
False.

3-14.   The risk manager maintains the risk register for the project manager.
True.

3-15.   Three levels of qualitative risk rating are positive, negative and neutral.
False.

3-16.   An excessive risk can be treated as if it will occur.
True.

3-17.   Delphi analysis takes more time than "brainstorming".
True.

3-18.   A risk management program should not raise risk awareness.
False.

3-19.   Once the risk horizon has passed, a risk can be removed from the risk register.
False.

3-20.   Managing project risks requires risk specialists.
False.

Chapter 4 Relating Organizations, Responsibility, and Work Scope

4-1.   Explain the role of the Responsibility Assignment Matrix, or RAM, in the project management process.

The Responsibility Assignment Matrix fulfills the key role of identifying the responsibility for all project scope. This intersection of scope and organization is then used to establish control accounts, the focal points of the entire management process.

4-2.   What is the fundamental difference between a WBS and an OBS?

A WBS defines WHAT has to be accomplished while the OBS defines WHO is responsible for performing that work.

4-3.   What is the role of the control account in the project management process?

The control account is the focal point of the entire management process. It is the point where scope is defined, responsibility is identified, and schedule and budget are established. It will be the point where actual costs are collected and reported, progress is measured, variance analysis is performed, corrective action initiated, and the estimate at completion assessed.

4-4.   What is the primary trade-off to be considered in the establishment of control accounts?

The primary trade-off is between increased project status visibility and cost of operating the system. As the number of control accounts proliferates, there is information that is more detailed but there is also more data to collect and analyze. This results in increased management monitoring costs.

4-5.   Name at least five factors that go into the determination of the proper level of detail for control accounts.

All seven of the following factors contribute to proper control account selection:

1. Work scope.

2. Associated risk (technical, schedule, and/or cost.)

3. Duration of the account.

4. Dollar value.

5. Performing organization.

6. Contract framework.

7. Information objectives.

True or False

4-6.   Since the Responsibility Assignment Matrix can be maintained in an automated system that indicates which accounts are valid charge numbers, there is not much cost impact if there were a large number of control accounts.

False. All of the data collection, reporting, and analysis activities are directly related to the number of control accounts.

4-7.   The Organization Breakdown Structure (OBS), is really just another name for the company's organization chart.

True.

4-8.   Use of a Responsibility Assignment Matrix (RAM) helps to ensure that someone is responsible for all elements of work while simultaneously ensuring that there is no duplication of responsibility.

True.

4-9.   A control account is the lowest level in the WBS/OBS matrix.

True.

Chapter 5 Work Teams

5-1.   List four advantages of using the work team concept.

A work team has many advantages, including an improved ability to get the job done efficiently and effectively. Communication and cooperation are improved by the elimination of traditional functional organization barriers. Morale typically improves. In addition to these qualitative improvements, there are objective quantifiable improvements as well. The number of control accounts can be greatly reduced, which results in decreased project management system costs throughout the life of the project.

5-2.   Which of the following is true about work teams?

D. All of the above are true.

True or False

5-3.   Work teams are organized in the RAM along the lines of the Organization Breakdown Structure (OBS).

False. They are organized primarily along product, or WBS, lines.

5-4.   Every work team has a work team lead.

True.

5-5.   A work team lead is always assigned by management.

False. He or she may be selected by the work team itself.

5-6.   The work team concept has been limited in its application to federal government contracts in the aerospace industry.

False. It has been widely applied in many industries.

5-7.   The work team approach looks at what the objective is (an end product or service) and organizes along those lines.

True.

5-8.   Some work teams are still applied along strictly functional lines because of inflexibility in the functional organizations.

True.

5-9.   Work teams are typically organized along a Work Breakdown Structure (WBS) because that is the manner of organizing work into manageable subdivisions.

True.

Section 1 Earned Value Project Management and Organization Quiz for Chapters 1 to 5

1.   What is the WBS Dictionary?

C. A document that describes each WBS element.

2.   A control account has four major characteristics. What are they?

B. Statement of work, budget, schedule, responsible person.

3.   A Work Breakdown Structure is:

B. A product-oriented subdivision of hardware, software, services, and facilities for a project.

4.   A Responsibility Assignment Matrix (RAM) is a matrix that depicts the intersection of the:

C. WBS and the contractor's organization.

5.   Control account levels are to be established where the contractor will actually manage the work.

True.

6.   List three factors that will impact the selection of project controls for a particular project application:

A. Project size and duration.

B. Technical risk.

C. Project contract type.

7.   The use of a firm fixed price contract will shift the emphasis from cost control to schedule control for the contractor.

     False.   A FFP contract will cause cost emphasis on the contractor's part.   It will, however, shift emphasis to schedule control for the owner or customer.

8.   What is needed even before the project work scope is identified?

     A. Project objectives.

9.   Cost and schedule objectives are more important than technical objectives.

     False. Technical objectives are at least as important as cost and schedule objectives. After all, the project exists to provide the product defined by the technical objectives.

10. The biggest impact of contract type is on the appropriate level of control for:

     A. Cost.

11. One of the biggest advantages of including a measure of accomplishment is the ability to forecast potential cost overruns and schedule slips early in the project.

     True. This knowledge allows timely management response to avoid the condition.

12. Work Breakdown Structures are only appropriate for large construction projects.

     False. There have been successful applications of the WBS concept on every type of project.

13. Which of the following statements are true about the Work Breakdown Structure Dictionary?

     D. All of the above.

14. The problem with an element of cost orientation for the WBS is:

     C. Costs associated with specific work scope end products are scattered throughout the WBS, complicating analysis.

15. The fact that engineering/construction efforts shift from an emphasis on systems to physical areas and back to systems again suggests that the best WBS approach would be:

     B. A different WBS for each project phase.

     C. A single project WBS with different legs (Level 2 WBS elements) corresponding to various project phases.

     Note: Selection B deserves partial credit since that is an approach frequently used. However, the entire project scope should still be maintained within a single WBS and that makes C a better answer.

16. A company should revise its organization structure in order to better support development of the Responsibility Assignment Matrix (RAM).

     False. The RAM should reflect the normal company organization so that the project can be managed most effectively.

17. The lowest level in the RAM is:

     C. The control account.

18. Selecting the proper level for the control account depends on:

     D. All of the above.

19. Summarizing the OBS to too high of a level causes problems because there is lost visibility of the status of the end products.

     False. The lost visibility occurs in the WBS, not the OBS.

20.   Use of work teams places more emphasis on organizational work areas than on end product development.
False.

21.   The use of work teams typically produces:
A. Increased productivity.
C. Improved communication.

22.   Which are the first three steps in the project management process?
D. Definition of project objectives, work scope definition, and responsibility assignment.

23.   A program may be made up of several projects.
True.

Chapter 6 What is Scheduling? Schedule Types

6-1.   Describe the functions of a schedule.
A schedule is a document which defines what work must be done to accomplish project objectives on time.

6-2.   What are the advantages of a formalized scheduling system?
Advantages include:
*   *Provides definition of the project plan.*
*   *Provides an excellent vehicle for project communication throughout the life of the project.*
*   *Provides a continuing basis for status reporting.*
*   *Identifies what staffing is needed to complete the work, allowing forward planning for hiring or transfer of personnel.*
*   *Facilitates time/cost trade-offs.*
*   *Provides a basis for exploring "What-if" scenarios.*
*   *Readily identifies Impact of delays on the project.*

6-3.   What are three ways in which schedule delays cause an increase in costs?
Reasons for cost increases include:
1. Escalation.
2. Delay of return on investment from the project.
3. Extended duration for support services such as management, administration, etc., during project execution.

6-4.   What are five information prerequisites for developing a valid schedule?
Information needed for schedule development includes:
1. The detailed scope of work.
2. Activity interrelationships.
3. Activity durations.
4. Resource requirements.
5. Assigned responsibilities.

6-5.   What are potential uses of scheduling system information in a project?
Schedules are used for:
*   *Development of a realistic baseline plan.*
*   *Priority definition.*

- *Status reporting.*
- *Problem area identification.*
- *Problem impact analysis.*
- *Corrective action plan support.*

6-6.   Describe how the "Combination Chart" is an improvement over the Milestone Chart or the Bar Chart for schedule status reporting.

The Combination Chart combines the best aspects of the Bar Chart and the Milestone Chart. It is an improvement over the Bar Chart because it provides for objective status indication at intermediate points along the activity duration, with milestones limiting the amount of subjective status reporting possible. It is an improvement over the Milestone Chart because it is possible to note when an activity should start to support the milestones, rather than being limited to a milestone completion date.

6-7.   Name at least three shortcomings of the Bar Chart when used for schedule status determination.

Significant shortcomings of the Bar Chart include the fact that it does not allow identification of problem areas; there is no capability for identifying the impact of slippages; there is no early warning capability; there is no way to see the inter-relationships among activities; and there is no way of objectively determining status of partially completed activities.

6-8.   Describe at least four types of information available from network scheduling systems that are not available from simpler scheduling techniques.

Network diagrams provide:
- *A complete listing of all activities.*
- *Exact interrelationships between activities.*
- *A method for identifying which activities are most critical.*
- *A basis for producing a trend analysis.*
- *Early warning of likely impacts to the project completion.*
- *Resource analysis capability.*
- *Capability of time/cost trade-offs.*
- *Ability to study the impacts of various alternative courses of action.*
- *A method for determining responsibility for schedule delays.*

NOTE: None of these capabilities is readily available with more primitive scheduling techniques, although Line of Balance will provide a few of them.

6-9.   Which of the following schedule techniques provide some indication of interrelationships between activities?

E.   B. (Modified Gantt/Milestone Chart), C. (Flow Process Chart) and D. (Network Diagrams).

True or False

6-10.   The first objective in the development of a project plan is preparation of a detailed schedule that includes all of the anticipated work activities.

False. There is insufficient information initially to develop a detailed schedule. Development of a summary schedule is one of the first project activities; however a great deal of planning precedes the development and release of the project schedule.

6-11.   Staffing requirements for supporting a scheduling system are affected most strongly by the level of detail selected for the schedule.

True. More activities not only means a larger schedule development effort, it also means much more time will be required in updating and analyzing results.

6-12.   Past similar jobs can be a "reality check" for current project schedules.

True. In fact, comparisons with similar past jobs should be a standard operating procedure.

6-13.   Schedules should initially be developed by the most experienced schedulers.

False. While experienced schedulers contribute much to the schedule development process, the primary responsibility remains with those responsible for actually accomplishing the work. They must decide the order of the work, how long it will take and what resources are necessary.

6-14.   Schedule status should be compared with an approved schedule baseline plan to identify variances.

True. Without comparison to the approved plan, trend analysis becomes meaningless.

6-15.   The simplest schedule reporting techniques also tend to be the least useful for successful management of a project.

True.

6-16.   One of the oldest and simplest forms of scheduling is the Gantt Chart.

True.

6-17.   The Bar Chart has no mechanism for forecasting revised completion dates.

False. Revised completion dates may be indicated.

6-18.   The Combination Chart combines useful traits of the Bar Chart and of schedule networks.

False. It combines useful traits of Bar Charts and Milestone Charts.

6-19.   In the Modified Gantt/Milestone Chart, true schedule status is compromised for the sake of a readable presentation.

True. It is impossible to accurately portray the many interfaces between activities in this presentation form.

6-20.   The Line of Balance scheduling technique is usually applied in the manufacturing environment.

True.

6-21.   One good application of a Bar Chart is to represent more complex information in a simple format, usually at a summary level.

True.

6-22.   PDM is a variation of the Line of Balance approach to scheduling.

False. PDM and Line of Balance are two applications of the CPM scheduling method.

Chapter 7   Introduction to Network Logic Development

7-1.   Explain the difference between finish-to-start and start-to-finish logic relationships. Which is more common?

A finish-to-start relationship produces sequential activities, with the second unable to start until the first finishes. A start-to-finish, on the other hand, states that the predecessor activity cannot finish until the successor activity starts. The most common of these by far is the finish-to-start. The start-to-finish has virtually no application, and some software packages do not even recognize it as an activity relationship.

7-2.   What are the four types of logic relationships?

    1. finish-to-start (FS).

    2. finish-to-finish (FF).

    3. start-to-start (SS).

    4. start-to-finish (SF).

True or False

7-3.   A start-to-start relationship means that the successor activity must start at the same time as its predecessor.

    False. The successor activity can start at any time after the predecessor but is does not have to.

7-4.   Both milestones and activities must have resources assigned to them.

    False. Activities are not required to have resources assigned unless the organization chooses to use this facility such as in an Earned Value Management environment and the schedule is the origin for cost calculation. If that were the case, then all activities must be resource loaded. Resources on milestones serve no purpose from a cost standpoint since milestones have zero duration.

Chapter 8 Critical Path Method Fundamentals

8-1.   Explain the forward pass through a network and what its results mean.

    The forward pass begins with the initiating activity and proceeds through the network to its completion, calculating the early start and early finish dates for each activity along with the overall project duration. The early start means that the date provided is the earliest that activity can possibly start, assuming the logic and durations are correct.

8-2.   Describe the backward pass through a network and what its results mean.

    The backward pass begins with the completion of the network, using the end date calculated from the forward pass through the network, or a directed date as per project requirements. It then proceeds backwards through the network logic, calculating the late start and late finish dates for each activity. The late dates represent the latest date on which that activity can start (or finish) and still support the completion date for the project.

8-3.   How do "total float" and "free float" differ?

    Total float is a measure of the flexibility of an activity to be delayed or extended without impacting the final project completion date identified in the network. It is a value shared along an activity path, so that any reduction in total float is reflected in all remaining activities along that path. Free float is associated with a single activity and represents the amount of time that activity may be delayed or extended without impacting any other activity in the network.

8-4.   List three absolute statements that are always true about the critical path.

    1. Is the longest activity path in the network.

    2. Defines the minimum project duration.

    3. Is the path with the lowest total float.

True or False

8-5.   "Critical path" refers to those activities that are most technically critical.

    False. This is a common misconception. Critical path only represents the longest path through the network, which may or may not be the most technically critical.

8-6.   On the forward pass through a network, converging paths require the use of the earliest early finish of the converging activities for the succeeding activity.

False. It requires the latest early finish, because both preceding activities must be complete before the next can start.

8-7.   Expending the total float of an activity has no impact on subsequent activities.

False. Total float is shared along an entire activity path and any reduction in total float affects the remaining activities in that path.

8-8.   "Slack" is another term for "float".

True. Slack was the term used in PERT and is used in some scheduling software.

8-9.   Changing the completion date for a project will affect the total float values for every activity in the entire network.

True.

8-10.   It is possible to have positive total float on the critical path.

True. Total float may be positive, negative, or zero on the critical path.

8-11.   Moving the completion date for the project network seven days earlier will result in all activities losing seven days of total float.

True.

8-12.   Free float and total float do not have to be equal for the same activity.

True. See Figure 8-15.

8-13.   The total float for any activity can be calculated by subtracting the early finish date from the late finish date.

True.

Chapter 9 Resource Loading and Leveling the Schedule

9-1.   Define several different types of resources.

Resources are anything required to complete the job: labor, material, equipment, subcontract, facilities, etc.

9-2.   Why is resource loading necessary as part of the schedule development process?

If resources are not loaded as part of the schedule development process, part of the project plan is missing. That is because no activity duration can be determined without some assumption of available resources. If these are not documented in the schedule, there will be no way of knowing later where the durations came from and if they are valid, or whether the plan is achievable.

9-3.   Explain the difference between resource loading and resource leveling.

Resource loading is simply the process of assigning resources to the individual activities. Resource leveling is a smoothing process that ensures that the resource profile can realistically be supported.

9-4.   What is meant by the statement, "This project is time critical"? How does this differ from being resource critical?

Every challenging resource loaded schedule, when it is resource leveled, will encounter problems. The question becomes "Which is more critical, finishing on time or not exceeding the resource limit?" If the project were "time critical," then the overriding concern should be to finish on time even if the resource peak were above the imposed limit. If it were "resource critical", then the maximum resource limit must not be exceeded even if it means delaying the completion date. Be aware that any deviation from the approved plan may have an impact on the project's cost because of the fluctuations of the amount of resource used.

9-5.   How does the leveled start/completion date relate to the early and late dates for the same activities?

The leveled start/completion is where the activity has been scheduled after the resource leveling process has been completed and the plan has been approved. For obvious reasons, it must be later than the early start date and earlier than the late finish date.

True or False

9-6.   Resource leveling is primarily a concern at the total project level.

False. Resource leveling at the bottom line of the project accomplishes almost nothing. Since technical skills are not interchangeable (i.e. an electrical engineer cannot complete the structural design if there happens to be an excess of electrical engineers when civil engineers are needed), each resource skill must be individually leveled to be of any use.

9-7.   The process and purpose of resource leveling is to help ensure that the necessary resources will be available when needed and that they can be used efficiently.

True.

9-8.   The use of nonlinear resource spreads on individual activities is usually not warranted.

True. This is a refinement that exceeds the accuracy of the data usually available for the resource loading process. If the resources are dramatically nonlinear, the activity should probably be split into more than one since it appears that the activity contains several phases.

9-9.   When resources are initially loaded in the schedule, the assumption should be that unlimited resources are available.

True. This is the only way to get a quick indication of how realistic that plan is.

9-10.   In order for resource leveling to be achieved, it will be necessary to delay the start and completion of some activities within the network.

True. This is the essence of resource leveling.

9-11.   An "early start" curve is a cumulative resource profile that represents what the resource requirements would be if all activities started on their earliest possible date.

True.

Chapter 10 Considerations for Developing a Useful, Quality Network Schedule

10-1.   Describe the "Top-Down" approach to schedule development.

The "Top-Down" approach to schedule development starts with the major milestones, such as the intended start and completion date for the project, and gradually expands the detail between these milestones as more information becomes available. This approach is typically used in the very early stages of a project, such as proposal generation.

10-2.   How does the "Bottom-Up" approach serve to validate the Top-Down schedule?

The "Bottom-Up" approach starts with the lowest level of detail and progressively summarizes it to higher levels. This is an entirely different way of looking at the schedule, and verifies the high level summary schedule by demonstrating how those milestones and summary durations can be supported by performing specific detailed activities. In most cases, revisions to one or both (summary and detail) schedules will be required for consistency to be achieved.

10-3.   Explain the differences between a hammock, a summary activity and a template.

A hammock is a single summary activity that encompasses a series of more detailed activities and their related logic. As such, a hammock is unique in that it only reflects its particular "children". A summary encompasses activities that are selected by code fields and are not necessarily connected to one another. Templates are standardized network modules of activities and logic that will be repeated many times in the overall network. The entire advantage of creating a template is that it be used as many times as possible to save time in network creation.

10-4.   How does a lag affect the network calculation?

A lag acts the same way as a separate activity with a duration. As such, it will affect the network calculations and will position subsequent activities in time according to its value.

10-5.   What does a negative lag between activities mean?

A negative lag between activities means that the "following" activity actually leads the preceding activity. Some people use the terminology lead/lag, depending on whether the value is positive or negative. A negative value turns a "lag" into a "lead". A negative lag on a start-to-start relationship from activity A to activity B would mean that B actually starts before A does.

10-6.   What scheduling considerations are important when assessing the value of a project schedule versus the use of organizational schedules?

The key considerations when assessing project schedules versus organizational schedules are integration of project information and size of network. The project schedule provides much better information and assures horizontal traceability, but also will result in many more activities in a single network file.

10-7.   Describe the advantages and disadvantages of using a conservative approach to developing the baseline schedule.

The main advantage is that a realistic schedule can be used that allows the ability to handle localized schedule slips without having to immediately develop alternative work-around plans. The main disadvantage is that a sense of urgency may be lost and the project duration may stretch to fill the available time.

10-8.   What is the major concern with use of an aggressive scheduling philosophy in baseline establishment?

An aggressive scheduling philosophy in establishment of a schedule baseline usually results in unrealistic schedules. If a schedule cannot be achieved and team members readily recognize that, the schedule is soon ignored and the project is operating without a schedule or with multiple functional schedules that no longer tie back to the official project schedule. In either event, this results in a lack of schedule visibility and control.

10-9.   What is the definition of an IMP?

An IMP is an event-based, top level plan consisting of a hierarchy of Program Events, with each Event being supported by specific Accomplishments, and each Accomplishment associated with specific Criteria to be satisfied for its completion.

10-10.   How is it possible to recognize qualitatively that a schedule is too detailed (i.e. has too many activities)?

A schedule is too detailed when the available staff spends so much time updating and producing the schedule reports that there is no time left for analysis and corrective action before the next update cycle must be supported.

10-11.   List the factors that must be considered when planning how detailed a schedule should be.

Factors to be considered in the selection of the appropriate level of schedule detail include project size/cost, project duration, and associated risk (technical, schedule, and cost).

10-12. What is one technique often used to limit the total number of activities maintained in a given project schedule file?

The use of hammocks is the easiest way to limit network size. The use of templates could also be considered.

10-13. What is the best way to ensure that schedule quality is maintained over the life of a project?

The frequent execution of a 14 point health check where the schedule is evaluated against a set of thresholds. The thresholds indicate whether the schedule has data integrity in its structure and data content. Full data audits at critical junctures are also recommended.

10-14. In the 14 point health check, what do leads, start to finish relationships and activities that start or finish in the future have in common?

The goal is to have none of them in any schedule.

True or False

10-15. Schedules that are developed using the "Top-Down" approach typically are too long in total duration.

False. Such schedules tend to be too short because they fail to recognize details that will interfere with the simple flow of information.

10-16. A "hammock" is a standardized network module used to describe a specific activity or series of activities.

False. That is the definition of a template.

10-17. Templates are used repeatedly within a large network file.

True.

10-18. Unlimited resources should be assumed in the first phase of resource loading.

True.

10-19. Resource loading a schedule assures efficient planning of staffing levels.

False. Resource leveling assures efficient staff planning.

10-20. Including contingency in schedule durations provides a further complication when schedule risk assessment is performed.

True. The contingency will need to be removed before performing the schedule risk assessment.

10-21. The level of detail to which a schedule should be developed depends on the amount of risk involved.

True. However, other factors should be considered as well.

10-22. Development of a schedule baseline requires a decision to either employ "top-down" scheduling or "bottom-up" scheduling.

False. Both of these techniques must be used in order to verify the feasibility of the proposed schedule.

10-23. Using a single, integrated project schedule helps keep the network small.

False. It makes it larger because of being all-inclusive.

10-24. When a schedule is being created, it is recommended that 90% or more of the activity relationships be start to finish.

False. 90% or more of the activity relationships should be Finish to Start.

10-25. Leads and lags should be limited to no more than 5% of the total number of activities in a schedule.

False. 5% applies to lags only. Leads should be 0%.

10-26. No more than 5% of activities should have a duration of greater than 44 days.

True.

Chapter 11 Crashing the Network

11-1.   Why is it important to recheck the critical path during a network crashing exercise?

As the crashing process proceeds, the critical path is continually being shortened until it is optimized. At that point, other paths become critical.

11-2.   What does it mean when the critical path is "fully crashed"?

A "fully crashed" critical path means that all of the activities along that path have been shortened as much as possible. That also means that the project has reached its minimum duration. Any additional expenditure of resources to expedite other network activities is a waste of resources.

11-3.   Define "crash time" and "crash cost."

"Crash time" is the shortest duration that any activity can be reduced, regardless of additional resources. "Crash cost" is the total cost associated with achieving "crash time."

11-4.   Explain why the cost slope is significant when performing a network crashing exercise.

The cost slope indicates the cost of reducing an activity's duration per time unit. This is significant since there are options as to which activity to shorten during the crashing process, and knowing the cost slope allows the cheapest alternative to be selected.

11-5.   What two occurrences will signal the end of a network crashing effort?

A network crashing effort is complete when either the objective has been fully reached or a critical path becomes "fully crashed."

True or False

11-6.   The network critical path must be known before a crashing exercise is begun.

True. The entire process focuses on shortening the critical path(s).

11-7.   Crashing a network is an effort of quantifying time/cost trade-offs.

True.

11-8.   Shortening a standard activity duration typically will cost less than the historical duration.

False. When accelerating activities, penalties associated with inefficiency are incurred. The "normal" duration consists of a trade-off between time and cost, with the low cost duration being the "normal" selection.

11-9.   A cost slope of $6,000 per week indicates that $6,000 will be saved for each week that the associated activity is shortened.

False. A $6,000 penalty will be incurred for each week that the activity is shortened.

11-10. Crashing all activities in a network will result in a higher cost than necessary for a fully crashed project schedule.

True. Once the critical path is fully crashed, any additional resource expenditure is wasted.

Chapter 12 Setting a Traceable Schedule Baseline

12-1. Define horizontal traceability.

Horizontal traceability means that schedules independently maintained by different divisions, departments, or contractors must reflect the same dates at interface points between schedules at the same level of detail.

12-2. Define vertical traceability.

Vertical traceability means that schedule dates are consistent between varying schedule levels. Specifically, lower level schedules must support the higher level milestones. This includes the possibility that the lower level, supporting activities, may be scheduled to finish earlier than the milestone dates.

12-3. Explain why traceability is important from a scheduling and management standpoint.

Traceability is essential because there is no schedule without it. Lack of traceability means that there are multiple schedules rather than one official schedule that the project team members are working towards. Without consistent schedules, there is no plan for managing the project.

12-4. Define what is meant by a "meaningful" milestone.

A meaningful milestone is one that can be clearly identified and is an objectively observable event that is understood, well documented, and agreed upon.

True or False

12-5. Once the schedule baseline has been approved, the emphasis for project schedule control should be on the late start curve.

False. The leveled start curve should receive the emphasis.

12-6. Baseline schedule dates should be revised if an activity starts later than planned.

False. That is merely an example of current status.

12-7. Repeated revising of schedule dates results in a moving target and meaningless trend indicators.

True. This is especially harmful if there were no baseline or the baseline itself is continually changing.

12-8. A true schedule baseline should include resources so that verification is available that required staffing to support the schedule can actually be met.

True.

12-9. Typically, requirements are for a schedule baseline to be in effect within 60-90 days after contract award.

True.

Chapter 13 Updating the Schedule

13-1. List four key inputs needed on a schedule update to allow accurate current status reporting.

1. Time Now.
2. Actual start date.
3. Actual completion date.
4. Remaining duration or percent complete (remaining duration preferred).

13-2.   A schedule has been updated to reflect current project status. One particular activity was reported as starting 5 days late, but its total duration has been shortened by 2 days. Before the update, this activity had 11 days of total float. How much float does it have now?

   8 days (11 - 5 + 2).

13-3.   What happens when activities have status reported that indicates they were performed out of sequence?

   The result is software dependent; however, the scheduler should determine the impact(s) of out of sequence work:

   1.   *Float anomalies exist?*

   2.   *Logic needs to be re-examined?*

   3.   *A scope change is imminent or has occurred?*

   4.   *Problems exist with others not meeting deadlines?*

   5.   *Is re-work a possibility?*

13-4.   Explain the "retained logic" method for addressing activities worked out of sequence.

   Retained logic, as its name suggests, attempts to change the logic as little as possible when out of sequence status is reported. A successor activity cannot be completed until its predecessor activity is completed. Note: Some scheduling software will accept an actual finish date on the successor activity and tie the completion of the predecessor to the activity following the successor. See Figure 13-11.

13-5.   Explain the "progress override" method for addressing activities worked out of sequence

   Progress override assumes that the previous logic was in error and the predecessor is rescheduled to minimize its impact. The predecessor's late finish will be set equal to the early finish date of the final project activity.   See Figure 13-12.

13-6.   Does it matter which of the two options (progress override or retained logic) is used within a scheduling software program? What are the implications for schedule analysis?

   Yes, it will have a major impact on total float calculations. See Figures 13-11 and 13-12.

13-7.   Why does remaining duration provide better information regarding schedule status than percent complete?

   From a scheduling standpoint, time is the key element. Remaining duration indicates the time it will take to complete the activity. With percent complete, a measure of the physical progress of the activity is provided. While percent complete is very useful for cost calculations, it has little to do with schedule status. It is not at all uncommon to have an activity virtually physically complete and yet still need weeks or months for completion because of a missing piece of design information or a missing part. There have been many examples of activities that are 95% complete and yet still have 50% of their total schedule duration ahead of them. If percent complete is used as the status reporting mechanism and this situation arises, the only alternative is to split the activity into multiple activities.

True or False

13-8.   Reported schedule status is always as of the "time now" date.

   True, by definition.

13-9.   For forecasting purposes, for an activity in progress as of the time now date, the actual start date is more important than the remaining duration.

   False. The remaining duration is the only significant item for forecasting purposes.

13-10. Once an actual date has been reported, the previously calculated early dates and late dates lose their significance.

True. The reported actual date will replace the previously calculated dates.

13-11. An actual start date can be chronologically later than "time now".

False. Most software has error checks to detect this unacceptable status.

13-12. With the "retained logic" option for handling activity status reported out of sequence, the out of sequence activity cannot be completed until the predecessor has been completed.

True, but see the note in response to question 13-4 above.

13-13. The main reason for needing to know the software default for out-of-sequence status is its impact on schedule analysis.

True. There may be substantial impacts on total float.

Chapter 14 Updating the Schedule

14-1.   Differentiate between current schedule updates and baseline changes.

Current schedule updates are those which are made to reflect current project status. Baseline changes are revisions to the approved project plan, i.e., scope changes.

14-2.   Why should baseline changes be treated differently than current schedule updates?

Baseline changes should only be incorporated after authorized review and approval. These are procedurally controlled changes. Current schedule updates can be made by anyone involved with the schedule update process based strictly on the input from the responsible individual and with no prior approval.

14-3.   Should activity duration changes for activities in progress be handled differently than duration changes for activities not yet started? Why?

Changes to activity durations currently in progress are necessary and expected since the remaining duration should be estimated, not calculated by subtraction. However, there is usually no reason to change activity durations for activities that have not begun. Doing so may indicate a CPM scheduling abuse: shortening future activity durations to compensate for current activity slippages. There should be some form of procedural control on future activity durations.

14-4.   Why does the frequency of the schedule update cycle have an impact on the definition of "significant" as it applies to total float?

Frequency is significant because total float disappears on a one-for-one basis as time elapses, assuming no progress is occurring on the activity. The result is that any activity with less total float than the time to the next update cycle will have negative float if no activity occurs during that time frame. That places these near-critical activities into a priority for attention now as much as negative path activities.

14-5.   What are the three most common approaches for "work-around" plans that must be implemented when contractual milestone dates cannot be met?

1.   Relax the technical specifications.

2.   Reallocate resources.

3.   Change the network logic.

14-6.   List the 5 conditions that could initiate a schedule baseline change.

1.   The schedule is impacted by approved scope changes.

2.   The project is delayed or accelerated or other owner direction is received.

3. *Rolling wave planning takes place where planning packages that approach the current period are converted to detailed work packages.*

4. *Management Reserve or Undistributed Budget is applied to the project and scheduling adjustments result.*

5. *When unrecoverable slippage has occurred, with owner approval.*

True or False

14-7.   Routine updates result from scope changes.
False.

14-8.   Shortening future activities can eliminate negative float on the critical path.
True. However, shortening future activities to compensate for execution is not a recommended scheduling practice.

14-9.   Adding or deleting activities is always considered a baseline change.
True. Schedule changes of these types need to be documented and approved.

14-10.   Total float is one of the best measures of schedule status.
True. In fact, it is the basis of the use of CPM as an exception reporting tool.

Chapter 15 Resolving Negative Float

15-1.   List at least three considerations that should be evaluated when schedule total float reports are issued. Specifically, what should be investigated?
The following five questions can be addressed:
1. What are the activity paths with the lowest total float?
2. Is the trend improving or deteriorating on these paths?
3. Which activities are causing the problem?
4. Why are those activities in trouble?
5. What can be done to resolve the problem?

15-2.   Why should activities with very high values of positive float be investigated at all?
Activities with very high positive total float are often not tied into the network logic properly or at all. It can be an indication that the network logic is not complete, with intermediate events and activities being tied to project completion instead of to intermediate events and activities as they should be.

15-3.   Should every activity with low/negative float be investigated, or just every activity path? Why?
Only the activity paths need to be analyzed and resolved, since total float is shared along an activity path. If any activity were corrected, the whole path would be resolved and not just that singular activity.

15-4.   In determining the cause of lost total float, baselines should be compared against what three pieces of information in the current network file?
Current/actual start date, current/actual completion date, and current/actual duration.

15-5.   Provide five methods that can be used to eliminate negative total float.
- *Expedite critical activities (i.e. shorten durations or provide additional resources).*
- *Revise the schedule logic (parallel instead of sequential).*
- *Redefine contract scope or procurement packages to eliminate the offending work   products that are late, including them in a later contract/bid or supplemental issue.*

- *Implement an Over Target Schedule.*
- *Correct schedule update input errors, if any, which may be the cause of the negative condition. Of course, it may be that no action is required because the results of the slip can be recovered later.*

15-6. Once the cause of float deterioration has been confirmed, what are the next steps to be taken?

The next steps include identification of the impact of the delay, an assessment of its seriousness, and then a plan of action for resolving the negative float condition, if warranted.

15-7. Identify one way to determine overall schedule performance that can be combined with the total float information to get a more accurate picture of overall status.

Simple product counts (actual versus scheduled) provide a wider perspective of status. Tracking the number of critical activities or the trend of the float value of the most critical activity path will also provide another view of the data.

True or False

15-8. Float analysis should be conducted by the scheduling group alone.

False. The input from the person responsible for the slipping activities is critically important.

15-9. A comparison of baseline total duration versus current duration will provide information about changing values of total float.

True.

15-10. If the duration of an activity on the critical path were reduced by one week, the project end date will be forecast to be one week earlier (assuming no other changes).

True.

15-11. Total product counts, scheduled versus actual, provide a form of schedule performance.

True.

15-12. Since the critical path method is a form of management by exception, there should be no real concern until after activities have total float values that are negative.

False. Management should be proactive rather than reactive. It would be far better if all negative path conditions could be averted so that the extra effort of resolution would never be required.

15-13. One approach to resolving negative float conditions is to see if the logic can be restructured so that more sequential activities are converted to parallel activities.

True.

Chapter 16 Special Networking Considerations

16-1. Define the "Not-Earlier-Than" (NET) directed date and discuss how it impacts the network calculation.

A "Not-Earlier-Than" date means that the activity to which it is assigned will not be allowed to start (or complete, depending on where the constraint is applied) any earlier than the assigned date, regardless of what is calculated in the CPM calculations. The NET directed date would impact the forward pass calculation through the network, truncating the early dates.

16-2. Discuss how secondary float differs from total float.

Total float is calculated from the overall project completion date. Secondary float is the same type of measure of schedule flexibility, but it is calculated from some intermediate point within the project logic rather than from the end date. Typically, secondary float would be computed from a contract milestone date. Scheduling software packages that cannot retain both of these types of float will replace the total float with the secondary float.

16-3.   What relationships cause some scheduling software to fail when handling multiple relationships between the same two activities?

There is greater complexity with this type of calculation. The dual relationships will imply different start and completion dates, and some software cannot handle this condition (low end products).

16-4.   What is the problem introduced with "Level of Effort" activities when they are included in a schedule network?

Level of Effort activities ordinarily extend for the entire duration of the project, with the unavoidable result that they appear as additional critical paths, which of course, is not correct. They are merely support activities and do not directly contribute to completion of the work products. Deleting them from the network file provides a different concern. Since they do consume resources, ignoring them will simply result in false resource curves.

16-5.   What is the "AM-PM" convention used by many scheduling software packages?

The "AM-PM" convention refers to the assumption that all activities begin at the beginning of the work day (or 12:01 A.M. in the absence of any other input) and end at the end of the work day (or 11:59 P.M., if the end is not defined). The result of this convention is that activities that are only one day in duration begin and end on the same date.

True or False

16-6.   Use of any directed date will supersede the normal network calculation.
True.

16-7.   Use of directed dates could make activities that are not critical appear to be critical.
True.

16-8.   There are no valid reasons to use a directed date.
False. The project completion date and contractual milestones are examples of dates that should be directed dates.

16-9.   It may be possible to shorten the total project duration by lengthening one of the activities.
True. See Figure 16-20 and the associated chapter discussion for an explanation.

16-10. The use of a "Not-Later-Than" (NLT) directed date would affect the backward pass calculation through the network, typically reducing the float value of that activity.
True.

Chapter 17 Schedule Risk Assessment

17-1.   Can the highest risk path for a logic network be different from the critical path? Explain.
Yes. The highest risk path is the one that has the potential to be the longest path, while the critical path is the one that is currently the longest identified path.

17-2.   Discuss the difference between the terms "uncertainty" and "risk."
"Uncertainty" refers to future events whose probability is unknown. "Risk" refers to future events whose probability is known. For that reason, risk may be thought of as measurable uncertainty.

17-3. Identify three important uses of schedule risk assessment.
1. *Quantify overrun potential for bid/no bid decisions.*
2. *Provide an estimate of required contingency to limit overrun risk to an acceptable level.*
3. *Provide advance warning of potential areas of high risk that are not on the critical path so that attention can be focused on them at an early stage.*

17-4. Identify the proper sequence of activities in a risk assessment by sequentially numbering the following steps in the order that they must occur:

4	Compute the activity path distribution
6	Initiate status monitoring
1	Create a CPM/PDM network
3	Calculate a duration distribution for activities
2	Develop activity duration estimates
5	Evaluate the results

17-5. Calculate the expected duration of the following activity, using a triangular distribution: minimum duration = 6 weeks, most likely duration = 8 weeks, maximum duration = 16 weeks.
Expected duration = 10 weeks. [(Low + Most Likely + High) / 3 = (6 + 8 + 16) / 3].

17-6. Explain how a cumulative probability curve of project durations can be used to recommend a value of schedule slippage reserve.
The cumulative probability curve displays the percent likelihood of any particular duration value being achieved. The current duration can then be read off the curve to determine its likelihood of being achieved. It is then possible to move along the Y-axis to the probability of achievement desired, and see what duration value that corresponds to on the X-axis. The difference between these values provides the number of days of schedule contingency that would be needed to improve the likelihood of achieving the completion date of the desired value.

17-7. How is schedule risk affected by the convergence of multiple activity paths in a network at a single point?
Converging activity paths in a network greatly increases the probability of schedule slippage beyond that point. This is true because if any of the converging paths are late, all of the subsequent paths beyond the convergence will be late.

17-8. Activity paths A, B, and C converge as common predecessors to milestone D. Paths A, B, and C have been analyzed using risk techniques. The cumulative percent likelihood curves for possible path durations of path A and B overlap, while path C does not. Path A has a 50% likelihood of completing within its assigned duration, while path B has a 60% chance and path C has a 95% chance. What is the likelihood that milestone D will be achieved on time?
30% (.6 X .5).

True or False

17-9. The highest risk path may be the one that actually determines the project duration, rather than the critical path.
True.

17-10. An advantage of a schedule risk assessment is that it allows the determination of a single point duration estimate for each activity.

False. CPM uses a single point; risk assessments provide a distribution of values for evaluation.

17-11. In most distributions, the expected duration and most likely duration are the same value.

False. This is only true in a symmetrical distribution, and most distributions of project schedule durations are not symmetrical.

17-12. A cumulative likelihood curve (S-curve) of a schedule risk assessment portrays the likelihood of each duration occurring.

False. A probability distribution would provide that type of information.

17-13. The bias in a schedule is the difference between the average duration and the nominal duration.

True.

17-14. Merge bias describes the tendency of schedulers to estimate short durations so that when the activity slips, it may still support the project completion date.

False.

17-15. The risk associated with completing an activity or total network may be greatly changed when directed dates are used.

True.

17-16. The use of late start scheduling greatly increases the risk in a project schedule.

True. There is a higher potential for multiple critical paths and much less flexibility when late dates are used.

17-17. PERT is an early risk assessment tool that heavily weights the most likely duration in the computation of average duration.

True.

17-18. "Expected duration" is another way of describing the average duration.

True.

17-19. High risk activities are identified in schedule risk studies, using the Monte Carlo approach, by the number of times they are determined to be on the critical path.

True.

Chapter 18 Scheduling in a Performance Measurement Environment

18-1. Describe the purpose of the System Description as it applies to the scheduling subsystem of an overall project management system.

The System description describes the intended operation of the scheduling subsystem for that project, just as it describes the intended operation of the other subsystems for the management of the project.

18-2. How do resource loaded schedules sometimes raise problems within an EVMSG (Earned Value Management System Guidelines) system application?

Once a resource loaded schedule exists, it must be verified against the integrated cost/schedule baseline for the project. What can happen is that the resource plan will be in significant disagreement with other cost documents produced from resource loaded plans at the lowest level of detail within the control account. Discrepancies raise doubt as to the validity of the entire management plan.

True or False

18-3.   Reported schedule status must be the same within the integrated schedule and the cost system.

True.

18-4.   If a detailed schedule milestone were scheduled earlier than the same milestone shown on a summary schedule, this is a violation of the requirement for vertical traceability.

False. If it is earlier, it can still meet the requirement that it support the summary level milestones.

18-5.   It is advantageous for a contractor to describe its best possible system in the System Description, since it can always be changed in the implementation phase of the contract.

False. This is a mistake contractors sometimes make: over-specifying their system capability. The system operation is defined in the System Description and becomes part of the bid evaluation process, the contractor is committed to abide by it.

Section 2 Scheduling
Quiz for Chapters 6 to 18

1.   A good schedule provides multiple benefits for the program. Which of the following is not true?
     D. Provides no project completion date.

2.   The Gantt Chart was the first computerized schedule system.
     False. PERT was first.

3.   Milestone charts are the most efficient tools to use to forecast schedule problems.
     False. Networks should be used to analyze status versus the baseline and to prepare forecasts.

4.   Which of the following do not define the critical path?
     C. The total float values are less than zero.
     D. The path with the highest technical risk.

5.   Which calculation is used to determine total float?
     A. LF - EF.
     B. LS - ES.

6.   Which set of dates is calculated from the forward pass?
     A. Early Start, Early Finish.

7.   Which set of dates is calculated from the backward pass?
     E. None of the above.

8.   What is the total float value for an activity that has the late finish equal to the early finish?
     A. Zero.

9.   What are resources?
     E. All of the above.

10.   Resources must be loaded into a CPM schedule.
       False. Schedules can be prepared without loading resources; however, this is not recommended.

11.   When using resource scheduling, what kinds of constraints are possible?
       A. Time constraints.
       B. Resource constraints.

12.   Can the resource leveling priority rules be changed during the life of the project?
       A. Yes.

13.   Which of the following are not used in resource leveling?
       E. Activity number.
       F. Level 3 WBS.
       H. Sick time.

14.   What happens to the CPM schedule dates after a resource schedule is calculated?
       A. The early dates are replaced by the resource dates.

15.   What is the bottom line result after accelerating (crashing) the schedule?
       A. Increased cost.
       B. Reduced time.

16.   Why does the project need a baseline schedule?
       A. Provides a saved set of planned dates.
       B. Allows for schedule variance analysis.
       D. Is part of the Performance Measurement Baseline.

17.   The baseline schedule changes each time a CPM calculation is performed.
       False. The baseline only changes with specific approval.

18.   You are reviewing a baseline schedule and find actual status for some activities. Is this a problem?
       A. Yes. Status should only be applied to the Current schedule.

19.   Vertical traceability is more important than horizontal traceability.
       False. They are equally important.

20.   Free float can be larger than total float.
       False. It can be equal or less, but never more.

21.   Which of the following are network development techniques?
       A. Top-Down.
       C. Bottom-Up.

22.   Top-Down schedule development typically over-estimates durations.
       False. Top-Down schedule development typically under-estimates durations.

23.   When should date constraints (if needed) be applied to a network?
       C. After the initial network is developed.

24.   Aggressive schedules can become unrealistic early in the project.
       True. All schedules should be prepared using realistic and achievable goals.

25.   Organizational schedules do not provide sufficient visibility for total program impacts.
       True. There are insufficient logic ties to promote visibility of inter-organizational impacts.

26.   What methods are available for statusing networks with out-of-sequence progress?
       A. Retained logic.
       E. Progress override.

27.   Which of the following are good practices to handle cyclic funding (e.g. annual) in a schedule?
       B. Stop and resume activities.

28.   Schedule status should be on the baseline schedule.
       False. Status is captured on the current schedule.

29.   Sources of project risk include:
       D. All of the above.

30.   Performing a risk assessment ensures good decisions.
       False.

31.   To combine distributions on a schedule network path, add:
       B. Average durations.

32.   Which of the following are risk assessment tools?
       A. PERT.
       B. Monte Carlo.

33.   In a performance measurement environment, activities do not need to be identified to a WBS element.
       False. All activities must be identifiable to a WBS element.

Questions 34 to 39 relate to Activity ABC which has the following pertinent information:

       Early Start   = Day 83
       Early Finish = Day 90
       Late Start   = Day 86
       Late Finish = Day 93

       Use the "AM-PM" convention to answer the questions (i.e. a 2-day duration activity beginning on day 3 ends on day 4).

34.   What is the total float?
       3 days.

35.   What is the activity's duration?
       6 days.

36.   Which of the following describes the free float:
       D. Cannot be determined from this information.

The schedule is updated to include progress and the actual start of Activity ABC is reported as Day 85.

37.   What is the revised total float?
       1 day.

38.   What is the planned duration?
       8 days.

39.   Can the project end date still be supported?
       Yes.

40.   What five types of information are needed to develop a baseline schedule?
       1. Scope of work, defined to the activity level.
       2. Activity interrelationships.
       3. Activity duration.
       4. Resource requirements.
       5. Assigned responsibilities.

41.   Name at least six uses of a scheduling system.
       1. Development of a realistic baseline plan.
       2. Priority definition.
       3. Status reporting.
       4. Problem area identification.
       5. Problem impact analysis.
       6. Corrective action plan support.

42.   Which of the following statements are true about hammocks?
       A. There is a single start date and end date for each hammock.
       C. It can be useful in "what-if" analysis.

43.   Templates are only useful in projects that contain more than 1,000 activities.
       False. Templates can be used in any size network.

44.   Which of the following statements are true about templates?
       A. They represent standard activity sequences repeatedly used in a large network diagram.
       B. They allow faster logic preparation time through the use of standard activity sequences.

45.   There is more than one hammock for an associated group of detailed activities.
       False.

Using Figure 1, answer questions 46 to 52.

Activity D has a "Start Not Earlier Than" directed date of day 7 applied to its start date.

Given this condition,

46.   What is the total float of Activity D?
       3 days.

47.   What is the total float of Activity G?
       3 days.

48.   What is the total float of Activity F?
       0 days.

49.   When is the expected finish of Activity D?
       Day 13.

50. When is the expected start of Activity G?
Day 14.

51. What is Activity E's total float?
8 days.

52. What is Activity E's free float?
5 days.

53. Based on Figure 2, Activity B CAN start:
C. On Day 3.

54. The schedule baseline should be changed:
D. All of the above.

55. The requirement that schedule dates at interface points between contractors or organizations must be consistent is known as vertical traceability.
False.

56. For recording schedule status, the choice of remaining duration versus activity percent complete for updating the schedule will always result in the same schedule position.
False.

57. A revised forecast completion date for an activity is a routine update and should not be considered a baseline change.
True.

58. Shortening durations for future activities is an accepted way of resolving negative float.
False. This is considered schedule abuse.

59. A "Not-Earlier-Than" directed date impacts:
A   The forward pass only.

60. All directed dates affect the total float calculation.
True.

61. A lag between activities may be positive or negative.
True.

62. Which of the following statements are true about secondary float?
A. It measures status against an intermediate milestone rather than against the project completion date.

63. A non-critical activity may be made to appear critical by inserting an imposed date.
True.

64. The highest risk path in a schedule network is always the critical path.
False.

65. A CPM network is a prerequisite for quantifying schedule risk.
True.

66. The advantages of the Bar Chart display include:
A. It is easy to prepare.
B. It is easy to understand.

67.   Fill in the meaning of the following common scheduling notations:

A. ES   **_Early Start_**

B. DU   **_Duration_**

C. FF   **_Free Float_**

D. LF   **_Late Finish_**

E. NET   **_Not Earlier Than_**

F. CPM   **_Critical Path Method_**

G. NLT   **_Not Later Than_**

H. AS   **_Actual Start_**

I. FS   **_Finish to Start_**

J. EF   **_Early Finish_**

K. SS   **_Start to Start_**

L. RD   **_Remaining Duration_**

M. PDM   **_Precedence Diagramming Method_**

N. TF   **_Total Float_**

O. AF   **_Actual Finish_**

P. LS   **_Late Start_**

Q. SF   **_Start to Finish_**

Chapter 19 The Estimating Process

19-1.   Discuss the problems associated with estimates which are (1) too low or (2) are too high.

The answer depends on whether it is looked at from the contractor's viewpoint or the owner's viewpoint.

1.   _For estimates which are too low, the contractor may lose money or even go bankrupt. The owner may find that the apparent bargain is no bargain at all if it becomes a battle over every nickel and dime scope change for the life of the contract (because the contractor needs the additional money from scope changes to survive). The financial failure of the contractor causes real problems to the owner as well: how will the project be finished? Hiring a new contractor to complete an ongoing project is an expensive venture._

2.   _If the estimate were too high, the contractor's problem is that business opportunities will be lost, because someone else will be awarded the contract. For the owner's part, it will mean that too much has been spent on the project. In all cases, having an inadequate estimate (too high or too low) will make the function of project management much more difficult._

19-2.   Discuss the difference in the owner/customer view and the contractor view of the bidding process.

The owner wants to get the best possible bargain from the bidding process while the contractor wants to win the contract award while still making a fair profit.

19-3.   How does shifting from a Firm Fixed Price contract to a Cost Plus contract shift the emphasis on cost between contractor and owner/customer?

On a cost plus contract, all of the motivation for controlling cost is with the owner. For a fixed price contract, the owner becomes less concerned about cost and more concerned with schedule while the contractor must become very cost-conscious or risk losing money.

19-4.   List four important prerequisites that should be in place before an estimate is produced.

1.   _Guidelines for estimate development are needed._

2. *Template Structure should be in place.*

3. *Work Breakdown Structure Dictionary.*

4. *Definition of standard estimate format.*

19-5. Why is it important to assure consistency of the templates with the WBS?

There must be some sort of translation table which will allow reconciliation of the two structures. They must be related to each other or actual costs can never be fairly compared with estimated costs, with the result that there is no feedback mechanism for improving estimate accuracy over time.

19-6. What are the three primary reasons for developing a Template Structure?

1. *To provide consistency between estimates, facilitating estimate comparisons.*

2. *To provide a summarization structure to ensure vertical traceability.*

3. *To provide a basis for establishing standard estimate formats.*

19-7. Discuss the trade-offs between visibility and accuracy in template structure detail.

Summary accounts in the estimate development process result in quicker estimates which can be reviewed more easily on an overview basis. This approach sacrifices visibility into the component detail, however, so that a problem in the rates of the detail cannot be detected. On the other hand, if the summary rate is accurate, variations in the components are not a big concern.

True or False

19-8. It is critically important that actual costs be collected in a way that they can be compared with estimated costs.

True, so that estimate accuracy can be improved.

19-9. The lowest level of construction cost estimating is the commodity level.

True.

19-10. Since the amount of available detail varies throughout the life of a project, estimates should be prepared in different formats depending on when in the project they were prepared.

False. They should be prepared in similar formats so that they can be compared, although the detail of the estimate will vary.

19-11. It is always in the best interests of the owner to award contracts at the lowest price offered.

False. See answer to question number 1 for this chapter.

19-12. Labor, equipment, subcontracts, ODC and material costs typically are combined in a single account and cannot be separately identified.

False. In fact, this would be a big problem because each is subject to differing factors and differing escalation rates; so they must be prepared separately and reviewed/analyzed individually.

19-13. Estimating procedures are not important since each project is a little different than the last one and the amount of available information for preparing the estimate varies on a case-by-case basis.

False. There needs to be a common approach precisely to provide some continuity in the estimating process.

Chapter 20 Types of Estimates

20-1. List four types of estimates.

    1. Conceptual Estimate.

    2. Preliminary Estimate.

    3. Detailed Estimate.

    4. Definitive Estimate.

20-2. Why is the Conceptual Estimate typically prepared by the owner/customer?

First of all, a contractor is usually not selected yet at the time of the Conceptual Estimate preparation. Secondly, this type of estimate is frequently involved in confidential studies and the intent is to limit their distribution to as few people as possible.

20-3. Explain why it is important for the different types of estimates to be defined in each company.

Not all estimates are created equal, and this is often forgotten by those requesting a rush estimate. Guidelines need to be established so that all who are involved in the estimating process understand what is expected and correctly interpret the limitations of the output.

True or False

20-4. Parametric guidelines are most likely to be used in the development of detailed estimates.

False. They are most frequently in Conceptual Estimates.

20-5. A Preliminary Estimate reflects project specific information.

True.

20-6. There should be reduced amounts of management reserve (cost risk) associated with each subsequent estimate.

True.

20-7. In an engineering/construction or development/production project, the Detailed Estimate is typically prepared during the bid/award process.

True.

20-8. Even for very large projects, a Conceptual Estimate is short in duration.

True.

20-9. An accurate definition of scope is an essential contributor to an accurate estimate.

True.

Chapter 21 Estimate Development

21-1. What is the first essential step in the estimating process?

An accurate scope of work must be developed and provided before an adequate estimate can be produced. Even for a Conceptual Estimate, there must be good understanding of the project's objectives and planned direction before acceptably accurate numbers can be generated.

21-2. Explain how material quantities are important for developing a cost estimate.

Material quantities determine how many labor hours are required for installation, which in turn determines how many labor dollars are necessary. The total quantity of each type of material is also needed so that unit prices can be applied to calculate the material cost.

21-3.   Identify and explain the three methods commonly used for developing estimates.

The Engineering Build-up Method requires specific project information at the lowest levels of the project structure. The Analogy Method requires data from similar projects that can be adjusted to fit the project being estimated. The Parametric Method requires historic cost data based on physical parameters such as weight, volume, and power.

21-4.   A final bottom line cost does not constitute an estimate by itself. What additional information must be provided, at a minimum, so that the estimate can be evaluated?

Cash flow, documented assumptions, risk analysis results.

21-5.   Why is the schedule important for developing the cost estimate?

The schedule is needed for multiple reasons, including:

*   *Escalation calculation.*
*   *Cash flow development.*
*   *Duration of support service costs.*

Note: Item 2 includes identification of delivery dates of large pieces of equipment (if applicable) to support cash flow development.

21-6.   What is a default, as applied to estimate development, and what is its role in estimate preparation?

A default is a standard assumption to be used in estimate development when specific project information is not available. Its role is to provide some standardization and to expedite estimate preparation by saving each estimator from having to decide on a new set of assumptions for each new estimate.

21-7.   Provide an example, from the text or from personal experience, of a parametric guideline.

This requires definition of a "cost driver," a variable which has a high correlation with cost. Examples might include cost versus size of equipment, pump flow rate, diameter of pipe, weight of steel, number of lines of code for a software development effort, barrels of waste to be processed, electric output for a power plant, steam output for a boiler/steam generator, fighter plane weight and speed, payload weight of satellite to be launched, heat exchanger surface area, or ambient air temperature.

21-8.   Which type of estimate, Preliminary or Definitive, would be prepared in more detail? Why?

A Definitive Estimate would be prepared in more detail because there is more available information. That translates into more accounts.

21-9.   Provide a general definition of indirect costs.

Indirect costs are costs that cannot be identified to any single project, but rather support multiple projects. As such, they are collected in an overhead account and distributed to individual projects on a prorated basis.

21-10. Why is it imperative that the "base date" of the estimate be identified; i.e., the date on which costs are based?

The cost estimate may or may not include escalation. In either event, the base date becomes a critical piece of information for interpreting the estimate. If escalation is included, the base date reveals the basis on which it was calculated. If escalation is not contained within the number, a base date must be defined for starting the escalation computations.

21-11. What are the five main sources of information needed for developing a cash flow for project material?

1. A summary project schedule.

2. Planned material delivery dates.

3. *Projected milestone payments.*
4. *Planned commodity installation curves.*
5. *Escalation tables.*

21-12. What are the two principal parameters that are used when estimating software costs?

Lines of code and function point estimates.

True or False

21-13. A composite labor rate is a rate that combines the direct labor rate with the indirect rates that apply to labor into one overall rate..

True, note that the composite rate may or may not include profit.

21-14. Accuracy in estimates is very important, so numbers should always be expressed in exact dollars.

False. An estimate is a prediction based on assumed factors. It is not an exact dollar figure. Estimates should express their inherent accuracy, this estimates are usually expressed in thousands of dollars for detailed estimates and possibly in millions of dollars for Conceptual Estimates.

21-15. One reason that it is important to isolate the labor and material components of a cost estimate is that they are each subject to separate escalation rates.

True.

21-16. There is no straightforward way to compare the relative costs of two projects that were built in different years with different capacities.

False. This type of effort is done routinely in "benchmarking" studies and is explained in the section, "Use of Other Escalation Factors," in this chapter.

21-17. "Rules of thumb" may be used for developing faster estimates and for quick summary review of an estimate.

True.

Chapter 22 Learning Curves

22-1.   What are the two types of learning curves?

Unit Learning Curves and Cumulative Average Learning Curves.

22-2.   Explain the concept of a learning curve.

The principle of the learning curve is that when a process or operation is done repetitively, those performing the operation will become more proficient over time and so the cost per unit will decrease.

22-3.   Unit 50 took 20 hours to complete and the average cost for the first 50 was 28 hours. Unit 100 required 16 hours to complete and the average cost for the first 100 was 23 hours. Calculate the learning curve slope for both types of learning curve.

The Unit Learning Curve slope would be 80% (16 / 20 x 100). The Cumulative Average Learning Curve would be 82% (23 / 28 x 100).

22-4.   What is the biggest contributor to the expected slope of the learning curve?

The degree to which the operation is automated.

22-5.   What are some of the factors (list at least 3) that must remain constant for learning curves to be meaningfully applied?

- *The work is similar.*
- *The same people and supervision are involved in the process.*
- *There should not be a change in work schedule or amount of overtime.*
- *There are no significant delays between projects or operations (start and stop, with time in the middle for proficiency to be lost).*

True or False

22-6.   Learning curves can be applied to any repetitive task or project for which conditions remain the same.

True.

22-7.   Typical learning curve values for aircraft manufacturing are in the 75%-80% range.

True.

22-8.   The standard definition of learning curves applies only to the doubling of the number of units in question.

True.

22-9.   Learning curves were introduced in the 1960's and have been widely applied since that time.

False. Learning curves have been around since the 1930's.

Chapter 23 Cost Risk Assessment

23-1.   Describe the difference between the Monte Carlo approach and the Latin Hypercube approach to risk assessment.

The Monte Carlo approach uses truly random sampling, but requires a large number of samples before the input distribution is truly representative. Latin Hypercube forces its random numbers to immediately come from all areas of the probability curve, achieving the representative solution in fewer trials (iterations).

23-2.   What is the expected accuracy of a Monte Carlo simulation with 25 iterations?

+/- 20%

23-3.   Explain what is meant by the "expected result" in the output distribution from a risk simulation.

The expected result is one that has a 50% chance of underrunning and a 50% chance of overrunning. It may not be the most likely individual result.

23-4.   How can alternatives be compared in risk simulations when all numbers are randomly generated and even the same set of conditions would result in slightly different answers?

Some programs allow the user to specify the use of a "seed", which causes the same set of random numbers generated for the first simulation to be used repeatedly in subsequent simulations so that they can be fairly compared while the variable in question changes.

23-5.   Describe what is meant by "skewness" of a distribution.

Skewness is the degree of asymmetry, with higher values indicating a greater degree of asymmetry. A distribution may be either left-skewed or right-skewed.

23-6.   What is the best distribution curve form to use when the range of values is known, but there is no information concerning the relative likelihood of values within the range?

Uniform Distribution.

23-7.   Why is a cost risk assessment used in estimate development?

A cost risk assessment is performed to determine the degree of variability in the estimated numbers and to use that information to make a recommendation regarding the actual estimate to be used.

23-8.   What are some reasons that risk assessments can go away?

Among others, the following can invalidate a risk assessment: bad assumptions, internal politics that dictate what the answer should be, suppressing real values, and unrealistic distributions (usually ranges that are too narrow). It is implementation, not the theory,that is flawed in all cases.

23-9.   In soliciting input for a risk distribution, how should the interviewer explain what is intended by the limits for minimum and maximum values?

The interviewer should indicate that it is not the absolute value that is being requested. The minimum value should be one that has a 95% chance of being exceeded, and the maximum value should have a 95% chance of being underrun. The extreme case, in which absurd conditions are hypothesized, is to be avoided because it adds little to the analysis and may falsely skew the results.

True or False

23-10.   There is not much difference in accuracy between a ten thousand iteration and a one million iteration risk simulation.
True.

23-11.   For most business applications, the normal distribution, uniform distribution, and triangular distribution will be sufficient for modeling the risk profile.
True.

23-12.   Most real life project applications, if asymmetrical, will be skewed left.
False. Because an absolute minimum cost always exists, but there is almost no absolute maximum cost, project applications are virtually always skewed right.

23-13.   Kurtosis is a measure of the shape of the probability distribution curve that measures how close the likely values congregate near the mean.
True.

23-14.   When a risk assessment of an estimate is accomplished, it does not matter whether it includes hedges against an overrun since that is what is being evaluated.
False. The inclusion of hedges confuses the issue and so must be removed prior to making the evaluation.

Chapter 24 Estimate Review

24-1.   Besides the estimate numbers and cash flow, what critical element of any estimate should always be carefully reviewed?

The assumptions require careful review, since they directly affect the estimate numbers. (Partial credit: the source documentation for the estimate, i.e. specific drawings, specifications, and their revision numbers).

24-2.   What is a "Check Estimate" and what is its function?

A Check Estimate is an estimate prepared by an independent third party using the same information that the estimator used. It is not used to check the accuracy of the original estimate, but rather to verify assumptions and to ensure that nothing has been overlooked in the preparation of the estimate. Typically such an estimate would only be requested when it is particularly critical or controversial.

24-3.   What is a "Fair Value Estimate" and what is its function?

A Fair Value Estimate is similar to a Check Estimate except that it is intended to verify bidders rather than another estimator. The estimator is given the exact package that was provided to the bidders and, in effect, asked to submit a bid under the same conditions. This implies that the estimator has the same amount of time to prepare the bid (no more or no less) as the bidders are allowed. One reason to do this is to identify areas of potential confusion internally so that clarification may be provided to the real bidders. Another reason is to identify either possible bidder collusion or low ball bids.

24-4.   Why is a team review of the estimate important?

The intent is to arrive at the most accurate estimate possible. This is facilitated by having all of the experts who provided input to the estimate development make one final check before it is submitted to ensure that the estimator incorporated and understood the various inputs.

True or False

24-5.   All estimates should be reviewed in the same manner.

False. Different types of estimates are also reviewed in different ways. A Definitive Estimate may include spot checks of the calculations and a review of particular source design documents, while a Conceptual Estimate will be limited to review of assumptions and reasonableness of the total value.

24-6.   One important reason for engineers to review the estimate is to verify the validity of the technical assumptions.

True.

24-7.   An advantage of limiting reviewers to their area of expertise is the reduction in battles over responsibility boundaries.

True.

24-8.   The value of an estimate is dependent in some part on the accuracy of its assumptions.

True.

Chapter 25 Tracking the Estimate

25-1.   What is the biggest challenge in comparing the final cost of a project to its original estimate?

The biggest challenge is to reconcile the scope that was estimated to the scope that was actually accomplished. Rarely will the original estimate accurately represent all of the later design decisions and adjustments that must be made in any type of project.

25-2.   What are the two main reasons for comparing a project's actual cost with the estimate?

1. To explain what happened.

2. To use the feedback to generate more accurate estimates in the future.

25-3.   Exact calculations from engineering design drawings of required material will still vary from the actual quantities that need to be bought. Why?

Material will need to be replaced because of damage, waste, failed inspections, loss and theft. Also, material may need to be purchased in lots because of Economic Order Quantities (EOQ).

25-4.   What is meant by vertical traceability in an estimate?

Vertical traceability in an estimate is the ability to accurately summarize data with no exclusions, no double counting, and correct summation totals.

25-5.   What is meant by historical traceability in an estimate?

Historical traceability is the ability to accurately track changes in an estimate over time so that all estimates can be related to each other and project scope and estimate scope are consistent.

25-6.   List at least 5 reasons why estimate totals change over time.

Estimates change over time because:
- *Scope changes are approved.*
- *Schedules change.*
- *Escalation rates change.*
- *Actual purchase orders and contracts vary versus the estimate.*
- *Cost risk is reevaluated.*
- *The estimate is refined (quantity or productivity variations etc.).*
- *Misunderstood scope is clarified; e.g., estimate omission or duplication is recognized.*

25-7.   Discuss what is meant by "estimate refinement."

Estimate refinement does not refer to scope changes and the term may look like a euphemism for errors. However, it is actually revision resulting from invalid estimate assumptions and from non-scope change revisions (quantity variations, productivity changes, changed market conditions).

25-8.   Explain the advantages of keeping escalation as a separate item.

If escalation is kept as a separate line item, this facilitates variance analysis because escalation changes are readily identifiable as a lump sum. If escalation rates change (which they will), only one number needs to be revised in the estimate rather that all numbers needing to be revised.

25-9.   Explain the advantages of including escalation within the individual estimate accounts.

If escalation is included within the associated cost line items, then the total cost is known for each item. When doing variance analysis on an item by item basis, the escalated value will be needed to make comparisons with the actual cost (which will include escalation).

True or False

25-10. Variance analysis of changes from one estimate to the next is important for achieving historical traceability.

True.

25-11. All possibilities for disaster should be included within an estimate to ensure that nothing is excluded.

False. Including all negative possibilities will make the estimate prohibitively high and will result in rejection of possible projects (from the owner) and loss of contracts (for the contractor).

25-12. Creating a document with a standard format for tracking costs is logical for supporting a database for future projects.

True.

Chapter 26 Automating the Estimating Function

26-1.   Describe some of the advantages of automating the estimating function.
- *Automation will provide consistency of results and approach.*
- *Allows documentation of defaults for all estimators to use.*
- *Will save time in generating future estimates.*
- *Databases can be organized and easily retrieved by others.*
- *Accuracy is automatic once the program is set up once.*
- *Standard formats will automatically be produced.*
- *Resorting of information is automatic.*
- *Global changes to the existing estimate are automatic.*

26-2.   Describe some of the problems with automating estimating.
Estimating is the most difficult project management function to automate. Every project is unique, standard productivity values have to be significantly changed depending on the type of application, assumptions drive the numbers, table look-up takes just as much time in a computer as in a hard copy on the shelf, and much of the estimating process requires judgment every step of the way that cannot be automated. In addition, many of the software packages are difficult to learn.

26-3.   Briefly describe five evaluation considerations for automating estimating.
See "Software Evaluation Considerations" in this chapter.

True or False

26-4.   Automation of estimating occurred on a widespread basis before scheduling was automated.
False.

26-5.   The availability of standard estimating databases commercially available makes estimating a "cook book" exercise.
False. The numbers in these databases must be substantially modified in many applications.

26-6.   Estimating standards may have to be modified by as much as 200-300% when applying them in different industries or applications.
True.

26-7.   A shortcoming of some estimating software packages is an inability to produce conceptual estimates because of a requirement to build the estimate from detailed tables and then total the entries.
True.

26-8.   The requirements of the estimating process should be defined and understood before automation is considered.
True, as with any automated system.

Section 3 Estimating
Quiz for Chapters 19 to 26

1.   Labor and material costs must be maintained separately because:
B. They must be calculated and analyzed individually.

2.   Which of the following are general requirements for estimate development?
A. A Template Structure and Dictionary.

B. Defined estimate formats.

3.   The overall project management process will be facilitated if there is a separate Cost Estimate Template Structure and Work Breakdown Structure.

False. This increases work by forcing reconciliations between the two cost structures.

4.   Summary estimate formats will usually include information on quantities to be installed by category.

False. At the summary levels, items with differing units of measure are frequently combined in a single account. This makes it impossible to list quantities.

5.   List 4 types of estimates:

A. *Conceptual.*

B. *Preliminary.*

C. *Detailed.*

D. *Definitive.*

6.   Which of the following is not used as a common estimating technique?

B. *Top-Down.*

7.   Which of the following is the most important input to the development of an estimate?

A. *Scope of work.*

8.   Indirect costs are:

C. *Costs that cannot be identified to a single project.*

9.   Which of the following would you accept as a conceptual estimate?

D. *$328,000,000, or*

E. *$300,000,000.*

Reason: Consider the accuracies these numbers imply. Answer A suggests an impossible accuracy for any estimate, including a Definitive Estimate. Answer D is the preferred one, rounded to the nearest million dollars. It is doubtful that any company would accept E, since it suggests the estimate can barely be calculated to the nearest hundred million dollars. However, this corresponds to an accuracy of +/- 33%, not too far from what should be expected for accuracy in a Conceptual Estimate.

10.   For estimating software development costs, which of the following techniques are used?

A. *Parametric.*

B. *Grassroots.*

11.   A 90% Unit Learning Curve means:

A. *It will take 90% as many labor hours for each successive doubling of the unit number being produced.*

12.   Using the Monte Carlo approach for cost risk assessment, which of the following increases in the number of iterations will result in the greatest improvement in accuracy?

A. *100 to 1,000*

Explanation: Since accuracy varies with the reciprocal of the square root of the number of iterations, choice A improves accuracy from 10% to 3%, far better than B which improves accuracy from 3% to 1%. Choices C and D realistically see no improvement at all.

13.   In a cost risk assessment, which of the following probability distributions should be used when the most likely value is known but it is equally likely to be underrun or overrun?

B. *Normal distribution.*

14.   Which of the following output statistics from a risk evaluation measures the degree of asymmetry of a probability distribution?

D. Skewness.

15.   A triangular distribution may be symmetrical or asymmetrical.

True.

The following output table resulted from a risk assessment. Answer questions 16 to 18 based on this information.

Cumulative % Probability	Value
0%	$100,000
10%	$150,000
20%	$175,000
30%	$200,000
40%	$215,000
50%	$225,000
60%	$235,000
70%	$250,000
80%	$270,000
90%	$295,000
100%	$400,000

16.   What is the likelihood of overrunning a budget of $175,000?

80%

17.   What is the most likely value of the probability distribution?

C. Cannot be determined from this data format.

18.   The estimate is $250,000 for this project. If management wants an 80% confidence level that the project will be completed within budget, how much should the budget be increased over the estimate?

$20,000

19.   A "check estimate" is:

B. A separate estimate developed independently by a third party to be compared with the original estimate.

20.   Estimate traceability includes which of the following concepts?

B. The ability to tally estimates from the detail to the summary totals accurately.

C. The ability to track a project from one estimate to the next on a comparable basis.

21.   Estimating is more difficult to automate than scheduling.

True

22.   Two of the main advantages of automating estimating include:

A. Consistency of results.

B. Ability to maintain a single database.

Explanation: While C and D should be true for automated estimates, they are not necessarily true. Estimate accuracy is primarily associated with a well-defined work scope, which has nothing to do with automation. Whether automated estimates are quicker or not is pure conjecture. At least half of the estimators in our experience believe estimates can be produced just as quick manually. However, in all cases, A and B are true. Everyone is working from the same starting point, presentation formats can be automated, and escalation formulae programmed. All of these help ensure consistency. And item B addresses a big problem in manual estimating systems: everyone has their own secret files they refer to when developing estimates.

23.   COCOMO, the Constructive Cost Model, is:

A. A parametric estimating technique used for preparing estimates for software development.

24.   It is possible to make fair cost comparisons between different size construction projects completed in different years.

True

25.   The schedule is a critical input to estimate development for a construction project. Name three pieces of information used for cash flow development that are derived from the schedule.

1. Escalation.

2. Duration of support activities.

3. Planned material delivery dates.

Acceptable Alternative: Milestone payments based on project/contract milestones.

Chapter 27 Earned Value

27-1.   What is earned value?

Earned value is the value of work completed as determined by the budget for that work.

27-2.   Why is earned value an important part of the project management process?

Earned value is a cornerstone of the project management process because it provides an objective measure of work accomplished. The management process includes the formulation of plans and then the measurement of work against that plan. Earned value provides that measurement.

27-3.   What two other cost/schedule status measures is earned value typically compared against?

Earned value is compared against the actual cost, and against the budget (or plan).

27-4.   What is the earned value of a completed task? Of a task that has not begun? Of a partially completed task?

The earned value of a completed task is 100% of that task's budget. The earned value for a task which has not yet started is zero. For partially completed work, the earned value is determined based on some measurement of completion status which is then applied against that task's approved budget.

27-5.   If earned value were higher than actual cost, what does that signify? What is likely to happen to the forecasted cost at completion compared to the approved budget?

Earned value higher than actual cost indicates that the work is proceeding better than originally budgeted. Put another way, work is being done more efficiently than anticipated. The implication of this is that a cost underrun may occur at project completion.

27-6.   If earned value were below the budget at a point in time, what does that mean in terms of status?

Earned value less than budget signifies that less work has been accomplished than planned at that point in time. This is an indication of behind schedule status, but the critical path schedule would need to be consulted to confirm that.

27-7.   Define cost variance and schedule variance.

Cost variance is earned value minus actual cost, meaning that a positive value is favorable and a negative value is unfavorable. Schedule variance is earned value minus budget, again meaning that a positive value indicates favorable status.

27-8.   What are the two most important characteristics of earned value?

Earned value's most important characteristics are that it is an objective measure of work performed and that it is based on the budgeted value, not the actual cost.

27-9.   From an earned value standpoint, why is it important that tasks be kept relatively short in duration?

As shown in Figure 27-5, it is most difficult to assess earned value when a task is partially complete. By keeping tasks short, this difficulty is minimized.

27-10. Explain how earned value can be used to provide early indication of final cost and schedule position on the project.

Indications of performance against budgeted efficiency and planned accomplishment are available when progress reporting starts. History has shown that projections based even on early results are accurate indicators of a contract's final relative position.

27-11. A control account has just been completed. Budget and actual costs were measured in labor hours. The budget for the account was 250 hours, the actual reported charges were 350 hours, and the account finished one month late on a three month schedule. What is the earned value?

250 hours

True or False

27-12. Earned value is also sometimes called Budgeted Cost for Work Performed, or BCWP.
True.

27-13. The concept of earned value was applied in industry even before the term "earned value" was created.
True.

27-14. Earned value can provide an accurate basis for assessing percent complete for a project.
True.

Chapter 28 The Brick Wall

True or False

28-1.   Earned value visibility can prevent schedule slippage and cost overruns as long as there is a stable statement of work.

False. Earned value will provide earlier and better visibility into project status, allowing better management decisions, but it cannot prevent schedule delays and cost overruns.

28-2. Budget versus actual cost data and detailed schedules are just as accurate for managing a project as the earned value approach but more time consuming, the cost is higher, and there is no common denominator.
False.

Chapter 29 Measuring Accomplishment

29-1. What is a work package?
A work package is a subset of a control account that consists of short duration jobs, including material items that are part of the identified scope of work.

29-2. Where does the work package fit within the framework of the Work Breakdown Structure?
The work package is at the lowest level, below the control account.

29-3. What are the important characteristics of a work package?
The important characteristics of a work package are listed in the "Work Packages" section of this chapter.

29-4. Give an example of a work package.
See "Typical Work Packages" in this chapter.

29-5. Identify the three types of work measurement.
1. Discrete effort
2. Apportioned effort
3. Level of Effort

29-6. Name the six earned value methods used for measuring discrete effort.
The following techniques are used for discrete effort work packages:
1. Incremental milestones
2. 50/50 Method
3. 0/100 Method
4. Equivalent Units
5. Units Complete
6. Percent Complete

29-7. Which earned value methods used for measuring discrete effort should not be used for work packages that are three months long or longer?
50/50 and 0/100.

29-8. For work packages such as inspection or testing that directly relate to the number of items being produced or inspected, what earned value technique would be an appropriate application?
Apportioned Effort.

29-9. When is earned value credit taken for labor?
Earned value is credited for labor when the work is accomplished.

29-10. When is earned value credit taken for material, equipment, and/or purchased services?
There are several possibilities for when earned value credit may be taken for material, equipment, and purchased services including when material is received, when it is placed in inventory, and when it is used.

True or False

29-11. It is at the work package level that cost and schedule should be formally tied together.
True.

29-12. A work package contains a series of control accounts.
False. A control account contains a series of work packages.

29-13. Actual costs must be captured at the work package level so that meaningful variance analysis can be performed.
False. They can be captured at the work package level and analysis is more effective if they are, but they will also support variance analysis if collected at the control account level.

29-14. The Equivalent Units earned value technique is a further refinement of the Units Complete technique.
True.

29-15. Because the earned value for a Level of Effort control account, by definition, always equals budget there will never be any cost variance or schedule variance.
False. There will never be a schedule variance, but there could be a cost variance.

29-16. When the Apportioned Effort earned value technique is used, it will always reflect a negative schedule variance if the direct account it is related to also has a negative schedule variance.
True.

29-17. Variations of the earned value techniques described in this chapter are possible by allowing partial percent complete between incremental milestones or by varying the start and completion values of the 50/50 technique.
True.

Chapter 30 Establishing the Performance Measurement Baseline

30-1. Explain the purpose of the performance measurement baseline (PMB).
The performance measurement baseline (PMB) is used as the master plan against which technical, schedule and cost performance are measured. Variances against the PMB will be analyzed and action taken to resolve them.

30-2. Work packages present the work scope in detail, so how can they be used to control very long duration projects when details are not known for work to be performed years in the future?
Work packages are only prepared for work scheduled to begin in the next 6-9 months (sometimes 12 months). Effort that is part of the project scope beyond that time frame is placed in larger, more summary, groupings called planning packages. The planning packages are converted into detailed work packages using the rolling wave process.

30-3. How far into the future should detailed planning extend?
Detailed planning should extend at least 6 months into the future, and preferably 9-12 months.

30-4. Explain the need for, and use of Management Reserve.
Project reserves are needed for unknown internal scope that has not been identified. It is not for contractual changes in scope or for management mistakes. Project reserves are essential for the project manager to have some flexibility to manage the project.

30-5. When should the performance measurement baseline be established?
The PMB should be established as soon as possible after contract award but at least within 60 to 90 days.

True or False

30-6. The time-phased PMB is the dollar value of work that is planned to be accomplished over time.

True.

30-7. The first step in the baseline establishment process is to develop the schedule.

False. The work scope must be defined first.

30-8. A primary distinguishing characteristic between undistributed budget and management reserve is that UB has an associated scope of work, while MR does not.

True.

30-9. The schedule baseline is a primary input to the establishment of the performance measurement baseline (PMB).

True.

30-10. A major benefit of the work authorization document within a project is that it serves as an in-house contract between the project manager and control account manager (CAM).

True.

Chapter 31 Collecting Actual Cost

31-1. With an earned value reporting system in place, why would a fundamental piece of data such as actual cost still be required?

There will always be management concern for the "bottom line". Actual costs are necessary to make comparisons with planned expenditures and with actual work accomplished. It is one of the three key components of a project management status reporting system.

31-2. How does the accounting view of cost differ from the project management view?

There are fundamental differences in the project orientation of accounting and project management. The accounting system ultimately must provide accurate reports to management and stockholders concerning revenue, profitability, net worth, and cash flow. Accounting's objective is to accurately reflect actual costs to the dollar (actually to the penny). The project management system must provide management and customers the status and projections for the cost and schedule objectives of a particular project. Project management operates on a management by exception philosophy, trying to identify significant cost concerns. Project management is primarily concerned with future costs while accounting is charged with maintaining accurate records of costs which have already been incurred.

31-3. Most accounting systems provide actual cost information too late to be useful in the project management process. Assuming accounting cannot provide its reports as needed by the project, what is a possible solution?

Project management should operate from preliminary, unaudited accounting records. These reports are typically 99% or more accurate anyway, which is already far more accurate than the other components with which it is being compared. They are also often available earlier than the final, official accounting reports. Adjustment may need to be made to the analysis after final actual costs are received.

31-4. Discuss the ways available to guard against incorrect labor time charges (i.e. correct totals but coded to the wrong individual accounts).

These are addressed in detail at the end of the "Accuracy of Reported Actual Costs" section of this chapter.

True or False

31-5.   When cash flow analyses are developed, they should consider material commitments.
True.

31-6.   The total labor cost of a project may be twice what the direct labor charges are because of indirect costs.
True.

31-7.   Estimated ACWP is used when earned value has been credited for a product or service while no actual costs have yet been incurred.
True.

31-8.   Careful coding of time reporting into the accounting system will ensure that charges have been collected to correct accounts.
False. There are many other possible sources of error, as discussed in the chapter. Additional precautions, such as those referenced in the answer to question 4 of this chapter, are necessary to increase confidence in the accuracy of the reported numbers.

Chapter 32 Performance Measurement Calculations and Estimates at Completion

32-1.   Explain how a graphical picture of trend analysis can be manipulated by switching between cost variance or schedule variance (numerical value) versus cost variance percent or schedule variance percent.
The cost variance or schedule variance may be increasing in size, but the percent variation may be decreasing because of the larger base in the denominator. For some projects, therefore, the status can be made to look more favorable by plotting the trend of CV% and SV% rather than the actual values of CV and SV.

32-2.   Explain what is meant by a CPI_E of 1.20.
A CPI_E of 1.20 means that work is being accomplished at 120% efficiency. Stated differently, $1.20 worth of work is accomplished for every dollar spent. This would strongly suggest a possible underrun to the final cost.

32-3.   What different information content is included in the CPI_E and $TCPI_{EAC}$?
The CPI_E looks at performance to date, while the TCPI expresses what the performance must be for the remainder of the control account or project in order to achieve the Estimate at Completion. Therefore, one is a look backwards and the other is a look forward.

32-4.   What information is indicated by a SPI of 0.80?
An SPI of 0.80 indicates that the budgeted work completed to date is only 80% of the budgeted work which was planned to be accomplished to this point.

32-5.   Describe generally how statistical Independent Estimates at Completion (IEACs) are generated to assess the validity of the reported EAC.
An independent Estimate at Completion is a calculated projection of what the final cost will be based on actual costs incurred to date plus a consideration of anticipated future performance and remaining work scope. The projection for future work is based on applying some performance factor expected for future work against the remaining work (i.e. BAC – earned value to date). This performance factor may reflect CPI_E to date, as one likely alternative.

32-6.   Discuss the difference in information content of the total float in CPM and schedule variance.

Total float in CPM can give an indication of how the most critical project work is proceeding on an exception basis while the schedule variance provides an overall indication of total project work completed, without regard to criticality.

32-7.   Explain why being far ahead of schedule may not be desirable in some cases.

In some cases, being too far ahead of schedule may actually cause problems. For example, accelerated work will mean higher cash flow payments earlier in the project if payments are tied to progress. This money may not be available. If something is being produced or manufactured, very early completion of a large number of items may mean storage problems. Lastly, there is a question of liability if design changes occur after items have been prematurely completed. If they had not been completed so early, the changes might have been incorporated instead of having completed items which now must be scrapped or reworked.

32-8.   What does it mean when total float is negative and SPI > 1.0?

With an SPI > 1, the indication is that more total work has been completed than planned. But if the critical items have not been completed, as indicated by the negative total float, then the "wrong" items are being worked on and priorities should be set to reflect criticality of the work effort. In summation, priorities are not being followed.

32-9.   What does it mean when total float is positive and SPI < 1.0?

Positive total float indicates that critical items are being successfully expedited. However, the SPI of less than 1 means that less total work is being accomplished than planned. While a nice job of priority establishment is occurring, the inevitable result if this continues is that more and more items will become critical over time until not all of them can be expedited to meet schedule.

32-10. What is the formula for calculating percent complete using earned value data?

Percent complete = BCWP / BAC x 100%

32-11. Discuss the meaning of price variance and usage variance as applied to material cost variances.

The price variance is the variation in price between budgeted price and actual costs realized. The usage variance reflects variations in quantities used versus quantities budgeted. The formula for price variance is PV = (Earned Value Unit Price – Actual Unit Price) x Actual Quantity and the formula for usage variance is UV = (Earned Value Quantity – Actual Quantity) x Earned Value Unit Price.

32-12. A control account has been completed with an actual cost of $500,000. The approved budget was $450,000 and the earned value is $450,000. The control account was supposed to take 6 months to complete but actually required 8 months. What is the schedule variance?

SV = 0, as it always does for any completed account regardless of how late it was completed.

32-13. Identify the factors that are to be considered in the development of an Estimate to Complete (ETC) and Estimate at Completion (EAC).

- *The "as of" date of the estimate.*
- *The current schedule to completion.*
- *Performance to date.*
- *Remaining work and its anticipated performance.*
- *Rates.*
- *Committed costs for material.*
- *Approved scope changes not yet incorporated in baseline.*

- *Pending scope changes.*
- *Funding constraints.*

True or False

32-14. Acceptable project status may be achieved many ways, including a favorable cost variance that is larger than an unfavorable schedule variance.
False. Cost variances and schedule variances cannot be added together to ascertain project status.

32-15. There are defined analytical approaches used to approximate the schedule variance in time instead of in dollars.
True.

32-16. Precise schedule status may be determined by dividing the cumulative schedule variance by the average earned value per month.
False. Critical path status must always be considered as well when assessing schedule status.

32-17. When using schedule variance conversion techniques to predict time variances, it is more accurate to use cumulative schedule variance divided by average planned accomplishment per month then to use cumulative schedule variance divided by average earned value per month.
False. It is always more accurate (in the general case) to base projections on what work has actually be done rather than on what work was planned to be done.

32-18. An approach sometimes used to interpret data is a rolling 3-month or 6-month average, because it is more stable than current period performance and more responsive to trends than cumulative to date performance.
True.

32-19. Cost variance percent is defined as CV/Earned Value x 100.
True.

32-20. A CPI_E of 0.7 would mean that work is being accomplished in 70% of the time defined in the CPM schedule.
False. An SPI of 0.70 would indicate that 70% of the planned work has been accomplished, without regard to the CPM schedule at all. There is also no indication of whether the same work was accomplished as planned or whether the critical work has been done.

32-21. The Estimate at Completion is a single point value of projected cost.
False. The EAC is a time-phased projection of future cost.

32-22. The Estimate at Completion is calculated by adding actual cost to date to the estimated cost to complete the remaining work scope.
True.

32-23. A comparison of CPI_E with $TCPI_{EAC}$ provides an insight into the validity of the Estimate at Completion.
True.

32-24. The Schedule Performance Index (SPI) and CPM analysis provide different views of schedule status which complement each other.
True.

32-25. An SPI of one means that the project is on schedule.

False. It only means that the total amount of work that should have been completed has been completed. It says nothing about whether the correct work was done. If critical work has been ignored, the project may be behind schedule.

32-26. If SPI > 1.00, that means that SV > 0.

True.

32-27. A Contract Performance Report can be prepared for summary information by organization or by Work Breakdown Structure.

True.

32-28. The following formula is always true for material cost variances: CV = PV + UV, where PV = price variance and UV = usage variance.

True.

32-29. There is no equivalent concept to material price variance and usage variance for labor analysis.

False. For labor analysis, rate variance and usage variance are used. This is directly analogous to material with labor rate replacing material unit cost as a variable.

32-30. There are two types of Estimates at Completion commonly prepared on a project: a monthly forecast which is part of the variance analysis process and a comprehensive EAC performed once or twice per year.

True.

Chapter 33 Variance Analysis and Corrective Action

33-1.   What is being compared through variance analysis?

The approved baseline plan, or Performance Measurement Baseline, is being compared with actual performance, or earned value, when variance analysis is discussed.

33-2.   What is referred to by the term "data traceability"?

"Data traceability" refers to the ability to "trace" a variance from a summary level in the organization or the Work Breakdown Structure down to its source. Conversely, the impact of a control account can be seen in the higher level summary accounts.

33-3.   How is a "significant" variance defined?

Significant variances are those variances which exceed a predetermined threshold that has been defined as being significant.

33-4.   Which of the following requires tighter thresholds:

A. Cumulative data or current month data? Cumulative.

B. Favorable or unfavorable variances? Unfavorable.

C. High WBS levels or low WBS levels? High WBS levels.

33-5.   Why bother to analyze very positive variances?

Unfortunately, very positive variances do not always mean that a very favorable condition exists. It may mean that time or cost is being charged incorrectly. It may also mean that the original budget was much too high, or that the scope was misunderstood. It may indicate a problem with the earned value technique chosen for monitoring that account.

33-6.   Explain the Top 5 approach for reporting variances.

The Top 5 approach refers to the limiting of the number of variances to be analyzed and reported to the owner/client for each reporting period. Rather than addressing a varying num-

ber of variances each month, an agreement is made to only address those variances which are most serious – whether five or ten or some other number. The intent is to allow a steady effort to be defined that can be handled in an effective manner.

33-7. A Variance Analysis Report (VAR) contains cost and schedule performance data. What type of information do the four sections on the VAR requiring narrative analysis need?

Problem analysis, impact of the problem, corrective action plan, and estimate at completion justification.

True or False

33-8. Variance thresholds may be set by considering the absolute value of a variance and/or the variance percent.

True.

33-9. The Estimate at Completion may require review if a significant schedule variance has occurred.

True. A large schedule variance will usually require additional resources to recover the slip, with a probable future cost impact.

33-10. In the "problem analysis" section of the VAR, a general description of the problem should be provided.

False. A description of the specific causes of the problem should be addressed.

33-11. In some instances, it may be appropriate to put a tighter threshold on a control account which is especially technically critical.

True.

Chapter 34 Baseline Revisions and Change Control

34-1. What is the difference between externally and internally driven changes? Which is a greater challenge to project management?

Externally driven changes are not within the defined contract work scope and are directed or authorized by the customer. Internally driven changes are either directed by the project manager or requested by a control account manager and are within the existing contract work scope.

34-2. List three generic requirements for all change control systems.

Three key elements of any change control program are:
* *Early identification of changes.*
* *Thorough evaluation of requested changes.*
* *Documented procedures for addressing, resolving, and incorporating them into the project plan.*

34-3. What is one of the best ways to control scope changes?

One of the most effective ways to control changes is to carefully define the exact scope of work in the contract.

34-4. Discuss at least four ways of controlling changes.

See the list of 9 ways to control changes and associated discussion under "How to Control Changes", in this chapter.

34-5.   Describe what is meant by an "internal replanning".

Internal replanning is a rescheduling of existing work without including any additional work scope. It revises the time-phasing of the work without revising the work itself.

34-6.   What is a "rubber baseline?" Is this an accepted technique for project management?

A rubber baseline is the bane of project control/management. With this approach, the plan is revised to match performance rather than performance expedited to match the plan. It defeats the purpose of a project management system, since the plan becomes a moving target and variance analysis loses its significance. No, this is not an accepted technique for project management.

34-7.   Discuss the proper procedure for closing a control account in progress and replacing it with a new control account.

The current budget of the control account being closed should be set equal to the earned value, because that represents the portion of the work which is actually complete. It also eliminates the schedule variance. This is entirely appropriate since SV is always equal to zero when a control account is complete. The actual costs should remain as is, since they are official corporate records supported by the accounting system. The new control account will have a total budget (or BAC) equal to the remaining budget from the closed account (i.e. BAC – cumulative earned value) plus any budget for new work authorized by the scope change. As the new account is opened, both the earned value and the actual cost will be zero. The planned work accomplishment (or "budget") will be time-phased over the period of performance of the new control account.

True or False

34-8.   The baseline plan, or PMB, is made up of all the time-phased control account budgets.
True.

34-9.   The performance measurement baseline (PMB) must always reflect the technical schedule and budget integrated baseline.
True.

34-10. Changes to the PMB must be identified to their lowest level of impact.
True.

34-11. Change control is an important element in the project management process.
True.

Chapter 35 Subcontract Management

35-1.   Why is it important to define subcontracts separate from material?

The EVMS Guidelines have specific requirements for material that do not apply to subcontracts. The most important difference is that material earned value cannot be taken prior to material delivery.

35-2.   What would be a good definition of major subcontracts?

A major subcontract is any subcontract that requires full compliance with the EVMS Guidelines.

35-3.   What contract type is the lowest risk to the customer? Why?

Firm Fixed Price because the cost risk is minimal. The only risk is that the subcontractor will go out of business, which is a low probability of occurrence.

35-4.   What is the most important consideration when integrating a subcontract into a prime contract? Why?

The WBS. Without a properly integrated WBS, earned value information cannot be accurately transferred to the prime contractor's EVMS

35-5.   Why is it important for the prime contractor CAM to understand the fee arrangement with a subcontractor?

Because the subcontractor's fee is cost to the prime contractor and, therefore, part of the CAM's budget.

35-6.   When a subcontractor has work scope that is contained in more than one of the prime contractor control accounts, how are common WBS elements such as data and project management treated by the prime contractor?

They are allocated to the prime contractor control accounts based on the size of the control account budgets. They should not be placed in the prime contractor's corresponding common WBS elements because they apply specifically to the product being provided by the subcontractor, not the entire product being supplied by the prime contractor. To put them in the prime contractor's common element WBS masks the total cost of the subcontractor's products in the prime contractor's cost summarization.

35-7.   How can the subcontractor's MR and UB be included in the prime contractor's Contract Budget Base?

Either by allocation to the relevant prime contractor control account or by making them part of the prime contractor's MR and UB, but earmarked for subcontractor use only.

35-8.   If the subcontractor were not required to submit a CPR, what are the basic elements of information a prime contractor should require to be submitted in order to comply with its EVMS requirement imposed by the customer?

Either a dollarized milestone plan or a time-phased budget/expenditure profile with a detailed network schedule.

35-9.   When does estimated ACWP need to be used and why?

It is used when the accounting system has not recorded the actual cost of work scope that has been earned or when the accounting system has recorded cost that has not been earned. The EVMSG requires that the actual cost of the work that has been performed be recorded in the same time period that the associated work scope has been performed to prevent inaccurate reporting of cost variance data.

35-10. What is factoring and when is it used?

Factoring is adjusting a subcontractor's budget data to be consistent with the prime contractor control account's authorized budget. It is used when the prime contractor does not have sufficient budget or MR to cover the subcontractor's authorized price. If factoring were not used, the prime contractor would be forced into a Formal Reprogramming action.

35-11. Why does an Inter-Divisional Work Authorization require special treatment?

Because of the possible double counting of corporate G&A and profits to the corporation.

35-12. What is the basic reason that makes a partnership (badgeless organization) difficult for satisfying EVMS reporting requirements to the customer?

Protection of company propriety and private data such as labor and indirect rates.

35-13. What are the three categories of subcontract revisions?

Directed changes, internal replanning, and formal reprogramming.

35-14. What is the condition that exists when an OTB is approved?

The performance measurement baseline (PMB) now exceeds the value of the negotiated contract.

35-15. Must a prime contractor conduct an Integrated Baseline Review on a major subcontract (a subcontract with EVMS flowdown) that already has acquired a Cognizant Federal Agency validation of its EVMS?

Yes.

True or False

35-16. All contracts equal to or greater than $20M are required to be compliant with the EVMS Guidelines.

True.

35-17. It is not required that an FFP contract establish an Integrated Master Schedule.

True, but it is recommended.

35-18. A subcontractor's fee is not part of the prime contractor's cost.

False.

35-19. The CPR DID requires that all subcontracts be identified in Format 2.

False, it requires that all major subcontracts be identified in Format 2.

35-20. A 40/60 incentive share ratio means that the subcontractor receives 60% of an underrun as an increase to its fee.

True.

35-21. The subcontractor's UB should always be contained in the prime contractor's UB, but earmarked for use only by the subcontractor.

False, it can be contained in an appropriate prime contractor control account.

35-22. The cost variance for a Firm Fixed Price subcontract is always zero.

True. If the prime contractor changes the contract payment options because the subcontractor might otherwise quit, it is no longer an FFP subcontract.

35-23. Estimated ACWP never needs to be used for subcontractors that submit CPRs.

False.

35-24. An OTS is always the result of an OTB.

False, an OTS is possible without an OTB.

35-25. A subcontractor's OTS must be included in the baseline schedule of the prime contractor.

True, but it may not cause the prime contractor to be in an OTS condition.

35-26. The prime contractor is responsible for all EVMSG compliance and surveillance activities for subcontracts that require EVMSG compliance without validation.

True.

Section 4 Earned Value
Quiz for Chapters 27 to 35

1.   The Schedule Variance is:

A. Earned Value - Planned Accomplishment.

2.   The Cost Variance is:

B.   *An indication of how well work is being accomplished against the budget for that work.*

3.   Which of the following is not an earned value technique?

D.   *Manpower loading.*

4.   Earned value differs from other cost and schedule control methods in what way?

B.   *Earned value integrates cost and schedule measures into a single value, allowing more accurate assessment of progress.*

5.   The Cost Performance Index (CPI) is a measure of:

A.   *Cost efficiency.*

6.   The To Complete Performance Index (TCPI) is a formula that:

D.   *Uses data from "time now" and calculates the projected efficiency required to support the reported estimate at completion.*

7.   Variance Analysis Reports need not include which of the following?

D.   *Contractor's profit for the reporting period.*

8.   The "Brick Wall" example showed that performance measurement:

D.   *Can give advance warning of cost and schedule problems.*

9.   In June, my budget was 50, my accomplishment was 45, and my actual cost was 48. How am I doing?

C.   *Behind schedule, overrunning cost.*

10.   A Schedule Variance of ($10,000) means that:

B.   *A behind schedule condition is occurring and the status is that $10,000 less budgeted value of work has been completed than planned.*

11.   The CPI_E measured to date is 0.85. Calculations show that the TCPI is 1.25. What should be concluded from this information?

E.   *None of the above.*

Note: This data states that the future performance must be much better than in the past in order for the project to achieve the estimate at completion. It does not indicate that the performance will be better in the future. What this data states is that the EAC is not realistic.

12.   The two most important characteristics of earned value are that it is an objective measure and that it is based on the **_budgeted_** value for the work.

13.   A work package within a control account is using the units complete technique for earned value. In March, 50 widgets were to be completed at a budgeted value of $1,000 per widget. Reported progress shows that 47 actually were completed. Which of the following is true?

C.   *The effort is behind schedule and the earned value for March is $47,000.*

14.   Establishing a budget baseline plan is an iterative 3-step process, including: 1) defining the work, 2) scheduling the work, and 3)?

C.   *Allocating the budgets.*

15.   What are the three classifications of work measurement?

B.   *Discrete, Apportioned Effort, and Level of Effort.*

16.   One unique aspect of Level of Effort work is that:

B.   *Earned value will always equal the scheduled budget value.*

17. A control account is behind schedule and continues to slip further behind schedule.   At completion, it had reached a status that had negatively impacted the total program schedule. What was the schedule variance (BCWP-BCWS) at completion?

Zero.

Note: The keyword in this question is "completion". When a control account is complete, the BCWP equals the BCWS and there is no schedule variance as all scheduled work has been performed.

18. Given the information below, what is the cumulative cost variance to date for this control account?

	January	February	March
Budget	1000	1500	1000
Earned Value	800	1400	1200
Actual cost	900	1600	1100

C. -200 (unfavorable).

19. Find the cumulative end of March status for the Level of Effort work package below.

	January	February	March	April
Budget	100	120	150	130
Actual cost	110	125	157	

B. Schedule variance is zero, cost variance is -22.

20. The cost variance for material can be broken down into what two parts?

C. Usage and price.

21. What is wrong with the following Variance Analysis Report's explanation of the cause of the variance?

"The cause of the May behind schedule and over cost conditions was that we were unable to meet our planned accomplishment and did not get the three Dyna-felt assembly housings built in time for delivery to the next assembly point. In addition, the tasks we did accomplish were performed at a 16% higher rate than expected."

D. It only restates there are problems, but gives no real causes.

22. List the meanings of the following common project management abbreviations/acronyms:

A. EAC   ***Estimate at Completion***
B. BAC   ***Budget at Completion***
C. CPI   ***Cost Performance Index***
D. VAR   ***Variance Analysis Report***
E. SV   ***Schedule Variance***
F. PMB   ***Performance Measurement Baseline***
G. LOE   ***Level of Effort***
H. RAM   ***Responsibility Assignment Matrix***
I.   WBS   ***Work Breakdown Structure***

23. What is the formula that is the basis for all other formulae that exist to derive a calculated EAC?

B. EAC = Actuals (cumulative) + ETC.

24.   The WBS includes all contract scope except LOE work.
      B. False.

25.   The company has a problem. Tom, who was in charge of a critical control account, quit and destroyed most of his cost records. All that could be salvaged were the following bits of information:

      BAC = $120,000
      Cumulative earned value = $40,000
      Cumulative cost variance = -$10,000
      Cumulative schedule variance = +$1,000
      Estimate to Complete = $86,000

      Help to reconstruct the status of Tom's control account by determining the following items. (Hint: These must be worked in the correct order.)

      A. Percent complete   **33%**   ($40,000/$120,000)
      B. Budget (cumulative)   **$39,000**   (from EV - Budget = SV)
      C. Actuals (cumulative)   **$50,000**   (from EV - Actuals = CV)
      D. EAC   **$136,000**   (from Actuals + ETC)
      E. Variance at Completion   **($16,000)**   (from BAC - EAC)
      F. CPI_E **0.80**   (from $40,000/50,000)
      G. $TCPI_{EAC}$ **0.93**   (from ($120,000-$40,000)/($136,000-$50,000)
      H. Calculate a projected EAC using the standard Independent EAC formula of EAC = Actual to date + ETC, where ETC = Work Remaining/CPI
          EAC =   **$150,000**   (from [$50,000 + ($120,000-$40,000)/0.80]

26.   Based on the $TCPI_{EAC}$ and the independent estimate at completion calculated in Question 25. G., and H., what does a brief analysis indicate?
      B. Efficiency must improve a lot just to achieve the EAC, but past performance indicates the reported EAC will be exceeded.

27.   A control account manager identified a conceptual engineering effort as level of effort. It was not until three months after the activity should have started that the manager finally hired the engineers to start the effort. This would be revealed in the control account data as:
      B. A cost underrun.

28.   Variations of the 0/100 and 50/50 earned value methods are not allowed (e.g. 60/40, 75/25 etc.)
      B. False.

29.   Earned value credit for labor is taken when:
      C. The work is accomplished.

30.   An apportioned effort account will always be behind schedule if the direct account it supports is behind schedule.
      A. True.

31.   If a significant schedule variance has occurred, which of the following should be considered as part of the total schedule analysis?
      E. All of the above.

32.   Variance thresholds may need to be changed during the life of a project.
      A. True.

33.   SPI is always greater than 1.00 when the SV is greater than 0.
       A. True.

34.   If total float were negative but SPI > 1.00, that indicates:
       A. There is a lack of proper prioritization.

35.   Using the Percent Complete earned value technique, a control account is reported as 50% complete. The actual cost to date is $300,000, the BAC is $500,000, and the EAC is $600,000. What is the earned value?
       B. $250,000.

36.   Variance analysis thresholds are being set for a project. Which of the following choices would cause you to set your thresholds a little wider than its alternate choice? Indicate by underlining your response.
       A. **_Incremental data_** vs. Cumulative data
       B. **_Favorable variance_** vs. Unfavorable variance
       C. **_Control account_** vs. Summary WBS element

37.   With the Equivalent Units earned value technique, it is possible to earn credit for completed units without any single product (unit) being completed.
       A. True.

38.   A work package is a subdivision of a control account. If a work package were 6 months long, which of the following earned value techniques should NOT be used?
       A. 50/50.
       B. 0/100.

39.   A work package using the 0/100 earned value technique is reported as 95% complete. What is its earned value?
       The earned value is zero.

40.   Level of Effort planning should always be a linear spread of resources since it is only reflecting planned staffing.
       B. False. Resources loading for LOE activities must always reflect the actual planned staffing and includes variable staffing levels between the beginning, peak, and end of the project as well as some possible part time staff.

41.   When is a typical requirement for having the performance measurement baseline available?
       C. 60-90 days after contract award.

42.   Which of the following are NOT used as a calculation method for predicting future performance?
       C. Staffing variance.
       D. CPM.

Chapter 36 Implementation of the Project Management Process

36-1. What is the single most important reason it takes top management support to successfully implement a new project management system?
       Top management support is essential because an implementation cuts across functional organizational lines, meaning that no single department can successfully implement the new system without broad support from above.

36-2.   What is the function of the system description?

The system description is intended to define how the project management system is integrated and functions. This allows common understanding of the roles and responsibilities of all people involved in the in the process. The system description is also used as a starting point for the preparation of detailed procedures.

36-3.   What is the value of a "storyboard" for a new system implementation?

A storyboard is used to assemble the entire process into a single flow of data and information using actual reports and forms as examples. This can be a powerful tool for the definition of the system since it visually depicts the integration of data from the beginning to the end of the process. Ordinarily, colored tape or string is used to connect the flow of data through the project management system. This serves as a tool for verifying the accurate function of the system as well as for process training.

True or False

36-4.   It is imperative that cost and schedule software be bought early in a project management system implementation so that procedures can be developed based on the software specific requirements.

False. This is one of the most common mistakes in system implementations. Software cannot be evaluated and selected until the company has defined the system requirements that the software will need to support.

36-5.   A project management system should never be defined and implemented without input from those who will use the system and its output.

True. Without the support of system users, successful implementation is will be difficult.

36-6.   Procedures should be initially issued in a draft form allowing opportunity for later revision to simplify the process and eliminate steps that are found to be unnecessary or should be changed.

True. This should always be true of procedures. If they cannot be revised when a better way is found, management is losing or restricting the opportunity for improvement.

36-7.   Temporary staff will be required for a new system implementation, with elimination of this staff occurring once routine operation is achieved.

True.

Earned Value Analysis Formulas

Refer to Chapter 32 for explanations of these formulas.

Variances

Cost Variance (CV) = EV - AC = BCWP - ACWP

    CV > 0 is favorable (underrun).

Schedule Variance (SV) = EV - PV = BCWP - BCWS

    SV > 0 is favorable (ahead of schedule).

Variance At Completion (VAC) = BAC - EAC

Variance Percentages

Schedule Variance % $= \dfrac{SV}{PV} \times 100 = \dfrac{SV}{BCWS} \times 100$

Cost Variance % $= \dfrac{CV}{EV} \times 100 = \dfrac{CV}{BCWP} \times 100$

Variance At Completion % $= \dfrac{VAC}{BAC} \times 100$

Performance Indices

There are two general concepts for cost: efficiency and performance. Either can apply to current data, cumulative data, or some increment in between, such as the last three months or the last six months.

Under the efficiency concept, the purpose of the Cost Performance Index (CPI_E) is to indicate the efficiency with which work has been accomplished. A CPI_E > 1.0 is favorable.

$$CPI_E = \frac{EV}{AC} = \frac{BCWP}{ACWP}$$

The formula for this CPI is merely the inverse of the one shown above. A CPI_P < 1.0 is favorable.

$$CPI_P = \frac{AC}{EV} = \frac{ACWP}{BCWP}$$

There is also a performance index for schedule which compares how much work has been accomplished against how much work had been planned to be accomplished. An SPI > 1.0 is favorable.

$$SPI = \frac{EV}{PV} = \frac{BCWP}{BCWS}$$

To Complete Performance Index (TCPI)

A TCPI > 1.0 is the required level of favorable cost performance in the future to achieve the EAC.

$$TCPI_{EAC} = \frac{BAC - EV_{cum}}{EAC - AC_{cum}} = \frac{BAC - BCWP_{cum}}{EAC - ACWP_{cum}}$$

Schedule Variance in Months

Two frequently used formulas are as follows.

1. $$SV\ (months) = \frac{SV_{cum}}{EV_{(Monthly\ Average)*}} = \frac{SV_{cum}}{BCWP_{(Monthly\ Average)*}}$$

2. $$SV\ (months) = \frac{SV_{cum}}{PV_{(Monthly\ Average)*}} = \frac{SV_{cum}}{BCWS_{(Monthly\ Average)*}}$$

*Monthly average can be the cumulative monthly average, current month, or a recent month average (e.g., last 3 month average).

Percent Complete, Percent Planned, and Percent Spent

$$Percent\ Complete = \frac{EV_{cum}}{BAC} \times 100 = \frac{BCWP_{cum}}{BAC} \times 100$$

$$Percent\ Planned = \frac{PV_{cum}}{BAC} \times 100 = \frac{BCWS_{cum}}{BAC} \times 100$$

$$Percent\ Spent = \frac{AC_{cum}}{EAC} \times 100 = \frac{ACWP_{cum}}{EAC} \times 100$$

Budgeted Cost of Work Remaining (BCWR)

$$BCWR = BAC - EV_{cum} = BAC - BCWP_{cum}$$

Estimate At Completion (EAC)

$$EAC = AC_{cum} + ETC = ACWP_{cum} + ETC$$

Independent Estimate At Completion (IEAC)

1. $$IEAC = \left(AC_{cum} + \frac{BAC - EV_{cum}}{(EV_{cum}/AC_{cum})}\right) = \left(ACWP_{cum} + \frac{BAC - BCWP_{cum}}{(BCWP_{cum}/ACWP_{cum})}\right)$$

Since earned value divided by actual cost is the CPI_E and the calculation assumes the same cost performance in the future as in the past, the calculation can be simplified to:

$$IEAC = \frac{BAC}{CPI_E}$$

2. $\text{IEAC} = \left(\text{AC}_{cum} + \dfrac{(\text{BAC} - \text{EV}_{cum})}{(80\% \times \text{CPI}_E) + (20\% \times \text{SPI})}\right) = \left(\text{ACWP}_{cum} + \dfrac{(\text{BAC} - \text{BCWP}_{cum})}{(80\% \times \text{CPI}_E) + (20\% \times \text{SPI})}\right)$

3. $\text{IEAC} = \left(\text{AC}_{cum} + \dfrac{(\text{BAC} - \text{EV}_{cum})}{(\text{CPI}_E \times \text{SPI})}\right) = \left(\text{ACWP}_{cum} + \dfrac{(\text{BAC} - \text{BCWP}_{cum})}{(\text{CPI}_E \times \text{SPI})}\right)$

4. $\text{IEAC} = \text{AC}_{cum} + (\text{BAC} - \text{EV}_{cum}) = \text{ACWP} + (\text{BAC} - \text{BCWP}_{cum})$

Independent Estimated Completion Date (IECD)

In calculating an Estimate at Completion (EAC), the date on which it is believed that the work will be completed, must also be estimated. There are several methods available to calculate the number of months required to complete the work remaining. The calculation may be based on:

- The current budget value,
- An average budget value,
- The current earned value,
- An average earned Value.

The Estimated Completion Date is determined by adding the estimated number of months required to complete the remaining work to the time now date.

Idependent Estimated Completion Date (IECD) = Time Now (in months) + Months to Complete

1. $\text{IECD} = \text{Time Now (months)} + \dfrac{\text{BAC} - \text{EV}_{cum}}{\text{PV}_{cur}} = \dfrac{\text{BAC} - \text{BCWP}_{cum}}{\text{BCWS}_{cur}}$

2. $\text{IECD} = \text{Time Now (months)} + \dfrac{\text{BAC} - \text{EV}_{cum}}{\text{PV}_{avg}} = \dfrac{\text{BAC} - \text{BCWP}_{cum}}{\text{BCWS}_{avg}}$

3. $\text{IECD} = \text{Time Now (months)} + \dfrac{\text{BAC} - \text{EV}_{cum}}{\text{EV}_{cur}} = \dfrac{\text{BAC} - \text{BCWP}_{cum}}{\text{BCWP}_{cur}}$

4. $\text{IECD} = \text{Time Now (months)} + \dfrac{\text{BAC} - \text{EV}_{cum}}{\text{EV}_{avg}} = \dfrac{\text{BAC} - \text{BCWP}_{cum}}{\text{BCWP}_{avg}}$

Performance to Date vs. Estimated Completion Dates (ECD)

$\text{Performance to Date (average)} = \dfrac{\text{EV}_{cum}}{\text{Months to Date}} = \dfrac{\text{BCWP}_{cum}}{\text{Months to Date}}$

$\text{Performance Required (average)} = \dfrac{\text{BAC} - \text{EV}_{cum}}{\text{ECD} - \text{Months to Date}} = \dfrac{\text{BAC} - \text{BCWP}_{cum}}{\text{ECD} - \text{Months to Date}}$

Labor Variances

Rate Variance = (EV Rate - AC Rate) x AC Hours
= (BCWP Rate - ACWP Rate) x ACWP Hours

Efficiency Variance = (EV Hours - AC Hours) x EV Rate
= (BCWP Hours - ACWP Hours) x BCWP Rate

Material Variances

Price Variance = (EV Unit Price - AC Unit Price) x AC Quantity
        = (BCWP Unit Price - ACWP Unit Price) x ACWP Quantity

Usage Variance = (EV Quantity - AC Quantity) x EV Unit Price
        = (BCWP Quantity - ACWP Quantity) x BCWP Unit Price

Abbreviations

AA	Advance Agreement
AC	Actual Cost
ACWP	Actual Cost of Work Performed
ADM	Arrow Diagramming Method
AE	Apportioned Effort
ANSI/EIA	American National Standard Institute/Electronic Industries Alliance
AUW	Authorized Unpriced Work
BAC	Budget at Completion
BCR	Baseline Change Request
BCWP	Budgeted Cost for Work Performed
BCWR	Budgeted Cost of Work Remaining
BCWS	Budgeted Cost for Work Scheduled
BEI	Baseline Execution Index
BOE	Basis of Estimate
CA	Control Account
CADS	Cost Accounting Disclosure Statement
CAM	Control Account Manager
CAP	Control Account Plan
CAS	Cost Accounting Standards
CBB	Contract Budget Base
CFA	Cognizant Federal Agency
COCOMO	Constructive Cost Model
COM	Cost of Money
CP	Critical Path
CPAF	Cost Plus Award Fee
CPFF	Cost Plus Fixed Fee
CPIF	Cost Plus Incentive Fee
CPI_E	Cost Performance Index Efficiency
CPI_P	Cost Performance Index Performance
CPLI	Critical Path Length Index
CPM	Critical Path Method
CPR	Contract Performance Report
CTC	Contract Target Cost
CTP	Contract Target Price
CV	Cost Variance
CWBS	Contract Work Breakdown Structure
DB	Distributed Budget
EAC	Estimate at Completion
ECD	Estimated Completion Date
EDI	Electronic Data Interchange

EF	Early Finish
EOC	Element of Cost
ES	Early Start
ETC	Estimate to Complete
EV	Earned Value
EVMIG	Earned Value Management Implementation Guide
EVMS	Earned Value Management System
EVMSG	Earned Value Management System Guidelines
EVT	Earned Value Technique
FF	Finish-to-Finish
FF	Free Float
FFP	Firm Fixed Price
FPI	Fixed Price Incentive
FS	Finish to Start
G & A	General and Administrative
GAO	Government Accountability Office
GASP	Generally Accepted Scheduling Principles
IEAC	Independent Estimate at Completion
IECD	Independent Estimated Completion Date
IMP	Integrated Master Plan
IMS	Integrated Master Schedule
IPT	Integrated Product Team (Work Team)
IPTL	Integrated Product Team Lead
LF	Late Finish
LOB	Line Of Balance
LOE	Level of Effort
LS	Late Start
MPS	Master Project Schedule
MR	Management Reserve
MTC	Months to Complete
MTD	Months to Date
NDIA	National Defense Industrial Association
OBS	Organization Breakdown Structure
ODC	Other Direct Costs
OH	Overhead
OTB	Over Target Baseline
OTS	Over Target Schedule
PASEG	Planning and Scheduling Excellence Guide
PDM	Precedence Diagramming Method
PERT	Program Evaluation and Review Technique
PM	Project Manager
PMB	Performance Measurement Baseline
PMO	Project Management Office
PMSC	Program Management Systems Committee

PP	Planning Package
PV	Planned Value
PV	Price Variance
PVR	Planned Value Remaining
RAM	Responsibility Assignment Matrix
RFI	Request for Information
RFP	Request for Proposal
RFQ	Request for Quotation
SF	Start-to-Finish
SLPP	Summary Level Planning Package
SOO	Statement of Objectives
SOW	Statement of Work
SPI	Schedule Performance Index
SQA	Software Quality Assurance
SRA	Schedule Risk Assessment
SS	Start-to-Start
SSI	Standard Surveillance Instruction
SV	Schedule Variance
TAB	Total Allocated Budget
TCPI	To Complete Performance Index
TF	Total Float
UB	Undistributed Budget
UV	Usage Variance
VAC	Variance at Completion
VAR	Variance Analysis Report
WBS	Work Breakdown Structure
WP	Work Package

Glossary

Accrued Costs. The concept of recognizing costs at the time of actual constructive receipt of goods and services, regardless of whether an invoice has been received and actual payment made.

Activity. A time and resource consuming component of a schedule.

Actual Cost (AC). See Actual Cost of Work Performed (ACWP).

Actual Cost of Work Performed (ACWP). The costs actually incurred and recorded in accomplishing the work performed within a given time period. The ACWP may include estimated actual costs or accruals of significant material items for which performance has been claimed but invoice payment has not been recorded in the accounting system.

Actual Direct Costs. Those costs identified specifically with a contract, based upon the contractor's cost identification and accumulation system.

Allocated Budget. See Total Allocated Budget.

American National Standard Institute, Electronic Industries Alliance (ANSI/EIA). ANSI/EIA-748 is the shortened title of the Government Electronics & Information Technology (GEIA) document containing the 32 Earned Value Management System Guidelines (EVMSG).

Applied Direct Cost. The actual direct costs recognized in the time period associated with the consumption of labor, material and other direct resources without regard to their date of commitment or the date of payment. These amounts are charged to work-in-process when any of the following takes place:

1. Labor, material and other direct resources are actually consumed.

2. Material resources are withdrawn from inventory for use.

3. Material resources are received that are uniquely identified to the contract and scheduled for use within sixty (60) days.

4. Major components or assemblies that are specifically and uniquely identified to single, serially numbered end-item that are received on a line flow basis.

5. Progress payments are made to suppliers for resources consumed.

Apportioned Effort. A method of planning and measuring the earned value for effort that is both (a) related in direct proportion to measured effort and (b) by itself is not readily measurable or broken into discrete work packages.

Authorized Unpriced Work (AUW). Work that the customer has authorized to be performed, but for which a formal proposal has not yet been submitted or negotiated.

Authorized Work. Effort that has been definitized and is on contract, plus that effort for which definitized contract costs have not been agreed to, but for which written authorization has been received.

Backward Pass. A method of analyzing the schedule by starting with the required end date and working backwards through the network to determine when prior activities must start and finish supporting the defined completion date. The Backward Pass determines the late dates, i.e. the latest any activity in the network can start or finish supporting the overall required completion date of the network. The Backward Pass also establishes the total float in the network.

Bar Chart. A schedule charting technique that graphically displays when specific activities are to take place. Also known as a Gantt Chart.

Baseline. The original plan for a project, control account, or work package plus or minus approved scope changes. Also see Performance Measurement Baseline.

Baseline Change. An approved scope, schedule, and/or budget revision to an approved baseline.

Baseline Change Request (BCR). Document authorizing a change to a control account work authorization. It explains the changes in the scope of work, schedule, and/or budget.

Baseline Execution Index (BEI). The BEI measures the activities that were completed as a percentage of the activities that should have been completed per the original (baseline) plan. Well executed schedules have a BEI of 0.95 or greater.

Basis of Estimate (BOE). The descriptive document to support the proposal's cost basis, including all necessary details; such as, technical aspects, labor and overhead rates, subcontractor estimates, material, etc.

Bill of Material (BOM). A list of the material requirements for the task or project.

Bottom-up Approach. The bottom-up scheduling technique begins schedule development at the lowest level of the network, i.e., at the activity level, and then summarizes to higher levels of the Work Breakdown Structure. This low level of definition illustrates the activities required to complete an established deliverable, goal or milestone, and identifies additional milestones that could affect the final outcome of the project.

Budget. The time-phased budgeted value for planned work. It is a plan for value of work to be accomplished and is compared with Earned Value to determine overall schedule position. Also referred to as Budgeted Cost for Work Scheduled (BCWS).

Budget At Completion (BAC). The sum of all performance budgets established for the contract. BAC is a term that may also be applied to lower levels, such as the PMB or at the control account level.

Budgeted Cost for Work Performed (BCWP). The value of completed work expressed as the value of the performance budget assigned to that work. This is equal to the sum of the budgets for completed work packages, completed portions of open work packages, apportioned effort earned on the base accounts, and the value of LOE activities. BCWP is synonymous with Earned Value.

Budgeted Cost for Work Scheduled (BCWS). The sum of the performance budgets for all work scheduled to be accomplished within a given time period. This includes detailed work packages, apportioned effort, LOE packages, planning packages, and Summary Level Planning Packages.

Budgeted Cost of Work Remaining (BCWR). The total of the performance budgets for all work yet to be accomplished.

Burden. The costs incurred by an organization for common or joint objectives that cannot be identified specifically with a particular project or activity and thus are distributed over the appropriate direct labor and/or material base (also known as indirect costs and overhead costs).

Check Estimate. Sometimes called "Fair Value Estimate," a Check Estimate may be requested when a second opinion is needed to evaluate an estimate or series of bids.

Combination Chart. A schedule presentation format that combines the Milestone Chart and the Bar Chart for better representation of status. By adding objective milestones along the schedule bars, it more clearly displays partial completion of activities.

Commitments. The incurrence of a liability for goods or services. It is that portion of the goods or services that have been ordered, but not received. The point where a company enters into an agreement with a supplier, generally when a purchase order is transmitted is considered the point of original commitment.

Contract Budget Base (CBB). The sum of the negotiated contract cost plus the estimated cost of authorized unpriced work (AUW).

Contract Performance Report (CPR). A contractually required customer report defined in Department of Defense Instruction 5000.02 and in Data Item Description (DID) DI-MGMT-81466A. Normally generated monthly to formally provide cost and schedule status information for project management and for the customer on major government projects. The CPR provides early identification of problems having significant cost, schedule and technical impact, effects of management actions and project status information for use in making and validating management decisions.

Contract Target Cost (CTC). The dollar value (excluding fee or profit) negotiated in the original contract plus the cumulative cost (excluding fee or profit) applicable to all definitized changes to the contract. It consists of the estimated cost negotiated for a cost plus fixed fee contract and the definitized target cost for an incentive contract. The contract target cost does not include the value of authorized unpriced work, and is thus equal to the contract budget base only when all authorized work has been negotiated/definitized.

Contract Target Price (CTP). The negotiated cost plus planned profit or fee.

Contract Work Breakdown Structure (CWBS). The complete WBS for a contract. It includes the government or customer approved WBS for reporting purposes and its discretionary extension to the lower levels by the contractor, in accordance with MIL-STD-881 (current version) and the contract statement of work. It includes all the elements for the hardware, software, data, and/or services that are the responsibility of the contractor.

Control Account (CA). A management control point at which budgets (resource plans) and actual costs are accumulated and compared to earned value for management control purposes. A control account is a natural management point for planning and control since it represents the work assigned to one responsible organizational element (or work team) for a single project WBS element.

Control Account Manager (CAM). A single manager within the organizational structure who has been given the authority and responsibility to manage one or more control accounts.

Control Account Plan (CAP). The detailed plan prepared by the CAM showing time phased planning of tasks, by element of cost (EOC), and the associated budgets for all work packages and planning packages within a control account.

Cost Element. Synonymous with Element of Cost (EOC). Cost elements are types of costs such as direct labor, direct material, subcontracts, and other direct costs.

Cost Accounting Disclosure Statement (CADS). A seven-part document designed to meet the requirements of Public Law 100-679, describing the contractor and its contract cost accounting practices.

Cost Accounting Standards (CAS). A set of 19 standards and rules designed to achieve uniformity and consistency in the measurement, assignment, and allocation of costs to government contracts.

Cost Performance Index (CPI$_E$). An indicator of the cost efficiency at which work is being performed. CPI = BCWP/ACWP. If the result is greater than 1.0, the CPI indicates that the work was performed in a more cost efficient manner and for less cost than was planned. Conversely, if the result is less than 1.0, the CPI indicates a less efficient use of resources at a cost greater than planned.

Cost Performance Index (CPI_P). The ratio of actual cost expenditure to earned value. It is the reciprocal of CPI_E and under the performance concept, the purpose of the CPI_P is to indicate the actual cost of each planned dollar of work accomplished.

Cost Plus Award Fee (CPAF). A type of cost plus contract that pays a fee based on the contractor's work performance. In some contracts, the fee is determined subjectively by an awards fee board; whereas in others the fee is based on objective performance metrics.

Cost Plus Fixed Fee (CPFF). A type of cost plus contract that pays a pre-determined fee that was agreed upon at the time of contract formation.

Cost Plus Incentive Fee (CPIF). A type of cost plus contract that has a larger fee awarded for contracts which meet or exceed performance targets, including any cost savings.

Cost Variance (CV). The difference between Budgeted Cost for Work Performed (BCWP) and Actual Cost of Work Performed (ACWP). CV = BCWP - ACWP. A positive value indicates a favorable position and a negative value indicates an unfavorable condition.

Crash Cost. To shorten the duration of activities, additional cost may be incurred. This cost may result from of overtime pay at premium rates, additional costs paid to expedite vendors when shops are full and orders are backlogged, using more expensive labor, or the result of reduced productivity because of the need to work excessive hours. Whatever the cause, an intelligent decision cannot be made about schedule acceleration until the cost for shortening the schedule is known.

Critical Path. A sequence of discrete work packages and planning packages (or lower level tasks/activities) in the network that has the longest total duration through an end point that is calculated by the schedule software application. Discrete work packages and planning packages (or lower level tasks/activities) along the critical path have the least amount of float/slack (scheduling flexibility) and cannot be delayed without delaying the finish time of the end point effort. 'Critical Path' has the same definition as 'Project Critical Path' with the exception that the end point can be a milestone or other point of interest in the schedule. Example: a critical path could be run to PDR, CDR, and/or first flight, etc. within a system development demonstration contract.

Critical Path Length Index (CPLI). The CPLI is an indicator of the likelihood of completing the schedule on time. A CPLI of 1.00 means the project must accomplish one day's worth of work for every day that passes. A CPLI less than 1.00 means the project schedule execution is inefficient with regard to the schedule completion (i.e., slipping from the baseline date). Likewise, a CPLI greater than 1.00 means that the project schedule is running efficiently in relationship to the schedule end (i.e., finishing before the baseline date).

Critical Path Method (CPM). A scheduling methodology/management technique that makes analytical use of information regarding the critical path and other sequential paths through the schedule logic network.

Decision Tree. A diagram depicting a set of possible alternative paths available to a decision maker. Assignment of probability estimates for the factors (cost, resources, etc.) allows consideration of all possible alternatives and the choice of the best alternatives.

Direct Cost. That portion of labor, material, and other direct costs (ODCs) incurred or expended to meet contractual specifications for an end product or other related service specifically identifiable to the contractually authorized task. These costs are charged directly and finally to the contract, without distribution to an overhead unit.

Direct Labor. That portion of labor expended in the actual design, tooling, testing and the physical application of labor to material altering its shape, form, nature, or fulfilling a contractual requirement for service.

Directed Dates. Specific dates applied to schedule network logic that supersede the network calculations.

Discrete Effort. Tasks that are directly related to the completion of project specific end-products or services, and can be directly planned and measured.

Distributed Budget. The budget divided into specific control accounts: discrete effort, apportioned effort, and level of effort work packages. The remainder of distributed budget may be assigned to long range planning packages that will later be divided into work packages in accordance with the rolling wave technique.

Early Finish (EF). The earliest an activity can finish based on the schedule logic and assigned durations. It assumes that all previous project activities start and finish on their earliest possible dates.

Early Start (ES). The earliest an activity can start based on the schedule logic and assigned durations. It assumes that all previous project activities start and finish on their earliest possible dates.

Earned Value (EV). The budget value for completed work. See Budgeted Cost for Work Performed.

Earned Value Management System (EVMS). The processes and procedures for managing certain contracts and projects.

Earned Value Management Implementation Guide (EVMIG). A document that provides guidance to be used during the implementation and surveillance of an EVMS established in compliance with DOD Guidelines.

Earned Value Management System Guidelines (EVMSG). The set of 32 guidelines established by the ANSI/EIA-748 that defines the requirements that an EVMS must meet.

Earned Value Technique (EVT). Defines the method used to earn budgeted value for work accomplished on a control account or work package. Examples of EVTs include weighted milestones, percent complete, 50/50, and level of effort.

Efficiency Variance. The efficiency variance is the difference between earned hours and actual hours, expended expressed in dollars. It is calculated by the formula: (earned hours - actual hours) x earned hourly rate.

Electronic Data Interchange (EDI). American National Standard Institute (ANSI) established an industry-wide electronic format to communicate common information.

Element of Cost (EOC). See Cost Element.

Equivalent Units Technique. This earned value technique is used for work packages that contain a series of like units with repetitive operations, with planning based on unit standards, standard hours and pay points. It is the most detailed method for earned value determination.

Estimate At Completion (EAC). The current projected cost of performing all authorized work at any level of the project; i.e., work package to total contract. It includes all actual direct costs, plus indirect costs allocable to the contract, plus the estimate of costs (direct and indirect) for authorized work remaining. EAC = Cumulative ACWP + Estimate to Complete.

Estimate To Complete (ETC). The value (in dollars and/or hours) developed to represent a realistic appraisal of the cost of the work still required to be accomplished in completing a task or the project.

Estimate Traceability. The ability to accurately summarize estimated costs (Vertical Traceability) as well as reconcile estimate changes over time (Historical Traceability).

Estimated Actual Costs. An adjustment to actual costs recorded in the accounting system to ensure that ACWP is being recorded in the same period as the BCWP is recorded. The adjustment can be positive or negative. The most common use of estimated actual costs is to account for the lag from receiving material (earning value) to accruing the cost in the accounting system.

External Change. Customer directed changes to the contract that can be in the form of a definitized change order or an authorized unpriced change order that calls for a change in the original plan, most often as a change in the scope of the contract in terms of a cost, schedule, or technical parameters or a combination thereof.

Event. A network component, usually a milestone that occurs at a particular instant in time and does not consume time or resources in a schedule network diagram.

Fair Value Estimate. An estimate developed by a third party using the same documentation and conditions utilized in the development of the original estimate. It is typically used to verify scope and reasonableness of assumptions in estimates developed by others. It may also be used to confirm bids in response to Requests for Proposals (RFP). Also known as a Check Estimate.

50/50 Technique. This earned value technique is used when work packages are scheduled to begin in one period and be completed within two consecutive accounting periods or less. The 50/50 technique is typically used when the work package begins in one reporting period and completes in the next reporting period.

Finish-To-Finish (FF). A relationship between two activities that states that one activity cannot finish until another activity finishes, although they may both start independent of each other.

Finish-To-Start (FS). A relationship between two activities that states that one activity cannot start until a prior activity finishes.

Firm Fixed Price (FFP). Also called Lump Sum. A specific price agreed to before award of the contract and not subject to adjustment except for customer approved changes in the scope of work.

Fixed Price Incentive Fee (FPIF). A type of fixed price contract that specifies a target cost, a target profit, a target price, a ceiling price, and one or more share ratios; i.e. the incentive fee.

Float. The amount of time that a task can be delayed without delaying the finish date of the schedule or succeeding task(s). Float is synonymous with slack.

Flow Process Chart. A graphical presentation used in Line Of Balance (LOB) scheduling that shows the cumulative delivery requirement for the product being manufactured. See "Setback Chart" and "Line Of Balance".

Formal Reprogramming. Replanning of the effort remaining in the contract, resulting in a new budget allocation and a performance measurement baseline (PMB) that exceeds the contact budget base (CBB). This process may adjust or eliminate cumulative schedule and cost variances. Formal reprogramming actions require customer coordination and/or approval prior to implementation. See also over target baseline (OTB).

Forward Pass. A calculation through the network logic to determine the earliest that each subsequent activity can start and the earliest that the project can finish. The Forward Pass determines the early dates for all activities.

Fragnets. Standardized network modules that describe a specific task or series of tasks, used repetitively as needed in the development of a network.

Free Float. Defines the amount of time an activity can be delayed or extended without impacting the succeeding activity in the network. It is determined by comparing the early finish of an activity and the early start of the next activity.

"Fully Crashed" Critical Path. A "fully crashed" critical path means that all of the activities along that path have been shortened as much as possible.

Functional Organization. An organization or group of organizations with a common operational orientation such as Quality Control, Engineering, Software Engineering, Manufacturing and Constructing Crafts, Purchasing, and Accounting.

Gantt Chart. A schedule charting technique that graphically displays when specific activities are to take place. Also known as a Bar Chart.

General and Administrative (G&A). Expenses incurred in the direction, control, and administration of a company. These expenses are spread over the total direct base as documented in the CAS Disclosure Statement.

Hammocks. A group or series of activities and their related logic. Duration is based upon the start of the first event and the finish of the last event in a series of sequential activities.

Historical Traceability. The ability to accurately track changes over time so that all estimates, scope, schedule, and budget can be related to each other and to the total project.

Horizontal Traceability. Horizontal traceability, or integration, means that schedules independently maintained by different divisions or departments, or between subcontractors, reflect the same schedule dates between schedules at the same level of detail. Horizontal integration is demonstrated by linking predecessor and successor relationships to a supportable and rational plan that summarizes vertically to support the higher level project plan.

Incremental Milestone Technique. This earned value technique is generally used when discrete work packages exceed two months in duration.

Independent Estimate at Completion (IEAC). A mathematically computed forecast based on performance to date and the mathematical projection of this performance to derive the estimated contract cost at completion.

Independent Estimated Completion Date (IECD). Mathmatically computed forecasts based on either performance (EV) or planned (PV) to derive an estimated completion date.

Indirect Budget. See Burden.

Indirect Costs. See Burden.

Integrated Master Plan (IMP). An event-based plan consisting of a hierarchy of project events, with each event supported by specific accomplishments, and each accomplishment associated with specific criteria to be satisfied for its completion. In many instances, IMP events are specified in a contract.

Integrated Master Schedule (IMS). A schedule network that contains all the detailed work packages (including activities and milestones) and planning packages to support the events, accomplishments, and criteria of the IMP (if applicable). It is directly traceable to the CWBS and the contract statement of work. The IMP and IMS are used to track and execute the project.

Integrated Product Team (IPT). A grouping of project personnel along project objective lines rather than along organizational lines. Integrated product teams are work teams that represent a transition from a functional organization structure to a multi-functional project objective arrangement.

Interim Budget. Budget furnished to projects or control accounts on an interim basis for contractually authorized tasks for which a firm bid or estimate may not yet have been completed. This budget may be for the baseline planning of work and/or to cover scope of the authorized work that must begin immediately. These amounts are entered into the Budget Logs until replaced by firm budget amounts. Interim budget will be replaced by firm budget amounts upon submittal of an estimate for the authorized work, and will be adjusted, if needed, upon negotiations with the customer.

Internal Replanning. Replanning actions performed by a project for remaining scope of work within the budget and schedule constraints of the contract. The company is required to notify the customer of all internal replanning actions (usually as part of the monthly performance report), but the customer has no approval/ disapproval authority over this action.

Internal Variance Thresholds. Variance thresholds established by the project manager, typically at the control account level, that may be equal to or more stringent than the contract reporting thresholds. The project manager may change internal variance thresholds during the period of contract performance.

Labor Efficiency or Usage Variance. The difference between earned hours and actual hours, expressed in dollars. When applied to labor cost variances, it is defined by the formula: (earned hours - actual Hours) x earned hourly rate.

Labor Rate Variances. The portion of a labor cost variance that is caused by a difference between the earned labor rate and the actual labor rate. Labor rate variance expressed as dollars = (earned rate - actual rate) x actual hours.

Lags. Introduction of a time delay between activities in a network. A lag may be positive or negative and indicates the amount time delay in an activity relationship. Lags may be used with any activity relationship.

Late Finish (LF). The latest that an activity can finish and still support the overall required completion date of the project based on the schedule logic and defined durations.

Late Start (LS). The latest that an activity can start and still support the overall required completion date of the project based on the schedule logic and defined durations.

Learning Curve. An adjustment to productivity rates in the development of an estimate that reflects the fact that the per unit cost of manufacturing or installing a unit decreases as the number of units increases.

Level of Effort (LOE). Effort of a general or supportive nature that does not produce finite end products and cannot be practically measured by discrete earned value techniques. Earned value is measured by the passage of time. For LOE activity, BCWP = BCWS.

Line Of Balance (LOB). A scheduling technique employed in manufacturing that relies on production rates at specific checkpoints in the manufacturing or production process, comparing planned and actual product counts.

Major Subcontractor. A subcontractor performing a complex portion of a contract that requires a flow down of EVMS and reporting requirements with various degrees of system integration, reviews, acceptance and control of subcontractor system and reporting. Major subcontractors are designated as a result of customer negotiation or by management direction.

Management Reserve (MR). An amount of the total allocated budget (TAB) withheld for management control purposes rather than designated for the accomplishment of a specific task or set of tasks. It is not a part of the performance measurement baseline (PMB), but it is included in the total allocated budget (TAB). Management reserve cannot be a negative value.

Master Project Schedule (MPS). A summary level schedule for a project depicting overall project phasing and interfaces, contractual milestones, and other significant project elements.

Material Price Variance. See Price Variance.

Material Usage Variance. See Usage Variance.

Milestone. A zero-duration schedule event or point in time such as "begin spacecraft integration," "release drawings," "pipe inspection complete." A milestone is measurable but does not consume time or resources.

Monte Carlo. A computer based simulation technique used for evaluating uncertainty.

Network Crashing. Also known as Schedule Acceleration. The process of shortening the schedule if the required duration is longer than the time actually available.

Negative Float. Negative float means that the project end date cannot be met based on the current status and the forecast plan for accomplishing the remaining work.

Negotiated Contract Cost. The estimated cost negotiated on a cost plus fixed fee contract or the negotiated contract target cost in either a fixed price incentive contract, a cost plus incentive fee contract, or a cost plus award fee contract. Also see contract target cost.

Network Schedule. A schedule format in which the activities and milestones are represented along with the interdependencies among activities, work packages and planning packages. It expresses the logic (i.e., predecessors and successors) of how the project is to be accomplished. Network schedules are the basis for critical path analysis, a method for identification and assessment of schedule priorities and impacts. Also see Integrated Master Schedule (IMS).

Organization Breakdown Structure (OBS). The hierarchical arrangement for an organization's management structure, graphically depicting the reporting relationships. Normally, the OBS is limited to showing only managerial positions down to the Control Account Manager, but may depict lower organizational levels.

Other Direct Costs (ODC). Costs other than labor and material that may be directly charged to a contract. Typical examples of ODC are such items as travel, computer time, and services.

Overhead Costs. See Burden.

Over Target Baseline (OTB). An established performance measurement baseline (PMB) that exceeds the value of the negotiated contract. An OTB results from a formal reprogramming process with the prior coordination or approval (as applicable) of the customer.

Over Target Schedule (OTS). An established baseline schedule that extends beyond the contract milestones or delivery dates. An OTS requires the prior coordination or approval (as applicable) of the customer.

Percent Complete Technique. The least desirable of the discrete earned value techniques as it is a subjective measure of status.

Performance Measurement Baseline (PMB). The time phased budget plan against which contract performance is measured. It consists of the time phased budgets assigned to scheduled control accounts and the applicable indirect budgets. For future effort, not planned to the control account level, the performance measurement baseline also includes budgets assigned to higher level CWBS elements and undistributed budgets. It equals the total allocated budget (TAB) less management reserve

Program Evaluation and Review Technique (PERT). An early network diagram technique and algorithm that allowed three time estimates for determining an activity's likely duration: an optimistic, a most likely, and a pessimistic duration.

Planned Value (PV). See Budgeted Cost for Work Scheduled (BCWS).

Planning Package (PP). If far-term effort in a control account cannot be subdivided into detailed work packages, it may be identified in larger planning packages for baseline control purposes. The budget for a planning package is identified specifically to the work that is intended, is time-phased to the extent possible, and has controls which prevent its use in performance of other work. Eventually, all work in planning packages will be planned to the appropriate level of detail in work packages before that work commences.

Precedence Diagramming Method (PDM). A scheduling technique that employs network diagrams displaying relationships between activities to portray a defined scope of work.

Price Variance (PV). The portion of a material cost variance that is caused by the difference between the planned/earned unit cost of a purchased item and its actual unit cost. Price variance is derived as follows: PV = (earned price per unit - actual price per unit) x actual quantity received or issued.

Program. A long-term undertaking that is usually made up of more than one project.

Project. A complex effort made up of interrelated tasks performed by various organizations, with a well-defined technical objective, schedule, and budget.

Project Risk Analysis. The system that provides a continuous analysis of identified risks, with respect to their impact on project cost, schedule and technical performance.

Rate Variance. See Labor Rate Variance.

Resource. Anything used in completing a project or program. Resources include people (labor), material and equipment. Ultimately, resources are measured in dollars (or appropriate currency) although labor resources may be measured in hours.

Resource Leveling. The process of analyzing resource usage over time and modifying it to make the distribution more efficient.

Responsibility Assignment Matrix (RAM). A graphic representation that reflects the integration of project participants (internal organizations, work teams, subcontractors) with individual CWBS elements to form control accounts.

Request for Information (RFI). A solicitation sent to a broad base of potential suppliers for the purpose of conditioning suppliers' minds, developing strategy, building a database, and preparing for an RFP or RFQ.

Request for Proposal (RFP). An early stage in a procurement process, issuing an invitation for suppliers, often through a bidding process, to submit a proposal on a specific commodity or service. The RFP process brings structure to the procurement decision and allows the risks and benefits to be identified clearly upfront.

Request for Quotation (RFQ). A standard business process whose purpose is to invite suppliers into a bidding process to bid on specific products or services.

Risk. The level of uncertainty associated with an outcome. In programs/projects, there are typically three components of risk: technical, schedule and cost.

Risk Assessment. An organized process to quantify risk so that it can be evaluated and adjustments in priorities made as appropriate.

Rolling Wave Planning. The progressive refinement of detailed work definition by continuous subdivision of planning packages into work packages. Budget and schedule planning details are developed for the near term and more summary allocations are made for future periods. Detail is developed for the future work as information becomes available.

Rubber Baseline. The practice of modifying the project plan to closely match the cumulative actual cost line (time-phased). The work to be done remains in the future while the budget for the work is moved into the near term. Essentially, the practice disintegrates work from its time phased budget.

Schedule Acceleration. In the process of developing the first project schedule, it is fairly common to find that the required duration is longer than the time desired or actually available. Even if the initial schedule does satisfy the required completion date, revised management direction may result in the need for a shorter schedule. In either of these cases, it is necessary to find a way to shorten the schedule. This process is also called schedule acceleration, "crashing" the network or fast tracking.

Schedule Baseline. The formally approved and resource leveled schedule that identifies what must be accomplished to support project objectives.

Schedule Performance Index (SPI). A performance indicator reflecting the relationship of earned value to budget. SPI = BCWP/BCWS. If the result is greater than 1.0, the SPI indicates that more work was accomplished than was planned. Conversely, if the result is less than 1.0, the SPI indicates that less work was accomplished than was planned.

Schedule Risk Assessment (SRA). A risk management process by which the project team uses multiple estimates for durations, etc. to predict the probability of completing the project on time.

Schedule Traceability. Consistency between schedule dates, status, and revisions at all levels of schedule detail (vertical traceability) and between schedules at the same level of detail (horizontal traceability).

Schedule Variance (SV). The difference between Budgeted Cost for Work Performed (BCWP) and Budgeted Cost for Work Scheduled (BCWS). SV = BCWP - BCWS. A positive value indicates a favorable condition and a negative value indicates an unfavorable condition.

Secondary Float. Similar to Total Float, but calculated from an intermediate event rather than from the project finish date.

Setback Chart. A plan for a single unit of production in the Line Of Balance scheduling technique. This chart is built by identifying events that represent the stages of completion of the product, and by putting them in sequence with the lead-time between events.

Slack. See "Float".

Statement of Objectives (SOO). A document that provides basic, top-level objectives of an acquisition and is provided in the request for proposal (RFP) in lieu of a government-written statement of work (SOW). It provides potential offerors the flexibility to develop cost-effective solutions and the opportunity to propose innovative alternatives meeting the objectives.

Start-To-Finish (SF). A relationship between two activities that states that an activity cannot finish until another activity starts. This is a rarely used PDM relationship that usually can be more appropriately shown using some other logic representation.

Start-To-Start (SS). A relationship between two activities that states that an activity cannot start until another activity starts.

Statement of Work (SOW). The document that defines the work scope requirements for a contract.

Subcontract. Effort on a given contract that has been issued to another manufacturer or supplier in accordance with the issuing contractor's design specification or directions for the end item. A subcontract may or may not have EVMS reporting as a flow down requirement based on the dollar value or criticality of the effort, or based on the agreement between the issuing contractor and its customer.

Summary Level Planning Package (SLPP). An aggregation of work for far-term efforts, not able to be identified to the control account level, that can be assigned to reporting level WBS elements (and is, therefore, not undistributed budget). These efforts have work scope, budget, a period of performance, and are planned in control accounts as soon as it is practicable.

Target Cost. See Contract Budget Base and Contract Target Cost.

Task. See Activity.

Template Structure Dictionary. The purpose of the dictionary is to define boundaries to work content. The purpose of the templates is to assist an estimator in cost element delineation within or beneath the WBS dictionary work content boundaries.

To Complete Performance Index (TCPI). The cost efficiency that would have to be attained in order to achieve the EAC value being used in the formula.

TCPI = Remaining budget/current Estimate to Complete

$$TCPI = \frac{BAC - BCWP_{cum}}{EAC - ACWP_{cum}}$$

Over 1.0 equals a projected favorable performance. Under 1.0 equals an unfavorable performance.

Top Down Approach. An approach in schedule development that uses high level milestones to identify key project schedule requirements or events that must occur in certain sequences and time frames..

Total Allocated Budget (TAB). The sum of all budgets allocated to the contract. Total allocated budget consists of the performance measurement baseline (PMB) and all management reserves. The TAB is equal to the contract budget base (CBB) unless an over target baseline (OTB) has been implemented (See Formal Reprogramming).

Total Float (TF). The amount of time an activity or path can be delayed or expanded before it impacts the project end date.

Traceability. A term used in both scheduling and estimating to indicate consistency of information. See also "Schedule Traceability," "Historical Traceability," "Horizontal Traceability," and "Vertical Traceability,"

Undistributed Budget (UB). A temporary holding account for authorized scope of work and its budget that has not yet been authorized to a control account or summary level planning package. UB cannot be a negative value.

Units Complete Technique. An earned value technique used when physical counts of products or completed output are the measurement of status.

Usage Variance (UV). The UV is the difference between earned quantity of materials and actual quantity used, expressed in dollars. UV is derived as follows: UV = (earned quantity - actual quantity) x earned unit price.

Variance. The value by which any schedule or cost performance varies from a specific plan. Significant variances are those differences between planned and actual performance that require further review, analysis, or action. See Cost Variance, Schedule Variance, and Variance at Completion.

Variance Analysis. The process of comparing actual results with planned results.

Variance Analysis Report (VAR). A report describing the nature, cause, impact, and corrective action for variances that exceed established thresholds.

Variance At Completion (VAC). The difference between budget at completion (BAC) and estimate at completion (EAC). A positive value indicates a projected underrun and a negative value indicates projected overrun.

Variance Threshold. Internal and external tolerances (or thresholds) established by contract or management direction. Variance conditions outside the threshold limits require investigation, analysis, corrective action, and reporting.

Vertical Traceability. In estimating, the ability to accurately summarize estimate data with no exclusions, no double counting, and correct summation totals. In scheduling, consistency of schedule dates, status and revisions at all levels of schedule detail.

Work Authorization. The document representing a bilateral agreement between the project manager and the manager of the responsible organization to accomplish and manage the authorized scope of work, schedule and budget.

Work Breakdown Structure (WBS). A product-oriented, family-tree composed of hardware, software, services, data and facilities and other project-unique tasks. A Work Breakdown Structure displays and defines the product(s) to be developed and/ or produced and relates the elements of work to be accomplished to each other and to the end product.

Work Breakdown Structure (WBS) Dictionary. A two-part document containing: 1) a listing of all WBS elements, and 2) the defined scope of each element. Work that is included, as well as closely related work that is excluded is normally contained in the definition of each WBS element.

Work Breakdown Structure (WBS) Index. An indentured listing of all CWBS elements in tabular form cross-referenced to the contract statement of work paragraph numbers. Other contract and funding related references (e.g., Contract Line Item Numbers) are also often included.

Work Package (WP). A work package is a natural subdivision of a control account. It is uniquely distinguishable from all other work packages and may be subdivided into activities or tasks. A work package is the point at which work is planned, progress is measured, and earned value is assessed. A work package has the following characteristics:

1. It represents units of work at levels where work is performed.

2. It is clearly distinguishable from all other tasks.

3. It is assignable to a single organizational element.

4. It has scheduled start and completion dates, and possibly interim milestones that are representative of physical accomplishment.

5. It has a budget expressed in dollars, work-hours, or other measurable units.

6. Its duration is limited to a relatively short span of time or is subdivided by discrete value milestones to facilitate the objective measurement of work performed.

7. It is integrated with detailed engineering, manufacturing, construction, or other schedules.

Work Team. Also known as Integrated Product Team. It is a grouping of project personnel along project objective lines rather than along organizational lines. Work teams represent a transition from a functional organization structure to a multi-functional project objective arrangement.

Bibliography

Chapter 1 Project Management Using Earned Value
Project Management Institute. *A Guide to the Project Management Body of Knowledge (PMBOK), Fourth Edition.* Newton Square, PA: Project Management Institute, 2008.

Chapter 4 Relating Organizations, Responsibility, and Work Scope
Project Management Institute. *A Guide to the Project Management Body of Knowledge (PMBOK), Fourth Edition.* Newtown Square, PA: Project Management Institute, 2008.

Chapter 5 Work Teams
Drucker, Peter F. *Management: Tasks, Responsibilities, Practices.* New York, NY: Harper & Row, 1974.

Chapter 6 What is Scheduling? Schedule Types
Fleming, Bronn, and Humphreys. *Project & Production Scheduling.* Chicago, IL: Probus Publishing Company, 1987.

Chapter 17 Schedule Risk Assessment
Dr. David T. Hulett contributed information for this chapter.

Chapter 21 Estimate Development
Federal Acquisition Regulations. *Part 2, Definition of Words and Terms.*
GEIA Standard, Earned Value Management Systems, EIA-748-B. July 2007.
Kemps, Robert R. *Fundamentals of Project Performance Measurement, Sixth Edition.* Orange, CA: Humphreys & Associates, Inc., 2011.
U.S. Department of Defense, OSD/PA&E/CAIG. Functional Cost-Hour Report, DI-FNCL-81566B. Washington, D.C., April 2007.
U.S. Government Accountability Office. *GAO-09-3SP, GAO Cost Estimating and Assessment Guide.* Washington, D.C., March 2009.

Chapter 22 Learning Curves
Synan, John F. and Larson, Frederick K. *Development and Application of Learning Curves.* American Association of Cost Engineers, 1989 Transactions, 33rd Annual Meeting, G.2.4.
Wright, T.P. *Factors Affecting the Cost of Airplanes.* Journal of Aeronautics Sciences, Vol. 3, No. 4, 1936.

Chapter 30 Establishing the Performance Measurement Baseline
Kemps, Robert R. *Fundamentals of Project Performance Measurement, Sixth Edition.* Orange, CA: Humphreys & Associates, Inc., 2011.

Chapter 32 Performance Measurement Calculations and Estimates at Completion
Christensen, David and Heise, Scott. *Cost Performance Index Stability.* Paper, www.suu.edu/faculty/christensend/evms/CPIstabilityNCMJ.pdf, 1993.
Christensen, David and Rees, David. *Is the CPI-Based EAC a Lower Bound to the Final Cost of Post A-12 Contracts?* Paper, Journal of Cost Analysis and Management, 2002.

Chapter 35 Subcontract Management
Federal Acquisition Regulations. *Subpart 16.601, Time-and-Materials Contracts.*
Fisher, Doug and Gasbarro, Jim. *Teaming Arrangements and EVMS Flowdown.* The Measurable News, Winter 2010 Issue 1, www.pmi-cpm.org/pages/measurable_news/documents/MN2010Issue1Feb4.pdf.

Index

About the Author

Mr. Gary C. Humphreys has over 35 years of program management experience in both government and commercial environments, specializing in earned value management systems (EVMS) design, development, and implementation. He was the first US Army Team Director to conduct an EVMS Tri-Service Demonstration. As both a Team Member and Team Director, he has assisted, evaluated, and directed review teams leading to successful system acceptance.

He has developed a successful consulting practice operating out of Orange, California. As the premier consultant in this field he has provided assistance in all phases of project management to over 800 clients from aerospace firms to utility companies, England's Inland Revenue Service (IRS), and Ship-building companies in North America, Australia, and Europe. Within the industry, no one has performed more on-site earned value cost/schedule performance work.

He was elected to the Nine Man Committee for Increasing the Cost Effectiveness of earned value and led the Fifteen Man Industry Committee to modify traditional documentation and interpretation of earned value to be more compatible with efficient, economical production management control techniques. As a member of the Integrated Program Management Initiative Joint Team, Mr. Humphreys received the DOD's highest acquisition award, the 1998 David Packard Excellence in Acquisition Award. He is also a recipient of the Whitey H. Driessnack Award for Outstanding Contributions to the Advancement of Performance Management.

He has served as Vice-Chair and Chair of the National Defense Industrial Association (NDIA) Program Management Systems Subcommittee (PMSC). As a direct result of his tenure as Chair, he took a fledgling committee and developed it into an influential, policy impacting committee with membership growing to over one hundred people. He was also instrumental in opening the lines of communication between the DOD's Performance Measurement Joint Executive Group (PMJEG) and industry by establishing the first dialogue interchange meetings between the two groups. It was through the NDIA PMSC that he orchestrated the first ever survey on EVMS. As a direct result of this survey's findings, the US Government conducted their own survey. These two independent surveys formed the genesis for subsequent revisions to numerous guides and reference material on EVMS.

Under his leadership, the Performance Management Association (PMA) (now the Project Management Institute's College of Performance Management) achieved importance as a policy-influencing group. He initiated international Chapters in Australia and new US Chapters. He served as leader of the Total Quality Management (TQM) Process Action Team (PAT) for streamlining business system descriptions for performance measurement and management applications.

He has been a guest and keynote speaker on a variety of performance measurement related subjects at the Air Force Institute of Technology (AFIT), Association for the Advancement of Cost Engineering International (AACE International), Certified Public Accountants (CPA) Government Contracts Conference, Defense Acquisition University (DAU), National Computer Conference (NCC) of American Federation of Information Processing Societies (AFIPS), PMI, CPM National and International Chapter meetings, and numerous software user groups.

Mr. Humphreys is a graduate of the University of California at Berkeley, with a Masters Degree in Business Administration from the University of Southern California.

He authored the first edition of *Project Management Using Earned Value* published in 2002. He was a co-author of *Project and Production Scheduling*, published in 1987. He has also written numerous articles on subjects related to project management and earned value.